Learning Bayesian Networks

**PRENTICE HALL SERIES
IN ARTIFICIAL INTELLIGENCE**
Stuart Russell and Peter Norvig, Editors

Learning Bayesian Networks

Richard E. Neapolitan

Northeastern Illinois University
Chicago, Illinois

PEARSON

Prentice
Hall

Upper Saddle River, NJ 07458

Library of Congress Cataloging-in-Publication Data Available

CIP DATA AVAILABLE.

Vice President and Editorial Director, ECS: *Marcia Horton*
Publisher: *Alan Apt*
Associate Editor: *Toni Holm*
Editorial Assistant: *Patrick Lindner*
Vice President and Director of Production and Manufacturing, ESM: *David W. Riccardi*
Executive Managing Editor: *Vince O'Brien*
Managing Editor: *Camille Trentacoste*
Production Editor: *Irwin Zucker*
Manufacturing Manager: *Trudy Pisciotti*
Manufacturing Buyer: *Lisa McDowell*
Director of Creative Services: *Paul Belfanti*
Creative Director: *Carole Anson*
Art Director: *Jayne Conte*
Cover Designer: *Kiwi Design*
Cover Illustration: Mark P. McKernin (adapted from an illustration © 1997 by Eric Horvitz)
Executive Marketing Manager: *Pamela Shaffer*
Marketing Assistant: *Barrie Reinhold*

© 2004 by Pearson Education, Inc.
Pearson Prentice Hall
Upper Saddle River, NJ 07458

About the Cover: The cover graphic was adapted from an illustration that was designed by Eric Horvitz, General Chair of the Thirteenth Conference on Uncertainty and Artificial Intelligence (UAI '97), for the UAI '97 web pages.

Printed in the United States of America

10   9   8   7   6   5   4   3   2   1

ISBN   0-13-012534-2

Pearson Education Ltd., *London*
Pearson Education Australia Pty. Ltd., *Sydney*
Pearson Education Singapore, Pte. Ltd.
Pearson Education North Asia Ltd., *Hong Kong*
Pearson Education Canada, Inc., *Toronto*
Pearson Educación de Mexico, S.A. de C.V.
Pearson Education—Japan, *Tokyo*
Pearson Education—Malaysia, Pte. Ltd.
Pearson Education, Inc., *Upper Saddle River, New Jersey*

In memory of my dad, a difficult, but loving, father who raised me well.

Preface

Bayesian networks are graphical structures for representing the probabilistic relationships among a large number of variables and for doing probabilistic inference with those variables. During the 1980s, a good deal of related research was done on developing Bayesian networks (belief networks, causal networks, influence diagrams), algorithms for performing inference with them, and applications that used them. However, the work was scattered throughout research articles. My purpose in writing the 1990 text *Probabilistic Reasoning in Expert Systems* was to unify this research and to establish a textbook and reference for the field which has come to be known as "Bayesian networks." The 1990s saw the emergence of excellent algorithms for learning Bayesian networks from data. However, by 2000 there still seemed to be no accessible source for "learning Bayesian networks." Similar to my purpose a decade ago, the goal of this text is to provide such a source.

In order to make this text a complete introduction to Bayesian networks, I discuss methods for doing inference in Bayesian networks and influence diagrams. However, there is no effort to be exhaustive in this discussion. For example, I give the details of only two algorithms for exact inference with discrete variables. These algorithms are Pearl's message-passing algorithm and D'Ambrosio and Li's symbolic probabilistic inference algorithm. It may seem odd that I present Pearl's algorithm, since it is one of the oldest. I have two reasons for doing this: (1) Pearl's algorithm corresponds to a model of human causal reasoning, which is discussed in this text; and (2) Pearl's algorithm extends readily to an algorithm for doing inference with continuous variables, which is also discussed in this text.

The content of the text is as follows. Chapters 1 and 2 cover basics. Specifically, Chapter 1 provides an introduction to Bayesian networks; Chapter 2 discusses further relationships between DAGs and probability distributions such as d-separation, the faithfulness condition, and the minimality condition. Chapters 3–5 concern inference. Chapter 3 covers Pearl's message-passing algorithm, D'Ambrosio and Li's symbolic probabilistic inference, and the relationship of Pearl's algorithm to human causal reasoning. Chapter 4 presents an algorithm for doing inference with continuous variables, an approximate inference algorithm, and an algorithm for abductive inference (finding the most probable explanation). Chapter 5 discusses influence diagrams, which are Bayesian networks augmented with decision nodes and a value node, and dynamic Bayesian networks and influence diagrams. Chapters 6–10 address learning. Chapters 6 and 7 are concerned with parameter learning. Since the notation for these learning algorithm is somewhat arduous, I introduce the algorithms by discussing binary variables in Chapter 6. I then generalize to multinomial variables in Chapter 7. Furthermore, in Chapter 7, I discuss learning parameters when the variables are continuous. Chapters 8, 9, and 10 are concerned with structure learning. Chapter 8 presents the Bayesian method for learning structure in the cases of both discrete and continuous variables, while Chapter 9 discusses the constraint-based method for learning structure. Chapter 10 compares the Bayesian and constraint-based methods, and it presents several real-world examples of learning Bayesian networks. The text ends by referencing applications of Bayesian networks in Chapter 11.

This is a text on learning Bayesian networks; it is not a text on artificial intelligence, expert systems, or decision analysis. However, since these are fields in which Bayesian networks find application, they emerge frequently throughout the text. Indeed, I have used the manuscript for this text in my course on expert systems at Northeastern Illinois University. In one semester, I have found that I can cover the core of the following chapters: 1, 2, 3, 5, 6, 7, 8, and 9.

I would like to thank those researchers who have provided valuable corrections, comments, and dialog concerning the material in this text. They include Bruce D'Ambrosio, David Maxwell Chickering, Gregory Cooper, Tom Dean, Carl Entemann, John Erickson, Finn Jensen, Clark Glymour, Piotr Gmytrasiewicz, David Heckerman, Xia Jiang, James Kenevan, Henry Kyburg, Kathryn Blackmond Laskey, Don LaBudde, David Madigan, Christopher Meek, Paul-André Monney, Scott Morris, Peter Norvig, Judea Pearl, Richard Scheines, Marco Valtorta, Alex Wolpert, and Sandy Zabell. I thank Sue Coyle for helping me draw the cartoon containing the robots. The idea for the cover design was motivated by Eric Horvitz's graphic for the UAI '97 web page. I thank Mark McKernin for creating a stunning cover using that idea as a seed.

Contents

About the Author

Richard E. Neapolitan has been a researcher in the area of uncertainty in artificial intelligence, in particular Bayesian networks, since the mid 1980s. In 1990 he wrote the seminal text *Probabilistic Reasoning in Expert Systems*, which helped to unify the field of Bayesian network. Dr. Neapolitan established the field further with his book *Learning Bayesian Network*, which appeared in 2003. Furthermore, he has co-authored the text *Foundations of Algorithms*, which is used in undergraduate and graduate algorithms courses. Besides authoring books, Dr. Neapolitan has published numerous cross-disciplinary articles spanning the fields of computer science, mathematics, philosophy of science, and psychology. Currently, he is professor and chair of Computer Science at Northeastern Illinois University.

Part I

Basics

Part 1

Chapter 1

Introduction to Bayesian Networks

Consider the situation in which one feature of an entity has a direct influence on another feature of that entity. For example, the presence or absence of a disease in a human being has a direct influence on whether a test for that disease turns out positive or negative. For decades, Bayes' theorem has been used to perform probabilistic inference in this type of situation. In the current example, we would use that theorem to compute the conditional probability of an individual having a disease when a test for the disease came back positive. Consider next the situation in which several features are related through inference chains. For example, whether or not an individual has a history of smoking has a direct influence both on whether or not that individual has bronchitis and on whether or not that individual has lung cancer. In turn, the presence or absence of each of these diseases has a direct influence on whether or not the individual experiences fatigue. Also, the presence or absence of lung cancer has a direct influence on whether or not a chest X-ray is positive. In this situation, we would want to do probabilistic inference involving features that are not related via a direct influence. We would want to determine, for example, the conditional probabilities both of bronchitis and of lung cancer when it is known that an individual smokes, is fatigued, and has a positive chest X-ray. Yet bronchitis has no direct influence (indeed no influence at all) on whether a chest X-ray is positive. Therefore, these conditional probabilities cannot be computed using a simple application of Bayes' theorem. There is a straightforward algorithm for computing them, but the probability values it requires are not ordinarily accessible; furthermore, the algorithm has exponential space and time complexity.

Bayesian networks were developed to address these difficulties. By exploiting conditional independencies entailed by influence chains, we are able to represent a large instance in a Bayesian network using little space, and we are often able to perform probabilistic inference among the features in an acceptable amount of time. In addition, the graphical nature of Bayesian networks gives us a much better intuitive grasp of the relationships among the features.

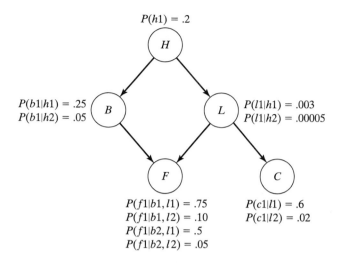

Figure 1.1: A Bayesian network.

Figure 1.1 shows a Bayesian network representing the probabilistic relationships among the features just discussed. The values of the features in that network represent the following:

Feature	Value	When the Feature Takes this Value
H	$h1$	There is a history of smoking
	$h2$	There is no history of smoking
B	$b1$	Bronchitis is present
	$b2$	Bronchitis is absent
L	$l1$	Lung cancer is present
	$l2$	Lung cancer is absent
F	$f1$	Fatigue is present
	$f2$	Fatigue is absent
C	$c1$	Chest X-ray is positive
	$c2$	Chest X-ray is negative

This Bayesian network is discussed in Example 1.36 in Section 1.4.3 after we provide the theory of Bayesian networks. Presently, we use it only to illustrate the nature and use of Bayesian networks. First, in this Bayesian network (called a causal network) the edges represent direct influences. For example, there is an edge from H to L because a history of smoking has a direct influence on the presence of lung cancer, and there is an edge from L to C because the presence of lung cancer has a direct influence on the result of a chest X-ray. There is no edge from H to C because a history of smoking has an influence on the result of a chest X-ray only through its influence on the presence of lung cancer. One way to construct Bayesian networks is by creating edges that represent direct influences as is done here; however, there are other ways. Second, the probabilities in the network are the conditional probabilities of the values of each feature, given every combination of values of the feature's parents in the network, except that in the case of roots they are prior probabilities. Third, probabilistic inference among the features can be accomplished using the Bayesian network. For example, we can compute the conditional probabilities both of bronchitis and of lung cancer when it is known that an individual smokes and has a positive chest X-ray. This Bayesian network is discussed again in Chapter 3 when we develop algorithms that do this inference.

The focus of this text is on learning Bayesian networks from data. For example, given that we had values of the five features just discussed (smoking history, bronchitis, lung cancer, fatigue, and chest X-ray) for a large number of individuals, the learning algorithms we develop might construct the Bayesian network in Figure 1.1. However, to provide a complete introduction to Bayesian networks, we do include a brief overview of methods for doing inference in Bayesian networks and for using Bayesian networks to make decisions. Chapters 1 and 2 cover properties of Bayesian networks which we need in order to discuss both inference and learning. Chapters 3–5 concern techniques for doing inference in Bayesian networks. Methods for learning Bayesian networks from data are discussed in Chapters 6–11. A number of successful expert systems (systems which make the judgments of an expert) have been developed which are based on Bayesian networks. Furthermore, Bayesian networks have been used to learn causal influences from data. Chapter 12 references some of these real-world applications. To see the usefulness of Bayesian networks, you may wish to review that chapter before proceeding.

Chapter 1 introduces Bayesian networks. Section 1.1 reviews basic concepts in probability. The enterprise of learning Bayesian networks from data relies on the notion of a probability as a relative frequency. So in Section 1.2 we review the relative frequency approach to probability and its relationship to another approach to probability called "subjective" or "Bayesian." Section 1.3 is concerned with the use of random variables in statistics. Section 1.4 shows the problem in representing large instances and introduces Bayesian networks as a solution to this problem. Finally, in Section 1.5 we discuss how Bayesian networks can often be constructed using causal edges.

1.1 Basics of Probability Theory

Next we review the probability calculus.

1.1.1 Probability Functions and Spaces

In 1933, A.N. Kolmogorov developed the set-theoretic definition of probability, which serves as a mathematical foundation for all applications of probability. We start by providing that definition.

Probability theory has to do with experiments that have a set of distinct **outcomes**. Examples of such experiments include drawing the top card from a deck of 52 cards, with the 52 outcomes being the 52 different faces of the cards;

flipping a two-sided coin with the two outcomes being "heads" and "tails"; picking a person from a population and determining whether the person is a smoker with the two outcomes being "smoker" and "non-smoker"; picking a person from a population and determining whether the person has lung cancer with the two outcomes being "having lung cancer" and "not having lung cancer"; after identifying 5 levels of serum calcium, picking a person from a population and determining the individual's serum calcium level with the 5 outcomes being each of the 5 levels; picking a person from a population and determining the individual's serum calcium level with the infinite number of outcomes being the continuum of possible calcium levels. The last two experiments illustrate two points. First, the experiment is not well-defined until we identify a set of outcomes. The same act (picking a person and measuring that person's serum calcium level) can be associated with many different experiments, depending on what we consider a distinct outcome. Second, the set of outcomes can be infinite. Once an experiment is well-defined, the collection of all outcomes is called the **sample space**. Mathematically, a sample space is a set and the outcomes are the elements of the set. To keep this review simple, we restrict ourselves to finite sample spaces in what follows. (You should consult a mathematical probability text such as Ash [1970] for a discussion of infinite sample spaces.). In the case of a finite sample space, every subset of the sample space is called an **event**. A subset containing exactly one element is called an **elementary event**. Once a sample space is identified, a probability function is defined as follows:

Definition 1.1 *Suppose we have a sample space Ω containing n distinct elements. That is,*

$$\Omega = \{e_1, e_2, \ldots, e_n\}.$$

*A function that assigns a real number $P(\mathsf{E})$ to each event $\mathsf{E} \subseteq \Omega$ is called a **probability function** on the set of subsets of Ω if it satisfies the following conditions:*

1. $0 \le P(\{e_i\}) \le 1$ for $1 \le i \le n$.

2. $P(\{e_1\}) + P(\{e_2\}) + \ldots + P(\{e_n\}) = 1$.

3. For each event $\mathsf{E} = \{e_{i_1}, e_{i_2}, \ldots, e_{i_k}\}$ that is not an elementary event,

$$P(\mathsf{E}) = P(\{e_{i_1}\}) + P(\{e_{i_2}\}) + \ldots + P(\{e_{i_k}\}).$$

*The pair (Ω, P) is called a **probability space**.*

We often just say that P is a probability function on Ω rather than saying that it is a probability function on the set of subsets of Ω.

Intuition for probability functions comes from considering games of chance as the following example illustrates.

Example 1.1 *Let the experiment be drawing the top card from a deck of* 52 *cards. Then* Ω *contains the faces of the* 52 *cards, and using the principle of indifference, we assign* $P(\{e\}) = 1/52$ *for each* $e \in \Omega$. *Therefore, if we let* kh *and* ks *stand for the king of hearts and king of spades respectively,* $P(\{kh\}) = 1/52$, $P(\{ks\}) = 1/52$, *and* $P(\{kh, ks\}) = P(\{kh\}) + P(\{ks\}) = 1/26$.

The **principle of indifference** (a term popularized by J.M. Keynes in 1921) says elementary events are to be considered equiprobable if we have no reason to expect or prefer one over the other. According to this principle, when there are n elementary events the probability of each of them is the ratio $1/n$. This is the way we often assign probabilities in games of chance, and a probability so assigned is called a **ratio**. Such probabilities are the ones used for illustration in this section. Other notions of probability are the focus of the next section.

It is straightforward to prove the following theorem concerning probability spaces.

Theorem 1.1 *Let* (Ω, P) *be a probability space. Then*

1. $P(\Omega) = 1$.

2. $0 \le P(\mathsf{E}) \le 1$ *for every* $\mathsf{E} \subseteq \Omega$.

3. *For* E *and* $\mathsf{F} \subseteq \Omega$ *such that* $\mathsf{E} \cap \mathsf{F} = \varnothing$,

$$P(\mathsf{E} \cup \mathsf{F}) = P(\mathsf{E}) + P(\mathsf{F}).$$

Proof. *The proof is left as an exercise.* ∎

The conditions in this theorem were labeled the **axioms of probability theory** by A.N. Kolmogorov in 1933. When Condition (3) is replaced by infinitely countable additivity, these conditions are used to define a probability space in mathematical probability texts.

Example 1.2 *Suppose we draw the top card from a deck of cards. Denote by* Queen *the set containing the 4 queens and by* King *the set containing the 4 kings. Then*

$$P(\mathsf{Queen} \cup \mathsf{King}) = P(\mathsf{Queen}) + P(\mathsf{King}) = 1/13 + 1/13 = 2/13$$

because Queen $\cap$ King $= \varnothing$. *Next denote by* Spade *the set containing the 13 spades. The sets* Queen *and* Spade *are not disjoint; so their probabilities are not additive. However, it is not hard to prove that, in general,*

$$P(\mathsf{E} \cup \mathsf{F}) = P(\mathsf{E}) + P(\mathsf{F}) - P(\mathsf{E} \cap \mathsf{F}).$$

So

$$
\begin{aligned}
P(\mathsf{Queen} \cup \mathsf{Spade}) &= P(\mathsf{Queen}) + P(\mathsf{Spade}) - P(\mathsf{Queen} \cap \mathsf{Spade}) \\
&= \frac{1}{13} + \frac{1}{4} - \frac{1}{52} = \frac{4}{13}.
\end{aligned}
$$

1.1.2   Conditional Probability and Independence

We have yet to discuss one of the most important concepts in probability theory, namely conditional probability. We do that next.

Definition 1.2 *Let* E *and* F *be events such that* $P(F) \neq 0$. *Then the **conditional probability** of* E *given* F, *denoted* $P(E|F)$, *is given by*

$$P(E|F) = \frac{P(E \cap F)}{P(F)}.$$

The initial intuition for conditional probability comes from considering probabilities that are ratios. In the case of ratios, $P(E|F)$, as defined above, is the fraction of items in F that are also in E. We show this as follows. Let n be the number of items in the sample space, n_F be the number of items in F, and n_{EF} be the number of items in $E \cap F$. Then

$$\frac{P(E \cap F)}{P(F)} = \frac{n_{EF}/n}{n_F/n} = \frac{n_{EF}}{n_F},$$

which is the fraction of items in F that are also in E. As far as meaning, $P(E|F)$ means the probability of E occurring given that we know F has occurred.

Example 1.3 *Again consider drawing the top card from a deck of cards, let* Queen *be the set of the 4 queens,* RoyalCard *be the set of the 12 royal cards, and* Spade *be the set of the 13 spades. Then*

$$P(\text{Queen}) = \frac{1}{13}$$

$$P(\text{Queen}|\text{RoyalCard}) = \frac{P(\text{Queen} \cap \text{RoyalCard})}{P(\text{RoyalCard})} = \frac{1/13}{3/13} = \frac{1}{3}$$

$$P(\text{Queen}|\text{Spade}) = \frac{P(\text{Queen} \cap \text{Spade})}{P(\text{Spade})} = \frac{1/52}{1/4} = \frac{1}{13}.$$

Notice in the previous example that $P(\text{Queen}|\text{Spade}) = P(\text{Queen})$. This means that finding out the card is a spade does not make it more or less probable that it is a queen. That is, the knowledge of whether it is a spade is irrelevant to whether it is a queen. We say that the two events are independent in this case, which is formalized in the following definition.

Definition 1.3 *Two events* E *and* F *are independent if one of the following holds:*

1. $P(E|F) = P(E)$ *and* $P(E) \neq 0, P(F) \neq 0.$

2. $P(E) = 0$ *or* $P(F) = 0.$

Notice that the definition states that the two events are independent even though it is based on the conditional probability of E given F. The reason is that independence is symmetric. That is, if $P(E) \neq 0$ and $P(F) \neq 0$, then $P(E|F) = P(E)$ if and only if $P(F|E) = P(F)$. It is straightforward to prove that E and F are independent if and only if $P(E \cap F) = P(E)P(F)$.

The following example illustrates an extension of the notion of independence.

Example 1.4 *Let* E $= \{kh, ks, qh\}$, F $= \{kh, kc, qh\}$, G $= \{kh, ks, kc, kd\}$, *where kh means the king of hearts, ks means the king of spades, and so forth. Then*

$$P(\mathsf{E}) = \frac{3}{52}$$

$$P(\mathsf{E}|\mathsf{F}) = \frac{2}{3}$$

$$P(\mathsf{E}|\mathsf{G}) = \frac{2}{4} = \frac{1}{2}$$

$$P(\mathsf{E}|\mathsf{F} \cap \mathsf{G}) = \frac{1}{2}.$$

So E *and* F *are not independent, but they are independent once we condition on* G.

In the previous example, E and F are said to be conditionally independent given G. Conditional independence is very important in Bayesian networks and will be discussed much more in the sections that follow. Presently, we have the definition that follows and another example.

Definition 1.4 *Two events* E *and* F *are **conditionally independent** given* G *if* $P(\mathsf{G}) \neq 0$ *and one of the following holds:*

1. $P(\mathsf{E}|\mathsf{F} \cap \mathsf{G}) = P(\mathsf{E}|\mathsf{G})$ *and* $P(\mathsf{E}|\mathsf{G}) \neq 0, P(\mathsf{F}|\mathsf{G}) \neq 0$.

2. $P(\mathsf{E}|\mathsf{G}) = 0$ *or* $P(\mathsf{F}|\mathsf{G}) = 0$.

Another example of conditional independence follows.

Example 1.5 *Let* Ω *be the set of all objects in Figure 1.2. Suppose we assign a probability of 1/13 to each object, and let* Black *be the set of all black objects,* White *be the set of all white objects,* Square *be the set of all square objects, and* One *be the set of all objects containing a "1." We then have*

$$P(\mathsf{One}) = \frac{5}{13}$$

$$P(\mathsf{One}|\mathsf{Square}) = \frac{3}{8}$$

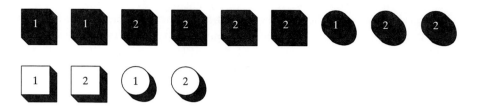

Figure 1.2: Containing a "1" and being a square are not independent events, but they are conditionally independent given the object is black and given it is white.

$$P(\text{One}|\text{Black}) \quad = \quad \frac{3}{9} = \frac{1}{3}$$

$$P(\text{One}|\text{Square} \cap \text{Black}) \quad = \quad \frac{2}{6} = \frac{1}{3}$$

$$P(\text{One}|\text{White}) \quad = \quad \frac{2}{4} = \frac{1}{2}$$

$$P(\text{One}|\text{Square} \cap \text{White}) \quad = \quad \frac{1}{2}.$$

So One *and* Square *are not independent, but they are conditionally independent given* Black *and given* White.

Next we discuss a very useful rule involving conditional probabilities. Suppose we have n events $\mathsf{E}_1, \mathsf{E}_2, \ldots \mathsf{E}_n$ such that $\mathsf{E}_i \cap \mathsf{E}_j = \varnothing$ for $i \neq j$ and $\mathsf{E}_1 \cup \mathsf{E}_2 \cup \ldots \cup \mathsf{E}_n = \Omega$. Such events are called **mutually exclusive and exhaustive**. Then the **law of total probability** says that for any other event F,

$$P(\mathsf{F}) = \sum_{i=1}^{n} P(\mathsf{F} \cap \mathsf{E}_i). \tag{1.1}$$

If $P(\mathsf{E}_i) \neq 0$, then $P(\mathsf{F} \cap \mathsf{E}_i) = P(\mathsf{F}|\mathsf{E}_i)P(\mathsf{E}_i)$. Therefore, if $P(\mathsf{E}_i) \neq 0$ for all i, the law is often applied in the following form:

$$P(\mathsf{F}) = \sum_{i=1}^{n} P(\mathsf{F}|\mathsf{E}_i)P(\mathsf{E}_i). \tag{1.2}$$

It is straightforward to derive both the axioms of probability theory and the rule for conditional probability when probabilities are ratios. However, they can also be derived in the relative frequency and subjectivistic frameworks (see Neapolitan [1990]), which are discussed in Section 1.2. These derivations make the use of probability theory compelling for handling uncertainty.

1.1.3   Bayes' Theorem

For decades conditional probabilities of events of interest have been computed from known probabilities using Bayes' theorem. We develop that theorem next.

Theorem 1.2 *(Bayes) Given two events* E *and* F *such that* $P(\mathsf{E}) \neq 0$ *and* $P(\mathsf{F}) \neq 0$, *we have*

$$P(\mathsf{E}|\mathsf{F}) = \frac{P(\mathsf{F}|\mathsf{E})P(\mathsf{E})}{P(\mathsf{F})}. \tag{1.3}$$

Furthermore, given n *mutually exclusive and exhaustive events* $\mathsf{E}_1, \mathsf{E}_2, \ldots \mathsf{E}_n$ *such that* $P(\mathsf{E}_i) \neq 0$ *for all* i, *we have for* $1 \leq i \leq n$,

$$P(\mathsf{E}_i|\mathsf{F}) = \frac{P(\mathsf{F}|\mathsf{E}_i)P(\mathsf{E}_i)}{P(\mathsf{F}|\mathsf{E}_1)P(\mathsf{E}_1) + P(\mathsf{F}|\mathsf{E}_2)P(\mathsf{E}_2) + \cdots P(\mathsf{F}|\mathsf{E}_n)P(\mathsf{E}_n)}. \tag{1.4}$$

Proof. *To obtain Equality 1.3, we first use the definition of conditional probability as follows:*

$$P(\mathsf{E}|\mathsf{F}) = \frac{P(\mathsf{E} \cap \mathsf{F})}{P(\mathsf{F})} \qquad and \qquad P(\mathsf{F}|\mathsf{E}) = \frac{P(\mathsf{F} \cap \mathsf{E})}{P(\mathsf{E})}.$$

Next we multiply each of these equalities by the denominator on its right side to show that

$$P(\mathsf{E}|\mathsf{F})P(\mathsf{F}) = P(\mathsf{F}|\mathsf{E})P(\mathsf{E})$$

because they both equal $P(\mathsf{E} \cap \mathsf{F})$. *Finally, we divide this last equality by* $P(\mathsf{F})$ *to obtain our result.*

To obtain Equality 1.4, we place the expression for F, *obtained using the rule of total probability (Equality 1.2), in the denominator of Equality 1.3.* ∎

Both of the formulas in the preceding theorem are called **Bayes' theorem** because they were originally developed by Thomas Bayes (published in 1763). The first enables us to compute $P(\mathsf{E}|\mathsf{F})$ if we know $P(\mathsf{F}|\mathsf{E})$, $P(\mathsf{E})$, and $P(\mathsf{F})$, while the second enables us to compute $P(\mathsf{E}_i|\mathsf{F})$ if we know $P(\mathsf{F}|\mathsf{E}_j)$ and $P(\mathsf{E}_j)$ for $1 \leq j \leq n$. An example of the use of Bayes' theorem follows:

Example 1.6 *Let* Ω *be the set of all objects in Figure 1.2, and assign each object a probability of* $1/13$. *Let* One *be the set of all objects containing a 1,* Two *be the set of all objects containing a 2, and* Black *be the set of all black objects. Then according to Bayes' theorem,*

$$
\begin{aligned}
P(\mathsf{One}|\mathsf{Black}) &= \frac{P(\mathsf{Black}|\mathsf{One})P(\mathsf{One})}{P(\mathsf{Black}|\mathsf{One})P(\mathsf{One}) + P(\mathsf{Black}|\mathsf{Two})P(\mathsf{Two})} \\
&= \frac{(\frac{3}{5})(\frac{5}{13})}{(\frac{3}{5})(\frac{5}{13}) + (\frac{6}{8})(\frac{8}{13})} = \frac{1}{3},
\end{aligned}
$$

which is the same value we get by computing $P(\mathsf{One}|\mathsf{Black})$ *directly.*

The previous example is not a very exciting application of Bayes' theorem since we can just as easily compute $P(\mathsf{One}|\mathsf{Black})$ directly. Section 1.2.2 shows useful applications of Bayes' theorem.

1.1.4 Random Variables and Joint Probability Distributions

We have one final concept to discuss in this overview, namely that of a random variable. The definition shown here is based on the set-theoretic definition of probability given in Section 1.1.1. In Section 1.3.2 we provide an alternative definition which is more pertinent to the way random variables are used in practice.

Definition 1.5 *Given a probability space (Ω, P), a **random variable** X is a function on Ω.*

That is, a random variable assigns a unique value to each element (outcome) in the sample space. The set of values random variable X can assume is called the **space** of X. A random variable is said to be **discrete** if its space is finite or countable. In general, we develop our theory assuming the random variables are discrete. Examples follow.

Example 1.7 *Let Ω contain all outcomes of a throw of a pair of six-sided dice, and let P assign $1/36$ to each outcome. Then Ω is the following set of ordered pairs:*

$$\Omega = \{(1,1), (1,2), (1,3), (1,4), (1,5), (1,6), (2,1), (2,2), \ldots, (6,5), (6,6)\}.$$

Let the random variable X assign the sum of each ordered pair to that pair, and let the random variable Y assign "odd" to each pair of odd numbers and "even" to a pair if at least one number in that pair is an even number. The following table shows some of the values of X and Y:

e	$X(e)$	$Y(e)$
$(1,1)$	2	*odd*
$(1,2)$	3	*even*
$\ldots$	$\ldots$	$\ldots$
$(2,1)$	3	*even*
$\ldots$	$\ldots$	$\ldots$
$(6,6)$	12	*even*

The space of X is $\{2,3,4,5,6,7,8,9,10,11,12\}$, and that of Y is $\{odd, even\}$.

For a random variable X, we use $X = x$ to denote the set of all elements $e \in \Omega$ that X maps to the value of x. That is,

$$X = x \quad \text{represents the event} \quad \{e \text{ such that } X(e) = x\}.$$

Note the difference between X and x. Small x denotes any element in the space of X, while X is a function.

Example 1.8 *Let Ω , P, and X be as in Example 1.7. Then*

$$X = 3 \qquad \text{represents the event} \qquad \{(1,2),(2,1)\} \text{ and}$$

$$P(X = 3) = \frac{1}{18}.$$

It is not hard to see that a random variable induces a probability function on its space. That is, if we define $P_X(\{x\}) \equiv P(X = x)$, then P_X is such a probability function.

Example 1.9 *Let Ω contain all outcomes of a throw of a single die, let P assign $1/6$ to each outcome, and let Z assign "even" to each even number and "odd" to each odd number. Then*

$$P_Z(\{even\}) = P(Z = even) = P(\{2,4,6\}) = \frac{1}{2}$$

$$P_Z(\{odd\}) = P(Z = odd) = P(\{1,3,5\}) = \frac{1}{2}.$$

We rarely refer to $P_X(\{x\})$. Rather we only reference the original probability function P, and we call $P(X = x)$ the **probability distribution** of the random variable X. For brevity, we often just say "distribution" instead of "probability distribution." Furthermore, we often use x alone to represent the event $X = x$, and so we write $P(x)$ instead of $P(X = x)$. We refer to $P(x)$ as "the probability of x."

Let Ω, P, and X be as in Example 1.7. Then if $x = 3$,

$$P(x) = P(X = x) = \frac{1}{18}.$$

If the space of random variable X is a subset of the real numbers, the **expected value** of X is given by

$$E(X) = \sum_x xP(x),$$

where $\sum_x$ means the sum as x goes through all values in the space of X.

Example 1.10 *Let Ω contain all outcomes of a throw of a single die, let P assign $1/6$ to each outcome, and let X assign the value of the outcome (number appearing on the die) to each outcome. Then*

$$E(X) = \sum_{x=1}^{6} xP(x) = \sum_{x=1}^{6} x\left(\frac{1}{6}\right) = \frac{7}{2}.$$

Given two random variables X and Y, defined on the same sample space Ω, we use $X = x, Y = y$ to denote the set of all elements $e \in \Omega$ that are mapped both by X to x and by Y to y. That is,

$X = x, Y = y$ represents the event

$$\{e \text{ such that } X(e) = x\} \cap \{e \text{ such that } Y(e) = y\}.$$

Example 1.11 *Let Ω, P, X, and Y be as in Example 1.7. Then*

$X = 4, Y = odd$ *represents the event* $\{(1,3),(3,1)\}$, *and*

$$P(X = 4, Y = odd) = 1/18.$$

Clearly, two random variables induce a probability function on the Cartesian product of their spaces. As is the case for a single random variable, we rarely refer to this probability function. Rather we reference the original probability function. That is, we refer to $P(X = x, Y = y)$, and we call this the **joint probability distribution** of X and Y. If $\mathsf{A} = \{X, Y\}$, we also call this the **joint probability distribution** of A. Furthermore, we often just say "joint distribution" or "probability distribution."

For brevity, we often use x, y to represent the event $X = x, Y = y$, and so we write $P(x, y)$ instead of $P(X = x, Y = y)$. This concept extends in a straightforward way to three or more random variables. For example, $P(X = x, Y = y, Z = z)$ is the joint probability distribution function of the variables X, Y, and Z, and we often write $P(x, y, z)$.

Example 1.12 *Let Ω, P, X, and Y be as in Example 1.7. Then if $x = 4$ and $y = odd$,*

$$P(x, y) = P(X = x, Y = y) = 1/18.$$

If, for example, we let $\mathsf{A} = \{X, Y\}$ and $\mathsf{a} = \{x, y\}$, we use

$\mathsf{A} = \mathsf{a}$ to represent $X = x, Y = y,$

and we often write $P(\mathsf{a})$ instead of $P(\mathsf{A} = \mathsf{a})$. The same notation extends to the representation of three or more random variables. For consistency, we set $P(\varnothing = \varnothing) = 1$, where $\varnothing$ is the empty set of random variables. Note that if $\varnothing$ is the empty set of events, $P(\varnothing) = 0$.

Example 1.13 *Let Ω, P, X, and Y be as in Example 1.7. If $\mathsf{A} = \{X, Y\}$, $\mathsf{a} = \{x, y\}$, $x = 4$, and $y = odd$,*

$$P(\mathsf{A} = \mathsf{a}) = P(X = x, Y = y) = 1/18.$$

This notation entails that if we have, for example, two sets of random variables $A = \{X, Y\}$ and $B = \{Z, W\}$, then

$A = a$, $B = b$ represents $X = x, Y = y, Z = z, W = w$.

Given a joint probability distribution, the law of total probability (Equality 1.1) implies that the probability distribution of any one of the random variables can be obtained by summing over all values of the other variables. It is left as an exercise to show this. For example, suppose we have a joint probability distribution $P(X = x, Y = y)$. Then

$$P(X = x) = \sum_y P(X = x, Y = y).$$

The probability distribution $P(X = x)$ is called the **marginal probability distribution** of X because it is obtained using a process similar to adding across a row or column in a table of numbers. This concept also extends in a straightforward way to three or more random variables. For example, if we have a joint distribution $P(X = x, Y = y, Z = z)$ of X, Y, and Z, the marginal distribution $P(X = x, Y = y)$ of X and Y is obtained by summing over all values of Z. If $A = \{X, Y\}$, we also call this the **marginal probability distribution** of A.

Example 1.14 *Let* Ω*,* P*,* X*, and* Y *be as in Example 1.7. Then*

$$
\begin{aligned}
P(X = 4) &= \sum_y P(X = 4, Y = y) \\
&= P(X = 4, Y = odd) + P(X = 4, Y = even) = \frac{1}{18} + \frac{1}{36} = \frac{1}{12},
\end{aligned}
$$

The following example reviews the concepts covered so far concerning random variables:

Example 1.15 *Let* Ω *be a set of 12 individuals, and let* P *assign 1/12 to each individual. Suppose the sexes, heights, and wages of the individuals are as follows:*

Case	Sex	Height (inches)	Wage ($)
1	*female*	64	30, 000
2	*female*	64	30, 000
3	*female*	64	40, 000
4	*female*	64	40, 000
5	*female*	68	30, 000
6	*female*	68	40, 000
7	*male*	64	40, 000
8	*male*	64	50, 000
9	*male*	68	40, 000
10	*male*	68	50, 000
11	*male*	70	40, 000
12	*male*	70	50, 000

Let the random variables S, H and W respectively assign the sex, height and wage of an individual to that individual. Then the distributions of the three variables are as follows (Recall that, for example, $P(s)$ represents $P(S = s)$.):

s	$P(s)$
female	1/2
male	1/2

h	$P(h)$
64	1/2
68	1/3
70	1/6

w	$P(w)$
30,000	1/4
40,000	1/2
50,000	1/4

The joint distribution of S and H is as follows:

s	h	$P(s,h)$
female	64	1/3
female	68	1/6
female	70	0
male	64	1/6
male	68	1/6
male	70	1/6

The following table also shows the joint distribution of S and H and illustrates that the individual distributions can be obtained by summing the joint distribution over all values of the other variable:

h	64	68	70	Distribution of S
s				
female	1/3	1/6	0	1/2
male	1/6	1/6	1/6	1/2
Distribution of H	1/2	1/3	1/6	

The table that follows shows the first few values in the joint distribution of S, H, and W. There are 18 values in all, of which many are 0.

s	h	w	$P(s,h,w)$
female	64	30,000	1/6
female	64	40,000	1/6
female	64	50,000	0
female	68	30,000	1/12
...	...	...	...

We have the following definition.

Definition 1.6 *Suppose we have a probability space (Ω, P), and two sets A and B containing random variables defined on Ω. Then the sets A and B are said to* be ***independent*** *if, for all values of the variables in the sets* a *and* b, *the events* A = a *and* B = b *are independent. That is, either* $P(a) = 0$ *or* $P(b) = 0$ *or*

$$P(a|b) = P(a).$$

When this is the case, we write

$$I_P(A, B),$$

where I_P *stands for independent in* P.

Example 1.16 *Let* Ω *be the set of all cards in an ordinary deck, and let* P *assign* $1/52$ *to each card. Define random variables as follows:*

Variable	Value	Outcomes Mapped to this Value
R	$r1$	*All royal cards*
	$r2$	*All nonroyal cards*
T	$t1$	*All tens and jacks*
	$t2$	*All cards that are neither tens nor jacks*
S	$s1$	*All spades*
	$s2$	*All nonspades*

Then we maintain that the sets $\{R, T\}$ *and* $\{S\}$ *are independent. That is,*

$$I_P(\{R, T\}, \{S\}).$$

To show this, we need to show for all values of r, t, *and* s *that*

$$P(r, t|s) = P(r, t).$$

(Note that we do not show brackets to denote sets in our probabilistic expression because in such an expression a set represents the members of the set. See the discussion following Example 1.12.) The following table shows this is the case:

s	r	t	$P(r, t\|s)$	$P(r, t)$
$s1$	$r1$	$t1$	$1/13$	$4/52 = 1/13$
$s1$	$r1$	$t2$	$2/13$	$8/52 = 2/13$
$s1$	$r2$	$t1$	$1/13$	$4/52 = 1/13$
$s1$	$r2$	$t2$	$9/13$	$36/52 = 9/13$
$s2$	$r1$	$t1$	$3/39 = 1/13$	$4/52 = 1/13$
$s2$	$r1$	$t2$	$6/39 = 2/13$	$8/52 = 2/13$
$s2$	$r2$	$t1$	$3/39 = 1/13$	$4/52 = 1/13$
$s2$	$r2$	$t2$	$27/39 = 9/13$	$36/52 = 9/13$

Another definition follows.

Definition 1.7 *Suppose we have a probability space* (Ω, P), *and three sets* A, B, *and* C *containing random variables defined on* Ω. *Then the sets* A *and* B *are said to be **conditionally independent given that the set** C *if, for all values* *of the variables in the sets* a, b, *and* c, *whenever* $P(c) \neq 0$, *the events* A $=$ a *and* B $=$ b *are conditionally independent given the event* C $=$ c. *That is, either* $P(a|c) = 0$ *or* $P(b|c) = 0$ *or*

$$P(a|b, c) = P(a|c).$$

When this is the case, we write

$$I_P(A, B|C).$$

Example 1.17 *Let* Ω *be the set of all objects in Figure 1.2 on page 8, and let* P *assign 1/13 to each object. Define random variables* S *(for shape),* V *(for value), and* C *(for color) as follows:*

Variable	Value	Outcomes Mapped to this Value
V	$v1$	*All objects containing a "1"*
	$v2$	*All objects containing a "2"*
S	$s1$	*All square objects*
	$s2$	*All round objects*
C	$c1$	*All black objects*
	$c2$	*All white objects*

Then we maintain that $\{V\}$ *and* $\{S\}$ *are conditionally independent given* $\{C\}$. *That is,*

$$I_P(\{V\}, \{S\}|\{C\}).$$

To show this, we need to show for all values of v, s, and c that

$$P(v|s, c) = P(v|c).$$

The results in Example 1.5 on page 7 show $P(v1|s1, c1) = P(v1|c1)$ *and* $P(v1|s1, c2) = P(v1|c2)$. *The table that follows shows that the equality holds for the other values of the variables too:*

c	s	v	$P(v|s, c)$	$P(v|c)$
$c1$	$s1$	$v1$	$2/6 = 1/3$	$3/9 = 1/3$
$c1$	$s1$	$v2$	$4/6 = 2/3$	$6/9 = 2/3$
$c1$	$s2$	$v1$	$1/3$	$3/9 = 1/3$
$c1$	$s2$	$v2$	$2/3$	$6/9 = 2/3$
$c2$	$s1$	$v1$	$1/2$	$2/4 = 1/2$
$c2$	$s1$	$v2$	$1/2$	$2/4 = 1/2$
$c2$	$s2$	$v1$	$1/2$	$2/4 = 1/2$
$c2$	$s2$	$v2$	$1/2$	$2/4 = 1/2$

For the sake of brevity, we sometimes say only "independent" rather than "conditionally independent." Furthermore, when a set contains only one item, we often drop the set notation and terminology. For example, in the preceding example, we might say V and S are independent given C and write $I_P(V, S|C)$.

Finally, we have the **chain rule** for random variables, which says that given n random variables $X_1, X_2, \ldots X_n$, defined on the same sample space Ω,

$$P(x_1, x_2, \ldots x_n) = P(x_n|x_{n-1}, x_{n-2}, \ldots x_1) \cdots \times P(x_2|x_1) \times P(x_1)$$

whenever $P(x_1, x_2, \ldots x_n) \neq 0$. It is straightforward to prove this rule using the rule for conditional probability.

1.2 Philosophical Foundations of Probability

As discussed at the beginning of this chapter, this text is concerned with learning Bayesian networks from data, and the enterprise of learning from data relies on the notion of a probability as a relative frequency. So we next review the relative frequency approach to probability, and we go over the "subjective" or "Bayesian" approach to handling probabilities that are relative frequencies.

1.2.1 The Relative Frequency Approach to Probability

In 1919 Richard von Mises developed the **relative frequency approach to probability**, which concerns repeatable identical experiments. First we review the fundamentals of von Mises' approach; then we discuss how we can learn something about relative frequencies from data; finally we discuss the need for the approach.

Fundamentals of the Approach

von Mises [1928] formalized the notion of repeatable identical experiments as follows:

> The term is "the **collective**", and it denotes a sequence of uniform events or processes which differ by certain observable attributes, say colors, numbers, or anything else [p. 12].

I, rather than von Mises, put the word "collective" in boldface in the preceding quotation. The classical example of a collective is an infinite sequence of tosses of the same coin. Each time we toss the coin, our knowledge about the conditions of the toss is the same (assuming we do not sometimes "cheat" by, for example, holding it close to the ground and trying to flip it just once). Of course, something is different in the tosses (e.g., the distance from the ground, the torque we put on the coin, and so on.) because otherwise the coin would always land heads or always land tails. But we are not aware of these differences. Our knowledge concerning the conditions of the experiment is always the same. Von Mises argued that, in such repeated experiments, the relative frequency of each outcome approaches a limit and he called that limit the probability of the outcome. We call such a probability a **relative frequency**.   Proponents of this approach to probability are sometimes called **frequentists**.

Note that the collective (infinite sequence) only exists in theory. We never will toss the coin indefinitely. Rather, the theory assumes there is a **propensity** for the coin to land heads, and as the number of tosses approaches infinity, the fraction of heads approaches that propensity. Since the probability is a physical property of the coin, it is also called a **physical probability**.

Example 1.18 *Suppose we toss a thumbtack and consider as outcomes the two ways it could land. It could land on its head, which we will call "heads," or it could land with the edge of the head and the end of the point touching the ground, which we will call "tails." Due to the lack of symmetry in a thumbtack, we would not assign a probability of 1/2 to each of these events. So we cannot compute the probability using ratios. However, according to the von Mises' theory, if p is the true $P(\{heads\})$,*

$$p = \lim_{m \to \infty} \frac{\#heads}{m}. \tag{1.5}$$

So, if we tossed the thumbtack 10,000 times and it landed heads 3373 times, we would estimate the probability of heads to be about .3373.

How are relative frequencies related to ratios? Intuitively, we would expect if, for example, we repeatedly shuffled a deck of cards and drew the top card, the ace of spades would come up about one out of every 52 times. In 1946 J. E. Kerrich conducted many such experiments using games of chance in which the principle of indifference seemed to apply (e.g. drawing a card from a deck). His results indicated that the relative frequency does appear to approach a limit and that limit is the ratio.

Another facet of von Mises' relative frequency approach is that a collective is only defined relative to a **random process**, which, in the von Mises theory, is defined to be a repeatable experiment for which the infinite sequence of outcomes is assumed to be a random sequence. Intuitively, a **random sequence** is one which shows no regularity or pattern. For example, the finite binary sequence "1011101100" appears random, whereas the sequence "1010101010" does not because it has the pattern "10" repeated five times. There is evidence that experiments like coin tossing and dice throwing are indeed random processes: in 1971, G.R. Iversen et al. ran many experiments with dice indicating that the sequence of outcomes is random. It is believed that unbiased sampling also yields a random sequence and is therefore a random process. See van Lambalgen [1987] for a thorough discussion of this matter, including a formal definition of random sequence. Neapolitan [1990] provides a more intuitive, less mathematical treatment. We close here with an example of a nonrandom process. This author prefers to exercise at his health club on Tuesday, Thursday, and Saturday. However, if he misses a day, he usually makes up for it the following day. If we track the days he exercises, we will find a pattern because the process is not random.

Under the assumption that the relative frequency approaches a limit and that a random sequence is generated, in 1928 von Mises was able to derive the rules of probability theory and the result that the trials are probabilistically independent. In terms of relative frequencies, what does it mean for the trials to be independent? The following example illustrates what it means. Suppose we develop sequences of length 20 (or any other number) by repeatedly tossing a coin 20 times. Then we separate the set of all these sequences into disjoint subsets such that the sequences in each subset all have the same outcomes on the first 19 tosses. Independence means the relative frequency of heads on the 20th toss is the same in all the subsets (in the limit).

Sampling

Sampling techniques estimate a relative frequency for a given collective from a finite set of observations. In accordance with standard statistical practice, we use the term **random sample** (or simply sample) to denote the set of observations, and we call a collective a **population**. Note the difference between a collective and a **finite population**. There are currently a finite number of smokers in the world. The fraction of them with lung cancer is the probability (in the sense of a ratio) of a current smoker having lung cancer. The propensity (relative frequency) of a smoker having lung cancer may not be exactly equal to this ratio. Rather the ratio is just an estimate of that propensity. When doing statistical inference, we sometimes want to estimate the ratio in a finite population from a sample of the population, and other times we want to estimate a propensity from a finite sequence of observations. For example, TV raters ordinarily want to estimate the actual fraction of people in a nation watching a show from a sample of those people. On the other hand, medical scientists want to estimate the propensity with which smokers have lung cancer from a finite sequence of smokers. One can create a collective from a finite population by returning a sampled item back to the population before sampling the next item. This is called "**sampling with replacement**." In practice it is rarely done, but ordinarily the finite population is so large that statisticians make the simplifying assumption it is done. That is, they do not replace the item, but still assume the ratio is unchanged for the next item sampled. In this text, we are always concerned with propensities rather than current ratios. So this simplifying assumption does not concern us.

Estimating a relative frequency from a sample seems straightforward. That is, we simply use S_m/m as our estimate, where m is the number of trials and S_m is the number of successes. However, there is a problem in determining our confidence in the estimate. That is, the von Mises theory says only that the limit in Expression 1.5 physically exists and is p. It is not a mathematical limit in that, given an $\epsilon > 0$, it offers no means for finding an $M(\epsilon)$ such that

$$\left| p - \frac{S_m}{m} \right| < \epsilon \qquad \text{for } m > M(\epsilon).$$

Mathematical probability theory enables us to determine confidence in our estimate of p. First, if we assume the trials are probabilistically independent and the probability for each trial is p, we can prove that S_m/m is the **maximum likelihood (ML)** value of p. That is, if d is a set of results of m trials, and $P(\mathrm{d}:\hat{p})$ denotes the probability of d if the probability of success were $\hat{p}$, then S_m/m is the value of $\hat{p}$ that maximizes $P(\mathrm{d}:\hat{p})$. Furthermore, we can prove the weak and strong laws of large numbers. The weak law says the following. Given $\epsilon, \delta > 0$

$$P\left(\left|p - \frac{S_m}{m}\right| < \epsilon\right) > 1 - \delta \qquad \text{for } m > \frac{2}{\delta\epsilon^2}.$$

So mathematically we have a means of finding an $M(\epsilon, \delta)$.

The weak law is not applied directly to obtain confidence in our estimate. Rather we obtain a confidence interval using the following result, which is obtained in a standard statistics text such as Brownlee [1965]. Suppose we have m independent trials, the probability of success on each trial is p, and we have k successes. Let

$$0 < \beta < 1$$

$$\alpha = (1 - \beta)/2$$

$$\theta_1 = \frac{kF_\alpha(2k, 2[m - k + 1])}{m - k + 1 + kF_\alpha(2x, 2[m - k + 1])}$$

$$\theta_2 = \frac{k}{(m - k + 1)F_{1-\alpha}(2[m - k + 1], 2k) + k},$$

where F is the F distribution. Then

$$(\theta_1, \theta_2) \qquad \text{is a } \beta \text{ \% confidence interval for } p.$$

This means β % of the time the interval generated will contain p.

Example 1.19 *Suppose we toss a thumbtack 30 times and it lands heads (i.e., on its head) 8 times. Then the following is a 95% confidence interval for p, the probability of heads:*

$$(.123, .459)$$

Since 95% of the time we will obtain an interval that contains p, we are pretty confident p is in this interval.

Need for the Approach

One should not conclude that mathematical probability theory somehow proves S_m/m will be close to p, and that, therefore, we have no need for the von Mises theory. Without some assumption about S_m/m approaching p, the mathematical result would say nothing about what is happening in the world. For example, without some such assumption, our explanation of confidence intervals would become the following. Suppose we have a sample space determined by m identically distributed independent discrete random variables, where p is the probability each of them assumes its first value. Consider the random variable whose possible values are the probability intervals obtained using the method for calculating a $\beta\%$ confidence interval. Then β is the probability that this random variable equals an interval that contains p. This result says nothing about what will happen when, for example, we toss a thumbtack m times. However, if we assume that the probability of an event is the limit of the relative frequency with which the event occurs in the world, this means that if we repeatedly did the experiment of tossing the thumbtack m times, in the limit 95% of the time we will generate an interval containing p, which is how we described confidence intervals above.

Some probabilists find fault with the von Mises theory because it assumes the observed relative frequency definitely approaches p. For example, Ash [1970], [p. 2] says,

> ... an attempt at a frequency definition of probability will cause trouble. If S_n is the number of occurrences of an event in n independent performances of an experiment, we expect physically that the relative frequency S_n/n should converge to a limit; however, we cannot assert that the limit exists in a mathematical sense. In the case of the tossing of an unbiased coin, we expect $S_n/n \to 1/2$, but a conceivable outcome of the process is that the coin will keep coming up heads forever. In other words, it is possible that $S_n/n \to 1$, or that $S_n/n \to$ any number between 0 and 1, or that S_n/n has no limit at all.

As mentioned previously, in 1946 J.E. Kerrich conducted many experiments using games of chance indicating that the relative frequency does appear to approach a limit. However, if it is only most likely this would happen, any such experiment may indicate that it does. So to resolve the objection posed by Ash, in 1992 R.E. Neapolitan obtained von Mises' results concerning the rules of probability by assuming $S_m/m \to p$ only in the sense of the weak law of large numbers.

1.2.2 The Subjective/Bayesian Approach to Probability

Next we discuss another approach to probability, which is called the "subjective" or "Bayesian" approach. First we describe probabilities according to this approach; then we show how its proponents use Bayes' theorem. Next we discuss relative frequencies in light of this approach. Finally we present a brief overview of the manner in which relative frequencies are learned from data using this approach.

Subjective Probabilities

We start with an example.

Example 1.20 *If you were going to bet on an upcoming basketball game between the Chicago Bulls and the Detroit Pistons, you would want to ascertain how probable it was that the Bulls would win. This probability is certainly not a ratio, and it is not a relative frequency, or even an estimate of a relative frequency, because the game cannot be repeated many times under exactly the same conditions (actually, with your knowledge of the conditions being the same). Rather, the probability represents only your belief concerning the Bulls chances of winning.*

A probability such as the one illustrated in the previous example is called a **degree of belief** or **subjective probability**. There are a number of ways of ascertaining such probabilities. One of the most popular methods is the following, which was suggested by D. V. Lindley in 1985. This method says an individual should liken the uncertain outcome to a game of chance by considering an urn containing white and black balls. The individual should determine for what fraction of white balls the individual would be indifferent between receiving a small prize if the uncertain outcome happened (or turned out to be true) and receiving the same small prize if a white ball was drawn from the urn. That fraction is the individual's probability of the outcome. Such a probability can be constructed using binary cuts. If, for example, you were indifferent when the fraction was .75, for you $P(\{bullswin\}) = .75$. If someone else were indifferent when the fraction was .6, for that individual $P(\{bullswin\}) = .6$. Neither individual is right or wrong. Subjective probabilities are unlike ratios and relative frequencies in that they do not have objective values upon which we all must agree. Indeed, that is why they are called subjective. Neapolitan [1996] discusses the construction of subjective probabilities further.

When we are able to compute ratios or relative frequencies, the probabilities obtained agree with most individuals' beliefs. For example, most individuals would assign a subjective probability of 1/13 to the top card being an ace because they would be indifferent between receiving a small prize if it were the ace and receiving that same small prize if a white ball were drawn from an urn containing one white ball out of 13 total balls.

The following example shows a subjective probability more relevant to applications of Bayesian networks.

Example 1.21 *After examining a patient and seeing the result of the patient's chest X-ray, Dr. Gloviak decides the probability that the patient has lung cancer is .9. This probability is Dr. Gloviak's subjective probability of that outcome.*

Although a physician may use estimates of relative frequencies (such as the fraction of times individuals with lung cancer have positive chest X-rays) and experience diagnosing many similar patients to arrive at the probability, it is still assessed subjectively. If asked, Dr. Gloviak may state that her subjective probability is her estimate of the relative frequency with which patients, who have these same symptoms, have lung cancer. However, there is no reason to believe her subjective judgement will converge, as she continues to diagnose patients with these same symptoms, to the actual relative frequency with which they have lung cancer.

Using Bayes' Theorem

The subjective probability approach is called "Bayesian" because its proponents use Bayes' theorem to infer unknown probabilities from known ones. The following examples illustrates this:

Example 1.22 *Suppose Joe has a routine diagnostic chest X-ray required of all new employees at Colonial Bank, and the X-ray comes back positive for lung cancer. Joe then becomes certain he has lung cancer and panics. But should he? Without knowing the accuracy of the test, Joe really has no way of knowing how probable it is that he has lung cancer. When he discovers the test is not absolutely conclusive, he decides to investigate its accuracy and he learns that it has a false negative rate of .4 and a false positive rate of .02. We represent this accuracy as follows. First we define these random variables:*

Variable	Value	When the Variable Takes This Value
Test	*positive*	*X-ray is positive*
	negative	*X-ray is negative*
LungCancer	*present*	*Lung cancer is present*
	absent	*Lung cancer is absent*

We then have these conditional probabilities:

$$P(Test = positive|LungCancer = present) = .6$$

$$P(Test = positive|LungCancer = absent) = .02.$$

Given these probabilities, Joe feels a little better. However, he then realizes he still does not know how probable it is that he has lung cancer. That is, the probability of Joe having lung cancer is $P(LungCancer = present|Test = positive)$, and this is not one of the probabilities previously listed above. Joe finally recalls Bayes' theorem and realizes he needs yet another probability to determine the probability of his having lung cancer. That probability is $P(LungCancer = present)$, which is the probability of his having lung cancer before any information on the test results were obtained. Even though this probability is not *based on any information concerning the test results, it is based on some information. Specifically, it is based on all information (relevant to lung cancer) known about Joe before he took the test. The only relevant information about Joe, before he took the test, was that he was one of a class of employees who took the test routinely required of new employees. So, when he learns that only 1 out of every 1000 new employees has lung cancer, he assigns .001 to P(LungCancer = present). He then employs Bayes' theorem as follows:*

$$P(present|positive)$$

$$= \frac{P(positive|present)P(present)}{P(positive|present)P(present) + P(positive|absent)P(absent)}$$

$$= \frac{(.6)(.001)}{(.6)(.001) + (.02)(.999)}$$

$$= .029.$$

So Joe now feels that the probability of his having lung cancer is only about .03, and he relaxes a bit while waiting for the results of further testing.

A probability like $P(LungCancer = present)$ is called a **prior probability** because, in a particular model, it is the probability of some event prior to updating the probability of that event, within the framework of that model, using new information. Do not mistakenly think it means a probability prior to any information. A probability like $P(LungCancer = present|Test = positive)$ is called a **posterior probability** because it is the probability of an event after its prior probability has been updated, within the framework of some model, based on new information. The following example illustrates how prior probabilities can change depending on the situation we are modeling.

Example 1.23 *Now suppose Sam is having the same diagnostic chest X-ray that Joe had. However, he is having the X-ray because he has worked in the mines for 20 years, and his employers became concerned when they learned that about 10% of all such workers develop lung cancer after many years in the mines. Sam also tests positive. What is the probability he has lung cancer? Based on the information known about Sam before he took the test, we assign a prior probability of .1 to Sam having lung cancer. Again using Bayes' theorem, we conclude that $P(LungCancer = present|Test = positive) = .769$ for Sam. Poor Sam concludes it is quite likely that he has lung cancer.*

The previous two examples illustrate that a probability value is relative to one's information about an event; it is not a property of the event itself. Both Joe and Sam either do or do not have lung cancer. It could be that Joe has it and Sam does not. However, based on our information, our degree of belief (probability) that Sam has it is much greater than our degree of belief that Joe has it. When we obtain more information relative to the event (e.g., whether Joe smokes or has a family history of cancer), the probability will change.

Another example of applying Bayes' theorem follows:

Example 1.24 *Suppose the Chicago Bulls are about to play in the seventh game of the NBA finals, and I assess the probability that they will win to be .6. I also feel there is a .9 probability there will be a big crowd celebrating at my favorite restaurant that night if they do win. However, even if they lose, I feel there might be a big crowd because a lot of people may show up to lick their wounds. So I assign a probability of .3 to a big crowd if they lose. Suppose I work all day, drive straight to my restaurant without finding out the result of the game, and see a big crowd overflowing into the parking lot. I can then use Bayes' theorem to compute my conditional probability they did indeed win. It is left as an exercise to do so.*

There is a difference in the probabilities in Example 1.24 and Example 1.22. Example 1.24 involves probabilities that are not estimates of relative frequencies (similar to the situation discussed in Example 1.20), whereas Example 1.22 involves estimates of relative frequencies. A frequentist would not consider the probabilities in Example 1.24 to be probabilities at all, and therefore would not even discuss their use. A frequentist would consider the probabilities in Example 1.22 probabilities (actually relative frequencies) and would be concerned with determining estimates of these relative frequencies. However, a strict frequentist (e.g., von Mises) could not infer the probability of Joe having lung cancer using Bayes' theorem. That is, from the data used to obtain the false negative rates, false positive rate, and prior probability, a strict frequentist could only obtain estimates of the relative frequencies and confidence intervals. The frequentist could not obtain degrees of belief (subjective probabilities) in the test results and the presence of lung cancer, and then use these subjective probabilities to compute the probability of Joe having lung cancer. The frequentist could only use Bayes' theorem when all known probabilities are obtained from either ratios or huge samples. On the other hand, using a subjective approach, Joe can obtain beliefs from the observed relative frequencies, regardless of the size of the samples, and can proceed using Bayes' theorem.

Bayesians and Relative Frequencies

A statistician who uses Bayes' theorem is sometimes called a **Bayesian**. Good [1983] shows there are 46,656 different Bayesian interpretations. (He notes that von Mises' view is not one of these.) He bases this on 11 different facets of the approach on which Bayesians can differ. Briefly, there is a descriptive Bayesian interpretation which maintains that humans reason using subjective probabilities and Bayes' theorem, there is a normative Bayesian interpretation that says humans should reason that way, and there is an empirical Bayesian interpretation that says, based on data, we can update our belief concerning a relative frequency using Bayes' theorem. Mulaik et al. [1997] discuss and criticize the first two views. The techniques discussed in this text are concerned mainly with the third interpretation, which we briefly illustrated in Example 1.22. In the next subsection we discuss that view further.

Before that, we note that one of the facets is the concept of "physical probability" as developed in Section 1.2.1. The three categories for this facet are (1) assumed to exist; (2) denied; and (3) used as if they exist, but without philosophical commitment. Both Good and I are in Category 3. Briefly, in applications such as sampling individuals and determining whether they have lung cancer, a limit seems to be approached. However, an infinite sequence of sampled items only exists as an idealization. That is, the circumstances of the experiment (e.g. pollution, changes in health care, and so forth) change as time passes. Even a coin's composition changes as we toss it. In these situations, it seems philosophically difficult to maintain that a physical probability, accurate to an arbitrary number of digits, exists at any given point in time. It appears that precise relative frequencies exist in very few applications. These include applications such as the repeated drawing of a top card from a deck of cards, the estimation of the ratio in a finite population from a sample of the population (See Section 1.2.1.), and perhaps some applications in physics such as statistical mechanics. In most real-world applications the notion of a relative frequency is an idealization, which can be used as a model for a subjective approach to probability. Henceforth, in this text we speak of relative frequencies as if they exist as objective entities in nature; however, we do so with the caveat that we are in Category 3 as indicated above.

Bayesian Learning of Relative Frequencies

At the end of Section 1.2.1 we discussed how a frequentist learns something about a relative frequency from data by obtaining a confidence interval for the relative frequency. The Bayesian approach is to put a prior subjective probability distribution on the value of the relative frequency and then update that distribution based on the data. The technique will be discussed in Section 6.1. Currently, we discuss only the use of prior distributions of relative frequencies because there is some controversy concerning this matter. We illustrate the issue with the following example:

Example 1.25 *Suppose we sampled 100 American males and the average height turned out to be 4 feet. Using a confidence interval, we would become highly confident the average height of American males is close to 4 feet.*

Good [1983] says we are "sweeping our prior experience under the carpet" in order to reach the absurd conclusion in the previous example. He maintains we should instead assign a prior probability distribution to the average height based on our prior knowledge, and then we should update this distribution based on the data. On the other hand, Mulaik et al. [1997] criticize the use of prior probabilities, when he says "at the outset, subjective/personal Bayesian inference based on these subjective/personal probabilities does not give what is just the evidentiary reasons to believe in something and is unable to separate in its inference what is subjective from what is objective and evidentiary." Both authors have their points. However, it seems their points involve different circumstances. Example 1.25 showed one situation in which we would not want to sweep our prior knowledge under the carpet. As another example, suppose we see a given coin land heads five times in a row. We would not want to sweep our prior knowledge about coins under the carpet and bet according to the belief it will most likely land heads on the next toss. Rather we would want to update our prior belief with the data consisting of the five heads. Of more practical interest, consider the development of a medical expert system, which is a system used to diagnose illnesses based on symptoms. Suppose we had access to the knowledge of a renowned medical authority. We would not want to sweep the authority's knowledge about the probabilistic relationships among the domain variables under the carpet and use only information from a data base in our system. Rather we would want to develop our system based both on the authority's knowledge and what could be learned from the data base. On the other hand, suppose a pharmaceutical company is testing the effectiveness of a new drug by performing a study using subjects, and they want to communicate their result to the scientific community. The scientific community would not be interested in their prior belief concerning the drug's effectiveness, but only in what the data had to say. So in this case, even if their prior belief was that the drug was effective, it would not be acceptable to base the stated result partly on that belief.

When we obtain an updated probability distribution for a relative frequency, we can obtain, for example, a 95% probability interval for the relative frequency. The **probability interval** is the Bayesian's counterpart of the confidence interval. In Section 6.3 we discuss the computation of probability intervals, while in Section 7.2 we show that in many cases, if we assume an improper prior distribution, the two intervals are mathematically identical.

1.3 Random Variables in Statistics

Look again at Example 1.22. In that example, we referred directly to the random variables *Test* and *LungCancer* without developing a sample space on which they were functions. This is a common practice in statistics; we discuss it next.

In general, the field of **statistics** is concerned with inferring something about the probability of an event. The term **"Classical" statistics** is usually associated with the relative frequency approach to probability and uses techniques such as confidence intervals to infer something about relative frequencies. The term **"Bayesian" statistics** is usually associated with the Bayesian approach to statistics, and uses techniques such as probability intervals to infer something about relative frequencies. It also use Bayes' theorem to infer unknown probabilities of events from known probabilities of other events. This is done both in cases in which the known probabilities are estimates of relative frequencies (e.g., Example 1.22) and in cases which they are not (e.g. Example 1.24).

In statistics, the probability space is usually not developed in the order outlined in Section 1.1. That is, we do not identify a sample space, determine probabilities of elementary events, determine random variables, and then compute values in joint probability distributions. Instead, we identify random variables directly. We first discuss the meaning of random variables and probabilities in statistics and we illustrate how they are identified directly. After that, we show how a joint probability distribution can be determined without first specifying a sample space.

1.3.1   Meaning of Random Variables

Although the definition of a random variable (Definition 1.5) given in Section 1.1.4 is mathematically elegant and, in theory, pertains to all applications of probability, it is not readily apparent how it applies to the use of random variables in statistics. In this subsection and the next we develop an alternative definition that clarifies this issue. We discussed random variables from the perspective of Bayesian statistics. However, the development pertains also to their use in classical statistics.

In statistics, there is some single entity, or set of entities, which has features, the states of which we wish to determine, but which we cannot determine for certain. So we settle for determining how likely it is that a particular feature is in a particular state. An example of a single entity is an instance in which we are considering the introduction of an economically beneficial chemical which might be carcinogenic. We would want to determine the relative risk of the chemical versus its benefits. An example of a set of entities is a set of patients with similar diseases and symptoms. In this case, we would want to diagnose diseases based on symptoms.

In these applications, a random variable represents some feature of the entity being modeled, and we are uncertain as to the value of this feature. In the case of a single entity, we are uncertain as to the value of the feature for that entity, while in the case of a set of entities, we are uncertain as to the value of the feature for some members of the set. To help resolve this uncertainty, we develop probabilistic relationships among the variables. When there is a set of entities, we assume the entities in the set all have the same probabilistic relationships concerning the variables used in the model. When this is not the case, our analysis is not applicable. In the case of the chemical introduction, features may include the amount of human exposure and the carcinogenic potential. If these are our features of interest, we identify the random variables *HumanExposure* and *CarcinogenicPotential*. (For simplicity, our illustrations include only a few variables. An actual application ordinarily includes many more than this.) In the case of a set of patients, features of interest might include whether or not a disease such as lung cancer is present, whether or not manifestations of diseases such as a chest X-ray are present, and whether or not causes of diseases such as smoking are present. Given these features, we would identify the random variables *ChestXray*, *LungCancer*, and *SmokingHistory*. After identifying the random variables, we distinguish a set of mutually exclusive and exhaustive values for each of them. The possible values of a random variable are the different states that the feature can take. For example, the state of *LungCancer* could be *present* or *absent*, the state of *ChestXray* could be *positive* or *negative*, and the state of *SmokingHistory* could be *yes* or *no*.

For simplicity, we have only distinguished two possible values for each of these random variables. However, in general they could have any number of possible values or they could even be continuous. For example, we might distinguish five different levels of smoking history (one pack or more per day for at least 10 years, two packs or more per day for at least 10 years, three packs or more per day for at least 10 years, and so forth.) The specification of the random variables and their values not only must be precise enough to satisfy the requirements of the particular situation being modeled, but also must be sufficiently precise to pass the **clarity test**, which was developed by Howard in 1988. That test is as follows: Imagine a clairvoyant who knows precisely the current state of the world (or future state if the model concerns events in the future). Would the clairvoyant be able to determine unequivocally the value of the random variable? For example, in the case of the chemical introduction, if we give $HumanExposure$ the values *low* and *high*, the clarity test is not passed because we do not know what constitutes high or low. However, if we define high as when the average (over all individuals) of the individual daily average skin contact, exceeds 6 grams of material, the clarity test is passed because the clairvoyant can answer precisely whether the contact exceeds that. In the case of a medical application, if we give $SmokingHistory$ only the values *yes* and *no*, the clarity test is not passed because we do not know whether *yes* means smoking cigarettes, cigars, or something else, and we have not specified how long smoking must have occurred for the value to be *yes*. On the other hand, if we say *yes* means the patient has smoked one or more packs of cigarettes every day during the past 10 years, the clarity test is passed.

After distinguishing the possible values of the random variables (i.e., their spaces), we judge the probabilities of the random variables having their values. However, in general we do not always determine prior probabilities; nor do we determine values in a joint probability distribution of the random variables. Rather we ascertain probabilities, concerning relationships among random variables, that are accessible to us. For example, we might determine the prior probability $P(LungCancer = present)$, and the conditional probabilities $P(ChestXray = positive|LungCancer = present)$, $P(ChestXray = positive|LungCancer = absent)$, $P(LungCancer = present| SmokingHistory = yes)$, and finally $P(LungCancer = present|SmokingHistory = no)$. We would obtain these probabilities either from a physician or from data or from both. Thinking in terms of relative frequencies, $P(LungCancer = present|SmokingHistory = yes)$ can be estimated by observing individuals with a smoking history, and determining what fraction of these have lung cancer. A physician is used to judging such a probability by observing patients with a smoking history. On the other hand, one does not readily judge values in a joint probability distribution such as $P(LungCancer = present, ChestXray = positive, SmokingHistory = yes)$. If this is not apparent, just think of the situation in which there are 100 or more random variables (which there are in some applications) in the joint probability distribution. We can obtain data and think in terms of probabilistic relationships among a few random variables at a time; we do not identify the joint probabilities of several events.

As to the nature of these probabilities, consider first the introduction of the toxic chemical. The probabilities of the values of $CarcinogenicPotential$ will be based on data involving this chemical and similar ones. However, this is certainly not a repeatable experiment like a coin toss, and therefore the probabilities are not estimates of relative frequencies. They are subjective probabilities based on a careful analysis of the situation. As to the medical application involving a set of entities, the probabilities are estimates of relative frequencies involving entities in the set. Hence, they are subjective probabilities obtained from data and prior belief about the relative frequencies.

Once we judge the probabilities for a given application, we can often obtain values in a joint probability distribution of the random variables. Theorem 1.5 in Section 1.4.2 provides a way to do this when there are many variables. Presently, we illustrate the case of two variables. Suppose we identify only the random variables $LungCancer$ and $ChestXray$, and we judge the prior probability $P(LungCancer = present)$, and the conditional probabilities $P(ChestXray = positive|LungCancer = present)$ and $P(ChestXray = positive|LungCancer = absent)$. Probabilities of values in a joint probability distribution can be obtained from these probabilities using the rule for conditional probability as follows:

$$P(present,\ positive) = P(positive|present)P(present)$$

$$P(present, negative) = P(negative|present)P(present)$$

$$P(absent, positive) = P(positive|absent)P(absent)$$

$$P(absent, negative) = P(negative|absent)P(absent).$$

Note that we used our abbreviated notation. We see then that at the outset we identify random variables and their probabilistic relationships, and values in a joint probability distribution can then often be obtained from the probabilities relating the random variables. So what is the sample space? We can think of the sample space as simply being the Cartesian product of the sets of all possible values of the random variables. For example, consider again the case where we only identify the random variables $LungCancer$ and $ChestXray$, and ascertain probability values in a joint distribution as in the preceding illustration above. We can define the following sample space:

$\Omega =$

$\{(present, positive), (present, negative), (absent, positive), (absent, negative)\}.$

We can consider each random variable a function on this space that maps each tuple into the value of the random variable in the tuple. For example,

LungCancer would map (*present, positive*) and (*present, negative*) each into *present*. We then assign each elementary event the probability of its corresponding event in the joint distribution. For example, we assign

$$\hat{P}(\{(present, positive)\}) = P(LungCancer = present, ChestXray = positive).$$

It is not hard to show that this does yield a probability function on Ω and that the initially assessed prior probabilities and conditional probabilities are the probabilities they notationally represent in this probability space. (This is a special case of Theorem 1.5.)

Since random variables are actually identified first and only implicitly become functions on an implicit sample space, it seems we could develop the concept of a joint probability distribution without the explicit notion of a sample space. Indeed, we do this next. Following this development, we give a theorem showing that any such joint probability distribution is a joint probability distribution of the random variables with the variables considered as functions on an implicit sample space. Definition 1.1 (of a probability function) and Definition 1.5 (of a random variable) can therefore be considered the fundamental definitions for probability theory because they pertain both to applications in which sample spaces are directly identified and to ones in which random variables are directly identified.

1.3.2 A Definition of Random Variables for Statistics

For the use of random variables in statistics, we can define a **random variable** X as a symbol representing any one of a set of **values**, called the **space** of X. For simplicity, we will assume the space of X is countable, but the theory extends naturally to the case where it is not. For example, we could identify the random variable *LungCancer* as having the space {*present, absent*}. We use the notation $X = x$ as a primitive which is used in probability expressions. That is, $X = x$ is not defined in terms of anything else. For example, in application *LungCancer = present* means the entity being modeled has lung cancer, but mathematically it is simply a primitive which is used in probability expressions. Given this definition and primitive, we have the following direct definition of a joint probability distribution:

Definition 1.8 *Let a set of n random variables $\mathsf{V} = \{X_1, X_2, \dots, X_n\}$ be specified such that each X_i has a countably infinite space. A function, that assigns a real number $P(X_1 = x_1, X_2 = x_2, \dots, X_n = x_n)$ to every combination of values of the x_i's such that the value of x_i is chosen from the space of X_i, is called a* **joint probability distribution** *of the random variables in V if it satisfies the following conditions:*

1. For every combination of values of the x_i's,

$$0 \le P(X_1 = x_1, X_2 = x_2, \dots, X_n = x_n) \le 1.$$

2. We have

$$\sum_{x_1,x_2,\dots,x_n} P(X_1 = x_1, X_2 = x_2, \dots, X_n = x_n) = 1.$$

The notation $\sum_{x_1,x_2,\dots,x_n}$ means the sum as the variables $x_1, \dots x_n$ go through all possible values in their corresponding spaces.

Note that a joint probability distribution, obtained by defining random variables as functions on a sample space, is one way to create a joint probability distribution that satisfies this definition. However, there are other ways as the following example illustrates:

Example 1.26 Let $V = \{X, Y\}$, let X and Y have spaces $\{x1, x2\}^1$ and $\{y1, y2\}$ respectively, and let the following values be specified:

$$P(X = x1) = .2 \qquad P(Y = y1) = .3$$
$$P(X = x2) = .8 \qquad P(Y = y2) = .7.$$

Next define a joint probability distribution of X and Y as follows:

$$P(X = x1, Y = y1) = P(X = x1)P(Y = y1) = (.2)(.3) = .06$$

$$P(X = x1, Y = y2) = P(X = x1)P(Y = y2) = (.2)(.7) = .14$$

$$P(X = x2, Y = y1) = P(X = x2)P(Y = y1) = (.8)(.3) = .24$$

$$P(X = x2, Y = y2) = P(X = x2)P(Y = y2) = (.8)(.7) = .56.$$

Since the values sum to 1, this is another way of specifying a joint probability distribution according to Definition 1.8. This is how we would specify the joint distribution if we felt X and Y were independent.

Notice that our original specifications, $P(X = xi)$ and $P(Y = yi)$, notationally look like marginal distributions of the joint distribution developed in Example 1.26. However, Definition 1.8 defines only a joint probability distribution P; it does not mention anything about marginal distributions. So the values initially specified do not represent marginal distributions of our joint distribution P according to that definition alone. The following theorem enables us to consider them marginal distributions in the classical sense and therefore justifies our notation:

---

[1]We use subscripted variables X_i to denote different random variables. So we do not subcript to denote a value of a random variable. Rather we write the index next to the variable.

Theorem 1.3 *Let a set of random variables* V *be given and let a joint probability distribution of the variables in* V *be specified according to Definition 1.8. Let* Ω *be the Cartesian product of the sets of all possible values of the random variables. Assign probabilities to elementary events in* Ω *as follows:*

$$\hat{P}(\{(x_1, x_2, \dots, x_n)\}) = P(X_1 = x_1, X_2 = x_2, \dots, X_n = x_n).$$

These assignments result in a probability function on Ω *according to Definition 1.1. Furthermore, if we let* $\hat{X}_i$ *denote a function (random variable in the classical sense) on this sample space that maps each tuple in* Ω *to the value of* x_i *in that tuple, then the joint probability distribution of the* $\hat{X}_i$ *'s is the same as the joint probability distribution originally specified.*

Proof. *The proof is left as an exercise.* ∎

Example 1.27 *Suppose we directly specify a joint probability distribution of* X *and* Y, *each with space* $\{x1, x2\}$ *and* $\{y1, y2\}$, *respectively, as done in Example 1.26. That is, we specify the following probabilities:*

$$P(X = x1, Y = y1)$$
$$P(X = x1, Y = y2)$$
$$P(X = x2, Y = y1)$$
$$P(X = x2, Y = y2).$$

Next we let $\Omega = \{(x1, y1), (x1, y2), (x2, y1), (x2, y2)\}$, *and we assign*

$$\hat{P}(\{(xi, yj)\}) = P(X = xi, Y = yj).$$

Then we let $\hat{X}$ *and* $\hat{Y}$ *be functions on* Ω *defined by the following tables:*

x	y	$\hat{X}((x,y))$
x1	y1	x1
x1	y2	x1
x2	y1	x2
x2	y2	x2

x	y	$\hat{Y}((x,y))$
x1	y1	y1
x1	y2	y2
x2	y1	y1
x2	y2	y2

Theorem 1.3 says the joint probability distribution of these random variables is the same as the joint probability distribution originally specified. Let's illustrate this:

$$\begin{aligned}
\hat{P}(\hat{X} = x1, \hat{Y} = y1) &= \hat{P}(\{(x1, y1), (x1, y2)\} \cap \{(x1, y1), (x2, y1)\}) \\
&= \hat{P}(\{(x1, y1)\}) \\
&= P(X = x1, Y = y1).
\end{aligned}$$

Due to Theorem 1.3, we need no postulates for probabilities of combinations of primitives not addressed by Definition 1.8. Furthermore, we need no new definition of conditional probability for joint distributions created according to that definition. We can just postulate that both obtain values according

to the set theoretic definition of a random variable. For example, consider
Example 1.26. Due to Theorem 1.3, $\hat{P}(\hat{X} = x1)$ is simply a value in a marginal
distribution of the joint probability distribution. So its value is computed as
follows:

$$
\begin{aligned}
\hat{P}(\hat{X} = x1) &= \hat{P}(\hat{X} = x1, \hat{Y} = y1) + \hat{P}(\hat{X} = x1, \hat{Y} = y2) \\
&= P(X = x1, Y = y1) + P(X = x1, Y = y2) \\
&= P(X = x1)P(Y = y1) + P(X = x1)P(Y = y2) \\
&= P(X = x1)[P(Y = y1) + P(Y = y2)] \\
&= P(X = x1)[1] = P(X = x1),
\end{aligned}
$$

which is the value originally specified. This result is a special case of
Theorem 1.5.

Note that the specified probability values are not by necessity equal to the
probabilities they notationally represent in the marginal probability distribution. However, since we used the rule for independence to derive the joint
probability distribution from them, they are in fact equal to those values. For
example, if we had defined $P(X = x1, Y = y1) = P(X = x2)P(Y = y1)$, the
specified probability values would not be equal to the probabilities they notationally represent. Of course we would not do this. In practice, all specified
values are always the probabilities they notationally represent in the resultant
probability space $(\Omega, \hat{P})$. Since this is the case, we will no longer show carats
over P or X when referring to the probability function in this space or a random
variable on the space.

Example 1.28 *Let* $V = \{X, Y\}$, *let* X *and* Y *have spaces* $\{x1, x2\}$ *and* $\{y1, y2\}$,
respectively, and let the following values be specified:

$$
\begin{array}{ll}
P(X = x1) = .2 & P(Y = y1|X = x1) = .3 \\
P(X = x2) = .8 & P(Y = y2|X = x1) = .7
\end{array}
$$

$$
\begin{array}{l}
P(Y = y1|X = x2) = .4 \\
P(Y = y2|X = x2) = .6.
\end{array}
$$

Next define a joint probability distribution of X *and* Y *as follows:*

$$P(X = x1, Y = y1) = P(Y = y1|X = x1)P(X = x1) = (.3)(.2) = .06$$

$$P(X = x1, Y = y2) = P(Y = y2|X = x1)P(X = x1) = (.7)(.2) = .14$$

$$P(X = x2, Y = y1) = P(Y = y1|X = x2)P(X = x2) = (.4)(.8) = .32$$

$$P(X = x2, Y = y2) = P(Y = y2|X = x2)P(X = x2) = (.6)(.8) = .48.$$

*Since the values sum to 1, this is another way of specifying a joint probability
distribution according to Definition 1.8. As we saw in Example 1.28 on page 34,
this is the way the values are specified in simple applications of Bayes' theorem.*

In the remainder of this text, we will create joint probability distributions
using Definition 1.8.

1.4 Large Instances / Bayesian Networks

Bayesian inference is fairly simple when it involves only two related variables as in Example 1.22. However, it becomes much more complex when we want to do inference with many related variables. We address this problem next. After discussing the difficulties inherent in representing large instances and in doing inference when there are a large number of variables, we describe a relationship, called the Markov condition, between graphs and probability distributions. Then we introduce Bayesian networks, which exploit the Markov condition in order to represent large instances efficiently.

1.4.1 The Difficulties Inherent in Large Instances

Recall the situation, discussed at the beginning of this chapter, in which several features (variables) are related through inference chains. We introduced the following example of this situation: Whether or not an individual has a history of smoking has a direct influence both on whether or not that individual has bronchitis and on whether or not that individual has lung cancer. In turn, the presence or absence of each of these features has a direct influence on whether or not the individual experiences fatigue. Also, the presence or absence of lung cancer has a direct influence on whether or not a chest X-ray is positive. We noted that, in this situation, we would want to do probabilistic inference involving features that are not related via a direct influence. We would want to determine, for example, the conditional probabilities both of having bronchitis and of having lung cancer when it is known that an individual smokes, is fatigued, and has a positive chest X-ray. Yet bronchitis has no influence on whether a chest X-ray is positive. Therefore, this conditional probability cannot readily be computed using a simple application of Bayes' theorem. So how could we compute it? Next we develop a straightforward algorithm for doing so, but we will show it has little practical value. First we define some notation. As done previously, we will denote random variables using capital letters such as X and use the corresponding lower case letters $x1$, $x2$, and so forth, to denote the values in the space of X. In the current example, we define the random variables that follow:

Variable	Value	When the Variable Takes this Value
H	$h1$	There is a history of smoking
	$h2$	There is no history of smoking
B	$b1$	Bronchitis is present
	$b2$	Bronchitis is absent
L	$l1$	Lung cancer is present
	$l2$	Lung cancer is absent
F	$f1$	Fatigue is present
	$f2$	Fatigue is absent
C	$c1$	Chest X-ray is positive
	$c2$	Chest X-ray is negative

Note that we presented this same table at the beginning of this chapter, but we called the random variables "features." We had not yet defined the term "random variable" at that point, so we used the informal term "feature." If we knew the joint probability distribution of these five variables, we could compute the conditional probability of an individual having bronchitis given that the individual smokes, is fatigued, and has a positive chest X-ray as follows:

$$P(b1|h1, f1, c1) = \frac{P(b1, h1, f1, c1)}{P(h1, f1, c1)} = \frac{\sum_{l} P(b1, h1, f1, c1, l)}{\sum_{b,l} P(b, h1, f1, c1, l)}, \qquad (1.6)$$

where $\sum_{b,l}$ means the sum as b and l go through all their possible values. There are a number of problems here. First, as noted previously, the values in the joint probability distribution are ordinarily not readily accessible. Second, there are an exponential number of terms in the sums in Equality 1.6. That is, there are 2^2 terms in the sum in the denominator, and, if there were 100 variables in the application, there would be 2^{97} terms in that sum. So, in the case of a large instance, even if we had some means of eliciting the values in the joint probability distribution, using Equality 1.6 simply requires determining too many such values and doing too many calculations with them. We see that this method has no practical value when the instance is large.

Bayesian networks address the problems of (1) representing the joint probability distribution of a large number of random variables and (2) doing Bayesian inference with these variables. Before introducing them in Section 1.4.3, we need to discuss the Markov condition.

1.4.2   The Markov Condition

First let's review some graph theory. Recall that a **directed graph** is a pair (V, E), where V is a finite, nonempty set whose elements are called **nodes** (or vertices), and E is a set of ordered pairs of distinct elements of V. Elements of E are called **edges** (or arcs), and if $(X, Y) \in E$, we say there is an edge from X to Y and that X and Y are each **incident** to the edge. If there is an edge from X to Y or from Y to X, we say X and Y are **adjacent**. Suppose we have a set of nodes $\{X_1, X_2, \ldots X_k\}$, where $k \geq 2$, such $(X_{i-1}, X_i) \in E$ for $2 \leq i \leq k$. We call the set of edges connecting the k nodes a **path** from X_1 to X_k, and we denote the path as $[X_1, X_2, \ldots, X_k]$ The nodes $X_2, \ldots X_{k-1}$ are called **interior nodes** on path $[X_1, X_2, \ldots X_k]$. The **subpath** of path $[X_1, X_2, \ldots X_k]$ from X_i to X_j is the path $[X_i, X_{i+1}, \ldots X_j]$ where $1 \leq i < j \leq k$. A **directed cycle** is a path from a node to itself. A **simple path** is a path containing no subpaths which are directed cycles. A directed graph $\mathbb{G}$ is called a directed acyclic graph (**DAG**) if it contains no directed cycles. Given a DAG $\mathbb{G} = (V, E)$ and nodes X and Y in V, Y is called a **parent** of X if there is an edge from Y to X, Y is called a **descendent** of X and X is called an **ancestor** of Y if there is a path from X to Y, and Y is called a **nondescendent** of X if Y is not a descendent of X. Note that in this text X is not considered a descendent of X because we require $k \geq 2$ in the definition of a path. Some texts say there is an empty path from X to X.

We can now state the following definition:

Definition 1.9 *Suppose we have a joint probability distribution P of the random variables in some set V and a DAG $\mathbb{G} = (\mathsf{V}, \mathsf{E})$. We say that $(\mathbb{G}, P)$ satisfies the **Markov condition** if for each variable $X \in \mathsf{V}$, $\{X\}$ is conditionally independent of the set of all its nondescendents given the set of all its parents. Using the notation established in Section 1.1.4, this means that if we denote the sets of parents and nondescendents of X by PA_X and ND_X respectively, then*

$$I_P(\{X\}, \mathsf{ND}_X | \mathsf{PA}_X).$$

When $(\mathbb{G}, P)$ satisfies the Markov condition, we say $\mathbb{G}$ and P satisfy the Markov condition with each other.

If X is a root, then its parent set PA_X is empty. So in this case the Markov condition means $\{X\}$ is independent of ND_X. That is, $I_P(\{X\}, \mathsf{ND}_X)$. It is not hard to show that $I_P(\{X\}, \mathsf{ND}_X | \mathsf{PA}_X)$ implies $I_P(\{X\}, \mathsf{B} | \mathsf{PA}_X)$ for any $\mathsf{B} \subseteq \mathsf{ND}_X$. It is left as an exercise to do this. Notice that $\mathsf{PA}_X \subseteq \mathsf{ND}_X$. So we could define the Markov condition by saying that X must be conditionally independent of $\mathsf{ND}_X - \mathsf{PA}_X$ given PA_X. However, it is standard to define it as we did previously. When discussing the Markov condition relative to a particular distribution and DAG (as in the following examples), we show just the conditional independence of X and $\mathsf{ND}_X - \mathsf{PA}_X$.

Example 1.29 *Let Ω be the set of objects in Figure 1.2 on page 8, and let P assign a probability of $1/13$ to each object. Let random variables V, S, and C be as defined as in Example 1.17 on page 16. That is, they are defined as follows:*

Variable	Value	Outcomes Mapped to this Value
V	$v1$	*All objects containing a "1"*
	$v2$	*All objects containing a "2"*
S	$s1$	*All square objects*
	$s2$	*All round objects*
C	$c1$	*All black objects*
	$c2$	*All white objects*

Then, as shown in Example 1.17, $I_P(\{V\}, \{S\} | \{C\})$. Therefore, $(\mathbb{G}, P)$ satisfies the Markov condition if $\mathbb{G}$ is the DAG in Figure 1.3 (a), (b), or (c). However, $(\mathbb{G}, P)$ does not satisfy the Markov condition if $\mathbb{G}$ is the DAG in Figure 1.3 (d) because $I_P(\{V\}, \{S\})$ is not the case.

Example 1.30 *Consider the DAG $\mathbb{G}$ in Figure 1.4. If $(\mathbb{G}, P)$ satisfied the Markov condition for some probability distribution P, we would have the following conditional independencies:*

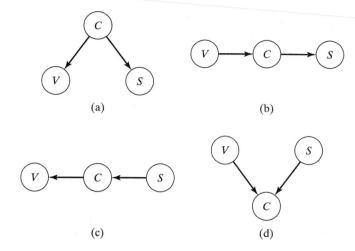

Figure 1.3: The probability distribution in Example 1.29 satisfies the Markov condition only with the DAGs in (a), (b), and (c).

Node	PA	Conditional Independency
C	$\{L\}$	$I_P(\{C\},\{H,B,F\}|\{L\})$
B	$\{H\}$	$I_P(\{B\},\{L,C\}|\{H\})$
F	$\{B,L\}$	$I_P(\{F\},\{H,C\}|\{B,L\})$
L	$\{H\}$	$I_P(\{L\},\{B\}|\{H\})$

Recall from Section 1.4.1 that the number of terms in a joint probability distribution is exponential in terms of the number of variables. So, in the case of a large instance, we could not fully describe the joint distribution by determining each of its values directly. Herein lies one of the powers of the Markov condition. Theorem 1.4, which follows shortly, shows that if $(\mathbb{G}, P)$ satisfies the Markov condition, then P equals the product of its conditional probability distributions of all nodes given values of their parents in $\mathbb{G}$, whenever these conditional distributions exist. After proving this theorem, we discuss

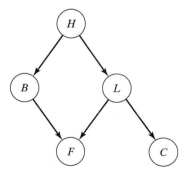

Figure 1.4: A DAG illustrating the Markov condition.

how this means we often need to ascertain far fewer values than if we had to determine all values in the joint distribution directly. Before proving it, we illustrate what it means for a joint distribution to equal the product of its conditional distributions of all nodes given values of their parents in a DAG $\mathbb{G}$. This would be the case for a joint probability distribution P of the variables in the DAG in Figure 1.4 if, for all values of f, c, b, l, and h,

$$P(f, c, b, l, h) = P(f|b, l)P(c|l)P(b|h)P(l|h)P(h), \tag{1.7}$$

whenever the conditional probabilities on the right exist. Notice that if one of them does not exist for some combination of the values of the variables, then $P(b, l) = 0$ or $P(l) = 0$ or $P(h) = 0$, which implies $P(f, c, b, l, h) = 0$ for that combination of values. However, there are cases in which $P(f, c, b, l, h) = 0$ and the conditional probabilities still exist. For example, this would be the case if all the conditional probabilities on the right existed and $P(f|b, l) = 0$ for some combination of values of f, b, and l. So Equality 1.7 must hold for all nonzero values of the joint probability distribution plus some zero values.

We now state the theorem:

Theorem 1.4 *If $(\mathbb{G}, P)$ satisfies the Markov condition, then P is equal to the product of its conditional distributions of all nodes given values of their parents, whenever these conditional distributions exist.*

Proof. *We prove the case where P is discrete. Order the nodes so that if Y is a descendent of Z, then Y follows Z in the ordering. Such an ordering is called an **ancestral ordering**. Examples of such an ordering for the DAG in Figure 1.4 are $[H, L, B, C, F]$ and $[H, B, L, F, C]$. Let $X_1, X_2, \ldots, X_n$ be the resultant ordering. For a given set of values of $x_1, x_2, \ldots, x_n$, let pa_i be the subset of these values containing the values of X_i's parents. We need to show that whenever $P(\mathsf{pa}_i) \neq 0$ for $1 \leq i \leq n$,*

$$P(x_n, x_{n-1}, \ldots, x_1) = P(x_n|\mathsf{pa}_n)P(x_{n-1}|\mathsf{pa}_{n-1}) \cdots P(x_1|\mathsf{pa}_1).$$

We show this by using induction on the number of variables in the network. Assume, for some combination of values of the x_i's, that $P(\mathsf{pa}_i) \neq 0$ for $1 \leq i \leq n$.

INDUCTION BASE: *Since PA_1 is empty,*

$$P(x_1) = P(x_1|\mathsf{pa}_1).$$

INDUCTION HYPOTHESIS: *Suppose for this combination of values of the x_i's that*

$$P(x_i, x_{i-1}, \ldots, x_1) = P(x_i|\mathsf{pa}_i)P(x_{i-1}|\mathsf{pa}_{i-1}) \cdots P(x_1|\mathsf{pa}_1).$$

INDUCTION STEP: *We need to show for this combination of values of the x_i's that*

$$P(x_{i+1}, x_i, \ldots, x_1) = P(x_{i+1}|\mathsf{pa}_{i+1})P(x_i|\mathsf{pa}_i) \cdots P(x_1|\mathsf{pa}_1). \tag{1.8}$$

There are two cases:

CASE 1: *For this combination of values*

$$P(x_i, x_{i-1}, \dots, x_1) = 0. \tag{1.9}$$

Clearly, Equality 1.9 implies

$$P(x_{i+1}, x_i, \dots, x_1) = 0.$$

Furthermore, due to Equality 1.9 and the induction hypothesis, there is some k, where $1 \le k \le i$, such that $P(x_k|\mathsf{pa}_k) = 0$. So Equality 1.8 holds.

CASE 2: *For this combination of values*

$$P(x_i, x_{i-1}, \dots, x_1) \ne 0.$$

In this case,

$$
\begin{aligned}
P(x_{i+1}, x_i, \dots, x_1) &= P(x_{i+1}|x_i, \dots, x_1)P(x_i, \dots, x_1) \\
&= P(x_{i+1}|\mathsf{pa}_{i+1})P(x_i, \dots, x_1) \\
&= P(x_{i+1}|\mathsf{pa}_{i+1})P(x_i|\mathsf{pa}_i) \cdots P(x_1|\mathsf{pa}_1).
\end{aligned}
$$

The first equality is due to the rule for conditional probability, the second is due to the Markov condition and the fact that $X_1, \dots X_i$ are all nondescendents of X_{i+1}, and the last is due to the induction hypothesis. ∎

Example 1.31 *Recall that the joint probability distribution in Example 1.29 satisfies the Markov condition with the DAG in Figure 1.3 (a). Therefore, owing to Theorem 1.4,*

$$P(v, s, c) = P(v|c)P(s|c)p(c), \tag{1.10}$$

and we need only determine the conditional distributions on the right in Equality 1.10 to uniquely determine the values in the joint distribution. We illustrate that this is the case for $v1$, $s1$, and $c1$:

$$P(v1, s1, c1) = P(\mathsf{One} \cap \mathsf{Square} \cap \mathsf{Black}) = \frac{2}{13}$$

$$
\begin{aligned}
P(v1|c1)P(s1|c1)P(c1) &= P(\mathsf{One}|\mathsf{Black}) \times P(\mathsf{Square}|\mathsf{Black}) \times P(\mathsf{Black}) \\
&= \frac{1}{3} \times \frac{2}{3} \times \frac{9}{13} = \frac{2}{13}.
\end{aligned}
$$

Figure 1.5 shows the DAG along with the conditional distributions.

The joint probability distribution in Example 1.29 also satisfies the Markov condition with the DAGs in Figures 1.3 (b) and (c). Therefore, the probability

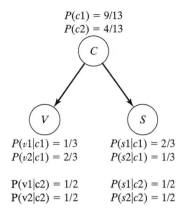

$P(c1) = 9/13$
$P(c2) = 4/13$

C

V   S

$P(v1|c1) = 1/3$ $P(s1|c1) = 2/3$
$P(v2|c1) = 2/3$ $P(s2|c1) = 1/3$

$P(v1|c2) = 1/2$ $P(s1|c2) = 1/2$
$P(v2|c2) = 1/2$ $P(s2|c2) = 1/2$

Figure 1.5: The probability distribution discussed in Example 1.31 is equal to the product of these conditional distributions.

distribution in that example equals the product of the conditional distributions for each of them. You should verify this directly.

Theorem 1.4 often enables us to reduce the problem of determining a huge number of probability values to that of determining relatively few. The number of values in the joint distribution is exponential in terms of the number of variables. However, each of these values is uniquely determined by the conditional distributions (due to the theorem), and if each node in the DAG does not have too many children, there are not many values in these distributions. For example, if each variable has two possible values and each node has at most one parent, we would need to ascertain less than $2n$ probability values to determine the conditional distributions when the DAG contains n nodes. On the other hand, we would need to ascertain $2^n - 1$ values to determine the joint probability distribution directly. In general, if each variable has two possible values and each node has at most k parents, we need to ascertain less than $2^k n$ values to determine the conditional distributions. So if k is not large, we have a manageable number of values.

Something may seem amiss to you. In Example 1.29, we started with an underlying sample space and probability function, specified some random variables, and showed that if P is the probability distribution of these variables and $\mathbb{G}$ is the DAG in Figure 1.3 (a), then $(P, \mathbb{G})$ satisfies the Markov condition. We can therefore apply Theorem 1.4 to conclude we need only determine the conditional distributions of the variables for that DAG to find any value in the joint distribution. We illustrated this in Example 1.31. However, as discussed in Section 1.3, in application we do not ordinarily specify an underlying sample space and probability function from which we can compute conditional distributions. Rather, we identify random variables and values in conditional distributions directly. For example, in an application involving the diagnosis of lung cancer, we identify variables like *SmokingHistory*, *LungCancer*, and *ChestXray*, and probabilities such as $P(SmokingHistory =$

yes), $P(LungCancer = present|SmokingHistory = yes)$, and $P(ChestXray = positive|\ LungCancer = present)$. How do we know the product of these conditional distributions is a joint distribution at all, much less one satisfying the Markov condition with some DAG? Theorem 1.4 tells us only that if we start with a joint distribution satisfying the Markov condition with some DAG, the values in that joint distribution will be given by the product of the conditional distributions. However, we must work in reverse. We must start with the conditional distributions and then be able to conclude the product of these distributions is a joint distribution satisfying the Markov condition with some DAG. The theorem that follows enables us to do just that.

Theorem 1.5 *Let a DAG $\mathbb{G}$ be given in which each node is a random variable, and let a discrete conditional probability distribution of each node given values of its parents in $\mathbb{G}$ be specified. Then the product of these conditional distributions yields a joint probability distribution P of the variables, and $(\mathbb{G}, P)$ satisfies the Markov condition.*

Proof. *Order the nodes according to an ancestral ordering. Let $X_1, X_2, \ldots, X_n$ be the resultant ordering. Next define*

$$P(x_1, x_2, \ldots, x_n) = P(x_n|\mathsf{pa}_n)P(x_{n-1}|\mathsf{pa}_{n-1}) \cdots P(x_2|\mathsf{pa}_2)P(x_1|\mathsf{pa}_1),$$

where PA_i is the set of parents of X_i in $\mathbb{G}$ and $P(x_i|\mathsf{pa}_i)$ is the specified conditional probability distribution. First we show this does indeed yield a joint probability distribution. Clearly, $0 \le P(x_1, x_2, \ldots x_n) \le 1$ for all values of the variables. Therefore, to show we have a joint distribution, Definition 1.8 and Theorem 1.3 imply we need only show that the sum of $P(x_1, x_2, \ldots x_n)$, as the variables range through all their possible values, is equal to one. To that end,

$$\sum_{x_1}\sum_{x_2} \cdots \sum_{x_{n-1}}\sum_{x_n} P(x_1, x_2, \ldots, x_n)$$

$$= \sum_{x_1}\sum_{x_2} \cdots \sum_{x_{n-1}}\sum_{x_n} P(x_n|\mathsf{pa}_n)P(x_{n-1}|\mathsf{pa}_{n-1}) \cdots P(x_2|\mathsf{pa}_2)P(x_1|\mathsf{pa}_1)$$

$$= \sum_{x_1}\left[\sum_{x_2}\left[\cdots \sum_{x_{n-1}}\left[\sum_{x_n} P(x_n|\mathsf{pa}_n)\right]P(x_{n-1}|\mathsf{pa}_{n-1}) \cdots \right]P(x_2|\mathsf{pa}_2)\right]P(x_1|\mathsf{pa}_1)$$

$$= \sum_{x_1}\left[\sum_{x_2}\left[\cdots \sum_{x_{n-1}} [1]P(x_{n-1}|\mathsf{pa}_{n-1}) \cdots \right]P(x_2|\mathsf{pa}_2)\right]P(x_1|\mathsf{pa}_1)$$

$$= \sum_{x_1}\left[\sum_{x_2}[\cdots 1 \cdots]P(x_2|\mathsf{pa}_2)\right]P(x_1|\mathsf{pa}_1)$$

$$= \sum_{x_1} [1]\, P(x_1|\mathsf{pa}_1) = 1.$$

It is left as an exercise to show that the specified conditional distributions are the conditional distributions they notationally represent in the joint distribution.

Finally, we show the Markov condition is satisfied. To do this, we need to show, for $1 \leq k \leq n$, that whenever $P(\mathsf{pa}_k) \neq 0$, if $P(\mathsf{nd}_k|\mathsf{pa}_k) \neq 0$ and $P(x_k|\mathsf{pa}_k) \neq 0$ then $P(x_k|\mathsf{nd}_k, \mathsf{pa}_k) = P(x_k|\mathsf{pa}_k)$, where ND_k is the set of non-descendents of X_k in $\mathbb{G}$. Since $\mathsf{PA}_k \subseteq \mathsf{ND}_k$, we need only show $P(x_k|\mathsf{nd}_k) = P(x_k|\mathsf{pa}_k)$.

First, for a given k, order the nodes so that all and only nondescendents of X_k precede X_k in the ordering. Note that this ordering depends on k, whereas the ordering in the first part of the proof does not. Clearly, then,

$$\mathsf{ND}_k = \{X_1, X_2, \dots, X_{k-1}\}.$$

Let

$$\mathsf{D}_k = \{X_{k+1}, X_{k+2}, \dots, X_n\}.$$

In what follows, $\sum_{\mathsf{d}_k}$ means the sum as the variables in d_k go through all their possible values. Furthermore, notation such as $\hat{x}_k$ means the variable has a particular value; notation such as $\hat{\mathsf{nd}}_k$ means all variables in the set have particular values; and notation such as pa_n means some variables in the set may not have particular values. We have

$$
\begin{aligned}
P(\hat{x}_k|\hat{\mathsf{nd}}_k) &= \frac{P(\hat{x}_k, \hat{\mathsf{nd}}_k)}{P(\hat{\mathsf{nd}}_k)} \\[2mm]
&= \frac{\displaystyle\sum_{\mathsf{d}_k} P(\hat{x}_1, \hat{x}_2, \dots, \hat{x}_k, x_{k+1}, \dots, x_n)}{\displaystyle\sum_{\mathsf{d}_k \cup \{x_k\}} P(\hat{x}_1, \hat{x}_2, \dots, \hat{x}_{k-1}, x_k, \dots, x_n)} \\[2mm]
&= \frac{\displaystyle\sum_{\mathsf{d}_k} P(x_n|\mathsf{pa}_n) \cdots P(x_{k+1}|\mathsf{pa}_{k+1}) P(\hat{x}_k|\hat{\mathsf{pa}}_k) \cdots P(\hat{x}_1|\hat{\mathsf{pa}}_1)}{\displaystyle\sum_{\mathsf{d}_k \cup \{x_k\}} P(x_n|\mathsf{pa}_n) \cdots P(x_k|\mathsf{pa}_k) P(\hat{x}_{k-1}|\hat{\mathsf{pa}}_{k-1}) \cdots P(\hat{x}_1|\hat{\mathsf{pa}}_1)} \\[2mm]
&= \frac{P(\hat{x}_k|\hat{\mathsf{pa}}_k) \cdots P(\hat{x}_1|\hat{\mathsf{pa}}_1) \displaystyle\sum_{\mathsf{d}_k} P(x_n|\mathsf{pa}_n) \cdots P(x_{k+1}|\mathsf{pa}_{k+1})}{P(\hat{x}_{k-1}|\hat{\mathsf{pa}}_{k-1}) \cdots P(\hat{x}_1|\hat{\mathsf{pa}}_1) \displaystyle\sum_{\mathsf{d}_k \cup \{x_k\}} P(x_n|\mathsf{pa}_n) \cdots P(x_k|\mathsf{pa}_k)} \\[2mm]
&= \frac{P(\hat{x}_k|\hat{\mathsf{pa}}_k)\,[1]}{[1]} = P(\hat{x}_k|\hat{\mathsf{pa}}_k).
\end{aligned}
$$

In the second-to-last step, the sums are each equal to unity for the following reason. Each is a sum of a product of conditional probability distributions specified for a DAG. In the case of the numerator, that DAG is the subgraph of our original DAG $\mathbb{G}$, consisting of the variables in D_k, and in the case of the denominator, it is the subgraph consisting of the variables in $\mathsf{D}_k \cup \{X_k\}$. Therefore, the fact that each sum equals unity follows from the first part of this proof. ∎

Notice that the theorem requires that specified conditional distributions be discrete. Often in the case of continuous distributions it still holds. For example, it holds for the Gaussian distributions introduced in Section 4.1.3. However, in

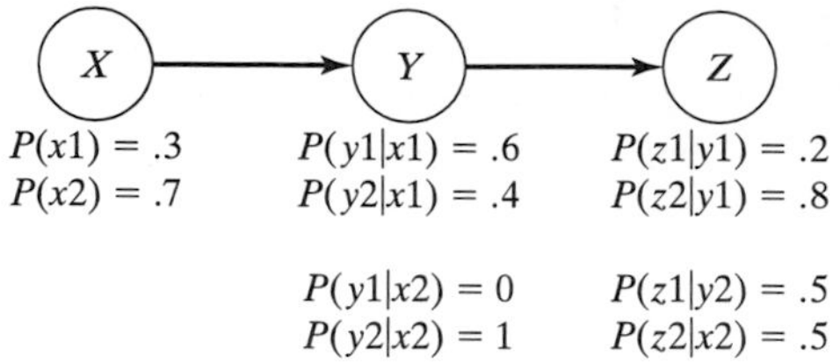

$$P(x1) = .3 \qquad P(y1|x1) = .6 \qquad P(z1|y1) = .2$$
$$P(x2) = .7 \qquad P(y2|x1) = .4 \qquad P(z2|y1) = .8$$

$$P(y1|x2) = 0 \qquad P(z1|y2) = .5$$
$$P(y2|x2) = 1 \qquad P(z2|y2) = .5$$

Figure 1.6: A DAG containing random variables, along with specified conditional distributions.

general, it does not hold for all continuous conditional distributions. See Dawid and Studeny [1999] for an example in which no joint distribution having the specified distributions as conditionals even exists.

Example 1.32 *Suppose we specify the DAG $\mathbb{G}$ shown in Figure 1.6, along with the conditional distributions shown in that figure. According to Theorem 1.5,*

$$P(x, y, z) = P(z|y)P(y|x)P(x)$$

satisfies the Markov condition with $\mathbb{G}$.

Note that the proof of Theorem 1.5 does not require that values in the specified conditional distributions be nonzero. The next example shows what can happen when we specify some zero values.

Example 1.33 *Consider first the DAG and specified conditional distributions in Figure 1.6. Because we have specified a zero conditional probability, namely $P(y1|x2)$, there are events in the joint distribution with zero probability. For example,*

$$P(x2, y1, z1) = P(z1|y1)P(y1|x2)P(x2) = (.2)(0)(.7) = 0.$$

However, there is no event with zero probability that is a conditioning event in one of the specified conditional distributions. That is, $P(x1)$, $P(x2)$, $P(y1)$, and $P(y2)$ are all nonzero. So the specified conditional distributions all exist.

Consider next the DAG and specified conditional distributions in Figure 1.7. We have

$$\begin{aligned} P(x1, y1) &= P(x1, y1|w1)P(w1) + P(x1, y1|w2)P(w2) \\ &= P(x1|w1)P(y1|w1)P(w1) + P(x1|w2)P(y1|w2)P(w2) \\ &= (0)(.8)(.1) + (.6)(0)(.9) = 0. \end{aligned}$$

The event $x1, y1$ is a conditioning event in one of the specified distributions, namely $P(zi|x1, y1)$, but it has zero probability, which means we can't condition on it. This poses no problem; it simply means we have specified some meaningless values, namely, $P(zi|x1, y1)$. The Markov condition is still satisfied because $P(z|w, x, y) = P(z|x, y)$ whenever $P(x, y) \neq 0$. (See the definition of conditional independence for sets of random variables in Section 1.1.4.)

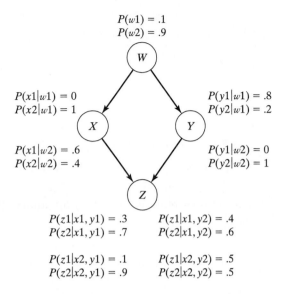

$P(w1) = .1$
$P(w2) = .9$

$P(x1|w1) = 0$
$P(x2|w1) = 1$

$P(y1|w1) = .8$
$P(y2|w1) = .2$

$P(x1|w2) = .6$
$P(x2|w2) = .4$

$P(y1|w2) = 0$
$P(y2|w2) = 1$

$P(z1|x1, y1) = .3$
$P(z2|x1, y1) = .7$

$P(z1|x1, y2) = .4$
$P(z2|x1, y2) = .6$

$P(z1|x2, y1) = .1$
$P(z2|x2, y1) = .9$

$P(z1|x2, y2) = .5$
$P(z2|x2, y2) = .5$

Figure 1.7: The event $x1, y1$ has 0 probability.

1.4.3 Bayesian Networks

Let P be a joint probability distribution of the random variables in some set
V, and $\mathbb{G} = (V, E)$ be a DAG. We call $(\mathbb{G}, P)$ a **Bayesian network** if $(\mathbb{G}, P)$
satisfies the Markov condition. Owing to Theorem 1.4, P is the product of its
conditional distributions in $\mathbb{G}$, and this is the way P is always represented in
a Bayesian network. Furthermore, owing to Theorem 1.5, if we specify a DAG
$\mathbb{G}$ and any discrete conditional distributions (and many continuous ones), we
obtain a Bayesian network. This is the way Bayesian networks are constructed
in practice. Figures 1.5, 1.6, and 1.7 all show Bayesian networks.

Example 1.34 *Figure 1.8 shows a Bayesian network containing the probability
distribution discussed in Example 1.22 on page 23.*

Example 1.35 *Recall the objects in Figure 1.2 on page 8 and the resultant joint
probability distribution P discussed in Example 1.29 on page 37. Example 1.31
developed a Bayesian network (namely the one in Figure 1.5) containing that
distribution. Figure 1.9 shows another Bayesian network whose conditional distributions are obtained from P. Does this Bayesian network contain P? No
it does not. Since P does not satisfy the Markov condition with the DAG in
that figure, there is no reason to suspect P would be the product of the conditional distributions in that DAG. It is a simple matter to verify that indeed it
is not. So, although the Bayesian network in Figure 1.9 contains a probability
distribution, it is not P.*

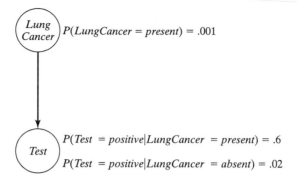

Figure 1.8: A Bayesian network representing the probability distribution discussed in Example 1.22.

Example 1.36 *Recall the situation discussed at the beginning of this section where we were concerned with the joint probability distribution of smoking history (H), bronchitis (B), lung cancer (L), fatigue (F), and chest X-ray (C). Figure 1.1, which appears again as Figure 1.10, shows a Bayesian network containing those variables in which the conditional distributions were estimated from actual data.*

Does the Bayesian network in the previous example contain the actual relative frequency distribution of the variables? Example 1.35 illustrates that, if we develop a Bayesian network from an arbitrary DAG and the conditionals of a probability distribution P relative to that DAG, in general the resultant Bayesian network does not contain P. Notice that, in Figure 1.10 we constructed the DAG using causal edges. For example, there is an edge from H to L because smoking causes lung cancer. In the next section, we argue that if we construct a DAG using causal edges, we often have a DAG that satisfies the Markov condition with the relative frequency distribution of the variables. Given this, owing to Theorem 1.4, the relative frequency distribution of the variables in Figure 1.10 should satisfy the Markov condition with the DAG in that

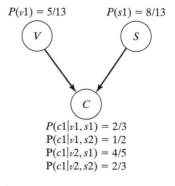

Figure 1.9: A Bayesian network.

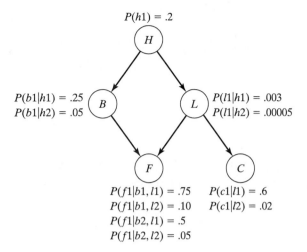

Figure 1.10: A Bayesian network. Each variable has only two values; so the probability of only one is shown.

figure. However, the situation is different than our urn example (Examples 1.29 and 1.31). Even if the values in the conditional distribution in Figure 1.10 are obtained from relative frequency data, they will only be estimates of the actual relative frequencies. Therefore, the resultant joint distribution is a different joint distribution than the joint relative frequency distribution of the variables. What distribution is it? It is our joint subjective probability distribution P of the variables obtained from our beliefs concerning conditional independencies among the variables (the structure of the DAG $\mathbb{G}$) and relative frequency data. Theorem 1.5 tells us that in the discrete case and in many continuous cases $(\mathbb{G}, P)$ satisfies the Markov condition and is therefore a Bayesian network. Note, that if we are correct about the conditional independencies, we will have convergence to the actual relative frequency distribution.

1.4.4 A Large Bayesian Network

So far in this section, we introduced Bayesian networks and we demonstrated their application using small textbook examples. To illustrate their practical use, we close by briefly discussing a large-scale Bayesian network used in a system called NasoNet.

NasoNet, Galán et al. [2002] is a system that performs diagnosis and prognosis of nasopharyngeal cancer, which is cancer involving the nasal passages. The Bayesian network used in NasoNet contains 15 nodes associated with tumors confined to the nasopharynx, 23 nodes representing the spread of tumors to nasopharyngeal surrounding sites, 4 nodes concerning distant metastases, 4 nodes indicating abnormal lymph nodes, 11 nodes expressing nasopharyngeal hemorrhages or infections, and 50 nodes representing symptoms or syndromes

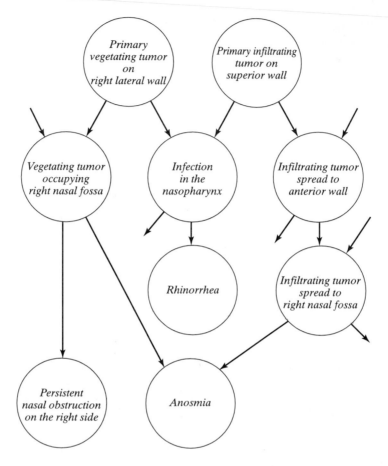

Figure 1.11: Part of the Bayesian network in NasoNet.

(combinations of symptoms). Figure 1.11 shows a portion of the Bayesian network. The feature shown in each node has a value of either present or absent.

NasoNet models the evolution of nasopharyngeal cancer in such a way that each arc represents a causal relation between the parent and the child. For example, in Figure 1.11 the presence of infection in the nasopharynx may cause rhinorrhea (excessive mucous secretion from the nose). The next section discusses why constructing a DAG with causal edges should often yield a Bayesian network.

1.5   Creating Bayesian Networks Using Causal Edges

Given a set of random variables V, if for every $X, Y \in V$ we draw an edge from X to Y if and only if X is a direct cause of Y relative to V, we call the resultant DAG a **causal DAG**. In this section, we illustrate why we feel the joint probability (relative frequency) distribution of the variables in a causal DAG often satisfies the Markov condition with that DAG, which means we can construct a Bayesian network by creating a causal DAG. Furthermore, we explain what we mean by "X is a direct cause of Y relative to V" (at least for one definition of causation). Before doing this, we first review the concept of causation and a method of determining causal influences.

1.5.1 Ascertaining Causal Influences Using Manipulation

Some of what follows is based on a similar discussion in Cooper [1999]. One dictionary definition of a cause is "the one, such as a person, an event, or a condition, that is responsible for an action or a result." Although useful, this simple definition is certainly not the last word on the concept of causation, which has been wrangled about philosophically for centuries (See e.g., Eells [1991], Hume [1748], Piaget [1966], Salmon [1994], and Spirtes et al. [1993, 2000].). The definition does, however, shed light on an **operational** method for identifying causal relationships. That is, if the action of making variable X take some value sometimes changes the value taken by variable Y, then we assume X is responsible for sometimes changing Y's value, and we conclude X is a cause of Y. More formally, we say we **manipulate** X when we force X to take some value, and we say X **causes** Y if there is some manipulation of X that leads to a change in the probability distribution of Y. We assume that if manipulating X leads to a change in the probability distribution of Y, then X obtaining a value by any means whatsoever also leads to a change in the probability distribution of Y. So we assume causes and their effects are statistically correlated. However, as we shall discuss soon, variables can be correlated without one causing the other. A manipulation consists of a randomized controlled experiment (**RCE**) using some specific population of entities (e.g., individuals with chest pain) in some specific context (e.g., they currently receive no chest pain medication and they live in a particular geographical area). The causal relationship discovered is then relative to this population and this context.

Let's discuss how the manipulation proceeds. We first identify the population of entities we wish to consider. Our random variables are features of these entities. Next we ascertain the causal relationship we wish to investigate. Suppose we are trying to determine if variable X is a cause of variable Y. We then sample a number of entities from the population. (See Section 1.2.1 for a discussion of sampling.) For every entity selected, we manipulate the value of X so that each of its possible values is given to the same number of entities. (If X is continuous, we choose the values of X according to a uniform distribution.) After the value of X is set for a given entity, we measure the value of Y for that entity. The more the resultant data shows a dependency between X and Y, the more the data supports that X causally influences Y. The manipulation of X can be represented by a variable M that is external to the system being studied. There is one value mi of M for each value xi of X, the probabilities of all values of M are the same, and when M equals mi, X equals xi. That is, the relationship between M and X is deterministic. The data supports that X

causally influences Y to the extent that the data indicates $P(yi|mj) \neq P(yi|mk)$ for $j \neq k$. Manipulation is actually a special kind of causal relationship that we assume exists primordially and is within our control so that we can define and discover other causal relationships.

An Illustration of Manipulation

We demonstrate these ideas with a comprehensive example concerning recent headline news. The pharmaceutical company Merck had been marketing its drug finasteride as medication for men for a medical condition. Based on anecdotal evidence, it seemed that there was a correlation between use of the drug and regrowth of scalp hair. Let's assume that Merck determined such a correlation does exist. Should they conclude finasteride causes hair regrowth and therefore market it as a cure for baldness? Not necessarily. There are quite a few causal explanations for the correlation of two variables. We discuss these next.

Possible Causal Relationships   Let F be a variable representing finasteride use and G be a variable representing scalp hair growth. The actual values of F and G are unimportant to the present discussion. We could use either continuous or discrete values. If F caused G, then indeed they would be statistically correlated, but this would also be the case if G caused F, or if they had some hidden common cause H. If we again represent a causal influence by a directed edge, Figure 1.12 shows these three possibilities plus two more. Figure 1.12 (a) shows the conjecture that F causes G, which we already suspect might be the case. However, it could be that G causes F (Figure 1.12 (b)). You may argue that, based on domain knowledge, this does not seem reasonable. However, in general we do not have domain knowledge when doing a statistical analysis. So

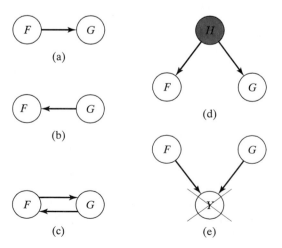

Figure 1.12: All five causal relationships could account for F and G being correlated.

from the correlation alone, the causal relationships in Figure 1.12 (a) and (b) are equally reasonable. Even in this domain, G causing F seems possible. A man may have used some other hair regrowth product such as minoxidil, which caused him to regrow hair, became excited about the regrowth, and decided to try other products such as finasteride which he heard might cause regrowth. As a third possibility, it could be both that finasteride causes hair regrowth and hair regrowth causes use of finasteride, meaning we could have a causal loop or feedback. Therefore, Figure 1.12 (c) is also a possibility. For example, finasteride may cause regrowth, and excitement about regrowth may cause use of finasteride. A fourth possibility, shown in Figure 1.12 (d), is that F and G have some hidden common cause H which accounts for their statistical correlation. For example, a man concerned about hair loss might try both finasteride and minoxidil in his effort to regrow hair. The minoxidil may cause hair regrowth, while the finasteride does not. In this case the man's concern is a cause of finasteride use and hair regrowth (indirectly through minoxidil use), while the latter two are not causally related. A fifth possibility is that we are observing a population in which all individuals have some (possibly hidden) effect of both F and G. For example, suppose finasteride and apprehension about lack of hair regrowth are both causes of hypertension[2], and we happen to be observing individuals who have hypertension Y. We say a node is **instantiated** when we know its value for the entity currently being modeled. So we are saying Y is instantiated to the same value for all entities in the population we are observing. This situation is depicted in Figure 1.12 (e), where the cross through Y means the variable is instantiated. Ordinarily, the instantiation of a common effect creates a dependency between its causes because each cause explains away the occurrence of the effect, thereby making the other cause less likely. Psychologists call this **discounting**. So, if this were the case, discounting would explain the correlation between F and G. This type of dependency is called **selection bias**. A final possibility (not depicted in Figure 1.12) is that F and G are not causally related at all. The most notable example of this situation is when our entities are points in time, and our random variables are values of properties at these different points in time. Such random variables are often correlated without having any apparent causal connection. For example, if our population consists of points in time, J is the Dow Jones Average at a given time, and L is Professor Neapolitan's hairline at a given time, then J and L are correlated. Yet they do not seem to be causally connected. Some argue there are hidden common causes beyond our ability to measure. We will not discuss this issue further here. We only wish to note the difficulty with such correlations. In light of all of the above, we see then that we cannot deduce the causal relationship between two variables from the mere fact that they are statistically correlated.

It may not be obvious why two variables with a common cause would be correlated. Consider the present example. Suppose H is a common cause of F and G and neither F nor G caused the other. Then H and F are correlated

---

[2]There is no evidence that either finasteride or apprehension about lack of hair regrowth cause hypertension. This is only for the sake of illustration.

because H causes F, H and G are correlated because H causes G, which implies F and G are correlated transitively through H. Here is a more detailed
explanation. For the sake of example, suppose $h1$ is a value of H that has a
causal influence on F taking value $f1$ and on G taking value $g1$. Then if F
had value $f1$, each of its causes would become more probable because one of
them should be responsible. So $P(h1|f1) > P(f1)$. Now since the probability
of $h1$ has gone up, the probability of $g1$ would also go up because $h1$ causes $g1$.
Therefore, $P(g1|f1) > P(f1)$, which means F and G are correlated.

Merck's Manipulation Study   Since Merck could not conclude finasteride
causes hair regrowth from their mere correlation alone, they did a manipulation
study to test this conjecture. The study was done on 1,879 men aged 18 to 41
with mild to moderate hair loss of the vertex and anterior midscalp areas. Half
of the men were given 1 mg. of finasteride, while the other half were given 1
mg. of placebo. Let's define variables for the study, including the manipulation
variable M:

Variable	Value	When the Variable Takes this Value
F	$f1$	Subject takes 1 mg. of finasteride.
	$f2$	Subject takes 1 mg. of placebo.
G	$g1$	Subject has significant hair regrowth.
	$e2$	Subject does not have significant hair regrowth.
M	$m1$	Subject is chosen to take 1mg of finasteride.
	$m2$	Subject is chosen to take 1mg of placebo.

Figure 1.13 shows the conjecture that F causes G and the RCE used to test
this conjecture. There is an oval around the system being modeled to indicate
the manipulation comes from outside that system. The edges in that figure
represent causal influences. The RCE supports the conjecture that F causes G
to the extent that the data support $P(g1|m1) \neq P(g1|m2)$. Merck decided that
"significant hair regrowth" would be judged according to the opinion of independent dermatologists. A panel of independent dermatologists evaluated photos

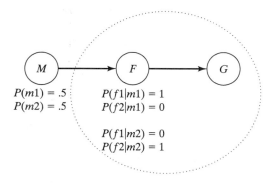

Figure 1.13: A manipulation investigating whether F causes G.

of the men after 24 months of treatment. The panel judged that significant hair regrowth was demonstrated in 66 percent of men treated with finasteride compared to 7 percent of men treated with placebo. Basing our probability on these results, we have $P(g1|m1) \approx .67$ and $P(g1|m2) \approx .07$. In a more analytical analysis, only 17 percent of men treated with finasteride demonstrated hair loss (defined as any decrease in hair count from baseline). In contrast, 72 percent of the placebo group lost hair, as measured by hair count. Merck concluded that finasteride does indeed cause hair regrowth, and on Dec. 22, 1997 announced that the U.S. Food and Drug Administration granted marketing clearance to Propecia(TM) (finasteride 1 mg.) for treatment of male pattern hair loss (androgenetic alopecia), for use in men only. See McClennan and Markham [1999] for more on this.

Causal Mediaries The action of finasteride is well known. That is, manipulation experiments have shown it significantly inhibits the conversion of testosterone to dihydro-testosterone (DHT). (See, e.g., Cunningham and Hirshkowitz [1995].). So without performing the study just discussed, Merck could assume finasteride (F) has a causal effect on DHT level (D). DHT is believed to be the androgen responsible for hair loss. Suppose we know for certain that a balding man, whose DHT level was set to zero, would regrow hair. We could then also conclude DHT level (D) has a causal effect on hair growth (G). These two causal relationships are depicted in Figure 1.14. Could Merck have used these causal relations to conclude for certain that finasteride would cause hair regrowth and avoid the expense of their study? No, they could not. Perhaps, a certain minimal level of DHT is necessary for hair loss, more than that minimal level has no further effect on hair loss, and finasteride is not capable of lowering DHT level below that level. That is, it may be that finasteride has a causal effect on DHT level, DHT level has a causal effect on hair growth, and yet finasteride has no effect on hair growth. If we identify that F causes D and D causes G, and F and G are probabilistically independent, we say the probability distribution of the variables is not faithful to the DAG representing their identified causal relationships. In general, we say $(\mathbb{G}, P)$ satisfies the **faithfulness** condition if $(\mathbb{G}, P)$ satisfies the Markov condition and the only conditional independencies in P are those entailed by the Markov condition. So, if F and G are independent, the probability distribution does not satisfy the faithfulness condition with the DAG in Figure 1.14 because this independence is not entailed by the Markov condition. Faithfulness, along with its role in causal DAGs, is discussed in detail in Chapter 2.

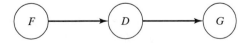

Figure 1.14: A causal DAG depicting that F causes D and D causes G.

Notice that if the variable D was not in the DAG in Figure 1.14, and if the probability distribution did satisfy the faithfulness condition (which we believe based on Merck's study), there would be an edge from F directly into G instead of the directed path through D. In general, our edges always represent only the relationships among the identified variables. It seems we can usually conceive of intermediate, unidentified variables along each edge. Consider the following example taken from Spirtes et al. [1993, 2000], [p. 42]:

> If C is the event of striking a match, and A is the event of the match catching on fire, and no other events are considered, then C is a direct cause of A. If, however, we added B; the sulfur on the match tip achieved sufficient heat to combine with the oxygen, then we could no longer say that C directly caused A, but rather C directly caused B and B directly caused A. Accordingly, we say that B is a causal mediary between C and A if C causes B and B causes A.

Note that, in this intuitive explanation, a variable name is used to stand also for a value of the variable. For example, A is a variable whose value is *on-fire* or *not-on-fire*, and A is also used to represent that the match is on fire. Clearly, we can add more causal mediaries. For example, we could add the variable D representing whether the match tip is abraded by a rough surface. C would then cause D, which would cause B, and so forth. We could go much further and describe the chemical reaction that occurs when sulfur combines with oxygen. Indeed, it seems we can conceive of a continuum of events in any causal description of a process. We see then that the set of observable variables is observer dependent. Apparently, an individual, given a myriad of sensory input, selectively records discernible events and develops cause–effect relationships among them. Therefore, rather than assuming there is a set of causally related variables out there, it seems more appropriate to only assume that, in a given context or application, we identify certain variables and develop a set of causal relationships among them.

Bad Manipulation

Before discussing causation and the Markov condition, we note some cautionary procedures of which one must be aware when performing a RCE. First, we must be careful that we do not inadvertently disturb the system other than the disturbance done by the manipulation variable M itself. That is, we must be careful we do not accidentally introduce any other causal edges into the system being modeled. The following is an example of this kind of bad manipulation (due to Greg Cooper [private correspondence]):

Example 1.37 *Suppose we want to determine the relative effectiveness of home treatment and hospital treatment for low-risk pneumonia patients. Consider those patients of Dr. Welby who are randomized to home treatment, but whom Dr. Welby normally would have admitted to the hospital. Dr. Welby may give more instructions to such home-bound patients than he would give to the typical* *home-bound patient. These instructions might influence patient outcomes. If those instructions are not measured, then the RCE may give biased estimates of the effect of treatment location (home or hospital) on patient outcome. Note, we are interested in estimating the effect of treatment location on patient outcomes, everything else being equal. The RCE is actually telling us the effect of treatment allocation on patient outcomes, which is not of interest here (although it could be of interest for other reasons). The manipulation of treatment allocation is a bad manipulation of treatment location because it not only results in a manipulation M of treatment location, but it also has a causal effect on physicians' other actions such as advice given. This is an example of what some call a "fat hand" manipulation, in the sense that one would like to manipulate just one variable, but one's hand is so fat that it ends up affecting other variables as well.*

Let's show with a DAG how this RCE inadvertently disturbs the system being modeled other than the disturbance done by M itself. If we let L represent treatment location, A represent treatment allocation, and M represent the manipulation of treatment location, we have these values:

Variable	Value	When the Variable Takes this Value
L	$l1$	*Subject is at home*
	$l2$	*Subject is in hospital*
A	$a1$	*Subject is allocated to be at home*
	$a2$	*Subject is allocated to be in hospital*
M	$m1$	*Subject is chosen to stay home*
	$m2$	*Subject is chosen to stay in hospital*

Other variables in the system include E representing the doctor's evaluation of the patient, T representing the doctor's treatments and other advice, and O representing patient outcome. Since these variables can have more than two values and their actual values are not important to the current discussion, we did not show their values in the preceding table. Figure 1.15 shows the relationships among the five variables. Note that A not only results in the desired manipulation, but there is another edge from A into the system being modeled, namely the edge into T. This edge is our inadvertent disturbance.

In many studies (whether experimental or observational) it often is difficult, if not impossible, to blind clinicians (and often patients) to the actions the clinicians have been randomized to take. Thus, a fat hand manipulation is a real possibility. Drug studies often are an important exception; however, there are many clinician actions we would like to study besides drug selection.

Besides fat hand manipulation, another kind of bad manipulation would be if we could not get complete control in setting the value of the variable we wish to manipulate. This manipulation is bad with respect to the objective we want to accomplish with the manipulation.

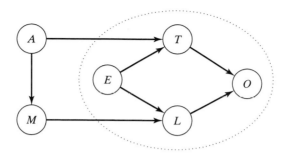

Figure 1.15: The action A has a causal arc into the system other than through M.

1.5.2   Causation and the Markov Condition

Recall from the beginning of Section 1.5 we stated the following: Given a set of variables V, if for every $X, Y \in$ V we draw an edge from X to Y if and only if X is a direct cause of Y relative to V, we call the resultant DAG a **causal DAG**. Given the manipulation definition of causation offered earlier, by "X being a direct cause of Y relative to V" we mean that a manipulation of X changes the probability distribution of Y, and that there is no subset $\mathsf{W} \subseteq \mathsf{V} - \{X, Y\}$ such that if we instantiate the variables in W a manipulation of X no longer changes the probability distribution of Y. When constructing a causal DAG containing a set of variables V, we call V "our set of observed variables." Recall further from the beginning of Section 1.5 we said we would illustrate why we feel the joint probability (relative frequency) distribution of the variables in a causal DAG often satisfies the Markov condition with that DAG. We do that first; then we state the causal Markov Assumption.

Why Causal DAGs Often Satisfy the Markov Condition

Consider first the situation concerning finasteride, DHT, and hair regrowth discussed in Section 1.5.1. In this case, our set of observed variables V is $\{F, D, G\}$. We learned that finasteride level has a causal influence on DHT level. So we placed an edge from F to D in Figure 1.14. We learned that DHT level has a causal influence on hair regrowth. So we placed an edge from D to G in Figure 1.14. We suspected that the causal effect finasteride has on hair regrowth is only through the lowering of DHT levels. So we did not place an edge from F to G in Figure 1.14. If there was another causal path from F to G (i.e., if F affected G by some means other than by decreasing DHT levels), we would also place an edge from F to G as shown in Figure 1.16. Assuming the only causal connection between F and G is as indicated in Fig 1.14, we would feel that F and G are conditionally independent given D because, once we knew the value of D, we would have a probability distribution of G based on this known value, and, since the value of F cannot change the known value of D and there is no other connection between F and G, it cannot change the probability

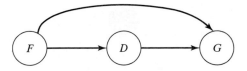

Figure 1.16: The causal relationships if F had a causal influence on G other than through D.

distribution of G. Manipulation experiments have substantiated this intuition. That is, there have been experiments in which it was established that X causes Y, Y causes Z, X and Z are not probabilistically independent, and X and Z are conditionally independent given Y. (See Lugg et al. [1995] for an example.) In general, when all causal paths from X to Y contain at least one variable in our set of observed variables V, X and Y do not have a common cause, there are no causal paths from Y back to X, and we do not have selection bias, then we feel X and Y are independent if we condition on a set of variables including at least one variable in each of the causal paths from X to Y. Since the set of all parents of Y is such a set, we feel the Markov condition is satisfied relative to X and Y.

We say X and Y have a **common cause** if there is some variable that has causal paths into both X and Y. If X and Y have a common cause C, there is often a dependency between them through this common cause. (But this is not necessarily the case. See Exercise 2.34.) However, if we condition on Y's parent in the path from C to Y, we feel we break this dependency for the same reasons previously discussed. So, as long as all common causes are in our set of observed variables V, we can still break the dependency between X and Y (assuming as before that there are no causal paths from Y to X) by conditioning on the set of parents of Y, which means the Markov condition is still satisfied relative to X and Y. A problem arises when at least one common cause is not in our set of observed variables V. Such a common cause is called a **hidden variable**. If two variables had a hidden common cause, then there would often be a dependency between them, which the Markov condition would identify as an independency. For example, consider the DAG in Figure 1.17. If we identified only the variables X, Y, and Z, and the causal relationships that X and Y each caused Z, we would draw edges from each of X and Y to Z. The Markov condition would entail that X and Y are independent. But if X and Y had a hidden common cause H, they would not ordinarily be independent. So, for us to assume the Markov condition is satisfied, either no two variables in the set of observed variables V can have a hidden common cause, or, if they do, it must have the same unknown value for every unit in the population under consideration. When this is the case, we say the set is **causally sufficient**.

Another violation of the Markov condition, similar to the failure to include a hidden common cause, is the case when there is selection bias present. Recall that, in the beginning of Section 1.5.1, we noted that if finasteride use (F) and apprehension about lack of hair regrowth (G) are both causes of hypertension

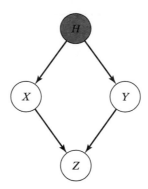

Figure 1.17: X and Y are not independent if they have a hidden common cause H.

(Y), and we happen to be observing individuals hospitalized for treatment of hypertension, we would observe a probabilistic dependence between F and G due to selection bias. This situation is depicted in Figure 1.12 (e). Note that in this situation our set of observed variables V is $\{F, G\}$. That is, Y is not observed. So if neither F nor G caused each other and they did not have a hidden common cause, a causal DAG containing only the two variables (i.e., one with no edges) would still not satisfy the Markov condition with the observed probability distribution, because the Markov condition says F and G are independent when indeed they are not for this population.

Finally, we must also make certain that if X has a causal influence on Y, then Y does not have a causal influence X. In this way we guarantee that the identified causal edges will indeed yield a DAG. Causal feedback loops (e.g., the situation identified in Figure 1.12 (c)) are discussed in Richardson and Spirtes [1999].

Before closing, we note that, if we mistakenly draw an edge from X to Y in a case where X's causal influence on Y is only through other variables in the model, we have not done anything to thwart the Markov condition being satisfied. For example, consider again the variables in Figure 1.14. If F's only influence on G was through D, we would not thwart the Markov condition by drawing an edge from F to G. That is, this does not result in the structure of the DAG entailing any conditional independencies that are not there. Indeed, the opposite has happened. That is, the DAG fails to entail a conditional independency (namely $I(\{F\}, \{G\}|\{D\})$) that is there. This is a violation of the faithfulness condition (discussed in Chapter 2), not the Markov condition. In general, we would not want to do this because it makes the DAG less informative and unnecessarily increases the size of the instance (which is important because, as we shall see in Section 3.6, the problem of doing inference in Bayesian networks is $\#P$-complete). However, a few mistakes of this sort are not that serious since we can still expect the Markov condition to be satisfied.

The Causal Markov Assumption

We've offered a definition of causation based on manipulation, and we've argued that, given this definition of causation, a causal DAG often satisfies the Markov condition with the probability distribution of the variables, which means we can construct a Bayesian network by creating a causal DAG. In general, given any definitions of "causation" and "direct causal influence," if we create a causal DAG $\mathbb{G} = (\mathsf{V}, \mathsf{E})$ and assume the probability distribution of the variables in V satisfies the Markov condition with $\mathbb{G}$, we say we are making the **causal Markov assumption**.

As previously discussed, if the following three conditions are satisfied, the causal Markov assumption is ordinarily warranted: (1) there must be no hidden common causes, (2) selection bias must not be present, and (3) there must be no causal feedback loops. In general, when constructing a Bayesian network using identified causal influences, one must take care that the causal Markov assumption holds.

Often we identify causes using methods other than manipulation. For example, most of us believe smoking causes lung cancer. Yet we have not manipulated individuals by making them smoke. We believe in this causal influence because smoking and lung cancer are correlated, the smoking precedes the cancer in time (a common assumption is that an effect cannot precede a cause), and there are biochemical changes associated with smoking. All of this could possibly be explained by a hidden common cause. (Perhaps a genetic defect causes both.) But domain experts essentially rule out this possibility. When we identify causes by any means whatsoever, ordinarily we feel they are ones that could be identified by manipulation if we were to perform a RCE, and we make the causal Markov assumption as long as we are confident exceptions such as conditions (1), (2), and (3) in the preceding paragraph are not present.

An example of constructing a causal DAG follows.

Example 1.38 *Suppose we have identified the following causal influences by some means: A history of smoking (H) has a causal effect both on bronchitis (B) and on lung cancer (L). Furthermore, each of these variables can cause fatigue (F). Lung Cancer (L) can cause a positive chest X-ray (C). Then the DAG in Figure 1.10 represents our identified causal relationships among these variables. If we believe (1) these are the only causal influences among the variables, (2) there are no hidden common causes, and (3) selection bias is not present, it seems reasonable to make the causal Markov assumption. Then if the conditional distributions specified in Figure 1.10 are our estimates of the conditional relative frequencies, that DAG along with those specified conditional distributions constitute a Bayesian network which represents our beliefs.*

Before closing we mention an objection to the causal Markov condition. That is, unless we abandon the "locality principle" the condition seems to be violated in some quantum mechanical experiments. See Spirtes et al. [1993, 2000] for a discussion of this matter.

The Markov Condition Without Causation

Using causal edges is just one way to develop a DAG and a probability distribution that satisfy the Markov condition. In Example 1.29 we showed the joint distribution of V (value), S (shape), and C (color) satisfied the Markov condition with the DAG in Figure 1.3 (a), but we would not say that the color of an object has a causal influence on its shape. The Markov condition is simply a property of the probabilistic relationships among the variables. Furthermore, if the DAG in Figure 1.3 (a) did capture the causal relationships among some causally sufficient set of variables and there was no selection bias present, the Markov condition would be satisfied not only with that DAG but also with the DAGS in Figures 1.3 (b) and (c). Yet we certainly would not say the edges in these latter two DAGs represent causal influence.

Some Final Examples

To solidify the notion that the Markov condition is often satisfied by a causal DAG, we close with three simple examples. We present these examples using an intuitive approach, which shows how humans reason qualitatively with the dependencies and conditional independencies among variables. In accordance with this approach, we again use the name of a variable to stand also for a value. For example, in modeling whether an individual has a cold, we use a variable C whose value is *present* or *absent*, and we also use C to represent that a cold is present.

Example 1.39 *If Alice's husband Ralph was planning a surprise birthday party for Alice with a caterer (C), this may cause him to visit the caterer's store (V). The act of visiting that store could cause him to be seen (S) visiting the store. So the causal relationships among the variables are the ones shown in Figure 1.18 (a). There is no direct path from C to S because planning the party with the caterer could only cause him to be seen visiting the store if it caused him to actually visit the store. If Alice's friend Trixie reported to her that she had seen Ralph visiting the caterer's store today, Alice would conclude that he may be planning a surprise birthday party because she would feel there is a good chance Trixie really did see Ralph visiting the store, and, if this actually was the case, there is a chance he may be planning a surprise birthday party. So C and S are not independent. If, however, Alice had al-*

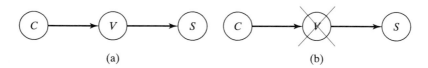

(a)   (b)

Figure 1.18: C and S are not independent in (a), but the instantiation of V in (b) renders them independent.

ready witnessed this same act of Ralph visiting the caterer's store, she would already suspect Ralph may be planning a surprise birthday party. Trixie's testimony would not affect her belief concerning Ralph's visiting the store and therefore would have no effect on her belief concerning his planning a party. So C and S are conditionally independent given V, as the Markov condition entails for the DAG in Figure 1.18 (a). The instantiation of V, which renders C and S independent, is depicted in Figure 1.18 (b) by placing a cross through V.

Example 1.40 *A cold (C) can cause both sneezing (S) and a runny nose (R). Assume neither of these manifestations causes the other and, for the moment, also assume there are no hidden common causes. (That is, this set of variables is causally sufficient.) The causal relationships among the variables are then the ones depicted in Figure 1.19 (a). Suppose now that Professor Patel walks into the classroom with a runny nose. You would fear she has a cold, and, if so, the cold may make her sneeze. So you back off from her to avoid the possible sneeze. We see then that S and R are not independent. Suppose next that Professor Patel calls school in the morning to announce she has a cold which will make her late for class. When she finally does arrive, you back off immediately because you feel the cold may make her sneeze. If you see that her nose is running, this has no effect on your belief concerning her sneezing because the runny nose no longer makes the cold more probable. (You know she has a cold.) So S and R are conditionally independent given C, as the Markov condition entails for the DAG in Figure 1.19 (a). The instantiation of C is depicted in Figure 1.19 (b).*

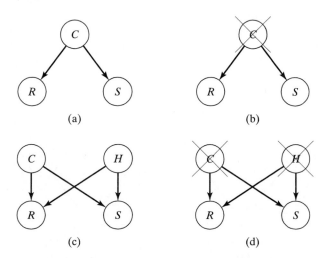

Figure 1.19: If C is the only common cause of R and S (a), we need to instantiate only C (b) to render them independent. If they have exactly two common causes, C and H (c), we need to instantiate both C and H (d) to render them independent.

There actually is at least one other common cause of sneezing and a runny nose, namely, hay fever (H). Suppose this is the only common cause missing from Figure 1.19 (a). The causal relationships among the variables would then be as depicted in Figure 1.19 (c). Given this, conditioning on C is not sufficient to render R and S independent, because R could still make S more probable by making H more probable. So we must condition on both C and H to render R and S independent. The instantiation of C and H is depicted in Figure 1.19 (d).

Example 1.41 *Antonio has observed that his burglar alarm (A) has sometimes gone off when a freight truck (F) was making a delivery to the Home Depot in back of his house. So he feels a freight truck can trigger the alarm. However, he also believes a burglar (B) can trigger the alarm. He does not feel that the appearance of a burglar might cause a freight truck to make a delivery or vice versa. Therefore, he feels that the causal relationships among the variables are the ones depicted in Figure 1.20 (a). Suppose Antonio sees a freight truck making a delivery in back of his house. This does not make him feel a burglar is more probable. So F and B are independent, as the Markov condition entails for the DAG in Figure 1.20 (a). Suppose next that Antonio is awakened at night by the sounding of his burglar alarm. This increases his belief that a burglar is present, and he begins fearing this is indeed the case. However, as he proceeds to investigate this possibility, he notices that a freight truck is making a delivery in back of his house. He reasons that this truck explains away the alarm, and therefore he believes a burglar probably is not present. So he relaxes a bit. Given the alarm has sounded, learning that a freight truck is present decreases the probability of a burglar. So the instantiation of A, as depicted in Figure 1.20 (b), renders F and B conditionally dependent. As noted previously, the instantiation of a common effect creates a dependence between its causes because each explains away the occurrence of the effect, thereby making the other cause less likely.*

Note that the Markov condition does not entail that F and B are conditionally dependent given A. Indeed, a probability distribution can satisfy the Markov condition for a DAG (See Exercise 2.18) without this conditional dependence occurring. However, if this conditional dependence does not occur, the distribution does not satisfy the faithfulness condition with the DAG. Faithfulness is defined earlier in this section and is discussed in Chapter 2.

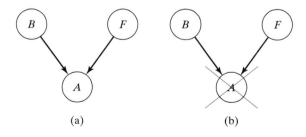

          (a)   (b)

Figure 1.20: B and F are independent in (a), but the instantiation of A in (b) renders them dependent.

EXERCISES

Section 1.1

Exercise 1.1 *Kerrich [1946] performed experiments such as tossing a coin many times, and he found that the relative frequency did appear to approach a limit. That is, for example, he found that after 100 tosses the relative frequency may have been .51, after 1000 it may have been .508, after 10,000 tosses it may have been .5003, and after 100,000 tosses, it may have been .50006. The pattern is that the 5 in the first place to the right of the decimal point remains in all relative frequencies after the first 100 tosses, the 0 in the second place remains in all relative frequencies after the first 1000 tosses, and so forth. Toss a thumbtack at least 1000 times and see if you obtain similar results.*

Exercise 1.2 *Pick some upcoming event. (It could be a sporting event or it could even be the event that you get an "A" in this course.) Determine your probability of the event using the Lindley [1985] method of comparing the uncertain event to a draw of a ball from an urn. (See the discussion following Example 1.20.)*

Exercise 1.3 *Prove Theorem 1.1.*

Exercise 1.4 *Example 1.3 showed that, in the draw of the top card from a deck, the event* Queen *is independent of the event* Spade. *That is, it showed $P(\text{Queen}|\text{Spade}) = P(\text{Queen})$.*

1. *Show directly that the event* Spade *is independent of the event* Queen. *That is, show $P(\text{Spade}|\text{Queen}) = P(\text{Spade})$. Show also that $P(\text{Queen} \cap \text{Spade}) = P(\text{Queen})P(\text{Spade})$.*

2. *Show, in general, that if $P(\text{E}) \neq 0$ and $P(\text{F}) \neq 0$, then $P(\text{E}|\text{F}) = P(\text{E})$ if and only if $P(\text{F}|\text{E}) = P(\text{F})$ and that each of these holds if and only if $P(\text{E} \cap \text{F}) = P(\text{E})P(\text{F})$.*

Exercise 1.5 *The complement of a set* E *consists of all the elements in Ω that are not in* E *and is denoted by $\overline{\text{E}}$.*

1. *Show that* E *is independent of* F *if and only if $\overline{\text{E}}$ is independent of* F, *which is true if and only if $\overline{\text{E}}$ is independent of $\overline{\text{F}}$.*

2. *Example 1.5 showed that, for the objects in Figure 1.2,* One *and* Square *are conditionally independent given* Black *and given* White. *Let* Two *be the set of all objects containing a "2" and* Round *be the set of all round objects. Use the result just obtained to conclude* Two *and* Square, One *and* Round, *and* Two *and* Round *are each conditionally independent given either* Black *or* White.

Exercise 1.6 *Example 1.4 showed that, in the draw of the top card from a deck, the event* $\mathsf{E} = \{kh, ks, qh\}$ *and the event* $\mathsf{F} = \{kh, kc, qh\}$ *are conditionally independent given the event* $\mathsf{G} = \{kh, ks, kc, kd\}$. *Determine whether* E *and* F *are conditionally independent given* $\overline{\mathsf{G}}$.

Exercise 1.7 *Prove the rule of total probability, which says if we have n mutually exclusive and exhaustive events $\mathsf{E}_1, \mathsf{E}_2, \dots \mathsf{E}_n$, then for any other event F,*

$$P(\mathsf{F}) = \sum_{i=1}^{n} P(\mathsf{F} \cap \mathsf{E}_i).$$

Exercise 1.8 *Let Ω be the set of all objects in Figure 1.2, and assign each object a probability of $1/13$. Let* **One** *be the set of all objects containing a 1, and* **Square** *be the set of all square objects. Compute $P(\mathsf{One}|\mathsf{Square})$ directly and using Bayes' theorem.*

Exercise 1.9 *Let a joint probability distribution be given. Using the law of total probability, show that the probability distribution of any one of the random variables is obtained by summing over all values of the other variables.*

Exercise 1.10 *Use the results in Exercise 1.5 (1) to conclude that it was only necessary in Example 1.16 to show that $P(r, t) = P(r, t|s1)$ for all values of r and t.*

Exercise 1.11 *Suppose we have two random variables X and Y with spaces $\{x1, x2\}$ and $\{y1, y2\}$, respectively.*

1. *Use the results in Exercise 1.5 (1) to conclude that we need only show $P(y1|x1) = P(y1)$ to conclude $I_P(X, Y)$.*

2. *Develop an example showing that if X and Y both have spaces containing more than two values, then we to need check whether $P(y|x) = P(y)$ for all values of x and y to conclude $I_P(X, Y)$.*

Exercise 1.12 *Consider the probability space and random variables given in Example 1.15.*

1. *Determine the joint distributions of S and W, of W and H, and the remaining values in the joint distribution of S, H, and W.*

2. *Show that the joint distribution of S and H can be obtained by summing the joint distribution of S, H, and W over all values of W.*

3. *Are H and W independent? Are H and W conditionally independent given S? If this small sample is indicative of the probabilistic relationships among the variables in some population, what causal relationships might account for this dependency and conditional independency?*

Exercise 1.13 *The chain rule states that given n random variables $X_1, X_2, \ldots,$ X_n, defined on the same sample space Ω,*

$$P(x_1, x_2, \ldots, x_n) = P(x_n | x_{n-1}, x_{n-2}, \ldots, x_1) \cdots \times P(x_2 | x_1) \times P(x_1)$$

whenever $P(x_1, x_2, \ldots x_n) \neq 0$. Prove this rule.

Section 1.2

Exercise 1.14 *Use Bayes' theorem to compute the conditional probability the Bulls won in Example 1.24.*

Exercise 1.15 *A forgetful nurse is supposed to give Mr. Nguyen a pill each day. The probability that she will forget to give the pill on a given day is .3. If he receives the pill, the probability he will die is .1. If he does not receive the pill, the probability he will die is .8. Mr. Nguyen died today. Use Bayes' theorem to compute the probability the nurse forgot to give him the pill.*

Exercise 1.16 *An oil well may be drilled on Professor Neapolitan's farm in Texas. Based on what has happened on similar farms, we judge the probability of oil being present to be .5, the probability of only natural gas being present to be .2, and the probability of neither being present to be .3. If oil is present, a geological test will give a positive result with probability .9; if only natural gas is present, it will give a positive result with probability .3; and if neither are present, the test will be positive with probability .1. Suppose the test comes back positive. Use Bayes' theorem to compute the probability oil is present.*

Section 1.3

Exercise 1.17 *Suppose we are developing a system for diagnosing viral infections, and one of our random variables is Fever. If we specify the possible values yes and no, is the clarity test passed? If not, further distinguish the values so it is passed.*

Exercise 1.18 *Prove Theorem 1.3.*

Exercise 1.19 *Let $\mathsf{V} = \{X, Y, Z\}$, let X, Y, and Z have spaces $\{x1, x2\}$, $\{y1, y2\}$, and $\{z1, z2\}$ respectively, and specify the following values:*

$$
\begin{array}{lll}
P(x1) = .2 & P(y1|x1) = .3 & P(z1|x1) = .1 \\
P(x2) = .8 & P(y2|x1) = .7 & P(z2|x1) = .9 \\
\\
& P(y1|x2) = .4 & P(z1|x2) = .5 \\
& P(y2|x2) = .6 & P(z2|x2) = .5.
\end{array}
$$

Define a joint probability distribution P of X, Y, and Z as the product of these values.

1. *Show that the values in this joint distribution sum to 1, and therefore this is a way of specifying a joint probability distribution according to Definition 1.8.*

2. *Show further that $I_P(Z, Y|X)$. Note that this conditional independency follows from Theorem 1.5 in Section 1.4.2.*

Section 1.4

Exercise 1.20 *Consider Figure 1.3.*

1. *The probability distribution in Example 1.29 satisfies the Markov condition with the DAGs in Figures 1.3 (b) and (c). Therefore, based on Theorem 1.4, that probability distribution is equal to the product of its conditional distributions for each of them. Show this directly.*

2. *Show that the probability distribution in Example 1.29 is not equal to the product of its conditional distributions for the DAG in Figure 1.3 (d).*

Exercise 1.21 *Create an arrangement of objects similar to the one in Figure 1.2, but with a different distribution of values, shapes, and colors, so that, if random variables V, S, and C are defined as in Example 1.29, then the only independency or conditional independency among the variables is $I_P(V, S)$. Does this distribution satisfy the Markov condition with any of the DAGs in Figure 1.3? If so, which one(s)?*

Exercise 1.22 *Complete the proof of Theorem 1.5 by showing that the specified conditional distributions are the conditional distributions they notationally represent in the joint distribution.*

Exercise 1.23 *Consider the objects in Figure 1.2 and the joint probability distribution of the random variables defined in Example 1.29. Suppose we compute its conditional distributions for the DAG in Figure 1.3 (d), and we take their product. Theorem 1.5 says this product is a joint probability distribution that constitutes a Bayesian network with that DAG. Is this the actual joint probability distribution of the variables?*

Section 1.5

Exercise 1.24 *Professor Morris investigated gender bias in hiring in the following way. He gave hiring personnel equal numbers of male and female resumes to review, and then he investigated whether their evaluations were correlated with gender. When he submitted a paper summarizing his results to a psychology journal, the reviewers rejected the paper because they said this was an example of fat hand manipulation. Explain why they might have thought this. Elucidate your explanation by identifying all relevant variables in the RCE and drawing a DAG like the one in Figure 1.15.*

Exercise 1.25 *Consider the following piece of medical knowledge taken from Lauritzen and Spiegelhalter [1988]: Tuberculosis and lung cancer can each cause shortness of breath (dyspnea) and a positive chest X-ray. Bronchitis is another cause of dyspnea. A recent visit to Asia can increase the probability of tuberculosis. Smoking can cause both lung cancer and bronchitis. Create a DAG representing the causal relationships among these variables. Complete the construction of a Bayesian network by determining values for the conditional probability distributions in this DAG, either based on your own subjective judgment or from data.*

Chapter 2

More DAG/Probability Relationships

The previous chapter introduced only one relationship between probability distributions and DAGs, namely the Markov condition. However, the Markov condition entails only independencies; it does not entail any dependencies. That is, when we know only that $(\mathbb{G}, P)$ satisfies the Markov condition, we know the absence of an edge between X any Y entails that there is no direct dependency between X any Y, but the presence of an edge between X and Y does not mean that there is a direct dependency. In general, we would want an edge to mean there is a direct dependency. In Section 2.3, we discuss another condition, namely the faithfulness condition, which does entail that there is a direct dependence. The concept of faithfulness is important to the methods of learning the structure of Bayesian networks from data, which are discussed in Chapters 8–11. For some probability distributions P, it is not possible to find a DAG with which P satisfies the faithfulness condition. In Section 2.4 we present the minimality condition, and we shall see that it is always possible to find a DAG $\mathbb{G}$ such that $(\mathbb{G}, P)$ satisfies the minimality condition. In Section 2.5 we discuss Markov blankets and Markov boundaries, which are sets of variables that render a given variable conditionally independent of all other variables. Finally, in Section 2.6 we show how the concepts addressed in this chapter relate to causal DAGs. Before any of this, in Section 2.1 we show what conditional independencies are entailed by the Markov condition, and in Section 2.2 we describe Markov equivalence, which groups DAGs into equivalence classes based on the conditional independencies they entail. Knowledge of the conditional independencies entailed by the Markov condition is needed to develop a message-passing inference algorithm in Chapter 3, while the concept of Markov equivalence is necessary to the structure learning algorithms developed in Chapters 8–11.

2.1 Entailed Conditional Independencies

If $(\mathbb{G}, P)$ satisfies the Markov condition, then each node in $\mathbb{G}$ is conditionally independent of the set of all its nondescendents given its parents. Do these conditional independencies entail any other conditional independencies? That is, if $(\mathbb{G}, P)$ satisfies the Markov condition, are there any conditional independencies which P must satisfy other than the one based on a node's parents? The answer is yes. Before explicitly stating these entailed independencies, we illustrate that one would expect them.

First we make the notion of "entailed conditional independency" explicit:

Definition 2.1 *Let $\mathbb{G} = (\mathsf{V}, \mathsf{E})$ be a DAG, where V is a set of random variables. We say that, based on the Markov condition, $\mathbb{G}$ **entails** conditional independency $I_P(\mathsf{A}, \mathsf{B}|\mathsf{C})$ for $\mathsf{A}, \mathsf{B}, \mathsf{C} \subseteq \mathsf{V}$ if*

$$I_P(\mathsf{A}, \mathsf{B}|\mathsf{C}) \ \textit{holds for every } P \in \mathsf{P},$$

*where P is the set of all probability distributions P such that $(\mathbb{G}, P)$ satisfies the Markov condition. We also say the Markov condition entails the conditional independency for $\mathbb{G}$ and that the conditional independency is **in** $\mathbb{G}$.*

In the previous definition, "random variable" does not designate a random variable with a particular space and probability distribution. Rather, it indicates a variable which can have any space and any distribution relative to that space.

2.1.1 Examples of Entailed Conditional Independencies

Suppose some distribution P satisfies the Markov condition with the DAG in Figure 2.1. Then we know $I_P(\{C\}, \{F, G\}|\{B\})$ because B is the parent of C, and F and G are nondescendents of C. Furthermore, we know $I_P(\{B\}, \{G\}|\{F\})$ because F is the parent of B, and G is a nondescendent of B. These are the only conditional independencies according to the statement of the Markov condition. However, can any other conditional independencies be deduced from them? For example, can we conclude $I_P(\{C\}, \{G\}|\{F\})$? Let's first give the variables meaning and the DAG a causal interpretation to see if we would expect this conditional independency.

Suppose we are investigating how professors obtain citations, and the variables represent the following:

$$
\begin{array}{ll}
G\text{:} & \text{Graduate Program Quality} \\
F\text{:} & \text{First Job Quality} \\
B\text{:} & \text{Number of Publications} \\
C\text{:} & \text{Number of Citations.}
\end{array}
$$

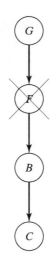

Figure 2.1: $I(\{C\}, \{G\}|\{F\})$ can be deduced from the Markov condition.

Further suppose the DAG in Figure 2.1 represents the causal relationships among these variables, there are no hidden common causes, and selection bias is not present.[1] Then it is reasonable to make the causal Markov assumption, and we would feel the probability distribution of the variables satisfies the Markov condition with the DAG. Given all this, if we learned that Professor La Budde attended a graduate program of high quality (that is, we found out that the value of G for Professor La Budde was "high quality"), we would expect his first job may well be of high quality, which means there should be a large number of publications, which in turn implies there should be a large number of citations. Therefore, we would not expect $I_P(C, G)$. If we learned that Professor Pellegrini's first job was of the high quality (that is, we found out that the value of F for Professor Pellegrini was "high quality"), we would expect his number of publications to be large, and in turn his number of citations to be large. That is, we would also not expect $I_P(C, F)$. If Professor Pellegrini then told us he attended a graduate program of high quality, would we expect the number of citations to be even higher than we previously thought? It seems not. The graduate program's high quality implies the number of citations is probably large because it implies the first job is probably of high quality. Once we already know the first job is of high quality, the information on the graduate program should be irrelevant to our beliefs concerning the number of citations. Therefore, we would expect C to be conditionally independent of G given not only its parent B, but also its grandparent F. Either one seems to block the dependency between G and C that exists through the chain $[G, F, B, C]$. So we would expect $I_P(\{C\}, \{G\}|\{F\})$.

---

[1]We make no claim this model accurately represents the causal relationships among the variables. See Spirtes et al. [1993, 2000] for a detailed discussion of this problem.

It is straightforward to show that the Markov condition does indeed entail $I_P(\{C\}, \{G\}|\{F\})$ for the DAG $\mathbb{G}$ in Figure 2.1. We illustrate this for the case where the variables are discrete. If $(\mathbb{G}, P)$ satisfies the Markov condition,

$$
\begin{aligned}
P(c|g, f) &= \sum_b P(c|b, g, f) P(b|g, f) \\
&= \sum_b P(c|b, f) P(b|f) \\
&= P(c|f).
\end{aligned}
$$

The second step is due to the Markov condition.

Suppose next we have an arbitrarily long directed linked list of variables and P satisfies the Markov condition with that list. In the same way as before, we can show that, for any variable in the list, the set of variables above it are conditionally independent of the set of variables below it given that variable.

Suppose now that P does not satisfy the Markov condition with the DAG in Figure 2.1 because there is a common cause A of G and B. For the sake of illustration, let's say A represents the following in the current example:

$$A: \qquad \text{Ability.}$$

Further suppose there are no other hidden common causes so that we would now expect P to satisfy the Markov condition with the DAG in Figure 2.2. Would we still expect $I_P(\{C\}, \{G\}|\{F\})$? It seems not. For example, suppose again that we initially learn Professor Pellegrini's first job was of high quality. As before, we would feel it probable that he has a high number of citations. Suppose again

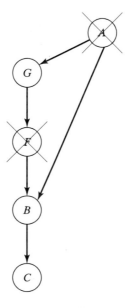

Figure 2.2: $I_P(\{C\}, \{G\}|\{A, F\})$ can be deduced from the Markov condition.

that we next learn his graduate program was of high quality. Given the current model, this fact is indicative of his having high ability, which can affect his publication rate (and thereby his citation rate) directly. So we would not feel $I_P(\{C\}, \{G\}|\{F\})$ as we did with the previous model. However, if we knew the state of Professor Pellegrini's ability, his attendance at a high quality graduate program could no longer be indicative of his ability, and therefore it would not affect our belief concerning his citation rate through the chain $[G, A, B, C]$. That is, this chain is blocked at A. So we would expect $I_P(\{C\}, \{G\}|\{A, F\})$. Indeed, it is possible to prove the Markov condition does entail $I_P(\{C\}, \{G\}|\{A, F\})$ for the DAG in Figure 2.2.

Finally, consider the conditional independency $I_P(\{F\}, \{A\}|\{G\})$. This independency is obtained directly by applying the Markov condition to the DAG in Figure 2.2. So we will not offer an intuitive explanation for it. Rather, we discuss whether we would expect the independency to be maintained if we also learned the state of B. That is, would we expect $I_P(\{F\}, \{A\}|\{B, G\})$? Suppose we first learn Professor Georgakis has a high publication rate (the value of B) and attended a high quality graduate program (the value of G). Then we later learned she also has high ability (the value of A). In this case, her high ability could explain away her high publication rate, thereby making it less probable she had a high quality first job. (As mentioned in Section 1.5.1, psychologists call this explaining away discounting.) So the chain $[A, B, F]$ is opened by instantiating B, and we would not expect $I_P(\{F\}, \{A\}|\{B, G\})$. Indeed, the Markov condition does not entail $I_P(\{F\}, \{A\}|\{B, G\})$ for the DAG in Figure 2.2. This situation is illustrated in Figure 2.3. Note that the in-

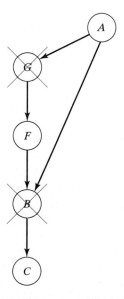

Figure 2.3: The Markov condition does not entail $I(\{F\}, \{A\}|\{B, G\})$.

stantiation of C should also open the chain $[A, B, F]$. That is, if we know the citation rate is high, then it is probable the publication rate is high, and each of the causes of B can explain away this high probability. Indeed, the Markov condition does not entail $I_P(\{F\}, \{A\}|\{C, G\})$ either. Note further that we are only saying that the Markov condition doe not entail $I_P(\{F\}, \{A\}|\{B, G\})$. We are not saying the Markov condition entails $\neg I_P(\{F\}, \{A\}|\{B, G\})$. Indeed, the Markov condition can never entail a dependency; it can only entail an independency. Exercise 2.18 shows an example in which this conditional dependency does not occur. That is, it shows a case in which there is no discounting.

2.1.2   d-Separation

We showed in Section 2.1.1 that the Markov condition entails $I_P(\{C\}, \{G\}|\{F\})$ for the DAG in Figure 2.1. This conditional independency is an example of a DAG property called "d-separation." That is, $\{C\}$ and $\{G\}$ are d-separated by $\{F\}$ in the DAG in Figure 2.1. Next we develop the concept of d-separation, and we show the following: (1) The Markov condition entails that all d-separations are conditional independencies, and (2) every conditional independency entailed by the Markov condition is identified by d-separation. That is, if $(\mathbb{G}, P)$ satisfies the Markov condition, every d-separation in $\mathbb{G}$ is a conditional independency in P. Furthermore, every conditional independency, which is common to all probability distributions satisfying the Markov condition with $\mathbb{G}$, is identified by d-separation.

All d-separations are Conditional Independencies

First we need to review more graph theory. Suppose we have a DAG $\mathbb{G} = (\mathsf{V}, \mathsf{E})$, and a set of nodes $\{X_1, X_2, \ldots, X_k\}$, where $k \geq 2$, such that $(X_{i-1}, X_i) \in \mathsf{E}$ or $(X_i, X_{i-1}) \in \mathsf{E}$ for $2 \leq i \leq k$. We call the set of edges connecting the k nodes a **chain** between X_1 and X_k. We denote the chain using both the sequence $[X_1, X_2, \ldots, X_k]$ and the sequence $[X_k, X_{k-1}, \ldots, X_1]$. For example, $[G, A, B, C]$ and $[C, B, A, G]$ represent the same chain between G and C in the DAG in Figure 2.3. Another chain between G and C is $[G, F, B, C]$. The nodes $X_2, \ldots, X_{k-1}$ are called **interior nodes** on chain $[X_1, X_2, \ldots, X_k]$. The **subchain** of chain $[X_1, X_2, \ldots, X_k]$ between X_i and X_j is the chain $[X_i, X_{i+1}, \ldots, X_j]$ where $1 \leq i < j \leq k$. A **cycle** is a chain between a node and itself. A **simple chain** is a chain containing no subchains that are cycles. We often denote chains by showing undirected lines between the nodes in the chain. For example, we would denote the chain $[G, A, B, C]$ as $G - A - B - C$. If we want to show the direction of the edges, we use arrows. For example, to show the direction of the edges, we denote the previous chain as $G \leftarrow A \rightarrow B \rightarrow C$. A chain containing two nodes, such as $X - Y$, is called a **link**. A directed link, such as $X \rightarrow Y$, represents an edge, and we will call it an edge. Given the edge $X \rightarrow Y$, we say the **tail** of the edge is at X and the **head** of the edge is Y. We also say the following:

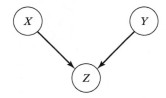

Figure 2.4: There is an uncoupled head-to-head meeting at Z.

- A chain $X \to Z \to Y$ is a **head-to–tail meeting**, the edges meet **head-to-tail** at Z, and Z is a **head-to-tail** node on the chain.

- A chain $X \leftarrow Z \to Y$ is a **tail-to–tail meeting**, the edges meet **tail-to-tail** at Z, and Z is a **tail-to-tail** node on the chain.

- A chain $X \to Z \leftarrow Y$ is a **head-to–head meeting**, the edges meet **head-to-head** at Z, and Z is a **head-to-head** node on the chain.

- A chain $X - Z - Y$, such that X and Y are not adjacent, is an **uncoupled meeting**.

Figure 2.4 shows an uncoupled head-to-head meeting.

We now have the following definition:

Definition 2.2 *Let* $\mathbb{G} = (\mathsf{V}, \mathsf{E})$ *be a DAG,* $\mathsf{A} \subseteq \mathsf{V}$, X *and* Y *be distinct nodes in* $\mathsf{V} - \mathsf{A}$, *and* ρ *be a chain between* X *and* Y. *Then* ρ *is **blocked** by* A *if one of the following holds:*

1. *There is a node* $Z \in \mathsf{A}$ *on the chain* ρ, *and the edges incident to* Z *on* ρ *meet head-to-tail at* Z.

2. *There is a node* $Z \in \mathsf{A}$ *on the chain* ρ, *and the edges incident to* Z *on* ρ *meet tail-to-tail at* Z.

3. *There is a node* Z, *such that* Z *and all of* Z's *descendents are not in* A, *on the chain* ρ, *and the edges incident to* Z *on* ρ *meet head-to-head at* Z.

We say the chain is blocked at any node in A *where one of the above meetings takes place. There may be more than one such node. The chain is called **active** given* A *if it is not blocked by* A.

Example 2.1 *Consider the DAG in Figure 2.5.*

1. *The chain* $[Y, X, Z, S]$ *is blocked by* $\{X\}$ *because the edges on the chain incident to* X *meet tail-to-tail at* X. *That chain is also blocked by* $\{Z\}$ *because the edges on the chain incident to* Z *meet head-to-tail at* Z.

2. *The chain* $[W, Y, R, Z, S]$ *is blocked by* $\varnothing$ *because* $R \notin \varnothing$, $T \notin \varnothing$, *and the edges on the chain incident to* R *meet head-to-head at* R.

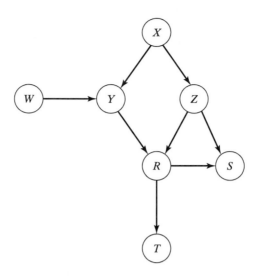

Figure 2.5: A DAG used to illustrate chain blocking.

3. *The chain* $[W, Y, R, S]$ *is blocked by* $\{R\}$ *because the edges on the chain incident to* R *meet head-to-tail at* R.

4. *The chain* $[W, Y, R, Z, S]$ *is not blocked by* $\{R\}$ *because the edges on the chain incident to* R *meet head-to-head at* R. *Furthermore, this chain is not blocked by* $\{T\}$ *because* T *is a descendent of* R.

We can now define d-separation.

Definition 2.3 *Let* $\mathbb{G} = (\mathsf{V}, \mathsf{E})$ *be a DAG,* $\mathsf{A} \subseteq \mathsf{V}$, *and* X *and* Y *be distinct nodes in* $\mathsf{V} - \mathsf{A}$. *We say* X *and* Y *are **d-separated** by* A *in* $\mathbb{G}$ *if every chain between* X *and* Y *is blocked by* A.

It is not hard to see that every chain between X and Y is blocked by A if and only if every simple chain between X and Y is blocked by A.

Example 2.2 *Consider the DAG in Figure 2.5.*

1. X *and* R *are d-separated by* $\{Y, Z\}$ *because the chain* $[X, Y, R]$ *is blocked at* Y, *and the chain* $[X, Z, R]$ *is blocked at* Z.

2. X *and* T *are d-separated by* $\{Y, Z\}$ *because the chain* $[X, Y, R, T]$ *is blocked at* Y, *the chain* $[X, Z, R, T]$ *is blocked at* Z, *and the chain* $[X, Z, S, R, T]$ *is blocked at* Z *and at* S.

3. W *and* T *are d-separated by* $\{R\}$ *because the chains* $[W, Y, R, T]$ *and* $[W, Y, X, Z, R, T]$ *are both blocked at* R.

4. Y *and* Z *are d-separated by* $\{X\}$ *because the chain* $[Y, X, Z]$ *is blocked at* X, *the chain* $[Y, R, Z]$ *is blocked at* R, *and the chain* $[Y, R, S, Z]$ *is blocked at* S.

5. W and S are d-separated by $\{R, Z\}$ because the chain $[W, Y, R, S]$ is blocked at R, the chains $[W, Y, R, Z, S]$ and $[W, Y, X, Z, S]$ are both blocked at Z.

6. W and S are also d-separated by $\{Y, Z\}$ because the chain $[W, Y, R, S]$ is blocked at Y, the chain $[W, Y, R, Z, S]$ is blocked at Y, R, and Z, and the chain $[W, Y, X, Z, S]$ is blocked at Z.

7. W and S are also d-separated by $\{Y, X\}$. You should determine why.

8. W and X are d-separated by $\varnothing$ because the chain $[W, Y, X]$ is blocked at Y, the chain $[W, Y, R, Z, X]$ is blocked at R, and the chain $[W, Y, R, S, Z, X]$ is blocked at S.

9. W and X are not d-separated by $\{Y\}$ because the chain $[W, Y, X]$ is not blocked at Y since $Y \epsilon \{Y\}$ and clearly it could not be blocked anywhere else.

10. W and T are not d-separated by $\{Y\}$ because, even though the chain $[W, Y, R, T]$ is blocked at Y, the chain $[W, Y, X, Z, R, T]$ is not blocked at Y since $Y \epsilon \{Y\}$ and this chain is not blocked anywhere else because no other nodes are in $\{Y\}$ and there are no other head-to-head meetings on it.

Definition 2.4 Let $\mathbb{G} = (\mathsf{V}, \mathsf{E})$ be a DAG, and A, B, and C be mutually disjoint subsets of V. We say A and B are d-separated by C in $\mathbb{G}$ if for every $X \in \mathsf{A}$ and $Y \in \mathsf{B}$, X and Y are d-separated by C. We write

$$I_{\mathbb{G}}(\mathsf{A}, \mathsf{B}|\mathsf{C}).$$

If $\mathsf{C} = \varnothing$, we write only

$$I_{\mathbb{G}}(\mathsf{A}, \mathsf{B}).$$

Example 2.3 Consider the DAG in Figure 2.5. We have

$$I_{\mathbb{G}}(\{W, X\}, \{S, T\}|\{R, Z\})$$

because every chain between W and S, W and T, X and S, and X and T is blocked by $\{R, Z\}$.

We write $I_{\mathbb{G}}(\mathsf{A}, \mathsf{B}|\mathsf{C})$ because, as we show next, d-separation identifies all and only those conditional independencies entailed by the Markov condition for $\mathbb{G}$. We need the following three lemmas to prove this:

Lemma 2.1 Let P be a probability distribution of the variables in V and $\mathbb{G} = (\mathsf{V}, \mathsf{E})$ be a DAG. Then $(\mathbb{G}, P)$ satisfies the Markov condition if and only if, for every three mutually disjoint subsets $\mathsf{A}, \mathsf{B}, \mathsf{C} \subseteq \mathsf{V}$, whenever A and B are d-separated by C, A and B are conditionally independent in P given C. That is, $(\mathbb{G}, P)$ satisfies the Markov condition if and only if

$$I_{\mathbb{G}}(\mathsf{A}, \mathsf{B}|\mathsf{C}) \implies I_P(\mathsf{A}, \mathsf{B}|\mathsf{C}). \tag{2.1}$$

Proof. *The proof that, if* $(\mathbb{G}, P)$ *satisfies the Markov condition, then each d-separation implies the corresponding conditional independency is quite lengthy and can be found in Verma and Pearl [1990] and in Neapolitan [1990].*

As to the other direction, suppose each d-separation implies a conditional independency. That is, suppose Implication 2.1 holds. It is not hard to see that a node's parents d-separate the node from all its nondescendents that are not its parents. That is, if we denote the sets of parents and nondescendents of X *by* PA_X *and* ND_X *respectively, we have*

$$I_{\mathbb{G}}(\{X\}, \mathsf{ND}_X - \mathsf{PA}_X | \mathsf{PA}_X).$$

Since Implication 2.1 holds, we can therefore conclude

$$I_P(\{X\}, \mathsf{ND}_X - \mathsf{PA}_X | \mathsf{PA}_X),$$

which clearly states the same conditional independencies as

$$I_P(\{X\}, \mathsf{ND}_X | \mathsf{PA}_X),$$

which means the Markov condition is satisfied.   ∎

According to the previous lemma, if A and B are d-separated by C in $\mathbb{G}$, the Markov condition entails $I_P(\mathsf{A}, \mathsf{B} | \mathsf{C})$. For this reason, if $(\mathbb{G}, P)$ satisfies the Markov condition, we say $\mathbb{G}$ is an **independence map** of P.

We close with an intuitive explanation for why every d-separation is a conditional independency. If $\mathbb{G} = (\mathsf{V}, \mathsf{E})$ and $(\mathbb{G}, P)$ satisfies the Markov condition, any dependency in P between two variables in V would have to be through a chain between them in $\mathbb{G}$ that has no head-to-head meetings. For example, suppose P satisfies the Markov condition with the DAG in Figure 2.5. Any dependency in P between X and T would have to be either through the chain $[X, Y, R, T]$ or the chain $[X, Z, R, T]$. There could be no dependency through the chain $[X, Z, S, R, T]$ due to the head-to-head meeting at S. If we instantiate a variable on a chain with no head-to-head meeting, we block the dependency through that chain. For example, if we instantiate Y we block the dependency between X and T through the chain $[X, Y, R, T]$, and if we instantiate Z we block the dependency between X and T through the chain $[X, Z, R, T]$. If we block all such dependencies, we render the two variables independent. For example, the instantiation of Y and Z render X and T independent. In summary, the fact that we have $I_{\mathbb{G}}(\{X\}, \{T\} | \{Y, Z\})$ means we have $I_P(\{X\}, \{T\} | \{Y, Z\})$. If every chain between two nodes contains a head-to-head meeting, there is no chain through which they could be dependent, and they are independent. For example, if P satisfies the Markov condition with the DAG in Figure 2.5, W and X are independent in P. That is, the fact that we have $I_{\mathbb{G}}(\{W\}, \{X\})$ means we have $I_P(\{W\}, \{X\})$. Note that we cannot conclude $I_P(\{W\}, \{X\} | \{Y\})$ from the Markov condition, and we do not have $I_{\mathbb{G}}(\{W\}, \{X\} | \{Y\})$.

Every Entailed Conditional Independency is Identified by d-separation

Could there be conditional independencies, other than those identified by d-separation, that are entailed by the Markov condition? The answer is no. The next two lemmas prove this. First we have a definition.

Definition 2.5 *Let* V *be a set of random variables, and* A_1, B_1, C_1, A_2, B_2, *and* C_2 *be subsets of* V. *We say conditional independency* $I_P(A_1, B_1|C_1)$ *is* **equivalent** *to conditional independency* $I_P(A_2, B_2|C_2)$ *if for every probability distribution* P *of* V, $I_P(A_1, B_1|C_1)$ *holds if and only if* $I_P(A_2, B_2|C_2)$ *holds.*

Lemma 2.2 *Any conditional independency entailed by a DAG, based on the Markov condition, is equivalent to a conditional independency among disjoint sets of random variables.*
Proof. *The proof is developed in Exercise 2.4.* ∎

Due to the preceding lemma, we need only discuss disjoint sets of random variables when investigating conditional independencies entailed by the Markov condition. The next lemma states that the only such conditional independencies are those that correspond to d-separations:

Lemma 2.3 *Let* $G = (V, E)$ *be a DAG, and* P *be the set of all probability distributions* P *such that* (G, P) *satisfies the Markov condition. Then for every three mutually disjoint subsets* $A, B, C \subseteq V$,

$$I_P(A, B|C) \text{ for all } P \in P \implies I_G(A, B|C).$$

Proof. *The proof can be found in Geiger and Pearl [1990].* ∎

Before stating the main theorem concerning d-separation, we need the following definition:

Definition 2.6 *We say conditional independency* $I_P(A, B|C)$ *is* **identified** *by d-separation in* G *if one of the following holds:*

1. $I_G(A, B|C)$.

2. A, B, *and* C *are not mutually disjoint,* A', B', *and* C' *are mutually disjoint,* $I_P(A, B|C)$ *and* $I_P(A', B'|C')$ *are equivalent, and we have* $I_G(A', B'|C')$.

Theorem 2.1 *Based on the Markov condition, a DAG* G *entails all and only those conditional independencies that are identified by d-separation in* G.

Proof. *The proof follows immediately from the preceding three lemmas.* ∎

You must be careful to interpret Theorem 2.1 correctly. A particular distribution P, that satisfies the Markov condition with G, may have conditional independencies that are not identified by d-separation. For example, consider the Bayesian network in Figure 2.6. It is left as an exercise to show that

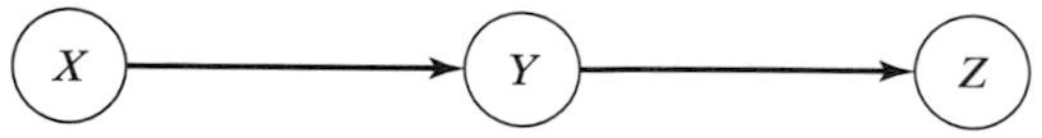

$P(x1) = a$ $P(y1|x1) = 1 - (b + c)$ $P(z1|y1) = e$

$P(x2) = 1 - a$ $P(y2|x1) = c$ $P(z2|y1) = 1 - e$

$P(y3|x1) = b$

$P(z1|y2) = e$

$P(y1|x2) = 1 - (b + d)$ $P(z2|y2) = 1 - e$

$P(y2|x2) = d$

$P(y3|x2) = b$ $P(z1|y3) = f$

$P(z2|y3) = 1 - f$

Figure 2.6: For this $(\mathbb{G}, P)$, we have $I_P(\{X\}, \{Z\})$ but not $I_{\mathbb{G}}(\{X\}, \{Z\})$.

$I_P(\{X\}, \{Z\})$ for the distribution P in that network. Clearly, $I_{\mathbb{G}}(\{X\}, \{Z\})$ is not the case. However, there are many distributions, which satisfy the Markov condition with the DAG in that figure, that do not have this independency. One such distribution is the one given in Example 1.29 on page 37 (with X, Y, and Z replaced by V, C, and S respectively). The only independency, that exists in all distributions satisfying the Markov condition with this DAG is $I_P(\{X\}, \{Z\}|\{Y\})$, and $I_{\mathbb{G}}(\{X\}, \{Z\}|\{Y\})$ is the case.

2.1.3 Finding d-Separations

Since d-separations entail conditional independencies, we want an efficient algorithm for determining whether two sets are d-separated by another set. We develop such an algorithm next. After that, we show a useful application of the algorithm.

An Algorithm for Finding d-Separations

We will develop an algorithm that finds the set of all nodes d-separated from one set of nodes B by another set of nodes A. To accomplish this, we will first find every node X such that there is at least one active chain given A between X and a node in B. This latter task can be accomplished by solving the following more general problem first. Suppose we have a directed graph (not necessarily acyclic), and we say that certain edges cannot appear consecutively in our paths of interest. That is, we identify certain ordered pairs of **edges** $(U \rightarrow V, V \rightarrow W)$ as **legal** and the remaining as illegal. We call a **path legal** if it does not contain any illegal ordered pairs of edges, and we say Y is **reachable** from X if there is a legal path from X to Y. Note that we are looking only for paths; we are not looking for chains that are not paths. We can find the set R of all nodes reachable from X as follows: We note that any node V such that the edge $X \rightarrow V$ exists is reachable. We label each such edge with a 1, and add each such V to R. Next for each such V, we check all unlabeled edges $V \rightarrow W$ and see if $(X \rightarrow V, V \rightarrow W)$ is a legal pair. We label each such edge with a 2 and we add each such W to R. We then repeat this procedure with V taking the place

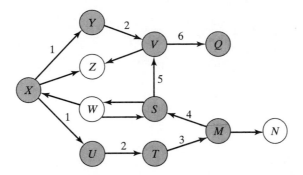

Figure 2.7: If the set of legal pairs is $\{(X \rightarrow Y, Y \rightarrow V), (X \rightarrow W, W \rightarrow S),$ $(X \rightarrow U, U \rightarrow T), (U \rightarrow T, T \rightarrow M), (T \rightarrow M, M \rightarrow S), (M \rightarrow S, S \rightarrow V),$ $(S \rightarrow V, V \rightarrow Q)\}$, and we are looking for the nodes reachable from $\{X\}$, Algorithm 2.1 labels the edges as shown. Reachable nodes are shaded.

of X and W taking the place of V. This time we label the edges found with a 3. We keep going in this fashion until we find no more legal pairs. This is similar to a breadth-first graph search except we are visiting links rather than nodes. In this way, we may investigate a given node more than once. Of course, we want to do this because there may be a legal path through a given node even though another edge reaches a dead end at the node. Figure 2.7 illustrates this method. The algorithm that follows, which is based on an algorithm in Geiger et al. [1990a], implements it.

Before starting the algorithm, we will discuss how we present algorithms. We use a very loose pseudocode similar to C++. That is, we use a good deal of simple English description, we ignore restrictions of the C++ language such as the inability to declare local arrays, and we freely use data types peculiar to the given application without defining them. Finally, when it will only clutter rather than elucidate the algorithm, we do not define variables. Our purpose is to present the algorithm using familiar, clear control structures rather than to adhere to the dictates of a programming language.

Algorithm 2.1 Find Reachable Nodes

Problem: Given a directed graph and a set of legal ordered pairs of edges, determine the set of all nodes reachable from a given set of nodes.

Inputs: a directed graph $\mathbb{G} = (V, E)$, a subset $B \subset V$, and a rule for determining whether two consecutive edges are legal.

Outputs: the subset $R \subset V$ of all nodes reachable from B.

void *find_reachable_nodes* (**directed_graph** $\mathbb{G} = (V, E)$,
         set-of-nodes B,
         set-of-nodes& R)

```
{
   for (each X ∈ B) {
      add X to R;
      for (each V such that the edge X → V exists) {
         add V to R;
         label X → V with 1;
      }
   }
   i = 1;
   found = true;
   while (found) {
      found = false;
      for (each V such that U → V is labeled i)
         for (each unlabeled edge V → W
         such that (U → V,V → W) is legal) {
            add W to R;
            label V → W with i + 1;
            found = true;
         }
      i = i + 1;
   }
}
```

Geiger et al. [1990b] proved that Algorithm 2.1 is correct. We analyze it next.

Analysis of Algorithm 2.1 (Find Reachable Nodes)

Let n be the number of nodes and m be the number of edges. In the worst case, each of the nodes can be reached from n entry points (Note that the graph is not necessarily a DAG; so there can be an edge from a node to itself.). Each time a node is reached, an edge emanating from it may need to be reexamined. For example, in Figure 2.7 the edge $V \rightarrow Q$ is examined twice. This means each edge may be examined n times, which implies that the worst-case time complexity is the following:

$$W(m, n) \in \theta(mn).$$

Next we address the problem of identifying the set of nodes D that are d-separated from B by A in a DAG $\mathbb{G} = (\mathsf{V}, \mathsf{E})$. First, we will find the set R such that $Y \in \mathsf{R}$ if and only if either $Y \in \mathsf{B}$ or there is at least one active chain given A between Y and a node in B. Once we find R, $\mathsf{D} = \mathsf{V} - (\mathsf{A} \cup \mathsf{R})$.

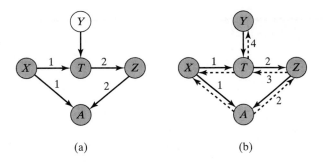

(a)   (b)

Figure 2.8: The directed graph $\mathbb{G}'$ in (b) is created from the DAG $\mathbb{G}$ in (a) by making each link go in both directions. The numbering of the edges in (a) is the result of applying a mimic of Algorithm 2.1 to $\mathbb{G}$, while the numbering of the edges in (b) is the result of applying Algorithm 2.1 to $\mathbb{G}'$.

If there is an active chain ρ between node X and some other node, then every 3-node subchain $U - V - W$ of ρ has one of the following properties:

1. $U - V - W$ is not head-to-head at V and V is not in A.

2. $U - V - W$ is head-to-head at V and V is or has a descendent in A.

Initially we may try to mimic Algorithm 2.1. We say we are mimicking Algorithm 2.1 because now we are looking for chains that satisfy certain conditions; we are not restricting ourselves to paths as Algorithm 2.1 does. We mimic Algorithm 2.1 as follows: We call a pair of adjacent links $(U - V, V - W)$ legal if and only if $U - V - W$ satisfies one of the two conditions above. Then we proceed from X as in Algorithm 2.1 numbering links and adding reachable nodes to R. This method finds only nodes that have an active chain between them and X, but it does not always find all of them. Consider the DAG in Figure 2.8 (a). Given A is the only node in A and X is the only edge in B, the edges in that DAG are numbered according to the method just described. The active chain $X \to A \leftarrow Z \leftarrow T \leftarrow Y$ is missed because the edge $T \to Z$ is already numbered by the time the chain $A \leftarrow Z \leftarrow T$ is investigated, which means the chain $Z \leftarrow T \leftarrow Y$ is never investigated. Since this is the only active chain between X and Y, Y is not be added to R.

We can solve this problem by creating from $\mathbb{G} = (\mathsf{V}, \mathsf{E})$ a new directed graph $\mathbb{G}' = (\mathsf{V}, \mathsf{E}')$, which has the links in $\mathbb{G}$ going in both directions. That is,

$$\mathsf{E}' = \mathsf{E} \cup \{U \to V \text{ such that } V \to U \ \in \mathsf{E}\}.$$

We then apply Algorithm 2.1 to $\mathbb{G}'$ calling $(U \to V, V \to W)$ legal in $\mathbb{G}'$ if and only if $U - V - W$ satisfies one of the two conditions in $\mathbb{G}$ stated previously. In this way every active chain between X and Y in $\mathbb{G}$ has associated with it a legal path from X to Y in $\mathbb{G}'$, and will therefore not be missed. Figure 2.8 (b) shows $\mathbb{G}'$, when $\mathbb{G}$ is the DAG in Figure 2.8 (a), along with the edges numbered according to this application of Algorithm 2.1. The following algorithm, taken from Geiger et al. [1990a], implements the method.

Algorithm 2.2 Find d-Separations

Problem: Given a DAG, determine the set of all nodes d-separated from one set of nodes by another set of nodes.

Inputs: a DAG $\mathbb{G} = (V, E)$ and two disjoint subsets $A, B \subset V$.

Outputs: the subset $D \subset V$ containing all nodes d-separated from every node in B by A. That is, $I_{\mathbb{G}}(B, D|A)$ holds and no superset of D has this property.

```
void find_d_separations (DAG G = (V, E),
                         set-of-nodes A, B,
                         set-of-nodes& D)
{
   DAG G' = (V, E');

   for (each V ∈ V) {
      if (V ∈ A)
         in[V] = true;
      else
         in[V] = false;
      if (V is or has a descendent in A)
         descendent[V] = true;
      else
         descendent[V] = false;
   }
   E' = E ∪ {U → V such that V → U ∈ E};
   // Call Algorithm 2.1 as follows:
   find_reachable_nodes(G' = (V, E'), B, R);
   // Use this rule to decide whether (U → V, V → W) is legal in G':
   // The pair (U → V, V → W) is legal if and only if U ≠ W
   // and one of the following hold:
   // 1) U − V − W is not head-to-head in G and in[V] is false;
   // 2) U − V − W is head-to-head in G and descendent[V] is true.
   D = V − (A ∪ R);      // We do not need to remove B because B ⊆ R.
}
```

Next we analyze the algorithm:

Analysis of Algorithm 2.2 (Find d-Separations)

Although Algorithm 2.1's worst-case time complexity is in $\theta(mn)$, where n is the number of nodes and m is the number of edges, we will show that this application of it requires only $\theta(m)$ time in the worst case. We can implement the construction of $descendent[V]$ as follows. Initially set $descendent[V]$ = true for all nodes in A. Then follow the incoming edges in A to their parents, their parents' parents, and so on, setting $descendent[V]$ = true for each node found along the way. In this way, each edge is examined at most once, and so the construction requires $\theta(m)$ time. Similarly, we can construct $in[V]$ in $\theta(m)$ time.

Next we show that the execution of Algorithm 2.1 can also be done in $\theta(m)$ time (assuming $m \geq n$). To accomplish this, we use the following data structure to represent $\mathbb{G}$. For each node we store a list of the nodes that point to that node. For example, this list for node T in Figure 2.8 (a) is $\{X, Y\}$. Call this list the node's **inlist**. We then create an **outlist** for each node, which contains all the node's to which a node points. For example, this list for node X in Figure 2.8 (a) is $\{A, T\}$. Clearly, these lists can be created from the inlists in $\theta(m)$ time. Now suppose Algorithm 2.1 is currently trying to determine for edge $U \rightarrow V$ in $\mathbb{G}'$ which pairs $(U \rightarrow V, V \rightarrow W)$ are legal. We simply choose all the nodes in V's inlist or outlist or both according to the following pseudocode:

```
if (U → V in G) {                    // U points to V in G.
    if (descendent[V] == true)
        choose all nodes W in V's inlist;
    if (in[V] == false)
        choose all nodes W in V's outlist;
}
else {                               // V points to U in G.
    if (in[V] == true)
        choose no nodes;
    else choose all nodes W in V's inlist and in V's outlist;
}
```

So for each edge $U \rightarrow V$ in $\mathbb{G}'$ we can find all legal pairs $(U \rightarrow V, V \rightarrow W)$ in constant time. Since Algorithm 2.1 looks only for these legal pairs at most once for each edge $U \rightarrow V$, the algorithm runs in $\theta(m)$ time.

Next we prove the algorithm is correct.

Theorem 2.2 *The set* D *returned by Algorithm 2.2 contains all and only nodes d-separated from every node in* B *by* A. *That is, we have* $I_{\mathbb{G}}(\mathsf{B}, \mathsf{D}|\mathsf{A})$ *and no superset of* D *has this property.*

Proof. *The set* R *determined by the algorithm contains all nodes in* B *(because Algorithm 2.1 initially adds nodes in* B *to* R*) and all nodes reachable from* B *via a legal path in* $\mathbb{G}'$*. For any two nodes* $X \in$ B *and* $Y \notin$ A $\cup$ B*, the chain*

$X - \cdots - Y$ *is active in* $\mathbb{G}$ *if and only if the path* $X \to \cdots \to Y$ *is legal in* $\mathbb{G}'$. *Thus* R *contains the nodes in* B *plus all and only those nodes that have active chains between them and a node in* B. *By the definition of d-separation, a node is d-separated from every node in* B *by* A *if the node is not in* A $\cup$ B *and there is no active chain between the node and a node in* B. *Thus* D = V − (A $\cup$ R) *is the set of all nodes d-separated from every node in* B *by* A. ■

An Application

In general, the inference problem in Bayesian networks is to determine $P(\mathsf{B}|\mathsf{A})$, where A and B are two sets of variables. In the application of Bayesian networks to decision theory, which is discussed in Chapter 5, we are often interested in determining how sensitive our decision is to each parameter in the network so that we do not waste effort trying to refine values which do not affect the decision. This matter is discussed more in Shachter [1988]. Next we show how Algorithm 2.2 can be used to determine which parameters are irrelevant to a given computation.

Suppose variable X has two possible values, $x1$ and $x2$, and we have not yet ascertained $P(x)$. We can create a variable P_X whose possible values lie in the interval $[0, 1]$, and represent $P(X = x)$ using the Bayesian network in Figure 2.9. In Chapter 6 we will discuss assigning probabilities to the possible values of P_x in the case in which the probabilities are relative frequencies. In general, we can represent the possible values of the parameters in the conditional distributions associated with a node using a set of auxiliary parent nodes. Figure 2.11 shows one such parent node for each node in the DAG in Figure 2.10. In general, each node can have more than one auxiliary parent node, and each auxiliary parent node can represent a set of random variables. However, this is not important to our present discussion, so we show only one node representing a single variable for the sake of simplicity. See Chapters 6 and 7 for the details of this representation. Let $\mathbb{G}''$ be the DAG obtained from $\mathbb{G}$ by adding these auxiliary parent nodes, and let P be the set of auxiliary parent nodes. Then, to determine which parameters are necessary to the calculation of $P(\mathsf{B}|\mathsf{A})$ in $\mathbb{G}$, we need only first use Algorithm 2.1 to determine D such that $I_{\mathbb{G}''}(\mathsf{B}, \mathsf{D}|\mathsf{A})$ and no superset of D has this property, and then take D $\cap$ P.

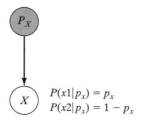

Figure 2.9: P_X is a variable whose possible values are the probabilities we may assign to $x1$.

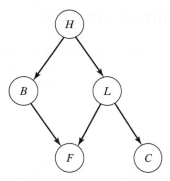

Figure 2.10: A DAG.

Example 2.4 *Let $\mathbb{G}$ be the DAG in Figure 2.10. Then $\mathbb{G}''$ is as shown in Figure 2.11. To determine $P(f)$ we need to ascertain all and only the values of P_H, P_B, P_L, and P_F because we have $I_{\mathbb{G}''}(\{F\}, \{P_X\})$, and P_X is the only auxiliary parent variable d-separated from $\{F\}$ by the empty set. To determine $P(f|b)$ we need to ascertain all and only the values of P_H, P_L, and P_F because we have $I_{\mathbb{G}''}(\{F\}, \{P_B, P_X\}|\{B\})$, and P_B and P_X are the only auxiliary parent variables d-separated from $\{F\}$ by $\{B\}$. To determine $P(f|b, x)$ we need to ascertain all and only the values of P_H, P_L, P_F, and P_X, because $I_{\mathbb{G}''}(\{F\}, \{P_B\}|\{B, X\})$, and P_B is the only auxiliary parent variable d-separated from $\{F\}$ by $\{B, X\}$.*

It is left as an exercise to write an algorithm implementing the method just described.

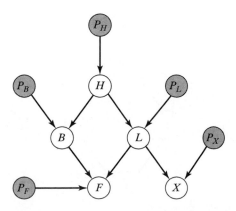

Figure 2.11: Each shaded node is an auxiliary parent node representing possible values of the parameters in the conditional distributions of the child.

2.2   Markov Equivalence

Many DAGs are equivalent in the sense that they have the same d-separations. For example, each of the DAGs in Figure 2.12 has the d-separations $I_\mathbb{G}(\{Y\}, \{Z\}| \{X\})$ and $I_\mathbb{G}(\{X\}, \{W\}| \{Y, Z\})$, and these are the only d-separations each has. After stating a formal definition of this equivalence, we give a theorem showing how it relates to probability distributions. Finally, we establish a criterion for recognizing this equivalence.

Definition 2.7 *Let* $\mathbb{G}_1 = (\mathsf{V}, \mathsf{E}_1)$ *and* $\mathbb{G}_2 = (\mathsf{V}, \mathsf{E}_2)$ *be two DAGs containing the same set of nodes* V. *Then* $\mathbb{G}_1$ *and* $\mathbb{G}_2$ *are called* **Markov equivalent** *if for every three mutually disjoint subsets* $\mathsf{A}, \mathsf{B}, \mathsf{C} \subseteq \mathsf{V}$, A *and* B *are d-separated by* C *in* $\mathbb{G}_1$ *if and only if* A *and* B *are d-separated by* C *in* $\mathbb{G}_2$. *That is*

$$I_{\mathbb{G}_1}(\mathsf{A}, \mathsf{B}|\mathsf{C}) \Longleftrightarrow I_{\mathbb{G}_2}(\mathsf{A}, \mathsf{B}|\mathsf{C}).$$

Although the previous definition relates only to graph properties, its application is in probability, due to the following theorem:

Theorem 2.3 *Two DAGs are Markov equivalent if and only if, based on the Markov condition, they entail the same conditional independencies.*

Proof. *The proof follows immediately from Theorem 2.1.*

Corollary 2.1 *Let* $\mathbb{G}_1 = (\mathsf{V}, \mathsf{E}_1)$ *and* $\mathbb{G}_2 = (\mathsf{V}, \mathsf{E}_2)$ *be two DAGs containing the same set of random variables* V. *Then* $\mathbb{G}_1$ *and* $\mathbb{G}_2$ *are Markov equivalent if and only if for every probability distribution* P *of* V, $(\mathbb{G}_1, P)$ *satisfies the Markov condition if and only if* $(\mathbb{G}_2, P)$ *satisfies the Markov condition.*

Proof. *The proof is left as an exercise.* ∎

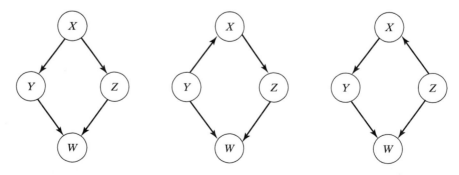

Figure 2.12: These DAGs are Markov equivalent, and there are no other DAGs Markov equivalent to them.

Next we develop a theorem that shows how to identify Markov equivalence. Its proof requires the following three lemmas:

Lemma 2.4 *Let* $\mathbb{G} = (\mathsf{V}, \mathsf{E})$ *be a DAG and* $X, Y \in \mathsf{V}$. *Then* X *and* Y *are adjacent in* $\mathbb{G}$ *if and only if they are not d-separated by some set in* $\mathbb{G}$.

Proof. *Clearly, if* X *and* Y *are adjacent, no set d-separates them since no set can block the chain consisting of the edge between them.*

In the other direction, suppose X *and* Y *are not adjacent. Either there is no path from* X *to* Y *or there is no path from* Y *to* X *for otherwise we would have a cycle. Without loss of generality, assume there is no path from* Y *to* X. *We will show that* X *and* Y *are d-separated by the set* PA_Y *consisting of all parents of* Y. *Clearly, any chain* ρ *between* X *and* Y, *such that the edge incident to* Y *has its head at* Y, *is blocked by* PA_Y. *Consider any chain* ρ *between* X *and* Y *such that the edge incident to* Y *has its tail at* Y. *There must be a head-to-head meeting on* ρ *because otherwise it would be a path from* Y *to* X. *Consider the head-to-head node* Z *closest to* Y *on* ρ. *The node* Z *cannot be a parent of* Y *because otherwise we would have a cycle. This implies that* ρ *is blocked by* PA_Y, *which completes the proof.* ∎

Corollary 2.2 *Let* $\mathbb{G} = (\mathsf{V}, \mathsf{E})$ *be a DAG and* $X, Y \in \mathsf{V}$. *Then if* X *and* Y *are d-separated by some set, they are d-separated either by the set consisting of the parents of* X *or the set consisting of the parents of* Y.

Proof. *The proof follows from the proof of Lemma 2.4.* ∎

Lemma 2.5 *Suppose we have a DAG* $\mathbb{G} = (\mathsf{V}, \mathsf{E})$ *and an uncoupled meeting* $X - Z - Y$. *Then the following are equivalent:*

1. $X - Z - Y$ *is a head-to-head meeting.*

2. *There exists a set not containing* Z *that d-separates* X *and* Y.

3. *All sets containing* Z *do not d-separate* X *and* Y.

Proof. *We will show* $1 \Rightarrow 2 \Rightarrow 3 \Rightarrow 1$.

Show $1 \Rightarrow 2$: *Suppose* $X - Z - Y$ *is a head-to-head meeting. Since* X *and* Y *are not adjacent, Lemma 2.4 says some set d-separates them. If it contained* Z, *it would not block the chain* $X - Z - Y$, *which means it would not d–separate* X *and* Y. *So it does not contain* Z.

Show $2 \Rightarrow 3$: *Suppose there exists a set* A *not containing* Z *that d-separates* X *and* Y. *Then the meeting* $X - Z - Y$ *must be head-to-head because otherwise the chain* $X - Z - Y$ *would not be blocked by* A. *However, this means any set containing* Z *does not block* $X - Z - Y$ *and therefore does not d-separate* X *and* Y.

Show $3 \Rightarrow 1$: *Suppose* $X - Z - Y$ *is not a head-to-head meeting. Since* X *and* Y *are not adjacent, Lemma 2.4 says some set d-separates them. That set must contain* Z *because it must block* $X - Z - Y$. *So it is not the case that all sets containing* Z *do not d-separate* X *and* Y. ∎

Lemma 2.6 *If $\mathbb{G}_1$ and $\mathbb{G}_2$ are Markov equivalent, then X and Y are adjacent in $\mathbb{G}_1$ if and only if they are adjacent in $\mathbb{G}_2$. That is, Markov equivalent DAGs have the same links (edges without regard for direction).*

Proof. *Suppose X and Y are adjacent in $\mathbb{G}_1$. Lemma 2.4 implies they are not d-separated in $\mathbb{G}_1$ by any set. Since $\mathbb{G}_1$ and $\mathbb{G}_2$ are Markov equivalent, this means they are not d-separated in $\mathbb{G}_2$ by any set. Lemma 2.4 therefore implies they are adjacent in $\mathbb{G}_2$. Clearly, we have the same proof with the roles of $\mathbb{G}_1$ and $\mathbb{G}_2$ reversed. This proves the lemma.* ∎

We now give the theorem that identifies Markov equivalence. This theorem was first stated in Pearl et al. [1989].

Theorem 2.4 *Two DAGs $\mathbb{G}_1$ and $\mathbb{G}_2$ are Markov equivalent if and only if they have the same links (edges without regard for direction) and the same set of uncoupled head-to-head meetings.*

Proof. *Suppose the DAGs are Markov equivalent. Lemma 2.6 says they have the same links. Suppose there is an uncoupled head-to-head meeting $X \rightarrow Z \leftarrow Y$ in $\mathbb{G}_1$. Lemma 2.5 says there is a set not containing Z that d-separates X and Y in $\mathbb{G}_1$. Since $\mathbb{G}_1$ and $\mathbb{G}_2$ are Markov equivalent, this means there is a set not containing Z that d-separates X and Y in $\mathbb{G}_2$. Again applying Lemma 2.5, we conclude $X - Z - Y$ is an uncoupled head-to-head meeting in $\mathbb{G}_2$.*

In the other direction, suppose two DAGs $\mathbb{G}_1$ and $\mathbb{G}_2$ have the same links and the same set of uncoupled head-to-head meetings. The DAGs are equivalent if two nodes X and Y are not d-separated in $\mathbb{G}_1$ by some set $\mathsf{A} \subset \mathsf{V}$ if and only if they are not d-separated in $\mathbb{G}_2$ by A. Without loss of generality, we need only show this implication holds in one direction because the same proof can be used to go in the other direction. If X and Y are not d-separated in $\mathbb{G}_1$ by A, then there is at least one active chain (given A) between X and Y in $\mathbb{G}_1$. If there is an active chain between X and Y in $\mathbb{G}_2$, then X and Y are not d-separated in $\mathbb{G}_2$ by A. So we need only show that the existence of an active chain between X and Y in $\mathbb{G}_1$ implies the existence of an active chain between X and Y in $\mathbb{G}_2$. To that end, let $\mathsf{N} = \mathsf{V} - \mathsf{A}$, label all nodes in N with an N, let ρ_1 be an active chain in $\mathbb{G}_1$, and let ρ_2 be the chain in $\mathbb{G}_2$ consisting of the same links. If ρ_2 is not active, we will show that we can create a shorter active chain between X and Y in $\mathbb{G}_1$. In this way, we can keep creating shorter active chains between X and Y in $\mathbb{G}_1$ until the corresponding chain in $\mathbb{G}_2$ is active, or until we create a chain with no intermediate nodes between X and Y in $\mathbb{G}_1$. In this latter case, X and Y are adjacent in both DAGs, and the direct link between them is our desired active chain in $\mathbb{G}_2$. Assuming ρ_2 is not active, we have two cases:
CASE 1: *There is at least one node $A \in \mathsf{A}$ responsible for ρ_2 being blocked. That is, there is a head-to-tail or tail-to-tail meeting at A on ρ_2. There must be a head-to-head meeting at A on ρ_1 because otherwise ρ_1 would be blocked. Since we've assumed the DAGs have the same set of uncoupled head-to-head meetings, this means there must be an edge connecting the nodes adjacent to A in the chains. Furthermore, these nodes must be in N because there is not a head-to-*

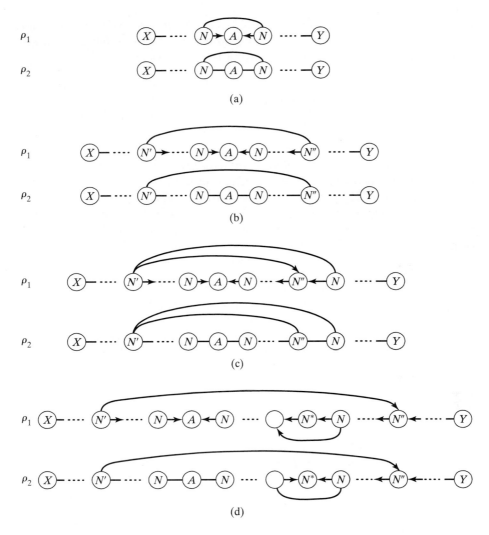

Figure 2.13: The figure used to prove Case 1 in Theorem 2.4.

head meeting at either of them on ρ_1. This is depicted in Figure 2.13 (a). By way of induction, assume we have sets of consecutive nodes in N on the chains on both sides of A, the nodes all point towards A on ρ_1, and there is an edge connecting the far two nodes N' and N'' in these sets. This situation is depicted in Figure 2.13 (b). Consider the chain σ_1 in $\mathbb{G}_1$ between X and Y obtained by using this edge to take a shortcut N'—N'' in ρ_1 around A. If there is not a head-to-head meeting on σ_1 at N' (note that this includes the case where N' is X), σ_1 is not blocked at N'. Similarly, if there is not a head-to-head meeting on σ_1 at N'', σ_1 is not blocked at N''. If σ_1 is not blocked at N' or N'', we are done because σ_1 is our desired shorter active chain. Suppose there is a head-to-head meeting at one of them in σ_1. Clearly, this could happen at most at one of them.

Without loss of generality, say it is at N''. This implies $N'' \neq Y$, which means there is a node to the right (closer to Y) on the chain. Consider the chain σ_2 in $\mathbb{G}_2$ consisting of the same links as σ_1. There are two cases:

1. *There is not a head-to-head meeting on σ_2 at N''. Consider the node to the right of N'' on the chains. This node cannot be in A because it points towards N'' on ρ_1. We have therefore created a new instance of the situation depicted in Figure 2.13 (b), and in this instance the node corresponding to N'' is closer on ρ_1 to Y. This is depicted in Figure 2.13 (c). Inductively, we must therefore eventually arrive at an instance in which one of the following is true: (1) There is not a head-to-head meeting at either side in $\mathbb{G}_1$ (i.e., at the nodes corresponding to N' and N'' on the chain corresponding to σ_1). This would at least happen when we reached both X and Y; or (2) there are head-to-head meetings on the same side in both $\mathbb{G}_1$ and $\mathbb{G}_2$. In the former situation we have found our shorter active path in $\mathbb{G}_1$, and in the latter we have the second case.*

2. *There is also a head-to-head meeting on σ_2 at N''. It is left as an exercise to show that in this case there must be a head-to-head meeting at a node $N^* \in \mathsf{N}$ somewhere between N' and N'' (including N'') on ρ_2, and there cannot be a head-to-head meeting at N^* on ρ_1. (Recall and ρ_1 is not blocked.) Therefore, there must be an edge connecting the nodes on either side of N^*. Without loss of generality, assume N^* is between A and Y. The situation is then as depicted in Figure 2.13 (d). We have not labeled the node to the left of N^* because it could be but is not necessarily A. The direction of the edge connecting the nodes on either side of N^* on ρ_1 must be towards A because otherwise we would have a cycle. When we take a shortcut around N^*, the node on N^*'s right still has an edge leaving it from the left and the node on N^*'s left still has an edge coming into it from the right. So this shortcut cannot be blocked in $\mathbb{G}_1$ at either of these nodes. Therefore, this shortcut must result in a shorter active chain in $\mathbb{G}_1$.*

CASE 2: *There are no nodes in A responsible for ρ_2 being blocked. Then there must be at least one node $N' \in \mathsf{N}$ responsible for ρ_2 being blocked, which means there must be a head-to-head meeting on ρ_2 at N'. Since ρ_1 is not blocked, there is not a head-to-head meeting on ρ_1 at N'. Since we've assumed the two DAGs have the same set of uncoupled head-to-head meetings, this means the nodes adjacent to N' on the chains are adjacent to each other. Since there is a head-to-head meeting on ρ_2 at N', there cannot be a head–to-head meeting on ρ_2 at either of these nodes (the ones adjacent to N' on the chains). These nodes therefore cannot be in A because we've assumed no nodes in A are responsible for ρ_2 being blocked. Since ρ_1 is not blocked, we cannot have a head-to-head meeting on ρ_1 at a node in N. Therefore, the only two possibilities (aside from symmetrical ones) in $\mathbb{G}_1$ are the ones depicted in Figures 2.14 (a) and (b). Clearly, in either case by taking the shortcut around N', we have a shorter active chain in $\mathbb{G}_1$.* ∎

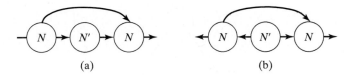

(a) (b)

Figure 2.14: In either case, taking the shortcut around N' results in a shorter active chain in $\mathbb{G}_1$.

Example 2.5 *The DAGs in Figure 2.15 (a) and (b) are Markov equivalent because they have the same links and the only uncoupled head-to-head meeting in both is $X \to Z \leftarrow Y$. The DAG in Figure 2.15 (c) is not Markov equivalent to the first two because it has the link $W - Y$. The DAG in Figure 2.15 (d) is not Markov equivalent to the first two because, although it has the same links, it does*

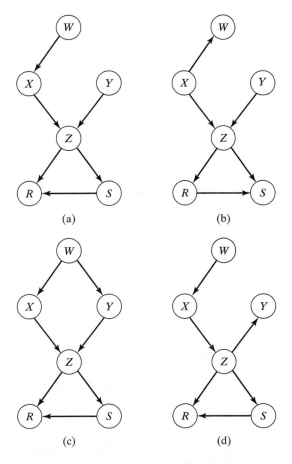

Figure 2.15: The DAGs in (a) and (b) are Markov equivalent. The DAGs in (c) and (d) are not Markov equivalent to the first two DAGs or to each other.

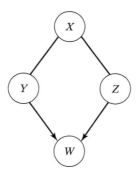

Figure 2.16: This DAG pattern represents the Markov equivalence class in Figure 2.12.

not have the uncoupled head-to-head meeting $X \to Z \leftarrow Y$. Clearly, the DAGs in Figure 2.15 (c) and (d) are not Markov equivalent to each other either.

It is straightforward that Theorem 2.4 enables us to develop a polynomial-time algorithm for determining whether two DAGs are Markov equivalent. We simply check to see if they have the same links and uncoupled head-to-head meetings. It is left as an exercise to write such an algorithm.

Furthermore, Theorem 2.4 gives us a simple way to represent a Markov equivalence class with a single graph. That is, we can represent a Markov equivalent class with a graph that has the same links and the same uncoupled head-to-head meeting as the DAGs in the class. Any assignment of directions to the undirected edges in this graph, that does not create a new uncoupled head-to-head meeting or a directed cycle, yields a member of the equivalence class. Often there are edges other than uncoupled head-to-head meetings which must be oriented the same in Markov equivalent DAGs. For example, if all DAGs in a given Markov equivalence class have the edge $X \to Y$, and the uncoupled meeting $X \to Y - Z$ is not head-to-head, then all the DAGs in the equivalence class must have $Y - Z$ oriented as $Y \to Z$. So we define a **DAG pattern** for a Markov equivalence class to be the graph that has the same links as the DAGs in the equivalence class and has oriented all and only the edges common to all of the DAGs in the equivalence class. The directed links in a DAG pattern are called **compelled edges**. The DAG pattern in Figure 2.16 represents the Markov equivalence class in Figure 2.12 on page 88. The DAG pattern in Figure 2.17 (b) represents the Markov equivalence class in Figure 2.17 (a). Notice that no DAG Markov equivalent to each of the DAGs in Figure 2.17 (a) can have $W - U$ oriented as $W \leftarrow U$ because this would create another uncoupled head-to-head meeting.

Since all DAGs in the same Markov equivalence class have the same d-separations, we can define d-separation for DAG patterns:

Definition 2.8 *Let gp be a dag pattern whose nodes are the elements of* V, *and* A, B, *and let* C *be mutually disjoint subsets of* V. *We say* A *and* B *are*

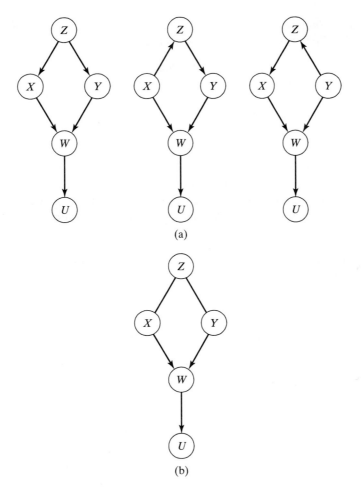

Figure 2.17: The DAG pattern in (b) represents the Markov equivalence class in (a).

d-separated *by* C *in gp if* A *and* B *are d-separated by* C *in any (and therefore every) DAG* G *in the Markov equivalence class represented by gp.*

Example 2.6 *For the DAG pattern gp in Figure 2.16, we have*

$$I_{gp}(\{Y\}, \{Z\}|\{X\})$$

because $\{Y\}$ *and* $\{Z\}$ *are d-separated by* $\{X\}$ *in the DAGs in Figure 2.12.*

The following lemmas follow immediately from the corresponding lemmas for DAGs:

Lemma 2.7 *Let gp be a DAG and X and Y be nodes in gp. Then X and Y are adjacent in gp if and only if they are not d-separated by some set in gp.*

Proof. *The proof follows from Lemma 2.4.* ∎

Lemma 2.8 *Suppose we have a DAG pattern gp and an uncoupled meeting* $X - Z - Y$. *Then the following are equivalent:*

1. $X - Z - Y$ *is a head-to-head meeting.*

2. *There exists a set not containing* Z *that d-separates* X *and* Y.

3. *All sets containing* Z *do not d-separate* X *and* Y.

Proof. *The proof follows from Lemma 2.5.*   ∎

Owing to Corollary 2.1, if $\mathbb{G}$ is an independence map of a probability distribution P (i.e., $(\mathbb{G}, P)$ satisfies the Markov condition), then every DAG Markov equivalent to $\mathbb{G}$ is also an independence map of P. In this case, we say the DAG pattern *gp* representing the equivalence class is an **independence map** of P.

2.3   Entailing Dependencies with a DAG

As noted at the beginning of this chapter, the Markov condition only entails independencies; it does not entail any dependencies. As a result, many uninformative DAGs can satisfy the Markov condition with a given distribution P. The following example illustrates this.

Example 2.7 *Let* Ω *be the set of objects in Figure 1.2 on page 8, and let* P, V, S, *and* C *be as defined in Example 1.29 on page 37. That is,* P *assigns a probability of* $1/13$ *to each object, and random variables* V, S, *and* C *are defined as follows:*

Variable	Value	Outcomes Mapped to this Value
V	$v1$	*All objects containing a "1"*
	$v2$	*All objects containing a "2"*
S	$s1$	*All square objects*
	$s2$	*All round objects*
C	$c1$	*All black objects*
	$c2$	*All white objects*

Then, as shown in Example 1.29, P *satisfies the Markov condition with the DAG in Figure 2.18 (a) because* $I_P(\{V\}, \{S\}|\{C\})$. *However,* P *also satisfies the Markov condition with the DAGs in Figures 2.18 (b) and (c) because the Markov condition does not entail any independencies in the case of these DAGs. This means that not only* P *but every probability distribution of* V, S, *and* C *satisfies the Markov condition with each of these DAGs.*

The DAGs in Figures 2.18 (b) and (c) are complete DAGs. Recall that a **complete DAG** $\mathbb{G} = (\mathsf{V}, \mathsf{E})$ is one in which there is an edge between every pair of nodes. That is, for every $X, Y \in \mathsf{V}$, either $(X, Y) \in \mathsf{E}$ or $(Y, X) \in \mathsf{E}$. In general, the Markov condition entails no independencies in the case of a complete DAG $\mathbb{G} = (\mathsf{V}, \mathsf{E})$, which means $(\mathbb{G}, P)$ satisfies the Markov condition

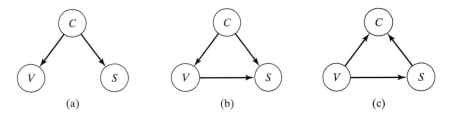

Figure 2.18: The probability distribution in Example 2.4 satisfies the Markov condition with each of these DAGs.

for every probability distribution P of the variables in V. We see then that $(\mathbb{G}, P)$ can satisfy the Markov condition without $\mathbb{G}$ telling us anything about P.

Given a probability distribution P of the variables in some set V and $X, Y \in V$, we say there is a **direct dependency** between X and Y in P if $\{X\}$ and $\{Y\}$ are not conditionally independent given any subset of V. The problem with the Markov condition alone is that it entails that the absence of an edge between X any Y means there is no direct dependency between X any Y, but it does not entail that the presence of an edge between X and Y means there is a direct dependency. That is, if there is no edge between X and Y, Lemmas 2.4 and 2.1 together tell us the Markov condition entails $\{X\}$ and $\{Y\}$ are conditionally independent given some set (possibly empty) of variables. For example, in Figure 2.18 (a), because there is no edge between V and C, we know from Lemma 2.4 they are d-separated by some set. It turns out that set is $\{C\}$. Lemma 2.1 therefore tells us $I_P(\{V\}, \{S\}|\{C\})$. On the other hand, if there is an edge between X and Y, the Markov condition does not entail that $\{X\}$ and $\{Y\}$ are not conditionally independent given some set of variables. For example, in Figure 2.18 (b), the edge between V and S does not mean that $\{V\}$ and $\{S\}$ are not conditionally independent given some set of variables. Indeed, we know they actually are.

2.3.1 Faithfulness

In general, we would want an edge to mean there is a direct dependency. As we shall see, the faithfulness condition entails this. We discuss it next.

Definition 2.9 *Suppose we have a joint probability distribution P of the random variables in some set V and a DAG $\mathbb{G} = (V, E)$. We say that $(\mathbb{G}, P)$ satisfies the **faithfulness condition** if, based on the Markov condition, $\mathbb{G}$ entails all and only conditional independencies in P. That is, the following two conditions hold:*

1. *$(\mathbb{G}, P)$ satisfies the Markov condition (This means $\mathbb{G}$ entails only conditional independencies in P.)*

2. *All conditional independencies in P are entailed by $\mathbb{G}$, based on the Markov condition.*

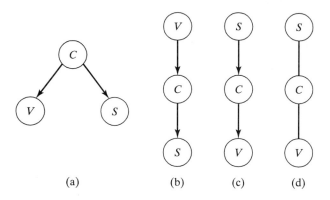

Figure 2.19: The probability distribution in Example 2.7 satisfies the faithfulness condition with each of the DAGs in (a), (b), and (c), and with the DAG pattern in (d).

When $(\mathbb{G}, P)$ satisfies the faithfulness condition, we say P and $\mathbb{G}$ are **faithful** to each other, and we say $\mathbb{G}$ is a **perfect map** of P. When $(\mathbb{G}, P)$ does not satisfy the faithfulness condition, we say they are **unfaithful** to each other.

Example 2.8 *Let P and V, S, and C be as in Example 2.7. Then, as shown in Example 1.29, $I_P(\{V\}, \{S\}|\{C\})$, which means $(\mathbb{G}, P)$ satisfies the Markov condition if $\mathbb{G}$ is the DAG in Figure 1.3 (a), (b), or (c). Those DAGs are shown again in Figure 2.19. It is left as an exercise to show that there are no other conditional independencies in P. That is, you should show*

$$\neg I_P(\{V\}, \{S\}) \qquad \neg I_P(\{V\}, \{C\}|\{S\})$$
$$\neg I_P(\{V\}, \{C\}) \qquad \neg I_P(\{C\}, \{S\}|\{V\})$$
$$\neg I_P(\{S\}, \{C\}).$$

(It is not necessary to show, for example, $\neg I_P(\{V\}, \{S, C\})$ because the first nonindependency listed above implies this one.) Therefore, $(\mathbb{G}, P)$ satisfies the faithfulness condition if $\mathbb{G}$ is any one of the DAGs in Figure 2.19.

The following theorems establish a criterion for recognizing faithfulness:

Theorem 2.5 *Suppose we have a joint probability distribution P of the random variables in some set V and a DAG $\mathbb{G} = (V, E)$. Then $(\mathbb{G}, P)$ satisfies the faithfulness condition if and only if all and only conditional independencies in P are identified by d-separation in $\mathbb{G}$.*
Proof. *The proof follows immediately from Theorem 2.1.*   ∎

Example 2.9 *Consider the Bayesian network $(\mathbb{G}, P)$ in Figure 2.6, which is shown again in Figure 2.20. As noted in the discussion following Theorem 2.1, for that network we have $I_P(\{X\}, \{Z\})$ but not $I_{\mathbb{G}}(\{X\}, \{Z\})$. Therefore, $(\mathbb{G}, P)$ does not satisfy the faithfulness condition.*

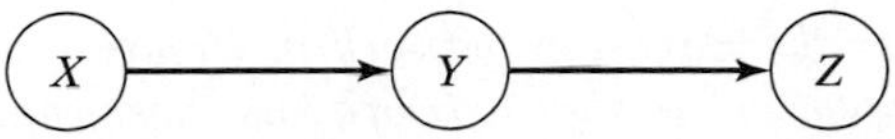

$$P(x1) = a \qquad P(y1|x1) = 1 - (b + c) \qquad P(z1|y1) = e$$
$$P(x2) = 1 - a \qquad P(y2|x1) = c \qquad P(z2|y1) = 1 - e$$
$$P(y3|x1) = b$$

$$P(z1|y2) = e$$
$$P(y1|x2) = 1 - (b + d) \qquad P(z2|y2) = 1 - e$$
$$P(y2|x2) = d$$
$$P(y3|x2) = b \qquad P(z1|y3) = f$$
$$P(z2|y3) = 1 - f$$

Figure 2.20: For this $(\mathbb{G}, P)$, we have $I_P(\{X\}, \{Z\})$ but not $I_\mathbb{G}(\{X\}, \{Z\})$.

We made very specific conditional probability assignments in Figure 2.20 to develop a distribution that is unfaithful to the DAG in that figure. If we just arbitrarily assign conditional distributions to the variables in a DAG, are we likely to end up with a joint distribution that is unfaithful to the DAG? The answer is no. A theorem to this effect in the case of linear models appears in Spirtes et al. [1993, 2000]. In a linear model, each variable is a linear function of its parents and an error variable. In this case, the set of possible conditional probability assignments to some DAG is a real space. The theorem says that the set of all points in this space, that yield distributions unfaithful to the DAG, form a set of Lebesgue measure zero. Intuitively, this means that almost all such assignments yield distributions faithful to the DAG. Meek [1995a] extends this result to the case of discrete variables.

The following theorem obtains the result that if P is faithful to some DAG, then P is faithful to an equivalence class of DAGs:

Theorem 2.6 *If $(\mathbb{G}, P)$ satisfies the faithfulness condition, then P satisfies this condition with all and only those DAGs that are Markov equivalent to $\mathbb{G}$. Furthermore, if we let gp be the DAG pattern corresponding to this Markov equivalence class, the d-separations in gp identify all and only conditional independencies in P. We say that gp and P are **faithful** to each other, and gp is a **perfect map** of P.*
Proof. *The proof follows immediately from Theorem 2.5.* ■

We say a distribution P **admits a faithful DAG representation** if P is faithful to some DAG (and therefore some DAG pattern). The distribution discussed in Example 2.8 admits a faithful DAG representation. Owing to the previous theorem, if P admits a faithful DAG representation, there is a unique DAG pattern with which P is faithful. In general, our goal is to find that DAG pattern whenever P admits a faithful DAG representation. Methods for doing this are discussed in Chapters 8–11. Presently, we show that not every P admits a faithful DAG representation.

Example 2.10 *Consider the Bayesian network in Figure 2.20. As mentioned in Example 2.9, the distribution in that network has these independencies:*

$$I_P(\{X\}, \{Z\}) \qquad I_P(\{X\}, \{Z\}|\{Y\}).$$

Suppose we specify values for the parameters so that these are the only independencies, and some DAG $\mathbb{G}$ is faithful to the distribution. (Note that $\mathbb{G}$ is not necessarily the DAG in Figure 2.20.) Due to Theorem 2.5, $\mathbb{G}$ has these and only these d-separations:

$$I_{\mathbb{G}}(\{X\}, \{Z\}) \qquad I_{\mathbb{G}}(\{X\}, \{Z\}|\{Y\}).$$

Lemma 2.4 therefore implies the links in $\mathbb{G}$ are $X - Y$ and $Y - Z$. This means $X - Y - Z$ is an uncoupled meeting. Since $I_{\mathbb{G}}(\{X\}, \{Z\})$, Condition (2) in Lemma 2.5 holds. This lemma therefore implies its Condition (3) holds, which means we cannot have $I_{\mathbb{G}}(\{X\}, \{Z\}|\{Y\})$. This contradiction shows there can be no such DAG.

Example 2.11 *Suppose we specify conditional distributions for the DAG in Figure 2.21 (a) so that the resultant joint distribution $P(v, s, c, l, f)$ satisfies the faithfulness condition with that DAG. Then the only independencies involving only the variables V, S, L, and F are the following:*

$$I_P(\{L\}, \{F, S\}) \qquad I_P(\{L\}, \{S\}) \qquad I_P(\{L\}, \{F\}) \qquad (2.2)$$
$$I_P(\{F\}, \{L, V\}) \qquad I_P(\{F\}, \{V\}).$$

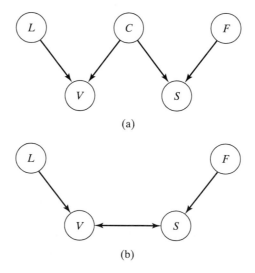

(a)

(b)

Figure 2.21: If P satisfies the faithfulness condition with the DAG in (a), the marginal distribution of V, S, L, and F cannot satisfy the faithfulness condition with any DAG. There would have to be arrows going both ways between V and S. This is depicted in (b).

Consider the marginal distribution $P(v, s, , l, f)$ of $P(v, s, c, l, f)$. We will show that this distribution does not admit a faithful DAG representation. Due to Theorem 2.5, if some DAG $\mathbb{G}$ was faithful to that distribution, it would have these and only these d-separations involving only the nodes V, S, L, and F:

$$I_{\mathbb{G}}(\{L\}, \{F, S\}) \qquad I_{\mathbb{G}}(\{L\}, \{S\}) \qquad I_{\mathbb{G}}(\{L\}, \{F\})$$
$$I_{\mathbb{G}}(\{F\}, \{L, V\}) \qquad I_{\mathbb{G}}(\{F\}, \{V\}).$$

Due to Lemma 2.4, the links in $\mathbb{G}$ are therefore $L - V$, $V - S$, and $S - F$. This means $L - V - S$ is an uncoupled meeting. Since $I_{\mathbb{G}}(\{L\}, \{S\})$, Lemma 2.5 therefore implies it is an uncoupled head-to-head meeting. Similarly, $V - S - F$ is an uncoupled head-to-head meeting. The resultant graph, which is shown in Figure 2.21 (b), is not a DAG. This contradiction shows $P(v, s, l, f)$ does not admit a faithful DAG representation. Exercise 2.20 shows an urn problem in which four variables have this distribution.

Pearl [1988] presents necessary but not sufficient conditions for a probability distribution to admit a faithful DAG representation.

Recall at the beginning of this subsection we stated that, in the case of faithfulness, an edge between two nodes means there is a direct dependency between the nodes. The theorem that follows includes this result and more.

Theorem 2.7 *Suppose we have a joint probability distribution P of the random variables in some set V and a DAG $\mathbb{G} = (\mathsf{V}, \mathsf{E})$. Then if P admits a faithful DAG representation, gp is the DAG pattern faithful to P if and only if the following two conditions hold:*

1. *X and Y are adjacent in gp if and only if there is no subset $\mathsf{S} \subseteq \mathsf{V}$ such that $I_P(\{X\}, \{Y\}|\mathsf{S})$. That is, X and Y are adjacent if and only if there is a direct dependency between X and Y.*

2. *$X - Z - Y$ is a head-to-head meeting in gp if and only if $Z \in \mathsf{S}$ implies $\neg I_P(\{X\}, \{Y\}|\mathsf{S})$.*

Proof. *Suppose gp is the DAG pattern faithful to P. Then due to Theorem 2.6, all and only the independencies in P are identified by d-separation in gp, which are the d-separations in any DAG $\mathbb{G}$ in the equivalence class represented by gp. Therefore, Condition (1) follows from Lemma 2.4, and Condition (2) follows from Lemma 2.5.*

In the other direction, suppose Conditions (1) and (2) hold for gp and P. Since we've assumed P admits a faithful DAG representation, there is some DAG pattern gp' faithful to P. By what was just proved, we know Conditions (1) and (2) also hold for gp' and P. However, this mean any DAG $\mathbb{G}$ in the Markov equivalence class represented by gp must have the same links and same set of uncoupled head-to-head meetings as any DAG $\mathbb{G}'$ in the Markov equivalence class represented by gp'. Theorem 2.4 therefore says $\mathbb{G}$ and $\mathbb{G}'$ are in the same Markov equivalence class, which means $gp = gp'$. ∎

2.3.2   Embedded Faithfulness

The distribution $P(v, s, l, f)$ in Example 2.11 does not admit a faithful DAG representation. However, it is the marginal of a distribution, namely $P(v, s, c, l, f)$, of one which does. This is an example of embedded faithfulness, which is defined as follows:

Definition 2.10 *Let P be a joint probability distribution of the variables in V where $V \subseteq W$, and let $G = (W, E)$ be a DAG. We say (G, P) satisfies the **embedded faithfulness condition** if the following two conditions hold:*

1. *Based on the Markov condition, G entails only conditional independencies in P for subsets including only elements of V.*

2. *All conditional independencies in P are entailed by G, based on the Markov condition.*

When (G, P) satisfies the embedded faithfulness condition, we say P is **embedded faithfully** in G. Notice that faithfulness is a special case of embedded faithfulness in which $W = V$.

Example 2.12 *Clearly, the distribution $P(v, s, l, f)$ in Example 2.11 is embedded faithfully in the DAG in Figure 2.21 (a).*

As was done in the previous example, we often obtain embedded faithfulness by taking the marginal of a faithful distribution. The following theorem formalizes this result:

Theorem 2.8 *Let P be a joint probability distribution of the variables in W with $V \subseteq W$, and $G = (W, E)$. If (G, P) satisfies the faithfulness condition, and P' is the marginal distribution of V, then (G, P') satisfies the embedded faithfulness condition.*
Proof. *The proof is obvious.*   ∎.

Definition 2.10 relates only to independencies entailed by a DAG. It says nothing about P being a marginal of a distribution of the variables in V. There are other cases of embedded faithfulness. Example 2.14 shows one such case. Before giving that example, we discuss embedded faithfulness further.

The following theorems are analogous to the corresponding ones concerning faithfulness:

Theorem 2.9 *Let P be a joint probability distribution of the variables in V with $V \subseteq W$, and $G = (W, E)$. Then (G, P) satisfies the embedded faithfulness condition if and only if all and only conditional independencies in P are identified by d-separation in G restricted to elements of V.*
Proof. *The proof is left as an exercise.*   ∎

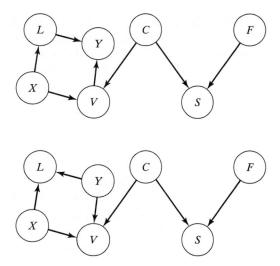

Figure 2.22: Suppose the only conditional independencies in a probability distribution P of V, S, L, and F are those in Equality 2.2, which appears in Example 2.11. Then P is embedded faithfully in both of these DAGs.

Theorem 2.10 *Let P be a joint probability distribution of the variables in* V *with* $\mathsf{V} \subseteq \mathsf{W}$*, and* $\mathbb{G} = (\mathsf{W}, \mathsf{E})$*. If* $(\mathbb{G}, P)$ *satisfies the embedded faithfulness condition, then P satisfies this condition with all those DAGs that are Markov equivalent to* $\mathbb{G}$*. Furthermore, if we let gp be the DAG pattern corresponding to this Markov equivalence class, the d-separations in gp, restricted to elements of* V*, identify all and only conditional independencies in P. We say P is* **embedded faithfully** *in gp.*
Proof. *The proof is left as an exercise.* ∎

Note that the theorem says "all those DAGS", but, unlike the corresponding theorem for faithfulness, it does not say "only those DAGs." If a distribution can be embedded faithfully, there are an infinite number of non-Markov equivalent DAGs in which it can be embedded faithfully. Trivially, we can always replace an edge by a directed linked list of new variables. Figure 2.22 shows a more complex example. The distribution $P(v, s, l, f)$ in Example 2.11 is embedded faithfully in both DAGs in that figure. However, even though the DAGs contain the same nodes, they are not Markov equivalent.

We say a probability distribution admits an **embedded faithful DAG representation** if it can be embedded faithfully in some DAG. Does every probability distribution admit an embedded faithful DAG representation? The following example shows the answer is no.

Example 2.13 *Consider the distribution in Example 2.10. Recall that it has these and only these conditional independencies:*

$$I_P(\{X\}, \{Z\}) \qquad I_P(\{X\}, \{Z\} | \{Y\}).$$

*Example 2.10 showed this distribution does not admit a faithful DAG represen-
tation. We show next that it does not even admit an embedded faithful DAG
representation. Suppose it can be embedded faithfully in some DAG $\mathbb{G}$. Due
to Theorem 2.9, $\mathbb{G}$ must have these and only these d-separations among the
variables X, Y, and Z:*

$$I_{\mathbb{G}}(\{X\},\{Z\})   \qquad I_{\mathbb{G}}(\{X\},\{Z\}|\{Y\}).$$

*There must be a chain between X and Y with no head-to-head meetings because
otherwise we would have $I_{\mathbb{G}}(\{X\},\{Y\})$. Similarly, there must be a chain between
Y and Z with no head-to-head meetings. Consider the resultant chain between X
and Z. If it had a head-to-head meeting at Y, it would not be blocked by $\{Y\}$ because it does not have a head-to-head meeting at a node not in $\{Y\}$. This means
if it had a head-to-head meeting at Y, we would not have $I_{\mathbb{G}}(\{X\},\{Z\}|\{Y\})$.
If it did not have a head-to-head meeting at Y, there would be no head-to-head
meetings on it at all, which means it would not be blocked by $\varnothing$, and we would
therefore not have $I_{\mathbb{G}}(\{X\},\{Z\})$. This contradiction shows there can be no such
DAG.*

We say P is **included** in DAG $\mathbb{G}$ if P is the probability distribution in a
Bayesian network containing $\mathbb{G}$ or P is the marginal of a probability distribution
in a Bayesian network containing $\mathbb{G}$. When a probability distribution is faithful
to some DAG $\mathbb{G}$, P is included in $\mathbb{G}$ by definition because the faithfulness
condition subsumes the Markov condition. In the case of embedded faithfulness,
things are not as simple. It is possible to embed a distribution P faithfully in
a DAG $\mathbb{G}$ without P being included in the DAG. The following example, taken
from Verma and Pearl [1991], shows such a case:

Example 2.14 *Let $\mathsf{V} = \{X,Y,Z,W\}$ and $\mathsf{W} = \{X,Y,Z,W,T\}$. The only
d-separation among the variables in V in the DAGs in Figures 2.23 (a) and (b),
is $I_{\mathbb{G}}(\{Z\},\{X\}|\{Y\})$. Suppose we assign conditional distributions to the DAG
in (a) so that the resultant joint distribution of W is faithful to that DAG. Then
the marginal distribution of V is faithfully embedded in both DAGs. The DAG
in (a) has the same edges as the one in (b) plus one more. So the DAG in (b)
has d-separations, (e.g., $I_{\mathbb{G}}(\{W\},\{X\}|\{Y,T\})$), which the one in (a) does not
have. We will show that as a result there are distributions which are embedded
faithfully in both DAGs but are only included in the DAG in (a).*

*To that end, for any marginal distribution $P(\mathsf{v})$ of a probability distribution
$P(\mathsf{w})$ satisfying the Markov condition with the DAG in (b), we have*

$$
\begin{aligned}
P(x,y,z,w) &= \sum_{t} P(w|z,t)P(z|y)P(y|x,t)P(x)P(t) \\
&= P(z|y)P(x)\sum_{t} P(w|z,t)P(y|x,t)P(t).
\end{aligned}
$$

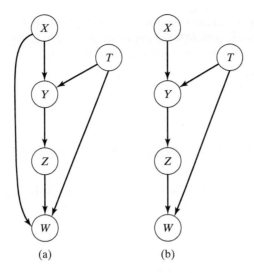

(a)   (b)

Figure 2.23: The DAG in (a) includes distributions of X, Y, Z, and W which the DAG in (b) does not.

Also, for any marginal distribution $P(\mathsf{v})$ of a probability distribution $P(\mathsf{w})$ satisfying the Markov condition with the DAGs in both figures, we have

$$
\begin{aligned}
P(x, y, z, w) &= P(w|x, y, z)P(z|x, y)P(y|x)p(x) \\
&= P(w|x, y, z)P(z|y)P(y|x)P(x).
\end{aligned}
$$

Equating these two expressions and summing over y yields

$$
\sum_y P(w|x, y, z)P(y|x) = \sum_t P(w|z, t)P(t).
$$

The left-hand side of the previous expression contains the variable x, whereas the right-hand side does not. Therefore, for a distribution of V to be the marginal of a distribution of W which satisfies the Markov condition with the DAG in (b), the distribution of V must have the left-hand side equal for all values of x. For example, for all values of w and z it would need to have

$$
\sum_y P(w|x_1, y, z)P(y|x) = \sum_y P(w|x_2, y, z)P(y|x). \tag{2.3}
$$

Repeating the preceding steps for the DAG in (a), we obtain that for any marginal distribution $P(\mathsf{v})$ of a probability distribution $P(\mathsf{w})$ satisfying the Markov condition with that DAG, we have

$$
\sum_y P(w|x, y, z)P(y|x) = \sum_t P(w|x, z, t)P(t). \tag{2.4}
$$

Note that now the variable x appears on both sides of the equality. Suppose we assign values to the conditional distributions in the DAG in (a) to obtain a distribution $P'(\mathsf{w})$ such that for some values of w and z

$$\sum_t P'(w|x_1, z, t)P'(t) \neq \sum_t P'(w|x_2, z, t)P'(t).$$

Then, because of Equality 2.4, we would have for the marginal distribution $P'(\mathsf{v})$

$$\sum_y P'(w|x_1, y, z)P'(y|x) \neq \sum_y P'(w|x_2, y, z)P'(y|x).$$

However, Equality 2.3 says these two expressions must be equal if a distribution of V *is to be the marginal of a distribution of* W *which satisfies the Markov condition with the DAG in (b). So the marginal distribution $P'(\mathsf{v})$ is not the marginal of a distribution of* W *which satisfies the Markov condition with the DAG in (b).*

Suppose further that we have made conditional distribution assignments so that $P'(\mathsf{w})$ is faithful to the DAG (a). Then, based on the discussion at the beginning of the example, $P'(\mathsf{v})$ is embedded faithfully in the DAG (b). So we have found a distribution of V *which is embedded faithfully in the DAG in (b) but is not included in it.*

2.4   Minimality

Consider again the Bayesian network in Figure 2.20. The probability distribution in that network is not faithful to the DAG because it has the independency $I_P(\{X\}, \{Z\})$ and the DAG does not have the d-separation $I_{\mathbb{G}}(\{X\}, \{Z\})$. In Example 2.10 we showed that it is not possible to find a DAG faithful to that distribution. So the problem was not in our choice of DAGs. Rather it is inherent in the distribution that there is no DAG with which it is faithful. Notice that, if we remove either of the edges from the DAG in Figure 2.20, the DAG ceases to satisfy the Markov condition with P. For example, if we remove the edge $X \to Y$, we have $I_{\mathbb{G}}(\{X\}, \{Y, Z\})$, but not $I_P(\{X\}, \{Y, Z\})$. So the DAG does have the property that it is minimal in the sense that we cannot remove any edges without the Markov condition ceasing to hold. Furthermore, if we add an edge between X and Z to form a complete graph, it would not be minimal in this sense. Formally, we have the following definition concerning the property just discussed:

Definition 2.11 *Suppose we have a joint probability distribution P of the random variables in some set* V *and a DAG* $\mathbb{G} = (\mathsf{V}, \mathsf{E})$. *We say that* $(\mathbb{G}, P)$ *satisfies the **minimality condition** if the following two conditions hold:*

1. *$(\mathbb{G}, P)$ satisfies the Markov condition.*

2. *If we remove any edges from* $\mathbb{G}$, *the resultant DAG no longer satisfies the Markov condition with P.*

Example 2.15 *Consider the distribution P in Example 2.7 on page 96. The only conditional independency is $I_P(\{V\}, \{S\}|\{C\})$. The DAG in Figure 2.18 (a) satisfies the minimality condition with P because if we remove the edge $C \to V$ we have $I_\mathbb{G}(\{V\}, \{C, S\})$, if we remove the edge $C \to S$ we have $I_\mathbb{G}(\{S\}, \{C, V\})$, and neither of these independencies hold in P. The DAG in Figure 2.18 (b) does not satisfy the minimality condition with P because if remove the edge $V \to S$, the only new d-separation is $I_\mathbb{G}(\{V\}, \{S\}|\{C\})$, and this independency does hold in P. Finally, the DAG in Figure 2.18 (c) does satisfy the minimality condition with P because no edge can be removed without creating a d-separation that is not an independency in P. For example, if we remove $V \to S$, we have $I_\mathbb{G}(\{V\}, \{S\})$, and this independency does not hold in P.*

The previous example illustrates that a DAG can satisfy the minimality condition with a distribution without being faithful to the distribution. Namely, the only DAG in Figure 2.18 that is faithful to P is the one in (a), but the one in (c) also satisfies the minimality condition with P. On the other hand, the reverse is not true. Namely, a DAG cannot be faithful to a distribution without satisfying the minimality with the distribution. The following theorem summarizes these results:

Theorem 2.11 *Suppose we have a joint probability distribution P of the random variables in some set V and a DAG $\mathbb{G} = (V, E)$. If $(\mathbb{G}, P)$ satisfies the faithfulness condition, then $(\mathbb{G}, P)$ satisfies the minimality condition. However, $(\mathbb{G}, P)$ can satisfy the minimality condition without satisfying the faithfulness condition.*

Proof. *Suppose $(\mathbb{G}, P)$ satisfies the faithfulness condition and does not satisfy the minimality condition. Since $(\mathbb{G}, P)$ does not satisfy the minimality condition. some edge (X, Y) can be removed and the resultant DAG will still satisfy the Markov condition with P. Due to Lemma 2.4, X and Y are d-separated by some set in this new DAG and therefore, due to Lemma 2.1, they are conditionally independent given this set. Since there is an edge between X and Y in $\mathbb{G}$, Lemma 2.4 implies X and Y are not d-separated by any set in $\mathbb{G}$. Since $(\mathbb{G}, P)$ satisfies the faithfulness condition, Theorem 2.5 therefore implies they are not conditionally independent given any set. This contradiction proves faithfulness implies minimality.*

The probability distribution in Example 2.7 along with the DAG in Figure 2.18 (c) shows minimality does not imply faithfulness. ∎

The following theorem shows that every probability distribution P satisfies the minimality condition with some DAG and gives a method for constructing one:

Theorem 2.12 *Suppose we have a joint probability distribution P of the random variables in some set V. Create an arbitrary ordering of the nodes in V. For each $X \in V$, let B_X be the set of all nodes that come before X in the ordering, and let PA_X be a minimal subset of B_X such that*

$$I_P(\{X\}, \mathsf{B}_X|\mathsf{PA}_X).$$

Create a DAG $\mathbb{G}$ *by placing an edge from each node in* PA_X *to* X. *Then* $(\mathbb{G}, P)$
satisfies the minimality condition. Furthermore, if P *is strictly positive (i.e.,*
there are no probability values equal 0), then PA_X *is unique relative to the or-*
dering.

Proof. *The proof is developed in Pearl [1988].*   ∎

Example 2.16 *Suppose* $V = \{X, Y, Z, W\}$ *and* P *is a distribution that is faith-*
ful to the DAG in Figure 2.24 (a). Then Figure 2.24 (b), (c), (d), and (e) show
four DAGs satisfying the minimality condition with P *obtained using the pre-*
ceding theorem. The ordering used to obtain each DAG is from top to bottom
as shown in the figure. If P *is strictly positive, each of these DAGs is unique*
relative to its ordering.

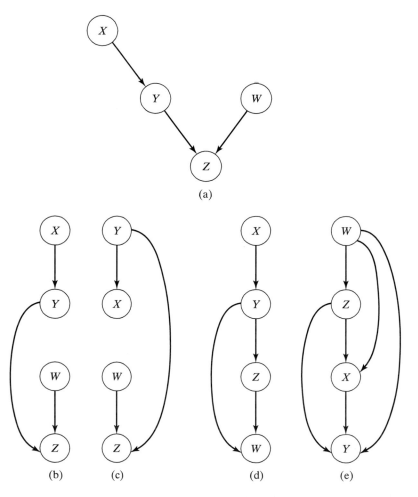

Figure 2.24: Four DAGs satisfying the minimality condition with P are shown
in (b), (c), (d), and (e) given that P is faithful to the DAG in (a).

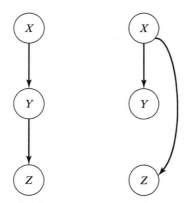

Figure 2.25: Two minimal DAG descriptions relative to the ordering $[X, Y, Z]$ when $P(y1|x1) = 1$ and $P(y2|x2) = 1$.

Notice from the previous example that a DAG satisfying the minimality condition with a distribution is not necessarily minimal in the sense that it contains the minimum number of edges needed to include the distribution. Of the DAGs in Figure 2.24, only the ones in (a), (b), and (c) are minimal in this sense. It is not hard to see that if a DAG is faithful to a distribution, then it is minimal in this sense.

Finally, we present an example showing that the method in Theorem 2.12 does not necessarily yield a unique DAG when the distribution is not strictly positive.

Example 2.17 *Suppose $V = \{X, Y, Z\}$ and P is defined as follows:*

$$P(x1) = a \qquad P(y1|x1) = 1 \qquad P(z1|x1) = b$$
$$P(x2) = 1 - a \qquad P(y2|x1) = 0 \qquad P(z2|x1) = 1 - b$$

$$P(y1|x2) = 0 \qquad P(z1|x2) = c$$
$$P(y2|x2) = 1 \qquad P(z2|x2) = 1 - c$$

Given the ordering $[X, Y, Z]$, both DAGs in Figure 2.25 are minimal descriptions of P obtained using the method in Theorem 2.12.

2.5 Markov Blankets and Boundaries

A Bayesian network can have a large number of nodes, and the probability of a given node can be affected by instantiating a distant node. However, it turns out that the instantiation of a set of close nodes can shield a node from the effect of all other nodes. The following definition and theorem show this:

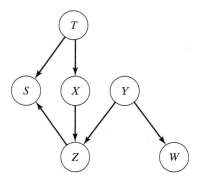

Figure 2.26: If P satisfies the Markov condition with this DAG, then $\{T, Y, Z\}$ is a Markov blanket of X.

Definition 2.12 *Let* V *be a set of random variables,* P *be their joint probability distribution, and* $X \in V$. *Then a **Markov blanket** M_X of X is any set of variables such that X is conditionally independent of all the other variables given M_X. That is,*

$$I_P(\{X\}, V - (M_X \cup \{X\})|M_X).$$

Theorem 2.13 *Suppose* $(\mathbb{G}, P)$ *satisfies the Markov condition. Then, for each variable* X, *the set of all parents of* X, *children of* X, *and parents of children of* X *is a Markov blanket of* X.

Proof. *It is straightforward that this set d-separates $\{X\}$ from the set of all other nodes in V. That is, if we call this set M_X,*

$$I_{\mathbb{G}}(\{X\}, V - (M_X \cup \{X\})|M_X).$$

The proof therefore follows from Theorem 2.1. ∎

Example 2.18 *Suppose* $(\mathbb{G}, P)$ *satisfies the Markov condition where* $\mathbb{G}$ *is the DAG in Figure 2.26. Then, due to Theorem 2.13* $\{T, Y, Z\}$ *is a Markov blanket of* X.

Example 2.19 *Suppose* $(\mathbb{G}, P)$ *satisfies the Markov condition where* $\mathbb{G}$ *is the DAG in Figure 2.26, and* $(\mathbb{G}', P)$ *also satisfies the Markov condition where* $\mathbb{G}'$ *is the DAG* $\mathbb{G}$ *in Figure 2.26 with the edge* $T \to X$ *removed. Then the Markov blanket* $\{T, Y, Z\}$ *is not minimal in the sense that its subset* $\{Y, Z\}$ *is also a Markov blanket of* X.

The last example leads to the following definition:

Definition 2.13 *Let* V *be a set of random variables,* P *be their joint probability distribution, and* $X \in V$. *Then a **Markov boundary** of X is any Markov blanket such that none of its proper subsets is a Markov blanket of X.*

We have the following theorem:

Theorem 2.14 *Suppose* $(\mathbb{G}, P)$ *satisfies the faithfulness condition. Then for each variable* X, *the set of all parents of* X, *children of* X, *and parents of children of* X *is the unique Markov boundary of* X.

Proof. *Let* M_X *be the set identified in this theorem. Due to Theorem 2.13,* M_X *is a Markov blanket of* X. *Clearly there is at least one Markov boundary for* X. *So if* M_X *is not the unique Markov boundary for* X, *there would have to be some other set* A *not equal to* M_X, *which is a Markov boundary of* X. *Since* $\mathsf{M}_X \neq \mathsf{A}$ *and* M_X *cannot be a proper subset of* A, *there is some* $Y \in \mathsf{M}_X$ *such that* $Y \notin \mathsf{A}$. *Since* A *is a Markov boundary for* X, *we have* $I_P(\{X\}, \{Y\}|\mathsf{A})$. *If* Y *is a parent or a child of* X, *we would not have* $I_G(\{X\}, \{Y\}|\mathsf{A})$, *which means we would have a conditional independence which is not a d-separation. But Theorem 2.5 says this cannot be. If* Y *is a parent of a child of* X, *let* Z *be their common child. If* $Z \in \mathsf{A}$, *we again would not have* $I_G(\{X\}, \{Y\}|\mathsf{A})$. *If* $Z \notin \mathsf{A}$, *we would have* $I_P(\{X\}, \{Z\}|\mathsf{A})$ *because* A *is a Markov boundary of* X, *but we do not have* $I_G(\{X\}, \{Z\}|\mathsf{A})$ *because* X *is a parent of* Z. *So again we would have a conditional independence which is not a d-separation. This proves there can be no such set* A. ∎

Example 2.20 *Suppose* $(\mathbb{G}, P)$ *satisfies the faithfulness condition where* $\mathbb{G}$ *is the DAG in Figure 2.26. Then due to Theorem 2.14* $\{T, Y, Z\}$ *is the unique Markov boundary of* X.

Theorem 2.14 holds for all probability distributions including ones that are not strictly positive. When a probability distribution is not strictly positive, there is not necessarily a unique Markov boundary. This is shown in the following example:

Example 2.21 *Let* P *be the probability distribution in Example 2.17. Then* $\{X\}$ *and* $\{Y\}$ *are both Markov boundaries of* $\{Z\}$. *Note that neither DAG in Figure 2.25 is faithful to* P.

Our final result is that in the case of strictly positive distributions the Markov boundary is unique:

Theorem 2.15 *Suppose* P *is a strictly positive probability distribution of the variables in* V. *Then for each* $X \in \mathsf{V}$ *there is a unique Markov boundary of* X.

Proof. *The proof can be found in Pearl [1988].* ∎

2.6 More on Causal DAGs

Recall from Section 1.5 that, if we create a causal DAG $\mathbb{G} = (\mathsf{V}, \mathsf{E})$ and assume the probability distribution of the variables in V satisfies the Markov condition with $\mathbb{G}$, we say we are making the **causal Markov assumption**. In that section

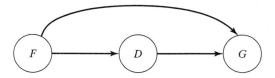

Figure 2.27: This DAG is not a minimal description of the probability distribution of the variables if the only influence of F on G is through D.

we argued that, if we define causation based on manipulation, this assumption is sometimes justified. Next we discuss three related causal assumptions, namely the causal minimality assumption, the causal faithfulness assumption, and the causal embedded faithfulness assumption.

2.6.1   The Causal Minimality Assumption

If we create a causal DAG $\mathbb{G} = (\mathsf{V}, \mathsf{E})$ and assume that the probability distribution of the variables in V satisfies the minimality condition with $\mathbb{G}$, we say we are making the **causal minimality assumption**. Recall that, if P satisfies the minimality condition with $\mathbb{G}$, then P satisfies the Markov condition with $\mathbb{G}$. So the causal minimality assumption subsumes the causal Markov assumption. If we define causation based on manipulation and we feel the causal Markov assumption is justified, would we also expect this assumption to be justified? In general, it seems we would. The only apparent exception to minimality could be if we included an edge from X to Y when X is only an indirect cause of Y through some other variable(s) in V. Consider again the situation concerning finasteride, DHT level, and hair growth discussed in Section 1.5. We noted that DHT level is a causal mediary between finasteride and hair growth with finasteride having no other causal path to hair growth. We concluded that hair growth (G) is independent of finasteride (F) conditional on DHT level (D). Therefore, if we represent the causal relationships among the variables by the DAG in Figure 2.27, the DAG would not be a minimal description of the probability distribution because we can remove the edge $F \rightarrow G$ and the Markov condition will still be satisfied. However, since we've defined a causal DAG (see the beginning of Section 1.5.2) to be one that contains only direct causal influences, the DAG containing the edge $F \rightarrow G$ is not a causal DAG according to our definition. So, given our definition of a causal DAG, this situation is not really an exception to the causal minimality assumption.

2.6.2   The Causal Faithfulness Assumption

If we create a causal DAG $\mathbb{G} = (\mathsf{V}, \mathsf{E})$ and assume the probability distribution of the variables in V satisfies the faithfulness condition with $\mathbb{G}$, we say we are making the **causal faithfulness assumption**. Recall that, if P satisfies the faithfulness condition with $\mathbb{G}$, then P satisfies the minimality condition with $\mathbb{G}$. So the causal faithfulness assumption subsumes the causal minimality as-

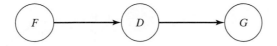

Figure 2.28: If D does not transmit an influence from F to G, this causal DAG will not be faithful to the probability distribution of the variables.

sumption. If we define causation based on manipulation and we feel the causal minimality assumption is justified, would we also expect this assumption to be justified? It seems in most cases we would. For example, if the manipulation of X leads to a change in the probability distribution of Y and to a change in the probability distribution of Z, we would ordinarily not expect Y and Z to be independent. That is, we ordinarily expect the presence of one effect of a cause should make it more likely that its other effects are present. Similarly, if the manipulation of X leads to a change in the probability distribution of Y, and the manipulation of Y leads to a change in the probability distribution of Z, we would ordinarily not expect X and Z to be independent. That is, we ordinarily expect a causal mediary to transmit an influence from its antecedent to its consequence. However, there are notable exceptions. Recall in Section 1.5.1 we offered the possibility that a certain minimal level of DHT is necessary for hair loss, more than that minimal level has no further effect on hair loss, and finasteride is not capable of lowering DHT level below that level. That is, it may be that finasteride (F) has a causal effect on DHT level (D), DHT level has a causal effect on hair growth (G), and yet finasteride has no effect on hair growth. Our causal DAG, which is shown in Figure 2.28, would then not be faithful to the distribution of the variables because its structure does not entail $I_P(\{G\}, \{F\})$. Figure 2.20 on page 99 shows actual probability values which result in this independence. Recall that it is not even possible to faithfully embed the distribution, which is the product of the conditional distributions shown in that figure.

This situation is fundamentally different than the problem encountered when we fail to identify a hidden common cause (discussed in Section 1.5.2 and more in the following subsection). If we fail to identify a hidden common cause, our problem is in our lack of identifying variables; and, if we did successfully identify all hidden common causes, we would ordinarily expect the Markov condition, and indeed the faithfulness condition, to be satisfied. In the current situation, the lack of faithfulness is inherent in the relationships among the variables themselves. There are other similar notable exceptions to faithfulness. Some are discussed in the exercises.

2.6.3 The Causal Embedded Faithfulness Assumption

In Section 1.5.2, we noted three important exceptions to the causal Markov assumptions. The first is that their can be no hidden common causes; the second is that selection bias cannot be present; and the third is that there can be no causal feedback loops. Since the causal faithfulness assumption subsumes the

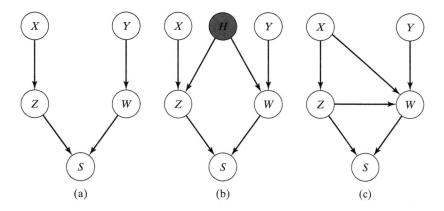

Figure 2.29: We would not expect the DAG in (a) to satisfy the Markov condition with the probability distribution of the five variables in that figure if Z and W had a hidden cause, as depicted by the shaded node H in (b). We would expect the DAG in (c) to be a minimal description of the distribution but not faithful to it.

causal Markov assumption, these are also exceptions to the causal faithfulness assumption. As discussed in the previous subsection, other exceptions to the causal faithfulness assumption include situations such as when a causal mediary fails to transmit an influence from its antecedent to its consequence. Of these exceptions, the first exception (hidden common causes) seems to be most prominent. Let's discuss that exception further.

Suppose we identify the following causal relationships with manipulation:

$$X \text{ causes } Z$$
$$Y \text{ causes } W$$
$$Z \text{ causes } S$$
$$W \text{ causes } S.$$

Then we would construct the causal DAG shown in Figure 2.29 (a). The Markov condition entails $I_P(Z, W)$ for that DAG. However, if Z and W had a hidden common cause as shown in Figure 2.29 (b), we would not ordinarily expect this independency. This was discussed in Section 1.5.2. So if we fail to identify a hidden common cause, ordinarily we would not expect the causal DAG to satisfy the Markov condition with the probability distribution of the variables, which means it would not satisfy the faithfulness condition with that distribution either. However, we would ordinarily expect faithfulness to the DAG that included all hidden common causes. For example, if H is the only hidden common cause among the variables in the DAG in Figure 2.29 (b), we would ordinarily expect the probability distribution of all six variables to satisfy the faithfulness condition with the DAG in that figure, which means the probability distribution of X, Y, Z, W, and S is embedded faithfully in that DAG. If we assume the probability distribution of the observed variables is embedded faithfully in a causal DAG containing these variables and all hidden common causes, we say we are making the **causal embedded faithfulness assumption**. It seems this assumption is often justified. Perhaps the most notable exception to it is the presence of selection bias. This exception is discussed further in Exercise 2.35 and in Section 9.1.2.

Note that if we assume faithfulness to the DAG in Figure 2.29 (b), and we add the adjacencies $Z \to W$ and $X \to W$ to the DAG in Figure 2.29 (a), the probability distribution of S, X, Y, Z, and W would satisfy the Markov condition with the resultant DAG (shown in Figure 2.29 (c)) because this new DAG does not entail $I_P(\{Z\}, \{W\})$ or any other independencies not entailed by the DAG in Figure 2.29 (b). The problem with the DAG in Figure 2.29 (c) is that it fails to entail independencies that are present. That is, we have $I_P(\{X\}, \{W\})$, and the DAG in Figure 2.29 (c) does not entail this independency. (Can you find others that it fails to entail?) This means it is not faithful to the probability distribution of S, X, Y, Z, and W. Indeed, similar to the result obtained in Example 2.11, no DAG is faithful to the distribution of only S, X, Y, Z, and W. Rather, this distribution can only be embedded faithfully as done in Figure 2.29 (b) with the hidden common cause. Regardless, the DAG in Figure 2.29 (c) is a minimal description of the distribution of only S, X, Y, Z, and W, and it constitutes a Bayesian network with that distribution. So any inference algorithms for Bayesian networks (discussed in Chapters 3, 4, and 5) are applicable to it. However, it is no longer a causal DAG.

EXERCISES

Section 2.1

Exercise 2.1 *Consider the DAG $\mathbb{G}$ in Figure 2.2. Prove that the Markov condition entails $I_P(\{C\}, \{G\}|\{A, F\})$ for $\mathbb{G}$.*

Exercise 2.2 *Suppose we add another variable R, an edge from F to R, and an edge from R to C to the DAG $\mathbb{G}$ in Figure 2.3. The variable R might represent the professor's initial reputation. State which of the following conditional independencies you would feel are entailed by the Markov condition for $\mathbb{G}$. For each that you feel is entailed, try to prove it actually is.*

1. *$I_p(\{R\}, \{A\})$.*

2. *$I_P(\{R\}, \{A\}|\{F\})$.*

3. *$I_P(\{R\}, \{A\}|\{F, C\})$.*

Exercise 2.3 *State which of the following d-separations are in the DAG in Figure 2.5:*

1. $I_{\mathbb{G}}(\{W\}, \{S\}|\{Y, X\})$.

2. $I_{\mathbb{G}}(\{W\}, \{S\}|\{Y, Z\})$.

3. $I_{\mathbb{G}}(\{W\}, \{S\}|\{R, X\})$.

4. $I_{\mathbb{G}}(\{W, X\}, \{S, T\}|\{R, Z\})$.

5. $I_{\mathbb{G}}(\{Y, Z\}, \{T\}|\{R, S\})$.

6. $I_{\mathbb{G}}(\{X, S\}, \{W, T\}|\{R, Z\})$.

7. $I_{\mathbb{G}}(\{X, S, Z\}, \{W, T\}|\{R\})$.

8. $I_{\mathbb{G}}(\{X, Z\}, \{W\})$.

9. $I_{\mathbb{G}}(\{X, S, Z\}, \{W\})$.

Are $\{X, S, Z\}$ and $\{W\}$ d-separated by any set in that DAG?

Exercise 2.4 Let A, B, and C be subsets of a set of random variables V. Show the following:

1. If $A \cap B = \varnothing$, $A \cap C \neq \varnothing$, and $B \cap C \neq \varnothing$, then $I_P(A, B|C)$ is equivalent to $I_P(A - C, B - C|C)$. That is, for every probability distribution P of V, $I_P(A, B|C)$ holds if and only $I_P(A - C, B - C|C)$ holds.

2. If $A \cap B \neq \varnothing$ and P is a probability distribution of V such that $I_P(A, B|C)$ holds, P is not positive definite. A probability distribution is **positive definite** if there are no 0 values in the distribution.

3. If the Markov condition entails a conditional independency, then the independency must hold in a positive definite distribution. Hint: Use Theorem 1.5.

Conclude Lemma 2.2 from these three facts.

Exercise 2.5 Show $I_P(\{X\}, \{Z\})$ for the distribution P in the Bayesian network in Figure 2.6.

Exercise 2.6 Use Algorithm 2.1 to find all nodes reachable from M in Figure 2.7. Show the labeling of the edges according to that algorithm.

Exercise 2.7 Implement Algorithm 2.1 in the computer language of your choice.

Exercise 2.8 Perform a more rigorous analysis of Algorithm 2.1 than that done in the text. That is, first identify basic operations. Then show $W(m, n) \in O(mn)$ for these basic operations, and develop an instance showing $W(m, n) \in \Omega(mn)$.

Exercise 2.9 Implement Algorithm 2.2 in the computer language of your choice.

Exercise 2.10 *Construct again a DAG representing the causal relationships described in Exercise 1.25, but this time include auxiliary parent variables representing the possible values of the parameters in the conditional distributions. Suppose we use the following variable names:*

$$\begin{array}{ll} A: & \textit{Visit to Asia} \\ B: & \textit{Bronchitis} \\ D: & \textit{Dyspnea} \\ L: & \textit{Lung Cancer} \\ H: & \textit{Smoking History} \\ T: & \textit{Tuberculosis.} \\ C: & \textit{Chest X-ray} \end{array}$$

Identify the auxiliary parent variables, whose values we need to ascertain, for each of the following calculations:

1. *$P(\{B\}|\{H, D\})$.*

2. *$P(\{L\}|\{H, D\})$.*

3. *$P(\{T\}|\{H, D\})$.*

Section 2.2

Exercise 2.11 *Prove Corollary 2.1.*

Exercise 2.12 *In Part 2 of Case 1 in the proof of Theorem 2.4 it was left as an exercise to show that if there is also a head-to-head meeting on σ_2 at N'', there must be a head-to-head meeting at a node $N^* \in \mathbb{N}$ somewhere between N' and N'' (including N'') on ρ_2, and there cannot be a head-to-head meeting at N^* on ρ_1. Show this. Hint: Recall ρ_1 is not blocked.*

Exercise 2.13 *Show all DAGs Markov equivalent to each of the following DAGs, and show the pattern representing the Markov equivalence class to which each of the following belongs:*

1. *The DAG in Figure 2.15 (a).*

2. *The DAG in Figure 2.15 (c).*

3. *The DAG in Figure 2.15 (d).*

Exercise 2.14 *Write a polynomial–time algorithm for determining whether two DAGs are Markov equivalent. Implement the algorithm in the computer language of your choice.*

Section 2.3

Exercise 2.15 *Show that all the nonindependencies listed in Example 2.8 hold for the distribution discussed in that example.*

Exercise 2.16 *Assign arbitrary values to the conditional distributions for the DAG in Figure 2.20, and see if the resultant distribution is faithful to the DAG. Try to find an unfaithful distribution besides ones in the family shown in that figure.*

Exercise 2.17 *Consider the Bayesian network in Figure 2.30.*

1. *Show that the probability distribution is not faithful to the DAG because we have $I_P(\{W\}, \{X\})$ and not $I_\mathbb{G}(\{W\}, \{X\})$.*

2. *Show further that this distribution does not admit a faithful DAG representation.*

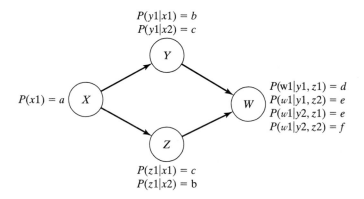

Figure 2.30: The probability distribution is not faithful to the DAG because $I_P(W, X)$ and not $I_\mathbb{G}(W, X)$. Each variable has only two possible values. So for simplicity the probability of only one is shown.

Exercise 2.18 *Consider the Bayesian network in Figure 2.31.*

1. *Show that the probability distribution is not faithful to the DAG because we have $I_P(\{X\}, \{Y\}|\{Z\})$ and not $I_\mathbb{G}(\{X\}, \{Y\}|\{Z\})$.*

2. *Show further that this distribution does not admit a faithful DAG representation.*

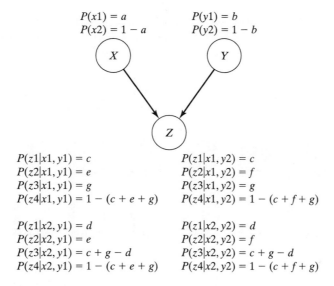

Figure 2.31: The probability distribution is not faithful to the DAG because $I_P(X, Y|Z)$ and not $I_{\mathbb{G}}(X, Y|Z)$.

Exercise 2.19 *Let* $V = \{X, Y, Z, W\}$ *and* P *be given by*

$$P(x, y, z, w) = k \times f(x, y) \times g(y, z) \times h(z, w) \times i(w, x),$$

where f, g, h, *and* i *are real-valued functions and* k *is a normalizing constant. Show that this distribution does not admit a faithful DAG representation. Hint: First show that the only conditional independencies are* $I_P(\{X\}, \{Z\}|\{Y, W\})$ *and* $I_P(\{Y\}, \{W\}|\{X, Z\})$.

Exercise 2.20 *Suppose we use the principle of indifference to assign probabilities to the objects in Figure 2.32. Let random variables* V, S, C, L, *and* F *be defined as follows:*

Variable	Value	Outcomes Mapped to this Value
V	$v1$	*All objects containing a "1"*
	$v2$	*All objects containing a "2"*
S	$s1$	*All square objects*
	$s2$	*All circular objects*
C	$c1$	*All grey objects*
	$c2$	*All white objects*
L	$l1$	*All objects covered with lines*
	$l2$	*All objects not covered with lines*
F	$f1$	*All objects containing a number in a large font*
	$f2$	*All objects containing a number in a small font*

Show that the probability distribution of $V, S, C, L,$ and F is faithful to the DAG in Figure 2.21 (a). The result in Example 2.11 therefore implies the marginal distribution of $V, S, L,$ and F is not faithful to any DAG.

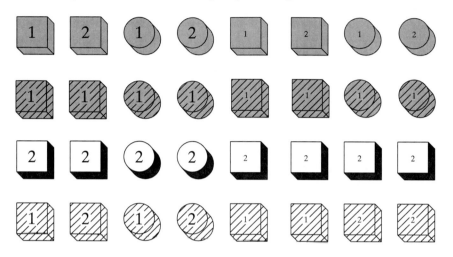

Figure 2.32: Objects with five properties.

Exercise 2.21 *Prove Theorem 2.9.*

Exercise 2.22 *Prove Theorem 2.10.*

Exercise 2.23 *Develop a distribution, other than the one given in Example 2.11, which admits an embedded faithful DAG representation but does not admit a faithful DAG representation.*

Exercise 2.24 *Show that the distribution discussed in Exercise 2.17 does not admit an embedded faithful DAG representation.*

Exercise 2.25 *Show that the distribution discussed in Exercise 2.18 does not admit an embedded faithful DAG representation.*

Exercise 2.26 *Show that the distribution discussed in Exercise 2.19 does not admit an embedded faithful DAG representation.*

Section 2.4

Exercise 2.27 *Obtain DAGs satisfying the minimality condition with P using other orderings of the variables discussed in Example 2.16.*

Section 2.5

Exercise 2.28 *Apply Theorem 2.13 to find a Markov blanket for each node in the DAG in Figure 2.26.*

Exercise 2.29 *Show that neither DAG in Figure 2.25 is faithful to the distribution discussed in Examples 2.17 and 2.21.*

Section 2.6

Exercise 2.30 *Besides $I_P(\{X\}, \{W\})$, are there other independencies entailed by the DAG in Figure 2.29 (b) that are not entailed by the DAG in Figure 2.29 (c)?*

Exercise 2.31 *Given that the joint distribution of X, Y, Z, W, S, and H is faithful to the DAG in Figure 2.29 (b), show that the marginal distribution of X, Y, Z, W, and S does not admit a faithful DAG representation.*

Exercise 2.32 *Typing experience increases with age but manual dexterity decreases with age. Experience results in better typing performance as does good manual dexterity. So it seems after an initial learning period, typing performance will stay about constant as age increases because the effects of increased experience and decreased manual dexterity will cancel each other out. Draw a DAG representing the causal influences among the variables, and discuss whether the probability distribution of the variables is faithful to the DAG. If it is not, show numeric values that could have this unfaithfulness. Hint: See Exercise 2.17.*

Exercise 2.33 *Exercise 2.18 showed that the probability distribution in Figure 2.31 is not faithful to the DAG in that figure because $I_P(\{X\}, \{Y\}|\{Z\})$ and not $I_G(\{X\}, \{Y\}|\{Z\})$. This means, if these are causal relationships, there is no discounting. (Recall discounting means one cause explains away a common effect, thereby making the other cause less likely.) Give an intuitive explanation for why this might be the case. Hint: Note that the probability of each of Z's values is dependent on only one of the variables. For example, $p(z1|x1, y1) = p(z1|x1, y2) = p(z1|x1)$ and $p(z1|x2, y1) = p(z1|x2, y2) = p(z1|x2)$.*

Exercise 2.34 *The probability distribution in Figure 2.20 does not satisfy the faithfulness condition with the DAG $X \leftarrow Y \rightarrow Z$. Explain why. If these edges describe causal influences, we would have two variables with a common cause that are independent. Give an example for how this might happen.*

Exercise 2.35 *Suppose the probability distribution P of X, Y, Z, W, and S is faithful to the DAG in Figure 2.33 and we are observing a subpopulation of individuals who have S instantiated to a particular value s (as indicated by the cross through S in the DAG). That is, selection bias is present. (See Section 1.5.1.) Let $P|s$ denote the probability distribution of X, Y, Z, and W conditional on $S = s$. Show that $P|s$ does not admit an embedded faithful DAG representation. Hint: First show that the only conditional independencies are $I_{P|s}(\{X\}, \{Z\}|\{Y, W\})$ and $I_{P|s}(\{Y\}, \{W\}|\{X, Z\})$. Note that these are the same conditional independencies as those obtained a different way in Exercise 2.19.*

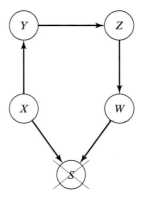

Figure 2.33: Selection bias is present.

Part II

Inference

Chapter 3

Inference: Discrete Variables

A standard application of Bayes' theorem (reviewed in Section 1.2) is inference in a two-node Bayesian network. As discussed in Section 1.4, larger Bayesian networks address the problem of representing the joint probability distribution of a large number of variables and doing Bayesian inference with these variables. For example, recall the Bayesian network discussed in Example 1.36 on page 46. That network, which is shown again in Figure 3.1, represents the joint probability distribution of smoking history (H), bronchitis (B), lung cancer (L), fatigue (F), and chest X-ray (C).

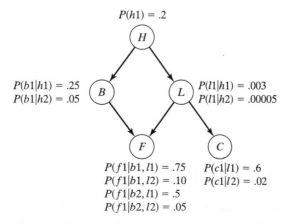

$P(h1) = .2$

$$P(b1|h1) = .25$$
$$P(b1|h2) = .05$$

$$P(l1|h1) = .003$$
$$P(l1|h2) = .00005$$

$$P(f1|b1, l1) = .75$$
$$P(f1|b1, l2) = .10$$
$$P(f1|b2, l1) = .5$$
$$P(f1|b2, l2) = .05$$

$$P(c1|l1) = .6$$
$$P(c1|l2) = .02$$

Figure 3.1: A Bayesian network. Each variable has only two values; so the probability of only one is shown.

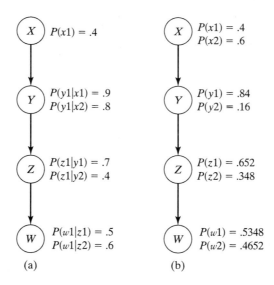

Figure 3.2: A Bayesian network is shown in (a), and the prior probabilities of the variables in that network are shown in (b). Each variable has only two values; so the probability of only one is shown in (a).

If a patient had a smoking history and a positive chest X-ray, we would be interested in the probability of that patient having lung cancer (i.e.. $P(l1|h1, c1)$) and having bronchitis (i.e., $P(b1|h1, c1)$). In this chapter, we develop algorithms that perform this type of inference.

In Section 3.1, we present simple examples showing why the conditional independencies entailed by the Markov condition enable us to do inference with a large number of variables. Section 3.2 develops the Pearl, [1986] message-passing algorithm for doing exact inference in Bayesian networks. This algorithm passes massages in the DAG to perform inference. In Section 3.3, we provide a version of the algorithm that more efficiently handles networks in which the noisy OR-gate model is assumed. Section 3.4 references other inference algorithms that also employ the DAG, while Section 3.5 presents the symbolic probabilistic inference algorithm which does not employ the DAG. Next Section 3.6 discusses the complexity of doing inference in Bayesian networks. Finally, Section 3.7 presents research relating Pearl's message-passing algorithm to human causal reasoning.

3.1   Examples of Inference

Next we present some examples illustrating how the conditional independencies entailed by the Markov condition can be exploited to accomplish inference in a Bayesian network.

Example 3.1 *Consider the Bayesian network in Figure 3.2 (a). The prior probabilities of all variables can be computed as follows:*

$$P(y1) \quad = \quad P(y1|x1)P(x1) + P(y1|x2)P(x2) = (.9)(.4) + (.8)(.6) = .84$$

$$P(z1) \quad = \quad P(z1|y1)P(y1) + P(z1|y2)P(y2) = (.7)(.84) + (.4)(.16) = .652$$

$$P(w1) \quad = \quad P(w1|z1)P(z1) + P(w1|z2)P(z2) = (.5)(.652) + (.6)(.348) = .5348.$$

These probabilities are shown in Figure 3.2 (b). Note that the computation for each variable requires information determined for its parent. We can therefore consider this method a message passing algorithm in which each node passes to its child a message needed to compute the child's probabilities. Clearly, this algorithm applies to an arbitrarily long linked list and to trees.

Suppose next that X is instantiated for x1. Since the Markov condition entails that each variable is conditionally independent of X given its parent, we can compute the conditional probabilities of the remaining variables by again passing messages down as follows:

$$P(y1|x1) \quad = \quad .9$$

$$
\begin{aligned}
P(z1|x1) \quad &= \quad P(z1|y1, x1)P(y1|x1) + P(z1|y2, x1)P(y2|x1) \\
&= \quad P(z1|y1)P(y1|x1) + P(z1|y2)P(y2|x1) \\
&= \quad (.7)(.9) + (.4)(.1) = .67
\end{aligned}
$$

$$
\begin{aligned}
P(w1|x1) \quad &= \quad P(w1|z1, x1)P(z1|x1) + P(w1|z2, x1)P(z2|x1) \\
&= \quad P(w1|z1)P(z1|x1) + P(w1|z2)P(z2|x1) \\
&= \quad P((.8)(.67) + (.6)(.33) = .734.
\end{aligned}
$$

Clearly, this algorithm also applies to an arbitrarily long linked list and to trees.

The preceding instantiation shows how we can use downward propagation of messages to compute the conditional probabilities of variables below the instantiated variable. Suppose now that W is instantiated for w1 (and no other variable is instantiated). We can use upward propagation of messages to compute the conditional probabilities of the remaining variables as follows. First we use Bayes' theorem to compute P(z1|w1):

$$P(z1|w1) = \frac{P(w1|z1)P(z1)}{P(w1)} = \frac{(.5)(.652)}{.5348} = .6096.$$

Then, to compute P(y1|w1), we again apply Bayes' theorem as follows:

$$P(y1|w1) = \frac{P(w1|y1)P(y1)}{P(w1)}.$$

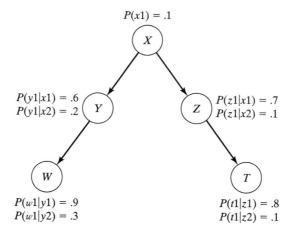

Figure 3.3: A Bayesian network that is a tree. Each variable has only two possible values. So the probability of only one is shown.

We cannot yet complete this computation because we do not know $P(w1|y1)$. However, we can obtain this value in the manner shown when we discussed downward propagation. That is,

$$P(w1|y1) = (P(w1|z1)P(z1|y1) + P(w1|z2)P(z2|y1).$$

After doing this computation, also computing $P(w1|y2)$ (because X will need this latter value), and then determining $P(y1|w1)$, we pass $P(w1|y1)$ and $P(w1|y2)$ to X. We then compute $P(w1|x1)$ and $P(x1|w1)$ in sequence as follows:

$$P(w1|x1) = (P(w1|y1)P(y1|x1) + P(w1|y2)P(y2|x1)$$

$$P(x1|w1) = \frac{P(w1|x1)P(x1)}{P(w1)}.$$

It is left as an exercise to perform these computations. Clearly, this upward propagation scheme applies to an arbitrarily long linked list.

The next example shows how to turn corners in a tree.

Example 3.2 *Consider the Bayesian network in Figure 3.3. Suppose W is instantiated for $w1$. We compute $P(y1|w1)$ followed by $P(x1|w1)$ using the upward propagation algorithm just described. Then we proceed to compute $P(z1|w1)$ followed by $P(t1|w1)$ using the downward propagation algorithm. It is left as an exercise to do this.*

3.2 Pearl's Message-Passing Algorithm

By exploiting local independencies as we did in the previous subsection, Pearl, [1986], Pearl [1988] developed a message-passing algorithm for inference in

Bayesian networks. Given a set **a** of values of a set **A** of instantiated variables, the algorithm determines $P(x|\mathbf{a})$ for all values x of each variable X the network. It accomplishes this by initiating messages from each instantiated variable to its neighbors. These neighbors in turn pass messages to their neighbors. The updating does not depend on the order in which we initiate these messages, which means the evidence can arrive in any order. First we develop the algorithm for Bayesian networks whose DAGs are rooted trees; then we extend the algorithm to singly connected networks.

3.2.1 Inference in Trees

Recall a **rooted tree** is a DAG in which there is a unique node called the root, which has no parent, every other node has precisely one parent, and every node is a descendent of the root.

The algorithm is based on the following theorem. It may be best to read the proof of the theorem before its statement as its statement is not very transparent without seeing it developed.

Theorem 3.1 *Let* $(\mathbb{G}, P)$ *be a Bayesian network whose DAG is a tree, where* $\mathbb{G} = (\mathsf{V}, \mathsf{E})$, *and let* **a** *be a set of values of a subset* $\mathsf{A} \subset \mathsf{V}$. *For each variable* X, *define* λ *messages,* λ *values,* π *messages, and* π *values as follows:*

1. *Define* λ *messages:*

   For each child Y *of* X, *for all values of* x,

   $$\lambda_Y(x) \equiv \sum_y P(y|x)\lambda(y).$$

2. *Define* λ *values:*

   If $X \in \mathsf{A}$ *and* X's *value is* $\hat{x}$,

   $$\begin{aligned} \lambda(\hat{x}) &\equiv 1 \\ \lambda(x) &\equiv 0 \qquad \text{for } x \neq \hat{x}. \end{aligned}$$

   If $X \notin \mathsf{A}$ *and* X *is a leaf, for all values of* x,

   $$\lambda(x) \equiv 1.$$

   If $X \notin \mathsf{A}$ *and* X *is a nonleaf, for all values of* x,

   $$\lambda(x) \equiv \prod_{U \in \mathsf{CH}_X} \lambda_U(x),$$

   where CH_X *denotes the set of children of* X.

3. *Define π messages:*

If Z is the parent of X, then for all values of z,

$$\pi_X(z) \equiv \pi(z) \prod_{U \in \mathsf{CH}_Z - \{X\}} \lambda_U(z).$$

4. *Define π values:*

If $X \in \mathsf{A}$ and X's value is $\hat{x}$,

$$\begin{aligned} \pi(\hat{x}) &\equiv 1 \\ \pi(x) &\equiv 0 \quad \text{for } x \neq \hat{x}. \end{aligned}$$

If $X \notin \mathsf{A}$ and X is the root, for all values of x,

$$\pi(x) \equiv P(x).$$

If $X \notin \mathsf{A}$, X is not the root, and Z is the parent of X, for all values of x,

$$\pi(x) \equiv \sum_z P(x|z)\pi_X(z).$$

5. *Given the foregoing definitions, for each variable X, we have, for all values of x,*

$$P(x|\mathsf{a}) = \alpha\lambda(x)\pi(x),$$

where α is a normalizing constant.

Proof. *We will prove the theorem for the case in which each node has precisely two children. The case of an arbitrary tree is then a straightforward generalization. Let D_X be the subset of A containing all members of A that are in the subtree rooted at X (therefore, including X if $X \in \mathsf{A}$), and N_X be the subset of A containing all members of A that are nondescendents of X. Recall that X is a nondescendent of X; so this set includes X if $X \in \mathsf{A}$. This situation is depicted in Figure 3.4. We have for each value of x,*

$$\begin{aligned} P(x|\mathsf{a}) &= P(x|\mathsf{d}_X, \mathsf{n}_X) &\qquad (3.1) \\ &= \frac{P(\mathsf{d}_X, \mathsf{n}_X|x)P(x)}{P(\mathsf{d}_X, \mathsf{n}_X)} \\ &= \frac{P(\mathsf{d}_X|x)P(\mathsf{n}_X|x)P(x)}{P(\mathsf{d}_X, \mathsf{n}_X)} \\ &= \frac{P(\mathsf{d}_X|x)P(x|\mathsf{n}_X)P(\mathsf{n}_X)P(x)}{P(x)P(\mathsf{d}_X, \mathsf{n}_X)} \\ &= \beta P(\mathsf{d}_X|x)P(x|\mathsf{n}_X), \end{aligned}$$

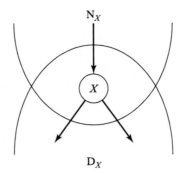

Figure 3.4: The set of instantiated variables $A = N_X \cup D_X$. If $X \in A$, X is in both N_X and D_X.

where β is a constant that does not depend on the value of x. The second and fourth equalities are due to Bayes' theorem. The third equality follows directly from d-separation (Lemma 2.1) if $X \notin A$. It is left as an exercise to show it still holds if $X \in A$.

We will develop functions $\lambda(x)$ and $\pi(x)$ such

$$\lambda(x) \;\simeq\; P(d_X|x)$$
$$\pi(x) \;\simeq\; P(x|n_X).$$

By $\simeq$ we mean "proportional to." That is, $\pi(x)$, for example, may not equal $P(x|n_X)$, but it equals a constant times $P(x|n_X)$, where the constant does not depend on the value of x. Once we do this, due to Equality 3.1, we will have

$$P(x|a) = \alpha\lambda(x)\pi(x),$$

where α is a normalizing constant that does not depend on the value of x.

1. Develop $\lambda(x)$: We need

$$\lambda(x) \simeq P(d_X|x). \tag{3.2}$$

CASE 1: $X \in A$ and X's value is $\hat{x}$. Since $X \in D_X$,

$$P(d_X|x) = 0 \qquad for\ x \neq \hat{x}.$$

So to achieve Proportionality 3.2, we can set

$$\lambda(\hat{x}) \;\equiv\; 1$$
$$\lambda(x) \;\equiv\; 0 \qquad for\ x \neq \hat{x}.$$

CASE 2: $X \notin A$ and X is a leaf. In this case $d_X = \varnothing$, the empty set of variables, and so

$$P(d_X|x) = P(\varnothing|x) = 1 \qquad for\ all\ values\ of\ x.$$

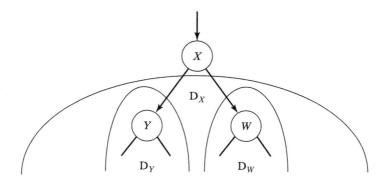

Figure 3.5: If X is not in A, then $\mathsf{D}_X = \mathsf{D}_Y \cup \mathsf{D}_W$.

So to achieve Proportionality 3.2, we can set

$$\lambda(x) \equiv 1 \qquad \textit{for all values of } x.$$

CASE 3: *$X \notin$ A and X is a nonleaf. Let Y be X's left child, W be X's right child. Then since $X \notin$ A,*

$$\mathsf{D}_X = \mathsf{D}_Y \cup \mathsf{D}_W.$$

This situation is depicted in Figure 3.5. We have

$$
\begin{aligned}
P(\mathsf{d}_X|x) &= P(\mathsf{d}_Y, \mathsf{d}_W|x) \\
&= P(\mathsf{d}_Y|x)P(\mathsf{d}_W|x) \\
&= \sum_y P(y|x)P(\mathsf{d}_Y|y) \sum_w P(w|x)P(\mathsf{d}_W|w) \\
&\backsimeq \sum_y P(y|x)\lambda(y) \sum_w P(w|x)\lambda(w).
\end{aligned}
$$

The second equality is due to d-separation and the third to the law of total probability. So we can achieve Proportionality 3.2 by defining for all values of x,

$$
\begin{aligned}
\lambda_Y(x) &\equiv \sum_y P(y|x)\lambda(y) \\
\lambda_W(x) &\equiv \sum_w P(w|x)\lambda(w),
\end{aligned}
$$

and setting

$$\lambda(x) \equiv \lambda_Y(x)\lambda_W(x) \qquad \textit{for all values of } x.$$

2. *Develop* $\pi(x)$: *We need*

$$\pi(x) \backsimeq P(x|\mathsf{n}_X). \tag{3.3}$$

CASE 1: *$X \in \mathsf{A}$ and X's value is $\hat{x}$. Due to the fact that $X \in \mathsf{N}_X$,*

$$
\begin{aligned}
P(\hat{x}|\mathsf{n}_X) &= P(\hat{x}|\hat{x}) = 1 \\
P(x|\mathsf{n}_X) &= P(x|\hat{x}) = 0 \qquad \text{for } x \neq \hat{x}.
\end{aligned}
$$

So we can achieve Proportionality 3.3 by setting

$$
\begin{aligned}
\pi(\hat{x}) &\equiv 1 \\
\pi(x) &\equiv 0 \qquad \text{for } x \neq \hat{x}.
\end{aligned}
$$

CASE 2: *$X \notin \mathsf{A}$ and X is the root. In this case $\mathsf{n}_X = \varnothing$, the empty set of random variables, and so*

$$P(x|\mathsf{n}_X) = P(x|\varnothing) = P(x) \qquad \text{for all values of } x.$$

So we can achieve Proportionality 3.3 by setting

$$\pi(x) \equiv P(x) \qquad \text{for all value of } x.$$

CASE 3: *$X \notin \mathsf{A}$ and X is not the root. Without loss of generality assume X is Z's right child, and let T be Z's left child. Then $\mathsf{N}_X = \mathsf{N}_Z \cup \mathsf{D}_T$. This situation is depicted in Figure 3.6. We have*

$$
\begin{aligned}
P(x|\mathsf{n}_X) &= \sum_z P(x|z)P(z|\mathsf{n}_X) \\
&= \sum_z P(x|z)P(x|\mathsf{n}_Z, \mathsf{d}_T) \\
&= \sum_z P(x|z)\frac{P(z|\mathsf{n}_Z)P(\mathsf{n}_Z)P(\mathsf{d}_T|z)P(z)}{P(z)P(\mathsf{n}_Z, \mathsf{d}_T)} \\
&= \gamma \sum_z P(x|z)\pi(z)\lambda_T(z).
\end{aligned}
$$

It is left as an exercise to obtain the third equality above using the same manipulations as in the derivation of Equality 3.1. So we can achieve Proportionality 3.3 by defining for all values of z,

$$\pi_X(z) \equiv \pi(z)\lambda_T(z),$$

and setting

$$\pi(x) \equiv \sum_z P(x|z)\pi_X(z) \qquad \text{for all values of } x.$$

This completes the proof. ∎

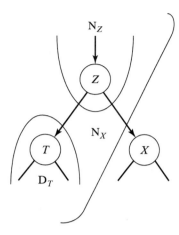

Figure 3.6: If X is not in E, then $\mathsf{N}_X = \mathsf{N}_Z \cup \mathsf{D}_T$.

Next we present an algorithm based on this theorem. It is left as an exercise to show that its correctness follows from the theorem. Clearly, the algorithm can be implemented as an object-oriented program, in which each node is an object that communicates with the other nodes by passing λ and π messages. However, our goal is to show the steps in the algorithm rather than to discuss implementation. So we present it using top-down design.

Before presenting the algorithm, we show how the routines in it are called. Routine *initial_tree* is first called as follows:

$initial\_tree((\mathbb{G}, P), \mathsf{A}, \mathsf{a}, P(x|\mathsf{a}));$

After this call, A and a are both empty, and for every variable X, for every value of x, $P(x|\mathsf{a})$ is the conditional probability of x given a, which, since a is empty, is the prior probability of x. Each time a variable V is instantiated for $\hat{v}$, routine *update-tree* is called as follows:

$update\_tree((\mathbb{G}, P), \mathsf{A}, \mathsf{a}, V, \hat{v}, P(x|\mathsf{a}));$

After this call, V has been added to A, $\hat{v}$ has been added to a, and for every variable X, for every value of x, $P(x|\mathsf{a})$ has been updated to be the conditional probability of x given the new value of a. The algorithm now follows.

Algorithm 3.1 Inference-in-Trees

Problem: Given a Bayesian network whose DAG is a tree, determine the probabilities of the values of each node conditional on specified values of the nodes in some subset.

Inputs: Bayesian network $(\mathbb{G}, P)$ whose DAG is a tree, where $\mathbb{G} = (\mathsf{V}, \mathsf{E})$, and a set of values a of a subset $\mathsf{A} \subseteq \mathsf{V}$.

Outputs: The Bayesian network $(\mathbb{G}, P)$ updated according to the values in a. The λ and π values and messages and $P(x|\mathsf{a})$ for each $X \in \mathsf{V}$ are considered part of the network.

```
void initial_tree  (Bayesian-network& (𝔾, P) where 𝔾 = (V, E),
                    set-of-variables& A, set-of-variable-values& a)

{
  A = ∅; a = ∅;
  for (each X ∈ V) {
    for (each value x of X)
      λ(x) = 1;                    // Compute λ values.
    for (the parent Z of X)        // Does nothing if X is the a root.
      for (each value z of Z)
        λ_X(z) = 1;                // Compute λ messages.
  }
  for (each value r of the root R) {
    P(r|a) = P(r);                 // Compute P(r|a).
    π(r) = P(r);                   // Compute R's π values.
  }
  for (each child X of R)
    send_π_msg(R, X);
}


void update_tree  (Bayesian-network& (𝔾, P) where 𝔾 = (V, E),
                   set-of-variables& A, set-of-variable-values& a,
                   variable V, variable-value v̂)

{
  A = A ∪ {V}; a = a ∪ {v̂};               // Add V to A.
  λ(v̂) = 1; π(v̂) = 1; P(v̂|a) = 1;        // Instantiate V to v̂.
  for (each value of v ≠ v̂) {
    λ(v) = 0; π(v) = 0; P(v|a) = 0;
  }
  if (V is not the root && V's parent Z ∉ A)
    send_λ_msg(V, Z);
  for (each child X of V such that X ∉ A)
    send_π_msg(V, X);
}
```

```
void send_λ_msg(node Y, node X)        // For simplicity (G, P) is
{                                      // not shown as input.
    for (each value of x) {
```
$$\lambda_Y(x) = \sum_y P(y|x)\lambda(y); \qquad \text{// } Y \text{ sends } X \text{ a } \lambda \text{ message.}$$

$$\lambda(x) = \prod_{U \in \mathsf{CH}_X} \lambda_U(x); \qquad \text{// Compute } X\text{'s } \lambda \text{ values.}$$

$$P(x|\mathsf{a}) = \alpha\lambda(x)\pi(x); \qquad \text{// Compute } P(x|\mathsf{a}).$$
```
    }
    normalize P(x|a);
    if (X is not the root and X's parent Z ∉ A)
        send_λ_msg(X, Z);
    for (each child W of X such that W ≠ Y and W ∉ A)
        send_π_msg(X, W);
}


void send_π_msg(node Z, node X)        // For simplicity (G, P) is
{                                      // not shown as input.
    for (each value of z)
```
$$\pi_X(z) = \pi(z) \prod_{Y \in \mathsf{CH}_Z - \{X\}} \lambda_Y(z); \qquad \text{// } Z \text{ sends } X \text{ a } \pi \text{ message.}$$

```
    for (each value of x) {
```
$$\pi(x) = \sum_z P(x|z)\pi_X(z); \qquad \text{// Compute } X\text{'s } \pi \text{ values.}$$

$$P(x|\mathsf{a}) = \alpha\lambda(x)\pi(x); \qquad \text{// Compute } P(x|\mathsf{a}).$$
```
    }
    normalize P(x|a);
    for (each child Y of X such that Y ∉ A)
        send_π_msg(X, Y);
}
```

Examples of applying the preceding algorithm follow:

Example 3.3 *Consider the Bayesian network in Figure 3.7 (a). It is the network in Figure 3.1 with node F removed. We will show the steps when the network is initialized.*

The call

$initial\_tree((\mathbb{G}, P), \mathsf{A}, \mathsf{a});$

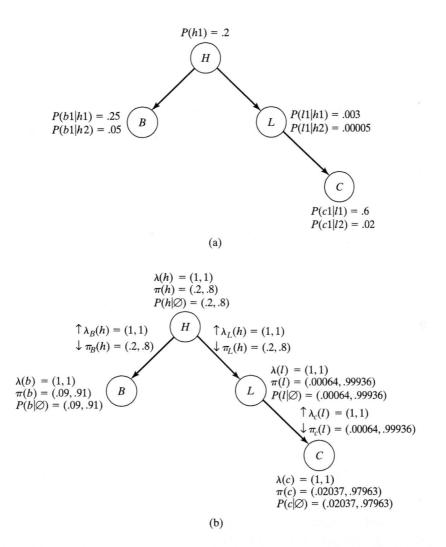

Figure 3.7: (b) shows the initialized network corresponding to the Bayesian network in (a). In (b) we write, for example, $P(h|\varnothing) = (.2, .8)$ instead of $P(h1|\varnothing) = .2$ and $P(h2|\varnothing) = .8$.

results in the following steps:

A = ∅;
a = ∅;

$\lambda(h1) = 1; \lambda(h2) = 1;$ // Compute λ values.
$\lambda(b1) = 1; \lambda(b2) = 1;$
$\lambda(l1) = 1; \lambda(l2) = 1;$
$\lambda(c1) = 1; \lambda(c2) = 1;$

$\lambda_B(h1) = 1; \lambda_B(h2) = 1;$ // Compute λ messages.
$\lambda_L(h1) = 1; \lambda_L(h2) = 1;$
$\lambda_C(l1) = 1; \lambda_C(l2) = 1;$

$P(h1|\varnothing) = P(h1) = .2;$ // Compute $P(h|\varnothing)$.
$P(h2|\varnothing) = P(h2) = .8;$

$\pi(h1) = P(h1) = .2;$ // Compute H's π values.
$\pi(h2) = P(h2) = .8;$

$send\_\pi\_msg(H, B);$
$send\_\pi\_msg(H, L);$

The call

$send\_\pi\_msg(H, B);$

results in the following steps:

$\pi_B(h1) = \pi(h1)\lambda_L(h1) = (.2)(1) = .2;$ // H sends B a π message.
$\pi_B(h2) = \pi(h2)\lambda_L(h2) = (.8)(1) = .8;$

$\pi(b1) = P(b1|h1)\pi_B(h1) + P(b1|h2)\pi_B(h2);$ // Compute B's π values.
$\quad = (.25)(.2) + (.05)(.8) = .09;$

$\pi(b2) = P(b2|h1)\pi_B(h1) + P(b2|h2)\pi_B(h2);$
$\quad = (.75)(.2) + (.95)(.8) = .91;$

$P(b1|\varnothing) = \alpha\lambda(b1)\pi(b1) = \alpha(1)(.09) = .09\alpha;$ // Compute $P(b|\varnothing)$.
$P(b2|\varnothing) = \alpha\lambda(b2)\pi(b2) = \alpha(1)(.91) = .91\alpha;$

$P(b1|\varnothing) = \frac{.09\alpha}{.09\alpha + .91\alpha} = .09;$

$P(b1|\varnothing) = \frac{.91\alpha}{.09\alpha + .91\alpha} = .91;$

The call

$send\_\pi\_msg(H, L);$

results in the following steps:

$\pi_L(h1) = \pi(h1)\lambda_B(h1) = (.2)(1) = .2;$ // *H sends L a* π

$\pi_L(h2) = \pi(h2)\lambda_B(h2) = (.8)(1) = .8;$ // *message.*

$\pi(l1) = P(l1|h1)\pi_L(h1) + P(l1|h2)\pi_L(h2);$ // *Compute L's* π

$\quad\quad = (.003)(.2) + (.00005)(.8) = .00064;$ // *values.*

$\pi(l2) = P(l2|h1)\pi_L(h1) + P(l2|h2)\pi_L(h2);$

$\quad\quad = (.997)(.2) + (.99995)(.8) = .99936;$

$P(l1|\varnothing) = \alpha\lambda(l1)\pi(l1) = \alpha(1)(.00064) = .00064\alpha;$ // *Compute* $P(l|\varnothing).$

$P(l2|\varnothing) = \alpha\lambda(l2)\pi(l2) = \alpha(1)(.99936) = .99936\alpha;$

$P(l1|\varnothing) = \frac{.00064\alpha}{.00064\alpha+.99936\alpha} = .00064;$

$P(l1|\varnothing) = \frac{.99936\alpha}{.00064\alpha+.99936\alpha} = .99936;$

$send\_\pi\_msg(L, C);$

The call

$send\_\pi\_msg(L, C);$

results in the following steps:

$\pi_C(l1) = \pi(l1) = .00064;$ // *L sends C a* π.

$\pi_C(l2) = \pi(l2) = .99936;$ // *message.*

$\pi(c1) = P(c1|l1)\pi_C(l1) + P(c1|l2)\pi_C(l2);$ // *Compute C's* π

$\quad\quad = (.6)(.00064) + (.02)(.99936) = .02037;$ // *values.*

$\pi(c2) = P(c2|l1)\pi_C(l1) + P(c2|l2)\pi_C(l2);$

$\quad\quad = (.4)(.00064) + (.98)(.99936) = .97963;$

$P(c1|\varnothing) = \alpha\lambda(c1)\pi(c1) = \alpha(1)(.02037) = .02037\alpha;$ // *Compute* $P(c|\varnothing).$

$P(c2|\varnothing) = \alpha\lambda(c2)\pi(c2) = \alpha(1)(.97963) = .97963\alpha;$

$P(c1|\varnothing) = \frac{.02037\alpha}{.02037\alpha+.97963\alpha} = .02037;$

$P(c1|\varnothing) = \frac{.97963\alpha}{.02037\alpha+.97963\alpha} = .97963;$

The initialization is now complete. The initialized network is shown in Figure 3.7 (b).

Example 3.4 *Consider again the Bayesian network in Figure 3.7 (a). Suppose B is instantiated for b1. That is, we find out the patient has bronchitis. Next we show the steps in the algorithm when the network's values are updated according to this instantiation.*

The call

$$update\_tree((\mathbb{G}, P), \mathsf{A}, \mathsf{a}, B, b1);$$

results in the following steps:

$\mathsf{A} = \varnothing \cup \{B\} = \{B\};$
$\mathsf{a} = \varnothing \cup \{b1\} = \{b1\};$

$\lambda(b1) = 1;\ \pi(b1) = 1;\ P(b1|\{b1\}) = 1;$ // *Instantiate B for b1.*
$\lambda(b2) = 0;\ \pi(b2) = 0;\ P(b2|\{b1\}) = 0;$

$send\_\lambda\_msg(B, H);$

The call

$$send\_\lambda\_msg(B, H);$$

results in the following steps:

$\lambda_B(h1) = P(b1|h1)\lambda(b1) + P(b2|h1)\lambda(b2);$ // *B sends H a λ*
$\qquad = (.25)(1) + .75(0) = .25;$ // *message.*

$\lambda_B(h2) = P(b1|h2)\lambda(b1) + P(b2|h2)\lambda(b2);$
$\qquad = (.05)(1) + .95(0) = .05;$

$\lambda(h1) = \lambda_B(h1)\lambda_L(h1) = (.25)(1) = .25;$ // *Compute H's λ*
$\lambda(h2) = \lambda_B(h2)\lambda_L(h2) = (.05)(1) = .05;$ // *values.*

$P(h1|\{b1\}) = \alpha\lambda(h1)\pi(h1) = \alpha(.25)(.2) = .05\alpha;$ // *Compute $P(h|\{b1\})$.*
$P(h2|\{b1\}) = \alpha\lambda(h2)\pi(h2) = \alpha(.05)(.8) = .04\alpha;$

$P(h1|\{b1\}) = \frac{.05\alpha}{.05\alpha + .04\alpha} = .5556;$

$P(h2|\{b1\}) = \frac{.04\alpha}{.04\alpha + .05\alpha} = .4444;$

$send\_\pi\_msg(H, L);$

The call

$send\_\pi\_msg(H, L);$

results in the following steps:

$$\pi_L(h1) = \pi(h1)\lambda_B(h1) = (.2)(.25) = .05; \qquad \text{// } H \text{ sends } L \text{ a } \pi$$
$$\pi_L(h2) = \pi(h2)\lambda_B(h2) = (.8)(.05) = .04; \qquad \text{// message.}$$

$$\pi(l1) = P(l1|h1)\pi_L(h1) + P(l1|h2)\pi_L(h2); \qquad \text{// Compute } L\text{'s } \pi$$
$$= (.003)(.05) + (.00005)(.04) = .00015; \quad \text{// values.}$$

$$\pi(l2) = P(l2|h1)\pi_L(h1) + P(l2|h2)\pi_L(h2);$$
$$= (.997)(.05) + (.99995)(.04) = .08985;$$

$$P(l1|\{b1\}) = \alpha\lambda(l1)\pi(l1) = \alpha(1)(.00015) = .00015\alpha; \quad \text{// Compute}$$
$$P(l2|\{b1\}) = \alpha\lambda(l2)\pi(l2) = \alpha(1)(.08985) = .08985\alpha; \quad \text{// } P(l|\{b1\}).$$

$$P(l1|\{b1\}) = \frac{.00015\alpha}{.00015\alpha+.08985\alpha} = .00167;$$

$$P(l2|\{b1\}) = \frac{.00015\alpha}{.00015\alpha+.08985\alpha} = .99833;$$

$send\_\pi\_msg(L, C);$

The call

$send\_\pi\_msg(L, C);$

results in the following steps:

$$\pi_C(l1) = \pi(l1) = .00015; \qquad\qquad\qquad \text{// } L \text{ sends } C \text{ a } \pi$$
$$\pi_C(l2) = \pi(l2) = .08985; \qquad\qquad\qquad \text{// message.}$$

$$\pi(c1) = P(c1|l1)\pi_C(l1) + P(c1|l2)\pi_C(l2); \qquad \text{// Compute } C\text{'s } \pi$$
$$= (.6)(.00015) + (.02)(.08985) = .00189; \quad \text{// values.}$$

$$\pi(c2) = P(c2|l1)\pi_C(l1) + P(c2|l2)\pi_C(l2);$$
$$= (.4)(.00015) + (.98)(.08985) = .08811;$$

$$P(c1|\{b1\}) = \alpha\lambda(c1)\pi(c1) = \alpha(1)(.00189) = .00189\alpha; \quad \text{// Compute}$$
$$P(c2|\{b1\}) = \alpha\lambda(c2)\pi(c2) = \alpha(1)(.08811) = .08811\alpha; \quad \text{// } P(c|\{b1\}).$$

$$P(l1|\{b1\}) = \frac{.00189\alpha}{.00189\alpha+.08811\alpha} = .021;$$

$$P(l2|\{b1\}) = \frac{.08811\alpha}{.00189\alpha+.08811\alpha} = .979;$$

The updated network in shown in Figure 3.8 (a). Notice that the probability of lung cancer increases slightly when we find out the patient has bronchitis. The reason is that they have the common cause smoking history, and the presence of bronchitis raises the probability of this cause, which in turn raises the probability of its other effect lung cancer.

Example 3.5 *Consider again the Bayesian network in Figure 3.7 (a). Suppose B has already been instantiated for b1, and C is now instantiated for c1. That is, we find out the patient has a positive chest X-ray. Next we show the steps in the algorithm when the network's values are updated according to this instantiation.*

The call

> $update\_tree((\mathbb{G}, P), \mathsf{A}, \mathsf{a}, C, c1);$

results in the following steps:

> $\mathsf{A} = \{B\} \cup \{C\} = \{B, C\};$
> $\mathsf{a} = \{b1\} \cup \{c1\} = \{b1, c1\};$

> $\lambda(c1) = 1;\ \pi(c1) = 1;\ P(c1|\{b1, c1\}) = 1;$ *// Instantiate C for c1.*
> $\lambda(c2) = 0;\ \pi(c2) = 0;\ P(c2|\{b1, c1\}) = 0;$

> $send\_\lambda\_msg(C, L);$

The call

> $send\_\lambda\_msg(C, L);$

results in the following steps:

> $\lambda_C(l1) = P(c1|l1)\lambda(c1) + P(c2|l1)\lambda(c2);$ *// C sends L a λ message.*
> $\quad\quad\quad = (.6)(1) + (.4)(0) = .6;$

> $\lambda_C(l2) = P(c1|l2)\lambda(c1) + P(c2|l2)\lambda(c2);$
> $\quad\quad\quad = (.02)(1) + .98(0) = .02;$

> $\lambda(l1) = \lambda_C(l1) = .6;$ *// Compute L's λ values.*
> $\lambda(l2) = \lambda_C(l2) = .02;$

> $P(l1|\{b1, c1\}) = \alpha\lambda(l1)\pi(l1) = \alpha(.6)(.00015) = .00009\alpha;$
> $P(l2|\{b1, c1\}) = \alpha\lambda(l2)\pi(l2) = \alpha(.02)(.08985) = .00180\alpha;$

> $P(l1|\{b1, c1\}) = \frac{.00009\alpha}{.00009\alpha + .00180\alpha} = .04762;$ *// Compute $P(l|\{b1, c1\})$.*

> $P(l2|\{b1, c1\}) = \frac{.00180\alpha}{.00009\alpha + .00180\alpha} = .95238;$

> $send\_\lambda\_msg(L, H);$

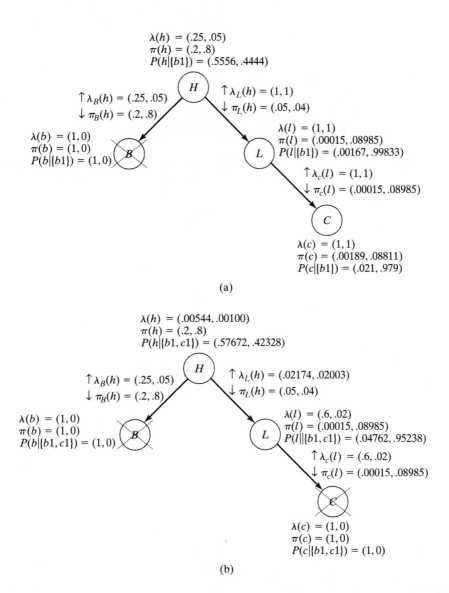

Figure 3.8: (a) shows the updated network after B is instantiated for $b1$. (b) shows the updated network after B is instantiated for $b1$ and C is instantiated for $c1$.

The call

$$send\_\lambda\_msg(L, H);$$

results in the following steps:

$$\lambda_L(h1) = P(l1|h1)\lambda(l1) + P(l2|h1)\lambda(l2); \qquad \textit{// L sends H a } \lambda$$
$$= (.003)(.6) + .997(.02) = .02174; \qquad \textit{// message.}$$

$$\lambda_L(h2) = P(l1|h2)\lambda(l1) + P(l2|h2)\lambda(l2);$$
$$= (.00005)(.6) + .99995(.02) = .02003;$$

$$\lambda(h1) = \lambda_B(h1)\lambda_L(h1) = (.25)(.02174) = .00544; \qquad \textit{// Compute H's } \lambda$$
$$\lambda(h2) = \lambda_B(h2)\lambda_L(h2) = (.05)(.02003) = .00100; \qquad \textit{// values.}$$

$$P(h1|\{b1, c1\}) = \alpha\lambda(h1)\pi(h1) = \alpha(.00544)(.2) = .00109\alpha;$$
$$P(h2|\{b1, c1\}) = \alpha\lambda(h2)\pi(h2) = \alpha(.00100)(.8) = .00080\alpha;$$

$$P(h1|\{b1, c1\}) = \frac{.00109\alpha}{.00109\alpha + .00080\alpha} = .57672; \quad \textit{// Compute } P(h|\{b1, c1\}).$$

$$P(h2|\{b1, c1\}) = \frac{.0008\alpha}{.00109\alpha + .00080\alpha} = .42328;$$

The updated network is shown in Figure 3.8 (b).

3.2.2 Inference in Singly Connected Networks

A DAG is called **singly connected** if there is at most one chain between any two nodes. Otherwise, it is called **multiply connected**. A Bayesian network is called **singly connected** if its DAG is singly connected and is called **multiply connected** otherwise. For example, the DAG in Figure 3.9 is not singly connected because there are two chains between a number of nodes including, for example, between B and L. The difference between a singly connected DAG,

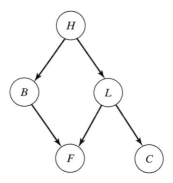

Figure 3.9: A DAG that is not singly connected.

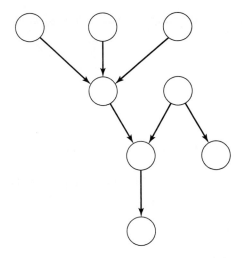

Figure 3.10: A singly connected network that is not a tree.

that is not a tree, and a tree is that in the latter a node can have more than one parent. Figure 3.10 shows a singly connected DAG that is not a tree. Next we present an extension of the algorithm for trees to one for singly connected DAGs. Its correctness is due to the following theorem, whose proof is similar to the proof of Theorem 3.1.

Theorem 3.2 *Let* $(\mathbb{G}, P)$ *be a Bayesian network that is singly connected, where* $\mathbb{G} = (\mathsf{V}, \mathsf{E})$, *and let* a *be a set of values of a subset* $\mathsf{A} \subset \mathsf{V}$. *For each variable* X, *define* λ *messages,* λ *values,* π *messages, and* π *values as follows:*

1. *Define* λ *messages:*

   For each child Y *of* X, *for all values of* x,

   $$\lambda_Y(x) \equiv \sum_y \left[\sum_{w_1, w_2, \dots, w_k} \left(P(y|x, w_1, w_2, \dots, w_k) \prod_{i=1}^{k} \pi_Y(w_i) \right) \right] \lambda(y).$$

   where $W_1, W_2, \dots, W_k$ *are the other parents of* Y.

2. *Define* λ *values:*

   If $X \in \mathsf{A}$ *and* X's *value is* $\hat{x}$,

   $$\begin{aligned} \lambda(\hat{x}) &\equiv 1 \\ \lambda(x) &\equiv 0 \qquad \text{for } x \neq \hat{x}. \end{aligned}$$

   If $X \notin \mathsf{A}$ *and* X *is a leaf, for all values of* x,

   $$\lambda(x) \equiv 1.$$

If $X \notin \mathsf{A}$ and X is a nonleaf, for all values of x,

$$\lambda(x) \equiv \prod_{U \in \mathsf{CH}_X} \lambda_U(x).$$

where CH_X is the set of all children of X.

3. Define π messages:

Let Z be a parent of X. Then for all values of z,

$$\pi_X(z) \equiv \pi(z) \prod_{U \in \mathsf{CH}_Z - \{X\}} \lambda_U(z).$$

4. Define π values:

If $X \in \mathsf{A}$ and X's value is $\hat{x}$,

$$\begin{aligned} \pi(\hat{x}) &\equiv 1 \\ \pi(x) &\equiv 0 \qquad \text{for } x \neq \hat{x}. \end{aligned}$$

If $X \notin \mathsf{A}$ and X is a root, for all values of x,

$$\pi(x) \equiv P(x).$$

If $X \notin \mathsf{A}$, X is a nonroot, and $Z_1, Z_2, \ldots, Z_j$ are the parents of X, for all values of x,

$$\pi(x) = \sum_{z_1, z_2, \ldots, z_j} \left(P(x | z_1, z_2, \ldots, z_j) \prod_{i=1}^{j} \pi_X(z_i) \right).$$

5. Given the definitions above, for each variable X, we have for all values of x,

$$P(x | \mathsf{a}) = \alpha \lambda(x) \pi(x),$$

where α is a normalizing constant.

Proof. *The proof is left as an exercise.* ∎

The algorithm based on the preceding theorem now follows.

Algorithm 3.2 Inference-in-Singly-Connected-Networks

Problem: Given a singly connected Bayesian network, determine the probabilities of the values of each node conditional on specified values of the nodes in some subset.

Inputs: Singly connected Bayesian network $(\mathbb{G}, P)$, where $\mathbb{G} = (\mathsf{V}, \mathsf{E})$, and a set of values a of a subset $\mathsf{A} \subseteq \mathsf{V}$.

Outputs: The Bayesian network $(\mathbb{G}, P)$ updated according to the values in a. The λ and π values and messages and $P(x|\mathsf{a})$ for each $X \in \mathsf{V}$ are considered part of the network.

```
void initial_net (Bayesian-network& (𝔾, P) where 𝔾 = (V, E),
                  set-of-variables& A, set-of-variable-values& a)
{
  A = ∅; a = ∅;
  for (each X ∈ V) {
    for (each value x of X)
      λ(x) = 1;                    // Compute λ values.
    for (each parent Z of X)       // Does nothing if X is the a root.
      for (each value z of Z)
        λ_X(z) = 1;                // Compute λ messages.
    for (each child Y of X)
      for (each value x of X)
        π_Y(x) = 1;               // Initialize π messages.
  }
  for each root R {
    for each value of r {
      P(r|a) = P(r);              // Compute P(r|a).
      π(r) = P(r);               // Compute R's π values.
    }
    for (each child X of R)
      send_π_msg(R, X);
  }
}

void update_tree (Bayesian-network (𝔾, P) where 𝔾 = (V, E),
                  set-of-variables& A, set-of-variable-values& a,
                  variable V, variable-value v̂)
{
  A = A ∪ {V}; a = a∪{v̂};          // Add V to A.
  λ(v̂) = 1; π(v̂) = 1; P(v̂|a) = 1; // Instantiate V for v̂.
  for (each value of v ≠ v̂) {
    λ(v) = 0; π(v) = 0; P(v|a) = 0;
  }
  for (each parent Z of V such that Z ∉ A)
    send_λ_msg(V, Z);
  for (each child X of V)
    send_π_msg(V, X);
}
```

```
void send_λ_msg(node Y, node X)    // (G, P) is not shown as input.
{                                   // Wᵢs are Y's other parents.
   for each value of x {            // Y sends X a λ message.
```

$$\lambda_Y(x) \equiv \sum_y \left[\sum_{w_1, w_2, \ldots, w_k} \left(P(y|x, w_1, w_2, \ldots, w_k) \prod_{i=1}^{k} \pi_Y(w_i) \right) \right] \lambda(y);$$

$$\lambda(x) = \prod_{U \in \mathsf{CH}_X} \lambda_U(x); \qquad\qquad \text{// Compute } X\text{'s } \lambda \text{ values.}$$

$$P(x|a) = \alpha\lambda(x)\pi(x); \qquad\qquad \text{// Compute } P(x|a).$$

```
   }
   normalize P(x|a);
   for (each parent Z of X such that Z ∉ A)
      send_λ_msg(X, Z);
   for (each child W of X such that W ≠ Y)
      send_π_msg(X, W);
}
```

```
void send_π_message(node Z, node X)    // (G, P) is not shown as
{                                       // input.
   for (each value of z)
```

$$\pi_X(z) = \pi(z) \prod_{Y \in \mathsf{CH}_Z - \{X\}} \lambda_Y(z); \qquad \text{// } Z \text{ sends } X \text{ a } \pi \text{ message.}$$

```
   if (X ∉ A) {
      for (each value of x) {              // the Zᵢs are X's parents.
```

$$\pi(x) = \sum_{z_1, z_2, \ldots, z_j} \left(P(x|z_1, z_2, \ldots, z_j) \prod_{i=1}^{j} \pi_X(z_i) \right);$$

$$P(x|a) = \alpha\lambda(x)\pi(x); \qquad\qquad \text{// Compute } X\text{'s } \pi \text{ values.}$$

```
      }
      normalize P(x|a);                    // Compute P(x|a).
      for (each child Y of X)
         send_π_msg(X, Y);
   }
   if not (λ(x) = 1 for all values of x)   // Do not send λ messages to
      for (each parent W of X              // X's other parents if X and
         such that W ≠ Z and W ∉ A)        // all of X's descendents are
            send_λ_msg(X, W);              // uninstantiated.
}
```

Notice that the comment in routine $send\text{-}\pi\text{-}message$ says "do not send λ messages to X's other parents if X and all of X's descendents are uninstantiated." The reason is that, if X and all X's descendents are uninstantiated, X d-separates each of its parents from every other parent. Clearly, if X and all X's descendents are uninstantiated, then all X's λ values are still equal to 1.

Examples of applying the preceding algorithm follow.

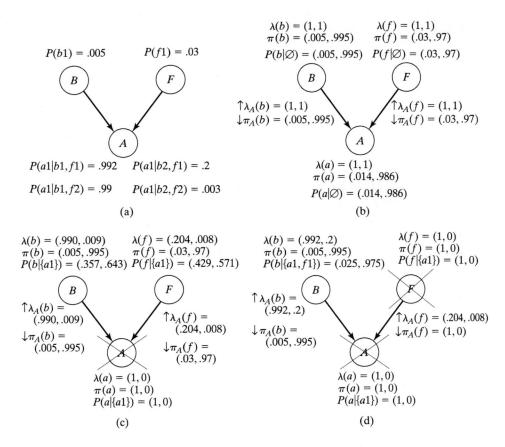

Figure 3.11: (b) shows the initialized network corresponding to the Bayesian network in (a). (c) shows the state of the network after A is instantiated for $a1$, and (d) shows its state after A is instantiated for $a1$ and F is instantiated for $f1$.

Example 3.6 *Consider the Bayesian network in Figure 3.11 (a). For the sake of concreteness, suppose the variables are the ones discussed in Example 1.41 on page 62. That is, they represent the following:*

Variable	Value	When the Variable Takes this Value
B	b1	A burglar breaks in house
	b2	A burglar does not break in house
F	f1	Freight truck makes a delivery
	f2	Freight truck does not make a delivery
A	a1	Alarm sounds
	m2	Alarm does not sound

We show the steps when the network is initialized.

The call

$initial\_tree((\mathbb{G}, P), \mathsf{A}, \mathsf{a});$

results in the following steps:

$\mathsf{A} = \varnothing;$
$\mathsf{a} = \varnothing;$

$\lambda(b1) = 1; \lambda(b2) = 1;$ // *Compute* λ *values.*
$\lambda(f1) = 1; \lambda(f2) = 1;$
$\lambda(a1) = 1; \lambda(a2) = 1;$

$\lambda_A(b1) = 1; \lambda_A(b2) = 1;$ // *Compute* λ *messages.*
$\lambda_A(f1) = 1; \lambda_A(f2) = 1;$

$\pi_A(b1) = 1; \pi_A(b2) = 1;$ // *Compute* π *messages.*
$\pi_A(f1) = 1; \pi_A(f2) = 1;$

$P(b1|\varnothing) = P(b1) = .005;$ // *Compute* $P(b|\varnothing)$.
$P(b2|\varnothing) = P(b2) = .995;$

$\pi(b1) = P(b1) = .005;$ // *Compute* B*'s* π *values.*
$\pi(b2) = P(b2) = .995;$

$send\_\pi\_msg(B, A);$

$P(f1|\varnothing) = P(f1) = .03;$ // *Compute* $P(f|\varnothing)$.
$P(f2|\varnothing) = P(f2) = .97;$

$\pi(f1) = P(f1) = .03;$ // *Compute* F*'s* π *values.*
$\pi(f2) = P(f2) = .97;$

$send\_\pi\_msg(F, A);$

The call

$send\_\pi\_msg(B, A);$

results in the following steps:

$\pi_A(b1) = \pi(b1) = .005;$ // *B sends A a* π *message.*
$\pi_A(b2) = \pi(b2) = .995;$

$$\begin{aligned} \pi(a1) &= P(a1|b1,f1)\pi_A(b1)\pi_A(f1) + P(a1|b1,f2)\pi_A(b1)\pi_A(f2) \\ &\quad + P(a1|b2,f1)\pi_A(b2)\pi_A(f1) + P(a1|b2,f2)\pi_A(b2)\pi_A(f2) \\ &= (.992)(.005)(1) + (.99)(.005)(1) \\ &\quad + (.2)(.995)(1) + (.003)(.995)(1) = .212; \end{aligned}$$

$$\begin{aligned} \pi(a2) &= P(a2|b1,f1)\pi_A(b1)\pi_A(f1) + P(a2|b1,f2)\pi_A(b1)\pi_A(f2) \\ &\quad + P(a2|b2,f1)\pi_A(b2)\pi_A(f1) + P(a2|b2,f2)\pi_A(b2)\pi_A(f2) \\ &= (.008)(.005)(1) + (.01)(.005)(1) \\ &\quad + (.8)(.995)(1) + (.997)(.995)(1) = 1.788; \end{aligned}$$

$P(a1|\varnothing) = \alpha\lambda(b1)\pi(b1) = \alpha(1)(.202) = .212\alpha;$ // Compute $P(a|\varnothing)$.
$P(a2|\varnothing) = \alpha\lambda(b2)\pi(b2) = \alpha(1)(2.788) = 1.788\alpha;$ // This will not be

$P(a1|\varnothing) = \frac{.212\alpha}{.212\alpha+1.788\alpha} = .106;$ // $P(a|\varnothing)$ until A

$P(a1|\varnothing) = \frac{1.788\alpha}{.212\alpha+1.788\alpha} = .894;$ // gets F's π message.

The call

$send\_\pi\_msg(F, A);$

results in the following steps:

$\pi_A(f1) = \pi(f1) = .03;$ // F sends A a π
$\pi_A(f2) = \pi(f2) = .97;$ // message.

$$\begin{aligned} \pi(a1) &= P(a1|b1,f1)\pi_A(b1)\pi_A(f1) + P(a1|b1,f2)\pi_A(b1)\pi_A(f2) \\ &\quad + P(a1|b2,f1)\pi_A(b2)\pi_A(f1) + P(a1|b2,f2)\pi_A(b2)\pi_A(f2) \\ &= (.992)(.005)(03) + (.99)(.005)(.97) \\ &\quad + (.2)(.995)(03) + (.003)(.995)(.97) = .014; \end{aligned}$$

$$\begin{aligned} \pi(a2) &= P(a2|b1,f1)\pi_A(b1)\pi_A(f1) + P(a2|b1,f2)\pi_A(b1)\pi_A(f2) \\ &\quad + P(a2|b2,f1)\pi_A(b2)\pi_A(f1) + P(a2|b2,f2)\pi_A(b2)\pi_A(f2) \\ &= (.008)(.005)(.03) + (.01)(.005)(.97) \\ &\quad + (.8)(.995)(.03) + (.997)(.995)(.97) = .986; \end{aligned}$$

$P(a1|\varnothing) = \alpha\lambda(b1)\pi(b1) = \alpha(1)(.014) = .014\alpha;$ // Compute $P(a|\varnothing)$.
$P(a2|\varnothing) = \alpha\lambda(b2)\pi(b2) = \alpha(1)(.986) = .986\alpha;$

$P(a1|\varnothing) = \frac{.014\alpha}{.014\alpha+.986\alpha} = .014;$

$P(a1|\varnothing) = \frac{.986\alpha}{.014\alpha+.986\alpha} = .986;$

The initialized network is shown in Figure 3.11 (b).

Example 3.7 *Consider again the Bayesian network in Figure 3.11 (a). Suppose A is instantiated for a1. That is, Antonio hears his burglar alarm sound. Next we show the steps in the algorithm when the network's values are updated according to this instantiation.*

The call

$\quad update\_tree((\mathbb{G}, P), \mathsf{A}, \mathsf{a}, A, a1);$

results in the following steps:

$\quad \mathsf{A} = \varnothing \cup \{A\} = \{A\};$
$\quad \mathsf{a} = \varnothing \cup \{a1\} = \{a1\};$

$\quad \lambda(a1) = 1;\ \pi(a1) = 1;\ P(a1|\{a1\}) = 1; \qquad$ // *Instantiate A for a1.*
$\quad \lambda(a2) = 0;\ \pi(a2) = 0;\ P(a2|\{a1\}) = 0;$

$\quad send\_\lambda\_msg(A, B);$
$\quad send\_\lambda\_msg(A, F);$

The call

$\quad send\_\lambda\_msg(A, B);$

results in the following steps:

$$\begin{aligned}
\lambda_A(b1) &= [P(a1|b1, f1)\pi_A(f1) + P(a1|b1, f2)\pi_A(f2)]\, \lambda(a1) \\
&= [P(a2|b1, f1)\pi_A(f1) + P(a2|b1, f2)\pi_A(f2)]\, \lambda(a2) \\
&= [(.992)(.03) + (.99)(.97)]\, 1 + [(.008)(.03) + (.01)(.97)]\, 0 \\
&= .990; \qquad\qquad\qquad\qquad\qquad \textit{// A sends B a } \lambda \textit{ message.}
\end{aligned}$$

$$\begin{aligned}
\lambda_A(b2) &= [P(a1|b2, f1)\pi_A(f1) + P(a1|b2, f2)\pi_A(f2)]\, \lambda(a1) \\
&= [P(a2|b2, f1)\pi_A(f1) + P(a2|b2, f2)\pi_A(f2)]\, \lambda(a2) \\
&= [(.2)(.03) + (.003)(.97)]\, 1 + [(.8)(.03) + (.997)(.97)]\, 0 \\
&= .009;
\end{aligned}$$

$\quad \lambda(b1) = \lambda_A(b1) = .990; \qquad\qquad$ // *Compute B's λ values.*
$\quad \lambda(b2) = \lambda_A(b2) = .009;$

$\quad P(b1|\{a1\}) = \alpha\lambda(b1)\pi(b1) = \alpha(.990)(.005) = .005\alpha; \quad .$
$\quad P(b2|\{a1\}) = \alpha\lambda(b2)\pi(b2) = \alpha(.009)(.995) = .009\alpha;$

$\quad P(b1|\{a1\}) = \frac{.005\alpha}{.005\alpha + .0009\alpha} = .357; \qquad$ // *Compute $P(b|\{a1\})$.*

$\quad P(b2|\{a1\}) = \frac{.009\alpha}{.005\alpha + .0009\alpha} = .643;$

The call

$send\_\lambda\_msg(A, F);$

results in the following steps:

$$\lambda_A(f1) = [P(a1|b1, f1)\pi_A(b1) + P(a1|b2, f1)\pi_A(b2)]\lambda(a1)$$
$$= [P(a2|b1, f1)\pi_A(b1) + P(a2|b2, f1)\pi_A(b2)]\lambda(a2)$$
$$= [(.992)(.005) + (.2)(.995)]\,1 + [(.008)(.005) + (.8)(.995)]\,0$$
$$= .204; \qquad\qquad // \text{ A sends F a } \lambda \text{ message.}$$

$$\lambda_A(f2) = [P(a1|b1, f2)\pi_A(b1) + P(a1|b2, f2)\pi_A(b2)]\lambda(a1)$$
$$= [P(a2|b1, f2)\pi_A(b1) + P(a2|b2, f2)\pi_A(b2)]\lambda(a2)$$
$$= [(.99)(.005) + (.003)(.995)]\,1 + [(.01)(.005) + (.997)(.995]\,0$$
$$= .008;$$

$$\lambda(f1) = \lambda_A(f1) = .204; \qquad\qquad // \text{ Compute F's } \lambda \text{ values.}$$
$$\lambda(f2) = \lambda_A(f2) = .008;$$

$$P(f1|\{a1\}) = \alpha\lambda(f1)\pi(f1) = \alpha(.204)(.03) = .006\alpha; \quad.$$
$$P(f2|\{a1\}) = \alpha\lambda(f2)\pi(f2) = \alpha(.008)(.97) = .008\alpha;$$

$$P(f1|\{a1\}) = \frac{.006\alpha}{.008\alpha + .006\alpha} = .429; \qquad // \text{ Compute } P(f|\{a1\}).$$

$$P(f2|\{a1\}) = \frac{.008\alpha}{.008\alpha + .006\alpha} = .571;$$

The state of the network after this instantiation is shown in Figure 3.11 (c). Notice the probability of a freight truck is greater than that of a burglar due to the former's higher prior probability.

Example 3.8 *Consider again the Bayesian network in Figure 3.11(a). Suppose after A is instantiated for a1, F is instantiated for f1. That is, Antonio sees a freight truck in back of his house. Next we show the steps in the algorithm when the network's values are updated according to this instantiation.*

The call

$update\_tree((\mathbb{G}, P), \mathsf{A}, \mathsf{a}, F, f1);$

results in the following steps:

$$\mathsf{A} = \{A\} \cup \{F\} = \{A, F\};$$
$$\mathsf{a} = \{a1\} \cup \{f1\} = \{a1, f1\};$$

$$\lambda(f1) = 1; \; \pi(f1) = 1; \; P(f1|\{f1\}) = 1; \qquad // \text{ Instantiate F for f1.}$$
$$\lambda(f2) = 0; \; \pi(f2) = 0; \; P(f2|\{f1\}) = 0;$$

$$send\_\pi\_msg(F, A);$$

The call

$send\_\pi\_msg(F, A);$

results in the following steps:

$\pi_A(f1) = \pi(f1) = 1;$ // F sends A a π message.
$\pi_A(f2) = \pi(f2) = 0;$

$send\_\lambda\_message(A, B);$

The call

$send\_\lambda\_msg(A, B);$

results in the following steps:

$$
\begin{aligned}
\lambda_A(b1) &= [P(a1|b1, f1)\pi_A(f1) + P(a1|b1, f2)\pi_A(f2)]\,\lambda(a1) \\
&= [P(a2|b1, f1)\pi_A(f1) + P(a2|b1, f2)\pi_A(f2)]\,\lambda(a2) \\
&= [(.992)(1) + (.99)(0)]\,1 + [(.008)(1) + (.01)(0)]\,0 \\
&= .992; \qquad\qquad\qquad\qquad\qquad \text{// A sends B a } \lambda \text{ message.}
\end{aligned}
$$

$$
\begin{aligned}
\lambda_A(b2) &= [P(a1|b2, f1)\pi_A(f1) + P(a1|b2, f2)\pi_A(f2)]\,\lambda(a1) \\
&= [P(a2|b2, f1)\pi_A(f1) + P(a2|b2, f2)\pi_A(f2)]\,\lambda(a2) \\
&= [(.2)(1) + (.003)(0)]\,1 + [(.8)(.03) + (.997)(.97)]\,0 \\
&= .2;
\end{aligned}
$$

$\lambda(b1) = \lambda_A(b1) = .992;$ // Compute B's λ values.
$\lambda(b2) = \lambda_A(b2) = .2;$

$P(b1|\{a1, f1\}) = \alpha\lambda(b1)\pi(b1) = \alpha(.992)(.005) = .005\alpha;$
$P(b2|\{a1, f1\}) = \alpha\lambda(b2)\pi(b2) = \alpha(.2)(.995) = .199\alpha;$

$P(b1|\{a1, f1\}) = \frac{.005\alpha}{.005\alpha + .199\alpha} = .025;$ // Compute $P(b|\{a1, f1\})$.

$P(b2|\{a1, f1\}) = \frac{.199\alpha}{.005\alpha + .199\alpha} = .975;$

The state of the network after this instantiation is shown in Figure 3.11 (d). Notice the discounting. The probability of a burglar drops from .357 to .025 when Antonio sees a freight truck in back of his house. However, since the two causes are not mutually exclusive conditional on the alarm, it does not drop to 0. Indeed, it does not even drop to its prior probability .005.

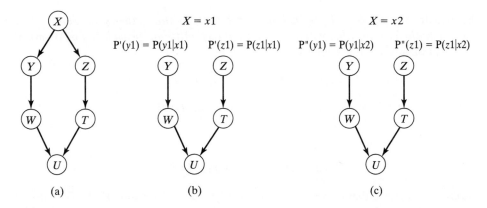

Figure 3.12: A multiply connected network is shown in (a). The singly connected networks obtained by instantiating X for $x1$ and for $x2$ are shown in (b) and (c), respectively.

3.2.3 Inference in Multiply Connected Networks

So far we have considered only singly connected networks. However, clearly there are real applications in which this is not the case. For example, recall that the Bayesian network in Figure 3.1 on page 125 is not singly connected. Next we show how to handle multiply connected networks using the algorithm for singly connected networks. The method we discuss is called **conditioning**.

We illustrate the method with an example. Suppose we have a Bayesian network containing a distribution P, whose DAG is the one in Figure 3.12 (a), and each random variable has two values. Algorithm 3.2 is not directly applicable because the network is multiply connected. However, if we remove X from the network, the network becomes singly connected. So we construct two Bayesian networks, one of which contains the conditional distribution P' of P given $X = x1$ and the other contains the conditional distribution P'' of P given $X = x2$. These networks are shown in Figures 3.12 (b) and (c), respectively. First we determine the conditional probability of every node given its parents for each of these networks. In this case, these conditional probabilities are the same as the ones in our original network except for the roots Y and Z. For those, we have

$$P'(y1) = P(y1|x1) \qquad P'(z1) = P(z1|x1)$$

$$P''(y1) = P(y1|x2) \qquad P'(z1) = P(z1|x2).$$

We can then do inference in our original network by using Algorithm 3.2 to do inference in each of these singly connected networks. The following examples illustrate the method:

Example 3.9 *Suppose U is instantiated for u1 in the network in Figure 3.12 (a) . For the sake of illustration, consider the conditional probability of W given this instantiation. We have*

$$P(w1|u1) = P(w1|x1, u1)P(x1|u1) + P(w1|x2, u1)P(x2|u1).$$

The values of $P(w1|x1, u1)$ and $P(w1|x2, u1)$ can be obtained by applying Algorithm 3.2 to the networks in Figures 3.12 (b) and (c), respectively. The value of $P(xi|u1)$ is given by

$$P(xi|u1) = \alpha P(u1|xi)P(xi),$$

where α is a normalizing constant equal to $1/P(u1)$. The value of $P(xi)$ is stored in the network since X is a root, and the value of $P(u1|xi)$ can be obtained by applying Algorithm 3.2 to the networks in Figures 3.12 (b) and (c). Thereby, we can obtain the value of $P(w1|u1)$. In the same way, we can obtain the conditional probabilities of all nonconditioning variables in the network. Note that along the way we have already computed the conditional probability (namely, $P(xi|u1)$) of the conditioning variable.

Example 3.10 *Suppose U is instantiated for u1 and Y is instantiated for y1 in the network in Figure 3.12 (a). We have*

$$P(w1|u1, y1) = P(w1|x1, u1, y1)P(x1|u1, y1) + P(w1|x2, u1, y1)P(x2|u1, y1).$$

The values of $P(w1|x1, u1, y1)$ and $P(w1|x2, u1, y1)$ can be obtained by applying Algorithm 3.2 to the networks in Figures 3.12 (b) and (c). The value of $P(xi|u1, y1)$ is given by

$$P(xi|u1, y1) = \alpha P(u1, y1|xi)P(xi),$$

where is α a normalizing constant equal to $\frac{1}{P(u1,y1)}$. The value of $P(xi)$ is stored in the network since X is a root. The value of $P(u1, y1|xi)$ cannot be computed directly using Algorithm 3.2. But the chain rule enables us to obtain it with that algorithm. That is,

$$P(u1, y1|xi) = P(u1|y1, xi)P(y1|xi).$$

The values on the right in this equality can both be obtained by applying Algorithm 3.2 to the networks in Figures 3.12 (b) and (c).

The set of nodes on which we condition is called a **loop-cutset**. It is not always possible to find a loop-cutset which contains only roots. Figure 3.18 in Section 3.6 shows a case in which we cannot. Suermondt and Cooper [1990] discuss criteria which must be satisfied by the conditioning nodes, and they present a heuristic algorithm for finding a set of nodes which satisfy these criteria. Furthermore, they prove the problem of finding a minimal loop-cutset is NP-hard.

The general method is as follows. We first determine a loop-cutset C. Let E be a set of instantiated nodes, and let e be their set of instantiations. Then for each $X \in \mathsf{V} - \{\mathsf{E} \cup \mathsf{C}\}$, we have

$$P(xi) = \sum_{\mathsf{c}} P(xi|\mathsf{e}, \mathsf{c})P(\mathsf{c}|\mathsf{e}),$$

where the sum is over all possible values of the variables in C. The values of $P(xi|\mathsf{e}, \mathsf{c})$ are computed using Algorithm 3.2. We determine $P(\mathsf{c}|\mathsf{e})$ using this equality:

$$P(\mathsf{c}|\mathsf{e}) = \alpha P(\mathsf{e}|\mathsf{c})P(\mathsf{c}).$$

To compute $P(\mathsf{e}|\mathsf{c})$ we first apply the chain rule as follows: If $\mathsf{e} = \{e_1, \ldots, e_k)$,

$$P(\mathsf{e}|\mathsf{c}) = P(e_k|e_{k-1}, e_{k-2}, \ldots, e_1, \mathsf{c})P(e_{k-1}|e_{k-2}, \ldots, e_1, \mathsf{c}) \cdots P(e_1|\mathsf{c}).$$

Then Algorithm 3.2 is used repeatedly to compute the terms in this product. The value of $P(\mathsf{c})$ is readily available if all nodes in C are roots. As mentioned previously, in general, the loop-cutset does not contain only roots. A way to compute $P(\mathsf{c})$ in the general case is developed in Suermondt and Cooper [1991].

Pearl [1988] discusses another method for extending Algorithm 3.2 to handle multiply connected networks called **clustering.**

3.2.4   Complexity of the Algorithm

Next we discuss the complexity of the algorithm. Suppose first the network is a tree. Let

$$n \;=\; \text{the number of nodes in the tree.}$$
$$k \;=\; \text{the maximum number of values for a node.}$$

Then there are $n-1$ edges. We need to store at most k^2 conditional probabilities at each node, two k-dimensional vectors (the π and λ values) at each node, and two k-dimensional vectors (the π and λ messages) at each edge. Therefore, an upper bound on the number of values stored in the tree is

$$n(k^2 + 2k) + 2(n - 1)k \in \theta(nk^2).$$

Let

$$c = \text{maximum number of children over all nodes.}$$

Then at most the number of multiplications needed to compute the conditional probability of a variable is k to compute the π message, k^2 to compute the λ message, k^2 to compute the π value, kc to compute the λ value, and k to compute the conditional probability. Therefore, an upper bound on the number of multiplications needed to compute all conditional probabilities is

$$n\left(2k^2 + 2k + kc\right) \in \theta(nk^2 + nkc).$$

It is not hard to see that, if a singly connected network is sparse (i.e., each node does not have many parents), the algorithm is still efficient in terms of space and time. However, if a node has many parents, the space complexity alone becomes intractable. In the next section, we discuss this problem and present a model that solves it under certain assumptions. In Section 3.6, we discuss the complexity in multiply connected networks.

3.3   The Noisy OR-Gate Model

Recall that a Bayesian network requires the conditional probabilities of each variable given all combinations of values of its parents. So, if each variable has only two values, and a variable has p parents, we must specify 2^p conditional probabilities for that variable. If p is large, not only does our inference algorithm become computationally infeasible, but the storage requirements alone become infeasible. Furthermore, even if p is not large, the conditional probability of a variable given a combination of values of its parents is ordinarily not very accessible. For example, consider the Bayesian network in Figure 3.1 (shown at the beginning of this chapter). The conditional probability of fatigue, given that both lung cancer and bronchitis are present, is not as accessible as the conditional probabilities of fatigue given that each is present by itself. Yet we need to specify this former probability. Next we develop a model which requires that we need only specify the latter probabilities. Not only are these probabilities more accessible, but there are only a linear number of them. After developing the model, we modify Algorithm 3.2 to execute efficiently using the model.

3.3.1   The Model

This model, called the **noisy OR-gate model**, concerns the case in which the relationships among variables ordinarily represent causal mechanisms, and each variable has only two values. A variable takes its first value if a feature is present and its second value otherwise. For the sake of notational simplicity, in this section we show the values only as 1 and 2. For example, if the variable B stands for bronchitis, it takes the value 1 if bronchitis is present and 2 otherwise.

We make the following three assumptions in this model:

1. **Causal inhibition**: This assumption entails that there is some mechanism that inhibits a cause from bringing about its effect, and the presence of the cause results in the presence of the effect if and only if this mechanism is disabled (turned off).

2. **Exception independence**: This assumption entails that the mechanism that inhibits one cause is independent of the mechanism that inhibits another causes.

3. **Accountability:** This assumption entails that an effect can happen only if at least one of its causes is present and is not being inhibited. Therefore,

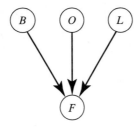

Figure 3.13: A DAG representing the causal relationships among bronchitis, lung cancer, other causes of fatigue, and fatigue.

all causes which are not stated explicitly must be lumped into one unknown cause.

Example 3.11 *Suppose bronchitis and lung cancer both cause fatigue. Let B stand for bronchitis, C for lung cancer, F for fatigue, and O for all other causes of fatigue. Then the DAG in Figure 3.13 represents the causal relationships among the variables. Causal inhibition implies that bronchitis will result in fatigue if and only if the mechanism that inhibits this from happening is not present. Exception independence implies that the mechanism that inhibits bronchitis from resulting in fatigue behaves independently of the mechanisms that inhibits lung cancer and other causes of fatigue from resulting in fatigue. Accountability implies fatigue cannot be present unless at least one of bronchitis, lung cancer, or one of the causes lumped into "other" is present.*

Given the assumptions in this model, the relationships among the variables can be represented by the Bayesian network in Figure 3.14. That figure shows the situation in which there are n causes $X_1, X_2, \ldots$ and X_n of Y. The variable I_j is the mechanism that inhibits X_j. The I_j's are independent owing to our assumption of exception independence. The variable A_j is on if and only if X_j is present (equal to 1) and is not being inhibited. Owing to our assumption of causal inhibition, this means Y should be present (equal to unity) if any one of the A_j's is present. Therefore, we have

$$P(Y = 2|A_j = \text{ON for some } j) = 0.$$

This is why it is called an "OR-gate" model. That is, we can think of the A_j's entering an OR-gate, whose exit feeds into Z. (It is called "noisy" because of the I_j's). Finally, the assumption of accountability implies we have

$$P(Y = 2|A_1 = \text{OFF}, A_2 = \text{OFF}, \ldots A_n = \text{OFF}) = 1.$$

We have the following theorem:

Theorem 3.3 *Suppose we have a Bayesian network representing the Noisy OR-gate model (i.e., Figure 3.14). Let*

$$\mathsf{W} = \{X_1, X_2, \ldots, X_n\},$$

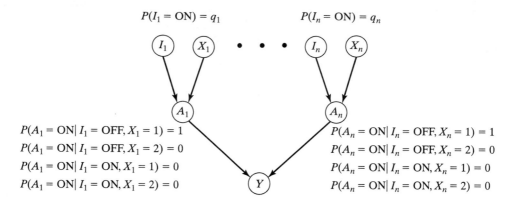

$$P(Y = 2|A_1 = \text{OFF}, A_2 = \text{OFF}, \dots A_n = \text{OFF}) = 1$$
$$P(Y = 2|A_j = \text{ON for some } j) = 0$$

Figure 3.14: A Bayesian network representing the assumptions in the noisy OR-gate model.

and let

$$\mathsf{w} = \{x_1, x_2, \dots, x_n\}$$

be a set of values of the variables in W. *Furthermore, let* S *be a set of indices such that* $j \in \mathsf{S}$ *if and only if* $X_j = 1$. *That is,*

$$\mathsf{S} = \{j \text{ such that } X_j = 1\}.$$

Then

$$P(Y = 2|\mathsf{W} = \mathsf{w}) = \prod_{j \in \mathsf{S}} q_j.$$

Proof. *We have*

$P(Y = 2|\mathsf{W} = \mathsf{w})$

$$= \sum_{a_1,\dots,a_n} P(Y = 2|A_1 = a_1, \dots, A_n = a_n)P(A_1 = a_1, \dots, A_n = a_n|\mathsf{W} = \mathsf{w})$$

$$= \sum_{a_1,\dots,a_n} P(Y = 2|A_1 = a_1, \dots, A_n = a_n)\prod_{j} P(A_j = a_j|X_j = x_j)$$

$$= \prod_{j} P(A_j = OFF|X_j = x_j)$$

$$= \prod_{j}[P(A_j = OFF|X_j = x_j, I_j = ON)P(I_j = ON) +$$

$$P(A_j = OFF|X_j = x_j, I_j = OFF)P(I_j = OFF)]$$

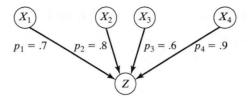

Figure 3.15: A Bayesian network using the Noisy OR-gate model.

$$= \left[\prod_{j \notin S} 1(q_j) + 1(1-q_j) \right] \left[\prod_{j \in S} 1(q_j) + 0(1-q_j) \right]$$

$$= \left[\prod_{j \notin S} 1 \right] \left[\prod_{j \in S} q_j \right] = \prod_{j \in S} q_j.$$

∎

Our actual Bayesian network contains Y and the X_j's but it does not contain the I_j's or A_j's. In that network, we need to specify the conditional probability of Y given each combination of values of the X_j's. Owing to the preceding theorem, we need only specify the values of q_j for all j. All necessary conditional probabilities can then be computed using Theorem 3.3. Instead, we often specify

$$p_j = 1 - q_j,$$

which is called the **causal strength** of X for Y. Theorem 3.3 implies

$$p_j = P(Y = 1 | X_j = 1, X_i = 2 \text{ for } i \neq j).$$

This value is relatively accessible. For example, we may have a reasonably large database of patients, whose only disease is lung cancer. To estimate the causal strength of lung cancer for fatigue, we need only determine how many of these patients are fatigued. On the other hand to directly estimate the conditional probability of fatigue given lung cancer, bronchitis, and other causes, we would need databases containing patients with all combinations of these diseases.

Example 3.12 *Suppose we have the Bayesian network in Figure 3.15, where the causal strengths are shown on the edges. Owing to Theorem 3.3,*

$$
\begin{aligned}
P(Y = 2 | X_1 = 1, X_2 = 2, X_3 = 1, X_4 = 1) &= (1 - p_1)(1 - p_3)(1 - p_4) \\
&= (1 - .7)(1 - .6)(1 - .9) \\
&= .012.
\end{aligned}
$$

So

$$P(Y = 1 | X_1 = 1, X_2 = 2, X_3 = 1, X_4 = 1) = 1 - .012 = .988.$$

3.3.2   Doing Inference with the Model

Even though Theorem 3.3 solves our specification problem, we still need to compute possibly an exponential number of values to do inference using Algorithm 3.2. Next we modify that algorithm to do inference more efficiently with probabilities specified using the noisy OR-gate model.

Assume the variables satisfy the noisy OR-gate model, and Y has n parents $X_1, X_2, \ldots$ and X_n. Let p_j be the causal strength of X_j for Y, and $q_j = 1 - p_j$. The situation with $n = 4$ is shown in Figure 3.15. Before proceeding, we alter our notation a little. That is, to denote that X_j is present, we use x_j^+ instead of 1; to denote that X_j is absent, we use x_j^- instead of 2.

Consider first the λ messages. Using our present notation, we must do the following computation in Algorithm 3.2 to calculate the λ message Y sends to X_j:

$$\lambda_Y(x_j) = \sum_y \left[\sum_{x_1, \ldots, x_{j-1}, x_{j+1}, \ldots, x_n} \left(P(y|x_1, x_2, \ldots, x_n) \prod_{i \neq j} \pi_Y(x_i) \right) \right] \lambda(y).$$

We must determine an exponential number of conditional probabilities to do this computation. It is left as an exercise to show that, in the case of the Noisy OR-gate model, this formula reduces to the following formulas:

$$\lambda_Y(x_j^+) = \lambda(y^-)q_j P_j + \lambda(y^+)(1 - q_j P_j) \tag{3.4}$$

$$\lambda_Y(x_j^-) = \lambda(y^-)P_j + \lambda(y^+)(1 - P_j) \tag{3.5}$$

where

$$P_j = \prod_{i \neq j} [1 - p_i \pi_Y(x_i^+)].$$

Clearly, this latter computation requires that we do only a linear number of operations.

Next consider the π values. Using our present notation, we must do the following computation in Algorithm 3.2 to compute the π value of Y:

$$\pi(y) = \sum_{x_1, x_2, \ldots, x_n} \left(P(y|x_1, x_2, \ldots, x_n) \prod_{j=1}^{n} \pi_Y(x_j) \right)$$

We must determine an exponential number of conditional probabilities to do this computation. It is also left as an exercise to show that, in the case of the Noisy OR-gate model, this formula reduces to the following formulas:

$$\pi(y^+) = 1 - \prod_{j=1}^{n} [1 - p_j \pi_Y(x_j^+)] \tag{3.6}$$

$$\pi(y^-) = \prod_{j=1}^{n}[1 - p_j \pi_Y(x_j^+)]. \tag{3.7}$$

Again, this latter computation requires that we do only a linear number of operations.

3.3.3 Further Models

A generalization of the Noisy OR-gate model to the case of more than two values appears in Srinivas [1993]. Other models for succinctly representing the conditional distributions use the **sigmoid** function (Neal [1992]) and the **logit** function (McLachlan and Krishnan [1997]). Another approach to reducing the number of parameter estimates is the use of **embedded Bayesian networks**, which is discussed in Heckerman and Meek [1997]. Note that their use of the term "embedded Bayesian network" is different than our use in Chapter 6.

3.4 Other Algorithms that Employ the DAG

Shachter [1988] created an algorithm that does inference by performing **arc reversal/node reduction** operations in the DAG. The algorithm is discussed briefly in Section 5.2.2; however, you are referred to the original source for a detailed discussion.

Based on a method originated in Lauritzen and Spiegelhalter [1988], Jensen et al. [1990] developed an inference algorithm that involves the extraction of an undirected triangulated graph from the DAG in a Bayesian network, and the creation of a tree whose vertices are the cliques of this triangulated graph. Such a tree is called a **junction tree**. Conditional probabilities are then computed by passing messages in the junction tree. You are referred to the original source and to Jensen [1996] for a detailed discussion of this algorithm, which we call the **Junction tree Algorithm**.

3.5 The SPI Algorithm

The algorithms discussed so far all do inference by exploiting the conditional independencies entailed by the DAG. Pearl's method does this by passing messages in the original DAG, while Jensen's method does it by passing messages in the junction tree obtained from the DAG. Li and D'Ambrosio [1994] took a different approach. They developed an algorithm that approximates finding the optimal way to compute marginal distributions of interest from the joint probability distribution. They call this **symbolic probabilistic inference (SPI)**. First we illustrate the method with an example.

Suppose we have a joint probability distribution determined by conditional distributions specified for the DAG in Figure 3.16 and all variables are binary.

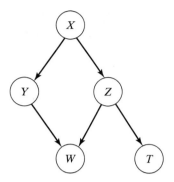

Figure 3.16: A DAG.

Then

$$P(x, y, z, w, t) = P(t|z)P(w|y, z)P(y|x)P(z|x)P(x).$$

Suppose further that we wish to compute $P(t|w)$ for all values of T and W. We have

$$P(t|w) = \frac{P(t, w)}{P(w)} = \frac{\sum_{x,y,z} P(x, y, z, w, t)}{\sum_{x,y,z,t} P(x, y, z, w, t)}$$

$$= \frac{\sum_{x,y,z} P(t|z)P(w|y, z)P(y|x)P(z|x)P(x)}{\sum_{x,y,z,t} P(t|z)P(w|y, z)P(y|x)P(z|x)P(x)}.$$

To compute the sums in the numerator and denominator of the last expression by the brute force method of individually computing all terms and adding them is computationally very costly. For specific values of T and W we would have to do $(2^3)\, 4 = 32$ multiplications to compute the sum in the numerator. Since there are four combinations of values of T and W, this means we would have to do 128 multiplications to compute all numerators. We can save time by not recomputing a product each time it is needed. For example, suppose we do the multiplications in the order determined by the factorization that follows:

$$P(t, w) = \sum_{x,y,z} \left[\left[\left[\left[P(t|z)P(w|y, z)\right] P(y|x)\right] P(z|x)\right] P(x)\right] \qquad (3.8)$$

The first product involves four variables, which means 2^4 multiplications are required to compute its value for all combinations of the variables; the second, third and fourth products each involve five variables, which means 2^5 multiplications are required for each. So the total number of multiplications required is 112, which means we saved 16 multiplications by not recomputing products. We can save more multiplications by summing over a variable once it no longer appears in remaining terms. Equality 3.8 then becomes

$$P(t, w) = \sum_{x} \left[P(x) \sum_{z} \left[P(z|x) \sum_{y} \left[\left[P(t|z)P(w|y, z)\right] P(y|x)\right]\right]\right]. \qquad (3.9)$$

The first product again involves four variables and requires 2^4 multiplications, and the second again involves five variables and requires 2^5 multiplications. However, we sum y out before taking the third product. So it involves only four variables and requires 2^4 multiplications. Similarly, we sum z out before taking the fourth product, which means it only involves three variables and requires 2^3 multiplications. Therefore, the total number of multiplications required is only 72.

Different factorizations can require different numbers of multiplications. For example, consider the factorization that follows:

$$P(t, w) = \sum_z \left[P(t|z) \sum_y \left[P(w|y, z) \sum_x [P(y|x) [P(z|x)P(x)]] \right] \right]. \qquad (3.10)$$

It is not hard to see that this factorization requires only 28 multiplications. To minimize the computational effort involved in computing a given marginal distribution, we want to find the factorization that requires the minimal number of multiplications. Li and D'Ambrosio [1994] called this the "optimal factoring problem." They formulated the problem for the case of binary variables (There is a straightforward generalization to multinomial variables.). After developing the formalization, we apply it to probabilistic inference.

3.5.1 The Optimal Factoring Problem

We start with a definition.

Definition 3.1 *A **factoring instance** $\mathbb{F} = (\mathsf{V}, \mathsf{S}, \mathsf{Q})$ consists of*

1. *a set V of size n;*

2. *A set S of m subsets $\{\mathsf{S}_{\{1\}}, \ldots, \mathsf{S}_{\{m\}}\}$ of V;*

3. *A subset $\mathsf{Q} \subseteq \mathsf{V}$ called the **target set**.*

Example 3.13 *The following is a factoring instance:*

1. *$n = 5$ and $\mathsf{V} = \{x, y, z, w, t\}$.*

2. *$m = 5$ and*

$$
\begin{aligned}
\mathsf{S}_{\{1\}} &= \{x\} \\
\mathsf{S}_{\{2\}} &= \{x, z\} \\
\mathsf{S}_{\{3\}} &= \{x, y\} \\
\mathsf{S}_{\{4\}} &= \{y, z, w\} \\
\mathsf{S}_{\{5\}} &= \{z, t\}.
\end{aligned}
$$

3. *$\mathsf{Q} = \{w, t\}$.*

Definition 3.2 *Let* $S = \{S_{\{1\}}, \ldots, S_{\{m\}}\}$. *A **factoring** α of* S *is a binary tree with the following properties:*

1. *All and only the members of* S *are leaves in the tree.*

2. *The parent of nodes* S_I *and* S_J *is denoted* $S_{I \cup J}$.

3. *The root of the tree is* $S_{\{1,\ldots,m\}}$.

We will apply factorings to factoring instances. However, note that a factoring is independent of the actual values of the $S_{\{i\}}$ in a factoring instance.

Example 3.14 *Suppose* $S = \{S_{\{1\}}, \ldots, S_{\{5\}}\}$. *Then three factorings of* S *appear in Figure 3.17.*

Given a factoring instance $\mathbb{F} = (V, S, Q)$ and a factoring α of S, we compute the **cost** $\mu_\alpha(\mathbb{F})$ as follows. Starting at the leaves of α, we compute the values of all nodes according to this formula:

$$S_{I \cup J} = S_I \cup S_J - W_{I \cup J}$$

where

$$W_{I \cup J} = \left\{ v : \left(\text{for all } k \notin I \cup J, v \notin S_{\{k\}} \right) \text{and } (v \notin Q) \right\}.$$

As the nodes' values are determined, we compute the cost of the nodes according to this formula:

$$\mu_\alpha(S_{\{j\}}) = 0 \qquad \text{for} \qquad 1 \le j \le m$$

and

$$\mu_\alpha(S_{I \cup J}) = \mu_\alpha(S_I) + \mu_\alpha(S_J) + 2^{|S_I \cup S_J|},$$

where $||$ is the number of elements in the set. Finally, we set

$$\mu_\alpha(\mathbb{F}) = \mu_\alpha(S_{\{1,\ldots,m\}}).$$

Example 3.15 *Suppose we have the factoring instance* $\mathbb{F}$ *in Example 3.13. Given the factoring α in Figure 3.17 (a), we have*

$$
\begin{aligned}
S_{\{1,2\}} &= S_{\{1\}} \cup S_{\{2\}} - W_{\{1,2\}} \\
&= \{x\} \cup \{x, z\} - \varnothing = \{x, z\}
\end{aligned}
$$

$$
\begin{aligned}
S_{\{1,2,3\}} &= S_{\{1,2\}} \cup S_{\{3\}} - W_{\{1,2,3\}} \\
&= \{x, z\} \cup \{x, y\} - \{x\} = \{y, z\}
\end{aligned}
$$

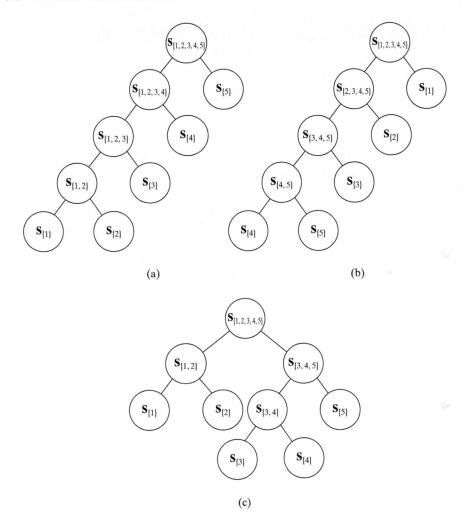

Figure 3.17: Three factorings of $S = \{S_{\{1\}}, \dots, S_{\{5\}}\}$.

$$
\begin{aligned}
S_{\{1,2,3,4\}} &= S_{\{1,2,3\}} \cup S_{\{4\}} - W_{\{1,2,3,4\}} \\
&= \{y, z\} \cup \{y, z, w\} - \{x, y\} = \{z, w\}
\end{aligned}
$$

$$
\begin{aligned}
S_{\{1,2,3,4,5\}} &= S_{\{1,2,3,4\}} \cup S_{\{5\}} - W_{\{1,2,3,4,5\}} \\
&= \{z, w\} \cup \{z, t\} - \{x, y, z\} = \{w, t\}.
\end{aligned}
$$

Next we compute the cost:

$$
\begin{aligned}
\mu_\alpha \left(S_{\{1,2\}} \right) &= \mu_\alpha \left(S_{\{1\}} \right) + \mu_\alpha \left(S_{\{2\}} \right) + 2^2 \\
&= 0 + 0 + 4 = 4
\end{aligned}
$$

$$\mu_\alpha\left(S_{\{1,2,3\}}\right) = \mu_\alpha\left(S_{\{1,2\}}\right) + \mu_\alpha\left(S_{\{3\}}\right) + 2^3$$
$$= 4 + 0 + 8 = 12$$

$$\mu_\alpha\left(S_{\{1,2,3,4\}}\right) = \mu_\alpha\left(S_{\{1,2,3\}}\right) + \mu_\alpha\left(S_{\{4\}}\right) + 2^3$$
$$= 12 + 0 + 8 = 20$$

$$\mu_\alpha\left(S_{\{1,2,3,4,5\}}\right) = \mu_\alpha\left(S_{\{1,2,3,4\}}\right) + \mu_\alpha\left(S_{\{5\}}\right) + 2^3$$
$$= 20 + 0 + 8 = 28.$$

So

$$\mu_\alpha\left(\mathbb{F}\right) = \mu_\alpha\left(S_{\{1,2,3,4,5\}}\right) = 28.$$

Example 3.16 *Suppose again we have the factoring instance* $\mathbb{F}$ *in Example 3.13. Given the factoring* β *in Figure 3.17 (b), we have*

$$S_{\{4,5\}} = S_{\{4\}} \cup S_{\{5\}} - W_{\{4,5\}}$$
$$= \{y, z, w\} \cup \{z, t\} - \varnothing = \{y, z, w, t\}$$

$$S_{\{3,4,5\}} = S_{\{4,5\}} \cup S_{\{3\}} - W_{\{3,4,5\}}$$
$$= \{y, z, w, t\} \cup \{x, y\} - \{y\} = \{x, z, w, t\}$$

$$S_{\{2,3,4,5\}} = S_{\{3,4,5\}} \cup S_{\{2\}} - W_{\{2,3,4,5\}}$$
$$= \{x, z, w, t\} \cup \{x, z\} - \{y, z\} = \{x, w, t\}$$

$$S_{\{1,2,3,4.5\}} = S_{\{2,3,4,5\}} \cup S_{\{1\}} - W_{\{1,2,3,4,5\}}$$
$$= \{x, w, t\} \cup \{x\} - \{x, y, z\} = \{w, t\}.$$

It is left as an exercise to show that

$$\mu_\beta\left(\mathbb{F}\right) = 72.$$

Example 3.17 *Suppose we have the following factoring instance* $\mathbb{F}'$:

1. $n = 5$ and $\mathsf{V} = \{x, y, z, w, t\}$.

2. $m = 5$ and

$$S_{\{1\}} = \{x\}$$
$$S_{\{2\}} = \{y\}$$
$$S_{\{3\}} = \{z\}$$
$$S_{\{4\}} = \{w\}$$
$$S_{\{5\}} = \{x, y, z, w, t\}.$$

3. $Q = \{t\}$.

Given the factoring γ in Figure 3.17 (c), we have

$$
\begin{aligned}
S_{\{1,2\}} &= S_{\{1\}} \cup S_{\{2\}} - W_{\{1,2\}} \\
&= \{x\} \cup \{y\} - \varnothing = \{x, y\}
\end{aligned}
$$

$$
\begin{aligned}
S_{\{3,4\}} &= S_{\{3\}} \cup S_{\{4\}} - W_{\{3,4\}} \\
&= \{z\} \cup \{w\} - \varnothing = \{z, w\}
\end{aligned}
$$

$$
\begin{aligned}
S_{\{3,4,5\}} &= S_{\{3,4\}} \cup S_{\{5\}} - W_{\{3,4,5\}} \\
&= \{z, w\} \cup \{x, y, z, w, t\} - \{z, w\} = \{x, y, t\}
\end{aligned}
$$

$$
\begin{aligned}
S_{\{1,2,3,4,5\}} &= S_{\{1,2\}} \cup S_{\{3,4,5\}} - W_{\{1,2,3,4,5\}} \\
&= \{x, y\} \cup \{x, y, t\} - \{x, y, z, w\} = \{t\}.
\end{aligned}
$$

Next we compute the cost:

$$
\begin{aligned}
\mu_\gamma \left(S_{\{1,2\}} \right) &= \mu_\gamma \left(S_{\{1\}} \right) + \mu_\gamma \left(S_{\{2\}} \right) + 2^2 \\
&= 0 + 0 + 4 = 4
\end{aligned}
$$

$$
\begin{aligned}
\mu_\gamma \left(S_{\{3,4\}} \right) &= \mu_\gamma \left(S_{\{3\}} \right) + \mu_\gamma \left(S_{\{4\}} \right) + 2^2 \\
&= 0 + 0 + 4 = 4
\end{aligned}
$$

$$
\begin{aligned}
\mu_\gamma \left(S_{\{3,4,5\}} \right) &= \mu_\gamma \left(S_{\{3,4\}} \right) + \mu_\gamma \left(S_{\{5\}} \right) + 2^5 \\
&= 4 + 0 + 32 = 36
\end{aligned}
$$

$$
\begin{aligned}
\mu_\gamma \left(S_{\{1,2,3,4,5\}} \right) &= \mu_\gamma \left(S_{\{1,2\}} \right) + \mu_\gamma \left(S_{\{3,4,5\}} \right) + 2^3 \\
&= 4 + 36 + 8 = 48.
\end{aligned}
$$

So

$$
\mu_\gamma \left(\mathbb{F}' \right) = \mu_\gamma \left(S_{\{1,2,3,4,5\}} \right) = 48.
$$

Example 3.18 *Suppose we have the factoring instance $\mathbb{F}'$ in Example 3.17. It is left as an exercise to show for the factoring β in Figure 3.17 (b) that*

$$
\mu_\beta \left(\mathbb{F}' \right) = 60.
$$

We now state the optimal factoring problem. The **optimal factoring problem** is to find a factoring α for a factoring instance $\mathbb{F}$ such that $\mu_\alpha \left(\mathbb{F} \right)$ is minimal.

3.5.2   Application to Probabilistic Inference

Notice that the cost $\mu_\alpha\,(\mathbb{F})$, computed in Example 3.15, is equal to the number of multiplications required by the factorization in Equality 3.10; and the cost $\mu_\beta\,(\mathbb{F})$, computed in Example 3.16, is equal to the number of multiplications required by the factorization in Equality 3.9. This is no coincidence. We can associate a factoring instance with every marginal probability computation in a Bayesian network, and any factoring of the set S in the instance corresponds to a factorization for the computation of that marginal probability. We illustrate the association next. Suppose we have the Bayesian network in Figure 3.16. Then

$$P(x, y, z, w, t) = P(t|z)P(w|y, z)P(y|x)P(z|x)P(x).$$

Suppose further that, as before, we want to compute $P(w, t)$ for all values of W and T. The factoring instance corresponding to this computation is the one shown in Example 3.13. Note that there is an element in S for each conditional probability expression in the product, and the members of an element are the variables in the conditional probability expression. Suppose we compute $P(w, t)$ using the factorization in Equality 3.10, which we now show again:

$$P(t, w) = \sum_z \left[P(t|z) \sum_y \left[P(w|y, z) \sum_x [P(y|x)\,[P(z|x)P(x)]] \right] \right].$$

The factoring α in Figure 3.17 (a) corresponds to this factorization. Note that the partial order in α of the subsets is the partial order in which the corresponding conditional probabilities are multiplied. Similarly, the factoring β in Figure 3.17 (b) corresponds to the factorization in Equality 3.9.

Li and D'Ambrosio [1994] show that, in general, if $\mathbb{F}$ is the factoring instance corresponding to a given marginal probability computation in a Bayesian network, then the cost $\mu_\alpha\,(\mathbb{F})$ is equal to the number of multiplications required by the factorization to which α corresponds. So if we solve the optimal factoring problem for a given factoring instance, we have found a factorization which requires a minimal number of multiplications for the marginal probability computation to which the factoring instance corresponds. They note that each graph-based inference algorithm corresponds to a particular factoring strategy. However, since a given strategy is constrained by the structure of the original DAG (or of a derived junction tree), it may be hard for the strategy to find an optimal factoring.

Li and D'Ambrosio [1994] developed a linear time algorithm which solves the Optimal factoring Problem when the DAG in the corresponding Bayesian network is singly connected. Furthermore, they developed a $\theta(n^3)$ approximation algorithm for the general case.

The total computational cost when doing probabilistic inference using this technique includes the time to find the factoring (called symbolic reasoning) and the time to compute the probability (called numeric computation). The algorithm for doing probabilistic inference, which consists of both the symbolic reasoning and the numeric computation, is called the **symbolic probabilistic inference (SPI) algorithm**.

The junction tree algorithm is considered overall to be the best graph-based algorithm. (There are, however, specific instances in which Pearl's algorithm is more efficient. See Neapolitan [1990] for examples.) If the task is to compute all marginals given all possible sets of evidence, it is believed one cannot improve on the junction tree algorithm (ignoring factorable local dependency models such as the noisy OR-gate model). However, even that has never been proven. Furthermore, for any specific pattern of evidence, one can often do much better than the generic evidence-independent junction tree. Li and D'Ambrosio [1994] compared the performance of the SPI algorithm with that of the junction tree algorithm using a number of different Bayesian networks and probability computations, and they found that the SPI algorithm performed dramatically fewer multiplications. Furthermore, they found that the time spent doing symbolic reasoning by the SPI algorithm was insignificant compared with the time spent doing numeric computation.

Before closing, we note that SPI is not the same as simply eliminating variables as early as possible. The following example illustrates this:

Example 3.19 *Suppose our joint probability distribution is*

$$P(t|x, y, z, w)P(w)P(z)P(y)P(x),$$

and we want to compute $P(t)$ for all values of T. The factoring instance $\mathbb{F}'$ in Example 3.17 corresponds to this marginal probability computation. The following factorization eliminates variables as early as possible:

$$\sum_x \left[P(x) \sum_y \left[P(y) \sum_z \left[P(z) \sum_w [P(t|x, y, z, w)P(w)] \right] \right] \right].$$

The factoring β in Figure 3.17 (b) corresponds to this factorization. As shown in Example 3.18 $\mu_\beta (\mathbb{F}') = 60$, which means this factorization requires 60 multiplications.

On the other hand, consider this factorization:

$$\sum_y \sum_x \left[[P(x)P(y)] \sum_z \sum_w [P(t|x, y, z, w) [P(w)P(z)]] \right].$$

The factoring γ in Figure 3.17 (c) corresponds to this factorization. As shown in Example 3.17 $\mu_\gamma (\mathbb{F}') = 48$, which means this factorization requires only 48 multiplications.

Bloemeke and Valtora [1998] developed a hybrid algorithm based on the junction tree and symbolic probabilistic methods.

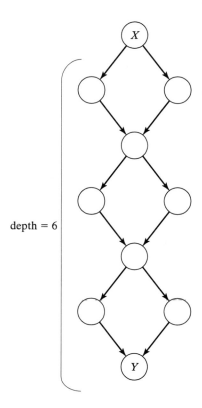

Figure 3.18: Our method of conditioning will require exponential time to compute $P(y1|x1)$.

3.6   Complexity of Inference

First we show that using conditioning and Algorithm 3.2 to handle inference in a multiply connected network can sometimes be computationally infeasible. Suppose we have a Bayesian network, whose DAG is the one in Figure 3.18. Suppose further that each variable has two values. Let k be the depth of the DAG. In the figure, $k = 6$. Using the method of conditioning presented in Section 3.2.3, we must condition on $k/2$ nodes to render the DAG singly connected. That is, we must condition on all the nodes on the far left side or the far right side of the DAG. Since each variable has two values, we must therefore perform inference in $\theta(2^{k/2})$ singly connected networks in order to compute $P(y1|x1)$.

   Although the junction tree and SPI algorithms are more efficient than Pearl's algorithm for certain DAGs, they too, in the worst-case, require nonpolynomial time. This is not surprising since the problem of inference in Bayesian networks has been shown to be NP-hard. Specifically, Cooper [1990] has obtained the result that, for the set of Bayesian networks that are restricted to having no more than two values per node and no more than two parents per node, with no restriction on the number of children per node, the problem of determining the conditional probabilities of remaining variables, given that certain variables have been instantiated, in multiply connected networks, is $\#P$-complete. $\#P$-complete problems are a special class of NP-hard algorithms—namely, the answer to a $\#P$-complete problem is the number of solutions to some NP-complete problem. In light of this result, researchers have worked on approximation algorithms for inference Bayesian networks. We show one such algorithm in Chapter 4.

3.7 Relationship to Human Reasoning

First we present the causal network model, which is a model of how humans reason with causes. Then we show results of studies testing this model.

3.7.1 The Causal Network Model

Recall from Section 1.5 that, if we identify direct cause-effect relationships (edges) by any means whatsoever, draw a causal DAG using the edges identified, and assume the probability distribution of the variables satisfies the Markov condition with this DAG, we are making the causal Markov assumption. We argued that, when causes are identified using manipulation, we can often make the causal Markov assumption, and hence the casual DAG, along with its conditional distributions, constitute a Bayesian network that pretty well models reality. That is, we argued that relationships, which we objectively define as causal, constitute a Bayesian network in external reality. Pearl, [1986], Pearl [1995] takes this argument a step further. He argues that a human internally structures his or her causal knowledge in his or her own personal Bayesian network, and that he or she performs inference using that knowledge in the same way as Algorithm 3.2. When the DAG in a Bayesian network is a causal DAG, the network is called a **causal network**. Henceforth, we will use this term, and we will call this model of human reasoning the **causal network model**. Pearl's argument is not that a globally consistent causal network exists at a cognitive level in the brain. "Instead, fragmented structures of causal organizations are constantly being assembled on the fly, as needed, from a stock of functional building blocks" [Pearl, 1995].

Figure 3.19 shows a causal network representing the reasoning involved when a Mr. Holmes learns that his burglar alarm has sounded. He knows that earthquakes and burglars can both cause his alarm to sound. So there are arcs from both *earthquake* and *burglar* to *alarm*. Only a burglar could cause footprints to be seen. So there is an arc only from *burglar* to *footprints*. The causal network model maintains that Mr. Holmes reasons as follows. If he were in his office at work and learned that his alarm had sounded at home, he would assemble the cause–effect relationship between *burglar* and *alarm*. He would reason along the arc from *alarm* to *burglar* to conclude that he had probably been burglarized. If he later learned of an earthquake, he would assemble the *earthquake–alarm* relationship. He would then reason that the earthquake explains away the alarm,

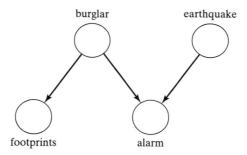

Figure 3.19: A causal network.

and therefore he had probably not been burglarized. Notice that according to this model, he mentally traces the arc from *earthquake* to *alarm*, followed by the one from *alarm* to *burglar*. If, when Mr. Holmes got home, he saw strange footprints in the yard, he would assemble the *burglar–footprints* relationship and reason along the arc between them. Notice that this tracing of arcs in the causal network is how Algorithm 3.2 does inference in Bayesian networks. The causal network model maintains that a human reasons with a large number of nodes by mentally assembling small fragments of causal knowledge in sequence. The result of reasoning with the link assembled in one time frame is used when reasoning in a future time frame. For example, the determination that he has probably been burglarized (when he learns of the alarm) is later used by Mr. Holmes when he sees and reasons with the footprints.

Tests on human subjects have been performed testing the accuracy of the causal network model. We discuss that research next.

3.7.2 Studies Testing the Causal Network Model

First we discuss "discounting" studies, which did not explicitly state they were testing the causal network model, but were doing so implicitly. Then we discuss tests that explicitly tested it.

Discounting Studies

Psychologists have long been interested in how an individual judges the presence of a cause when informed of the presence of one of its effect, and whether and to what degree the individual becomes less confident in the cause when informed that another cause of the effect was present. Kelly [1972] called this inference **discounting**. Several researchers, (Jones [1979], Quattrone [1982], Einhorn and Hogarth [1983], and McClure [1989]) have argued that studies indicate that in certain situations people discount less than is warranted. On the other hand, arguments that people discount more than is warranted also have a long history. (See Mill [1843], Kanouse [1972], and Nisbett and Ross [1980].)

In many of the discounting studies, individuals were asked to state their feelings about the presence of a particular cause when informed another cause was present. For example, a classic finding is that subjects who read an essay defending Fidel Castro's regime in Cuba ascribe a pro-Castro attitude to the essay writer even when informed that the writer was instructed to take a pro-Castro stance. Researchers interpreted these results as indicative of underdiscounting. Morris and Larrick [1995] argue that the problem in these studies is that the researchers assume that subjects believe a cause is sufficient for an effect when actually the subjects do not believe this. That is, the researchers assumed the subjects believed the probability is 1 that an effect is present conditional on one of its causes being present. Morris and Larrick [1995] repeated the Castro studies, but used subjective probability testing instead of assuming, for example, that the subject believes an individual will always write a pro-Castro essay whenever told to do so. (They found that subjects only felt it was highly probable this would happen.) When they replaced deterministic relationships by probabilistic ones, they found that subjects discounted **normatively**. That is, using as a benchmark the amount of discounting implied by applying Bayes' rule, they found that subjects discounted about correctly. Since the causal network model implies subjects would reason normatively, their results support that model.

Plach's Study

While research on discounting is consistent with the causal network model, the inference problems considered in this research involved very simple networks (e.g., one effect and two causes). One of the strengths of causal networks is the ability to model complex relationships among a large number of variables. Therefore, research was needed to examine whether human causal reasoning involving more complex problems can be modeled effectively using a causal network. To this end, Plach [1997] examined human reasoning in larger networks modeling traffic congestion. Participants were asked to judge the probabilities of various traffic-related events (weather, accidents, and so forth), and were then asked to update their estimates of the probability of traffic congestion as additional evidence was made available. The results revealed a high correspondence between subjective updating and normative values implied by the network. However, there were several limitations to this study. All analyses were performed on probability estimates, which had been averaged across subjects. To the extent that individuals differ in their subjective beliefs, these averages may obscure important individual differences. Second, participants were asked only to consider two pieces of evidence at a time. Thus, it is unclear whether the result would generalize to more complex problems with larger amounts of evidence. Finally, participants were asked to make inferences from cause to effect, which is distinct from the diagnostic task in which inferences must be made from effects to causes.

Morris and Neapolitan's Study

Morris and Neapolitan [2000] utilized an approach similar to Plach's to explore causal reasoning in computer debugging. However, they examined individuals' reasoning with more complex causal relationships and with more evidence. We discuss their study in more detail.

Methodology   First we give the methodology.

   Participants   The participants were 19 students in a graduate-level computer science course. All participants had some experience with the type of program used in the study. Most participants (88%) rated their programming skill as either okay or good, while the remainder rated their skill level as expert.

   Procedure   The study was conducted in three phases. In the first phase, two causal networks were presented to the participants and discussed at length to familiarize participants with the content of the problem. The causal networks had been developed based on interviewing an experienced computer programmer and observing him while he was debugging code. Both networks described potential causes of an error in a computer program, which was described as follows:

> One year ago, your employer asked you to create a program to verify and insert new records into a database. You finished the program and it compiled without errors. However, the project was put on hold before you had a chance to fully test the program. Now, one year later, your boss wants you to implement the program. While you remember the basic function of the program (described below), you can't recall much of the detail of your program. You need to make sure the program works as intended before the company puts it into operation.
>
> The program is designed to take information from a data file (the Input File) and add it to a database. The database is used to track shipments received from vendors, and contains information relating to each shipment (e.g., date of arrival, mode of transportation, etc.), as well as a description of one or more packages within each shipment (e.g., product type, count, invoice number, etc.). Each shipment is given a unique Shipment Identification code (SID), and each package is given a unique Package Identification code (PID).
>
> The database has two relations (tables). The Shipment Table contains information about the entire shipment, and the Package Table contains information about individual packages. SID is the primary key for the Shipment Table and a foreign key in the Package Table. PID is the primary key for the Package Table.
>
> If anything goes wrong with the insertion of new records (e.g., there are missing or invalid data), the program writes the key infor-

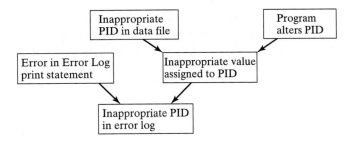

Figure 3.20: Causal network for a simple debugging problem.

mation to a file called the Error Log. This is not a problem as long as records are being rejected because they are invalid. However, you need to verify that errors are written correctly to the Error Log.

Two debugging tasks were described. The first problem was to determine why inappropriate PID values were found in the Error Log. The causal network for this problem was fairly simple, containing only five nodes. (See Figure 3.20.) The second problem was to determine why certain records were not added to the database. The causal network for this problem was considerably more complex, containing 14 variables. (See Figure 3.21.)

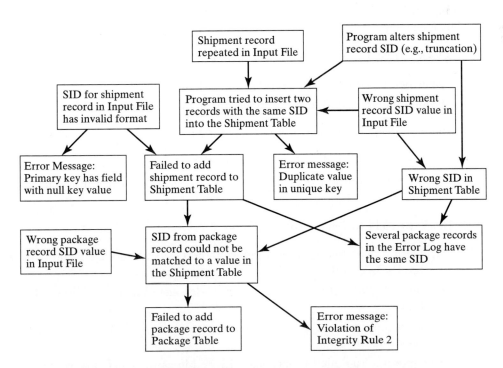

Figure 3.21: Causal network for a complex debugging problem.

In the second phase, participants' prior beliefs about the events in each network were measured. For events with no causes, participants were asked to indicate the prior probability, which was defined as the probability of the event occurring when no other information is known. For events that were caused by other events in the network, participants were asked to indicate the conditional probabilities. Participants indicated the probability of the effect, given that each cause was known to have occurred in isolation, assuming that no other causes had occurred. In addition, participants rated the probability of the effect occurring when none of the causes was present. From this data, all conditional probabilities were computed using the noisy OR-gate model.

All probabilities were obtained using the method described in Plach [1997]. Participants were asked to indicate the number of times, out of 100, that an event would occur. So probabilities were measured on a scale from 0 to 100. Examples of both prior and conditional probabilities were presented to participants and discussed to ensure that everyone understood the rating task.

In the third phase of the study, participants were asked to update the probabilities of events as they received evidence about the values of particular nodes. Participants were first asked to ascertain the prior probabilities of the values of every node in the network. They were then informed of the value of a particular node, and they were asked to determine the conditional probabilities of the values of all other nodes given this evidence. Several pieces of additional evidence were given in each block of trials. Four blocks of trials were conducted, two involving the first network, and two involving the second network.

The following evidence was provided in each block:

1. Block 1 (refers to the network in Figure 3.20)

    Evidence 1. You find an inappropriate PID in the error log.

    Evidence 2. You find an error in the Error Log print statement.

2. Block 2 (refers to the network in Figure 3.20)

    Evidence 1. You find an inappropriate PID in the error log.

    Evidence 2. You find that there are no inappropriate PIDs in the data file.

3. Block 3 (refers to the network in Figure 3.21)

    Evidence 1. You find there is a failure to add several package records to the Package Table.

    Evidence 2. You get the message "Error Message: Violation of integrity rule 2."

    Evidence 3. You find that several package records in the Error Log have the same SID.

    Evidence 4. You get the message "Error Message: Duplicate value in unique key."

4. Block 4 (refers to the network in Figure 3.21)

>   Evidence 1. You find there is a failure to add a shipment record to the Shipment Table.

>   Evidence 2. You get the message "Error Message: Primary key has field with null key value."

Statistical Analysis   The first step in the analysis was to model participants' subjective causal networks. A separate Bayesian network was developed for each participant based on the subjective probabilities gathered in Phase 2. Each of these networks was constructed using the Bayesian network inference program, Hugin. (See Olesen et al. [1992].) Then nodes in the network were instantiated using the same evidence as was provided to participants in Phase 3 of the study. The updated probabilities produced by Hugin were used as normative values for the conditional probabilities.

The second step in the analysis was to examine the correspondence between participants and the Bayesian networks, which was defined as the correlation between subjective and normative probabilities. In addition, the analysis included an examination of the extent to which correspondence changed as a function of (1) the complexity of the network, (2) the amount of evidence provided, and (3) the participant providing the judgments.

The correspondence between subjective and normative ratings was examined using hierarchical linear model (HLM) analysis (Bryk and Raudnebush [1992]). The primary result of interest was the determination of the correlation between normative and subjective probabilities. These results are shown in Figure 3.22.

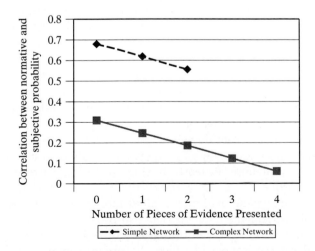

Figure 3.22: The combined effect of network complexity and amount of evidence on the correlation between subjective and normative probability.

Conclusions   The results offer some limited support for the causal network model. Some programmers were found to update their beliefs normatively; however, others did not. In addition, the degree of correspondence declined as the complexity of the inference increased.

Normative reasoning was more likely on simple problems, and less likely when the causal network was large, or when the participants had to integrate multiple pieces of evidence. With a larger network, there will tend to be more links to traverse to form an inference. Similarly, when multiple pieces of evidence are provided, the decision maker must reason along multiple paths in order to update the probabilities. In both cases, the number of computations would increase, which may result in less accurate subjective judgments.

Research on human problem solving consistently shows that decision makers have limited memory and perform limited search of the problem space. (See Simon [1955].) In complex problems, rather than applying normative decision rules, it seems people may rely on heuristics. (See Kahneman et al. [1982].) The use of heuristic information processing is more likely when the problem becomes too complex to handle efficiently using normative methods. Therefore, while normative models may provide a good description of human reasoning with simple problems (e.g., as in the discounting studies described in Morris and Larrick [1995]), normative reasoning in complex problems may require computational resources beyond the capacity of humans. Consistent with this view, research on discounting has shown that normative reasoning occurs only when the participants are able to focus on the judgment task, and that participants insufficiently discount for alternate causes when forced to perform multiple tasks simultaneously. (See Gilbert et al. [1988].)

Considerable variance in the degree of correspondence was also observed across participants, suggesting that individual differences may play a role in the use of Bayes' rule. Normative reasoning may be more likely among individuals with greater working memory, more experience with the problem domain, or certain decision-making styles. For example, individuals who are high in need for cognition, seem more likely than others to carefully consider multiple factors before reaching a decision. (See Petty and Cacioppo [1986].) Future research should investigate such factors as the manner in which working memory might moderate the relationship (correspondence) between normative and subjective probabilities. That is, it should investigate whether the relationship increases with the amount of working memory.

Experience in the problem domain is possibly a key determinant of normative reasoning. As individuals develop expertise in a domain, it seems they learn to process information more efficiently, freeing up the cognitive resources needed for normative reasoning. (See Ackerman [1987].) A limitation of the current study was that participants had only limited familiarity with the problem domain. While all participants had experience in programming, and were at least somewhat familiar with the type of programs involved, they were not familiar with the details of the system in which the program operated. When working on a program of his or her own creation, a programmer will probably have a much deeper and more easily accessible knowledge base about the potential problems. Therefore, complex reasoning about causes and effects may be more easy to perform, and responses may more closely match normative predictions. An improvement for future research would be to involve the participants in the definition of the problem.

EXERCISES

Section 3.1

Exercise 3.1 *Compute $P(x1|w1)$ assuming the Bayesian network in Figure 3.2.*

Exercise 3.2 *Compute $P(t1|w1)$ assuming the Bayesian network in Figure 3.3.*

Section 3.2

Exercise 3.3 *Relative to the proof of Theorem 3.1, show*

$$\sum_z P(x|z)P(x|\mathsf{n}_Z, \mathsf{d}_T) = \sum_z P(x|z)\frac{P(z|\mathsf{n}_Z)P(\mathsf{n}_Z)P(\mathsf{d}_T|z)P(z)}{P(z)P(\mathsf{n}_Z, \mathsf{d}_T)}.$$

Exercise 3.4 *Given the initialized Bayesian network in Figure 3.7 (b), use Algorithm 3.1 to instantiate H for h1 and then C for c2.*

Exercise 3.5 *Prove Theorem 3.2.*

Exercise 3.6 *Given the initialized Bayesian network in Figure 3.11 (b), instantiate B for b1 and then A for a2.*

Exercise 3.7 *Given the initialized Bayesian network in Figure 3.11 (b), instantiate A for a1 and then B for b2.*

Exercise 3.8 *Consider Figure 3.1, which appears at the beginning of this chapter. Use the method of conditioning to compute the conditional probabilities of all other nodes in the network when F is instantiated for f1 and C is instantiated for c1.*

Section 3.3

Exercise 3.9 *Assuming the Bayesian network in Figure 3.15, compute the following:*

1. $P(Z = 1|X_1 = 1, X_2 = 2, X_3 = 2, X_4 = 2)$.

2. $P(Z = 1|X_1 = 2, X_2 = 1, X_3 = 1, X_4 = 2)$.

3. $P(Z = 1|X_1 = 2, X_2 = 1, X_3 = 1, X_4 = 1)$.

Exercise 3.10 *Derive Formulas 3.4, 3.5, 3.6, and 3.7.*

Section 3.5

Exercise 3.11 *Show what was left as an exercise in Example 3.16.*

Exercise 3.12 *Show what was left as an exercise in Example 3.18.*

Chapter 4

More Inference Algorithms

In this chapter, we further investigate algorithms for doing inference in Bayesian networks. So far we have considered only discrete random variables. However, as illustrated in Section 4.1, in many cases it is an idealization to assume that a variable can have only discrete values. After illustrating the use of continuous variables in Bayesian networks, that section develops an algorithm for doing inference with continuous variables. Recall from Section 3.6 that the problem of inference in Bayesian networks is NP-hard. So for some networks none of our exact inference algorithms will be efficient. In light of this, researchers have developed approximation algorithms for inference in Bayesian networks. Section 4.2 shows an approximate inference algorithm. Besides being interested in the conditional probabilities of every variable given a set of findings, we are often interested in the most probable explanation for the findings. The process of determining the most probable explanation for a set of findings is called abductive inference and is discussed in Section 4.3.

4.1 Continuous Variable Inference

Suppose a medical application requires a variable that represents a patient's calcium level. If we feel that it takes only three ranges to model significant differences in patients' reactions to calcium level, we may assign the variable three values as follows:

Value	Serum Calcium Level (mg/100ml)
decreased	less than 9
normal	9 to 10.5
increased	above 10.5

If we later realized that three values do not adequately model the situation, we may decide on five values, seven values, or even more. Clearly, the more values assigned to a variable the slower the processing time. At some point it would be more prudent to simply treat the variable as having a continuous range.

Next, we develop an inference algorithm for the case in which the variables are continuous. Before giving the algorithm, we show a simple example illustrating how inference can be done with continuous variables. Since our algorithm manipulates normal (Gaussian) density functions, we first review the normal distribution and give a theorem concerning it.

4.1.1 The Normal Distribution

Recall the definition of the normal distribution:

Definition 4.1 *The **normal density function with parameters** μ and σ, where $-\infty < \mu < \infty$ and $\sigma > 0$, is*

$$\rho(x) = \frac{1}{\sqrt{2\pi}\sigma} e^{-\frac{(x-\mu)^2}{2\sigma^2}} \qquad -\infty < x < \infty, \qquad (4.1)$$

and is denoted $N(x; \mu, \sigma^2)$.

*A random variable X that has this density function is said to have a **normal distribution.***

If the random variable X has the normal density function, then

$$E(X) = \mu \quad \text{and} \quad V(X) = \sigma^2.$$

The density function $N(x; 0, 1^2)$ is called the **standard normal density function**. Figure 4.1 shows this density function.

The following theorem states properties of the normal density function needed to do Bayesian inference with variables that have normal distributions:

Theorem 4.1 *These equalities hold for the normal density function:*

$$N(x; \mu, \sigma^2) = N(\mu; x, \sigma^2) \qquad (4.2)$$

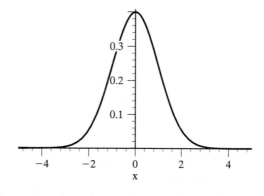

Figure 4.1: The standard normal density function.

$$N(ax; \mu, \sigma^2) = \frac{1}{a} N\left(x; \frac{\mu}{a}, \frac{\sigma^2}{a^2}\right) \qquad (4.3)$$

$$N(x; \mu_1, \sigma_1^2) N(x; \mu_2, \sigma_2^2) = kN\left(x; \frac{\sigma_2^2 \mu_1 + \sigma_1^2 \mu_2}{\sigma_1^2 + \sigma_2^2}, \frac{\sigma_1^2 \sigma_2^2}{\sigma_1^2 + \sigma_2^2}\right), \qquad (4.4)$$

where k does not depend on x.

$$\int_x N(x; \mu_1, \sigma_1^2) N(x; y, \sigma_2^2) dx = N(y; \mu_1, \sigma_1^2 + \sigma_2^2). \qquad (4.5)$$

Proof. The proof is left as an exercise.   ∎

4.1.2   An Example Concerning Continuous Variables

Next we present an example of Bayesian inference with continuous random variables.

Example 4.1 *Suppose you are considering taking a job that pays $10 an hour and you expect to work 40 hours per week. However, you are not guaranteed 40 hours, and you estimate the number of hours actually worked in a week to be normally distributed with mean 40 and standard deviation 5. You have not yet fully investigated the benefits such as bonus pay and nontaxable deductions such as contributions to a retirement program, and so forth. However, you estimate these other influences on your gross taxable weekly income also to be normally distributed with mean 0 (i.e., you feel they about offset one another.) and standard deviation 30. Furthermore, you assume that these other influences are independent of your hours worked.*

First let's determine your expected gross taxable weekly income and its standard deviation. The number of hours worked X is normally distributed with density function $\rho_X(x) = N(x; 40, 5^2)$, the other influences W on your pay are normally distributed with density function $\rho_W(w) = N(w; 0, 30^2)$, and X and W are independent. Your gross taxable weekly income Y is given by

$$y = w + 10x.$$

Let $\rho_Y(y|x)$ denote the conditional density function of Y given $X = x$. The results just obtained imply $\rho_Y(y|x)$ is normally distributed with expected value and variance as follows:

$$
\begin{aligned}
E(Y|x) &= E(W|x) + 10x \\
&= E(W) + 10x \\
&= 0 + 10x = 10x
\end{aligned}
$$

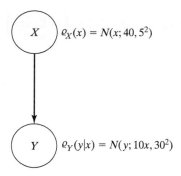

$$\varrho_X(x) = N(x; 40, 5^2)$$

$$\varrho_Y(y|x) = N(y; 10x, 30^2)$$

Figure 4.2: A Bayesian network containing continuous random variables.

and

$$
\begin{aligned}
V(Y|x) &= V(W|x) \\
&= V(W) \\
&= 30^2.
\end{aligned}
$$

The second equality in both cases is due to the fact that X and W are independent. We have shown that $\rho_Y(y|x) = N(y; 10x, 30^2)$. The Bayesian network in Figure 4.2 summarizes these results. Note that W is not shown in the network. Rather W is represented implicitly in the probabilistic relationship between X and Y. Were it not for W, Y would be a deterministic function of X. We compute the density function $\rho_Y(y)$ for your weekly income from the values in that network as follows:

$$
\begin{aligned}
\rho_Y(y) &= \int_x \rho_Y(y|x)\rho_X(x)dx \\[2mm]
&= \int_x N(y; 10x, 30^2)N(x; 40, 5^2)dx \\[2mm]
&= \int_x N(10x; y, 30^2)N(x; 40, 5^2)dx \\[2mm]
&= \frac{1}{10}\int_x N\left(x; \frac{y}{10}, \frac{30^2}{10^2}\right) N(x; 40, 5^2)dx \\[2mm]
&= \frac{1}{10}N\left(\frac{y}{10}; 40, 5^2 + \frac{30^2}{10^2}\right) \\[2mm]
&= \frac{10}{10}N\left(y; (10)(40), 10^2\left[5^2 + \frac{30^2}{10^2}\right]\right) \\[2mm]
&= N(y; 400, 3400).
\end{aligned}
$$

The third through sixth equalities above are due to Equalities 4.2, 4.3, 4.5, and 4.3, respectively. We conclude that the expected value of your gross taxable weekly income is $400 and the standard deviation is $\sqrt{3400} \approx 58$.

Example 4.2 *Suppose next that your first check turns out to be for $300, and this seems low to you. That is, you don't recall exactly how many hours you worked, but you feel that it should have been enough to make your income exceed $300. To investigate the matter, you can determine the distribution of your weekly hours given that the income has this value, and decide whether this distribution seems reasonable. Towards that end, we have*

$$
\begin{aligned}
\rho_X(x|Y=300) &= \frac{\rho_Y(300|x)\rho_X(x)}{\rho_Y(300)} \\
&= \frac{N(300;10x,30^2)N(x;40,5^2)}{\rho_Y(300)} \\
&= \frac{N(10x;300,30^2)N(x;40,5^2)}{\rho_Y(300)} \\
&= \frac{\frac{1}{10}N\left(x;\frac{300}{10},\frac{30^2}{10^2}\right)N(x;40,5^2)}{\rho_Y(300)} \\
&= \frac{\frac{1}{10}N\left(x;30,3^2\right)N(x;40,5^2)}{\rho_Y(300)} \\
&= \frac{k}{10\rho_Y(300)}N\left(x;\frac{5^2 30+3^2 40}{3^2+5^2},\frac{3^2 5^2}{3^2+5^2}\right) \\
&= N\left(x;32.65,6.62\right).
\end{aligned}
$$

The third equality is due to Equality 4.2, the fourth is due to Equality 4.3, the sixth is due to Equality 4.4, and the last is due to the fact that $\rho_X(x|Y=300)$ and $N(x;32.65,6.62)$ are both density functions, which means their integrals over x must both equal unity, and therefore $\frac{k}{10^2\rho_Y(300)}=1$. So, the expected value of the number of hours you worked is 32.65 and the standard deviation is $\sqrt{6.62} \approx 2.57$.

4.1.3 An Algorithm for Continuous Variables

We will show an algorithm for inference with continuous variables in singly connected Bayesian networks in which the value of each variable is a linear function of the values of its parents. That is, if PA_X is the set of parents of X, then

$$
x = w_X + \sum_{Z \in \text{PA}_X} b_{XZ}z, \tag{4.6}
$$

where W_X has density function $N(w;0,\sigma_{W_X}^2)$, and W_X is independent of each Z. The variable W_X represents the uncertainty in X's value given values of

X's parents. For each root X, we specify its density function $N(x; \mu_X, \sigma_X^2)$. A density function equal to $N(x; \mu_X, 0)$ means we know the root's value, while a density function equal to $N(x; 0, \infty)$ means complete uncertainty as to the root's value. Note that $\sigma_{W_X}^2$ is the variance of X conditional on values of its parents. So the conditional density function of X is

$$\rho(x|\mathsf{pa}_X) = N(x, \sum_{Z \in \mathsf{PA}_X} b_{XZ} z, \sigma_{W_X}^2).$$

When an infinite variance is used in an expression, we take the limit of the expression containing the infinite variance. For example, if $\sigma^2 = \infty$ and σ^2 appears in an expression, we take the limit as σ^2 approaches ∞ of the expression. Examples of this appear after we give the algorithm. All infinite variances represent the same limit. That is, if we specify $N(x; 0, \infty)$ and $N(y; 0, \infty)$, in both cases ∞ represents a variable t in an expression for which we take the limit as $t \to \infty$ of the expression. The assumption is that our uncertainty as to the value of X is exactly the same as our uncertainty as to the value of Y. Given this, if we wanted to represent a large, but not infinite, variance for both variables, we would not use a variance of say $1,000,000$ to represent our uncertainty as to the value of X and a variance of $ln(1,000,000)$ to represent our uncertainty as to the value of Y. Rather, we would use $1,000,000$ in both cases. In the same way, our limits are assumed to be the same. Of course, if it better models the problem, the calculations could be done using different limits, and we would sometimes get different results.

The type of Bayesian network just described is called a **Gaussian Bayesian network**. The linear relationship (Equality 4.6) used in Gaussian Bayesian networks has been used in causal models in economics (Joereskog [1982]), in structural equations in psychology (Bentler [1980]), and in path analysis in sociology and genetics (Kenny [1979]; Wright [1921]).

Before giving the algorithm, we show the formulas used in it. To avoid clutter, in the following formulas we use σ to represent a **variance** rather than a standard deviation.

The formula for X is as follows:

$$x = w_X + \sum_{Z \in \mathsf{PA}_X} b_{XZ} z.$$

The λ and π values for X are as follows:

$$\sigma_X^\lambda = \left[\sum_{U \in \mathsf{CH}_X} \frac{1}{\sigma_{UX}^\lambda} \right]^{-1}$$

$$\mu_X^\lambda = \sigma_X^\lambda \sum_{U \in \mathsf{CH}_X} \frac{\mu_{UX}^\lambda}{\sigma_{UX}^\lambda}$$

$$\sigma_X^\pi = \sigma_{W_X} + \sum_{Z \in \mathsf{PA}_X} b_{XZ}^2 \sigma_{XZ}^\pi$$

$$\mu_X^\pi = \sum_{Z \in \mathsf{PA}_X} b_{XZ} \mu_{XZ}^\pi.$$

The variance and expectation for X are as follows:

$$\sigma_X = \frac{\sigma_X^\pi \sigma_X^\lambda}{\sigma_X^\pi + \sigma_X^\lambda}$$

$$\mu_X = \frac{\sigma^\pi \mu_X^\lambda + \sigma_X^\lambda \mu_X^\pi}{\sigma_X^\pi + \sigma_X^\lambda}.$$

The π messages Z sends to a child X is as follows:

$$\sigma_{XZ}^\pi = \left[\frac{1}{\sigma_Z^\pi} + \sum_{Y \in \mathsf{CH}_Z - \{X\}} \frac{1}{\sigma_{YZ}^\lambda} \right]^{-1}$$

$$\mu_{XZ}^\pi = \frac{\dfrac{\mu_Z^\pi}{\sigma_Z^\pi} + \displaystyle\sum_{Y \in \mathsf{CH}_Z - \{X\}} \dfrac{\mu_{YZ}^\lambda}{\sigma_{YZ}^\lambda}}{\dfrac{1}{\sigma_Z^\pi} + \displaystyle\sum_{Y \in \mathsf{CH}_Z - \{X\}} \dfrac{1}{\sigma_{YZ}^\lambda}}.$$

The λ messages X sends to a parent Y are as follows:

$$\sigma_{YX}^\lambda = \frac{1}{b_{YX}^2} \left[\sigma_Y^\lambda + \sigma_{W_Y} + \sum_{Z \in \mathsf{PA}_Y - \{X\}} b_{YZ}^2 \sigma_{YZ}^\pi \right]$$

$$\mu_{YX}^\lambda = \frac{1}{b_{YX}} \left[\mu_Y^\lambda - \sum_{Z \in \mathsf{PA}_Y - \{X\}} b_{YZ} \mu_{YZ}^\pi \right].$$

When V is instantiated for $\hat{v}$, we set

$$\sigma_V^\pi = \sigma_V^\lambda = \sigma_V = 0$$

$$\mu_V^\pi = \mu_V^\lambda = \mu_V = \hat{v}.$$

Next we present the algorithm. You are asked to prove that it is correct in Exercise 4.2. The proof proceeds in a manner similar to that presented in Section 3.2.1, and can be found in Pearl [1988].

Algorithm 4.1 Inference With Continuous Variables

Problem: Given a singly connected Bayesian network containing continuous variables, determine the expected value and variance of each node conditional on specified values of nodes in some subset.

Inputs: Singly connected Bayesian network $(\mathbb{G}, P)$ containing continuous variables, where $\mathbb{G} = (\mathsf{V}, \mathsf{E})$, and a set of values a of a subset $\mathsf{A} \subseteq \mathsf{V}$.

Outputs: The Bayesian network $(\mathbb{G}, P)$ updated according to the values in a. All expectations and variances, including those in messages, are considered part of the network.

```
void initial_net  (Bayesian-network& (G, P) where G = (V, E),
                       set-of-variables& A,
                       set-of-variable-values& a)
{
  A = ∅; a = ∅;
  for (each X ∈ V) {
      σ_X^λ = ∞; μ_X^λ = 0;              // Compute λ values.

         for (each parent Z of X)      // Do nothing if X is a root.
             σ_XZ^λ = ∞; μ_XZ^λ = 0;   // Compute λ messages.

         for (each child Y of X)
             σ_YX^π = ∞; μ_YX^π = 0;    // Initialize π messages.
  }
  for (each root R) {                    // Compute variance and
      σ_R|a = σ_R; μ_R|a = μ_R;          // expectation for R.

      σ_R^π = σ_R; μ_R^π = μ_R;          // Compute R's π values.

         for (each child X of R)
             send-π-msg(R, X);
  }
}
```

```
void update_tree  (Bayesian-network& (G, P) where G = (V, E),
                       set-of-variables& A,
                       set-of-variable-values& a,
                       variable V, variable-value v̂)
```

$\{$

$\quad$ A = A $\cup \{V\}$; a = a$\cup\{\hat{v}\}$; $\qquad$ // Add V to A.

$\quad \sigma_V^\pi = 0$; $\sigma_V^\lambda = 0$; $\sigma_{V|\mathsf{a}} = 0$; $\qquad$ // Instantiate V for $\hat{v}$.

$\quad \mu_V^\pi = \hat{v}$; $\mu_V^\lambda = \hat{v}$; $\mu_{V|\mathsf{a}} = \hat{v}$;

$\quad$ **for** (each parent Z of V such that $Z \notin$ A)

$\qquad$ *send-λ-msg*(V, Z);

$\quad$ **for** (each child X of V)

$\qquad$ *send-π-msg*(V, X);

$\}$

void *send_λ_msg*(**node** Y, **node** X) $\qquad$ // For simplicity $(\mathbb{G}, P)$

$\{$ $\qquad\qquad\qquad\qquad\qquad\qquad\qquad\qquad\quad$ // is not shown as input.

$\quad \sigma_{YX}^\lambda = \frac{1}{b_{YX}^2}\left[\sigma_Y^\lambda + \sigma_{W_Y} + \sum_{Z\in\mathsf{PA}_Y - \{X\}} b_{YZ}^2 \sigma_{YZ}^\pi\right]$; $\quad$ // Y sends X a λ message.

$\quad \mu_{YX}^\lambda = \frac{1}{b_{YX}}\left[\mu_Y^\lambda - \sum_{Z\in\mathsf{PA}_Y - \{X\}} b_{YZ}\mu_{YZ}^\pi\right]$;

$\quad \sigma_X^\lambda = \left[\sum_{U\in\mathsf{CH}_X} \frac{1}{\sigma_{UX}^\lambda}\right]^{-1}$; $\qquad\qquad$ // Compute X's λ values.

$\quad \mu_X^\lambda = \sigma_X^\lambda \sum_{U\in\mathsf{CH}_X} \frac{\mu_{UX}^\lambda}{\sigma_{UX}^\lambda}$;

$\quad \sigma_{X|\mathsf{a}} = \frac{\sigma_X^\pi \sigma_X^\lambda}{\sigma_X^\pi + \sigma_X^\lambda}$; $\qquad\qquad\qquad$ // Compute variance

$\qquad\qquad\qquad\qquad\qquad\qquad\qquad$ // and

$\quad \mu_{X|\mathsf{a}} = \frac{\sigma_X^\pi \mu_X^\lambda + \sigma_X^\lambda \mu_X^\pi}{\sigma_X^\pi + \sigma_X^\lambda}$; $\qquad\qquad$ // expectation for X.

$\quad$ **for** (each parent Z of X such that $Z \notin$ A)

$\qquad$ *send_λ_msg*(X, Z);

$\quad$ **for** (each child W of X such that $W \neq Y$)

$\qquad$ *send_π_msg*(X, W);

$\}$

void *send_π_message*(**node** Z, **node** X) $\quad$ // For simplicity $(\mathbb{G}, P)$

$\{$ $\qquad\qquad\qquad\qquad\qquad\qquad\qquad\qquad$ // is not shown as input.

$\quad \sigma_{XZ}^\pi = \left[\frac{1}{\sigma_Z^\pi} + \sum_{Y\in\mathsf{CH}_Z - \{X\}} \frac{1}{\sigma_{YZ}^\lambda}\right]^{-1}$; $\quad$ // Z sends X a π message.

$$\mu_{XZ}^\pi = \frac{\dfrac{\mu_Z^\pi}{\sigma_Z^\pi} + \displaystyle\sum_{Y\in\mathsf{CH}_Z - \{X\}} \dfrac{\mu_{YZ}^\lambda}{\sigma_{YZ}^\lambda}}{\dfrac{1}{\sigma_Z^\pi} + \displaystyle\sum_{Y\in\mathsf{CH}_Z - \{X\}} \dfrac{1}{\sigma_{YZ}^\lambda}};$$

if $(X \notin A)$ {
$\quad \sigma_X^\pi = \sigma_{W_X} + \sum_{Z \in PA_X} b_{XZ}^2 \sigma_{XZ}^\pi;$ // Compute X's π values.

$\quad \mu_X^\pi = \sum_{Z \in PA_X} b_{XZ} \mu_{XZ}^\pi;$

$\quad \sigma_{X|a} = \frac{\sigma_X^\pi \sigma_X^\lambda}{\sigma_X^\pi + \sigma_X^\lambda};$ // Compute variance
                                           // and
$\quad \mu_{X|a} = \frac{\sigma_X^\pi \mu_X^\lambda + \sigma_X^\lambda \mu_X^\pi}{\sigma_X^\pi + \sigma_X^\lambda};$ // expectation for X.

$\quad$ **for** (each child Y of X)
$\quad\quad$ $send\_\pi\_msg(X, Y);$
}

$\quad$ **if not** $(\sigma_X = \infty)$ // Do not send λ messages
$\quad\quad$ **for** (each parent W of X // to X's other parents if X
$\quad\quad$ such that $W \neq Z$ **and** $W \notin A$)   // and all of X's descendents
$\quad\quad\quad$ $send\_\lambda\_msg(X, W);$ // are uninstantiated.
}

As mentioned previously, the calculations with ∞ in Algorithm 4.1 are done by taking limits, and every specified infinity represents the same variable approaching ∞. For example, if $\sigma_P^\pi = \infty$, $\mu_P^\lambda = 8000$, $\sigma_P^\lambda = \infty$, and $\mu_P^\pi = 0$, then

$$
\begin{aligned}
\frac{\sigma_P^\pi \mu_P^\lambda + \sigma_P^\lambda \mu_P^\pi}{\sigma_P^\pi + \sigma_P^\lambda} &= \lim_{t \to \infty} \frac{t \times 8000 + t \times 0}{t + t} \\
&= \lim_{t \to \infty} \frac{1 \times 8000 + 1 \times 0}{1 + 1} \\
&= \lim_{t \to \infty} \frac{8000}{2} = 4000.
\end{aligned}
$$

As mentioned previously,we could let different infinite variances represent different limits, and thereby possibly get different results. For example, we could replace σ_P^π by t and σ_P^λ by $ln(t)$. If we did this, we would obtain

$$
\begin{aligned}
\frac{\sigma_P^\pi \mu_P^\lambda + \sigma_P^\lambda \mu_P^\pi}{\sigma_P^\pi + \sigma_P^\lambda} &= \lim_{t \to \infty} \frac{t \times 8000 + \ln(t) \times 0}{t + \ln(t)} \\
&= \lim_{t \to \infty} \frac{1 \times 8000 + \frac{\ln(t)}{t} \times 0}{1 + \frac{\ln(t)}{t}} \\
&= 8000.
\end{aligned}
$$

Henceforth, our specified infinite variances always represent the same limit.

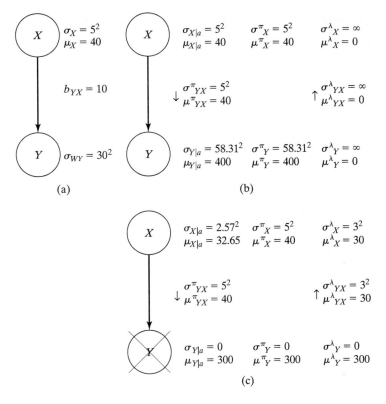

Figure 4.3: A Bayesian network modeling the relationship between hours work and taxable income is shown in (a), the initialized network is shown in (b), and the network after Y is instantiated for 300 is shown in (c).

Since λ and π messages and values are used in other computations, we assign variables values that are multiplies of infinity when it is indicated. For example, if

$$\sigma^\lambda_{DP} = 0 + 300^2 + \infty + \infty,$$

we would make 2∞ the value of σ^λ_{DP} so that $2t$ would be used in an expression containing σ^λ_{DP}.

Next we show examples of applying Algorithm 4.1.

Example 4.3 *We will redo the determinations in Example 4.1 using Algorithm 4.1 rather than directly as was done in the previous example. Figure 4.3 (a) shows the same network as Figure 4.2; however, it explicitly shows the parameters specified for a Gaussian Bayesian network. The values of the parameters in Figure 4.2, which are the ones in the general specification of a Bayesian network, can be obtained from the parameters in Figure 4.3 (a). Indeed, we did that in Example 4.1. In general, we show Gaussian Bayesian networks as in Figure 4.3 (a).*

First we show the steps when the network is initialized.

The call

$\quad$ $initial\_tree((\mathbb{G}, P), \mathsf{A}, \mathsf{a})$;

results in the following steps:

$\quad$ $\mathsf{A} = \varnothing$;
$\quad$ $\mathsf{a} = \varnothing$;

$\quad$ $\sigma_X^\lambda = \infty; \mu_X^\lambda = 0$; $\quad$ // Compute λ values.

$\quad$ $\sigma_Y^\lambda = \infty; \mu_Y^\lambda = 0$

$\quad$ $\sigma_{YX}^\lambda = \infty; \mu_{YX}^\lambda = 0$; $\quad$ // Compute λ messages.

$\quad$ $\sigma_{YX}^\pi = \infty; \mu_{YX}^\pi = 0$; $\quad$ // Compute π messages.

$\quad$ $\sigma_{X|\mathsf{a}} = 5^2; \mu_{X|\mathsf{a}} = 40$; $\quad$ // Compute $\mu_X|\mathsf{a}$ and $\sigma_X|\mathsf{a}$.

$\quad$ $\sigma_X^\pi = 5^2; \mu_R^\pi = 40$; $\quad$ // Compute X's π values.

$\quad$ $send\_\pi\_msg(X, Y)$;

The call

$\quad$ $send\_\pi\_msg(X, Y)$;

results in the following steps:

$$\sigma_{YX}^\pi = \left[\frac{1}{\sigma_X^\pi}\right]^{-1} = \sigma_X^\pi = 5^2; \qquad\qquad\qquad // X \text{ sends } Y \text{ a } \pi \text{ message.}$$

$$\mu_{YX}^\pi = \frac{\frac{\mu_X^\pi}{\sigma_X^\pi}}{\frac{1}{\sigma_X^\pi}} = \mu_X^\pi = 40;$$

$$\sigma_Y^\pi = \sigma_{W_Y} + b_{YX}^2 \sigma_{YX}^\pi \qquad\qquad\qquad\qquad // \text{ Compute } Y\text{'s } \pi \text{ value.}$$

$$= 30^2 + 10^2 \times 5^2 = 3400 = 58.31^2;$$

$$\mu_Y^\pi = b_{YX}\mu_{YX}^\pi = 10 \times 40 = 400;$$

$$\sigma_{Y|\mathsf{a}} = \frac{\sigma_Y^\pi \sigma_Y^\lambda}{\sigma_Y^\pi + \sigma_Y^\lambda} = \lim_{t \to \infty} \frac{3400 \times t}{3400 + t} = 3400; \qquad // \text{ Compute variance}$$
$$\qquad\qquad\qquad\qquad\qquad\qquad\qquad\qquad\qquad // \text{ and expectation for } Y.$$

$$\mu_{Y|\mathsf{a}} = \frac{\sigma_Y^\pi \mu_Y^\lambda + \sigma_Y^\lambda \mu_Y^\pi}{\sigma_Y^\pi + \sigma_Y^\lambda} = \lim_{t \to \infty} \frac{3400 \times 0 + t \times 400}{3400 + t} = 400;$$

The initialized network is shown in Figure 4.3 (b). Note that we obtained the same result as in Example 4.1.

Next we instantiate Y for 300 in the network shown in Figure 4.3 (b).

The call

$update\_tree((\mathbb{G}, P), \mathsf{A}, \mathsf{a}, Y, 300);$

results in the following steps:

$\mathsf{A} = \varnothing \cup \{Y\} = \{Y\};$
$\mathsf{a} = \varnothing \cup \{300\} = \{300\};$

$\sigma_Y^\pi = \sigma_Y^\lambda = \sigma_{Y|\mathsf{a}} = 0;$ *// Instantiate Y for 300.*

$\mu_Y^\pi = \mu_Y^\lambda = \mu_{Y|\mathsf{a}} = 300;$

$send\_\lambda\_msg(Y, X);$

The call

$send\_\lambda\_msg(Y, X);$

results in the following steps:

$\sigma_{YX}^\lambda = \frac{1}{b_{YX}^2} \left[\sigma_Y^\lambda + \sigma_{W_Y} \right] = \frac{1}{100} [0 + 900] = 9;$ *// Y sends X a λ*
                                                      // message.

$\mu_{YX}^\lambda = \frac{1}{b_{YX}} \left[\mu_Y^\lambda \right] = \frac{1}{10} [300] = 30;$

$\sigma_X^\lambda = \left[\frac{1}{\sigma_{YX}^\lambda} \right]^{-1} = 9;$ *// Compute X's λ*
                                                      // values.

$\mu_X^\lambda = \sigma_X^\lambda \frac{\mu_{YX}^\lambda}{\sigma_{YX}^\lambda} = 9 \frac{30}{9} = 30;$

$\sigma_{X|\mathsf{a}} = \frac{\sigma_X^\pi \sigma_X^\lambda}{\sigma_X^\pi + \sigma_X^\lambda} = \frac{25 \times 9}{25 + 9} = 6.62 = 2.57^2;$ *// Compute variance*
                                                      // and expectation

$\mu_{X|\mathsf{a}} = \frac{\sigma_X^\pi \mu_X^\lambda + \sigma_X^\lambda \mu_X^\pi}{\sigma_X^\pi + \sigma_X^\lambda} = \frac{25 \times 30 + 9 \times 40}{25 + 9} = 32.65;$ *// for X.*

The updated network is shown in Figure 4.3 (c). Note that we obtained the same result as in Example 4.2.

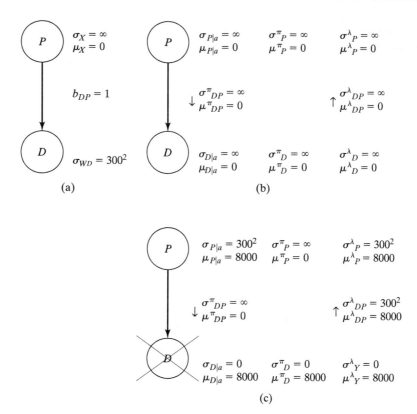

Figure 4.4: The Bayesian network in (a) models the relationship between a car dealer's asking price for a given vehicle and the wholesale price of the vehicle. The network in (b) is after initialization, and the one in (c) is after D is instantiated for $\$8,000$.

Example 4.4 *This example is based on an example in Pearl [1988]. Suppose we have the following random variables:*

Variable	What the Variable Represents
P	Wholesale price
D	Dealer's asking price

We are modeling the relationship between a car dealer's asking price for a given vehicle and the wholesale price of the vehicle. We assume

$$d = w_D + p \qquad \sigma_{W_D} = 300^2,$$

where W_D is distributed $N(w_D; 0, \sigma_{W_D})$. The idea is that in past years, the dealer has based its asking price on the mean profit from the last year, but there has been variation, and this variation is represented by the variables W_D. The Bayesian network representing this model appears in Figure 4.4 (a). Fig-

ure 4.4 (b) shows the network after initialization. We show the result of learning that the asking price is $8,000.

The call

$$update\_tree((\mathbb{G}, P), \mathsf{A}, \mathsf{a}, D, 8000);$$

results in the following steps:

$$\mathsf{A} = \varnothing \cup \{D\} = \{D\};$$
$$\mathsf{a} = \varnothing \cup \{8000\} = \{8000\};$$

$$\sigma_D^\pi = \sigma_D^\lambda = \sigma_{D|\mathsf{a}} = 0; \qquad \textit{// Instantiate D for 8000.}$$

$$\mu_D^\pi = \mu_D^\lambda = \mu_{D|\mathsf{a}} = 8000;$$

$$send\_\lambda\_msg(D, P);$$

The call

$$send\_\lambda\_msg(D, P);$$

results in the following steps:

$$\sigma_{DP}^\lambda = \frac{1}{b_{DP}^2} \left[\sigma_D^\lambda + \sigma_{W_D} \right] = \frac{1}{1} \left[0 + 300^2 \right] = 300^2; \quad \textit{// D sends P a } \lambda$$
$$\textit{// message.}$$

$$\mu_{DP}^\lambda = \frac{1}{b_{DP}} \left[\mu_D^\lambda \right] = \frac{1}{1} \left[8000 \right] = 8000;$$

$$\sigma_P^\lambda = \left[\frac{1}{\sigma_{DP}^\lambda} \right]^{-1} = 300^2; \qquad \textit{// Compute P's } \lambda$$
$$\textit{// values.}$$

$$\mu_P^\lambda = \sigma_P^\lambda \frac{\mu_{DP}^\lambda}{\sigma_{DP}^\lambda} = 300^2 \frac{8000}{300^2} = 8000;$$

$$\sigma_{P|\mathsf{a}} = \frac{\sigma_P^\pi \sigma_P^\lambda}{\sigma_P^\pi + \sigma_P^\lambda} = \lim_{t \to \infty} \frac{t \times 300^2}{t + 300^2} = 300^2; \qquad \textit{// Compute variance}$$
$$\textit{// and expectation}$$

$$\mu_{P|\mathsf{a}} = \frac{\sigma_P^\pi \mu_P^\lambda + \sigma_P^\lambda \mu_P^\pi}{\sigma_P^\pi + \sigma_P^\lambda} = \lim_{t \to \infty} \frac{t \times 8000 + 300^2 \times 0}{t + 300^2} = 8000; \quad \textit{// for P.}$$

The updated network is shown in Figure 4.4 (c). Note that the expected value of P is the value of D, and the variance of P is the variance owing to the variability W.

Example 4.5 *Suppose we have the following random variables:*

Variable	What the Variable Represents
P	Wholesale price
M	Mean profit per car realized by Dealer in past year
D	Dealer's asking price

We are now modeling the situation in which the car dealer's asking price for a given vehicle is based both on the wholesale price of the vehicle and the mean profit per car realized by the dealer in the past year. We assume

$$d = w_D + p + m \qquad\qquad \sigma_D = 300^2,$$

where W_D is distributed $N(w_D; 0, \sigma_{W_D})$. The Bayesian network representing this model appears in Figure 4.5 (a). We do not show the initialized network since its appearance should now be apparent. We show the result of learning that the asking price is $\$8,000$.

The call
$$update\_tree((\mathbb{G}, P), \mathsf{A}, \mathsf{a}, D, 8000);$$
results in the following steps:

$\mathsf{A} = \varnothing \cup \{D\} = \{D\};$
$\mathsf{a} = \varnothing \cup \{8000\} = \{8000\};$

$\sigma_D^\pi = \sigma_D^\lambda = \sigma_{D|\mathsf{a}} = 0;$ // *Instantiate D for 8000.*

$\mu_D^\pi = \mu_D^\lambda = \mu_{D|\mathsf{a}} = 8000;$

$send\_\lambda\_msg(D, P);$
$send\_\lambda\_msg(D, M);$

The call
$$send\_\lambda\_msg(D, P);$$
results in the following steps:

$\sigma_{DP}^\lambda = \frac{1}{b_{DP}^2}\left[\sigma_D^\lambda + \sigma_{W_D} + b_{DM}^2 \sigma_{DM}^\pi\right]$ // *D sends P a*

$\qquad = \lim_{t\to\infty} \frac{1}{1}\left[0 + 300^2 + 1 \times t\right] = \infty;$ // *λ message.*

$\mu_{DP}^\lambda = \frac{1}{b_{DP}}\left[\mu_D^\lambda - b_{DM}\mu_{DM}^\pi\right]$

$\qquad = \frac{1}{1}\left[8000 - 1 \times 0\right] = 8000;$

$$\sigma_P^\lambda = \left[\frac{1}{\sigma_{DP}^\lambda}\right]^{-1} = \lim_{t\to\infty} \left[\frac{1}{t}\right]^{-1} = \infty; \qquad \text{// Compute } P\text{'s}$$
$$\text{// } \lambda \text{ values.}$$

$$\mu_P^\lambda = \sigma_P^\lambda \frac{\mu_{DP}^\lambda}{\sigma_{DP}^\lambda} = \lim_{t\to\infty} \left[t\frac{8000}{t}\right] = 8000;$$

$$\sigma_{P|a} = \frac{\sigma_P^\pi \sigma_P^\lambda}{\sigma_P^\pi + \sigma_P^\lambda} = \lim_{t\to\infty} \frac{t\times t}{t+t} = \lim_{t\to\infty} \frac{t}{2} = \frac{\infty}{2}; \qquad \text{// Compute variance}$$
$$\text{// and expectation}$$

$$\mu_{P|a} = \frac{\sigma_P^\pi \mu_P^\lambda + \sigma_P^\lambda \mu_P^\pi}{\sigma_P^\pi + \sigma_P^\lambda} \qquad \text{// for } P.$$

$$= \lim_{t\to\infty} \frac{t\times 8000 + t\times 0}{t+t} = \frac{8000}{2} = 4000;$$

Clearly, the call *send_λ_msg(D, M)* results in the same values for M as we just calculated for P.

The updated network is shown in Figure 4.5 (b). Note that the expected values of P and M are both 4000, which is half the value of D. Note further that each variable still has infinite variance owing to uncertainty as to the value of the other variable.

Notice in the previous example that D has two parents, and each of their expected values is half of the value of D. What would happen if D had a third parent F, $b_{DF} = 1$, and F also had an infinite prior variance? In this case,

$$\sigma_{DP}^\lambda = \frac{1}{b_{DP}^2} \left[\sigma_D^\lambda + \sigma_{W_D} + b_{DM}^2 \sigma_{DM}^\pi + b_{DF}^2 \sigma_{DF}^\pi\right]$$
$$= \lim_{t\to\infty} \frac{1}{1} \left[0 + 300^2 + 1\times t + 1\times t\right] = 2\infty.$$

This means σ_P^λ also equals 2∞, and therefore,

$$\mu_{P|a} = \frac{\sigma_P^\pi \mu_P^\lambda + \sigma_P^\lambda \mu_P^\pi}{\sigma_P^\pi + \sigma_P^\lambda}$$
$$= \lim_{t\to\infty} \frac{t\times 8000 + 2t\times 0}{t + 2t} = \frac{8000}{3} = 2667.$$

It is not hard to see that if there are k parents of D, all b_{DX}'s are 1 and all prior variances are infinite, and we instantiate D for d, then the expected value of each parent is d/k.

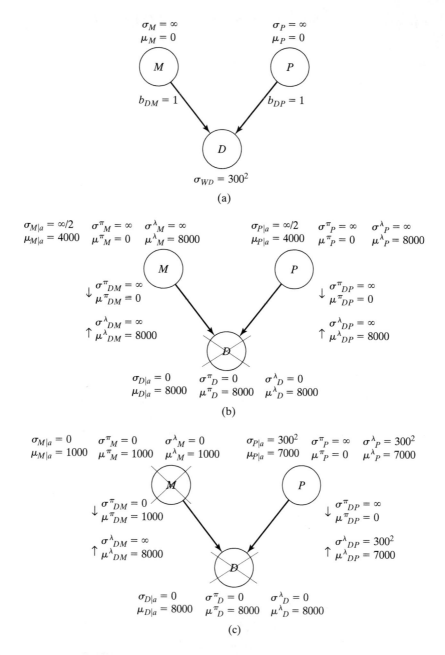

Figure 4.5: The Bayesian network in (a) models the relationships among a car dealer's asking price for a given vehicle, the wholesale price of the vehicle, and the dealer's mean profit in the past year. The network in (b) is after initialization and after D is instantiated for $8,000$, and the network in (c) is after M is also instantiated for 1000.

Example 4.6 *Next we instantiate M for 1000 in the network in Figure 4.5 (b).*

The call

$$update\_tree((\mathbb{G}, P), \mathsf{A}, \mathsf{a}, M, 1000);$$

results in the following steps:

$\mathsf{A} = \{D\} \cup \{M\} = \{D, M\};$
$\mathsf{a} = \{8000\} \cup \{1000\} = \{8000, 1000\};$

$\sigma_M^\pi = \sigma_M^\lambda = \sigma_{M|\mathsf{a}} = 0;$ // *Instantiate M for*
                                                            // *1000.*

$\mu_M^\pi = \mu_M^\lambda = \mu_{M|\mathsf{a}} = 1000;$

$send\_\pi\_msg(M, D);$

The call

$$send\_\pi\_msg(M, D);$$

results in the following steps:

$\sigma_{DM}^\pi = \left[\frac{1}{\sigma_M^\pi}\right]^{-1} = \sigma_M^\pi = 0;$ // *M sends D a π message.*

$\mu_{DM}^\pi = \dfrac{\frac{\mu_M^\pi}{\sigma_M^\pi}}{\frac{1}{\sigma_M^\pi}} = \mu_M^\pi = 1000;$

$send\_\lambda\_msg(D, P);$

The call

$$send\_\lambda\_msg(D, P);$$

results in the following steps:

$\sigma_{DP}^\lambda = \frac{1}{b_{DP}^2}\left[\sigma_D^\lambda + \sigma_{W_D} + b_{DP}^2 \sigma_{DM}^\pi\right] = \frac{1}{1}\left[0 + 300^2 + 0\right] = 300^2;$

$\mu_{DP}^\lambda = \frac{1}{b_{DP}}\left[\mu_D^\lambda - b_{DM}m\mu_{DM}^\pi\right] = \frac{1}{1}[8000 - 1000] = 7000;$

$\sigma_P^\lambda = \left[\frac{1}{\sigma_{DP}^\lambda} + \frac{1}{\sigma_{EP}^\lambda}\right]^{-1} = \lim_{t \to \infty}\left[\frac{1}{300^2} + \frac{1}{t}\right]^{-1} = 300^2;$

$$\mu_P^\lambda = \sigma_P^\lambda \left[\frac{\mu_{DP}^\lambda}{\sigma_{DP}^\lambda} + \frac{\mu_{EP}^\lambda}{\sigma_{EP}^\lambda} \right] = 300^2 \lim_{t \to \infty} \left[\frac{7000}{300^2} + \frac{10000}{t} \right] = 7000;$$

$$\sigma_{P|a} = \frac{\sigma_P^\pi \sigma_P^\lambda}{\sigma_P^\pi + \sigma_P^\lambda} = \lim_{t \to \infty} \frac{t \times 300^2}{t + 300^2} = 300^2;$$

$$\mu_{P|a} = \frac{\sigma_P^\pi \mu_P^\lambda + \sigma_P^\lambda \mu_P^\pi}{\sigma_P^\pi + \sigma_P^\lambda} = \lim_{t \to \infty} \frac{t \times 7000 + 300^2 \times 0}{t + 300^2} = 7000;$$

The final network is shown in Figure 4.5 (c). Note that the expected value of P is the difference between the value of D and the value of M. Note further that the variance of P is now simply the variance of W_D.

Example 4.7 *Suppose we have the following random variables:*

Variable	What the Variable Represents
P	Wholesale price
D	Dealer-1's asking price
E	Dealer-2's asking price

We are now modeling the situation in which there are two dealers, and for each the asking price is based only on the wholesale price and not on the mean profit realized in the past year. We assume

$$d = w_D + p \qquad\qquad \sigma_{W_D} = 300^2$$

$$e = w_E + p \qquad\qquad \sigma_{W_E} = 1000^2,$$

where W_D is distributed $N(w_D; 0, \sigma_{W_D})$ and W_E is distributed $N(w_E; 0, \sigma_{W_E})$. The Bayesian network representing this model appears in Figure 4.6 (a). Figure 4.6 (b) shows the network after we learn that the asking prices of Dealer-1 and Dealer-2 in the past year are $8,000 and $10,000, respectively. We do not show the calculations of the message values in that network because these calculations are just like those in Example 4.4. We show only the computations done when P receives both its λ messages. They are as follows:

$$\sigma_P^\lambda = \left[\frac{1}{\sigma_{DP}^\lambda} + \frac{1}{\sigma_{EP}^\lambda} \right]^{-1} = \left[\frac{1}{300^2} + \frac{1}{1000^2} \right]^{-1} = 287^2;$$

$$\mu_P^\lambda = \sigma_P^\lambda \left[\frac{\mu_{DP}^\lambda}{\sigma_{DP}^\lambda} + \frac{\mu_{EP}^\lambda}{\sigma_{EP}^\lambda} \right] = 300^2 \left[\frac{8000}{300^2} + \frac{10000}{1000^2} \right] = 8145;$$

$$\sigma_{P|a} = \frac{\sigma_P^\pi \sigma_P^\lambda}{\sigma_P^\pi + \sigma_P^\lambda} = \lim_{t \to \infty} \frac{t \times 287^2}{t + 297^2} = 287^2;$$

$$\mu_{P|a} = \frac{\sigma_P^\pi \mu_P^\lambda + \sigma_P^\lambda \mu_P^\pi}{\sigma_P^\pi + \sigma_P^\lambda} = \lim_{t \to \infty} \frac{t \times 8145 + 287^2 \times 0}{t + 287^2} = 8145;$$

Notice that the expected value of the wholesale price is closer to the asking price for the dealer with less variability.

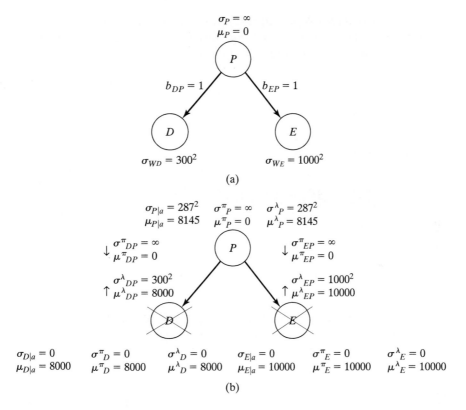

Figure 4.6: The Bayesian network in (a) models the relationship between two car dealers' asking price for a given vehicle and the wholesale price of the vehicle. The network in (b) is after initialization and D and E are instantiated for $8,000 and $10,000, respectively.

Example 4.8 *Suppose we have the following random variables:*

Variable	What the Variable Represents
P	Wholesale price
M	Mean profit per car realized by Dealer-1 in past year
D	Dealer-1's asking price
N	Mean profit per car realized by Dealer-2 in past year
E	Dealer-2's asking price

We are now modeling the situation in which we have two dealers and, for each, the asking price is based both on the wholesale price and the mean profit per car realized by the dealer in the past year. We assume

$$d = w_D + p + m \qquad \sigma_{W_D} = 300^2$$

$$e = w_E + p + n \qquad \sigma_{W_E} = 1000^2,$$

where W_D is distributed $N(w_D; 0, \sigma_{W_D})$ and W_E is distributed $N(w_E; 0, \sigma_{W_E})$. The Bayesian network representing this model appears in Figure 4.7 (a). Figure 4.7 (b) shows the network after initialization and after we learn the asking prices of Dealer-1 and Dealer-2 in the past year are $\$8,000$ and $\$10,000$, respectively. For that network, we show only the computations when P receives its λ messages because all other computations are exactly like those in Example 4.5. They are as follows:

$$\sigma_P^\lambda = \left[\frac{1}{\sigma_{DP}^\lambda} + \frac{1}{\sigma_{EP}^\lambda} \right]^{-1} = \lim_{t\to\infty} \left[\frac{1}{t} + \frac{1}{t} \right]^{-1} = \frac{\infty}{2};$$

$$\mu_P^\lambda = \sigma_P^\lambda \left[\frac{\mu_{DP}^\lambda}{\sigma_{DP}^\lambda} + \frac{\mu_{EP}^\lambda}{\sigma_{EP}^\lambda} \right] = \lim_{t\to\infty} \frac{t}{2} \left[\frac{8000}{t} + \frac{10000}{t} \right] = 9000;$$

$$\sigma_{P|a} = \frac{\sigma_P^\pi \sigma_P^\lambda}{\sigma_P^\pi + \sigma_P^\lambda} = \lim_{t\to\infty} \frac{t \times \frac{t}{2}}{t + \frac{t}{2}} = \frac{\infty}{3};$$

$$\mu_{P|a} = \frac{\sigma_P^\pi \mu_P^\lambda + \sigma_P^\lambda \mu_P^\pi}{\sigma_P^\pi + \sigma_P^\lambda} = \lim_{t\to\infty} \frac{t \times 9000 + \frac{t}{2} \times 0}{t + \frac{t}{2}} = 6000;$$

Note in the previous example that the expected value of the wholesale price is greater than half of the asking price of either dealer. What would happen of D had a third parent F, $b_{DF} = 1$, and F also had an infinite prior variance? In this case,

$$\sigma_{DP}^\lambda = \frac{1}{b_{DP}^2} \left[\sigma_D^\lambda + \sigma_{W_D} + b_{DM}^2 \sigma_{DM}^\pi + b_{DF}^2 \sigma_{DF}^\pi \right]$$

$$= \lim_{t\to\infty} \frac{1}{1} \left[0 + 300^2 + 1 \times t + 1 \times t \right] = 2\infty.$$

So

$$\sigma_P^\lambda = \left[\frac{1}{\sigma_{DP}^\lambda} + \frac{1}{\sigma_{EP}^\lambda} \right]^{-1} = \lim_{t\to\infty} \left[\frac{1}{2t} + \frac{1}{t} \right]^{-1} = \frac{2\infty}{3}$$

$$\mu_P^\lambda = \sigma_P^\lambda \left[\frac{\mu_{DP}^\lambda}{\sigma_{DP}^\lambda} + \frac{\mu_{EP}^\lambda}{\sigma_{EP}^\lambda} \right] = \lim_{t\to\infty} \frac{2t}{3} \left[\frac{8000}{2t} + \frac{10000}{t} \right] = 9333,$$

and

$$\mu_{P|a} = \frac{\sigma_P^\pi \mu_P^\lambda + \sigma_P^\lambda \mu_P^\pi}{\sigma_P^\pi + \sigma_P^\lambda} = \lim_{t\to\infty} \frac{t \times 9333 + \frac{2t}{3} \times 0}{t + \frac{2t}{3}} = 5600.$$

Notice that the expected value of the wholesale price has decreased. It is not hard to see that, as the number of such parents of D approaches infinity, the expected value of the wholesale price approaches half the value of E.

Example 4.9 Next we instantiate both M and N for 1000 in the network in Figure 4.7 (b). The resultant network appears in Figure 4.7 (c). It is left as an exercise to obtain that network.

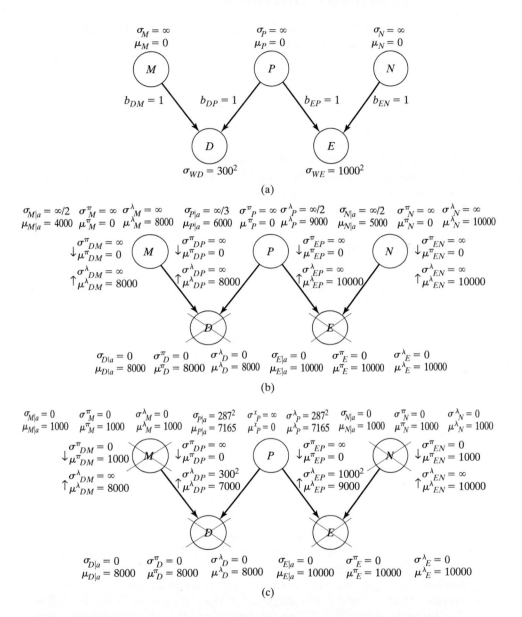

Figure 4.7: The Bayesian network in (a) models the relationships among two car dealers' asking price for a given vehicle, the wholesale price of the vehicle, and the mean profit per car realized by each dealer in the past year. The network in (b) is after initialization and D and E are instantiated for \$8,000 and \$10,000, respectively, and the one in (c) is after M and N are also instantiated for \$1,000.

4.2   Approximate Inference

As mentioned at the beginning of this chapter, since the problem of inference in Bayesian networks is NP-hard, researchers have developed approximation algorithms for inference in Bayesian networks. One way to do approximate inference is by sampling data items, using a pseudorandom number generator, according to the probability distribution in the network, and then approximating the conditional probabilities of interest using this sample. This method is called **stochastic simulation**. We discuss this method here. Another method is to use **deterministic search**, which generates the sample systematically. (See Castillo et al. [1997] for a discussion of that method.)

After showing a basic sampling algorithm called logic sampling, we improve the basic algorithm. Note that these sampling techniques are methods in classical statistics. (See Section 1.3.)

4.2.1   Logic Sampling

Suppose p is the fraction of black balls in an urn containing white and black balls. We could sample with replacement from the urn and, according to the theory discussed in the previous section, use k/m as an estimate of p, where of m balls sampled k are black. Alternatively, assuming we have a function *random* that returns a pseudorandom number between 0 and 1 according to the uniform distribution, we could write the following computer simulation of sampling m balls:

```
k = 0;
for (i = 1; i <= m; i + +)
   if random() < p
      k + +;
p̂ = k/m;
```

Our estimate of p is $\hat{p}$. This is called a **simulation** because we are not sampling from an actual distribution, but rather are using pseudorandom numbers to imitate the process of sampling. Of course, the previous simulation has no value because, if we knew p, we would have no need to estimate it. The purpose of discussing this simulation is for illustration.

Suppose next that we have the Bayesian network in Figure 4.8 and we wish to compute $P(y1)$. Instead of computing it directly, we could do the following simulation to estimate it. First we determine all probabilities in the joint distribution as follows:

$$
\begin{aligned}
P(x1, y1) &= P(y1|x1)P(x1) = (.2)(.5) = .1 \\
P(x1, y2) &= P(y2|x1)P(x1) = (.8)(.5) = .4 \\
P(x2, y1) &= P(y1|x2)P(x2) = (.6)(.5) = .3 \\
P(x2, y2) &= P(y2|x2)P(x2). = (.4)(.5) = .2.
\end{aligned}
$$

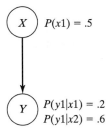

Figure 4.8: A Bayesian Network.

Next we use our pseudorandom number generator to obtain m values of (x, y) according to this distribution. If we let k be the number of tuples containing $y1$, we then have the following estimate:

$$\hat{P}(y1) = \frac{k}{m}.$$

Example 4.10 *Suppose we have the Bayesian network in Figure 4.8, $m = 7$, and we generate the data in the following table:*

Case	X	Y
1	$x2$	$y1$
2	$x1$	$y1$
3	$x1$	$y2$
4	$x2$	$y1$
5	$x1$	$y2$
6	$x2$	$y1$
7	$x2$	$y2$

Since $y1$ occurs in four cases, our estimate is

$$\hat{P}(y1) = \frac{k}{m} = \frac{4}{7}.$$

In a large network, we could never compute all the values in the joint distribution. So instead of using the method just described, we could obtain each case by first generating a value $\tilde{x}$ of X using $P(x)$, and then generating a value $\tilde{y}$ of Y using $P(y|\tilde{x})$. For each tuple $(\tilde{x}, \tilde{y})$, $\tilde{x}$ will occur $P(\tilde{x})$ fraction of the time in the limit; of those occurrences, $\tilde{y}$ will occur $P(\tilde{y}|\tilde{x})$ fraction of the time in the limit. So $(\tilde{x}, \tilde{y})$ will occur $P(\tilde{y}|\tilde{x})P(\tilde{x}) = P(\tilde{x}, \tilde{y})$ fraction of the time in the limit, which is what we want. The following is a high-level algorithm describing this method:

```
k = 0;
for (i = 1; i <= m; i + +) {
    generate a value x̃ of X using P(x);
    generate a value ỹ of Y using P(y|x̃);
    if (ỹ == y1)
        k + +;
}
P̂(y1) = k/m;
```

Example 4.11 *Suppose we have the Bayesian network in Figure 4.8, and m =
3. The following shows one possible outcome of our simulation:*

1. *We generate a value of X using $P(x1) = .5$. Suppose we find that $x1$
   occurs. We then generate a value for Y using $P(y1|x1) = .2$. Suppose we
   find that $y2$ occurs. We do not increment k.*

2. *We generate a value for X using $P(x1) = .5$. Suppose we find that $x2$
   occurs. We then generate a value for Y using $P(y1|x2) = .6$. Suppose we
   find that $y1$ occurs. We increment k to 1.*

3. *We generate a value for X using $P(x1) = .5$. Suppose we find that $x1$
   occurs. We then generate a value for Y using $P(y1|x1) = .2$. Suppose we
   find that $y1$ occurs. We increment k to 2.*

Our final estimate is

$$\hat{P}(y1) = 2/3.$$

We can also use the method just presented to estimate $P(x1|y1)$. However,
we must throw out any cases that have $Y = y2$. The following high-level
algorithm does this:

```
k = 0;
for (i = 1; i <= m; i + +) {
    repeat
        generate a value x̃ of X using P(x1);
        generate a value ỹ of Y using P(y1|x̃);
    until (ỹ == y1);
    if (x̃ == x1)
        k + +;
}
P̂(x1|y1) = k/m;
```

Example 4.12 *Suppose we have the Bayesian network in Figure 4.8, $m = 5$, and the preceding algorithm generates the data in the following table:*

Case	X	Y
1	$x2$	$y1$
2	$x1$	$y1$
3	$x1$	$y2$
4	$x2$	$y1$
5	$x1$	$y1$
6	$x2$	$y1$
7	$x2$	$y2$

Cases 3 and 7 are rejected because $Y = y2$. So $k = 2$, and we have

$$\hat{P}(x1|y1) = \frac{k}{m} = \frac{2}{5}.$$

You may wonder why we regenerate a new value for X when we generate a value of $y2$ for Y. That is, you may ask why can't we just retain our old value, and keep generating a value of Y until we get $y1$. If we did this, in the limit we would simply get X generated according to its prior probability because the X values we kept have nothing to do with the Y values we generate. Recall we want to generate X values according to $P(x1|y1)$. The following table shows values our algorithm would generate if the first 10 generated cases corresponded exactly to the distribution in Figure 4.8:

Case	X	Y
1	$x1$	$y1$
2	$x1$	$y2$
3	$x1$	$y2$
4	$x1$	$y2$
5	$x1$	$y2$
6	$x2$	$y1$
7	$x2$	$y1$
8	$x2$	$y1$
9	$x2$	$y2$
10	$x2$	$y2$

Our algorithm will reject Cases 2, 3, 4, 5, 9, and 10, and it will estimate $P(x1|y1)$ to be $1/4$ (using a value of 4 for m), which you can confirm as the correct value. However, if we simply kept all X values and kept generating Y values until we got $y1$, our estimate would be $5/10$ (using a value of 10 for m).

The method just outlined is easily extended to an algorithm for doing approximate inference in Bayesian networks. The algorithm first orders the nodes according to an **ancestral ordering**, which you should recall is an ordering of the nodes such that, if Z is a descendent of Y, then Z follows Y in the ordering. The algorithm, called **logic sampling**, was developed in Henrion [1988].

Algorithm 4.2 Approximate Inference Using Logic Sampling

Problem: Given a Bayesian network, determine the probabilities of the values
of each node conditional on specified values of the nodes in some subset.

Inputs: Bayesian network $(\mathbb{G}, P)$, where $\mathbb{G} = (\mathsf{V}, \mathsf{E})$, and a set of values a of
a subset $\mathsf{A} \subseteq \mathsf{V}$.

Outputs: Estimates of the conditional probabilities of the values of each node
in $\mathsf{V} - \mathsf{A}$ given $\mathsf{A} = \mathsf{a}$.

```
void logic_sampling (Bayesian-network& (G, P) where G = (V, E),
                     set-of-variables A,
                     set-of-variable-values a,
                     estimates& P̂(xⱼ|a))
{
    order the n nodes in V in an ancestral ordering;
    for (each Xⱼ ∈ V − A)
        for (k = 1; k <= # of values in Xⱼ's space; k + +)    // xⱼₖ is
            set # of occurrences of xⱼₖ to 0;                  // the kth
    for (i = 1; i <= m; i + +) {                               // value in
        j = 1;                                                 // Xⱼ's space.
        while (j <= n) {
            generate a value x̃ⱼ for Xⱼ using
            P(xⱼ|p̃aⱼ) where p̃aⱼ is the
            set of values generated for Xⱼ's parents;
            if (Xⱼ ∈ A && x̃ⱼ ≠ the value of Xⱼ ∈ a)
                j = 1;
            else
                j + +;
        }
    }


    for (each Xⱼ ∈ V − A)
        for (k = 1; k <= # of values in Xⱼ's space; k + +)
            if (xⱼₖ == x̃ⱼ)
                add 1 to # of occurrences of xⱼₖ;
    }


    for (each Xⱼ ∈ V − A)
        for (k = 1; k <= # of values in Xⱼ's space; k + +)
            P̂(xⱼₖ|a) = (# of occurrences of xⱼₖ)/m;
}
```

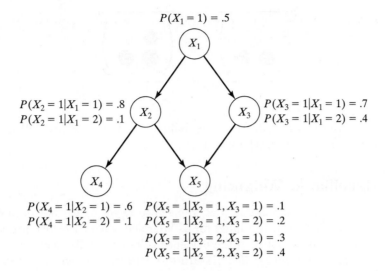

$P(X_1 = 1) = .5$

X_1

$P(X_2 = 1|X_1 = 1) = .8$
$P(X_2 = 1|X_1 = 2) = .1$ X_2

X_3 $P(X_3 = 1|X_1 = 1) = .7$
$P(X_3 = 1|X_1 = 2) = .4$

X_4 X_5

$P(X_4 = 1|X_2 = 1) = .6$ $P(X_5 = 1|X_2 = 1, X_3 = 1) = .1$
$P(X_4 = 1|X_2 = 2) = .1$ $P(X_5 = 1|X_2 = 1, X_3 = 2) = .2$
$P(X_5 = 1|X_2 = 2, X_3 = 1) = .3$
$P(X_5 = 1|X_2 = 2, X_3 = 2) = .4$

Figure 4.9: The Bayesian network discussed in Example 4.13.

Example 4.13 *Suppose we have the Bayesian network in Figure 4.9. Note that we are using 1 and 2 as the values of all variables. If we instantiate X_3 to 1 and X_4 to 2, then $\mathsf{A} = \{X_3, X_4\}$ and $\mathsf{a} = \{1, 2\}$. An application of the preceding algorithm with $m = 4$ may yield the following data:*

Case	X_1	X_2	X_3	X_4	X_5
1	1	2	1	2	2
2	1	2	2		
3	1	2	1	2	1
4	2	1	1	1	
5	2	2	1	2	2
6	2	1	2		
7	1	1	1	2	1

Note that Case 2 never obtained values for X_4 or X_5 because the value generated for X_3 was not its value in a. We had similar results for Cases 4 and 6. The resultant estimates are as follows:

$$\hat{P}(X_1 = 1|X_3 = 1, X_4 = 2) = \frac{3}{4}$$

$$\hat{P}(X_2 = 1|X_3 = 1, X_4 = 2) = \frac{1}{4}$$

$$\hat{P}(X_5 = 1|X_3 = 1, X_4 = 2) = \frac{2}{4}.$$

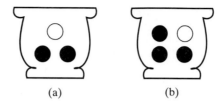

(a)   (b)

Figure 4.10: We can estimate the probability of picking a black ball from the urn in (a) by sampling from the urn in (b).

4.2.2   Likelihood Weighting

A problem with logic sampling is that we need to reject cases that do not have the evidence variables A instantiated for a. We reject each case with probability $1 - P(a)$. So if the probability of the evidence is low, we will reject many cases. Next we present a method called **likelihood weighting**, which circumvents this problem. Before showing how the method is used in Bayesian networks, we present a simple example illustrating the method.

Consider the two urns shown in Figure 4.10. Let $Color$ be a random variable whose value is $black$ if we pick a black ball and whose value is $white$ if we pick a white ball. Furthermore, let $P(black)$ be the probability $Color = black$ for the urn in Figure 4.10 (a), and let $P'(black)$ be the probability $Color = black$ for the urn in Figure 4.10 (b). We will show how to estimate $P(black)$ by sampling with replacement from the urn in Figure 4.10 (b). Suppose we create a sample of size m by sampling from that urn, and k of the balls are black. Instead of adding 1 each time we sample a black ball, we add $score(black)$, where

$$score(black) = \frac{P(black)}{P'(black)}.$$

By adding $score(black)$ each time we sample a black ball and then dividing the result by m, we obtain

$$\frac{k \times score(black)}{m}.$$

In the limit, we have

$$
\begin{aligned}
\lim_{m \to \infty} \frac{k \times score(black)}{m} &= \lim_{m \to \infty} \frac{k \left(\frac{P(black)}{P'(black)} \right)}{m} \\
&= \left(\frac{P(black)}{P'(black)} \right) \lim_{m \to \infty} \frac{k}{m} \\
&= \left(\frac{P(black)}{P'(black)} \right) P'(black) = P(black),
\end{aligned}
$$

which is what we want. Therefore, if we use $[k \times score(black)]/m$ as an estimate of $P(black)$, we will have convergence. However, for any finite sample, we would not necessarily have

$$\frac{k \times score(black)}{m} + \frac{(m-k) \times score(white)}{m} = 1.$$

So instead we simply determine $k \times score(black)$ and $(m-k) \times score(white)$, and then normalize to obtain our estimate. The following example illustrates this.

Example 4.14 *Suppose we sample* 100 *balls with replacement from the urn in Figure 4.10 (b) and* 72 *are black. We have*

$$score(black) = \frac{P(black)}{P'(black)} = \frac{2/3}{3/4} = 8/9$$

$$score(white) = \frac{P(white)}{P'(white)} = \frac{1/3}{1/4} = 4/3.$$

$$k \times score(black) = 72(8/9) = 64$$

$$(m-k) \times score(white) = 28(4/3) = \frac{112}{3},$$

So our estimate of $P(black)$ is given by

$$\hat{P}(black) = \frac{64}{64 + 112/3} = .632.$$

The previous sampling strategy for estimating $P(black)$ has no practical value because we had to know $P(black)$ to do the estimation. However, next we show how the method can be applied to Bayesian networks in a case in which we do not know the probabilities of interest.

Let $(\mathbb{G}, P)$, where $\mathbb{G} = (\mathsf{V}, \mathsf{E})$, be a Bayesian network, $\mathsf{V} = \{X_1, X_2, \ldots X_n\}$, $\mathsf{A} \subseteq \mathsf{V}$, $\mathsf{W} = \mathsf{V} - \mathsf{A}$, a and w be sets of values of the variables in A and W, respectively, and $\mathsf{v} = \mathsf{w} \cup \mathsf{a}$. Then

$$
\begin{aligned}
P(\mathsf{w}|\mathsf{a}) &= \frac{P(\mathsf{w}, \mathsf{a})}{P(\mathsf{a})} \\
&= \alpha P(\mathsf{v}) \\
&= \alpha P(x_n|\mathsf{pa}_n) P(x_{n-1}|\mathsf{pa}_{n-1}) \cdots P(x_2|\mathsf{pa}_2) P(x_1|\mathsf{pa}_1),
\end{aligned}
$$

where x_i and pa_i are, respectively, the values of X_i and its parents PA_i in v, and α is a normalizing constant. Now suppose we let $P'(\mathsf{w})$ be the probability distribution obtained by taking the product of the conditional distributions in the Bayesian network of only the variables in W with the evidence variables A clamped to a. That is,

$$P'(\mathsf{w}) = \prod_{X_i \in \mathsf{W}} P(x_i|\mathsf{pa}_i),$$

where again the values of all variables are their values in v. We now define

$$score(\mathsf{w}) \equiv \frac{P(\mathsf{w}|\mathsf{a})}{\alpha P'(\mathsf{w})}$$

$$= \frac{\alpha P(x_n|\mathsf{pa}_n)P(x_{n-1}|\mathsf{pa}_{n-1})\cdots P(x_2|\mathsf{pa}_2)P(x_1|\mathsf{pa}_1)}{\alpha \prod_{X_i \in \mathsf{W}} P(x_i|\mathsf{pa}_i)}$$

$$= \prod_{X_i \in \mathsf{A}} P(x_i|\mathsf{pa}_i).$$

Notice that we have eliminated the normalizing constant α in the score. Since we eventually normalize to obtain our probability estimates from the scores, there is no reason to include the constant. Before giving an algorithm for this method, we show an example.

Example 4.15 *Suppose we have the Bayesian network in Figure 4.9. To estimate $P(X_j = x_j|X_3 = 1, X_4 = 2)$ for $j = 1, 2,$ and 5 using the method just described, we first clamp X_3 to 1 and X_4 to 2. Then we generate values of the other variables according to the distributions in the network. For example, the first case is generated as follows: We initially generate a value of X_1 according to $P(X_1 = 1) = .5$. Let's say we get a value of 2 for X_1. We then generate a value of X_2 according to $P(X_2 = 1|X_1 = 2) = .1$. Let's say we get a value of 2 for X_2. Finally, we generate a value of X_5 according to $P(X_5 = 1|X_2 = 2, X_3 = 1) = .3$. Note that the value of X_2 is 2 because this is the value that was generated, while the value of X_3 is 1 because X_3 is clamped to this value. Let's say we get a value of 1 for X_5. The score score' of a case is defined to be the score of the value of w for that case. For example, the score of the first case (just discussed) is given by*

$$score'(Case\ 1) = score(X_1 = 2, X_2 = 2, X_5 = 1)$$
$$= P(X_4 = 2|X_2 = 2)P(X_3 = 1|X_1 = 2)$$
$$= (.9)(.4) = .36.$$

The following table shows possible data for the first four cases and the corresponding scores:

Case	X_1	X_2	X_3	X_4	X_5	score'
1	2	2	1	2	1	.36
2	1	1	1	2	2	.28
3	2	1	1	2	2	.16
4	1	1	1	2	1	.28

Finally we estimate the conditional probability of the value of any particular variable by normalizing the sum of the scores for the cases containing that value. For example,

$$\hat{P}(X_1 = 1|X_3 = 1, X_4 = 2) \propto [score'(Case\ 2) + score'(Case\ 4)]$$
$$\propto [.28 + .28] = .56$$

$$\hat{P}(X_1 = 2 | X_3 = 1, X_4 = 2) \quad \propto \quad [score'(Case\ 1) + score'(Case\ 3)]$$
$$\propto \quad [.36 + .16] = .52.$$

So

$$\hat{P}(X_1 = 1 | X_3 = 1, X_4 = 2) = \frac{.56}{.56 + .52} = .52.$$

It is left as an exercise to do the computations that estimate the conditional probabilities of the other variables.

Next we give an algorithm for the likelihood weighing method.

Algorithm 4.3 Approximate Inference Using Likelihood Weighting

Problem: Given a Bayesian network, determine the probabilities of the values of each node conditional on specified values of the nodes in some subset.

Inputs: Bayesian network $(\mathbb{G}, P)$, where $\mathbb{G} = (\mathsf{V}, \mathsf{E})$, and a set of values a of a subset $\mathsf{A} \subseteq \mathsf{V}$.

Outputs: Estimates of the conditional probabilities of the values of each node in $\mathsf{V} - \mathsf{A}$ given $\mathsf{A} = \mathsf{a}$.

```
void like_weight (Bayesian-network& (G, P) where G = (V, E),
                  set-of-variables A,
                  set-of-variable-values a,
                  estimates& P̂(x_j|a))
{
    order the n nodes in V in an ancestral order;
    for (each X_j ∈ V − A)
        for (k = 1; k <= # of values in X_j's space; k + +)    // x_jk is
            P̂(x_jk|a) = 0;                                       // the kth
    for (each X_j ∈ A)                                          // value in
        set x̃_j to the value of X_j in a;                       // X_j's space.
    for (i = 1; i <= m; i + +) {
        for (j = 1; j <= n; j + +) {
            if (X_j ∉ A)
                generate a value x̃_j for X_j using               // Use all
                P(x_jk|p̃a_j) where p̃a_j is the                  // values of k.
                set of values generated for X_j's parents;
    }
```

$$score = \prod_{X_j \in A} P(\tilde{x}_j | \tilde{p}a_j);$$

```
    for (each X_j ∈ V − A);
        for (k = 1; k <= # of values in X_j's space; k++)
            if (x_jk == x̃_j)
                P̂(x_jk|a) = P̂(x_jk|a) + score;
}
    for (each X_j ∈ V − A)
        for (k = 1; k <= # of values in X_j's space; k++)
        normalize P̂(x_jk|a);
}
```

Algorithm 4.3 was developed independently in Fung and Chang [1990] and Shachter and Peot [1990]. It is proven in Dagum and Luby [1993] that the problem of approximate inference in Bayesian networks is NP-hard. However, there are restricted classes of Bayesian networks which are provably amenable to a polynomial–time solution. (See Dagum and Chavez [1993].) Indeed, a variant of the likelihood weighting algorithm, which is worst-case polynomial time as long as the network does not contain extreme conditional probabilities, was developed in Pradham and Dagum [1996].

4.3   Abductive Inference

First we describe abductive inference in Bayesian networks; then we present an algorithm for it.

4.3.1   Abductive Inference in Bayesian Networks

Recall the Bayesian network discussed in Example 1.36 on page 46. That network is shown again in Figure 4.11. Recall further that the variables represent the following:

Variable	Value	When the Variable Takes this Value
H	$h1$	Patient has a smoking history
	$h2$	Patient does not have a smoking history
B	$b1$	Patient has bronchitis
	$b2$	Patient does not have bronchitis
L	$l1$	Patient has lung cancer
	$l2$	Patient does not have lung cancer
F	$f1$	Patient is fatigued
	$f2$	Patient is not fatigued
C	$c1$	Patient has a positive chest X-ray
	$c2$	Patient has a negative chest X-ray

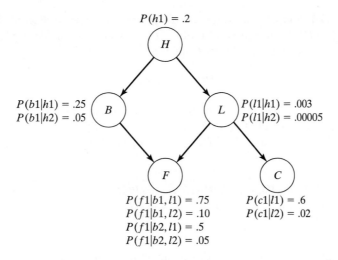

$P(h1) = .2$

H

$P(b1|h1) = .25$
$P(b1|h2) = .05$

B

L

$P(l1|h1) = .003$
$P(l1|h2) = .00005$

F

C

$P(f1|b1,l1) = .75$
$P(f1|b1,l2) = .10$
$P(f1|b2,l1) = .5$
$P(f1|b2,l2) = .05$

$P(c1|l1) = .6$
$P(c1|l2) = .02$

Figure 4.11: A Bayesian network.

We discussed this network again in the beginning of Chapter 3. We noted that if a patient had a smoking history and a positive chest X-ray, we would be interested in the probability of that patient having lung cancer (i.e., $P(l1|h1, c1)$) and having bronchitis (i.e., $P(b1|h1, c1)$). We went on to develop algorithms that perform this type of inference. Besides being interested in these conditional probabilities, a physician would be interested in the most probable explanation for the symptoms. That is, the physician would be interested in whether it is most probable that the patient has both lung cancer and bronchitis, has lung cancer and does not have bronchitis, does not have lung cancer and has bronchitis, or does not have either lung cancer or bronchitis. In general, the physician is interested in the most probable set of diseases given some symptoms. Similarly, in the case of an electronic circuit, we would be interested in the most probable explanation for a failure at some point in the circuit. Another example is the determination for the most probable cause of failure of an automobile to function properly. This process of determining the most probable explanation for a set of findings is called **abductive inference**. We have the following definition specific to Bayesian networks:

Definition 4.2 *Let* $(\mathbb{G}, P)$ *where* $\mathbb{G} = (\mathsf{V}, \mathsf{E})$ *be a Bayesian network, let* $\mathsf{M} \subseteq \mathsf{V}$, $\mathsf{D} \subseteq \mathsf{V}$, *and* $\mathsf{M} \cap \mathsf{D} = \varnothing$. M *is called the* ***manifestation set*** *and* D *is called the* ***explanation set***. *Let* m *be a set of values of the variables in* M. *Then a set of values of the variables in* D *that maximizes*

$$P(\mathsf{d}|\mathsf{m})$$

is called a ***most probable explanation (MPE)*** *for* m. *The process of determining such a set is called* ***abductive inference***.

Example 4.16 *Suppose we have the Bayesian network in Figure 4.11,* M = {H, C}, D = {B, L} *and* m = {h1, c1}. *Then a most probable explanation for* m *contains values of B and H that maximize*

$$P(bi, lj|h1, c1).$$

The chain rule gives us a straightforward algorithm for determining a most probable explanation. That is, if $D = \{D_1, D_2, \ldots, D_k\}$, $M = \{M_1, M_2, \ldots, M_j\}$, $m = \{m_1, m_2, \ldots, m_j\}$, and $d = \{d_1, d_2, \ldots, d_k\}$ is a set of values of the variables in D, then

$$
\begin{aligned}
P(\mathsf{d}|\mathsf{m}) &= P(d_1, d_2, d_3, \ldots, d_k|m_1, m_2, \ldots, m_j) \\
&= P(d_1|d_2, \ldots, d_k, m_1, m_2, \ldots, m_j)P(d_2|d_3, \ldots, d_k, m_1, m_2, \ldots, m_j) \\
&\quad \cdots P(d_k|m_1, m_2, \ldots, m_j).
\end{aligned}
$$

We can compute all the probabilities in the expression on the right in the equality above using our algorithms for doing inference in Bayesian networks. So, to determine a most probable explanation, we simply use this method to compute the conditional probabilities of all of the explanations, and then we take the maximum.

Example 4.17 *To compute a most probable explanation for the instance in Example 4.16, we need to compute the following four conditional probabilities:*

$$P(b1, l1|h1, c1) = P(b1|l1, h1, c1)P(l1|h1, c1)$$

$$P(b1, l2|h1, c1) = P(b1|l2, h1, c1)P(l2|h1, c1)$$

$$P(b2, l1|h1, c1) = P(b2|l1, h1, c1)P(l1|h1, c1)$$

$$P(b2, l2|h1, c1) = P(b2|l2, h1, c1)P(l2|h1, c1).$$

After doing this, we take the maximum to determine a most probable explanation.

The problem with the simple algorithm just described is that it has exponential time complexity. For example, if each variable has only two values and their are k variables in the explanation set, we must determine the conditional probability of 2^k explanations. Cooper [1990] has shown that the problem of abductive inference in Bayesian networks is NP-hard. One way to handle optimization problems such as abductive inference is to use best-first search with branch-and-bound pruning. For many instances this technique avoids generating most of the possible explanations and is therefore efficient. This is the method presented here. Zhaoyu and D'Ambrosio [1993] develop an algorithm for finding the r most probable explanations in an arbitrary Bayesian network, which does not use search.

4.3.2 A Best-First Search Algorithm for Abductive Inference

The best-first search with branch-and-bound pruning technique is used to solve problems in which a set of items needs to be chosen so as to maximize or minimize some function of the items. Neapolitan and Naimipour [1998] present a general introduction to the technique. Here we only develop an algorithm for abductive inference using the technique.

For the sake of focus, we will use medical terminology. We assume that the explanation set consists of k possible diseases, each of which may or may not be present in the patient. That is,

$$\mathsf{D} = \{D_1, D_2, \ldots, D_k\},$$

We know that the patient has a certain set of values m of certain symptoms M. Our goal is to find the set of diseases that is most probably present. Note that these assumptions entail that each variable in the explanation set has only two values. Let $\mathsf{A} = D_{i_1}, D_{i_2}, \ldots, D_{i_j}$ be a subset of D. We will denote the event that the diseases in A are present and all other diseases are absent by

$$\mathsf{A}$$

and by

$$D_{i_1}, D_{i_2}, \ldots, D_{i_j}.$$

For example, suppose there are four diseases. Then

$$D_1, D_3$$

represents the event

$$D_1 = \text{present}, D_2 = \text{absent}, D_3 = \text{present}, D_4 = \text{absent}.$$

We call

$$P(D_1, D_3|\mathsf{m})$$

the **conditional probability of the diseases**. Note that this is not consistent with the usual use of this terminology because ordinarily it means these diseases are present and it is not known whether others are also. Here it entails that no other diseases are present.

We can solve the problem of determining the most probable set of diseases (conditional on the information that some symptoms are present) by constructing a **state space tree**, such that each node in the tree contains a subset of

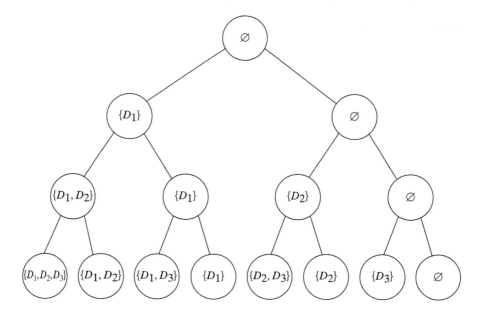

Figure 4.12: The state space tree for abductive inference when there are three possible diseases.

D, as follows: The root of the tree contains the empty set, the left child of the root contains $\{D_1\}$, and the right child of the root contains the empty set. The left child of the root's left child contains $\{D_1, D_2\}$, and its right child contains $\{D_1\}$. In general, we go to the left of a node a level i to include disease D_{i+1} and we go to the right to not include it. (Note that the root is at level 0.) Each leaf in the state space tree represents a possible solution (that is, the set of diseases that have been included up to the leaf). To solve the problem, we compute the conditional probability of the set of diseases at each leaf, and then we determine which conditional probability is largest. The tree for the case of three possible diseases is shown in Figure 4.12.

Our goal is to avoid generating most nodes in the tree. We can often accomplish this by determining a bounding function, which, at each node, puts an upper bound on the conditional probabilities of the sets of diseases in all descendents of the node. As we generate nodes starting from the root, we compute both the conditional probability of the disease set at the node and the bound for the node. We use the bound for two purposes. First, we prune any node whose bound is less than the greatest conditional probability found so far. Second, we always next expand the node with the current best bound. In this way, we can often arrive at an optimal solution faster than we would if we visited the nodes in some predetermined order. This technique is called **best-first search with branch-and-bound pruning**. Before we can illustrate the technique, we need to find a bounding function. The following theorem accomplishes this for a large class of instances.

Theorem 4.2 *If* A *and* A′ *are two sets of diseases such that*

$$P(A') \leq P(A),$$

then

$$P(A'|m) \leq \frac{P(A)}{P(m)}.$$

Proof. *According to Bayes' theorem*

$$
\begin{aligned}
P(A'|m) \;&=\; \frac{P(m|A')P(A')}{P(m)} \\[2mm]
&\leq\; \frac{P(m|A')P(A)}{P(m)} \\[2mm]
&\leq\; \frac{P(A)}{P(m)}.
\end{aligned}
$$

The first inequality is due to the assumption in the theorem, and the second is due to the fact that any probability is less than or equal to 1. This proves the theorem. ∎

For a given node, let A be the set of diseases that have been included up to the node, and for some descendent of that node, let A′ be the set of diseases that have been included up to that descendent. Then $A \subseteq A'$. Often it is reasonable to assume that

$$P(A') \leq P(A) \qquad \text{when} \qquad A \subseteq A'.$$

The reason is that usually it is at least as probable that a patient has a set of diseases as it is that the patient has that set plus even more diseases. (Recall that these are prior probabilities before any symptoms are observed.) If we make this assumption, Theorem 4.2 implies that

$$P(A'|m) \leq \frac{P(A)}{P(m)}.$$

Therefore, $P(A)/P(m)$ is an upper bound on the conditional probability of the set of diseases in any descendent of the node.

Next we show an example that uses this bound to prune branches. First we need some additional terminology. When the bound for a given node is no better than the value of the best solution found so far, the node is called **nonpromising**. Otherwise, it is called **promising**.

Example 4.18 *Suppose there are four diseases D_1, D_2, D_3, and D_4 in our explanation set* D, *and we have a set of values* m *of the variables in our symptom set* M. *The input to this example would also include a Bayesian network that contains the probabilistic relationships among the diseases and the symptoms. The probabilities used in this example would be computed from this Bayesian network using an algorithm for inference in a Bayesian network. Therefore, do not think that there is a place in this text where they are computed. We are assigning arbitrary probabilities to illustrate the best-first search algorithm.*

Figure 4.13 is the pruned state space tree produced by a best-first search with branch-and-bound pruning. Probabilities have been given arbitrary values in the tree. The conditional probability is on the top and the bound is on the bottom at each node. The shaded node is where the best solution is found. Nodes are labeled according to their depth and position from the left in the tree. The steps that produce the tree follow. The value of the variable Best *is the current best solution, while* $P(\text{Best}|\text{m})$ *is its conditional probability. Our goal is to determine a value of* Best *that maximizes this conditional probability. It is also assumed arbitrarily that*

$$p(\text{m}) = .01.$$

1. **Visit node (0,0) (the root).**

   (a) *Compute its conditional probability.* {∅ *is the empty set. This means no diseases are present.*}

   $$P(∅|\text{m}) \quad = \quad .1. \quad \{\textit{The computation would be done by another}\}$$
   $$\{\textit{algorithm. We are assigning arbitrary values.}\}$$

   (b) *Set*

   $$\text{Best} = ∅$$
   $$P(\text{Best}|\text{m}) = .1.$$

   (c) *Compute its prior probability and bound.*

   $$P(∅) = .9.$$

   $$bound = \frac{P(∅)}{P(\text{m})} = \frac{.9}{.01} = 90.$$

2. **Visit node (1,1).**

   (a) *Compute its conditional probability.*

   $$P(D_1|\text{m}) = .4.$$

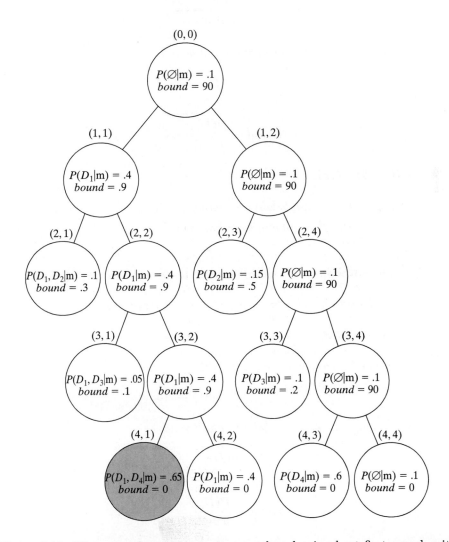

Figure 4.13: The pruned state space tree produced using best-first search with branch-and-bound pruning in Example 4.18. At each node, the conditional probability of the diseases included up to that node is at the top, and the bound on the conditional probability that could be obtained by expanding beyond the node is at the bottom. The shaded node is the one at which a most probable explanation is found.

(b) *Since .4 is greater than* $P(\text{Best}|m)$, *set*

$$\text{Best} = \{D_1\}$$
$$P(\text{Best}|m) = .4.$$

(c) *Compute its prior probability and bound.*

$$P(D_1) = .009$$

$$bound = \frac{P(D_1)}{P(m)} = \frac{.009}{.01} = .9.$$

3. **Visit node (1,2).**

   (a) *Its conditional probability is simply that of its parent, namely .1.*

   (b) *Its prior probability and bound are simply those of its parent, namely .9 and 90.*

4. **Determine promising, unexpanded node with largest bound.**

   (a) *That node is node (1,2). We visit its children next.*

5. **Visit node (2,3).**

   (a) *Compute its conditional probability.*

   $$P(D_2|m) = .15.$$

   (b) *Compute its prior probability and bound.*

   $$P(D_2) = .005.$$

   $$bound = \frac{P(D_2)}{P(m)} = \frac{.005}{.01} = .5.$$

6. **Visit node (2,4).**

   (a) *Its conditional probability is simply that of its parent, namely .1.*

   (b) *Its prior probability and bound are simply those of its parent, namely .9 and 90.*

7. **Determine promising, unexpanded node with largest bound.**

   (a) *That node is node (2,4). We visit its children next.*

8. **Visit node (3,3).**

   (a) *Compute its conditional probability.*

   $$P(D_3|m) = .1.$$

   (b) *Compute its prior probability and bound.*

   $$P(D_3) = .002.$$

   $$bound = \frac{P(D_3)}{P(m)} = \frac{.002}{.01} = .2.$$

   (c) *Determine it is nonpromising because its bound .2 is less than .4, the value of $P(\text{Best}|m)$.*

9. **Visit node (3,4).**

   (a) *Its conditional probability is simply that of its parent, namely .1.*

   (b) *Its prior probability and bound are simply those of its parent, namely .9 and 90.*

10. **Determine promising, unexpanded node with the largest bound.**

    (a) *That node is node (3,4). We visit its children next.*

11. **Visit node (4,3).**

    (a) *Compute its conditional probability.*

    $$P(D_4|m) = .6.$$

    (b) *Since $.6 > P(\text{Best}|m)$, set*

    $$\begin{aligned} \text{Best} &= \{D_4\} \\ P(\text{Best}|m) &= .6. \end{aligned}$$

    (c) *Set its bound to 0 because it is a leaf in the state space tree.*

    (d) *At this point the node (2,3) becomes nonpromising because its bound .5 less than or equal to .6, the new value of $P(\text{Best}|m)$.*

12. **Visit node (4,4).**

    (a) *Its conditional probability is simply that of its parent, namely .1.*

    (b) *Set its bound to 0 because it is a leaf in the state space tree.*

13. **Determine promising, unexpanded node with largest bound.**

   (a) *That node is node (1,1). We visit its children next.*

14. **Visit node (2,1).**

   (a) *Compute its conditional probability.*

   $$P(D_1, D_2|\mathsf{m}) = .1.$$

   (b) *Compute its prior probability and bound.*

   $$P(D_1, D_2) = .003$$

   $$bound = \frac{P(D_1, D_2)}{P(\mathsf{m})} = \frac{.003}{.01} = .3.$$

   (c) *Determine it is nonpromising because its bound .3 less than or equal to .6, the value of $P(\mathsf{Best}|\mathsf{m})$.*

15. **Visit node (2,2).**

   (a) *Its conditional probability is simply that of its parent, namely .4.*

   (b) *Its prior probability and bound are simply those of its parent, namely .009 and .9.*

16. **Determine promising, unexpanded node with greatest bound.**

   (a) *The only promising, unexpanded node is node (2,2). We visit its children next.*

17. **Visit node (3,1).**

   (a) *Compute its conditional probability.*

   $$P(D_1, D_3|\mathsf{m}) = .05.$$

   (b) *Compute its prior probability and bound.*

   $$P(D_1, D_3) = .001$$

   $$bound = \frac{P(D_1, D_3)}{P(\mathsf{m})} = \frac{.001}{.01} = .1.$$

   (c) *Determine it is nonpromising because its bound .1 less than or equal to .6, the value of $P(\mathsf{Best}|\mathsf{m})$.*

18. **Visit node (3,2).**

    (a) *Its conditional probability is simply that of its parent, namely .4.*

    (b) *Its prior probability and its bound are simply those of its parent, namely .009 and .9.*

19. **Determine promising, unexpanded node with largest bound.**

    (a) *The only promising, unexpanded node is node (3,2). We visit its children next.*

20. **Visit node (4,1).**

    (a) *Compute its conditional probability.*

    $$P(D_1, D_4|\mathsf{m}) = .65.$$

    (b) *Since .65 is greater than $P(\mathsf{Best}|\mathsf{m})$, set*

    $$\begin{aligned} \mathsf{Best} &= \{D_1, D_4\} \\ P(\mathsf{Best}|\mathsf{m}) &= .66. \end{aligned}$$

    (c) *Set its bound to 0 because it is a leaf in the state space tree.*

21. **Visit node (4,2).**

    (a) *Its conditional probability is simply that of its parent, namely .4.*

    (b) *Set its bound to 0 because it is a leaf in the state space tree.*

22. **Determine promising, unexpanded node with largest bound.**

    (a) *There are no more promising, unexpanded nodes. We are done.*

We have determined that the most probable set of diseases is $\{D_1, D_4\}$ and that $P(D_1, D_4|\mathsf{m}) = .65$.

A reasonable strategy in this problem would be to initially sort the diseases in nondecreasing order according to their prior probabilities. There is no guarantee, however, that this strategy will minimize the search time. We did not do this in the previous example and there were 15 nodes checked. In the exercises, you will establish that, if the diseases were sorted, there would be 23 nodes checked.

We present the algorithm shortly. However, first we need to discuss our implementation of best-first search. This implementation uses a priority queue. In a **priority queue**, the element with the highest priority is always removed next. In best-first search applications, the element with the highest priority is the node with the best bound. A priority queue can be implemented as a linked list, but more efficiently as a heap. We manipulate the priority queue PQ with the following two procedures:

$$Insert(PQ, X)$$

is a procedure that adds X to the priority queue PQ, while

$$Remove(PQ, X)$$

is a procedure that removes the node with the best bound and assigns its value to X. When removing a node from PQ, we have a check which determines if the bound for the node is still better than Best. This is how we determine that a node has become nonpromising after visiting the node. For example, node (2,3) in Figure 4.13 is promising at the time we visit it. In our implementation, this is when we insert it in PQ. However, it becomes nonpromising when Best takes the value .6. In our implementation, this is before we remove it from PQ. We learn this by comparing its bound to Best after removing it from PQ. In this way, we avoid visiting children of a node that becomes nonpromising after it is visited. Since we need the bound for a node at insertion time, at removal time, and to order the nodes in the priority queue, we store the bound at the node. The declaration is as follows:

```
struct node
{
    int level;                // the node's level in the tree
    set-of-indices A;
    float bound;
};
```

The value of the field A is the set of indices of the diseases included up to the node. The algorithm now follows. It has come to be known as **Cooper's algorithm**, because it was developed by Greg Cooper in Cooper [1984].

Algorithm 4.4 Cooper's Best-First Search Algorithm for Abductive Inference

Problem: Determine a most probable set of diseases (explanation) given a set of symptoms. It is assumed that, if a set of diseases A is a subset of a set of diseases A', then

$$P(\mathsf{A}') \leq P(\mathsf{A}).$$

Inputs: Positive integer n, Bayesian network $(\mathbb{G}, P)$ where $\mathbb{G} = (\mathsf{V}, \mathsf{E})$, ordered subset D of V containing n disease variables, and set of values m of the variables in a subset M of V.

Outputs: A set Best that contains the indices of the diseases in a most probable explanation, and a variable *Pbest* that is the probability of Best given that M = m.

```
void Cooper (int n,
             Bayesian-network& (𝔾, P) where 𝔾 = (V, E),
             ordered-set-of-diseases D,
             set-of-symptoms M,
             set-of-symptom-values m,
             set-of-indices& Best, float& Pbest)


{
  priority-queue-of-node PQ;
  node X, Y;

  X.level = 0;                        // Set X to the root.
  X.A = ∅;                            // Store empty set at root.
  Best = ∅;
  Pbest = P(Best|m);
  X.bound = bound(X);
  insert(PQ, X);
  while (!empty(PQ)){
    remove(PQ, X);                    // Remove node with best bound.
    if (X.bound > Pbest){
      Y.level = X.level + 1;          // Set Y to a child of X.
      Y.A = X.A;                      // Set Y to the child that includes
      put Y.level in Y.A;             // the next disease.
      if (P(Y.A|m) > Pbest){
        Best = Y.A;
        Pbest = P(Y.A|m);
      }
      Y.bound = bound(Y);
      if (Y.bound > Pbest)
        insert(PQ, Y);
      Y.A = X.A;                      // Set Y to the child that does
      Y.bound = bound(Y);             // not include the next disease.
      if (Y.bound > Pbest)
        insert(PQ, Y);
    }
  }
}


int bound (node Y)
{
  if (Y.level == n)                   // A leaf is nonpromising.
    return 0;
  else
    return (P(Y.A)/P(m));
}
```

The notation $P(A)$ stands for the prior probability of A, $P(m)$ stands for the prior probability of m, and $P(A|m)$ stands for the conditional probability of A given m. These values would be computed from the Bayesian network $(\mathbb{G}, P)$ using an algorithm for inference in a Bayesian network.

We have written the algorithm strictly according to guidelines for writing best-first search algorithms. An improvement is possible. First, there is no need to call function *bound* for the right child of a node. The reason is that the right child contains the same set of diseases as the node itself, which means its bound is the same. Therefore, the right child will be pruned only if we change *Pbest* to a value greater than or equal to this bound at the left child. We can modify our algorithm to prune the right child when this happens, and to expand to the right child when it does not happen

If there is more than one best solution, Algorithm 4.4 produces only one of them. It is straightforward to modify the algorithm to produce all the best solutions. It is also possible to modify it to produce the r most probable solutions, where r is any positive integer. This modification is discussed in Neapolitan [1990], which, furthermore, analyzes the algorithm in detail.

EXERCISES

Section 4.1

Exercise 4.1 *Prove Theorem 4.1.*

Exercise 4.2 *Prove that Algorithm 4.1 is correct.*

Exercise 4.3 *Obtain the network in Figure 4.7 (c).*

Exercise 4.4 *This exercise involves an expanded model of the auto pricing problem discussed in Example 4.8. Suppose we have the following random variables:*

Variable	What the Variable Represents
P	Wholesale price
M	Mean profit per car realized by Dealer-1 in past year
D	Dealer-1's asking price
N	Mean profit per car realized by Dealer-2 in past year
E	Dealer-2's asking price
C	Production cost
K	Marketing cost
X	An expert's estimate of the production cost
R	An expert's estimate of the marketing cost
I	Manufacturer's profit

Suppose further that the relationships among the variables are modeled by the Bayesian network in Figure 4.14.

a) Initialize this network.

b) Suppose we learn that the expert estimates the production cost to be $5,000 and the marketing cost to be $2,000. That is, we have the following instantiations:

$$X = 5000$$
$$R = 2000.$$

Update the network based on this information.

c) Suppose next we learn that Dealer-1 has an asking price of $8,000 and Dealer-2 has an asking price of $10,000. That is, we now also have the following instantiations:

$$D = 8000$$
$$E = 10000.$$

Update the network based on this additional information.

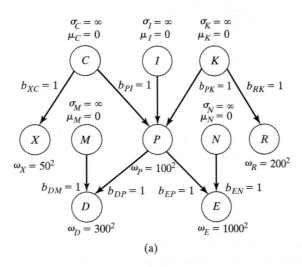

(a)

Figure 4.14: A Bayesian network representing an expanded model of the auto pricing problem.

Section 4.2

Exercise 4.5 *Suppose we have the Bayesian network in Figure 4.9. If we instantiate X_2 to 2 and X_5 to 1, then $A = \{X_2, X_5\}$ and $a = \{2, 1\}$. Suppose an application of Algorithm 4.2 with $m = 5$ yields the following data:*

Item	X_1	X_2	X_3	X_4	X_5
I_1	1	2	1	2	1
I_2	1	1			
I_3	2	2	1	2	1
I_4	1	2	2	1	1
I_5	2	2	1	2	2
I_6	2	1			
I_7	1	2	1	2	1
I_8	2	2	2	1	1

Show the resultant estimates of the conditional probabilities of the remaining variables.

Exercise 4.6 *In Example 4.15, it was left as an exercise to compute the conditional probabilities of the remaining variables besides X_1. Do so.*

Exercise 4.7 *Suppose we have the Bayesian network in Figure 4.9. If we instantiate X_2 to 2 and X_5 to 1, then $A = \{X_2, X_5\}$ and $a = \{2, 1\}$. Suppose an application of Algorithm 4.3 with $m = 5$ yields the following data:*

Item	X_1	X_2	X_3	X_4	X_5
I_1	2	2	1	2	1
I_2	1	2	2	1	1
I_3	2	2	2	2	1
I_4	1	2	1	1	1
I_5	2	2	1	2	1

Compute the score of each item and the estimates of the conditional probabilities.

Section 4.3

Exercise 4.8 *Sort the diseases in Example 4.18 in nondecreasing order according to their prior probabilities, and then apply Algorithm 4.4 to find a most probable explanation. How many nodes were generated? Is it more or less than the number of nodes generated when we did not sort them in Example 4.18?*

Chapter 5

Influence Diagrams

Consider again the Bayesian network in Figure 4.11. If a patient was, for example, a smoker and had a positive chest X-ray, a physician might consult that network to determine how probable it was that the patient had lung cancer or had bronchitis, or to determine the most probable explanation. The physician would then use this and other information to arrive at a decision as to how to treat the patient. In general, the information obtained by doing inference in a Bayesian network can be used to arrive at a decision even though the Bayesian network itself does not recommend a decision. In this chapter, we extend the structure of a Bayesian network so that the network actually does recommend a decision. Such a network is called an influence diagram. Before discussing influence diagrams in Section 5.2, we present decision trees in Section 5.1, which are mathematically equivalent to influence diagrams, and which are often simpler when the problem instance is small. After all this, Section 5.3 introduces dynamic Bayesian networks and influence diagrams.

5.1 Decision Trees

After presenting some simple examples of decision trees, we discuss several issues regarding their use.

5.1.1 Simple Examples

We start with the following example:

Example 5.1 *Suppose your favorite stock NASDIP is downgraded by a reputable analyst and it plummets from $40 to $10 per share. You feel this is a good buy, but there is a lot of uncertainty involved. NASDIP's quarterly earnings are about to be released and you think they will be good, which should positively influence its market value. However, you also think there is a good chance the whole market will crash, which will negatively influence NASDIP's market value. In an attempt to quantify your uncertainty, you decide there is a .25*

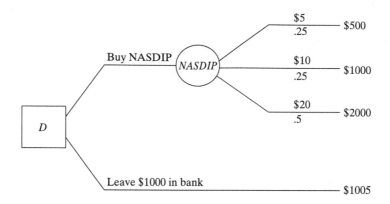

Figure 5.1: A decision tree representing the problem instance in Example 5.1.

probability the market will crash, in which case you feel NASDIP will go to $5 by the end of the month. If the market does not crash, you feel by the end of the month NASDIP will be either at $10 or at $20 depending on the earnings report. You think it is twice as likely it will be at $20 as at $10. So you assign a .5 probability to NASDIP being at $20 and a .25 probability to it being at $10 at month end. Your decision now is whether to buy 100 shares of NASDIP for $1000 or to leave the $1000 in the bank where it will earn .005 interest in the next month.

One way to make your decision is to determine the expected value of your investment if you purchase NASDIP and compare that value to the amount of money you would have if you put the money in the bank. Let X be a random variable, whose value is the worth of your $1000 investment in one month if you purchase NASDIP. If NASDIP goes to $5, your investment will be worth $500, if it stays at $10, your investment will be worth $1000, and if it goes to $20, it will be worth $2000. Therefore,

$$E(X) \quad = \quad .25(\$500) + .25(\$1000) + .5(\$2000)$$
$$= \quad \$1375.$$

If you leave the money in the bank, your investment with be worth

$$1.005(\$1000) = \$1005.$$

*If you are what is called an **"expected value maximizer,"** your decision would be to buy NASDIP.*

The problem instance in the previous example can be represented by a decision tree. That tree is shown in Figure 5.1. A **decision tree** contains two kinds of nodes: **chance (or uncertainty) nodes** representing random variables; and **decision nodes** representing decisions to be made. We depict these nodes as follows:

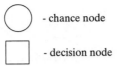

- chance node

- decision node

A **decision** represents a set of mutually exclusive and exhaustive actions the decision maker can take. Each action is called an **alternative** in the decision. There is an edge emanating from a decision node for each alternative in the decision. In Figure 5.1, we have the decision node D with the two alternatives "Buy NASDIP" and "Leave $1000 in bank." There is one edge emanating from a chance node for each possible outcome (value) of the random variable. We show the probability of the outcome on the edge and the utility of the outcome to the right of the edge. The **utility** of the outcome is the value of the outcome to the decision maker. When an amount of money is small relative to one's total wealth, we can usually take the utility of an outcome to be the amount of money realized given the outcome. Currently, we make that assumption. Handling the case in which we do not make that assumption is discussed in Section 5.1.2. So, for example, if you buy 100 shares of NASDIP and NASDIP goes to $20, we assume the utility of that outcome to you is $2000. In Figure 5.1, we have the chance node $NASDIP$ with three possible outcome utilities, namely $500, $1000, and $2000. The **expected utility** EU of a chance node is defined to be the expected value of the utilities associated with its outcomes. The expected utility of a decision alternative is defined to be the expected utility of the chance node encountered if that decision is made. If there is certainty when the alternative is taken, this expected utility is the value of that certain outcome. So

$$EU(\text{Buy NASDIP}) = EU(NASDIP) \quad = \quad .25(\$500) + .25(\$1000) + .5(\$2000)$$
$$= \quad \$1375$$

$$EU(\text{Leave \$1000 in bank}) = \$1005.$$

Finally, the expected utility of a decision node is defined to be the maximum of the expected utilities of all its alternatives. So

$$EU(D) = \max(\$1375, \$1005) = \$1375.$$

The alternative chosen is the one with the largest expected utility. The process of determining these expected utilities is called **solving the decision tree**. After solving it, we show expected utilities above nodes and an arrow to the alternative chosen. The solved decision tree, given the decision tree in Figure 5.1, is shown in Figure 5.2.

Another example follows.

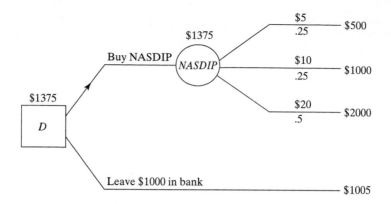

Figure 5.2: The solved decision tree given the decision tree in Figure 5.1.

Example 5.2 *Suppose you are in the same situation as in Example 5.1 except, instead of considering leaving your money in the bank, your other choice is to buy an option on NASDIP. The option costs $1000, and it allows you to buy 500 shares of NASDIP at $11 per share in one month. So if NASDIP is at $5 or $10 per share in one month, you would not exercise your option and you would lose $1000. However, if NASDIP is at $20 per share in one month, you would exercise your option, and your $1000 investment would be worth*

$$500(\$20 - \$11) = \$4500.$$

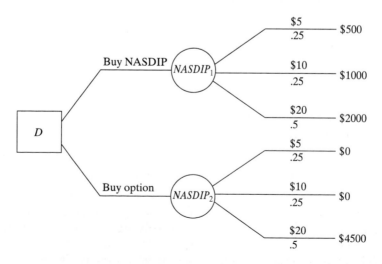

Figure 5.3: The decision tree modeling the investment decision concerning NAS-DIP, when the other choice is to buy an option on NASDIP.

Figure 5.3 shows a decision representing this problem instance. From that tree, we have

$$EU(Buy\ option) = EU(NASDIP_2) \quad = \quad .25(\$0) + .25(\$0) + .5(\$4500)$$
$$= \quad \$2250.$$

Recall that EU(Buy NASDIP) is only \$1375. So our decision would be to buy the option. It is left as an exercise to show the solved decision tree.

Notice that the decision tree in Figure 5.3 is symmetrical, whereas the one in Figure 5.2 is not. The reason is that we encounter the same uncertain event regardless of which decision is made. Only the utilities of the outcomes are different.

5.1.2 Probabilities, Time, and Risk Attitudes

Before proceeding, we address some concerns you may have. First, you may be wondering how an individual could arrive at the probabilities of .25, .5, and .25 in Example 5.1. These probabilities are not relative frequencies; rather they are subjective probabilities that represent an individual's reasonable numeric beliefs. The individual arrives at them by a careful analysis of the situation. Methods for assessing subjective beliefs were discussed briefly in Section 1.2.2 and are discussed in more detail in Neapolitan [1996]. Even so, you may argue that the individual surely must believe there are many possible future values for a share of NASDIP. How can the individual claim the only possible values are \$5, \$10 and \$20? You are correct. Indeed, this author is the individual in this example, which concerns a recent investment decision of his. Although I believe there are many possible future values, I feel the values \$5, and \$10, and \$20 with probabilities .25, .5, and .25 are sufficient to represent my beliefs as far as influencing my decision. That is, I feel that further refinement of my beliefs would not affect my decision.

Second, you many wonder why we based the decision on the outcome in one month. Why not two months or a year, for example? When using decision analysis in problems such as these, the decision maker must base the decision on the outcome at some point in the future. It is up to the decision maker's preferences to determine that point. This was my decision, and I based my decision on my status one month into the future.

Finally, you may wonder why we chose the alternative with the largest expected value. Surely, a person who is very risk-averse might prefer the sure \$1005 over the possibility of ending up with only \$500. This is absolutely true, and it is possible to incorporate one's attitude towards risk into the decision. We modeled the situation in which the utility of the outcome is the same as the amount of money realized given the outcome. As mentioned previously, many people maximize expected value when the amount of money is small relative to their total wealth. The idea is that in the long run one will end up better off by so doing. On the other hand, in the current example, I would not invest \$100,000 in NASDIP because that is too much money relative to my total wealth.

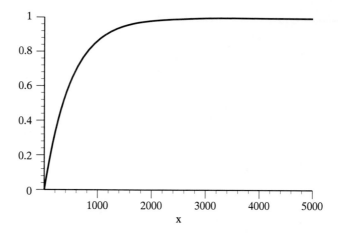

Figure 5.4: The $U_{500}(x) = 1 - e^{-x/500}$ function.

One way to model an individual's attitude towards risk is with a **utility function**, which is a function that maps dollar amounts to utilities. An example is the **exponential utility function**:

$$U_R(x) = 1 - e^{-x/R}.$$

In this function the parameter R, called the **risk tolerance**, determines how risk-averse the function is. As R becomes smaller, the function becomes more risk-averse. Figure 5.4 shows $U_{500}(x)$, while Figure 5.5 shows $U_{1000}(x)$. Notice that both functions are concave (opening downward) and the one in Figure 5.5 is closer to being a straight line. The more concave, the more risk-averse the function is; a straight line is risk neutral, and a convex (opening upward) function is risk-seeking. The following example illustrates the use of this function.

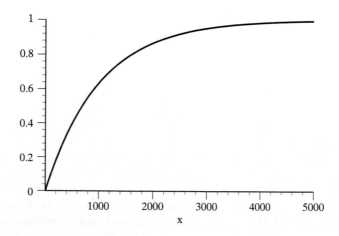

Figure 5.5: The $U_{1000}(x) = 1 - e^{-x/1000}$ function.

Example 5.3 *Suppose we are making the decision in Example 5.1, and we use the exponential utility function with $R = 500$. Then*

$$
\begin{aligned}
EU(Buy\ NASDIP) &= EU(NASDIP) \\
&= .25U_{500}(\$500) + .25U_{500}(\$1000) + .5U_{500}(\$2000) \\
&= .25\left(1 - e^{-500/500}\right) + .25\left(1 - e^{-1000/500}\right) \\
&\quad +.5\left(1 - e^{-2000/500}\right) \\
&= .86504.
\end{aligned}
$$

$$
EU(Leave\ \$1000\ in\ bank) = U_{500}(\$1005) = 1 - e^{-1005/500} = .86601.
$$

If we modeled some individual's attitude towards risk with this utility function, that individual would choose to leave the money in the bank. It is left as an exercise to show that using $R = 1000$ leads to the decision to buy NASDIP.

One way to determine your personal value of R is to consider a lottery in which you will win $\$x$ with probability .5 and lose $-\$x/2$ with probability .5. Your value of R is the largest value of x for which you would choose the lottery over doing nothing.

Modeling risk attitudes are discussed much more in Clemen [1996]. Henceforth, we simply assume the utility of an outcome is the same as the amount of money realized given the outcome.

5.1.3 Solving Decision Trees

Next we show the general method for solving decision trees. There is a time ordering from left to right in a decision tree. That is, any node to the right of another node, occurs after that node in time. The tree is solved as follows:

> Starting at the right,
>> proceed to the left
>>> passing expected utilities to chance nodes;
>>> passing maxima to decision nodes;
>> until the root is reached.

5.1.4 More Examples

We now present more complex examples of modeling with decision trees.

Example 5.4 *Suppose Xia is a high roller and she is considering buying 10,000 shares of ICK for $10 a share. This number of shares is so high that if she purchases them, it could affect market activity and bring up the price of ICK. She also believes the overall value of the DOW industrial average will affect the* *price of ICK. She feels that, in one month, the DOW will be at either 10,000 or 11,000, and ICK will be at either $5 or $20 per share. Her other choice is to buy an option on ICK for $100,000. The option will allow her to buy 50,000 shares of ICK for $15 a share in one month. To analyze this problem instance, she constructs the following probabilities:*

$$P(ICK = \$5|Decision \ = \ Buy\ ICK, DOW = 11,000) = .2$$

$$P(ICK = \$5|Decision \ = \ Buy\ ICK, DOW = 10,000) = .5$$

$$P(ICK = \$5|Decision \ = \ Buy\ option, DOW = 11,000) = .3$$

$$P(ICK = \$5|Decision \ = \ Buy\ option, DOW = 10,000) = .6.$$

Furthermore, she assigns

$$P(DOW = 11,000) = .6.$$

This problem instance is represented by the decision tree in Figure 5.6. Next we solve the tree:

$$EU(ICK_1) = (.2)(\$50,000) + (.8)(\$200,000) = \$170,000$$

$$EU(ICK_2) = (.5)(\$50,000) + (.5)(\$200,000) = \$125,000$$

$$EU(Buy\ ICK) = EU(DOW_1) = (.6)(\$170,000) + (.4)(\$125,000) = \$152,000$$

$$EU(ICK_3) = (.3)(\$0) + (.7)(\$250,000) = \$175,000$$

$$EU(ICK_4) = (.6)(\$0) + (.4)(\$250,000) = \$100,000$$

$$EU(Buy\ option) = EU(DOW_2) = (.6)(\$175,000) + (.4)(\$100,000) = \$145,000$$

$$EU(D) = \max(\$152,000, \$145,000) = \$152,000.$$

The solved decision tree is shown in Figure 5.7. The decision is buy ICK.

The previous example illustrates a problem with decision trees. That is, the representation of a problem instance by a decision tree grows exponentially with

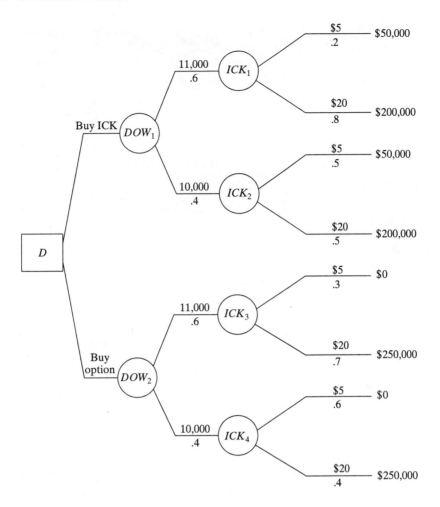

Figure 5.6: A decision tree representing Xia's decision as to whether to buy ICK or an option on ICK.

the size of the instance. Notice that the instance in Example 5.4 has only one more element in it than the instance in Example 5.2. That is, it includes that uncertainty about the DOW. Yet its representation is twice as large. So it is quite difficult to represent a large instance with a decision tree. We will see in the next section that influence diagrams do not have this problem. Before that, we show more examples.

Example 5.5 *Sam has the opportunity to buy a 1996 Spiffycar automobile for* $10,000, *and he has a prospect who would be willing to pay* $11,000 *for the auto if it is in excellent mechanical shape. Sam determines that all mechanical parts except for the transmission are in excellent shape. If the transmission is bad, it will cost Sam* $3000 *to repair it, and he would have to repair it before the prospect*

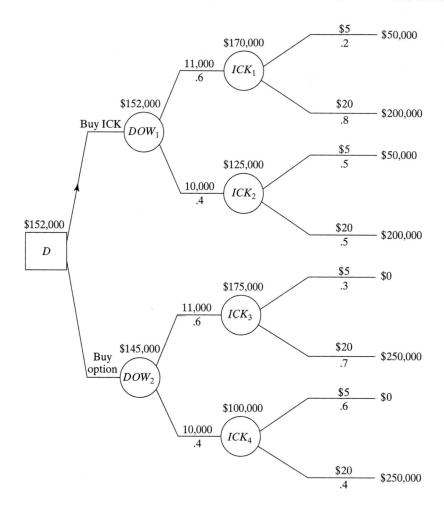

Figure 5.7: The solved decision tree given the decision tree in Figure 5.6.

would buy it. So he would only end up with $8000 if he bought the vehicle and
its transmission was bad. He cannot determine the state of the transmission
himself. However, he has a friend who can run a test on the transmission.
The test is not absolutely accurate. Rather 30% of the time it judges a good
transmission to be bad and 10% of the time it judges a bad transmission to be
good. To represent this relationship between the transmission and the test, we
define the random variables which follow.

Variable	Value	When the Variable Takes This Value
Test	*positive*	*Test judges the transmission is bad*
	negative	*Test judges the transmission is good*
Tran	*good*	*Transmission is good*
	bad	*Transmission is good*

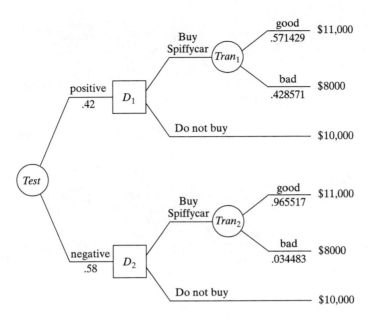

Figure 5.8: The decision tree representing the problem instance in Example 5.5.

The previous discussion implies we have these conditional probabilities:

$$P(Test = positive|Tran = good) = .3$$

$$P(Test = positive|Tran = bad) = .9.$$

Furthermore, Sam knows that 20% of the 1996 Spiffycars have bad transmissions. That is,

$$P(Tran = good) = .8.$$

Sam is going to have his friend run the test for free, and then he will decide whether to buy the car.

This problem instance is represented in the decision tree in Figure 5.8. Notice first that, if he does not buy the vehicle, the outcome is simply $10,000. This is because the point in the future is so near that we can neglect interest as negligible. Note further that the probabilities in that tree are not the ones stated in the example. They must be computed from the stated probabilities. We do that next. The probability on the upper edge emanating from the Test node is the prior probability that the test is positive. It is computed it follows (note that we use our abbreviated notation):

$$
\begin{aligned}
P(positive) &= P(positive|good)P(good) + P(positive|bad)P(bad) \\
&= (.3)(.8) + (.9)(.2) = .42.
\end{aligned}
$$

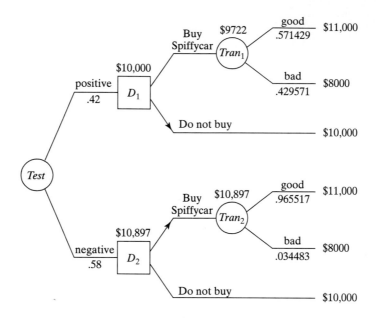

Figure 5.9: The solved decision tree given the decision tree in Figure 5.8.

The probability on the upper edge emanating from the $Tran_1$ node is the probability the transmission is good given the test is positive. We compute it using Bayes' theorem as follows:

$$P(good|positive) \quad = \quad \frac{P(positive|good)P(good)}{P(positive)}$$

$$= \quad \frac{(.3)(.8)}{.42} = .571429.$$

It is left as an exercise to determine the remaining probabilities in the tree. Next we solve the tree:

$$EU(Tran_1) = (.571429)(\$11,000) + (.428571)(\$8000) = \$9714$$

$$EU(D_1) = \max(\$9714, \$10,000) = \$10,000$$

$$EU(Tran_2) = (.965517)(\$11,000) + (.034483)(\$8000) = \$10,897$$

$$EU(D_2) = \max(\$10,897, \$10,000) = \$10,897.$$

We need not compute the expected value of the Test node because there are no decisions to the left of it. The solved decision tree is shown in Figure 5.9. The decision is to not buy the vehicle if the test is positive and to buy it if the test is negative.

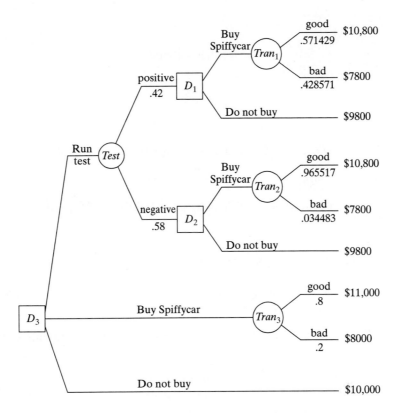

Figure 5.10: The decision tree representing the problem instance in Example 5.6.

The previous example illustrates another problem with decision trees. That is, the probabilities needed in a decision tree are not always the ones that are readily available to us. So we must compute them using the law of total probability and Bayes' theorem. We will see that influence diagrams do not have this problem either.

More examples follow.

Example 5.6 *Suppose Sam is in the same situation as in Example 5.5 except that the test is not free. Rather it costs $200. So Sam must decide whether to run the test, buy the car without running the test, or keep his $10,000. The decision tree representing this problem instance is shown in Figure 5.10. Notice that the outcomes when the test is run are all $200 less than their respective outcomes in Example 5.5. This is because it cost $200 to run the test. Note further that, if the vehicle is purchased without running the test, the probability of the transmission being good is simply its prior probability .8. This is because no test was run. So our only information about the transmission is our prior information. Next we solve the decision tree. It is left as an exercise to show* *that*

$$EU(D_1) = \$9800$$

$$EU(D_2) = \$10,697.$$

Therefore,

$$EU(Test) = (.42)(\$9800) + (.58)(\$10,697) = \$10,320.$$

Furthermore,

$$EU(Tran_3) = (.8)(\$11,000) + (.2)(\$8000) = \$10,400.$$

Finally,

$$EU(D_3) = \max(\$10,320,\$10,400,\$10,000) = \$10,400.$$

So Sam's decision is to buy the vehicle without running the test. It is left as an exercise to show the solved decision tree.

The following two examples illustrate cases in which the outcomes are not numeric.

Example 5.7 *Suppose Leonardo has just bought a new suit, he is about to leave for work, and it looks like it might rain. Leonardo has a long walk from the train to his office. So he knows if it rains and he does not have his umbrella, his suit will be ruined. His umbrella will definitely protect his suit from the rain. However, he hates the inconvenience of lugging the umbrella around all day. Given he feels there is a .4 probability it will rain, should he bring his umbrella? A decision tree representing this problem instance is shown in Figure 5.11. We cannot solve this tree yet because its outcomes are not numeric. We can give them numeric utilities as follows. Clearly, the ordering of the outcomes from worst to best is as follows:*

  1. *suit ruined*
  2. *suit not ruined, inconvenience*
  3. *suit not ruined.*

We assign a utility of 0 to the worst outcome and a utility of 1 to the best outcome. So

$$U(suit\ ruined) = 0$$

$$U(suit\ not\ ruined) = 1.$$

Then we consider lotteries (chance nodes) L_p in which Leonardo gets outcome "suit not ruined" with probability p and outcome "suit ruined" with probability

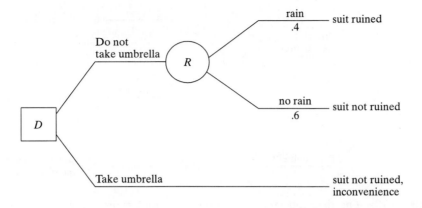

Figure 5.11: The decision tree representing the problem instance in Example 5.7.

$1 - p$. *The utility of "suit not ruined, inconvenience" is defined to be the expected utility of the lottery $L_{p'}$ for which Leonardo would be indifferent between lottery $L_{p'}$ and being assured of "suit not ruined, inconvenience." We then have*

$$
\begin{aligned}
U(\text{suit not ruined, inconvenience}) &\equiv EU(L_{p'}) \\
&= p'U(\text{suit not ruined}) \\
&\quad +(1 - p')U(\text{suit ruined}) \\
&= p'(1) + (1 - p')0 = p'.
\end{aligned}
$$

Let's say Leonardo decides $p' = .8$. Then

$$U(\text{suit not ruined, inconvenience}) = .8$$

The decision tree with these numeric values is shown in Figure 5.12. We solve that decision tree next:

$$EU(R) = (.4)(0) + (.6)(1) = .6$$

$$EU(D) = \max(.6, .8) = .8.$$

So the decision is to take the umbrella.

The method used to obtain numeric values in the previous example easily extends to the case in which there are more than three outcomes. For example, suppose there was a fourth outcome "suit goes to cleaners" in between "suit not ruined, inconvenience" and "suit not ruined" in the preference ordering. We consider lotteries L_q in which Leonardo gets outcome "suit not ruined" with probability q and outcome "suit not ruined, inconvenience" with probability $1 - q$. The utility of "suit goes to cleaners" is defined to be the expected utility

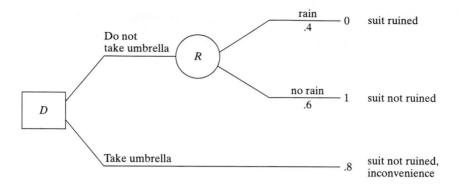

Figure 5.12: The decision tree with numeric values representing the problem instance in Example 5.7.

of the lottery $L_{q'}$ for which Leonardo would be indifferent between lottery $L_{q'}$ and being assured of "suit goes to cleaners." We then have

$$
\begin{aligned}
U(\text{suit goes to cleaners}) &\equiv EU(L_{q'}) \\
&= q'U(\text{suit not ruined}) \\
&\quad +(1-q')U(\text{suit not ruined, inconvenience}) \\
&= q'(1) + (1-q')(.8) = .8 + .2q'.
\end{aligned}
$$

Let's say Leonardo decides $q' = .6$. Then

$$
U(\text{suit goes to cleaners}) = .8 + (.2)(.6) = .92.
$$

Next we give an example from the medical domain.

Example 5.8 [1]*Amit, a 15 year old high school student, has been definitively diagnosed with streptococcal infection, and he is considering having a treatment which is known to reduce the number of days with a sore throat from 4 to 3. He learns however that the treatment has a .000003 probability of causing death due to anaphylaxis. Should he have the treatment?*

*You may argue that, if he may die from the treatment, he certainly should not have it. However, the probability of dying is extremely small, and we daily accept small risks of dying in order to obtain something of value to us. For example, many people take a small risk of dying in a car accident in order to arrive at work. We see then that we cannot discount the treatment based solely on that risk. So what should Amit do? Next we apply decision analysis to recommend a decision to him. Figure 5.13 shows a decision tree representing Amit's decision. To solve this problem instance we need to quantify the outcomes in that tree. We can do this using **quality adjusted life expectancies (QALE)**. We ask*

---

[1]This example is based on an example in Nease and Owens [1997]. Although the information is not fictitious, some of it is controversial.

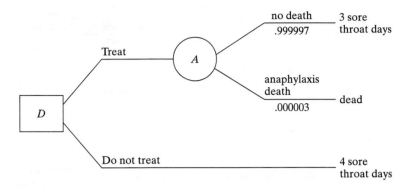

Figure 5.13: A decision tree modeling Amit's decision concerning being treated for streptococcal infection.

Amit to determine what one year of life with a sore throat is worth relative to one year of life without one. We will call such years "well years." Let's say he says it is worth .9 well years. That is, for Amit,

      1 year with sore throat   is equivalent to   .9 well years.

   *We then assume a **constant proportional trade-off**. That is, we assume the time trade-off associated with having a sore throat is independent of the time spent with one. (The validity of this assumption and alternative models are discussed in Nease and Owens [1997].) Given this assumption, for Amit,*

      t years with sore throat   is equivalent to   .9t well years.

*The value .9 is called the **time-trade-off quality adjustment** for a sore throat. Another way to look at it is that Amit would give up .1 years of life to avoid having a sore throat for .9 years of life. Now, if we let t be the amount of time Amit will have a sore throat due to this infection, and l be Amit's remaining life expectancy, we define his quality **QALE** as follows:*

$$QALE(l, t) = (l - t) + .9t.$$

From life expectancy charts, we determine Amit's remaining life expectancy is 60 years. Converting days to years, we have the following:

$$3 \text{ days} = .008219 \text{ years}$$

$$4 \text{ days} = .010959 \text{ years}.$$

Therefore, Amit's QALE are as follows:

$$
\begin{aligned}
QALE(60 \text{ yrs, 3 sore throat days}) &= 60 - .008219 + .9(.008219) \\
&= 59.999178
\end{aligned}
$$

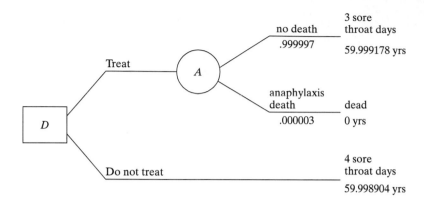

Figure 5.14: The decision tree in Figure 5.13 with the actual outcomes augmented by QALE.

$$QALE(60 \ yrs, \ 4 \ sore \ throat \ days) = 60 - .010959 + .9(.010959)$$
$$= 59.998904.$$

Figure 5.14 shows the decision tree in Figure 5.13 with the actual outcomes augmented with QALE. Next we solve that tree:

$$EU(Treat) = EU(A) = (.999997)(59.998998) + (.000003)(0)$$
$$= 59.998998$$

$$EU(Do \ not \ treat) = 59.998904$$

$$EU(D) = \max(59.998998, 59.998904) = 59.998998.$$

So the decision is to treat, but just barely.

Example 5.9 *This example is an elaboration of the previous one. Actually, streptococcus infection can lead to rheumatic heart disease (RHD), which is less probable if the patient is treated. Specifically, if we treat a patient with streptococcus infection, the probability of rheumatic heart disease is .000013, while if we do not treat the patient, the probability is .000063. The rheumatic heart disease would be for life. So Amit needs to take all this into account. First he must determine time trade-off quality adjustments both for having rheumatic heart disease alone and for having it along with a sore throat. Suppose he determines the following:*

$$1 \ year \ with \ RHD \quad is \ equivalent \ to \quad .15 \ well \ years.$$

$$1 \ year \ with \ sore \ throat \ and \ RHD \quad is \ equivalent \ to \quad .1 \ well \ years.$$

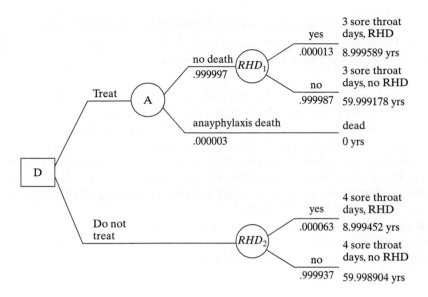

Figure 5.15: A decision tree modeling Amit's decision concerning being treated for streptococcal infection when rheumatic heart disease is considered.

We then have

$$QALE(60 \text{ yrs, RHD, 3 sore throat days}) = \left(60 - \frac{3}{365}\right)(.15) + \left(\frac{3}{365}\right)(.1)$$
$$= 8.999589$$

$$QALE(60 \text{ yrs, RHD, 4 sore throat days}) = \left(60 - \frac{4}{365}\right)(.15) + \left(\frac{4}{365}\right)(.1)$$
$$= 8.999452.$$

We have already computed QALE for 3 or 4 days with only a sore throat in the previous example. Figure 5.15 shows the resultant decision tree. We solve that decision tree next:

$$EU(RHD_1) = (.000013)(8.999569) + (.999987)(59.999178)$$
$$= 59.998515$$

$$EU(Treat) = EU(A) = (.999997)(59.998515) + (.000003)(0)$$
$$= 59.998335$$

$$EU(Do \text{ not treat}) = EU(RHD_2)$$
$$= (.000063)(8.999452) + (.999937)(59.998904)$$
$$= 59.995691$$

$$EU(D) = \max(59.998335, 59.995691) = 59.998335.$$

So again the decision is to treat, but again barely.

You may argue that, in the previous two examples, the difference in the expected utilities is negligible because the number of significant digits needed to express it is far more than the number of significant digits in Amit's assessments. This argument is reasonable. However, the utilities of the decisions are so close because the probabilities of both anaphylaxis death and rheumatic heart disease are so small. In general, this situation is not always the case. It is left as an exercise to rework the previous example with the probability of rheumatic heart disease being .13 instead of .000063.

Another consideration in medical decision making is the financial cost of the treatments. In this case, the value of an outcome is a function of both the QALE and the financial cost associated with the outcome.

5.2   Influence Diagrams

In the previous section, we noted the following two difficulties with decision trees. First, the representation of a problem instance by a decision tree grows exponentially with the size of the instance. Second, the probabilities needed in a decision tree are not always the ones that are readily available to us. Next we present an alternative representation of decision problem instances, namely influence diagrams, which do not have either of these difficulties. First we discuss representing problem instances with influence diagrams; then we discuss solving influence diagrams.

5.2.1   Representing with Influence Diagrams

An **influence diagram** contains three kinds of nodes: **chance (or uncertainty) nodes** representing random variables; **decision nodes** representing decisions to be made; and one **utility node**, which is a random variable whose possible values are the utilities of the outcomes. We depict these nodes as follows:

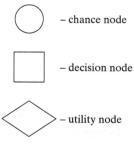

– chance node

– decision node

– utility node

The edges in an influence diagram have the following meaning:

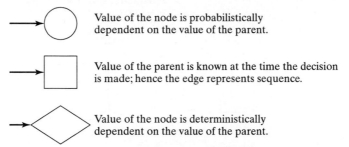

The chance nodes in an influence diagram satisfy the Markov condition with the probability distribution. That is, for each chance node X, $\{X\}$ is conditionally independent of the set of all its nondescendents given the set of all its parents. So an influence diagram is actually a Bayesian network augmented with decision nodes and a utility node. There must be an ordering of the decision nodes in an influence diagram based on the order in which the decisions are made. The order is specified using the edges between the decision nodes. For example, if we have the order

$$D_1, D_2, D_3,$$

then there are edges from D_1 to D_2 and D_3, and an edge from D_2 to D_3.

To illustrate influence diagrams, we next represent the problem instances, in the examples in the section on decision trees, by influence diagrams.

Example 5.10 *Recall Example 5.1 in which you felt there is a .25 probability NASDIP will be at $5 at month's end, a .5 probability it will be at $20, and a .25 probability it will be at $10. Your decision is whether to buy 100 shares of NASDIP for $1000 or to leave the $1000 in the bank where it will earn .005 interest. Figure 5.16 shows an influence diagram representing this problem instance. Notice a few things about that diagram. There is no edge from D to NASDIP because your decision as to whether to buy NASDIP has no affect on its performance. (We assume your 100 shares is not enough to affect market activity.) There is no edge from NASDIP to D because at the time you make your decision you do not know NASDIP's value in one month. There are edges from both NASDIP and D to U because your utility depends both on whether NASDIP goes up and whether you buy it. Notice that if you do not buy it, the utility is the same regardless of what happens to NASDIP. This is why we write $U(d2, n) = \$1005$. The variable n represents any possible value of NASDIP.*

Example 5.11 *Recall Example 5.2, which involved the same situation as Example 5.1, except that your choices were either to buy NASDIP or to buy an option on NASDIP. Recall further, that if NASDIP is at $5 or $0 per share in one month, you would not exercise your option and you would lose your $1000;*

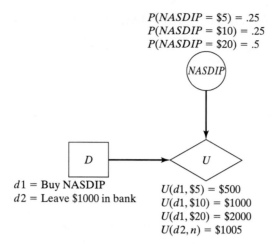

Figure 5.16: An influence diagram modeling your decision as to whether to buy NASDIP.

and, if NASDIP is at $20 per share in one month, you would exercise your option and your $1000 investment would be worth $4500. Figure 5.17 shows an influence diagram representing this problem instance. Recall that when we represented this instance with a decision tree (Figure 5.3) that tree was symmetrical because we encounter the same uncertain event regardless of which decision is made. This symmetry manifests itself in the influence diagram in that the value

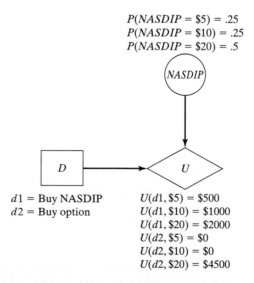

Figure 5.17: An influence diagram modeling your decision as to whether to buy NASDIP when the other choice is to buy an option.

of U depends on the value of the chance node NASDIP regardless of the value of the decision node D.

Example 5.12 *Recall Example 5.4 in which Xia is considering either buying 10,000 shares of ICK for $10 a share, or buying an option on ICK for $100,000 which would allow her to buy 50,000 shares of ICK for $15 a share in one month. Recall further that she believes that, in one month, the DOW will be either at 10,000 or at 11,000, and ICK will be either at $5 or at $20 per share. Finally, recall that she assigns the following probabilities:*

$$P(ICK = \$5|DOW = 11,000, Decision = Buy\ ICK) = .2$$

$$P(ICK = \$5|DOW = 11,000, Decision = Buy\ option) = .3$$

$$P(ICK = \$5|DOW = 10,000, Decision = buy\ ICK) = .5$$

$$P(ICK = \$5|DOW = 10,000, Decision = Buy\ option) = .6$$

$$P(DOW = \$11,000) = .6.$$

Figure 5.18 shows an influence diagram representing this problem instance. Notice that the value of ICK depends not only on the value of the DOW but also on the decision D. This is because Xia's purchase can affect market activity.

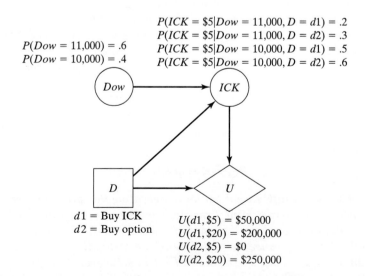

$$P(ICK = \$5|Dow = 11,000, D = d1) = .2$$
$$P(ICK = \$5|Dow = 11,000, D = d2) = .3$$
$$P(ICK = \$5|Dow = 10,000, D = d1) = .5$$
$$P(ICK = \$5|Dow = 10,000, D = d2) = .6$$

$$P(Dow = 11,000) = .6$$
$$P(Dow = 10,000) = .4$$

d1 = Buy ICK
d2 = Buy option

$U(d1, \$5) = \$50,000$
$U(d1, \$20) = \$200,000$
$U(d2, \$5) = \$0$
$U(d2, \$20) = \$250,000$

Figure 5.18: An influence diagram modeling Xia's decision concerning buying ICK or an option on ICK.

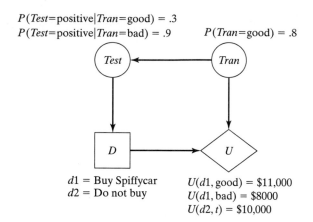

$P(Test=\text{positive}|Tran=\text{good}) = .3$
$P(Test=\text{positive}|Tran=\text{bad}) = .9$

$P(Tran=\text{good}) = .8$

$d1$ = Buy Spiffycar
$d2$ = Do not buy

$U(d1, \text{good}) = \$11{,}000$
$U(d1, \text{bad}) = \$8000$
$U(d2, t) = \$10{,}000$

Figure 5.19: An influence diagram modeling Sam's decision concerning buying the Spiffycar.

Note further that this instance has one more component than the instance in Example 5.11, and we needed to add only one more node to represent it with an influence diagram. So the representation grew linearly with the size of the instance. By contrast, recall that, when we represented the instances with decision trees, the representation grew exponentially.

Example 5.13 Recall Example 5.5 in which Sam has the opportunity to buy a 1996 Spiffycar automobile for $10,000$, and he has a prospect who would be willing to pay $11,000$ for the auto if it is in excellent mechanical shape. Recall further that, if the transmission is bad, Sam will have to spend 3000 to repair it before he could sell the vehicle. So he would end up only with 8000 if he bought the vehicle and its transmission was bad. Finally, recall he has a friend who can run a test on the transmission, and we have the following:

$$P(Test = positive|Tran = good) = .3$$

$$P(Test = positive|Tran = bad) = .9$$

$$P(Tran = good) = .8.$$

Figure 5.19 shows an influence diagram representing this problem instance. Notice that there is an arrow from Tran to Test because the value of the test is probabilistically dependent on the state of the transmission, and there is an arrow from Test to D because the outcome of the test will be known at the time the decision is made. That is, D follows Test in sequence. Note further that the probabilities in the influence diagram are the ones we know. We did not need to use the law of total probability and Bayes' theorem to compute them, as we did when we represented the instance with a decision tree.

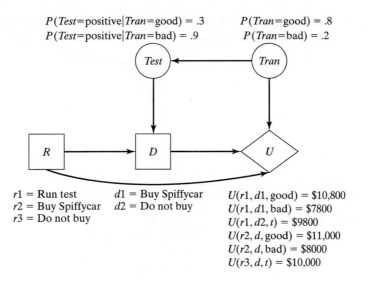

$P(Test{=}positive|Tran{=}good) = .3$ $P(Tran{=}good) = .8$
$P(Test{=}positive|Tran{=}bad) = .9$ $P(Tran{=}bad) = .2$

$r1$ = Run test $d1$ = Buy Spiffycar $U(r1, d1, good) = \$10{,}800$
$r2$ = Buy Spiffycar $d2$ = Do not buy $U(r1, d1, bad) = \$7800$
$r3$ = Do not buy $U(r1, d2, t) = \$9800$
                        $U(r2, d, good) = \$11{,}000$
                        $U(r2, d, bad) = \$8000$
                        $U(r3, d, t) = \$10{,}000$

Figure 5.20: An influence diagram modeling Sam's decision concerning buying the Spiffycar when he must pay for the test.

Example 5.14 *Recall Example 5.6 in which Sam is in the same situation as in Example 5.5 except that the test is not free. Rather, it costs $200. So Sam must decide whether to run the test, buy the car without running the test, or keep his $10,000. Figure 5.20 shows an influence diagram representing this problem instance. Notice that there is an edge from R to D because decision R is made before decision D. Note further that again the representation of the instance grew linearly with the size of the instance.*

You may wonder why there is no edge from R to Test since the value of Test is dependent on the decision R in the sense that the test will not be run if Sam's choice is r2 or r3. If a decision only affects whether the "experiment" at a chance node takes place, and does not affect the outcome of the experiment if it does take place, there is no need to draw an edge from the decision node to the chance node. The reason is as follows: To each influence diagram there corresponds a decision tree, which represents the same problem instance as the influence diagram. By not including an edge from R to Test, we get a decision tree that is symmetrical concerning the Test node rather than the one in Figure 5.10. For the choices that do not run the test, the utilities of the outcomes will be the same for both values of the Test node. So the solution to this decision tree will be the same as the solution to the one in Figure 5.10. Contrast this with the situation in Example 5.12, in which Xia's decision does affect the value of ICK. So we must have an arrow from the decision node D to the chance node ICK.

Next we show a more complex instance, which we did not represent with a decision tree.

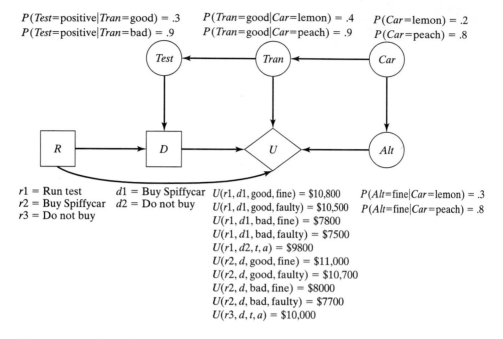

$P(Test=\text{positive}|Tran=\text{good}) = .3$ $P(Tran=\text{good}|Car=\text{lemon}) = .4$ $P(Car=\text{lemon}) = .2$
$P(Test=\text{positive}|Tran=\text{bad}) = .9$ $P(Tran=\text{good}|Car=\text{peach}) = .9$ $P(Car=\text{peach}) = .8$

$r1$ = Run test $d1$ = Buy Spiffycar $U(r1, d1, \text{good}, \text{fine}) = \$10,800$ $P(Alt=\text{fine}|Car=\text{lemon}) = .3$
$r2$ = Buy Spiffycar $d2$ = Do not buy $U(r1, d1, \text{good}, \text{faulty}) = \$10,500$ $P(Alt=\text{fine}|Car=\text{peach}) = .8$
$r3$ = Do not buy $U(r1, d1, \text{bad}, \text{fine}) = \$7800$
                                              $U(r1, d1, \text{bad}, \text{faulty}) = \$7500$
                                              $U(r1, d2, t, a) = \$9800$
                                              $U(r2, d, \text{good}, \text{fine}) = \$11,000$
                                              $U(r2, d, \text{good}, \text{faulty}) = \$10,700$
                                              $U(r2, d, \text{bad}, \text{fine}) = \$8000$
                                              $U(r2, d, \text{bad}, \text{faulty}) = \$7700$
                                              $U(r3, d, t, a) = \$10,000$

Figure 5.21: An influence diagram modeling Sam's decision concerning buying the Spiffycar when the alternator may be faulty.

Example 5.15 *Suppose Sam is in the same situation as in Example 5.14, but with the following modifications. First, Sam knows that 20% of the Spiffycars were manufactured in a plant that produced lemons and 80% of them were man- ufactured in a plant that produced peaches. Furthermore, he knows 40% of the lemons have good transmissions and 90% of the peaches have good transmis- sions. Also, 30% of the lemons have fine alternators and 80% of the peaches have fine alternators. If the alternator is faulty (not fine), it will cost Sam \$300 to repair it before he can sell he vehicle. Figure 5.21 shows an influence diagram representing this problem instance. Notice that the set of chance nodes in the influence diagram constitute a Bayesian network. For example, Tran and Alt are not independent, but they are conditionally independent given Car.*

We close with a large problem instance in the medical domain.

Example 5.16 *This example is taken from Nease and Owens [1997]. Suppose a patient has a non-small-cell carcinoma of the lung. The primary tumor is 1 cm. in diameter, a chest X-ray indicates the tumor does not abut the chest wall or mediastinum, and additional workup shows no evidence of distant metas- tases. The preferred treatment in this situation is thoracotomy. The alternative treatment is radiation. Of fundamental importance in the decision to perform thoracotomy is the likelihood of mediastinal metastases. If mediastinal metas- tases are present, thoracotomy would be contraindicated because it subjects the* patient to a risk of death with no health benefit. If mediastinal metastases are absent, thoracotomy offers a substantial survival advantage as long as the primary tumor has not metastasized to distant organs.

We have two tests available for assessing the involvement of the mediastinum. They are computed tomography (CT scan) and mediastinoscopy. This problem instance involves three decisions. First, should the patient undergo a CT scan? Second, given this decision and any CT results, should the patient undergo mediastinoscopy? Third, given these decisions and any test results, should the patient undergo thoracotomy.

The CT scan can detect mediastinal metastases. The test is not absolutely accurate. Rather, if we let MedMet be a variable whose values are present and absent depending on whether or not mediastinal metastases are present, and CTest be a variable whose values are cpos and cneg depending on whether or not the CT scan is positive, we have

$$P(CTest = cpos | MedMet = present) = .82$$

$$P(CTest = cpos | MedMet = absent) = .19.$$

The mediastinoscopy is an invasive test of mediastinal lymph nodes for determining whether the tumor has spread to those nodes. If we let Mtest be a variable whose values are mpos and mneg depending on whether or not the mediastinoscopy is positive, we have

$$P(MTest = mpos | MedMet = present) = .82$$

$$P(MTest = mpos | MedMet = absent) = .005.$$

The mediastinoscopy can cause death. If we let M be the decision concerning whether to have mediastinoscopy, m1 be the choice to have it, m2 be the choice not to have it, and MedDeath be a variable whose values are mdie and mlive depending on whether the patient dies from the mediastinoscopy, we have

$$P(MedDeath = mdie | M = m1) = .005$$

$$P(MedDeath = mdie | M = m2) = 0.$$

The thoracotomy has a greater chance of causing death than the alternative treatment radiation. If we let T be the decision concerning which treatment to have, t1 be the choice to undergo thoracotomy, t2 be the choice to undergo radiation, and Thordeath be a variable whose values are tdie and tlive depending on whether the patient dies from the treatment, we have

$$P(ThorDeath = tdie | T = t1) = .037$$

$$P(ThorDeath = tdie | T = t2) = .002.$$

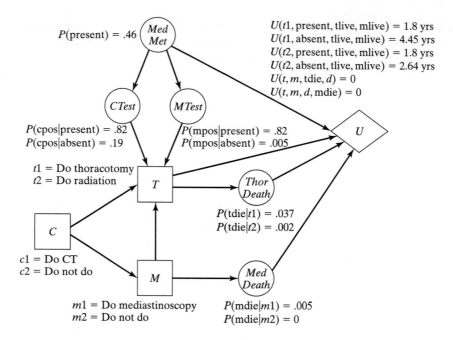

Figure 5.22: An influence diagram modeling the decision as to whether to be treated with thoracotomy.

Finally, we need the prior probability that mediastinal metastases are present. We have

$$P(MedMet = present) = .46.$$

Figure 5.22 shows an influence diagram representing this problem instance. Note that we considered quality adjustments to life expectancy (QALE) and financial costs to be insignificant in this example. The value node is only in terms of life expectancy.

5.2.2   Solving Influence Diagrams

We illustrate how influence diagrams can be solved using examples.

Example 5.17 *Consider the influence diagram in Figure 5.16, which was developed in Example 5.10. To solve the influence diagram, we need to determine which decision choice has the largest expected utility. The expected utility of a* *decision choice is the expected value E of U given the choice is made. We have*

$$
\begin{aligned}
EU(d1) &= E(U|d1) \\
&= P(\$5|d1)U(d1,\$5) + P(\$10|d1)U(d1,\$10) + P(\$20|d1)U(d1,\$20) \\
&= (.25)(\$500) + (.25)(\$1000) + (.5)(\$2000) \\
&= \$1375
\end{aligned}
$$

$$
\begin{aligned}
EU(d2) &= E(U|d2) \\
&= P(\$5|d2)U(d2,\$5) + P(\$10|d2)U(d2,\$10) + P(\$20|d2)U(d2,\$20) \\
&= (.25)(\$1005) + (.25)(\$1005) + (.5)(\$1005) \\
&= \$1005.
\end{aligned}
$$

The utility of our decision is therefore

$$
\begin{aligned}
EU(D) &= \max(EU(d1), EU(d2)) \\
&= \max(\$1375, \$1005) = \$1375,
\end{aligned}
$$

and our decision choice is d1.

Notice in the previous example that the probabilities do not depend on the decision choice. This is because there is no edge from D to $NASDIP$. In general, this is not always the case as the next example illustrates.

Example 5.18 *Consider the influence diagram in Figure 5.18, which was developed in Example 5.12. We have*

$$
\begin{aligned}
EU(d1) &= E(U|d1) \\
&= P(\$5|d1)U(d1,\$5) + P(\$20|d1)U(d1,\$20) \\
&= (.32)(\$50,000) + (.68)(\$200,000) \\
&= \$152,000
\end{aligned}
$$

$$
\begin{aligned}
EU(d2) &= E(U|d2) \\
&= P(\$5|d2)U(d2,\$5) + P(\$20|d2)U(d2,\$20) \\
&= (.42)(\$0) + (.58)(\$250,000) \\
&= \$145,000
\end{aligned}
$$

$$
\begin{aligned}
EU(D) &= \max(EU(d1), EU(d2)) \\
&= \max(\$152,000, \$145,000) = \$152,000,
\end{aligned}
$$

and our decision choice is d1. You may wonder where we obtained the values of P(\$5|d1) and P(\$5|d2). Once we instantiate the decision node, the chance nodes comprise a Bayesian network. We then call a Bayesian network inference *algorithm to compute the needed conditional probabilities. For example, that algorithm would do the following computation:*

$$P(\$5|d1) \;=\; P(\$5|11,000,d1)P(11,000) + P(\$5|10,000,d1)P(10,000)$$
$$=\; (.2)(.6) + (.5)(.4) = .32.$$

Henceforth, we will not usually show the computations done by the Bayesian network inference algorithm. We will only show the results.

Example 5.19 *Consider the influence diagram in Figure 5.19, which was developed in Example 5.13. Since there is an arrow from Test to D, the value of Test will be known when the decision is made. So we need to determine the expected value of U given each value of Test. We have*

$$
\begin{aligned}
EU(d1|\,\text{positive}) \;&=\; E(U|d1,\text{positive}) \\
&=\; P(good|d1,\text{positive})U(d1,good) \\
&\quad +P(bad|d1,\text{positive})U(d1,bad) \\
&=\; (.571429)(\$11,000) + (.428571)(\$8000) \\
&=\; \$9714
\end{aligned}
$$

$$
\begin{aligned}
EU(d2|\,\text{positive}) \;&=\; E(U|d2,\text{positive}) \\
&=\; P(good|d2,\text{positive})U(d2,good) \\
&\quad +P(bad|d2,\text{positive})U(d2,bad) \\
&=\; (.571429)(\$10,000) + (.428571)(\$10,000) \\
&=\; \$10,000
\end{aligned}
$$

$$
\begin{aligned}
EU(D|\,\text{positive}) \;&=\; \max(EU(d1|\,\text{positive}), EU(d2|\,\text{positive})) \\
&=\; \max(\$9714, \$10,000) = \$10,000,
\end{aligned}
$$

and our decision choice is d2. As in the previous example, the needed conditional probabilities are obtained from a Bayesian network inference algorithm.

It is left as an exercise to compute $EU(D|\,\text{negative})$.

Example 5.20 *Consider the influence diagram in Figure 5.20, which was developed in Example 5.14. Now we have two decisions, R and D. Since there is an edge from R to D, decision R is made first and the EU of this decision is the one we need to compute. We have*

$$
\begin{aligned}
EU(r1) \;&=\; E(U|r1) \\
&=\; P(d1,good|r1)U(r1,d1,good) + P(d1,bad|r1)U(r1,d1,bad) \\
&\quad +P(d2,good|r1)U(r1,d2,good) + P(d2,bad|r1)U(r1,d2,bad)
\end{aligned}
$$

We need to compute the conditional probabilities in this expression. D and $Tran$ are not dependent on R. (Decision R determines the value of decision D only in *the sense that decision D does not take place for some values of R.) Therefore, we no longer show $r1$ to the right of the conditioning bar. We use an inference algorithm for Bayesian networks to do these computations. For illustration, we show them:*

$$
\begin{aligned}
P(d1, good) &= P(d1|good)P(good) \\
&= [P(d1|\text{positive})P(\text{positive }|good) \\
&\quad + P(d1|\text{negative})P(\text{negative }|good)]P(good) \\
&= [(0)P(\text{positive }|good) + (1)P(\text{negative }|good)]\,P(good) \\
&= P(\text{negative }|good)P(good) \\
&= (.7)(.8) = .56.
\end{aligned}
$$

The second equality above is obtained because D and $Tran$ are independent conditional on $Test$. The values of $P(d1|\text{positive})$ and $P(d1|\text{negative})$ were obtained by first computing expected utilities as in Example 5.19, and then setting the conditional probability to 1 if the decision choice is the one that maximizes expected utility and to 0 otherwise. It is left as an exercise to show that the other three probabilities are .02, .24, and .18 respectively. We therefore have

$$
\begin{aligned}
EU(r1) &= E(U|r1) \\
&= P(d1, good)U(r1, d1, good) + P(d1, bad)U(r1, d1, bad) \\
&\quad + P(d2, good)U(r1, d2, good) + P(d2, bad)U(r1, d2, bad) \\
&= (.56)(\$10,800) + (.02)(\$7800) + (.24)(\$9800) + (.18)(\$9800) \\
&= \$10320.
\end{aligned}
$$

It is left as an exercise to show that

$$
EU(r2) = \$10,400
$$

$$
EU(r3) = \$10,000.
$$

So

$$
\begin{aligned}
EU(R) &= \max(EU(r1), EU(r2), EU(r2)) \\
&= \max(\$10320, \$10,400, \$10,000) = \$10,400,
\end{aligned}
$$

and our decision choice is $r2$.

Next we show another method for solving the influence diagram which, although it may be less elegant than the previous method, corresponds more to the way decision trees are solved. In this method, with decision R fixed at each of its choices we solve the resultant influence diagram for decision D, and then we use these results to solve for R.

First, fixing R at $r1$, we solve the influence diagram for D. The steps are the same as those in Example 5.19. That is, since there is an arrow from $Test$

to D, the value of Test will be known when the decision is made. So we need to determine the expected value of U given each value of Test. We have

$$
\begin{aligned}
EU(d1|r1, \text{positive}) &= E(U|r1, d1, \text{positive}) \\
&= P(good|\text{positive})U(r1, d1, good) \\
&\quad + P(bad|\text{positive})U(r1, d1, bad) \\
&= (.571429)(11000) + (.429571)(8000) \\
&= \$9522
\end{aligned}
$$

$$
\begin{aligned}
EU(d2|r1, \text{positive}) &= E(U|r1, d2, \text{positive}) \\
&= P(good|\text{positive})U(r1, d2, good) \\
&\quad + P(bad|\text{positive})U(r1, d2, bad) \\
&= (.571429)(\$9800) + (.429571)(\$9800) \\
&= \$9800
\end{aligned}
$$

$$
\begin{aligned}
EU(D|r1, \text{positive}) &= \max(EU(d1|r1, \text{positive}), EU(d2|r1, \text{positive})) \\
&= \max(\$9522, \$9800) = \$9800
\end{aligned}
$$

$$
\begin{aligned}
EU(d1|r1, \text{negative}) &= E(U|r1, d1, \text{negative}) \\
&= P(good|\text{negative})U(r1, d1, good) \\
&\quad + P(bad|\text{negative})U(r1, d1, bad) \\
&= (.965517)(\$10,800) + (.034483)(\$7800) \\
&= \$10,697
\end{aligned}
$$

$$
\begin{aligned}
EU(d2|r1, \text{negative}) &= E(U|r1, d2, \text{negative}) \\
&= P(good|\text{negative})U(r1, d2, good) \\
&\quad + P(bad|\text{negative})U(r1, d2, bad) \\
&= (.965517)(\$9800) + (.034483)(\$9800) \\
&= \$9800
\end{aligned}
$$

$$
\begin{aligned}
EU(D|r1, \text{negative}) &= \max(EU(d1|r1, \text{negative}), EU(d2|r1, \text{negative})) \\
&= \max(\$10,697, \$9800) = \$10,697.
\end{aligned}
$$

As before, the conditional probabilities are obtained from a Bayesian network inference algorithm. Once we have the expected utilities of D, we can compute the expected utility of R as follows:

$$
\begin{aligned}
EU(r1) &= EU(D|r1, \text{positive})P(\text{positive}) + EU(D|r1, \text{negative})P(\text{negative}) \\
&= \$9800(.42) + \$10,697(.58) \\
&= \$10,320.
\end{aligned}
$$

Note that this is the same value we obtained using the other method. We next proceed to compute $EU(r2)$ and $EU(r3)$ in the same way. It is left as an exercise to do so.

The second method illustrated in the previous example extends readily to an algorithm for solving influence diagrams. For example, if we had three decision nodes D_1, D_2, and D_3 in that order, we would first instantiate D_1 to its first decision choice. Then, with D_2 instantiated to its first decision choice, we would solve the influence diagram for D_3. We would then compute the expected utility of D_2's first decision choice. After doing this for all of D_2's decision choices, we would solve the influence diagram for D_2. We would then compute the expected utility of D_1's first decision choice. This process would be repeated for each of D_1's decision choices. It is left an exercise to write an algorithm that implements this method.

The algorithm just illustrated solves the influence diagram by converting it on the fly to a decision tree. Shachter [1988] describes a way to evaluate an influence diagram without transforming it to a decision tree. The method operates directly on the influence diagram by performing arc reversal/node reduction operations. These operations successively transform the diagram, ending with a diagram with only one utility node that holds the utility of the optimal decision. Shenoy [1992] describes another approach for evaluating influence diagrams. The influence diagram is converted to a valuation network, and the nodes are removed from this network by fusing the valuations bearing on the node to be removed. Shenoy's algorithm is slightly more efficient than Shachter's algorithm because it maintains valuations, while Shachter's algorithm maintains conditional probabilities. Additional operations are required to keep the probability distributions normalized. Shachter and Ndilikijlikeshav [1993] modified the arc reversal/node reduction algorithm to avoid these extra operations. The result is an algorithm that has the same efficiency as Shenoy's algorithm. Jensen et al. [1994] developed an algorithm which transforms an influence diagram to a junction tree. (See Section 3.4.) The algorithm is a based on the work in Shenoy [1992] and Jensen et al. [1990].

5.3 Dynamic Networks

After introducing dynamic Bayesian networks, we discuss dynamic influence diagrams.

5.3.1 Dynamic Bayesian Networks

First we develop the theory; then we give an example.

Formulation of the Theory

Bayesian networks do not model temporal relationships among variables. That is, a Bayesian network represents only the probabilistic relationships among a set of variables at some point in time. It does not represent how the value of some variable may be related to its value and the values of other variables at previous points in time. In many problems, however, the ability to model temporal relationships is very important. For example, in medicine it is often important to represent and reason about time in tasks such as diagnosis, prognosis, and treatment options. Capturing the dynamic (temporal) aspects of the problem is also important in artificial intelligence, economics, and biology. Next we discuss dynamic Bayesian networks, which do model the temporal aspects of a problem.

First we need to define a random vector. Given random variables $X_1, \ldots$ and X_n, the column vector

$$\mathbf{X} = \begin{pmatrix} X_1 \\ \vdots \\ X_n \end{pmatrix}$$

is called a **random vector**. A **random matrix** is defined in the same manner. We use $\mathbf{X}$ to denote both a random vector and the set of random variables that constitute $\mathbf{X}$. Similarly, we use $\mathbf{x}$ to denote both a vector value of $\mathbf{X}$ and the set of values that constitute $\mathbf{x}$. The meaning is clear from the context. Given this convention and a random vector $\mathbf{X}$ with dimension n, $P(\mathbf{x})$ denotes the joint probability distribution $P(x_1, \ldots, x_n)$. Random vectors are called **independent** if the sets of variables that constitute them are independent. A similar definition holds for conditional independence.

Now we can define a dynamic Bayesian network, which extends the Bayesian network to model temporal processes. We assume changes occur between discrete time points, which are indexed by the nonnegative integers, and we have some finite number T of points in time. Let $\{X_1, \ldots, X_n\}$ be the set of features whose values change over time, let $X_i[t]$ be a random variable representing the value of X_i at time t for $0 \leq t \leq T$, and let

$$\mathbf{X}[t] = \begin{pmatrix} X_1[t] \\ \vdots \\ X_n[t] \end{pmatrix}.$$

For all t, each $X_i[t]$ has the same space, which depends on i, and we call it the space of X_i. A **simple dynamic Bayesian network** is a Bayesian network containing the variables that constitute the T random vectors $\mathbf{X}[t]$, and which is determined by the following specifications:

1. An initial Bayesian network consisting of (a) an initial DAG $\mathbb{G}_0$ containing the variables in $\mathbf{X}[0]$; and (b) an initial probability distribution P_0 of these variables.

2. A transition Bayesian network that is a template consisting of (a) a transition DAG $\mathbb{G}_\rightarrow$ containing the variables in $\mathbf{X}[t] \cup \mathbf{X}[t+1]$; and (b) a

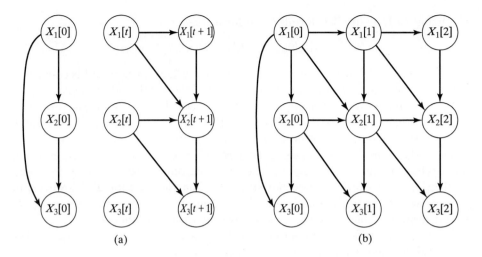

Figure 5.23: Prior and transition Bayesian networks are shown in (a). The resultant dynamic Bayesian network for $T = 2$ is shown in (b). Note that the probability distributions are not shown.

transition probability distribution $P_{\to}$ that assigns a conditional probability to every value of $\mathbf{X}[t+1]$ given every value of $\mathbf{X}[t]$. That is, for every value $\mathbf{x}[t+1]$ of $\mathbf{X}[t+1]$ and value $\mathbf{x}[t]$ of $\mathbf{X}[t]$, we specify

$$P_{\to}(\mathbf{X}[t+1] = \mathbf{x}[t+1]|\mathbf{X}[t] = \mathbf{x}[t]).$$

Since for all t each X_i has the same space, the vectors $\mathbf{x}[t+1]$ and $\mathbf{x}[t]$ both represent values from the same set of spaces. The index in each indicates the random variable that has the value. We showed the random variables above; henceforth we will not show them.

3. The dynamic Bayesian network containing the variables that constitute the T random vectors consists of (a) the DAG composed of the DAG $\mathbb{G}_0$ and for $0 \leq t \leq T - 1$ the DAG $\mathbb{G}_{\to}$ evaluated at t; and (b) the following joint probability distribution:

$$P(\mathbf{x}[0], \dots, \mathbf{x}[T]) = P_0 (\mathbf{x}[0]) \prod_{t=0}^{T-1} P_{\to}(\mathbf{x}[t+1]|\mathbf{x}[t]). \qquad (5.1)$$

Figure 5.23 shows an example. The transition probability distribution entailed by the network in that figure is

$$P_{\to}(\mathbf{x}[t+1]|\mathbf{x}[t]) = \prod_{i=0}^{n} P_{\to}(x_i[t+1]|\mathsf{pa}_i[t+1]),$$

where $\mathsf{pa}_i[t+1]$ denotes the values of the parents of $X_i[t+1]$. Note that there are parents in both $\mathbf{X}[t]$ and $\mathbf{X}[t+1]$.

Owing to Equality 5.1, for all t and for all $\mathbf{x}$,

$$P(\mathbf{x}[t+1]|\mathbf{x}[0],\dots,\mathbf{x}[t]) = P(\mathbf{x}[t+1]|\mathbf{x}[t]).$$

That is, all the information needed to predict a world state at time t is contained in the description of the world at time $t-1$. No information about earlier times is needed. Owing to this feature, we say the process has the **Markov** property. Furthermore, the process is **stationary**. That is, $P(\mathbf{x}[t+1]|\mathbf{x}[t])$ is the same for all t. In general, it is not necessary for a dynamic Bayesian network to have either of these properties. However, they reduce the complexity of representing and evaluating the networks, and they are reasonable assumptions in many applications. The process need not stop at an particular time T. However, in practice we reason only about some finite amount of time. Furthermore, we need a terminal time value to properly specify a Bayesian network.

Probabilistic inference in a dynamic Bayesian network can be done using the standard algorithms discussed in Chapter 3. However, since the size of a dynamic Bayesian network can become enormous when the process continues for a long time, the algorithms can be quite inefficient. There is a special subclass of dynamic Bayesian networks in which this computation can be done more efficiently. This subclass includes Bayesian networks in which the networks in different time steps are connected only through nonevidence variables. An example of such a network is shown in Figure 5.24. The variables labeled with an E are the evidence variables and are instantiated in each time step. We lightly shade nodes representing them. An application that uses such a dynamic Bayesian network is shown in the next subsection. Presently, we illustrate how updating can be done effectively in such networks.

Let $\mathbf{e}[t]$ be the set of values of the evidence variables at time step t, and $\mathbf{f}[t]$ be the set of values of the evidence variables up to and including time step t. Suppose for each value $\mathbf{x}[t]$ of $\mathbf{X}[t]$ we know that

$$P(\mathbf{x}[t]|\mathbf{f}[t]).$$

We now want to compute $P(\mathbf{x}[t+1]|\mathbf{f}[t+1])$. First we have

$$
\begin{aligned}
P(\mathbf{x}[t+1]|\mathbf{f}[t]) &= \sum_{\mathbf{x}[t]} P(\mathbf{x}[t+1]|\mathbf{x}[t],\mathbf{f}[t])P(\mathbf{x}[t]|\mathbf{f}[t]). \\
&= \sum_{\mathbf{x}[t]} P(\mathbf{x}[t+1]|\mathbf{x}[t])P(\mathbf{x}[t]|\mathbf{f}[t]). \qquad (5.2)
\end{aligned}
$$

Using Bayes' theorem, we then have

$$
\begin{aligned}
P(\mathbf{x}[t+1]|\mathbf{f}[t+1]) &= P(\mathbf{x}[t+1]|\mathbf{f}[t],\mathbf{e}[t+1]) \\
&= \alpha P(\mathbf{e}[t+1]|\mathbf{x}[t+1],\mathbf{f}[t])P(\mathbf{x}[t+1]|\mathbf{f}[t]) \\
&= \alpha P(\mathbf{e}[t+1]|\mathbf{x}[t+1])P(\mathbf{x}[t+1]|\mathbf{f}[t]), \qquad (5.3)
\end{aligned}
$$

where α is a normalizing constant. The value of $P(\mathbf{e}[t+1]|\mathbf{x}[t+1])$ can be computed using an inference algorithm for Bayesian networks. We start the

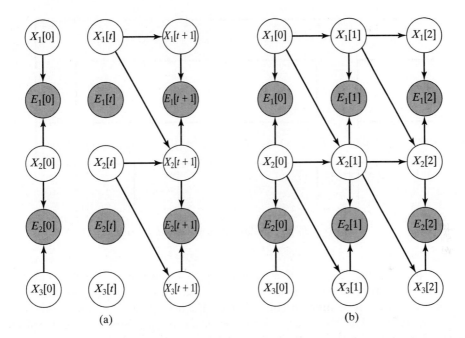

Figure 5.24: Prior and transition Bayesian networks, for the case in which the networks in different time slots are connected only through nonevidence variables, are shown in (a). The resultant dynamic Bayesian network for $T = 2$ is shown in (b).

process by computing $P(\mathbf{x}[0]|\mathbf{f}[0]) = P(\mathbf{x}[0]|\mathbf{e}[0])$. Then at each time step $t + 1$ we compute $P(\mathbf{x}[t + 1]|\mathbf{f}[t + 1])$ using Equalities 5.2 and 5.3 in sequence. Note that to update the probability for the current time step we need only values computed at the previous time step and the evidence at the current time step. We can throw out all previous time steps, which means we need keep only enough network structure to represent two time steps.

A simple way to view the process is as follows: We define

$$P'(\mathbf{x}[t + 1]) \equiv P(\mathbf{x}[t + 1]|\mathbf{f}[t]),$$

which is the probability distribution of $\mathbf{X}[t+1]$ given the evidence in the first t time steps. We determine this distribution at the beginning of time step $t + 1$ using Equality 5.2, and then we discard all previous information. Next we obtain the evidence in the time step $t + 1$ and update P' using Equality 5.3.

An Example: Mobile Target Localization

We show an application of dynamic Bayesian networks to mobile target localization, which was developed by Basye et al. [1993]. The **mobile target localization problem** involves tracking a target while maintaining knowledge of one's own location. Basye et al. [1993] developed a world in which a target

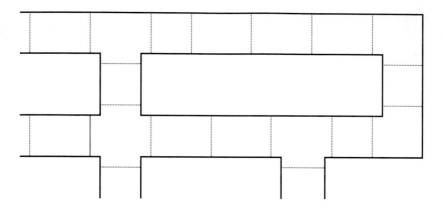

Figure 5.25: Tessellation of corridor layout.

and a robot reside. The robot is supplied with a map of the world, which is divided into corridors and junctions. Figure 5.25 shows a portion of one such world tessellated according to this scheme. Each rectangle in that figure is a different region. The state space for the location of the target is the set of all the regions shown in the figure, and the state space for the location of the robot is the set of all these regions augmented with four quadrants to represent the directions in which the robot can face. Let L_R and L_A be random variables whose values are the locations of the robot and the target respectively.

Both the target and the robot are mobile, and the robot has sensors it uses to maintain knowledge of its own location and to track the target's location. Specifically, the robot has a sonar ring consisting of eight sonar transducers, configured in pairs pointing forward, backward, and to each side of the robot. Each sonar gives a reading between 30 and 6000 millimeters, where 6000 means 6000 or more. Figure 5.26 shows one set of readings obtained from the sonars on entering a T-junction. We want the sensors to tell us what kind of region we

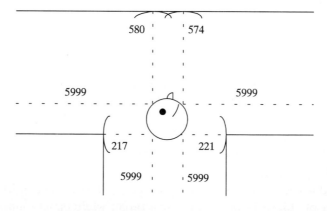

Figure 5.26: Sonar readings upon entering a T-junction.

are in. So we need a mapping from the raw sensor data to an abstract sensor space consisting of the following: corridor, T-junction, L-junction, dead end, open space, and crossing. This mapping could be deterministic or probabilistic. Basye et al. [1993] discuss methods for developing it. Sonar data is notoriously noisy and difficult to disambiguate. A sonar that happens to be pointed at an angle of greater than 70 degrees to a wall, will likely not see that wall at all. So we will assume the relationship is probabilistic. The robot also has a forward pointing camera to identify the presence of its target. The camera can detect the presence of a blob identified to be the target. If it does not detect a suitable blob, this evidence is reported. If it does find a suitable blob, the size of the blob is used to estimate its distance from the robot, which is reported in rather gross units (i.e., within 1 meter, between 2 and 3 meters, and so forth). The detection of a blob at a given distance is only probabilistically dependent on the actual presence of the target at that distance. Let E_R be a random variable whose value is the sonar reading, which tells the robot something about its own location, and let E_A be a random variable whose value is the camera reading, which tells the robot something about the target's location relative to the robot. It follows from the previous discussion that E_R is probabilistically dependent on L_R, and E_A is probabilistically dependent on both L_R and L_A. At each time step, the robot obtains readings from its sonar ring and camera. For example, it may obtain the sonar readings in Figure 5.26, and its camera may inform it that the target is visible at a certain distance.

The actions available to the robot and to the target are as follows: travel down the corridor the length of one region, turn left around the corner, turn around, and so forth. In the dynamic Bayesian network model, these actions are simply performed in some preprogrammed probabilistic way, which is not related to the sensor data. So the location of the robot at time $t + 1$ is a probabilistic function of its location at time t. When we model the problem with a dynamic influence diagram in the Section 5.3.2, the robot will decide on its action based on the sensor data. The target's movement could be determined by a person or could also be preprogrammed probabilistically.

In summary, the random variables in the problem are as follows:

Variable	What the Variable Represents
L_R	Location of the robot
L_A	Location of the target
E_R	Sensor reading regarding location of robot
E_A	Camera reading regarding location of target relative to robot

Figure 5.27 shows a dynamic Bayesian network that models this problem (without showing any actual probability distributions). The prior probabilities in the prior network represent information initially known about the location of the robot and the target. The conditional probabilities in the transition Bayesian network can be obtained from data. For example, $P(e_A|l_R, l_A)$ can be obtained by repeatedly putting the robot and the target in positions l_R and l_A, respectively, and seeing how often reading e_A is obtained.

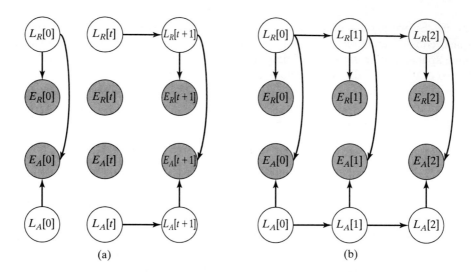

Figure 5.27: The prior and transition Bayesian networks for the mobile target mobilization problem are shown in (a). The resultant dynamic Bayesian network for $T = 2$ is shown in (b).

Note that although the robot can sometimes view the target, the robot makes no effort to track. That is, the robot moves probabilistically according to some scheme. Our goal is for the robot to track the target. However, to do this it must decide on where to move next based on the sensor data and camera reading. As mentioned, we need dynamic influence diagrams to produce such a robot. They are discussed next.

5.3.2   Dynamic Influence Diagrams

Again we first develop the theory, and then we give an example.

Formulation of the Theory

To create a **dynamic influence diagram** from a dynamic Bayesian network we need only add decision nodes and a value node. Figure 5.28 shows the high level structure of such a network for $T = 2$. The chance node at each time step in that figure represents the entire DAG at that time step, and so the edges represent sets of edges. There is an edge from the decision node at time t to the chance nodes at time $t + 1$ because the decision made at time t can affect the state of the system at time $t + 1$. The problem is to determine the decision at each time step that maximizes expected utility at some point in the future. Figure 5.28 represents the situation in which we are determining the decision at time 0 that maximizes expected utility at time 2. The final utility could, in general, be based on the earlier chance nodes and even the decision nodes. However, we do not show such edges to simplify the diagram. Furthermore, the

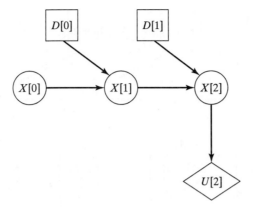

Figure 5.28: The high-level structure of a dynamic influence diagram.

final expected utility is often a weighted sum of expected utilities independently computed for each time step up to the point in the future we are considering. Such a utility function is called **time-separable**.

In general, dynamic influence diagrams can be solved using the algorithm presented in Section 5.2.2. The next section contains an example.

An Example: Mobile Target Localization Revisited

After we present the model, we show some results concerning a robot constructed according to the model.

The Model Recall the robot discussed in Section 5.3.1. Our goal is for the robot to track the target by deciding on its move at time t based on its evidence at time t. So now we allow the robot to make a decision $D[t]$ at time t as to which action it will take, where the value of $D[t]$ is a result of maximizing some expected utility function based on the evidence in time step t. We assume there is error in the robot's movement. So the location of the robot at time $t + 1$ is a probabilistic function of its location at the previous time step and the action taken. The conditional probability distribution of L_R is obtained from data as discussed at the end of Section 5.3.1 That is, we repeatedly place the robot in a location, perform an action, and then observe its new location.

The dynamic influence diagram, which represents the decision at time t and in which the robot is looking three time steps into the future, is shown in Figure 5.29. Note that there are crosses through the evidence variables at time t to indicate that their values are already known. We need to maximize expected utility using the probability distribution conditional on these values and the values of all previous evidence variables. Recall that at the end of Section 5.3.1 we called this probability distribution P' and we discussed how it can be obtained. First we need to define a utility function. Suppose we decide

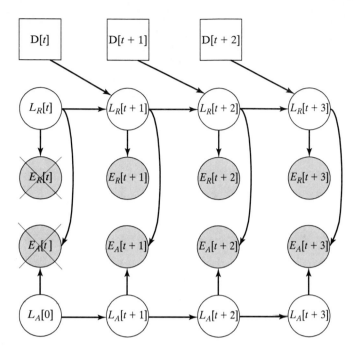

Figure 5.29: The dynamic influence diagram modeling the robot's decision as to which action to take at time t.

to determine the decision at time t by looking M time steps into the future. Let

$$\mathsf{d}_M = \{d[t], d[t+1], \dots, d[t+M-1]\}$$

be a set of values of the next M decisions including the current one and

$$\mathsf{f}_M = \{e_R[t+1], e_A[t+1], e_R[t+2], e_A[t+2], \dots, e_R[t+M], e_A[t+M]\}$$

be a set of values of the evidence variables observed after the decisions are made. For $1 \le k \le M$ let d_k and f_k respectively be the first k decisions and evidence pairs in each of these sets. Define

$$U_k(\mathsf{f}_k, \mathsf{d}_k) = -\min_u \sum_v dist(u,v) P'(L_A[t+k]=v)|\mathsf{f}_k, \mathsf{d}_k), \qquad (5.4)$$

where $dist$ is the Euclidean distance, the sum is taken over all values v in the space of L_A, and the minimum is calculated over all values u in the space of L_A. Recall from the beginning of Section 5.3.1 that the robot is supplied with a map of the world. It uses this map to find every element in the space of L_A. The idea is that if we make these decisions and obtain these observations at time $t+k$, the sum in Equality 5.4 is the expected value of the distance between the target and a given location u. The smaller this expected value is the more likely it is the target is close to u. The location $\breve{u}$ which has the minimum expected value is then our best guess at where the target is if we make these decisions and obtain these observations. So the utility of the decisions and the observations is the expected value for $\breve{u}$. The minus sign occurs because we maximize expected utility.

We then have

$$EU_k(\mathsf{d}_k) = \sum_{\mathsf{f}_k} U_k(\mathsf{f}_k, \mathsf{d}_k) P'(\mathsf{f}_k | \mathsf{d}_k). \qquad (5.5)$$

This expected utility involves only the situation k time steps into the future. To take into account all time steps up to and including time $t + M$, we use a utility function that is a weighted sum of the utilities at each time step. We then have

$$EU(\mathsf{d}_M) = \sum_{k=1}^{M} \gamma_k EU_k(\mathsf{d}_k), \qquad (5.6)$$

where γ_k decreases with k to discount the impact of future consequences. Note that implicitly $\gamma_k = 0$ for $k > M$. Note further that we have a time-separable utility function. We choose the decision sequence that maximizes this expected utility in Equality 5.6, and we then make the first decision in this sequence at time step t.

In summary, the process proceeds as follows: In time step t the robot updates its probability distribution based on the evidence (sensor and camera readings) obtained in that step. Then the expected utility of a sequence of decisions (actions) is evaluated. This is repeated for other decision sequences, and the one that maximizes expected utility is chosen. The first decision (action) in that sequence is executed, the sensor and camera readings in time step $t + 1$ are obtained, and the process repeats.

The computation of $P'(\mathsf{f}_k | \mathsf{d}_k)$ in Equality 5.5 for all values of f can be quite expensive. Dean and Wellman [1991] discuss ways to reduce the complexity of the decision evaluation.

Result: Emergent Behavior Basye et al. [1993] developed a robot using the model just described, and they observed some interesting, unanticipated emergent behavior. By **emergent behavior** we mean behavior that is not purposefully programmed into the robot, but that emerges as a consequence of the model. For example, when the target moves towards a fork, the robot stays close behind it, since this will enable it to determine which branch the target takes. However, when the target moves towards a cul-de-sac, the robot keeps fairly far away, whereas Basye et al. [1993] expected it to remain close behind. Analyzing the probability distributions and results of the value function, they discovered that the model allows for the possibility that the target might slip behind the robot, leaving the robot unable to determine the location of the target without additional actions. If the robot stays some distance away, regardless of what action the target takes, the observations made by the robot

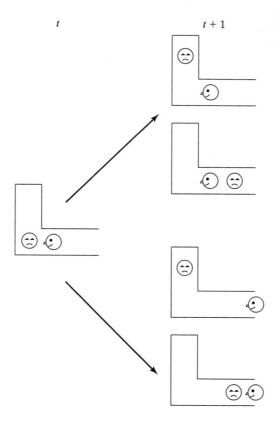

Figure 5.30: Staying close to the target may not be optimal.

are sufficient to determine the target's location. Figure 5.30 illustrates the situation. In time step t the robot is close to the target as the target is about to enter the cul-de-sac. If the robot stays close as illustrated by the top path, in time step $t+1$ it is just as likely that the target will slip behind the robot as it is that the target will move up the cul–de–sac. If the target does slip behind the robot, it will no longer be visible. However, if the robot backs off, as illustrated by the bottom path, the robot will be able determine the location of the target regardless of what the target does. When considering its possible observations in time step $t+1$, the observation "target not visible" would not give the robot a good idea as to the target's location. So the move to stay put is less valued than the move to back off.

Larger-Scale Systems   The method used to control our robot could be applied to a more complex system. Consider the following example taken from Russell and Norvig [1995]. An autonomous vehicle uses a vision-based lane-position sensor to keep it in the center of its lane. The position sensor's accuracy is directly affected by rain and also by an uneven road surface. Furthermore,

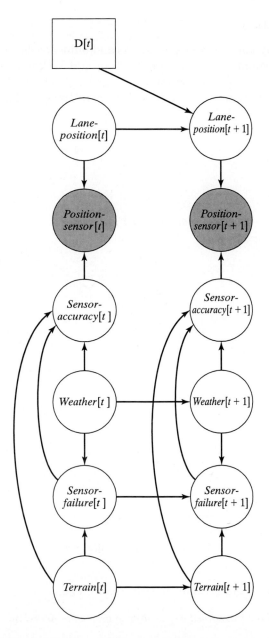

Figure 5.31: Two time steps in a dynamic influence diagram, which models the decision faced by an autonomous vehicle.

both rain and a bumpy road could cause the position sensor to fail. Sensor failure of course affects the sensor's accuracy. Two time steps in a dynamic influence diagram, which models this situation, appear in Figure 5.31.

Other Applications

Applications of dynamic Bayesian networks and influence diagrams include planning under uncertainty (e.g., our robot) Dean and Wellman [1991], analysis of freeway traffic using computer vision Huang et al. [1994], modeling the stepping patterns of the elderly to diagnose falls Nicholson [1996], and audiovisual speech recognition Nefian et al. [2002].

EXERCISES

Section 5.1

Exercise 5.1 *Solve the decision tree in Figure 5.32.*

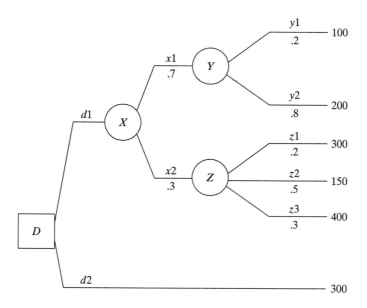

Figure 5.32: A decision tree.

Exercise 5.2 *Solve the decision tree in Figure 5.33.*

Exercise 5.3 *Show the solved decision tree given the decision tree in Figure 5.3.*

Exercise 5.4 *Show that if we use $R = 1000$ in Example 5.3 the decision will be to buy NASDIP.*

Exercise 5.5 *Compute the conditional probabilities in the tree in Figure 5.8 from the conditional probabilities given in Example 5.5.*

Exercise 5.6 *Show that $EU(D_1) = \$9820$ and $EU(D_2) = \$10,697$ for the decision tree in Figure 5.10.*

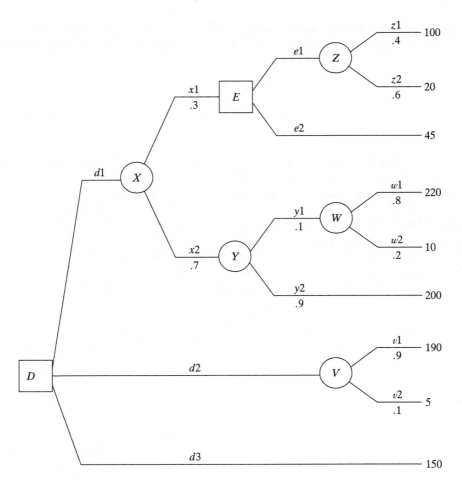

Figure 5.33: A decision tree with three alternatives.

Exercise 5.7 *Consider Example 5.7. Suppose Leonardo has the opportunity to consult the weather forecast before deciding on whether to take his umbrella. Suppose further that the weather forecast says it will rain on 90% of the days it actually does rain, and 20% of the time it says it will rain on days it does not rain. That is,*

$$P(Forecast = rain | R = rain) = .9$$

$$P(Forecast = rain | R = no\ rain) = .2.$$

As before, suppose Leonardo judges that

$$P(R = rain) = .4.$$

Show the decision tree representing this problem instance assuming the utilities in Example 5.7. Solve that decision tree.

Exercise 5.8 *Consider again Example 5.7. Assume that, if it rains, there is a .7 probability the suit will only need to go to the cleaners, and a .3 probability it will be ruined. Assume again that*

$$P(R = rain) = .4.$$

Assess your own utilities for this situation, show the resultant decision tree, and solve that tree.

Exercise 5.9 *Consider Example 5.9. Assume that your life expectancy from birth is 75 years. Assess your own QALE for the situation described in that example, show the resultant decision tree, and solve that tree.*

Exercise 5.10 *Suppose Jennifer is a young, potential capitalist with $1000 to invest. She has heard glorious tales of many who have made fortunes in the stock market. So she decides to do one of three things with her $1000. She could buy an option on Techjunk which would allow her to buy 1000 shares of Techjunk for $22 a share in one month. She could use the $1000 to buy shares of Techjunk. Finally, she could leave the $1000 in the bank earning .07% annually. Currently, Techjunk is selling for $20 a share. Suppose further that she feels there is a .5 chance the NASDAQ will be at 1500 in two months and a .5 chance it will be at 2000. She feels that, if it is at 1500, there is a .3 chance Techjunk will be at $23 a share and a .7 chance it will be at $15 a share. She feels that, if the NASDAQ is at 2000, there is a .7 chance Techjunk will be at $26 a share and a .3 chance it will be $20 a share. Show a decision tree that represents this decision and solve that decision tree.*

Let $P(NASDAQ = 1500) = p$ and $P(NASDAQ = 2000) = 1 - p$. Determine the maximal value of p for which the decision would be to buy the option. Is there any value of p for which the decision would be to buy the stock?

Exercise 5.11 *This exercise is based on an example in Clemen [1996]. In 1984, Penzoil and Getty Oil agreed to a merger. However, before the deal was closed, Texaco offered Getty a better price. So Gordon Getty backed out of the Penzoil deal and sold to Texaco. Penzoil immediately sued, won the case, and was awarded $11.1 billion. A court order reduced the judgment to $2 billion, but interest and penalties drove the total back up to $10.3 billion. James Kinnear, Texaco's chief executive officer, said he would fight the case all the way up to the U.S. Supreme Court because, he argued, Penzoil had not followed Security and Exchange Commission regulations when negotiating with Getty. In 1987, just before Penzoil was to begin filing liens against Texaco, Texaco offered to give Penzoil $2 billion to settle the entire case. Hugh Liedke, chairman of Penzoil, indicated that his advisors told him a settlement between $3 billion and $5 billion would be fair.*

What should Liedke do? Two obvious choices are 1) he could accept the $2 billion; and 2) he could turn it down. Let's say that he is also considering counteroffering $5 billion. If he does, he judges that Texaco will accept the counteroffer with probability .17, refuse the counteroffer with probability .5, or *counter back in the amount of $3 billion with probability .33. If Texaco does counter back, Liedke will then have the decision as to whether to refuse or accept the counteroffer. Liedke assumes that, if he simply turns down the $2 billion with no counteroffer, or if Texaco refuses his counteroffer, or if he refuses their return counteroffer, the matter will end up in court. If it does go to court, he judges that there is .2 probability Penzoil will be awarded $10.3 billion, a .5 probability they will be awarded $5 billion, and a .3 probability they will get nothing.*

Show a decision tree that represents this decision, and solve that tree.

What finally happened? Liedke simply refused the $2 billion. Just before Penzoil began to file liens on Texaco's assets, Texaco filed for protection from creditors under Chapter 11 of the federal bankruptcy code. Penzoil then submitted a financial reorganization plan on Texaco's behalf. Under the plan, Penzoil would receive about $4.1 billion. Finally, the two companies agreed on $3 billion as part of Texaco's financial reorganization.

Section 5.2

Exercise 5.12 *Solve the influence diagram in Figure 5.17, which was developed in Example 5.11.*

Exercise 5.13 *Represent the problem instance in Exercise 5.7 with an influence diagram. Solve that influence diagram.*

Exercise 5.14 *Represent the problem instance in Exercise 5.8 with an influence diagram. Solve that influence diagram.*

Exercise 5.15 *Represent the problem instance in Exercise 5.9 with an influence diagram. Solve that influence diagram.*

Section 5.3

Exercise 5.16 *Assign parameter values to the dynamic Bayesian network in Figure 5.27, and compute the conditional probability of the locations of the robot and the target at time 1 given certain evidence at times 0 and 1.*

Exercise 5.17 *Assign parameter values to the dynamic influence diagram in Figure 5.29, and determine the decision at time 0 based on certain evidence at time 0 and by looking 1 time step into the future.*

Part III

Learning

Chapter 6

Parameter Learning: Binary Variables

Initially, the DAG in a Bayesian network was hand-constructed by a domain expert. Then the conditional probabilities were assessed by the expert, learned from data, or obtained using a combination of both techniques. For example, the DAG in the Bayesian network in Figures 1.10 on page 47 was hand-constructed, and its conditional probabilities were learned from data. Eliciting Bayesian networks from experts can be a laborious and difficult procedure in the case of large networks. So researchers developed methods that could learn the DAG from data; furthermore, they formalized methods for learning the conditional probabilities from data. We present these methods in the chapters that follow. In a Bayesian network, the DAG is called the **structure** and the values in the conditional probability distributions are called the **parameters**. In this chapter and the next, we address the problem of learning the parameter values from data. This chapter assumes that each random variable has a space of size 2 (i.e., the variables are binary), while Chapter 7 concerns multinomial and continuous variables. Chapters 8–11 discuss learning the structure from data. Chapters 8 and 9 present a Bayesian method for learning structure, while Chapter 10 presents an alternative method called constraint-based. Furthermore, in that chapter we show how causal influences can be learned from data. Chapter 11 compares the methods and presents several examples of learning both Bayesian networks and causal influences.

We can learn parameter values only from data when the probabilities are relative frequencies, which were discussed in Section 1.2.1. We will use the term **relative frequency** to refer to such probabilities. The term **probability** will ordinarily refer to a subjective probability (degree of belief) as discussed in Section 1.2.2. We will represent our belief concerning the value of a relative frequency using a subjective probability distribution.

This chapter proceeds as follows: In Section 6.1 we discuss learning a single parameter, which means we obtain an estimate of a single relative frequency.

Section 6.2 further discusses the beta density function, which is introduced in Section 6.1. Section 6.3 shows how to compute a probability interval for a relative frequency, which enables us to express our confidence in its estimate. Section 6.4 addresses the problem of learning all the parameters in a Bayesian network. Learning parameters in the case of missing data items is covered in Section 6.5. Finally, Section 6.6 shows a method for determining the variance in the probability distribution of an inferred relative frequency in a Bayesian network from the probability distributions of the parameters specified in the network.

6.1   Learning a Single Parameter

After discussing subjective probability distributions of relative frequencies, we develop a method for estimating a relative frequency from data.

6.1.1   Probability Distributions of Relative Frequencies

First we discuss developing a probability distribution of a relative frequency when all numbers in $[0,1]$ are considered equally likely to be the relative frequency. Then we introduce a family of density functions that can be used to represent an instance in which we do not feel all numbers in $[0,1]$ are equally likely to be the relative frequency. Finally, we present the general method for representing belief concerning a relative frequency using a subjective probability distribution.

All Relative Frequencies Equally Probable

We present an urn example illustrating a probability distribution of a relative frequency. First we discuss the case in which the number of possible relative frequencies are discrete; then we address the continuous case.

The Discrete Case   Suppose we have 101 coins in an urn, each with a different propensity for landing heads. The propensity for the first coin is .00, for the second it is .01, for the third it is .02, ... and for the last it is 1.00. This situation is depicted in Figure 6.1. This means that, if we tossed, for example, the second coin many times, the relative frequency with which it landed heads would approach .01. Suppose next that I pick a coin at random from the urn and I am about to toss it. What probability should I assign to it landing heads? It seems most would agree that, if we knew the relative frequency with which the coin landed heads, our probability of it landing heads would be that relative frequency. For example, if we knew we were tossing the second coin, our probability[1] would be .01 because this is the relative frequency with which the second coin lands heads. Let *Side* be a random variable whose values are the

---
[1]Henceforth, I will simply refer to probabilities as "our probablity," meaning only my belief. It is simplest to state things that way. No one is compelled to agree.

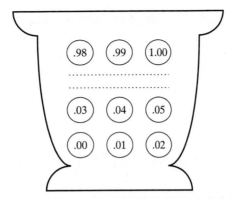

Figure 6.1: An urn containing 101 coins, each with a different propensity for landing heads.

outcomes of the toss, namely, *heads* and *tails*, and let F be a random variable whose range consists of the 101 values of the relative frequencies. Then

$$P(Side = heads | f) = f.$$

Note that we used f to denote $F = f$, but we did not use shorthand notation for $Side = heads$. This is consistent with the policy discussed in Section 1.1.4. If we use the principle of indifference (see Section 1.1.1) to assign equal probabilities to all relative frequencies (coins), we can represent our probability distribution by the Bayesian network in Figure 6.2. Such a Bayesian network is called an **augmented Bayesian network** because it includes a node representing our belief about a relative frequency. Note that we shade that node. "Augmented

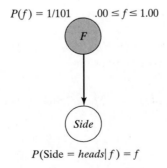

Figure 6.2: A Bayesian network representing our belief concerning tossing a coin picked at random from the urn in Figure 6.1

Bayesian network" is formally defined in Section 6.4.2. We have, then,

$$P(Side = heads) = \sum_{f=.00}^{1.00} P(Side = heads | f) P(f)$$

$$= \sum_{f=.00}^{1.00} f \left(\frac{1}{101} \right)$$

$$= \left(\frac{1}{100 \times 101} \right) \sum_{f=0}^{100} f = \left(\frac{1}{100 \times 101} \right) \left(\frac{100 \times 101}{2} \right) = \frac{1}{2}.$$

It is not surprising that the probability turns out to be .5 since the relative frequencies are distributed evenly on both sides of .5. What is this probability value of .5? It is unlikely that it is the relative frequency with which the sampled coin will land heads as that would be the case only if we picked the coin with a propensity of .5. Rather it is our subjective probability (degree of belief) of the coin landing heads on the first toss just as .6 was our subjective probability of whether the Bulls won (discussed in Section 1.2.2). Just as to how we would be indifferent between receiving a small prize if the Bulls won and receiving the same small prize if a white ball was drawn from an urn containing 60% white balls, we would be indifferent between receiving a small prize if the coin landed heads and receiving the same small prize if a white ball was drawn from an urn containing 50% white balls. Note that the value .5 is also the relative frequency with which heads will occur if we repeatedly sample coins with replacement and toss each sampled coin once.

The Continuous Case   Suppose now that there is a continuum of coins in the urn, for every real number f between 0 and 1 there is exactly one coin with a propensity of f for landing heads, and we again pick a coin at random. Then our probability distribution of the random variable, whose values are the relative frequencies with which the coins land heads, is given by the uniform density function. That is,

$$\rho(f) = 1.$$

This density function is shown in Figure 6.3. In this case, our probability of landing heads on the first toss is given by

$$P(Side = heads) = \int_0^1 P(Side = heads | f) \rho(f) df$$

$$= \int_0^1 f(1) df = \frac{1}{2}.$$

Again, this result is not surprising.

Now consider some repeatable experiment such as the tossing of a thumbtack, or sampling dogs and determining whether or not they eat the potato chips I

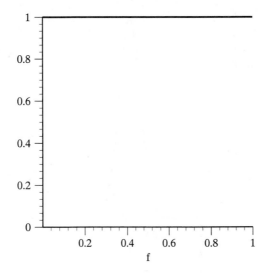

Figure 6.3: The uniform density function.

offer them. (I choose this example because I have no idea whether a particular dog would eat potato chips.) If we feel all numbers in $[0,1]$ are equally likely to be the value of the relative frequency, then we can model our belief concerning the relative frequency using the uniform density function, just as we did in the case of the coins in the urns.

All Relative Frequencies Not Equally Probable

In many, if not most, cases we do not feel all numbers in $[0,1]$ are equally likely to be the value of a relative frequency. Even in the case of tossing a thumbtack, I would not feel extreme values as probable as ones nearer the middle. More notably, if I tossed a coin from my pocket, I would think it most probable that the relative frequency is around .5. In this case, I would want a density function similar to the one in Figure 6.4. If I sampled individuals in the United States and determined whether they brushed their teeth, I would think it most probable that the relative frequency would be around .9. In this case, I would want a density function like the one in Figure 6.5. Next, we develop such density functions. Namely, we discuss a family of density functions called the beta density functions, which provide a natural way for quantifying prior beliefs about relative frequencies and updating these beliefs in the light of evidence.

Before proceeding, we need review the **gamma function**, which is defined as follows:

$$\Gamma(x) = \int_0^\infty t^{x-1} e^{-t} dt.$$

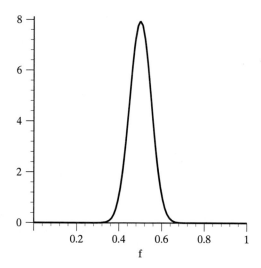

Figure 6.4: The $beta(f; 50, 50)$ density function.

The integral on the right converges if and only if $x > 0$. If x is an integer ≥ 1, it is possible to show that

$$\Gamma(x) = (x - 1)!.$$

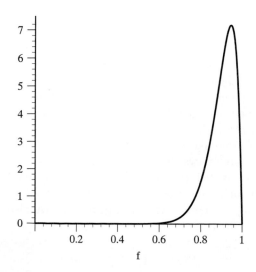

Figure 6.5: The $beta(f; 18, 2)$ density function.

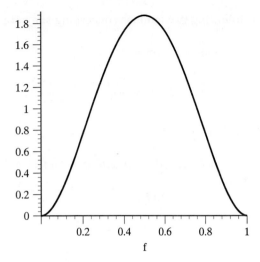

Figure 6.6: The $beta(f; 3, 3)$ density function.

So the gamma function is a generalization of the factorial function. The following lemma deals with the gamma function:

Lemma 6.1 *We have*

$$\frac{\Gamma(x+1)}{\Gamma(x)} = x.$$

Proof. *The proof is left as an exercise.* ∎

Now we can define the beta density function.

Definition 6.1 *The **beta density function** with parameters a, b, $N = a + b$, where a and b are real numbers > 0, is*

$$\rho(f) = \frac{\Gamma(N)}{\Gamma(a)\Gamma(b)} f^{a-1}(1-f)^{b-1} \qquad 0 \le f \le 1.$$

*A random variable F that has this density function is said to have a **beta distribution**.*

We refer to the beta density function as $beta(f; a, b)$.

The uniform density function in Figure 6.3 is $beta(f; 1, 1)$. Figures 6.4, 6.5, and 6.6 show other beta density functions. Notice that the larger the values of a and b, the more the mass is concentrated around $a/(a+b)$. For this and other reasons, when a and b are integers, we often say the values of a and b are such that the probability assessor's experience is equivalent to having seen the first outcome occur a times in $a + b$ trials. The results in Section 6.1.2 give further justification for this statement.

We will need the following two lemmas concerning the beta density function:

Lemma 6.2 *If a and b are real numbers > 0 then*

$$\int_0^1 f^a(1-f)^b df = \frac{\Gamma(a+1)\Gamma(b+1)}{\Gamma(a+b+2)}.$$

Proof. *The proof is left as an exercise.* ∎

Lemma 6.3 *If F has a beta distribution with parameters $a, b, N = a+b$, then*

$$E(F) = \frac{a}{N}.$$

Proof. *We have*

$$
\begin{aligned}
E(F) &= \int_0^1 f\rho(f)df \\[6pt]
&= \int_0^1 f \frac{\Gamma(N)}{\Gamma(a)\Gamma(b)} f^{a-1}(1-f)^{b-1}df \\[6pt]
&= \frac{\Gamma(N)}{\Gamma(a)\Gamma(b)} \int_0^1 f^a(1-f)^{b-1}df \\[6pt]
&= \frac{\Gamma(N)}{\Gamma(a)\Gamma(b)} \frac{\Gamma(a+1)\Gamma(b)}{\Gamma(a+b-1+2)} \\[6pt]
&= \frac{\Gamma(N)}{\Gamma(a)\Gamma(b)} \frac{\Gamma(a+1)\Gamma(b)}{\Gamma(N+1)} \\[6pt]
&= \frac{a}{N}.
\end{aligned}
$$

The fourth equality above is due to Lemma 6.2 and the last is due to Lemma 6.1.

∎

Representing Belief Concerning a Relative Frequency

Next we formalize and generalize the notions introduced in the preceding discussion. Suppose we have some two-outcome random process such as the tossing of a thumbtack, and we let X be a random variable whose values, 1 and 2, are the outcomes of the experiment[2]. We assume that we can represent our belief concerning the relative frequency with which X equals 1 using a random variable F whose space consists of numbers in the interval $[0,1]$[3]. The expected value

---

[2] Recall that in previous chapters we ordinarily used $x1$ and $x2$ as the values of variable X when we do not use names that have semantic connotations. For the sake of notational simplicity, in this chapter we simply use 1 and 2 as the values of all variables.

[3] It is somewhat standard to use theta (θ) for a random variable whose value is a relative frequency. However, owing to the similarity of capital and small theta, we find it more lucid to use F for relative frequency.

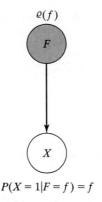

$\varrho(f)$

$P(X = 1|F = f) = f$

Figure 6.7: The probability distribution of F represents our belief concerning the relative frequency with which X equals 1.

$E(F)$ is defined to be our **estimate of the relative frequency**. We further assume our beliefs are such that

$$P(X = 1|f) = f. \qquad (6.1)$$

That is, if we knew for a fact that the relative frequency with which X equals 1 was f, our belief concerning the occurrence of 1 in the first execution of the experiment would be f. This situation is represented by the Bayesian network in Figure 6.7. Given this assumption, the theorem that follows shows that our subjective probability for the first trial is the same as our estimate of the relative frequency.

Theorem 6.1 *Suppose X is a random variable with two values 1 and 2, and F is another random variable such that*

$$P(X = 1|f) = f.$$

Then

$$P(X = 1) = E(F),$$

where E stands for expected value.

Proof. *We prove the case from which F is continuous. Owing to the law of total probability,*

$$
\begin{aligned}
P(X = 1) &= \int_0^1 P(X = 1|f)\rho(f)df \\
&= \int_0^1 f\rho(f)df \\
&= E(F).
\end{aligned}
$$

∎

Corollary 6.1 *If the conditions in Theorem 6.1 hold, and F has a beta distribution with parameters $a, b, N = a + b$, then*

$$P(X = 1) = \frac{a}{N}.$$

Proof. *The proof follows immediately from Theorem 6.1 and Lemma 6.3.*   ∎

Example 6.1 *Suppose I am going to repeatedly toss a coin from my pocket. Since I would feel it highly probable that the relative frequency is around .5, I might feel my prior experience is equivalent to having seen 50 heads in 100 tosses. Therefore, I could represent my belief concerning the relative frequency with the beta(f; 50, 50) density function, which is shown in Figure 6.4. Due to the previous corollary, for the first toss of the coin,*

$$P(Side = heads) = \frac{50}{50 + 50} = .5.$$

Furthermore, .5 is our estimate of the relative frequency with which the coin will land heads.

Example 6.2 *Suppose I am going to repeatedly toss a thumbtack. Based on its structure, I might feel it should land heads about half the time, but I would not be nearly so confident as I would with the coin from my pocket. So I might feel my prior experience is equivalent to having seen 3 heads (landing on its flat side) in 6 tosses, which means I could represent my belief concerning the relative frequency with the beta(f; 3, 3) density function, which is shown in Figure 6.6. Due to the previous corollary, for the first toss of the thumbtack,*

$$P(Side = heads) = \frac{3}{3 + 3} = .5.$$

Furthermore, .5 is our estimate of the relative frequency with which the thumbtack will land heads.

Example 6.3 *Suppose I am going to sample individuals in the United States and determine whether they brush their teeth. In this case, I might feel my prior experience is equivalent to having seen 18 individuals brush their teeth out of 20 sampled. Therefore, I could represent my belief concerning the relative frequency with the beta(f; 18, 2) density function, which is shown in Figure 6.5. Due to the previous corollary, for the first individual sampled,*

$$P(Teeth = brushed) = \frac{18}{18 + 2} = .9.$$

Furthermore, .9 is our estimate of the relative frequency of individuals who brush their teeth.

6.1.2   Learning a Relative Frequency

Recall the coins in the urn in Figure 6.1. We determined that, if we picked a coin at random and tossed it, our probability of landing heads on that toss would be .5. Suppose now that we've tossed it 20 times and it landed heads 18 times. Would we still assign a probability of .5 to the next toss? We would not because we would now feel it more probable that the coin is one of the coins with propensity around .9 than we would that it is one of the coins with a small propensity. Next we discuss how to quantify such a change in belief.

Suppose we perform M trials of a random process. Let $X^{(h)}$ be a random variable whose value is the outcome of the hth trial, and let F be a random variable whose probability distribution represents our belief concerning the relative frequency. We assume that if we knew the value of F for certain, then we would feel the $X^{(h)}$s are mutually independent, and our probability for each trial would be that relative frequency. That is, if, for example, we were tossing a coin whose propensity we knew to be .5, then our probability for the hth toss would be .5 regardless of the outcomes of the first $h - 1$ tosses.

Why should we make the assumption in the previous paragraph? First, there is evidence that separate trials are independent as far as the actual relative frequencies are concerned. That is, as discussed in Section 1.2.1, in 1946 J.E. Kerrich conducted many experiments indicating that the relative frequency appears to approach a limit; in 1971 G.R. Iversen et al. ran many experiments with dice indicating that what we call random processes do indeed generate random sequences; and in 1928 R. von Mises proved that separate trials are independent if we assume that the relative frequency approaches a limit and a random sequence is generated.

If one denies that objective relative frequencies exist, one may not find the preceding argument so compelling as to why separate trials should be independent conditional on F as far as our beliefs go. Bruno de Finetti developed a purely subjective argument for having such beliefs concerning separate trials. His argument is as follows: He assumed **exchangeability**, which means an individual assigns the same probability to all sequences of the same length containing the same number of each outcome. For example, if we denote a heads by a 1 and a tails by 2, the individual assigns the same probability to these two sequences:

$$1212121222 \quad \text{and} \quad 1221122212.$$

Furthermore, this same probability is assigned to all other sequences of length ten that have precisely four 1's and six 0's. De Finetti's assumption of exchangeability is similar to von Mises' assumption that the sequence of outcomes is a random sequence (See Section 1.2.1.). However, exchangeability has to do with an individual's beliefs, whereas randomness has to do with an objective property of nature. Exchangeability could serve as a Bayesian definition of "random process." That is, a repeatable experiment is considered a **random process** by an individual if the individual's beliefs (probabilities) concerning sequences of outcomes of the experiment satisfy exchangeability. Given the assumption of

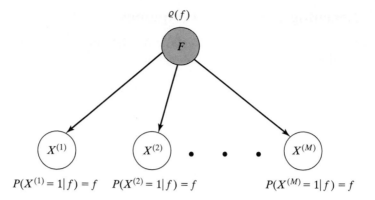

$$\varrho(f)$$

$$P(X^{(1)} = 1|f) = f \quad P(X^{(2)} = 1|f) = f \qquad P(X^{(M)} = 1|f) = f$$

Figure 6.8: A Bayesian network representing the fact that the $X^{(h)}$s are independent conditional on F.

exchangeability, in 1937, B. de Finetti proved that there must be some random variable that renders the individual's beliefs concerning the trials independent. These matters are discussed more in Good [1965].

Given all of the preceding, we will assume that the $X^{(h)}$s are mutually independent conditional on the value of the relative frequency. This independence is represented by the Bayesian network in Figure 6.8.

Next we give formal definitions concerning the notion just developed.

Definition 6.2 *Suppose*

1. *We have a set of random variables (or random vectors)* $D = \{X^{(1)}, X^{(2)},$
   $\dots, X^{(M)}\}$ *such that each* $X^{(h)}$ *has the same space;*

2. *There is a random variable* F *with density function* ρ *such that the* $X^{(h)}$s
   are mutually independent conditional on F, *and for all values* f *of* F, *all*
   $X^{(h)}$ *have the same probability distribution conditional on* f.

Then D *is called a **sample** of size M with parameter* F.

Given a sample, the density function ρ is called the **prior density function of the parameters** relative to the sample. It represents our prior belief concerning the unknown parameters. Given a sample, the marginal distribution of each $X^{(h)}$ is the same. This distribution is called the **prior distribution** relative to the sample. It represents our prior belief concerning each trial.

In general, F is a set containing more than one element, at least one of which is a random variable. Furthermore, the members of D may be random vectors. Such a case is discussed in Section 6.4.3. (Random vectors were defined in Section 5.3.1.) However, in the case of binomial samples, which are discussed next, F contains only one element and the members of D are random variables.

Definition 6.3 *Suppose we have a sample of size M such that*

  1. each $X^{(h)}$ has space $\{1, 2\}$;

  2. $\mathsf{F} = \{F\}$, F has space $[0, 1]$, and for $1 \leq h \leq M$

$$P(X^{(h)} = 1|f) = f. \tag{6.2}$$

  *Then D is called a **binomial sample** of size M with parameter F.*

Example 6.4 *Suppose we sample a coin from the urn in Figure 6.1 and toss it twice. Let 1 be the outcome if a heads occurs, 2 be the outcome if a tails occurs, and $X^{(h)}$'s value be the outcome of the hth toss. Clearly, the density function for F is beta$(f; 1, 1)$. So $\mathsf{D} = \{X^{(1)}, X^{(2)}\}$ is a binomial sample of size 2 with parameter F. Owing to Theorem 6.1 and Corollary 6.1, the prior distribution relative to the sample is*

$$P(X^{(h)} = 1) = E(F) = \frac{1}{1 + 1} = \frac{1}{2}.$$

Example 6.5 *Suppose we toss a thumbtack 10 times. Let 1 be the outcome if a heads occurs, 2 be the outcome if a tails occurs, and $X^{(h)}$'s value be the outcome of the hth toss. Furthermore, let the density function for F be beta$(f; 3, 3)$. So $\mathsf{D} = \{X^{(1)}, X^{(2)}, \ldots, X^{(10)}\}$ is a binomial sample of size 10 with parameter F. Owing to Theorem 6.1 and Corollary 6.1, the prior distribution relative to the sample is*

$$P(X^{(h)} = 1) = E(F) = \frac{3}{3 + 3} = \frac{1}{2}.$$

Before developing theory that enables us to update our belief about the next trial from a binomial sample, we present two more lemmas.

Lemma 6.4 *Suppose F has a beta distribution with parameters $a, b, N = a + b$, s and t are two integers ≥ 0, and $M = s + t$. Then*

$$E\left(F^s[1 - F]^t\right) = \frac{\Gamma(N)}{\Gamma(N + M)} \frac{\Gamma(a + s)\Gamma(b + t)}{\Gamma(a)\Gamma(b)}.$$

Proof. We have

$$
\begin{aligned}
E\left(F^s[1 - F^t]\right) &= \int_0^1 f^s(1 - f)^t \rho(f) df \\
&= \int_0^1 f^s(1 - f)^t \frac{\Gamma(N)}{\Gamma(a)\Gamma(b)} f^{a-1}(1 - f)^{b-1} df \\
&= \frac{\Gamma(N)}{\Gamma(a)\Gamma(b)} \int_0^1 f^{a+s-1}(1 - f)^{b+t-1} df \\
&= \frac{\Gamma(N)}{\Gamma(a)\Gamma(b)} \frac{\Gamma(a + s)\Gamma(b + t)}{\Gamma(a + s + b + t)} \\
&= \frac{\Gamma(N)}{\Gamma(N + M)} \frac{\Gamma(a + s)\Gamma(b + t)}{\Gamma(a)\Gamma(b)}.
\end{aligned}
$$

The fourth equality is due to Lemma 6.2.   ∎

Lemma 6.5 *Suppose F has a beta distribution with parameters $a, b, N = a+b$, and s and t are two integers ≥ 0. Then*

$$\frac{f^s(1-f)^t\rho(f)}{E(F^s[1-F]^t)} = beta(f; a+s, b+t).$$

Proof. *Let $M = s+t$. We have*

$$
\begin{aligned}
\frac{f^s(1-f)^t\rho(f)}{E(F^s[1-F]^t)} &= \frac{f^s(1-f)^t\frac{\Gamma(N)}{\Gamma(a)\Gamma(b)}f^{a-1}(1-f)^{b-1}}{\frac{\Gamma(N)}{\Gamma(N+M)}\frac{\Gamma(a+s)\Gamma(b+t)}{\Gamma(a)\Gamma(b)}} \\
&= \frac{\Gamma(N+M)}{\Gamma(a+s)\Gamma(b+t)}f^{a+s-1}(1-f)^{b+t-1} \\
&= beta(f; a+s, b+t).
\end{aligned}
$$

The first equality is due to Lemma 6.4. ∎

We now obtain results enabling us to update our belief from a binomial sample.

Theorem 6.2 *Suppose*

1. *D is a binomial sample of size M with parameter F;*

2. *we have a set of values*

$$\mathsf{d} = \{x^{(1)}, x^{(2)}, \ldots, x^{(M)}\}$$

   *of the variables in D [the set d is called our **data set** (or simply data)];*

3. *s is the number of variables in d equal to 1; and*

4. *t is the number of variables in d equal to 2.*

   Then

$$P(\mathsf{d}) = E(F^s[1-F]^t).$$

Proof. *We prove the case for which F is continuous. We have*

$$
\begin{aligned}
P(\mathsf{d}) &= \int_0^1 P(\mathsf{d}|f)\rho(f)df \\
&= \int_0^1 \prod_{h=1}^M P(x^{(h)}|f)\rho(f)df \\
&= \int_0^1 f^s(1-f)^t\rho(f)df \\
&= E(F^s[1-F]^t).
\end{aligned}
$$

The second equality results from the fact that the variables in D are conditionally independent conditional on F, and the third equality is obtained by repeatedly applying Equality 6.2 in Definition 6.3. ∎

Recall from Section 1.2.1 that we also use the word "sample" for the set of observations, which is our data set d. It is clear from the context which we mean.

Corollary 6.2 *If the conditions in Theorem 6.2 hold, and F has a beta distribution with parameters $a, b, N = a + b$, then*

$$P(\mathsf{d}) = \frac{\Gamma(N)}{\Gamma(N + M)} \frac{\Gamma(a + s)\Gamma(b + t)}{\Gamma(a)\Gamma(b)}.$$

Proof. *The proof follows immediately from Theorem 6.2 and Lemma 6.4.* ∎

Example 6.6 *Suppose we have the binomial sample in Example 6.4, and*

$$\mathsf{d} = \{1, 2\}.$$

Then $a = b = 1$, $N = 2$, $s = 1$, $t = 1$, $M = 2$, and due to the preceding theorem,

$$P(\mathsf{d}) = \frac{\Gamma(2)}{\Gamma(2 + 2)} \frac{\Gamma(1 + 1)\Gamma(1 + 1)}{\Gamma(1)\Gamma(1)} = \frac{1}{6}.$$

Similarly, if $\mathsf{d}' = \{1, 1\}$, $P(\mathsf{d}') = 1/3$. You may wonder why the probability of two heads is twice the probability of a head followed by a tail. Note that

$$P(\mathsf{d}) = P(X^{(1)} = 1, X^{(2)} = 2) = P(X^{(2)} = 2|X^{(1)} = 1)P(X^{(1)} = 1)$$

while

$$P(\mathsf{d}') = P(X^{(1)} = 1, X^{(2)} = 1) = P(X^{(2)} = 1|X^{(1)} = 1)P(X^{(1)} = 1).$$

Intuitively, $P(X^{(2)} = 1|X^{(1)} = 1)$ is greater than $P(X^{(2)} = 2|X^{(1)} = 1)$, because once the first toss results in heads, it becomes more likely we have a coin with propensity for landing heads. So the probability of heads on the second toss is increased.

Note that in the previous example, $P(\mathsf{d})$ is the relative frequency with which we will obtain data d when we repeatedly sample a coin with replacement from the urn and toss it twice.

Example 6.7 *Suppose we have the binomial sample in Example 6.5, and*

$$\mathsf{d} = \{1, 1, 2, 1, 1, 1, 1, 1, 2, 1\}.$$

Then $a = b = 3$, $N = 6$, $s = 8$, $t = 2$, $M = 10$, and due to the preceding corollary,

$$P(\mathsf{d}) = \frac{\Gamma(6)}{\Gamma(6 + 10)} \frac{\Gamma(3 + 8)\Gamma(3 + 2)}{\Gamma(3)\Gamma(3)} = .001998.$$

Theorem 6.3 *If the conditions in Theorem 6.2 hold, then*

$$\rho(f|\mathsf{d}) = \frac{f^s(1-f)^t\rho(f)}{E(F^s[1-F]^t)},$$

where $\rho(f|\mathsf{d})$ *is the density function of* F *conditional on* $\mathsf{D} = \mathsf{d}$.
Proof. *We have*

$$
\begin{aligned}
\rho(f|\mathsf{d}) &= \frac{P(\mathsf{d}|f)\rho(f)}{P(\mathsf{d})} \\
&= \frac{f^s(1-f)^t\rho(f)}{E(F^s[1-F]^t)}.
\end{aligned}
$$

The first equality is due to Bayes' theorem. The second equality is due to the fact that the variables in D *are independent conditional on* F, *Equality 6.2, and Theorem 6.2.* ∎

Corollary 6.3 *Suppose the conditions in Theorem 6.2 hold, and* F *has a beta distribution with parameters* $a, b, N = a + b$. *That is,*

$$\rho(f) = beta(f; a, b).$$

Then

$$\rho(f|\mathsf{d}) = beta(f; a + s, b + t).$$

Proof. *The proof follows immediately from Theorem 6.3 and Lemma 6.5.* ∎

Given a sample, the density function of F conditional on data d is called the **updated density function of the parameters** relative to the sample and the data d. It represents our posterior belief concerning the unknown parameters. The previous corollary shows that when we update a beta density function relative to a binomial sample, we obtain another beta density function. For this reason, we say the set of all beta density functions is a **conjugate family of density functions** for binomial sampling.

Example 6.8 *Suppose we have the binomial sample in Example 6.5 and the data in Example 6.7. Then* $a = b = 3$, $s = 8$, *and* $t = 2$. *Due to the preceding corollary,*

$$\rho(f|\mathsf{d}) = beta(f; 3 + 8, 3 + 2) = beta(f; 11, 5).$$

Figure 6.9 shows the original density function and the updated density function.

Suppose we have a sample D of size M, a set d of values (data) of the variables in D, and we create a sample of size $M + 1$ by adding another variable $X^{(M+1)}$ to the sample. Then the conditional probability distribution of $X^{(M+1)}$ given d is called the **updated distribution** relative to the sample and the data d. It represents our posterior belief concerning the next trial.

In the case of binomial samples, $E(F|\mathsf{d})$ is our **posterior estimate of the relative frequency** with which $X = 1$. The following theorem shows that it is the same as $P(X^{(M+1)} = 1|\mathsf{d})$.

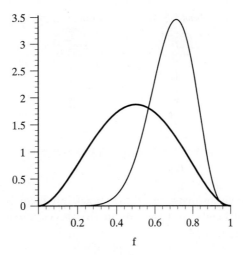

Figure 6.9: The thickly plotted density function is $beta(f; 3, 3)$ and represents our prior belief concerning the relative frequency of heads. The thinly plotted one is $beta(f; 11, 5)$, and represents our posterior belief after we have seen 8 heads in 10 trials.

Theorem 6.4 *Suppose the conditions in Theorem 6.2 hold, and we create a binomial sample of size $M + 1$ by adding another variable $X^{(M+1)}$. Then, if* D *is the binomial sample of size M, the updated distribution relative to the sample and data* d *is given by*

$$P\left(X^{(M+1)} = 1 | \mathbf{d}\right) = E(F|\mathbf{d}).$$

Proof. *We have*

$$
\begin{aligned}
P\left(X^{(M+1)} = 1 | \mathbf{d}\right) &= \int_0^1 P(X^{(M+1)} = 1 | f, \mathbf{d}) \rho(f | \mathbf{d}) df \\
&= \int_0^1 P(X^{(M+1)} = 1 | f) \rho(f | \mathbf{d}) df \\
&= \int_0^1 f \rho(f | \mathbf{d}) df \\
&= E(F | \mathbf{d}).
\end{aligned}
$$

The second equality results from the fact that $X^{(M+1)}$ is independent of the variables in D *conditional on F, and the third equality is obtained by applying Equality 6.2 in Definition 6.3.* ∎

Corollary 6.4 *If the conditions in Theorem 6.4 hold and F has a beta distribution with parameters $a, b, N = a + b$, then*

$$P\left(X^{(M+1)} = 1 | \mathbf{d}\right) = \frac{a + s}{N + M}.$$

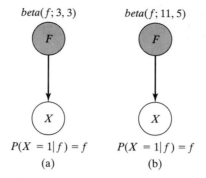

Figure 6.10: The Bayesian network in (a) shows our prior belief concerning the relative frequency of heads, and the one in (b) shows our posterior belief after we have seen 8 heads in 10 trials.

Proof. *The proof follows immediately from Theorem 6.4, Corollary 6.3, and Lemma 6.3.*   ∎

Notice that, as $M \to \infty$, our probability (which is also our estimate of the relative frequency) converges to the relative frequency.

Example 6.9 *Suppose we have the binomial sample in Example 6.5 and the data in Example 6.7. Then $a = 3$, $N = 6$, $s = 8$, and $M = 10$. Due to the preceding corollary, the probability of heads for the 11th toss is given by*

$$P\left(X^{(M+1)} = 1 | \mathbf{d}\right) = \frac{3+8}{6+10} = .6875.$$

Furthermore, .6875 is our new estimate of the relative frequency with which the coin will land heads.

In a Bayesian network representation of our posterior beliefs based on a sample, we often drop the superscript on X and represent our beliefs as shown in Figure 6.10. That figure shows our prior beliefs and posterior beliefs in the case of the previous examples.

6.2   More on the Beta Density Function

First, we discuss the case in which the parameters a and b in the beta density function are not integers. Then we present guidelines for assessing the values of a and b. Finally, we show an argument for using the beta density function to quantify our beliefs.

6.2.1   Nonintegral Values of a and b

So far we have shown only examples in which a and b are both integers ≥ 1. Next we discuss nonintegral values. Figure 6.11 shows the $beta(f; .2, .2)$ density func-

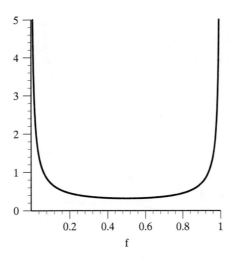

Figure 6.11: The *beta*$(f; .2, .2)$ density function.

tion. As that figure illustrates, as a and b approach 0, we become increasingly certain the relative frequency is either 0 or 1.

You may wonder when we would ever use nonintegral values of a and b. The following example gives such a case.

Example 6.10 *This example is taken from Berry [1996]. Glass panels in high-rise buildings sometimes break and fall to the ground. A particular case involved 39 broken panels. In their quest for determining why the panels broke, the owners wanted to analyze the broken panels, but they could only recover three of them. These three were found to contain nickel sulfide (NiS), a manufacturing flaw which can cause panels to break. In order to determine whether they should hold the manufacturer responsible, the owners then wanted to determine how probable it was that all 39 panels contained NiS. So they contacted a glass expert.*

The glass expert testified that among glass panels that break, only 5% contain NiS. However, NiS tends to be pervasive in production lots. So, given that the first panel sampled, from a particular production lot of broken panels, contains NiS, the expert felt the probability is .95 that the second panel sampled also does. It was known all 39 panels came from the same production lot. Let $X^{(h)}$'s value be either NiS or ⌐NiS depending on whether the hth panel contains NiS. Given the preceding, the expert's probabilities are as follows (all probabilities are conditional on the panels breaking and coming from the same production lot):

$$P\left(X^{(1)} = NiS\right) = .05$$

$$P\left(X^{(2)} = NiS | X^{(1)} = NiS\right) = .95.$$

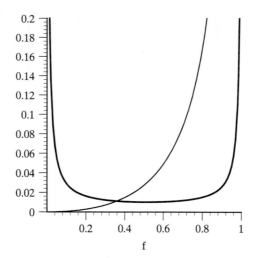

Figure 6.12: The thickly plotted density function represents an expert's prior belief concerning the relative frequency of NiS in glass panels, while the thinly plotted one represents his belief after he learns 3 window panels contain NiS.

So, if we model the expert's beliefs with a beta density function, Corollaries 6.1 and 6.4 imply that

$$\frac{a}{a+b} = .05 \qquad and \qquad \frac{a+1}{a+1+b} = .95.$$

Solving for a and b yields

$$a = \frac{1}{360} \qquad b = \frac{19}{360}.$$

This is an alternative technique for assessing a and b. Namely, we assess the probability for the first trial. Then we assess the conditional probability for the second trial given the first one is a "success." So the expert's belief concerning the relative frequency of NiS is beta(f; 1/360, 19/360). Therefore, after sampling three windows and seeing that they all contain NiS, due to Corollary 6.3, his updated belief is beta(f; 3 + 1/360, 19/360). The original density function and the updated one are shown in Figure 6.12. Notice how his belief changes from believing that the relative frequency is either very low or very high (with more density on the low end) to believing it is most likely very high.

Furthermore, due to Corollary 6.4, we have that the probability that any one of the other 36 panels (the next one sampled) contains NiS is given by

$$\frac{a+s}{N+M} = \frac{\frac{1}{360}+3}{\frac{20}{360}+3} = .983.$$

We are really most interested in whether all 36 remaining panels contain NiS. We can determine the probability of this event as follows. The expert's

current belief, based on the three windows sampled, is beta(f; $3+1/360$, $19/360$).
Therefore, owing to Corollary 6.2, the probability of the next 36 containing NiS
is equal to

$$\frac{\Gamma\left(3+\frac{20}{360}\right)}{\Gamma\left(3+\frac{20}{360}+36\right)} \frac{\Gamma\left(3+\frac{1}{360}+36\right)\Gamma\left(\frac{19}{360}+0\right)}{\Gamma\left(3+\frac{1}{360}\right)\Gamma\left(\frac{19}{360}\right)} = .866.$$

6.2.2 Assessing the Values of a and b

Next, we give the following guidelines for choosing the size of a and b in the beta density function, when we are assessing our beliefs concerning a relative frequency:

- $a = b = 1$: These values mean we consider all numbers in $[0, 1]$ equally likely to be the relative frequency with which the random variable assumes each of its values. We would use these values when we feel we have no knowledge at all concerning the value of the relative frequency. We might also use these values to try to achieve objectivity in the sense that we impose none of our beliefs concerning the relative frequency on the learning algorithm. We only impose the fact that we know at most two things can happen. An example might be when we are learning the probability of lung cancer given smoking from data, and we want to communicate our result to the scientific community. The scientific community would not be interested in our prior belief, but in what the data had to say. Note that we might not actually believe a priori that all relative frequencies are equally probable, but our goal is not to impose this belief on the learning algorithm. Essentially, the posterior probability represents the belief of an agent that has no prior belief concerning the relative frequency.

- $a, b > 1$: These values mean we feel it more probable that the relative frequency with which the random variable assumes its first value is around $a/(a + b)$. The larger the values of a and b, the more we believe this. We would use such values when we want to impose our beliefs concerning the relative frequency on the learning algorithm. For example, if we were going to toss a coin taken from the pocket, we might take $a = b = 50$.

- $a, b < 1$: These values mean we feel it more probable that the relative frequency with which the random variable assumes one of its values is low, although we are not committed to which it is. If we take $a = b \approx 0$ (almost 0), then we are almost certain the relative frequency with which it assumes one value is very close to 1. We would also use values like these when we want to impose our beliefs concerning the relative frequency on the learning algorithm. Example 6.10 shows a case in which we would choose values less than 1. Notice that such prior beliefs are quickly overwhelmed by data. For example, if $a = b = .1$, and our data d consists of seeing X

take the value 1 in a single trial,

$$P\left(X^{(M+1)} = 1 | \mathbf{d}\right) = \frac{.1 + 1}{.2 + 1} = .917. \tag{6.3}$$

Intuitively, we thought a priori that the relative frequency with which X assumes one of its values is high. The fact that it took the value 1 once makes us believe it is probably that value.

- $a < 1, b > 1$: These values mean we feel it is more probable the relative frequency with which X assumes its first value is low. We would also use values like these when we want to impose our beliefs concerning the relative frequency on the learning algorithm

You may wonder why, when we assume no knowledge at all about the relative frequency ($a = b = 1$), and the data $\mathbf{d}$ contains s occurrences of 1 in N trials, we have, due to Corollary 6.4, that

$$P\left(X^{(M+1)} = 1 | \mathbf{d}\right) = \frac{1 + s}{2 + N}.$$

You may feel the answer should be s/N because this is all the data has to say. An intuition for this is obtained by looking at an example in which our sample size is one. Suppose I am going to sample dogs and determine whether or not they eat the potato chips I offer them. Since I have no idea whether a particular dog would eat potato chips, I assign $a = b = 1$. Suppose further that it turns out the first dog sampled eats the potato chips. Using Equality 6.3, we obtain a probability of .67, whereas $s/N = 1$. The first value (.67) seems to more accurately model my belief for the next trial. In terms of a comparison to an urn lottery, it means I would be indifferent between receiving a small prize if the next dog sampled ate the potato chips and receiving the same small prize if a white ball were drawn from an urn containing 67% white balls. However, the second value (1) means I would be indifferent between receiving a small prize if the next dog sampled ate the potato chips and receiving the same small prize if a white ball were drawn from an urn containing 100% white balls. I would feel this way only if I were certain the next dog would eat potato chips, and I would not be certain of this after one trial. Note that if I take $a = b \approx 0$ (almost 0), then my updated belief after one trial would be almost 1. This makes sense since, in this case, my prior belief was that I was almost certain that either all dogs would eat potato chips or all would not. So after, seeing one dog eat them, I become almost certain all will eat them.

6.2.3   Why the Beta Density Function?

The use of the beta distribution to represent our beliefs concerning a relative frequency is intuitively appealing and has a long tradition. Indeed, in 1889 the actuary G.F. Hardy and in 1897 the mathematician W.A. Whitworth proposed quantifying prior beliefs with beta distributions. However, are there any cogent arguments we should use such distributions? Next we present two such arguments.

First, if we initially consider all numbers in $[0, 1]$ equally likely to be the relative frequency and therefore use the uniform density function to represent our prior beliefs, it is a mathematical consequence of the theory that the updated density function is beta.

Second, in 1982 Sandy Zabell proved that, if we make certain assumptions about an individual's beliefs, then that individual must use the beta density function to quantify any prior beliefs about a relative frequency. Zabell's theorem actually concerns the Dirichlet distribution, which is a generalization of the beta distribution. So before giving the theorem, we briefly review the Dirichlet distribution. This distribution is discussed in detail in the next chapter.

Definition 6.4 *The **Dirichlet density function** with parameters $a_1, a_2, \ldots, a_r$, $N = \sum_{k=1}^{r} a_k$, where $a_1, a_2, \ldots, a_r$ are integers ≥ 1, is*

$$\rho(f_1, f_2, \ldots, f_{r-1}) = \frac{\Gamma(N)}{\prod_{k=1}^{r} \Gamma(a_k)} f_1^{a_1-1} f_2^{a_2-1} \cdots f_r^{a_r-1} \quad 0 \leq f_k \leq 1, \ \sum_{k=1}^{r} f_k = 1.$$

*Random variables $F_1, F_2, \ldots, F_r$, that have this density function, are said to have a **Dirichlet distribution**.*

The Dirichlet density function is denoted $Dir(f_1, f_2, \ldots, f_{r-1}; a_1, a_2, \ldots, a_r)$.

Note that the value of F_r is uniquely determined by the values of the first $r - 1$ variables (i.e., $f_r = 1 - \sum_{h=1}^{r-1} f_h$). That is why ρ is a function of only $r - 1$ variables. Let's show that the beta density function is the same as the Dirichlet density function for $r = 2$. In this case, the Dirichlet density function is

$$\begin{aligned} \rho(f_1) &= \frac{\Gamma(N)}{\Gamma(a_1)\Gamma(a_2)} f_1^{a_1-1} f_2^{a_2-1} & 0 \leq f_k \leq 1, \ f_1 + f_2 = 1 \\ &= \frac{\Gamma(N)}{\Gamma(a_1)\Gamma(a_2)} f_1^{a_1-1} (1 - f_1)^{a_2-1} & 0 \leq f_1 \leq 1, \end{aligned}$$

which is the beta density function.

As already mentioned, we show examples of Dirichlet density functions and prove properties of the Dirichlet family in the next chapter. Presently, we give only Zabell's theorem. First, we need some definitions and discussion. We start with a formal definition of exchangeability:

Definition 6.5 *Let $\mathsf{D} = \{X^{(1)}, X^{(2)}, \ldots, X^M\}$ be an ordered set (sequence) of random variables, each with space $\{1, 2, \ldots, r\}$. If, for every two sets of values d' and d'' of the variables in D, such that each of the r values occurs the same number of times in d' and d'', we have*

$$P(\mathsf{d}') = P(\mathsf{d}''),$$

*the sequence is said to be **finite exchangeable**.*

Note that P represents an individual's beliefs. So exchangeability is relative to an individual.

Example 6.11 *Suppose* $\mathsf{D} = \{X^{(1)}, X^{(2)}, \ldots, X^{(7)}\}$ *represent the outcomes of seven throws of a six-sided die. Then, if we assume the sequence is finite exchangeable, it follows that*

$$P(\{1, 3, 2, 1, 4, 2, 1\}) = P(\{1, 1, 1, 2, 2, 3, 4\})$$

because in both sets 1 *occurs three times,* 2 *occurs twice,* 3 *and* 4 *each occur once, and* 5 *and* 6 *do not occur at all.*

Definition 6.6 *Let* $X^{(1)}, X^{(2)}, X^{(3)}, \ldots$ *be an infinite sequence of random variables, each with space* $\{1, 2, \ldots, r\}$. *If for every* M, *the sequence of the first* M *variables is finite exchangeable, the sequence is said to be* **infinite exchangeable**.

Exchangeability seems to be a minimal assumption in the case of experiments that are in some sense considered random processes. (Indeed, recall that we offered exchangeability as a Bayesian definition of "random process" in Section 6.1.2.) For example, it seems many individuals would assign the same probability to the two sequences of die throws in Example 6.11.

Definition 6.7 *Let* $X^{(1)}, \ldots, X^{(M)}, X^{(M+1)}$ *be a sequence of random variables, each with space* $\{1, 2, \ldots, r\}$, *and let* $\mathsf{D} = \{X^{(1)}, X^{(2)}, \ldots, X^{(M)}\}$. *Suppose for every set of values* d *of the variables in* D, *we have*

$$P(X^{(M+1)} = k | \mathsf{d}) = g_k(s_k, M),$$

where s_k *is the number of times* k *occurs in* d. *That is, the probability the next variable is equal to* k *is a function* g_k *only of how many times* k *occurs in* d *and the number of variables in* D. *Then* **Johnson's sufficientness postulate** *is said to hold for the sequence.*

Example 6.12 *Suppose we throw a six-sided die seven times and we have the following set of outcomes:*

$$\mathsf{d} = \{2, 3, 1, 2, 1, 2, 4\}.$$

Since we repeat the experiment seven times, M *is equal to seven and since* 2 *occurs three times,* s_2 *is equal to three. Johnson's sufficientness postulate says our probability of the eighth throw landing* 2 *can be determined using a two-argument function evaluated at three (the value of* s_2*) and seven (the value of* M*).*

Johnson's sufficientness hypothesis also seems to be a minimal assumption in the case of experiments that are in some sense considered to be random processes. That is, the probability of a given outcome for the next trial can be computed using the same function for all possible outcomes, and this function needs only the number of previous trials and the number of times the outcome occurred. However, given only this hypothesis and the assumption of exchangeability, we get the surprising result that an individual's prior beliefs concerning the relative frequency must be represented by a Dirichlet distribution. We give that theorem after a lemma:

Lemma 6.6 *Suppose Johnson's sufficientness postulate holds for $X^{(1)}, \ldots, X^{(M)}$, $X^{(M+1)}$ and the number of values r in their space is greater than 2. Then there exist constants $a_1, a_2, \ldots, a_r \geq 0$ and b such that, for every set of values d of the variables in $\mathsf{D} = \{X^{(1)}, X^{(2)}, \ldots, X^{(M)}\}$,*

$$P\left(X^{(M+1)} = k|\mathsf{d}\right) = a_k + bs_k,$$

where s_k is the number of times k occurs in d.
Proof. *The proof can be found in Zabell [1982].* ∎

Theorem 6.5 *Suppose $X^{(1)}, X^{(2)}, X^{(3)}, \ldots$ is an infinite exchangeable sequence of random variables, which are not independent, such that for every M, there exists constants $a_1, a_2, \ldots, a_r \geq 0$ and b such that for every set of values d of the variables in $\mathsf{D} = \{X^{(1)}, X^{(2)}, \ldots, X^{(M)}\}$,*

$$P\left(X^{(M+1)} = k|\mathsf{d}\right) = a_k + bs_k, \qquad (6.4)$$

where s_k is the number of times k occurs in d. (Note that the values of the constants depend on M even though we do not explicitly denote that.) Let $F_1, F_2, \ldots, F_r$ be random variables such that for each value f_k of F_k such that $0 \leq f_k \leq 1$

$$P\left(X^{(1)} = k|f_k\right) = f_k. \qquad (6.5)$$

Then the distribution of the F_ks is Dirichlet.
Proof. *The proof can be found in Zabell [1982].* ∎

Lemma 6.6 and Theorem 6.5 together show that if $r > 2$, then the assumptions of exchangeability, Johnson's sufficientness postulate, and Equality 6.5 imply that the prior distribution of the relative frequencies must be Dirichlet. If $r = 2$, we can conclude that the prior distributions must be beta from exchangeability and the linearity condition in Equality 6.4.

Johnson's sufficientness postulate seems most plausible. However, there are situations in which it seems to be too strong an assumption. For example, while engaged in cryptanalytic work for the British government in World War II, the logician Alan Turing noticed that the frequencies of the frequencies may contain information relative to the probability of each value. That is, Turing noticed the following. Let c_i be the number of frequencies equal to i. For example, suppose there are $r = 5$ values and we observe the sequence

$$\{2, 1, 5, 3, 4, 2, 3, 4, 2, 1, 2\}.$$

Then $c_1 = 1$ because 5 occurs once, $c_2 = 3$ because 1, 3, and 4 each occur twice, $c_3 = 0$ because no value occurs three times, and $c_4 = 1$ because 2 occurs four times. Although it is not obvious, the c_i's can sometimes be used to determine probabilities of the values. (See Good [1965].)

The use of the Dirichlet distribution to quantify our prior beliefs concerning relative frequencies concerns only the case in which we know the number of values of the variable in advance. For example, we know a thumbtack can land two ways, we know a die can land six ways, we know a patient either does or does not have lung cancer. In some cases, we know the variable but we do not know how many values it can have. For example, if I were about to be stranded on a desert island, I would expect to find some species there, but I would not know how many different species there might be. After seeing one creature of a given species, I might want to attach a probability to the event the next creature seen will be of that same species and one minus that probability to the event that it will be of a new species. If the next creature turns out to be of a new species, I would have three possibilities for the third creature, and so on. This situation, which is not as relevant to Bayesian networks, is discussed in detail in Zabell [1996].

A derivation of the Dirichlet distribution, based on assumptions different than those of Zabell, can be found in Geiger and Heckerman [1997].

6.3   Computing a Probability Interval

Given a distribution (either prior or posterior) of a random variable F, which represents our belief concerning a relative frequency, Theorem 6.1 tells us the expected value of F, which is our estimate of the relative frequency, is also our probability for the next trial. We would not only be interested in this expected value, but also in how probable it is that the true relative frequency is close to this expected value. For example, we may want a value c such that

$$P\left(f \in (E(F) - c, E(F) + c)\right) = .95.$$

The interval $(E(F) - c, E(F) + c)$ is called a 95% **probability interval** for F. Probability intervals can be computed directly from the distribution of F as the following examples illustrate.

Example 6.13 *Suppose we have the binomial sample in Example 6.5 on page 297. Then, due to Lemma 6.3, the prior expected value is given by*

$$E(F) = \frac{3}{3+3} = .5.$$

A prior 95% probability interval can therefore be found by solving the following equation for c:

$$\int_{.5-c}^{.5+c} \frac{\Gamma(6)}{\Gamma(3)\Gamma(3)} f^2 (1-f)^2 df = .95.$$

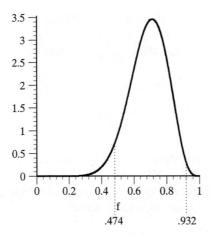

Figure 6.13: The $beta(f; 11, 5)$ density function. The dotted lines show a 95% probability interval for F. This means 95% of the area under the curve is between .474 and .932.

Using the mathematics package Maple, we obtain the solution $c = .353$. So our 95% probability interval is

$$(.5 - .353, .5 + .353) = (.147, .853).$$

Note that we are not all that confident that the relative frequency really is around .5.

Suppose now we have the data in Example 6.7. Due to Corollary 6.3, the posterior density function is $beta(f; 3+8, 3+2) = beta(f; 11, 5)$. Therefore, our posterior expected value is given by

$$E(F|\mathbf{d}) = \frac{11}{11 + 5} = .688,$$

and a posterior 95% probability interval can be found by solving

$$\int_{.688-c}^{.688+c} \frac{\Gamma(16)}{\Gamma(11)\Gamma(5)} f^{10}(1 - f)^4 df = .95.$$

Using Maple, we obtain the solution $c = .214$. So our 95% probability interval is

$$(.688 - .214, .688 + .214) = (.474, .902).$$

Note that the width of our interval has decreased significantly in light of the data. This interval is shown in Figure 6.13.

Example 6.14 *Suppose $a = 31$ and $b = 1$. Then*

$$E(F) = \frac{31}{31 + 1} = .969.$$

If we try to obtain a 95% probability interval by solving

$$\int_{.969-c}^{.969+c} \frac{\Gamma(32)}{\Gamma(31)\Gamma(1)} f^{30}(1 - f)^0 df = .95,$$

we obtain $c = .033$ and our 95% probability interval is $(.936, 1.002)$. The reason we obtain this result is that $.969$ is too close to 1 for there to be an interval, centered at $.969$ and contained in the interval $(0, 1)$, that yields 95% of the area under the curve. In this case, we should solve

$$\int_{.969-c}^{1} \frac{\Gamma(32)}{\Gamma(31)\Gamma(1)} f^{30}(1 - f)^0 df = .95$$

to obtain $c = .061$, which yields a 95% probability interval of

$$(.969 - .061, 1) = (.908, 1).$$

We obtain a 95% probability interval that is not centered at $.969$ but at least has $.969$ as close to its center as possible.

In general, the procedure for obtaining a *perc* % probability interval is as follows:

Computing a *perc* % Probability Interval for $E(F)$

Solve the following equation for c:

$$\int_{.E(F)-c}^{E(F)+c} \rho(f) df = .perc.$$

Case $(E(F) - c, E(F) + c) \subseteq (0, 1)$:
  A *perc*% probability interval is given by

$$(E(F) - c, E(F) + c).$$

Case $(E(F) - c, E(F) + c) \not\subseteq (0, 1)$ and $E(F) > .5$:
  Solve the following equation for c:

$$\int_{.E(F)-c}^{1} \rho(f) df = .perc.$$

A *perc*% probability interval is given by

$$(E(F) - c, 1).$$

Case $(E(F) - c, E(F) + c) \not\subseteq (0, 1)$ **and** $E(F) < .5$:

Solve the following equation for c:

$$\int_{.0}^{E(F)+c} \rho(f)df = .perc.$$

A *perc* % probability interval is given by

$$(0, E(F) + c).$$

Example 6.15 *Suppose the density function for F is beta$(f; 2, 51)$, and we want a 95% probability interval. We have*

$$E(F) = \frac{2}{2 + 51} = .038.$$

Solving

$$\int_{.038-c}^{.038+c} \frac{\Gamma(53)}{\Gamma(2)\Gamma(51)} f^1 (1 - f)^{50} df = .95$$

yields $c = -.063$. Since $(.038 - [-.063], .038 + [-.063]) = (.101, -.025) \not\subseteq (0, 1)$ and $E(F) < .5$, we solve

$$\int_0^{.038+c} \frac{\Gamma(53)}{\Gamma(2)\Gamma(51)}, f^1 (1 - f)^{50} df = .95$$

which yields $c = .050$. A 95% probability interval is therefore given by

$$(0, .038 + .050) = (0, .088).$$

As we shall see in Section 6.6, sometimes we do not have a simple expression for the density function of F, but we do know the expected value and the variance. In such cases we can obtain a probability interval using the normal density function to approximate the given density function. We present that approximation next.

Computing a *perc* % Probability Interval for $E(F)$
Using the Normal Approximation

The **normal approximation** to a *perc* % probability interval for F is given by

$$(E(F) - z_{perc}\sigma(F), E(F) + z_{perc}\sigma(F)),$$

where $\sigma(F)$ is the standard deviation of F, and z_{perc} is the z-score obtained from the standard normal table. The following are some typical values for z_{perc}:

perc	z_{perc}
80	1.28
95	1.96
99	2.58

Before giving an example of the above approximation, we present a lemma that enables us to compute the variance of a random variable that has the beta distribution.

Lemma 6.7 *Suppose the random variables F has the beta$(f; a, b)$ density function. Then*

$$E(F^2) = \left(\frac{a+1}{a+b+1}\right)\left(\frac{a}{a+b}\right).$$

Proof. *The proof is left as an exercise.* ■

Example 6.16 *Suppose F has density function beta$(f; 11, 5)$. Then, due to the preceding lemma,*

$$E(F^2) = \left(\frac{11+1}{11+5+1}\right)\left(\frac{11}{11+5}\right) = \frac{33}{68},$$

which means the variance of F is given by

$$V(F) = E(F^2) - [E(F)]^2 = \frac{33}{68} - \left(\frac{11}{16}\right)^2 = .012638,$$

and therefore

$$\sigma(F) = \sqrt{V(F)} = \sqrt{.012638} = .112.$$

The normal approximation therefore yields the following 95% probability interval:

$$(.688 - (1.96)(.112), .688 + (1.96)(.112)) = (.468, .908).$$

Compare this with the exact answer of $(.474, .902)$ obtained in Example 6.13.

The normal density function becomes a better approximation of beta$(f; a, b)$ as a and b become larger and as they become closer to being equal. If a and b are each at least 5, it is usually a reasonable approximation.

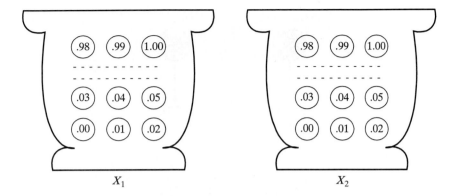

Figure 6.14: Each urn contains 101 coins, each with a different propensity for landing heads.

6.4 Learning Parameters in a Bayesian Network

Next we extend the theory for learning a single parameter to learning all the parameters in a Bayesian network. First, we motivate the theory by presenting urn examples in which we have only two variable networks. Then, we formally introduce augmented Bayesian networks, and we show how they can be used to learn parameters in a Bayesian network.

6.4.1 Urn Examples

Recall that Figure 6.1 showed an urn containing 101 coins, each with a different propensity (relative frequency) for landing heads. The propensities were uniformly distributed between 0 and 1. Suppose now we have two such urns as shown in Figure 6.14, we sample a coin from each urn, we toss the coin from the urn labeled X_1, and then we toss the coin from the urn labeled X_2. For the sake of simplicity assume that the distributions are each the uniform continuous distribution rather than a discrete distribution. Let X_1 be a random variable whose value is the result of the first toss, and let X_2 be a random variable whose value is the result of the second toss. If we let 1 stand for heads and 2 stand for tails, the Bayesian network in Figure 6.15 (a) represents the probability distribution associated with this experiment. Recall from Section 6.1.1 that such a Bayesian network is called an **augmented Bayesian network** because it includes nodes (which we shade) representing our beliefs about relative frequencies. The probability distribution of F_{11} is our belief concerning the relative frequency with which the first coin lands heads, while the probability distribution of F_{21} is our belief concerning the relative frequency with which the second coin lands heads.

It is not hard to see that the Bayesian network, whose specified conditional distributions are the marginal distributions of X_1 and X_2, contains the joint distribution of X_1 and X_2. We say this Bayesian network is **embedded** in

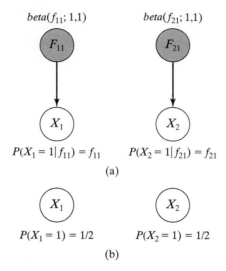

Figure 6.15: A Bayesian network representing the probability distribution concerning the experiment of sampling and tossing coins from the urns in Figure 6.14 is shown in (a); a Bayesian network containing the marginal distribution of X_1 and X_2 is shown in (b).

the augmented Bayesian network. "Embedded Bayesian network" is defined formally in Section 6.4.2. Owing to Corollary 6.1, this network is the one in Figure 6.15 (b). From that network, we have

$$P(X_1 = 1, X_2 = 1) = P(X_1 = 1)P(X_2 = 1) = \left(\frac{1}{2}\right)\left(\frac{1}{2}\right) = \frac{1}{4}$$

$$P(X_1 = 1, X_2 = 2) = P(X_1 = 1)P(X_2 = 2) = \left(\frac{1}{2}\right)\left(\frac{1}{2}\right) = \frac{1}{4}$$

$$P(X_1 = 2, X_2 = 1) = P(X_1 = 2)P(X_2 = 1) = \left(\frac{1}{2}\right)\left(\frac{1}{2}\right) = \frac{1}{4}$$

$$P(X_1 = 2, X_2 = 2) = P(X_1 = 2)P(X_2 = 2) = \left(\frac{1}{2}\right)\left(\frac{1}{2}\right) = \frac{1}{4}.$$

Note that these probabilities are not the relative frequencies with which the outcomes will occur (unless we sample the two coins with propensity .5). Rather, they are our beliefs concerning the first outcome. They are also the relative frequencies with which the outcomes will occur if we repeatedly sample coins with replacement and toss each sample pair once.

Suppose now we repeatedly toss the coins we sampled. Our goal is to update the probability distributions in the augmented Bayesian network (and therefore

Case	X_1	X_2
1	1	1
2	1	1
3	1	1
4	1	2
5	2	1
6	2	1
7	2	2

Table 6.1: Data on 6 cases

the parameters in the embedded network) based on the data obtained from these tosses. Intuitively, we might expect, we could update the distributions of F_{11} and F_{21} separately using the techniques developed in Section 6.1.2, and we could compute the probability of data by multiplying the probability of the data on X_1 by the probability of the data on X_2. The theory developed in Section 6.4.3 justifies doing this. Presently, we illustrate the technique in an example.

Example 6.17 *Suppose we sample coins from the urns in Figure 6.14, we toss the coins seven times, and we obtain the data* **d** *in Table 6.1. In that table, the ith row shows the outcome for the ith pair of tosses. Recall that 1 stands for heads and 2 for tails. Let*

1. *s_{11} be the number of times X_1 equals 1;*

2. *t_{11} be the number of times X_1 equals 2;*

3. *s_{21} be the number of times X_2 equals 1;*

4. *t_{21} be the number of times X_2 equals 2.*

Updating the distributions of X_1 and X_2 separately, we have, due to Corollary 6.3,

$$
\begin{aligned}
\rho(f_{11}|\mathbf{d}) &= beta(f_{11}; a_{11} + s_{11}, b_{11} + t_{11}) \\
&= beta(f_{11}; 1 + 4, 1 + 3) = beta(f_{11}; 5, 4)
\end{aligned}
$$

$$
\begin{aligned}
\rho(f_{21}|\mathbf{d}) &= beta(f_{21}; a_{21} + s_{21}, b_{21} + t_{21}) \\
&= beta(f_{21}; 1 + 5, 1 + 2) = beta(f_{21}; 6, 3).
\end{aligned}
$$

The updated augmented and embedded Bayesian networks appear in Figure 6.16 (a) and (b), respectively. According to the embedded Bayesian network,

$$
P(X_1 = 1, X_2 = 1) = P(X_1 = 1)P(X_2 = 1) = \left(\frac{5}{9}\right)\left(\frac{2}{3}\right) = \frac{10}{27}
$$

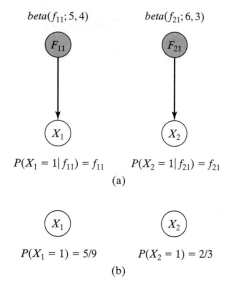

$$beta(f_{11}; 5, 4) \qquad beta(f_{21}; 6, 3)$$

$$P(X_1 = 1 | f_{11}) = f_{11} \qquad P(X_2 = 1 | f_{21}) = f_{21}$$

(a)

$$P(X_1 = 1) = 5/9 \qquad P(X_2 = 1) = 2/3$$

(b)

Figure 6.16: A Bayesian network containing the posterior probability distribution given data obtained by performing the experiment of sampling and tossing coins from the urns in Figure 6.14 is shown in (a); a Bayesian network containing the posterior marginal distribution of X_1 and X_2 is shown in (b).

$$P(X_1 = 1, X_2 = 2) = P(X_1 = 1)P(X_2 = 2) = \left(\frac{5}{9}\right)\left(\frac{1}{3}\right) = \frac{5}{27}$$

$$P(X_1 = 2, X_2 = 1) = P(X_1 = 2)P(X_2 = 1) = \left(\frac{4}{9}\right)\left(\frac{2}{3}\right) = \frac{8}{27}$$

$$P(X_1 = 2, X_2 = 2) = P(X_1 = 2)P(X_2 = 2) = \left(\frac{4}{9}\right)\left(\frac{1}{3}\right) = \frac{4}{27},$$

which is the probability given the data d.

Furthermore, assuming that we can compute the probability of the data by multiplying the probability of the data on X_1 by the probability of the data on X_2, then, owing to Corollary 6.2, we have

$$
\begin{aligned}
P(\mathsf{d}) &= \left[\frac{\Gamma(N_{11})}{\Gamma(N_{11}+M_{11})}\frac{\Gamma(a_{11}+s_{11})\Gamma(b_{11}+t_{11})}{\Gamma(a_{11})\Gamma(b_{11})}\right]\left[\frac{\Gamma(N_{21})}{\Gamma(N_{21}+M_{21})}\frac{\Gamma(a_{21}+s_{21})\Gamma(b_{21}+t_{21})}{\Gamma(a_{21})\Gamma(b_{21})}\right] \\
&= \left[\frac{\Gamma(2)}{\Gamma(2+7)}\frac{\Gamma(1+4)\Gamma(1+3)}{\Gamma(1)\Gamma(1)}\right]\left[\frac{\Gamma(2)}{\Gamma(2+7)}\frac{\Gamma(1+5)\Gamma(1+2)}{\Gamma(1)\Gamma(1)}\right] \\
&= 2.125\,9 \times 10^{-5}.
\end{aligned}
$$

Note that $P(\mathsf{d})$ is the relative frequency with which we will obtain data d *when we repeatedly sample coins with replacement from the urns and toss each sample pair seven times.*

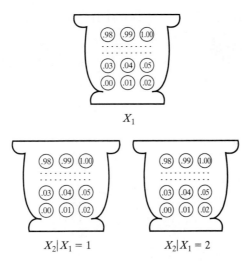

Figure 6.17: Each urn contains 101 coins, each with a different propensity for landing heads.

Suppose now we have three urns, each containing coins with propensities uniformly distributed between 0 and 1, as shown in Figure 6.17. Again assume the distributions are each the uniform continuous distribution. Suppose further that we sample a coin from each urn. We then toss the coin from the urn labeled X_1. If the result is heads (1), we toss the coin from the urn labeled $X_2|X_1 = 1$, and if the result is tails (2), we toss the coin from the urn labeled $X_2|X_1 = 2$. Let X_1 be a random variable whose value is the result of the first toss, and let X_2 be a random variable whose value is the result of the second toss. The Bayesian network in Figure 6.18 (a) represents the probability distribution associated with this experiment. The probability distribution of F_{11} is our belief concerning the relative frequency with which the first coin lands heads, the probability distribution of F_{21} is our belief concerning the relative frequency with which the second coin lands heads when the first coin lands heads, and the probability distribution of F_{22} is our belief concerning the relative frequency with which the second coin lands heads when the first coin lands tails. Note the difference between the network in Figure 6.18 (a) and the one in Figure 6.15 (a). In our second experiment, a result of tossing the coin picked from the urn labeled $X_2|X_1 = 1$ tells us nothing about the coin picked from the urn labeled $X_2|X_1 = 2$. So F_{21} and F_{22} are independent in Figure 6.18 (a). However, in our first experiment, the same coin is used in the second toss regardless of the value of X_1. So in this case F_{21} and F_{22} are completely dependent (deterministically related) and are therefore collapsed into one node in Figure 6.15 (a). (It is also labeled F_{21} in that figure.)

It is not hard to see that the Bayesian network, whose specified conditional distributions are the marginal distributions of X_1, of X_2 conditional on $X_1 = 1$, and of X_2 conditional on $X_1 = 2$, contains the joint distribution of X_1 and X_2.

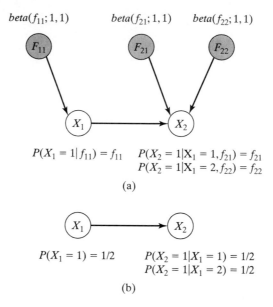

$$P(X_1 = 1|f_{11}) = f_{11} \quad P(X_2 = 1|X_1 = 1, f_{21}) = f_{21}$$
$$P(X_2 = 1|X_1 = 2, f_{22}) = f_{22}$$

(a)

$$P(X_1 = 1) = 1/2 \quad P(X_2 = 1|X_1 = 1) = 1/2$$
$$P(X_2 = 1|X_1 = 2) = 1/2$$

(b)

Figure 6.18: A Bayesian network representing the probability distribution for the experiment (as discussed in the text) of sampling and tossing coins from the urns in Figure 6.17 is shown in (a); a Bayesian network containing the marginal distribution of X_1 and X_2 is shown in (b).

This network is shown in Figure 6.15 (b). From that network, we have

$$P(X_1 = 1, X_2 = 1) = P(X_2 = 1|X_1 = 1)P(X_1 = 1) = \left(\frac{1}{2}\right)\left(\frac{1}{2}\right) = \frac{1}{4}$$

$$P(X_1 = 1, X_2 = 2) = P(X_2 = 2|X_1 = 1)P(X_1 = 1) = \left(\frac{1}{2}\right)\left(\frac{1}{2}\right) = \frac{1}{4}$$

$$P(X_1 = 2, X_2 = 1) = P(X_2 = 1|X_1 = 2)P(X_1 = 2) = \left(\frac{1}{2}\right)\left(\frac{1}{2}\right) = \frac{1}{4}$$

$$P(X_1 = 2, X_2 = 2) = P(X_2 = 2|X_1 = 2)P(X_1 = 2) = \left(\frac{1}{2}\right)\left(\frac{1}{2}\right) = \frac{1}{4}.$$

Suppose now we repeatedly toss the coins we sampled according to the rules of the new experiment just discussed. Our goal again is to update the probability distributions in the augmented network (and therefore the parameters in the embedded network) based on the data obtained from these tosses. Again, we might expect that we could update the distributions F_{11}, F_{21}, and F_{22} separately using the techniques developed in Section 6.1.2, and that we could compute the probability of data by multiplying the probability of the data on X_1, the probability of the data on X_2 when $X_1 = 1$, and the probability of the data on X_2 when $X_1 = 2$. The theory developed in Section 6.4.3 justifies doing this. Presently, we illustrate the technique in an example.

Example 6.18 *Suppose we sample coins from the urns in Figure 6.17, we toss the coins seven times according to the rules of the current experiment, and we again obtain the data* d *in Table 6.1. Let*

1. *s_{11} be the number of times X_1 equals 1;*

2. *t_{11} be the number of times X_1 equals 2;*

3. *s_{21} be the number of times X_2 equals 1 when X_1 equals 1;*

4. *t_{21} be the number of times X_2 equals 2 when X_1 equals 1;*

5. *s_{22} be the number of times X_2 equals 1 when X_1 equals 2;*

6. *t_{22} be the number of times X_2 equals 2 when X_1 equals 2.*

Updating the distributions separately, from Corollary 6.3, we have

$$
\begin{aligned}
\rho(f_{11}|\mathbf{d}) &= beta(f_{11}; a_{11} + s_{11}, b_{11} + t_{11}) \\
&= beta(f_{11}; 1 + 4, 1 + 3) = beta(f_{11}; 5, 4)
\end{aligned}
$$

$$
\begin{aligned}
\rho(f_{21}|\mathbf{d}) &= beta(f_{21}; a_{21} + s_{21}, b_{21} + t_{21}) \\
&= beta(f_{21}; 1 + 3, 1 + 1) = beta(f_{21}; 4, 2)
\end{aligned}
$$

$$
\begin{aligned}
\rho(f_{22}|\mathbf{d}) &= beta(f_{22}; a_{22} + s_{22}, b_{22} + t_{22}) \\
&= beta(f_{22}; 1 + 2, 1 + 1) = beta(f_{22}; 3, 2).
\end{aligned}
$$

The updated augmented and embedded Bayesian networks appear in Figure 6.19 (a) and (b), respectively. According to the embedded Bayesian network,

$$
P(X_1 = 1, X_2 = 1) = P(X_2 = 1|X_1 = 1)P(X_1 = 1) = \left(\frac{2}{3}\right)\left(\frac{5}{9}\right) = \frac{10}{27}
$$

$$
P(X_1 = 1, X_2 = 2) = P(X_2 = 2|X_1 = 1)P(X_1 = 1) = \left(\frac{1}{3}\right)\left(\frac{5}{9}\right) = \frac{5}{27}
$$

$$
P(X_1 = 2, X_2 = 1) = P(X_2 = 1|X_1 = 2)P(X_1 = 2) = \left(\frac{3}{5}\right)\left(\frac{4}{9}\right) = \frac{4}{15}
$$

$$
P(X_1 = 2, X_2 = 2) = P(X_2 = 2|X_1 = 2)P(X_1 = 2) = \left(\frac{2}{5}\right)\left(\frac{4}{9}\right) = \frac{8}{45}.
$$

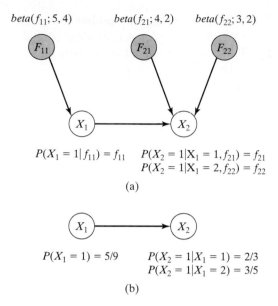

Figure 6.19: A Bayesian network containing the posterior probability distribution given data obtained by performing the experiment (as discussed in the text) of sampling and tossing coins from the urns in Figure 6.17 is shown in (a); a Bayesian network containing the posterior marginal distribution of X_1 and X_2 is shown in (b).

Note that this is not the same distribution as the one obtained in Example 6.17 even though the prior distributions are the same.

Furthermore, assuming that we can compute the probability of the data by multiplying the probability of the data on X_1, the probability of the data on X_2 when $X_1 = 1$, and the probability of the data on X_2 when $X_1 = 2$, owing to Corollary 6.2 we have

$$
\begin{aligned}
P(\mathsf{d}) &= \left[\frac{\Gamma(N_{11})}{\Gamma(N_{11}+M_{11})} \frac{\Gamma(a_{11}+s_{11})\Gamma(b_{11}+t_{11})}{\Gamma(a_{11})\Gamma(b_{11})} \right] \\
&\quad \times \left[\frac{\Gamma(N_{21})}{\Gamma(N_{21}+M_{21})} \frac{\Gamma(a_{21}+s_{21})\Gamma(b_{21}+t_{21})}{\Gamma(a_{21})\Gamma(b_{21})} \right] \left[\frac{\Gamma(N_{22})}{\Gamma(N_{22}+M_{22})} \frac{\Gamma(a_{22}+s_{22})\Gamma(b_{22}+t_{22})}{\Gamma(a_{22})\Gamma(b_{22})} \right] \\
&= \left[\frac{\Gamma(2)}{\Gamma(2+7)} \frac{\Gamma(1+4)\Gamma(1+3)}{\Gamma(1)\Gamma(1)} \right] \left[\frac{\Gamma(2)}{\Gamma(2+4)} \frac{\Gamma(1+3)\Gamma(1+1)}{\Gamma(1)\Gamma(1)} \right] \left[\frac{\Gamma(2)}{\Gamma(2+3)} \frac{\Gamma(1+2)\Gamma(1+1)}{\Gamma(1)\Gamma(1)} \right] \\
&= 1.488\,1 \times 10^{-5}.
\end{aligned}
$$

Note that $P(\mathsf{d})$ is the relative frequency with which we will obtain data d when we repeatedly sample coins with replacement from the urns and toss them seven times according to the rules of the experiment. Note further that it is not the same as the $P(\mathsf{d})$ obtained in Example 6.17.

6.4.2 Augmented Bayesian Networks

Next we formalize the notions introduced in the previous subsection.

Definition 6.8 *An **augmented Bayesian network** $(\mathbb{G}, \mathsf{F}, \rho)$ is a Bayesian network determined by the following:*

1. *A DAG $\mathbb{G} = (\mathsf{V}, \mathsf{E})$ where $\mathsf{V} = \{X_1, X_2, \ldots, X_n\}$ and each X_i is a random variable.*

2. *For every i, an auxiliary parent variable F_i of X_i and a density function ρ_i of F_i. Each F_i is a root and has no edge to any variable except X_i. The set of all $\mathsf{F}_i s$ is denoted by F. That is,*

$$\mathsf{F} = \mathsf{F}_1 \cup \mathsf{F}_2 \cup \cdots \mathsf{F}_n.$$

3. *For every i, for all values pa_i of the parents PA_i in V of X_i, and all values f_i of F_i, a probability distribution of X_i conditional on pa_i and f_i.*

In general, in an augmented Bayesian network the distributions of the $\mathsf{F}_i s$ need not be continuous. However, since in the ones we consider they are, we denote them that way. Furthermore, the conditional distribution of the $X_i s$ may be either continuous or discrete. Still, we denote the joint distribution of the $X_i s$ by P.

The idea in an augmented Bayesian network is that we know conditional independencies among a set of variables, and we are able to represent these conditional independencies using a DAG $\mathbb{G}$. We then want to represent our beliefs concerning the unknown conditional relative frequencies (parameters) needed for that DAG. We do this using the nodes in F. F_i is a set of random variable representing our belief concerning the relative frequencies of the values of X_i given values of the parents of X_i.

Clearly, an augmented Bayesian network is simply a Bayesian network. It is only the notation that distinguishes it.

Since the $\mathsf{F}_i s$ are all roots in a Bayesian network, they are mutually independent. Therefore, we have **global parameter independence**:

$$\rho(\mathsf{f}_1, \mathsf{f}_2, \ldots, \mathsf{f}_n) = \rho_1(\mathsf{f}_1)\rho_2(\mathsf{f}_2) \cdots \rho_n(\mathsf{f}_n). \tag{6.6}$$

Subscripting both ρ and f creates clutter. So from now on we will just write the joint distribution in Equality 6.8 as follows:

$$\rho(\mathsf{f}_1)\rho(\mathsf{f}_2) \cdots \rho(\mathsf{f}_n)$$

It's clear from the subscript on f which density function each ρ represents.

We have the following theorem:

Theorem 6.6 *Let an augmented Bayesian network* $(\mathbb{G}, \mathsf{F}, \rho)$ *be given. Then the marginal distribution* P *of* $\{X_1, X_2, \ldots, X_n\}$ *constitutes a Bayesian network with* $\mathbb{G}$. *We say* $(\mathbb{G}, \mathsf{F}, \rho)$ *embeds* $(\mathbb{G}, P)$.

Proof. *It is left as an exercise to show that, in general, when we marginalize by summing (integrating) over the values of a set of roots in a Bayesian network, such that each root in the set has only one child, the marginal distribution of the remaining variables constitutes a Bayesian network with the subgraph containing those variables.* ∎

After developing an augmented Bayesian network, its embedded network is the one used to do inference with the variables in V since this latter network contains our probability distribution of those variables.

The following augmented Bayesian networks are discussed in this chapter:

Definition 6.9 *A **binomial augmented Bayesian network*** $(\mathbb{G}, \mathsf{F}, \rho)$ *is an augmented Bayesian network with the following properties:*

1. *For every* i, X_i *has space* $\{1, 2\}$.

2. *For every* i, *there is an ordering* $[\mathsf{pa}_{i1}, \mathsf{pa}_{i2}, \ldots, \mathsf{pa}_{iq_i}]$ *of all instantiations of the parents* PA_i *in* V *of* X_i, *where* q_i *is the number of different instantiations of these parents. Furthermore, for every* i,

$$\mathsf{F}_i = \{F_{i1}, F_{i2}, \ldots, F_{iq_i}\},$$

where each F_{ij} *is a root, has no edge to any variable except* X_i, *and has density function*

$$\rho_{ij}(f_{ij}) \qquad 0 \leq f_{ij} \leq 1.$$

3. *For every* i *and* j, *and all values* $\mathsf{f}_i = \{f_{i1}, \ldots, f_{ij}, \ldots, f_{iq_i}\}$ *of* F_i,

$$P(X_i = 1 | \mathsf{pa}_{ij}, f_{i1}, \ldots, f_{ij}, \ldots, f_{iq_i}) = f_{ij}. \qquad (6.7)$$

If X_i is a root, PA_i is empty. In this case, $q_i = 1$ and pa_{ij} does not appear in Equality 6.7.

Since the F_{ij}s are all roots in a Bayesian network, they are mutually independent. So, besides the global parameter independence of the sets F_i, we have **local parameter independence** of their members F_{ij}. That is, for $1 \leq i \leq n$,

$$\rho(f_{i1}, f_{i2}, \ldots, f_{iq_i}) = \rho(f_{i1})\rho(f_{i2}) \cdots \rho(f_{iq_i}).$$

Global and local independence together imply that

$$\rho(f_{11}, f_{12}, \ldots, f_{nq_n}) = \rho(f_{11})\rho(f_{12}) \cdots \rho(f_{nq_n}). \qquad (6.8)$$

Note that, again, to avoid clutter we did not subscript the density functions.

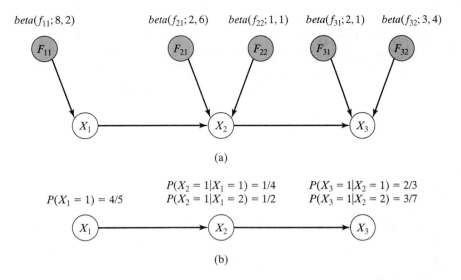

Figure 6.20: A binomial augmented Bayesian network is shown in (a), and its embedded Bayesian network is shown in (b).

Figure 6.20 (a) shows a binomial augmented Bayesian network. Note that we shade the nodes in F. Note further that to avoid clutter in this and future figures we do not show the conditional distributions in the augmented network. They are all given by Equality 6.7. In the network in Figure 6.20 (a), $q_1 = 1$, $q_2 = 2$, $q_3 = 2$, and

$$PA_1 = \varnothing \qquad pa_{11} = \varnothing$$

$$PA_2 = \{X_1\} \qquad pa_{21} = \{1\}$$
$$pa_{22} = \{2\}$$

$$PA_3 = \{X_2\} \qquad pa_{31} = \{1\}$$
$$pa_{32} = \{2\}.$$

In a binomial augmented Bayesian network, F_{ij} is a random variable whose probability distribution represents our belief concerning the relative frequency with which X_i is equal to 1 given that the parents of X_i are in their jth instantiation. For example, in Figure 6.20 (a), the probability distribution of F_{11} represents our belief concerning the relative frequency with which X_1 is equal to 1, the probability distribution of F_{21} represents our belief concerning the relative frequency with which X_2 is equal to 1 given that $X_1 = 1$, and the probability distribution of F_{22} represents our belief concerning the relative frequency with which X_2 is equal to 1 given that $X_1 = 2$. Furthermore, Equality 6.7 is the same assumption we made in Section 6.1 — namely, if we knew a relative frequency for certain, then that relative frequency would be our probability.

Given a binomial augmented Bayesian network $(\mathbb{G}, \mathsf{F}, \rho)$, the following theorem proves that the conditional probabilities in the embedded Bayesian network $(\mathbb{G}, P)$ are equal to the expected values of the variables in F.

Theorem 6.7 *Let a binomial augmented Bayesian network $(\mathbb{G}, \mathsf{F}, \rho)$ be given. Then for each i and each j, the ijth conditional distribution in the embedded Bayesian network $(\mathbb{G}, P)$ is given by*

$$P(X_i = 1|\mathsf{pa}_{ij}) = E(F_{ij}). \qquad (6.9)$$

Proof. *We have*

$P(X_i = 1|\mathsf{pa}_{ij})$

$$
\begin{aligned}
&= \int_0^1 \cdots \int_0^1 P(X_i = 1|\mathsf{pa}_{ij}, f_{i1}, \ldots, f_{iq_i})\rho(f_{i1})\cdots\rho(f_{iq_i})df_{i1}\cdots df_{iq_i} \\
&= \int_0^1 \cdots \int_0^1 f_{ij}\rho(f_{i1})\cdots\rho(f_{iq_i})df_{i1}\cdots df_{iq_i} \\
&= \int_0^1 f_{ij}\rho(f_{ij})df_{ij} \\
&= E(F_{ij}).
\end{aligned}
$$

The first equality is due to the law of total probability and the fact that F is independent of PA_i, the second is due to Equality 6.7, and the third is obtained by integrating over all density functions other than $\rho(f_{ij})$. ∎

Corollary 6.5 *Let a binomial augmented Bayesian network be given. If each F_{ij} has a beta distribution with parameters $a_{ij}, b_{ij}, N_{ij} = a_{ij} + b_{ij}$, then for each i and each j the ijth conditional distribution in the embedded network $(\mathbb{G}, P)$ is given by*

$$P(X_i = 1|\mathsf{pa}_{ij}) = \frac{a_{ij}}{N_{ij}}.$$

Proof. *The proof follows directly from Theorem 6.7 and Lemma 6.3.* ∎

Example 6.19 *Consider the augmented Bayesian network in Figure 6.20 (a). We have*

$$
\begin{aligned}
E(F_{11}) &= \frac{8}{8+2} = \frac{4}{5} \\
E(F_{21}) &= \frac{2}{2+6} = \frac{1}{4} \\
E(F_{22}) &= \frac{1}{1+1} = \frac{1}{2} \\
E(F_{31}) &= \frac{2}{2+1} = \frac{2}{3} \\
E(F_{32}) &= \frac{3}{3+4} = \frac{3}{7}.
\end{aligned}
$$

Therefore, that augmented Bayesian network embeds the Bayesian network in Figure 6.20 (b).

As mentioned previously, the embedded Bayesian network is the one used to do inference with the variables in V. For example, after developing the binomial augmented Bayesian network in Figure 6.20 (a), we do inference using the network in Figure 6.20 (b).

Before ending this subsection, we discuss the assumption concerning our beliefs entailed by a binomial augmented Bayesian network. The assumption is that the variables, whose probability distributions represent our belief concerning the relative frequencies, are independent. This assumption holds for the urn examples presented in Section 6.4.1. In many cases, however, it seems it does not hold. For example, suppose in a given population, we find out that the relative frequency of lung cancer given smoking is .99. This unusually high value should make us suspect there is some other carcinogenic present in the population, which means we should now believe the relative frequency of lung cancer given nonsmoking is higher than we previously thought. Nevertheless, even if the assumption does not hold in a strict sense, we can still make it because, regardless of our personal beliefs, the learning algorithm in the next section will converge to the true joint distribution of the relative frequencies as long as the conditional independencies entailed by the DAG are correct. We might say that our model represents the beliefs of an agent that has no prior knowledge about the variables other than these conditional independencies. Note that we can create arcs among the F_{ij}s or introduce hidden variables that connect them, and thereby model our beliefs concerning dependence of these variables. However, this method will not be discussed in this text.

6.4.3 Learning Using an Augmented Bayesian Network

Next we develop theory which entails that we can update probability distributions as illustrated in Section 6.4.1. Random vectors (defined in Section 5.3.1) are used in this development.

We start with the following definitions:

Definition 6.10 *Suppose we have a sample of size M as follows:*

1. We have the random vectors

$$\mathbf{X}^{(1)} = \begin{pmatrix} X_1^{(1)} \\ \vdots \\ X_n^{(1)} \end{pmatrix} \qquad \mathbf{X}^{(2)} = \begin{pmatrix} X_1^{(2)} \\ \vdots \\ X_n^{(2)} \end{pmatrix} \qquad \cdots \qquad \mathbf{X}^{(M)} = \begin{pmatrix} X_1^{(M)} \\ \vdots \\ X_n^{(M)} \end{pmatrix}$$

$$\mathsf{D} = \left\{ \mathbf{X}^{(1)}, \mathbf{X}^{(2)}, \ldots, \mathbf{X}^{(M)} \right\}$$

such that, for every i, each $X_i^{(h)}$ has the same space.

2. *There is an augmented Bayesian network* $(\mathbb{G}, \mathsf{F}, \rho)$, *where* $\mathbb{G} = (\mathsf{V}, \mathsf{E})$, *such that, for* $1 \leq h \leq M$

$$\{X_1^{(h)}, \dots, X_n^{(h)}\}$$

constitutes an instance of V *in* $\mathbb{G}$ *resulting in a distinct augmented Bayesian network.*

Then the sample D *is called a* **Bayesian network sample** *of size M with parameter* $(\mathbb{G}, \mathsf{F})$.

Definition 6.11 *Suppose we have a Bayesian network sample of size M such that*

1. *for every i, each $X_i^{(h)}$ has space $\{1, 2\}$;*

2. *its augmented Bayesian network $(\mathbb{G}, \mathsf{F}, \rho)$ is binomial.*

Then D *is called a* **binomial Bayesian network sample** *of size M with parameter* $(\mathbb{G}, \mathsf{F})$.

Note that the network $(\mathbb{G}, \mathsf{F}, \rho)$ is used as a schema for representing other augmented Bayesian networks. Note further that in application each $\mathbf{X}^{(h)}$ is a case; that is, it is a random vector whose value is data on one individual sampled. Finally, note that a Bayesian network sample is itself a big Bayesian network, and that for each h, the subgraph, consisting of the variables in F united with the set of variables that make up each $\mathbf{X}^{(h)}$, constitutes an augmented Bayesian network with ρ. This is illustrated in Figure 6.21. From that figure, we see that the $\mathbf{X}^{(h)}$s are mutually independent conditional on F because F d-separates all of them. A binomial sample (Definition 6.3) is a binomial Bayesian network sample in which $\mathbb{G}$ contains only one node.

The idea in a Bayesian network sample is that we know the conditional independencies in the relative frequency distribution of a set of variables, and we are able to represent these independencies and our beliefs concerning the relative frequencies of the variables using an augmented Bayesian network. Then we obtain data consisting of a set of cases (different instantiations of those variables). Our goal is to update our beliefs concerning the relative frequencies from the data. To that end, we first obtain results that apply to all Bayesian network samples. After that, we obtain results pertaining specifically to binomial Bayesian network samples.

Results for all Bayesian Network Samples

Lemma 6.8 *Suppose*

1. D *is a Bayesian network sample of size M with parameter* $(\mathbb{G}, \mathsf{F})$;

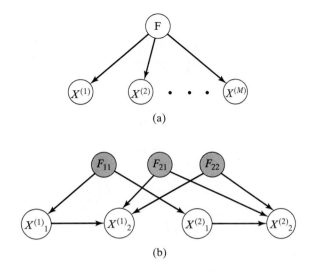

(a)

(b)

Figure 6.21: The high-level structure of a Bayesian network sample is given by the DAG in (a). In that DAG, each node and arc actually represents a set of nodes and arcs respectively. The detailed structure in the case of a binomial augmented Bayesian network sample when $m = n = 2$ is shown in (b).

2. *we have a set of values (data) of the* $\mathbf{X}^{(h)}s$ *as follows:*

$$\mathbf{x}^{(1)} = \begin{pmatrix} x_1^{(1)} \\ \vdots \\ x_1^{(1)} \end{pmatrix} \qquad \mathbf{x}^{(2)} = \begin{pmatrix} x_1^{(2)} \\ \vdots \\ x_n^{(2)} \end{pmatrix} \qquad \cdots \qquad \mathbf{x}^{(M)} = \begin{pmatrix} x_1^{(M)} \\ \vdots \\ x_n^{(M)} \end{pmatrix}$$

$$\mathsf{d} = \{\mathbf{x}^{(1)}, \mathbf{x}^{(2)}, \dots, \mathbf{x}^{(M)}\}.$$

Then

$$P(\mathsf{d}|\mathsf{f}_1, \dots, \mathsf{f}_n) = \prod_{i=1}^{n} \prod_{h=1}^{M} P(x_i^{(h)}|\mathsf{pa}_i^{(h)}, \mathsf{f}_i),$$

where $\mathsf{pa}_i^{(h)}$ *contains the values of the parents of* X_i *in the hth case.*

Proof. *We have*

$$
\begin{aligned}
P(\mathsf{d}|\mathsf{f}_1,\dots,\mathsf{f}_n) &= \prod_{h=1}^{M} P(\mathbf{x}^{(h)}|\mathsf{f}_1,\dots,\mathsf{f}_n) \\
&= \prod_{h=1}^{M} \frac{P(\mathbf{x}^{(h)},\mathsf{f}_1,\dots,\mathsf{f}_n)}{\rho(\mathsf{f}_1,\dots,\mathsf{f}_n)} \\
&= \prod_{h=1}^{M} \left(\frac{\prod_{i=1}^{n} P(x_i^{(h)}|\mathsf{pa}_i^{(h)},\mathsf{f}_i) \prod_{i=1}^{n}\rho(\mathsf{f}_i)}{\prod_{i=1}^{n}\rho(\mathsf{f}_i)} \right) \\
&= \prod_{h=1}^{M}\prod_{i=1}^{n} P(x_i^{(h)}|\mathsf{pa}_i^{(h)},\mathsf{f}_i) \\
&= \prod_{i=1}^{n}\prod_{h=1}^{M} P(x_i^{(h)}|\mathsf{pa}_i^{(h)},\mathsf{f}_i).
\end{aligned}
$$

The first equality is true because the $\mathbf{X}^{(h)}s$ *are mutually independent given* F; *the denominator in the third equality is due to global parameter independence.* ∎

Lemma 6.9 *Suppose we have the conditions in Lemma 6.8. Then for each* i,

$$
P(\mathsf{d}|\mathsf{f}_i) = \prod_{h=1}^{M} P(x_i^{(h)}|\mathsf{pa}_i^{(h)},\mathsf{f}_i) \prod_{j\neq i}\int_{\mathsf{f}_j}\prod_{h=1}^{M} P(x_j^{(h)}|\mathsf{pa}_j^{(h)},\mathsf{f}_j)\rho(\mathsf{f}_j)d\mathsf{f}_j.
$$

Proof. *We have*

$$
\begin{aligned}
P(\mathsf{d}|\mathsf{f}_i) &= \int_{\mathsf{f}_j\neq\mathsf{f}_i} P(\mathsf{d}|\mathsf{f}_1,\dots,\mathsf{f}_n)\prod_{j\neq i}[\rho(\mathsf{f}_j)d\mathsf{f}_j] \\
&= \int_{\mathsf{f}_j\neq\mathsf{f}_i}\prod_{j=1}^{n}\prod_{h=1}^{M} P(x_j^{(h)}|\mathsf{pa}_j^{(h)},\mathsf{f}_j)\prod_{j\neq i}[\rho(\mathsf{f}_j)d\mathsf{f}_j] \\
&= \prod_{h=1}^{M} P(x_i^{(h)}|\mathsf{pa}_i^{(h)},\mathsf{f}_i)\int_{\mathsf{f}_j\neq\mathsf{f}_i}\prod_{j\neq i}\prod_{h=1}^{M} P(x_j^{(h)}|\mathsf{pa}_j^{(h)},\mathsf{f}_j)\prod_{j\neq i}[\rho(\mathsf{f}_j)d\mathsf{f}_j] \\
&= \prod_{h=1}^{M} P(x_i^{(h)}|\mathsf{pa}_i^{(h)},\mathsf{f}_i)\prod_{j\neq i}\int_{\mathsf{f}_j}\prod_{h=1}^{M} P(x_j^{(h)}|\mathsf{pa}_j^{(h)},\mathsf{f}_j)\rho(\mathsf{f}_j)d\mathsf{f}_j.
\end{aligned}
$$

The first equality is due to the law of total probability and global parameter independence, and the second is due to Lemma 6.8. ∎

Theorem 6.8 *Suppose we have the conditions in Lemma 6.8. Then*

$$P(\mathsf{d}) = \prod_{i=1}^{n} \left(\int_{\mathsf{f}_i} \prod_{h=1}^{M} P(x_i^{(h)} | \mathsf{pa}_i^{(h)}, \mathsf{f}_i) \rho(\mathsf{f}_i) d\mathsf{f}_i \right).$$

Proof. *We have*

$$\begin{aligned}
P(\mathsf{d}) &= \int_{\mathsf{f}_1} \cdots \int_{\mathsf{f}_n} P(\mathsf{d}|\mathsf{f}_1, \dots, \mathsf{f}_n) \rho(\mathsf{f}_1) \cdots \rho(\mathsf{f}_n) d\mathsf{f}_1 \cdots d\mathsf{f}_n \\
&= \int_{\mathsf{f}_1} \cdots \int_{\mathsf{f}_n} \prod_{i=1}^{n} \prod_{h=1}^{M} P(x_i^{(h)} | \mathsf{pa}_i^{(h)}, \mathsf{f}_i) \rho(\mathsf{f}_1) \cdots \rho(\mathsf{f}_n) d\mathsf{f}_1 \cdots d\mathsf{f}_n \\
&= \prod_{i=1}^{n} \left(\int_{\mathsf{f}_i} \prod_{h=1}^{M} P(x_i^{(h)} | \mathsf{pa}_i^{(h)}, \mathsf{f}_i) \rho(\mathsf{f}_i) d\mathsf{f}_i \right).
\end{aligned}$$

The second equality is due to Lemma 6.8. ∎

Theorem 6.9 (Posterior Global Parameter Independence) *Suppose we have the conditions in Lemma 6.8. Then the F_is are mutually independent conditional on D. That is,*

$$\rho(\mathsf{f}_1, \dots, \mathsf{f}_n | \mathsf{d}) = \prod_{i=1}^{n} \rho(\mathsf{f}_i | \mathsf{d}).$$

Proof. *We have*

$$\begin{aligned}
\rho(\mathsf{f}_1, \dots, \mathsf{f}_n | \mathsf{d}) &= \frac{P(\mathsf{d}|\mathsf{f}_1, \dots, \mathsf{f}_n) \prod_{i=1}^{n} \rho(\mathsf{f}_i)}{P(\mathsf{d})} \\
&= \frac{\prod_{i=1}^{n} \prod_{h=1}^{M} P(x_i^{(h)} | \mathsf{pa}_i^{(h)}, \mathsf{f}_i) \prod_{i=1}^{n} \rho(\mathsf{f}_i)}{P(\mathsf{d})}.
\end{aligned} \tag{6.10}$$

The first equality is due to Bayes' theorem and global parameter independence, and the second is due to Lemma 6.8.

We have further that, for each i,

$$\prod_{i=1}^{n} \rho(f_i|d)$$

$$= \prod_{i=1}^{n} \frac{P(d|f_i)\rho(f_i)}{P(d)}$$

$$= \prod_{i=1}^{n} \frac{\left(\prod_{h=1}^{M} P(x_i^{(h)}|pa_i^{(h)}, f_i) \prod_{j \neq i} \int \prod_{h=1}^{M} P(x_j^{(h)}|pa_j^{(h)}, f_j)\rho(f_j)df_j \right) \rho(f_i)}{P(d)}$$

$$= \frac{\prod_{i=1}^{n} \prod_{h=1}^{M} P(x_i^{(h)}|pa_i^{(h)}, f_i) \left(\prod_{i=1}^{n} \prod_{j \neq i} \int \prod_{h=1}^{M} P(x_j^{(h)}|pa_j^{(h)}, f_j)\rho(f_j)df_j \right) \prod_{i=1}^{n} \rho(f_i)}{[P(d)]^n}$$

$$= \frac{\prod_{i=1}^{n} \prod_{h=1}^{M} P(x_i^{(h)}|pa_i^{(h)}, f_i) [P(d)]^{n-1} \prod_{i=1}^{n} \rho(f_i)}{[P(d)]^n}.$$

$$= \frac{\prod_{i=1}^{n} \prod_{h=1}^{M} P(x_i^{(h)}|pa_i^{(h)}, f_i) \prod_{i=1}^{n} \rho(f_i)}{P(d)} \qquad (6.11)$$

The first equality is due to Bayes' theorem, the second is due to Lemma 6.9, and the fourth is obtained by rearranging terms and applying Theorem 6.8.

Since Expressions 6.10 and 6.11 are equal, the theorem is proven. ∎

Before giving our final theorem concerning Bayesian network samples, we have the following definition:

Definition 6.12 *Suppose we have the conditions in Lemma 6.8. Then the augmented Bayesian network $(\mathbb{G}, F, \rho|d)$ is called the **updated augmented Bayesian network** relative to the Bayesian network sample and the data d. The network it embeds is called the **updated embedded Bayesian network** relative to the Bayesian network sample and the data d.*

Note that $\rho|d$ denotes the density function $\rho(f_1, \ldots, f_n|d)$.

Theorem 6.10 *Suppose the conditions in Lemma 6.8 hold, and we create a Bayesian network sample of size $M + 1$ by including another random vector*

$$\mathbf{X}^{(M+1)} = \begin{pmatrix} X_1^{(M+1)} \\ \vdots \\ X_n^{(M+1)} \end{pmatrix}.$$

Then if D *is the Bayesian network sample of size* M, *the updated distribution*

$$P(x_1^{(M+1)}, \dots, x_n^{(M+1)} | \mathsf{d})$$

is the probability distribution in the updated embedded Bayesian network.
Proof. *We have, due to that law of total probability,*

$$P(x_1^{(M+1)}, \dots, x_n^{(M+1)} | \mathsf{d})$$

$$= \int_{\mathsf{f}_1} \cdots \int_{\mathsf{f}_n} P(x_1^{(M+1)}, \dots, x_n^{(M+1)} | \mathsf{f}_1, \dots, \mathsf{f}_n, \mathsf{d}) \rho(\mathsf{f}_1, \dots, \mathsf{f}_n | \mathsf{d}) d\mathsf{f}_1 \cdots d\mathsf{f}_n$$

$$= \int_{\mathsf{f}_1} \cdots \int_{\mathsf{f}_n} P(x_1^{(M+1)}, \dots, x_n^{(M+1)} | \mathsf{f}_1, \dots, \mathsf{f}_n) \rho(\mathsf{f}_1, \dots, \mathsf{f}_n | \mathsf{d}) d\mathsf{f}_1 \cdots d\mathsf{f}_n.$$

The second equality is true because $\mathbf{X}^{(M+1)}$ *is independent of* D *conditional on* F. *This proves the theorem since this last expression is the probability distribution in the updated embedded Bayesian network.* ■

Due to Theorem 6.10, the updated embedded Bayesian network is the one used to do inference for the $M + 1$st case. When doing inference for that case, we ordinarily do not use the superscript but rather use just the notation X_i. Furthermore, we do not show the conditioning on $\mathsf{D} = \mathsf{d}$. Essentially, we simply use the updated embedded network as always representing our current belief for the next case.

Results for Binomial Bayesian Network Samples

Next, we apply the previous results to binomial Bayesian network samples.

Lemma 6.10 *Suppose*

1. D *is a binomial Bayesian network sample of size* M *with parameter* $(\mathbb{G}, \mathsf{F})$;

2. *we have a set of values (data) of the* $\mathbf{X}^{(h)}s$ *as follows:*

$$\mathbf{x}^{(1)} = \begin{pmatrix} x_1^{(1)} \\ \vdots \\ x_1^{(1)} \end{pmatrix} \qquad \mathbf{x}^{(2)} = \begin{pmatrix} x_1^{(2)} \\ \vdots \\ x_n^{(2)} \end{pmatrix} \qquad \cdots \qquad \mathbf{x}^{(M)} = \begin{pmatrix} x_1^{(M)} \\ \vdots \\ x_n^{(M)} \end{pmatrix}$$

$$\mathsf{d} = \{\mathbf{x}^{(1)}, \mathbf{x}^{(2)}, \dots, \mathbf{x}^{(M)}\};$$

3. M_{ij} is the number of $\mathbf{x}^{(h)}s$ in which $X_i^{(h)}$'s parents are in their jth instantiation, and of these M_{ij} cases, s_{ij} is the number in which $x_i^{(h)}$ is equal to 1 and t_{ij} is the number in which it equals 2.

Then

$$\prod_{h=1}^{M} P(x_i^{(h)}|\mathsf{pa}_i^{(h)}, \mathsf{f}_i) = \prod_{j=1}^{q_i} (f_{ij})^{s_{ij}} (1 - f_{ij})^{t_{ij}}.$$

Proof. Let H_{ij} be the set of all indices h such that $X_i^{(h)}$'s parents are in their jth instantiation pa_{ij}.

We have

$$\begin{aligned}
\prod_{h=1}^{M} P(x_i^{(h)}|\mathsf{pa}_i^{(h)}, \mathsf{f}_i) &= \prod_{h=1}^{M} P(x_i^{(h)}|\mathsf{pa}_i^{(h)}, f_{i1}, \dots, f_{iq_i}) \\
&= \prod_{j=1}^{q_i} \prod_{h \in \mathsf{H}_{ij}} P(x_i^{(h)}|\mathsf{pa}_{ij}, f_{i1}, \dots, f_{iq_i}) \\
&= \prod_{j=1}^{q_i} (f_{ij})^{s_{ij}} (1 - f_{ij})^{t_{ij}}.
\end{aligned}$$

The first equality is obtained by substituting the members of f_i, the second is obtained by rearranging terms, and the third is due to Equality 6.7.   ∎

Lemma 6.11 *Suppose we have the conditions in Lemma 6.10. Then*

$$P(\mathsf{d}|f_{11}, \dots, f_{nq_n}) = \prod_{i=1}^{n} \prod_{j=1}^{q_i} (f_{ij})^{s_{ij}} (1 - f_{ij})^{t_{ij}}.$$

Proof. We have

$$\begin{aligned}
P(\mathsf{d}|f_{11}, \dots, f_{nq_n}) &= P(\mathsf{d}|\mathsf{f}_1, \dots, \mathsf{f}_n) \\
&= \prod_{i=1}^{n} \prod_{h=1}^{M} P(x_i^{(h)}|\mathsf{pa}_i^{(h)}, \mathsf{f}_i) \\
&= \prod_{i=1}^{n} \prod_{j=1}^{q_i} (f_{ij})^{s_{ij}} (1 - f_{ij})^{t_{ij}}.
\end{aligned}$$

The first equality is obtained by replacing the members of the $\mathsf{f}_i s$ by these sets, the second is due to Lemma 6.8, and the third is due to Lemma 6.10.   ∎

Theorem 6.11 *Suppose we have the conditions in Lemma 6.10. Then*

$$P(\mathsf{d}) = \prod_{i=1}^{n} \prod_{j=1}^{q_i} E(F_{ij}{}^{s_{ij}} [1 - F_{ij}]^{t_{ij}}).$$

Proof. *We have*

$$
\begin{aligned}
P(\mathsf{d}) &= \prod_{i=1}^{n} \left(\int_{\mathsf{f}_i} \prod_{h=1}^{M} P(x_i^{(h)} | \mathsf{pa}_i^{(h)}, \mathsf{f}_i) \rho(\mathsf{f}_i) d\mathsf{f}_i \right) \\
&= \prod_{i=1}^{n} \left(\int_{\mathsf{f}_i} \prod_{j=1}^{q_i} (f_{ij})^{s_{ij}} (1 - f_{ij})^{t_{ij}} \rho(\mathsf{f}_i) d\mathsf{f}_i \right) \\
&= \prod_{i=1}^{n} \prod_{j=1}^{q_i} \int_0^1 (f_{ij})^{s_{ij}} (1 - f_{ij})^{t_{ij}} \rho(f_{ij}) df_{ij} \\
&= \prod_{i=1}^{n} \prod_{j=1}^{q_i} E(F_{ij}{}^{s_{ij}} [1 - F_{ij}]^{t_{ij}}).
\end{aligned}
$$

The first equality is due to Theorem 6.8, and the second is due Lemma 6.10.
■

Corollary 6.6 *Suppose we have the conditions in Lemma 6.10 and each F_{ij} has a beta distribution with parameters $a_{ij}, b_{ij}, N_{ij} = a_{ij} + b_{ij}$. Then*

$$P(\mathsf{d}) = \prod_{i=1}^{n} \prod_{j=1}^{q_i} \frac{\Gamma(N_{ij})}{\Gamma(N_{ij} + M_{ij})} \frac{\Gamma(a_{ij} + s_{ij})\Gamma(b_{ij} + t_{ij})}{\Gamma(a_{ij})\Gamma(b_{ij})}.$$

Proof. *The proof follows immediately from Theorem 6.11 and Lemma 6.4.*
■

Example 6.20 *Suppose we have a binomial Bayesian network sample whose parameter is the augmented Bayesian network in Figure 6.22 (a). For the sake of concreteness, let's say the variables represent the following:*

Variable	Value	When the Variable Takes this Value
X_1	1	*There is a history of smoking*
	2	*There is no history of smoking*
X_2	1	*Lung Cancer is present*
	2	*Lung Cancer is absent*

Suppose further that we obtain the data (values of X_1 and X_2) on eight individuals (cases) shown in Table 6.2. Then

$$\mathbf{x}^{(1)} = \begin{pmatrix} 1 \\ 2 \end{pmatrix} \qquad \mathbf{x}^{(2)} = \begin{pmatrix} 1 \\ 1 \end{pmatrix} \qquad \mathbf{x}^{(3)} = \begin{pmatrix} 2 \\ 1 \end{pmatrix} \qquad \mathbf{x}^{(4)} = \begin{pmatrix} 2 \\ 2 \end{pmatrix}$$

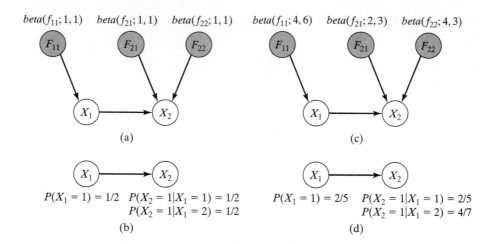

Figure 6.22: An augmented Bayesian network is shown in (a) and its embedded Bayesian network is shown in (b). Updated networks are shown in (c) and (d).

$$\mathbf{x}^{(5)} = \begin{pmatrix} 2 \\ 1 \end{pmatrix} \qquad \mathbf{x}^{(6)} = \begin{pmatrix} 2 \\ 1 \end{pmatrix} \qquad \mathbf{x}^{(7)} = \begin{pmatrix} 1 \\ 2 \end{pmatrix} \qquad \mathbf{x}^{(8)} = \begin{pmatrix} 2 \\ 2 \end{pmatrix}$$

$$\mathsf{d} = \{\mathbf{x}^{(1)}, \mathbf{x}^{(2)}, \dots, \mathbf{x}^{(8)}\}.$$

Counting yields $s_{11} = 3$, $t_{11} = 5$, $s_{21} = 1$, $t_{21} = 2$, $s_{22} = 3$, $t_{22} = 2$. From Figure 6.22 (a), we see for all i and j that $a_{ij} = b_{ij} = 1$. Therefore, due to the preceding corollary,

$$
\begin{aligned}
P(\mathsf{d}) &= \left(\frac{\Gamma(2)}{\Gamma(2+8)} \frac{\Gamma(1+3)\Gamma(1+5)}{\Gamma(1)\Gamma(1)} \right) \left(\frac{\Gamma(2)}{\Gamma(2+3)} \frac{\Gamma(1+1)\Gamma(1+2)}{\Gamma(1)\Gamma(1)} \right) \left(\frac{\Gamma(2)}{\Gamma(2+5)} \frac{\Gamma(1+3)\Gamma(1+2)}{\Gamma(1)\Gamma(1)} \right) \\
&= 2.7557 \times 10^{-6}.
\end{aligned}
$$

Case	X_1	X_2
1	1	2
2	1	1
3	2	1
4	2	2
5	2	1
6	2	1
7	1	2
8	2	2

Table 6.2: Data on eight cases

Theorem 6.12 *(Posterior Local Parameter Independence) Suppose we have the conditions in Lemma 6.10. Then the $F_{ij}s$ are mutually independent conditional on* D. *That is,*

$$\rho(f_{11}, f_{12}, \ldots, f_{nq_n}|\mathsf{d}) = \prod_{i=1}^{n} \prod_{j=1}^{q_i} \rho(f_{ij}|\mathsf{d}).$$

Furthermore,

$$\rho(f_{ij}|\mathsf{d}) = \frac{(f_{ij})^{s_{ij}}(1 - f_{ij})^{t_{ij}}\rho(f_{ij})}{E(F_{ij}{}^{s_{ij}}[1 - F_{ij}]^{t_{ij}})}.$$

Proof. *We have*

$$
\begin{aligned}
\rho(f_{11}, \ldots, f_{nq_n}|\mathsf{d}) &= \frac{P(\mathsf{d}|f_{11}, \ldots, f_{nq_n})\rho(f_{11})\cdots\rho(f_{nq_n})}{P(\mathsf{d})} \\[2mm]
&= \frac{\left(\prod_{i=1}^{n}\prod_{j=1}^{q_i}(f_{ij})^{s_{ij}}(1 - f_{ij})^{t_{ij}}\right)\rho(f_{11})\cdots\rho(f_{nq_n})}{P(\mathsf{d})} \\[2mm]
&= \frac{\prod_{i=1}^{n}\prod_{j=1}^{q_i}(f_{ij})^{s_{ij}}(1 - f_{ij})^{t_{ij}}\rho(f_{ij})}{P(\mathsf{d})} \\[2mm]
&= \frac{\prod_{i=1}^{n}\prod_{j=1}^{q_i}(f_{ij})^{s_{ij}}(1 - f_{ij})^{t_{ij}}\rho(f_{ij})}{\prod_{i=1}^{n}\prod_{j=1}^{q_i}E(F_{ij}{}^{s_{ij}}[1 - F_{ij}]^{t_{ij}})} \\[2mm]
&= \prod_{i=1}^{n}\prod_{j=1}^{q_i}\frac{(f_{ij})^{s_{ij}}(1 - f_{ij})^{t_{ij}}\rho(f_{ij})}{E(F_{ij}{}^{s_{ij}}[1 - F_{ij}]^{t_{ij}})}.
\end{aligned}
$$

The first equality is due to Bayes' theorem, the second is due to Lemma 6.11, the third is obtained by rearranging terms, and the fourth is due to Theorem 6.11.

We have further that for each u and each v,

$$\rho(f_{uv}|\mathbf{d}) = \frac{P(\mathbf{d}|f_{uv})\rho(f_{uv})}{P(\mathbf{d})}$$

$$= \frac{\left(\int_0^1 \cdots \int_0^1 P(\mathbf{d}|f_{11}, \ldots, f_{nq_n}) \prod_{ij \neq uv} [\rho(f_{ij})df_{ij}] \right) \rho(f_{uv})}{P(\mathbf{d})}$$

$$= \frac{(f_{uv})^{s_{uv}}(1 - f_{uv})^{t_{uv}} \left(\prod_{ij \neq uv} \int_0^1 (f_{ij})^{s_{ij}}(1 - f_{ij})^{t_{ij}} \rho(f_{ij})df_{ij} \right) \rho(f_{uv})}{P(\mathbf{d})}$$

$$= \frac{(f_{uv})^{s_{uv}}(1 - f_{uv})^{t_{uv}} \left(\prod_{ij \neq uv} E(F_{ij}{}^{s_{ij}}[1 - F_{ij}]^{t_{ij}}) \right) \rho(f_{uv})}{\prod_{i=1}^{n} \prod_{j=1}^{q_i} E(F_{ij}{}^{s_{ij}}[1 - F_{ij}]^{t_{ij}})}$$

$$= \frac{(f_{uv})^{s_{uv}}(1 - f_{uv})^{t_{uv}} \rho(f_{uv})}{E(F_{uv}{}^{s_{uv}}[1 - F_{uv}]^{t_{uv}})}.$$

The first equality is due to Bayes' theorem, the second is due to the law of total probability and the fact that the F_{ij}s are independent, the third is obtained by applying Lemma 6.11 and rearranging terms, and the fourth is due to Theorem 6.11.

This proves the theorem. ∎

Corollary 6.7 *Suppose we have the conditions in Lemma 6.10 and each F_{ij} has a beta distribution with parameters $a_{ij}, b_{ij}, N_{ij} = a_{ij} + b_{ij}$. That is, for each i and each j,*

$$\rho(f_{ij}) = beta(f_{ij}; a_{ij}, b_{ij}).$$

Then

$$\rho(f_{ij}|\mathbf{d}) = beta(f_{ij}; a_{ij} + s_{ij}, b_{ij} + t_{ij}).$$

Proof.   *The proof follows immediately from Theorem 6.12 and Lemma 6.5.* ∎

Example 6.21 *Suppose we have the binomial Bayesian network sample in Example 6.20. Then since $a_{ij} = b_{ij} = 1$ for all i and j, and $s_{11} = 3$, $t_{11} = 5$, $s_{21} = 1$, $t_{21} = 2$, $s_{22} = 3$, $t_{22} = 2$, we have*

$$\rho(f_{11}|\mathbf{d}) = beta(f_{11}; 1 + 3, 1 + 5) = beta(f_{11}; 4, 6)$$
$$\rho(f_{21}|\mathbf{d}) = beta(f_{21}; 1 + 1, 1 + 2) = beta(f_{21}; 2, 3)$$
$$\rho(f_{22}|\mathbf{d}) = beta(f_{22}; 1 + 3, 1 + 2) = beta(f_{22}; 4, 3).$$

Recall that Definition 6.12 says the augmented Bayesian network $(\mathbb{G}, \mathsf{F}, \rho | \mathsf{d})$ is called the updated augmented Bayesian network relative to the Bayesian network sample and the data d, and the network it embeds is called the updated embedded Bayesian network. The following example shows updated networks.

Example 6.22 *Given the binomial Bayesian network sample in Example 6.20, the updated networks are the ones shown in Figures 6.22 (c) and (d).*

Recall that, due to Theorem 6.10, the updated embedded Bayesian network is the one used to do inference for the $M + 1$st case, and we do not show the conditioning on $\mathsf{D} = \mathsf{d}$. That is, we simply use the updated embedded network as always representing our current belief for the next case.

Example 6.23 *As discussed in Example 6.22, given the binomial Bayesian network sample in Example 6.20, the updated networks are the ones shown in Figures 6.22 (c) and (d). Therefore, due to Theorem 6.10, the network in Figure 6.22 (d) is the one used to do inference for the 9th case. For example, we compute $P(X_2 = 1)$ for the 9th case as follows:*

$$
\begin{aligned}
P(X_2 = 1) &= P(X_2 = 1 | X_1 = 1)P(X_1 = 1) + P(X_2 = 1 | X_1 = 2)P(X_1 = 2) \\
&= \left(\frac{2}{5}\right)\left(\frac{2}{5}\right) + \left(\frac{4}{7}\right)\left(\frac{3}{5}\right) = .50286.
\end{aligned}
$$

Note in the previous example that we dropped the superscript and the conditioning on $\mathsf{D} = \mathsf{d}$.

6.4.4   A Problem with Updating; Using an Equivalent Sample Size

Let's compute $P(X_2 = 1)$ using the original embedded Bayesian network in Figure 6.22 (b). We have

$$
P(X_2 = 1) = \left(\frac{1}{2}\right)\left(\frac{1}{2}\right) + \left(\frac{1}{2}\right)\left(\frac{1}{2}\right) = .5.
$$

As shown in Example 6.23, after updating using the data in Table 6.2, we have

$$
P(X_2 = 1) = .50286. \tag{6.12}
$$

Something may seem amiss. We initially had $P(X_2 = 1)$ equal to .5. Then we updated our belief using a sample that had four occurrences in which $X_2 = 1$ and four occurrences in which $X_2 = 2$, and our $P(X_2 = 1)$ changed to .50286. Even if this seems odd, it is a mathematical consequence of assigning uniform prior distributions to all three parameters. That is, if the situation being modeled is the experiment discussed in Section 6.4.1 concerning the three urns in Figure 6.1.1, then this is the correct probability. It is correct in that if we repeated the experiment of sampling coins and tossing them nine times, the probability

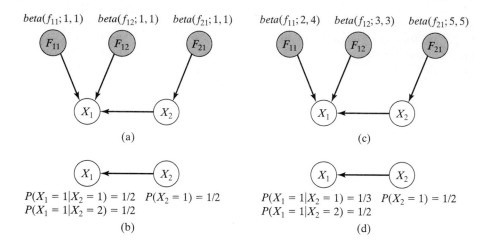

Figure 6.23: An augmented Bayesian network is shown in (a) and its embedded Bayesian network is shown in (b). Updated networks are shown in (c) and (d).

in Equality 6.12 is the relative frequency of the second coin landing heads when the first eight tosses yield the data in Table 6.2. Although the coin tossing example clearly illustrates a probability distribution of the value of a relative frequency, it does not seem to be a good metaphor for applications. Rather it seems more reasonable to use the metaphor which says that our prior belief concerning the relative frequency is obtained from a prior sample. That is, we take the specified values of a_{ij} and b_{ij} as meaning our prior experience is equivalent to having seen a sample in which the first value occurred a_{ij} times in $a_{ij} + b_{ij}$ trials. Given this, since F_{11} has the $beta(f_{11}; 1, 1)$ density function in Figure 6.22 (a), our prior experience is equivalent to having seen X_1 take the value 1 *once* in two trials. However, since F_{21} also has the $beta(f_{21}; 1, 1)$ density function, our prior experience is equivalent to having seen X_2 take the value 1 once out of the *two* times X_1 took the value 1. Of course, this is not a very reasonable representation of one's prior belief. It happened because we have specified four prior occurrences at node X_2 (two in each beta density function), but only two prior occurrences at node X_1. As a result, we use mixed sample sizes in the computation of $P(X_2 = 1)$. We therefore end up with strange results because we do not cling to the originally specified probabilities at node X_1 as much as the specifications at node X_2 indicate we should.

Another problem arises for the same reason. Suppose we simply reverse the arc between X_1 and X_2, try again to specify prior indifference by using all $beta(f; 1, 1)$ density functions, and update using the data in Table 6.2. The results are shown in Figure 6.23. As Figure 6.23 (d) shows, now after updating, we have

$$P(X_2 = 1) = .5.$$

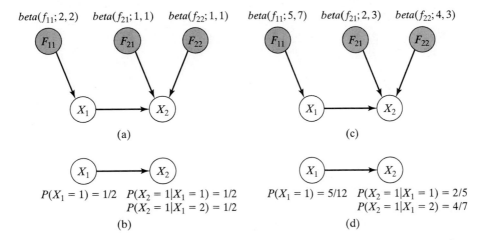

Figure 6.24: An augmented Bayesian network is shown in (a) and its embedded Bayesian network is shown in (b). Updated networks are shown in (c) and (d).

We see that our updated probabilities depend on which equivalent DAG we use to represent the independencies. Recall that our assumption in a Bayesian network sample is that we know the conditional independencies among the variables, and we are merely using the DAG to represent these independencies. So our results should not depend on which equivalent DAG we use.

Prior Equivalent Sample Size

It seems we could remedy these problems by specifying the same prior sample size at each node. That is, given the network $X_1 \rightarrow X_2$, if we specify four occurrences at X_2 using two $beta(f; 1, 1)$ distributions, then we should specify four occurrences at X_1 using a $beta(f; 2, 2)$ distribution[4]. Figure 6.24 shows the result when we do this and subsequently update using the data in Table 6.2. Let's compute $P(X_2 = 1)$ using the updated network in Figure 6.24 (d):

$$P(X_2 = 1) = \left(\frac{2}{5}\right)\left(\frac{5}{12}\right) + \left(\frac{4}{7}\right)\left(\frac{7}{12}\right) = .5.$$

So now we get the value we would expect. Furthermore, if we reverse the arrow between X_1 and X_2, specify a $beta(f; 2, 2)$ density function at X_2 and two $beta(f; 1, 1)$ density functions at X_1, and update using the same data, we get

---

[4]If our prior beliefs are based only on past cases with no missing data, then an equivalent sample size models our prior beliefs, and this remedy to the noted problems seems appropriate. However, if our prior beliefs come from different knowledge sources, it may not be appropriate. For example, our knowledge of the distribution of X_1 may be based on seeing $X_1 = 1$ once in two trials. However, our knowledge of $X_2 = 1$ given $X_1 = 1$ may be based on a distribution of some population we read about in a research paper. In this case an equivalent sample size would not model our prior beliefs. I thank Gregory Cooper for this observation.

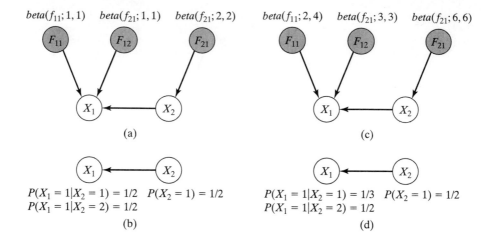

Figure 6.25: An augmented Bayesian network is shown in (a) and its embedded Bayesian network structure is shown in (b). Updated networks are shown in (c) and (d).

the updated network in Figure 6.25 (d). Clearly, in that network we also have

$$P(X_2 = 1) = .5.$$

Indeed the entire updated joint distribution for the network with the edge $X_2 \rightarrow X_1$ is the same as that for the network with the edge $X_1 \rightarrow X_2$. Example 6.29, which follows shortly, shows this. So the updated distribution now does not depend on which equivalent DAG we use. This result is a special case of Theorem 6.13, which we present shortly. First, we need a definition.

Definition 6.13 *Suppose we have a binomial augmented Bayesian network in which the density functions are beta$(f_{ij}; a_{ij}, b_{ij})$ for all i and j. If there is a number N such that, for all i and j*

$$N_{ij} = a_{ij} + b_{ij} = P(\mathsf{pa}_{ij}) \times N, \tag{6.13}$$

*then the network is said to have **equivalent sample size** N.*

Recall that in the case of a root, PA_i is empty and $q_i = 1$. So in this case, $P(\mathsf{pa}_{i1}) = 1$. If a binomial augmented Bayesian network has n nodes and equivalent sample size N, we have for $1 \le i \le n$,

$$\sum_{j=1}^{q_i} N_{ij} = \sum_{j=1}^{q_i} \left[P(\mathsf{pa}_{ij}) \times N \right] = N \times \sum_{j=1}^{q_i} P(\mathsf{pa}_{ij}) = N.$$

The idea in an equivalent sample size is that we specify values of a_{ij} and b_{ij} that could actually occur in a sample that exhibit the conditional independencies entailed by the DAG. Some examples follow:

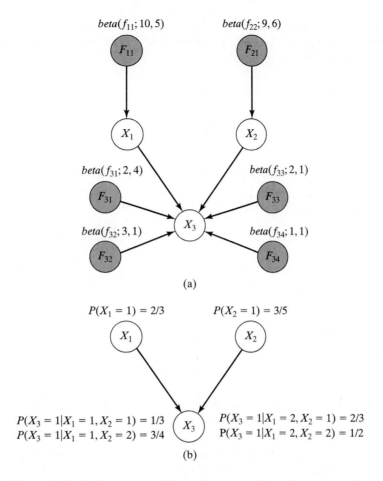

Figure 6.26: A binomial augmented Bayesian network with an equivalent sample size of 15 is shown in (a). It's embedded network is shown in (b).

Example 6.24 *Figure 6.26 shows a binomial augmented Bayesian network with an equivalent sample size of* 15. *We prove that this is the case by showing that Equality 6.13 holds. To that end,*

$$a_{11} + b_{11} = 10 + 5 = 15$$

$$P(\mathbf{pa}_{11}) \times N = (1)(15) = 15$$

$$a_{31} + b_{31} = 2 + 4 = 6$$

$$P(\mathbf{pa}_{31}) \times N = P(X_1 = 1, X_2 = 1) \times N = \left(\frac{2}{3}\right)\left(\frac{3}{5}\right) 15 = 6.$$

It is left as an exercise to compute the remaining four pairs of values.

Example 6.25 *Figure 6.20 shows a binomial augmented Bayesian network with an equivalent sample size of 10. We prove that this is the case by showing that Equality 6.13 holds. To that end,*

$$a_{31} + b_{31} = 2 + 1 = 3$$

$P(\mathsf{pa}_{31}) \times N$

$$
\begin{aligned}
&= P(X_2 = 1) \times N \\
&= [P(X_2 = 1|X_1 = 1)P(X_1 = 1) + P(X_2 = 1|X_1 = 2)P(X_1 = 2)] \times N \\
&= \left[\left(\frac{1}{4} \right) \left(\frac{4}{5} \right) + \left(\frac{1}{2} \right) \left(\frac{1}{5} \right) \right] \times 10 = 3.
\end{aligned}
$$

It is left as an exercise to compute the remaining four pairs of values.

It is unlikely that we would arrive at a network with an equivalent sample size simply by making up values of a_{ij} and b_{ij}. The next two theorems give common ways for constructing one.

Theorem 6.13 *Suppose we specify* $\mathbb{G}$, F, *and* N *and assign for all* i *and* j

$$a_{ij} = b_{ij} = \frac{N}{2q_i}.$$

Then the resultant augmented Bayesian network has equivalent sample size N, *and the probability distribution in the resultant embedded Bayesian network is uniform.*

Proof. *It is left as an exercise to show that, with these specifications,* $P(\mathsf{pa}_{ij}) = 1/q_i$ *for all values of* i *and* j. *Therefore,*

$$a_{ij} + b_{ij} = \frac{N}{2q_i} + \frac{N}{2q_i} = \left(\frac{1}{q_i} \right) \times N = P(\mathsf{pa}_{ij}) \times N.$$

It is also left as an exercise to show that the probability distribution in the resultant embedded Bayesian network is uniform. This proves the theorem. ∎

Example 6.26 *The specifications in the previous theorem simply spread the value of* N *evenly among all the values specified at a node. This is how the networks in Figures 6.24 (a) and 6.25 (a) were developed.*

Theorem 6.14 *Suppose we specify* $\mathbb{G}$, F, N, *a Bayesian network* $(\mathbb{G}, P)$, *and assign for all* i *and* j

$$a_{ij} = P(X_i = 1|\mathsf{pa}_{ij}) \times P(\mathsf{pa}_{ij}) \times N$$

$$b_{ij} = P(X_i = 2|\mathsf{pa}_{ij}) \times P(\mathsf{pa}_{ij}) \times N.$$

Then the resultant augmented Bayesian network has equivalent sample size N. Furthermore, it embeds the originally specified Bayesian network.

Proof. *Let P' be the probability distribution in the resultant embedded network. Clearly,*

$$a_{ij} + b_{ij} = P(\mathsf{pa}_{ij}) \times N.$$

So if we can show that P' is the same distribution as P, Equality 6.13 is satisfied and we are done. To that end, due to Corollary 6.5, we have

$$
\begin{aligned}
P'(X_i = 1|\mathsf{pa}_{ij}) &= \frac{a_{ij}}{a_{ij} + b_{ij}} \\
&= \frac{P(X_i = 1|\mathsf{pa}_{ij}) \times P(\mathsf{pa}_{ij}) \times N}{P(\mathsf{pa}_{ij}) \times N} \\
&= P(X_i = 1|\mathsf{pa}_{ij}).
\end{aligned}
$$

This proves the theorem. ∎

Example 6.27 *If we specify the Bayesian network in Figure 6.26 (b), $N = 15$, and values of a_{ij} and b_{ij} according to the previous theorem, we obtain the augmented network in Figure 6.26 (a). It is left as an exercise to do this.*

After a definition, a lemma and an example, we prove the theorem to which we alluded earlier. In what follows we need to refer to two augmented Bayesian networks. So we show the dependence of F and ρ on $\mathbb{G}$ by representing an augmented Bayesian network as $(\mathbb{G}, \mathsf{F}^{(\mathbb{G})}, \rho|\mathbb{G})$. The notation $\rho|\mathbb{G}$ denotes the density function in the augmented Bayesian network containing the DAG $\mathbb{G}$. It does not entail that the DAG $\mathbb{G}$ is an event.

Definition 6.14 *Binomial augmented Bayesian networks $(\mathbb{G}_1, \mathsf{F}^{(\mathbb{G}_1)}, \rho|\mathbb{G}_1)$ and $(\mathbb{G}_2, \mathsf{F}^{(\mathbb{G}_2)}, \rho|\mathbb{G}_2)$ are called **equivalent** if they satisfy the following:*

1. *$\mathbb{G}_1$ and $\mathbb{G}_2$ are Markov equivalent.*

2. *The probability distributions in their embedded Bayesian networks are the same.*

3. *The specified density functions in both are beta.*

4. *They have the same equivalent sample size.*

Lemma 6.12 *(**Likelihood Equivalence**) Suppose we have two equivalent binomial augmented Bayesian network $(\mathbb{G}_1, \mathsf{F}^{(\mathbb{G}_1)}, \rho|\mathbb{G}_1)$ and $(\mathbb{G}_2, \mathsf{F}^{(\mathbb{G}_2)}, \rho|\mathbb{G}_2)$. Let D be a set of random vectors as specified in Definition 6.11. Then for every set d of values of the vectors in D,*

$$P(\mathsf{d}|\mathbb{G}_1) = P(\mathsf{d}|\mathbb{G}_2),$$

where $P(\mathsf{d}|\mathbb{G}_1)$ and $P(\mathsf{d}|\mathbb{G}_2)$ are the probabilities of d when D is considered a binomial Bayesian network sample with parameters $(\mathbb{G}_1, \mathsf{F}^{(\mathbb{G}_1)})$ and $(\mathbb{G}_2, \mathsf{F}^{(\mathbb{G}_2)})$, respectively.

Proof. *The proof can be found in Heckerman et al. [1995].* ∎

Example 6.28 Let $(\mathbb{G}_1, \mathsf{F}^{(\mathbb{G}_1)}, \rho|\mathbb{G}_1)$ be the augmented Bayesian network in Figure 6.24 (a) and $(\mathbb{G}_2, \mathsf{F}^{(\mathbb{G}_2)}, \rho|\mathbb{G}_2)$ be the one in Figure 6.25 (a). Clearly, they are equivalent. Given the data d in Table 6.2, we have, due to Corollary 6.2,

$$
\begin{aligned}
P(\mathsf{d}|\mathbb{G}_1) &= \left(\frac{\Gamma(4)}{\Gamma(4+8)} \frac{\Gamma(2+3)\Gamma(2+5)}{\Gamma(2)\Gamma(2)} \right) \left(\frac{\Gamma(2)}{\Gamma(2+3)} \frac{\Gamma(1+1)\Gamma(1+2)}{\Gamma(1)\Gamma(1)} \right) \left(\frac{\Gamma(2)}{\Gamma(2+5)} \frac{\Gamma(1+3)\Gamma(1+2)}{\Gamma(1)\Gamma(1)} \right) \\
&= 3.6075 \times 10^{-6}.
\end{aligned}
$$

$$
\begin{aligned}
P(\mathsf{d}|\mathbb{G}_2) &= \left(\frac{\Gamma(4)}{\Gamma(4+8)} \frac{\Gamma(2+4)\Gamma(2+4)}{\Gamma(2)\Gamma(2)} \right) \left(\frac{\Gamma(2)}{\Gamma(2+4)} \frac{\Gamma(1+2)\Gamma(1+2)}{\Gamma(1)\Gamma(1)} \right) \left(\frac{\Gamma(2)}{\Gamma(2+4)} \frac{\Gamma(1+3)\Gamma(1+1)}{\Gamma(1)\Gamma(1)} \right) \\
&= 3.6075 \times 10^{-6}.
\end{aligned}
$$

The values are the same as the lemma implies. It is left as an exercise to show that they are not the same for the networks in Figures 6.22 (a) and 6.23 (a).

Theorem 6.15 Suppose we have two equivalent binomial augmented Bayesian networks $(\mathbb{G}_1, \mathsf{F}^{(\mathbb{G}_1)}, \rho|\mathbb{G}_1)$ and $(\mathbb{G}_2, \mathsf{F}^{(\mathbb{G}_2)}, \rho|\mathbb{G}_2)$. Let D be a set of random vectors as specified in Definition 6.11. Then, given any set d of values of the vectors in D, the updated embedded Bayesian network relative to D and the data d, obtained by considering D a binomial Bayesian network sample with parameter $(\mathbb{G}_1, \mathsf{F}^{(\mathbb{G}_1)})$, contains the same probability distribution as the one obtained by considering D a binomial Bayesian network sample with parameter $(\mathbb{G}_2, \mathsf{F}^{(\mathbb{G}_2)})$. **Proof.** We have

$$
\begin{aligned}
P(\mathbf{x}^{(M+1)}|\mathsf{d}, \mathbb{G}_1) &= \frac{P(\mathsf{d}, \mathbf{x}^{(M+1)}|\mathbb{G}_1)}{P(\mathsf{d}|\mathbb{G}_1)} \\
&= \frac{P(\mathsf{d}, \mathbf{x}^{(M+1)}|\mathbb{G}_2)}{P(\mathsf{d}|\mathbb{G}_2)} \\
&= P(\mathbf{x}^{(M+1)}|\mathsf{d}, \mathbb{G}_2).
\end{aligned}
$$

The second equality is true because Lemma 6.12 implies that the values in the numerators and denominators are the same. Since Theorem 6.10 says $P(\mathbf{x}^{(M+1)}|\mathsf{d}, \mathbb{G}_i)$ is the probability distribution contained in the updated embedded Bayesian network relative to D and the data d, the theorem is proven. ■

Corollary 6.8 Suppose we have two equivalent binomial augmented Bayesian networks $(\mathbb{G}_1, \mathsf{F}^{(\mathbb{G}_1)}, \rho|\mathbb{G}_1)$ and $(\mathbb{G}_2, \mathsf{F}^{(\mathbb{G}_2)}, \rho|\mathbb{G}_2)$. Then, given any set d of values of the vectors in D, the updated embedded Bayesian network relative to D and the data d, obtained by considering D a binomial Bayesian network sample with parameter $(\mathbb{G}_1, \mathsf{F}^{(\mathbb{G}_1)})$, is equivalent to the one obtained by considering D a binomial Bayesian network sample with parameter $(\mathbb{G}_2, \mathsf{F}^{(\mathbb{G}_2)})$. **Proof.** The proof follows easily from the preceding theorem. ■

Example 6.29 Consider augmented Bayesian networks discussed in Example 6.28 and their updated embedded Bayesian networks which appear in Figures 6.24 (d) and 6.25 (d). For the one in Figure 6.24 (d), we have

$$
P(X_1 = 1, X_2 = 1) = \left(\frac{2}{5} \right) \left(\frac{5}{12} \right) = .16667.
$$

For the one in Figure 6.25 (d), we have

$$P(X_1 = 1, X_2 = 1) = \left(\frac{1}{3}\right)\left(\frac{1}{2}\right) = .16667.$$

The values are the same as the theorem implies. It is left as an exercise to check the other three values.

Due to the preceding theorem, as long as we use an equivalent sample size, our updated probability distribution does not depend on which equivalent DAG we use to represent a set of conditional independencies. So henceforth, we will always use an equivalent sample size.

Expressing Prior Indifference with a Prior Equivalent Sample Size

Recall from Section 6.2.2 that we take $a = b = 1$ when we feel all numbers in $[0, 1]$ equally likely to be the relative frequency with which the random variable assumes each of its values. We use these values when we feel we have no knowledge at all concerning the value of the relative frequency, and also to try to achieve objectivity in the sense that we impose none of our beliefs concerning the relative frequency on the learning algorithm. We tried doing this with the specifications in the augmented Bayesian network in Figure 6.22 (a), and ended up with unacceptable results. We eliminated these unacceptable results by using the network with an equivalent sample size in Figure 6.24 (a). However, in that network, we no longer assign equal density to all possible values of the relative frequency with which $X_1 = 1$. By the mere fact of including X_1 in a network with X_2, we have become more confident that the relative frequency with which X_1 equals 1 is around .5! So what equivalent sample size should we use to express prior indifference? We can shed light on this question by looking again at the two equivalent DAGs $X_1 \rightarrow X_2$ and $X_2 \rightarrow X_1$. If we used the former DAG, we would want to specify a $beta(f_{11}; 1, 1)$ density function for F_{11}. That is, we would want to use a prior sample size of two at node X_1. If we merely reverse the arrows, it seems that there is no reason we should change that sample size. So it seems we should still use a prior sample size of two at X_1, only now we must spread it over two density functions, namely $beta(f_{11}; .5, .5)$ and $beta(f_{12}; .5, .5)$. In general, it seems a good way to express prior indifference is to use an equivalent sample size of two, and for each node to distribute the sample evenly among all specified values. In this way, the total "sample" size at each node is always two, even though for nonroots the specified ones are fractional. Figure 6.27 shows an example.

Our Beliefs When Using a Prior Equivalent Sample Size

At the end of Section 6.4.2, we mentioned that the assumption when using an augmented Bayesian network is that the variables representing our belief concerning relative frequencies are independent. However, when we use a different equivalent binomial augmented Bayesian network, different variables are

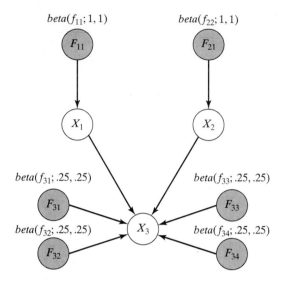

Figure 6.27: We express prior indifference to the values of all relative frequencies using a prior equivalent sample size of two.

assumed to be independent. For example, in Figure 6.24, it is assumed that the variable representing our belief concerning the relative frequency with which $X_2 = 1$ given $X_1 = 1$ is independent of the variable representing our belief concerning the relative frequency with which $X_2 = 1$ given $X_1 = 2$. However, in Figure 6.25, it is assumed that the variable whose probability distribution represents our belief concerning the relative frequency with which $X_1 = 1$ given $X_2 = 1$ is independent of the variable whose probability distribution represents our belief concerning the relative frequency with which $X_1 = 1$ given $X_2 = 2$. As we have seen, all our results are the same as long as we use equivalent bino-mial Bayesian networks. So perhaps our assumptions should be stated relative to using equivalent augmented Bayesian networks rather than a particular one. We could state this as follows: Given a repeatable experiment whose outcome determines the state of n random variables, the assumption, when using a bino-mial augmented Bayesian network, is that our belief, concerning the probability of the outcome of repeated executions of the experiment, is entailed by any augmented Bayesian network equivalent to the one used.

6.5   Learning with Missing Data Items

So far we have considered data sets in which every value of every variable is recorded in every case. Next we consider the case in which some data items might be omitted. How might they be omitted? A common way, and indeed a way that is relatively easy to handle, is that they are simply random omissions due to recording problems or some similar error. First we discuss this case.

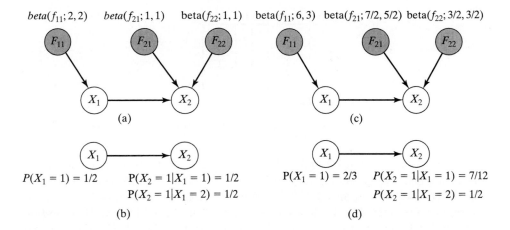

Figure 6.28: The network in (a) has been updated to the network in (c) using a first pass of the EM Algorithm.

6.5.1 Data Items Missing at Random

Suppose data items are missing at random. Before discussing how to update based on such data, let's review how we update when no data items are missing. Suppose we want to update the network in Figure 6.28 (a) with the data d in Table 6.3. Recall that s_{21} is the number of cases that have X_1 equal to 1 and X_2 equal to 1, while t_{21} is the number of cases that have X_1 equal to 1 and X_2 equal to 2. So we have

$$s_{21} = 3$$
$$t_{21} = 1.$$

Owing to Corollary 6.7,

$$\rho(f_{21}|\mathbf{d}) = beta(f_{21}; a_{21} + s_{21}, b_{21} + t_{21})$$
$$= beta(f_{21}; 1 + 3, 1 + 1)$$
$$= beta(f_{21}; 4, 2).$$

Suppose next that we want to update the network in Figure 6.28 (a) with the data d in Table 6.4. These data contain missing data items. We do not know

Case	X_1	X_2
1	1	1
2	1	1
3	1	1
4	1	2
5	2	2

Table 6.3: Data on five cases

Case	X_1	X_2
1	1	1
2	1	?
3	1	1
4	1	2
5	2	?

Table 6.4: Data on five cases with some data items missing

the value of X_2 for cases 2 and 5. It seems reasonable to "estimate" the value of X_2 in these cases using $P(X_2 = 1|X_1 = 1)$. That is, since this probability equals 1/2, we say X_2 has a 1/2 occurrence of 1 in each of cases 2 and 5. So we replace the data $\mathbf{d}$ in Table 6.4 by the data $\mathbf{d}'$ in Table 6.5. We then update our density functions using the number of occurrences listed in Table 6.5. So we have

$$
\begin{aligned}
s'_{21} &= 1 + \tfrac{1}{2} + 1 = \tfrac{5}{2} \\
t'_{21} &= \tfrac{1}{2} + 1 = \tfrac{3}{2},
\end{aligned}
\tag{6.14}
$$

$$
\begin{aligned}
s'_{22} &= \tfrac{1}{2} \\
t'_{22} &= \tfrac{1}{2},
\end{aligned}
\tag{6.15}
$$

where s'_{21}, t'_{21}, s'_{22}, and t'_{22} denote the counts in data $\mathbf{d}'$ (shown in Table 6.5). We then have

$$
\begin{aligned}
\rho(f_{21}|\mathbf{d}') &= beta(f_{21}; a_{21} + s'_{21}, b_{21} + t'_{21}) \\
&= beta\left(f_{21}; 1 + \tfrac{5}{2}, 1 + \tfrac{3}{2}\right) \\
&= beta\left(f_{21}; \tfrac{7}{2}, \tfrac{5}{2}\right)
\end{aligned}
$$

and

$$
\begin{aligned}
\rho(f_{22}|\mathbf{d}') &= beta(f_{21}; a_{22} + s'_{22}, b_{22} + t'_{22}) \\
&= beta\left(f_{21}; 1 + \tfrac{1}{2}, 1 + \tfrac{1}{2}\right) \\
&= beta\left(f_{21}; \tfrac{3}{2}, \tfrac{3}{2}\right).
\end{aligned}
$$

The updated network is shown in Figure 6.28 (c).

Case	X_1	X_2	# Occurences
1	1	1	1
2	1	1	1/2
2	1	2	1/2
3	1	1	1
4	1	2	1
5	2	1	1/2
5	2	2	1/2

Table 6.5: Estimates of missing values

If we consider s_{ij} and t_{ij} random variables, the method just outlined estimates the actual values of s_{ij} and t_{ij} by their expected values relative to the joint distribution of X_1 and X_2 conditional on the data and on the variables in F having their prior expected values. That is, if we set

$$\mathsf{f'} = \{f'_{11}, f'_{21}, f'_{22}\} = \{f_{11}, f_{21}, f_{22}\} = \{1/2, 1/2, 1/2\}$$

(the reason for defining $\mathsf{f'}$ will become clear shortly), then

$$
\begin{aligned}
s'_{21} = E(s_{21}|\mathsf{d}, \mathsf{f'}) &= \sum_{h=1}^{5} 1 \times P(X_1^{(h)} = 1, X_2^{(h)} = 1|\mathsf{d}, \mathsf{f'}) \qquad (6.16) \\
&= \sum_{h=1}^{5} P(X_1^{(h)} = 1, X_2^{(h)} = 1|\mathbf{x}^{(h)}, \mathsf{f'}) \\
&= \sum_{h=1}^{5} P(X_1^{(h)} = 1, X_2^{(h)} = 1|x_1^{(h)}, x_2^{(h)}, \mathsf{f'}) \\
&= 1 + \tfrac{1}{2} + 1 + 0 + 0 = \tfrac{5}{2}.
\end{aligned}
$$

Similarly,

$$t'_{21} = E(t_{21}|\mathsf{d}, \mathsf{f'}) = 0 + \tfrac{1}{2} + 0 + 1 + 0 = \tfrac{3}{2}.$$

Furthermore,

$$
\begin{aligned}
s'_{22} = E(s_{22}|\mathsf{d}, \mathsf{f'}) &= \sum_{h=1}^{5} 1 \times P(X_1^{(h)} = 1, X_2^{(h)} = 2|\mathsf{d}, \mathsf{f'}) \\
&= \sum_{h=1}^{5} P(X_1^{(h)} = 1, X_2^{(h)} = 2|\mathbf{x}^{(h)}, \mathsf{f'}) \\
&= \sum_{h=1}^{5} P(X_1^{(h)} = 1, X_2^{(h)} = 2|x_1^{(h)}, x_2^{(h)}, \mathsf{f'}) \\
&= 0 + 0 + 0 + 0 + \tfrac{1}{2} = \tfrac{1}{2}
\end{aligned}
$$

and

$$t'_{22} = E(t_{22}|\mathsf{d}, \mathsf{f'}) = 0 + 0 + 0 + 0 + \tfrac{1}{2} = \tfrac{1}{2}.$$

Note that these are the same values obtained in Equalities 6.14 and 6.15.

Using these expected values to estimate our density functions seems reasonable. However, note that our estimates are based only on the "data" in our prior sample. They are not based on the data d. That is, we say X_2 has a 1/2 occurrence of 1 in each of cases 2 and 5 because $P(X_2 = 1|X_1 = 1) = 1/2$ according to our prior sample. However, the data d "prefers" the event $X_1 = 1, X_2 = 1$ to the event $X_1 = 1, X_2 = 2$ because the former event occurs twice while the latter event occurs only once. To incorporate the data $\mathbf{d}$ in our estimates we can now repeat the computation in Expression 6.16 using the probability distribution in the updated network [Figures 6.28 (c) and (d)]. That is, we now set

$$\mathbf{f}' = \{f'_{11}, f'_{21}, f'_{22}\} = \{2/3, 7/12, 1/2\}$$

and compute

$$
\begin{aligned}
s'_{21} = E(s_{21}|\mathbf{d}, \mathbf{f}') &= \sum_{h=1}^{5} 1 \times P(X_1^{(h)} = 1, X_2^{(h)} = 1|\mathbf{d}, \mathbf{f}') \\
&= \sum_{h=1}^{5} P(X_1^{(h)} = 1, X_2^{(h)} = 1|\mathbf{x}^{(h)}, \mathbf{f}') \\
&= \sum_{h=1}^{5} P(X_1^{(h)} = 1, X_2^{(h)} = 1|x_1^{(h)}, x_2^{(h)}, \mathbf{f}') \\
&= 1 + \tfrac{7}{12} + 1 + 0 + 0 = 2\tfrac{7}{12}.
\end{aligned}
$$

Similarly,

$$t'_{21} = E(t_{21}|\mathbf{d}, \mathbf{f}') = 0 + \tfrac{5}{12} + 0 + 1 + 0 = 1\tfrac{5}{12}.$$

We recompute s'_{22} and t'_{22} in the same manner.

Clearly, we can keep repeating the previous two steps. Suppose we reiterate these steps, let $s_{ij}^{(v)}$ and $t_{ij}^{(v)}$ be the values of s'_{ij} and t'_{ij} after the vth iteration, and take the

$$\lim_{v \to \infty} f'_{ij} = \lim_{v \to \infty} \frac{a_{ij} + s_{ij}^{(v)}}{a_{ij} + s_{ij}^{(v)} + b_{ij} + t_{ij}^{(v)}}. \tag{6.17}$$

Then under certain regularity conditions, the limit that is approached by $\mathbf{f}' = \{f'_{i1}, \dots, f'_{ij}, \dots, f'_{nq_n}\}$ is a value of $\mathbf{f}$ that locally maximizes $\rho(\mathbf{f}|\mathbf{d})$[5].

The procedure we have just described is an application of the EM algorithm (Dempster et al. [1977]; McLachlan and Krishnan [1997]). In this algorithm, the step in which we recompute s'_{ij} and t'_{ij} is called the **expectation step**, and the step in which we recompute the value of $\mathbf{f}'$ is called the **maximization step** because we are approaching a local maximum.

The value $\tilde{\mathbf{f}}$ which maximizes $\rho(\mathbf{f}|\mathbf{d})$ is called the **maximum a posterior probability (MAP)** value of $\mathbf{f}$. We want to arrive at this value rather than at a local maximum. After presenting the algorithm, we discuss a way to avoid a local maximum.

---

[5]The maximizing values actually depend on the coordinate systems used to express the parameters. The ones given here correspond to the canonical coordinate system for the multinomial distribution. (See, e.g., Bernardo and Smith [1994].)

Algorithm 6.1 EM-MAP-determination

Problem: Given a binomial augmented Bayesian network in which the density functions are beta, and data d containing some missing data items, estimate $\rho(\mathsf{f}|\mathsf{d})$ and the MAP value of the parameter set f.

Inputs: binomial augmented Bayesian network $(\mathbb{G}, \mathsf{F}, \rho)$ and data d containing some incomplete data items.

Outputs: estimate $\rho(\mathsf{f}|\mathsf{d}')$ of $\rho(\mathsf{f}|\mathsf{d})$ and estimate f' of the MAP value of the parameter set f.

> **void** EM_MAP (**augmented-Bayesian-network** $(\mathbb{G}, \mathsf{F}, \rho)$,
> **data** d,
> **int** k,   // number of
> **density-function&** $\rho(\mathsf{f}|\mathsf{d}')$,   // iterations
> **MAP-estimate&** f')

```
{
    float s'_ij, t'_ij ;

    for (i = 1; i <= n; i ++)
        for (j = 1; j <= q_i; j ++)
            assign f'_ij a value in the interval (0, 1);
    repeat (k times) {
        for (i = 1; i <= n; i ++)                    // expectation
            for (j = 1; j <= q_i; j ++) {            // step
```

$$s'_{ij} = E(s_{ij}|\mathsf{d}, \mathsf{f}') = \sum_{h=1}^{M} P(X_i^{(h)} = 1, \mathsf{pa}_{ij}|\mathbf{x}^{(h)}, \mathsf{f}');$$
$$t'_{ij} = E(t_{ij}|\mathsf{d}, \mathsf{f}' = \sum_{h=1}^{M} P(X_i^{(h)} = 2, \mathsf{pa}_{ij}|\mathbf{x}^{(h)}, \mathsf{f}');$$

```
        }
        for (i = 1; i <= n; i ++)                    // maximiza-
            for (j = 1; j <= q_i; j ++)              // tion step
```

$$f'_{ij} = \frac{a_{ij} + s'_{ij}}{a_{ij} + s'_{ij} + b_{ij} + t'_{ij}};$$

```
    }
```
$$\rho(f_{ij}|\mathsf{d}') = beta(f_{ij}; a_{ij} + s'_{ij}, b_{ij} + t'_{ij});$$
```
}
```

Note that in the algorithm we initialized the algorithm by saying "assign f'_{ij} a value in the interval $(0, 1)$" rather than setting $f'_{ij} = a_{ij}/(a_{ij} + b_{ij})$ as we did in our illustration. We want to end up with the MAP value $\tilde{\mathsf{f}}$ of f; however, in general, we could end up with a local maximum when starting with any particular configuration of f'. So we do not start at only one particular configuration. Rather, we use multiple restarts of the algorithm. The following is a multiple-restart strategy discussed in Chickering and Heckerman [1997]. We sample 64 prior configurations of the variables in F according to a uniform distribution. By a configuration of the variables we mean an assignment of values to the variables. Next we perform one expectation and one maximization step, and we retain the 32 initial configurations that yielded the 32 values of f' with the largest values of $\rho(f'|d)$. Then we perform two expectation and maximization steps, and we retain 16 initial configurations using this same rule. We continue in this manner, in each iteration doubling the number of expectation–maximization steps, until only one configuration remains. You may wonder how we could determine which values of f' had the largest values of $\rho(f'|d)$ when we do not know this density function. For any value of f, we have

$$\rho(f|d) = \alpha\rho(d|f)\rho(f),$$

which means we can determine whether $\rho(f'|d)$ or $\rho(f''|d)$ is larger by comparing $\rho(d|f')\rho(f')$ and $\rho(d|f'')\rho(f'')$. To compute $\rho(d|f)\rho(f)$, we simply calculate $\rho(f)$ and determine $\rho(d|f) = \prod_{h=1}^{M} P(\mathbf{x}^{(h)}|f)$ using a Bayesian network inference algorithm.

The **maximum likelihood (ML)** value $\hat{f}$ of f is the value such that $P(d|f)$ is a maximum. (Recall that we introduced this value in Section 1.2.1.) Algorithm 6.1 can be modified to produce the ML value. We simply update as follows:

$$f'_{ij} = \frac{s'_{ij}}{s'_{ij} + t'_{ij}}.$$

A parameterized EM algorithm, which has faster convergence, is discussed in Bauer et al. [1997]. The EM Algorithm is not the only method for handling missing data items. Other methods include Monte Carlo techniques, in particular Gibb's sampling, which is discussed in Section 8.3.1.

6.5.2   Data Items Missing Not at Random

The method we outlined in the previous subsection is appropriate only when the absence of a data item does not depend on the states (values) of other variables. This is true if the data items are missing at random. It is also true if a variable is never observed in any cases. However, there are situations in which missing data is not independent of state. For example, in a drug study a patient may become too sick, due to a side effect of the drug, to complete the study. So the fact that the result variable is missing depends directly on the value of the side effect variable. Cooper [1995a], Spirtes et al. [1995], and Ramoni and Sebastiani [1999] discuss handling this more complicated situation.

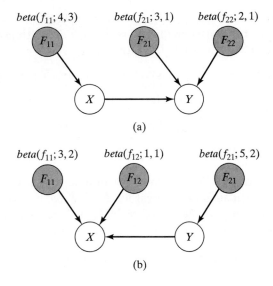

Figure 6.29: $E(F_{y1}^2) = 3/10$ regardless of which network we use to compute it.

6.6 Variances in Computed Relative Frequencies

Next we discuss how to compute the uncertainty (variance) in a relative frequency for which we have not directly assessed a belief. Rather, the relative frequency estimate is computed from relative frequencies for which we have assessed beliefs.

For the sake of space and notational simplicity, in this section we will again represent variables by unsubscripted letters like X, Y, and Z, and values of those variables by small letters. For example, the values of X will be $x1$ and $x2$.

6.6.1 A Simple Variance Determination

Consider the Bayesian network in Figure 6.29 (a). The probability distribution of the random variable F_{11} represents our belief concerning the relative frequency with which $x1$ occurs, the probability distribution of F_{21} represents our belief concerning the relative frequency with which Y takes the value $y1$ given that $X = x1$, and the probability distribution of F_{22} represents our belief concerning the relative frequency with which Y takes the value $y1$ given that $X = x2$. Consider now the space determined by the joint distribution of the F_{ij}s. We assume our belief concerning the relative frequency with which Y takes the value $y1$ is represented by the random variable F_{y1} which assigns

$$P(y1|f)$$

to each set of values $f = \{f_{11}, f_{21}, f_{22}\}$ of the variables in $\mathsf{F} = \{F_{11}, F_{21}, F_{22}\}$, and our estimate of the relative frequency is $E(F_{y1})$. Note that this is consistent with Equality 6.1 in Section 6.1.1. We have

$$
\begin{aligned}
P(y1|\mathsf{f}) &= P(y1|x1, \mathsf{f})P(x1|\mathsf{f}) + P(y1|x2, \mathsf{f})P(x2|\mathsf{f}) \\
&= f_{21}f_{11} + f_{22}(1 - f_{11}).
\end{aligned}
$$

The second equality is due to Equality 6.7. Therefore,

$$
F_{y1} = F_{21}F_{11} + F_{22}(1 - F_{11}). \tag{6.18}
$$

In Section 6.3 we showed how to compute probability intervals for the F_{ij}s, but how can we obtain such an interval for F_{y1}? Next we prove two theorems which enable us to compute the variance $V(F_{y1})$, from which we can at least approximate such an interval using a normal approximation.

Theorem 6.16 *Suppose F has the beta$(f; a, b)$ density function. Then*

$$
E(F) = \frac{a}{a + b}
$$

$$
E(F^2) = \left(\frac{a + 1}{a + b + 1}\right)\left(\frac{a}{a + b}\right)
$$

$$
E(F[1 - F]) = \frac{ab}{(a + b + 1)(a + b)}.
$$

Proof. *The proof is left as an exercise.* ∎

Theorem 6.17 *Suppose the random variable F_{y1} is defined as in Expression 6.18, and the F_{ij}s are mutually independent. Then*

$$
E(F_{y1}) = E(F_{21})E(F_{11}) + E(F_{22})E(1 - F_{11})
$$

$$
\begin{aligned}
E(F_{y1}^2) &= E(F_{21}^2)E(F_{11}^2) + 2E(F_{21})E(F_{22})E(F_{11}[1 - F_{11}]) \\
&\quad + E(F_{22}^2)E([1 - F_{11}]^2).
\end{aligned}
$$

Proof. *The proof is left as an exercise.* ∎.

Example 6.30 *Let's now compute $V(F_{y1})$ for the network in Figure 6.29. Due to Theorem 6.16,*

$$
E(F_{11}) = E(1 - F_{11}) = E(F_{21}) = E(F_{22}) = \frac{1}{1 + 1} = \frac{1}{2}
$$

$$
E(F_{11}^2) = E([1 - F_{11}]^2) = \left(\frac{2 + 1}{2 + 2 + 1}\right)\left(\frac{2}{2 + 2}\right) = \frac{3}{10}
$$

$$E(F_{21}^2) = E(F_{22}^2) = \left(\frac{1+1}{1+1+1}\right)\left(\frac{1}{1+1}\right) = \frac{1}{3}$$

$$E(F_{11}[1 - F_{11}]) = \frac{(2)(2)}{(2+2+1)(2+2)} = \frac{1}{5}.$$

Therefore, due to Theorem 6.17,

$$
\begin{aligned}
E(F_{y1}) &= E(F_{21})E(F_{11}) + E(F_{22})E(1 - F_{11}) \\
&= \left(\frac{1}{2}\right)\left(\frac{1}{2}\right) + \left(\frac{1}{2}\right)\left(\frac{1}{2}\right) = \frac{1}{2}.
\end{aligned}
$$

$$
\begin{aligned}
E(F_{y1}^2) &= E(F_{21}^2)E(F_{11}^2) + 2E(F_{21})E(F_{22})E(F_{11}[1 - F_{11}]) \\
&\quad + E(F_{22}^2)E([1 - F_{11}]^2) \\
&= \left(\frac{1}{3}\right)\left(\frac{3}{10}\right) + 2\left(\frac{1}{2}\right)\left(\frac{1}{2}\right)\left(\frac{1}{5}\right) + \left(\frac{1}{3}\right)\left(\frac{3}{10}\right) = \frac{3}{10}.
\end{aligned}
$$

So we have

$$V(F_{y1}) = E(F_{y1}^2) - [E(F_{y1})]^2 = \frac{3}{10} - \left(\frac{1}{2}\right)^2 = .05.$$

6.6.2 The Variance and Equivalent Sample Size

We introduce this subsection with an example.

Example 6.31 *Consider the augmented Bayesian network in Figure 6.29 (b). It is equivalent to the one in Figure 6.29 (a). Therefore, intuitively we would expect $E(F_{y1}^2)$ would be the same when computed using either network. Since, clearly, in that network $F_{y1} = F_{21}$, we have, due to Theorem 6.16,*

$$E(F_{y1}^2) = E(F_{21}^2) = \left(\frac{2+1}{2+2+1}\right)\left(\frac{2}{2+2}\right) = \frac{3}{10},$$

which is the same as the value obtained using Figure 6.29 (a). It is left as an exercise to show that the expected values are also equal, which means the variances are equal.

It is also left as an exercise to show that $E(F_{y1}^2)$ is not the same for the networks in Figures 6.29 (a) and (b) if we specify all $beta(f; 1, 1)$ density functions in both networks. Is there a theorem concerning equivalent sample sizes and variances corresponding to Theorem 6.15? That is, is a variance the same when computed using two equivalent augmented Bayesian networks? Although we have no proof of this, we conjecture it is true. Before formally stating this conjecture, we investigate more examples which substantiate it. We will compare only the expected values of squares of our random variables since, if they are equal, the variances are equal. The reason is that the expected values of our random variables are always equal to the corresponding probabilities. Before giving a theorem to this effect, we motivate the theorem with two examples.

Example 6.32 *Consider a two-node network such as the one in Figure 6.29 (a). Let F_{y1} be a random variable that assigns $P(y1|\mathsf{f})$ to each set of values f of the variables in F. We have due to the law of total probability,*

$$E(F_{y1}) = \int_{\mathsf{f}} P(y1|\mathsf{f})\rho(\mathsf{f})d\mathsf{f}$$
$$= P(y1).$$

Example 6.33 *Consider again a two-node network such as the one in Figure 6.29 (a). Let $F_{x1|y1}$ be a random variable that assigns $P(x1|y1,\mathsf{f})$ to each set of values f of the variables in F. We have*

$$E(F_{x1|y1}|y1) = \int_{\mathsf{f}} P(x1|y1,\mathsf{f})\rho(\mathsf{f}|y1)d\mathsf{f}$$
$$= P(x1|y1).$$

The second equality is due to the law of total probability.

The method in the previous examples can be used to prove a theorem.

Theorem 6.18 *Let a binomial augmented Bayesian network be given, and let A and B be two disjoint subsets of V and a and b be values of the variables in these sets. Let $F_{\mathsf{a}|\mathsf{b}}$ be a random variable which assigns $P(\mathsf{a}|\mathsf{b},\mathsf{f})$ to each set of values f of the variables in F. Then*

$$E(F_{\mathsf{a}|\mathsf{b}}|\mathsf{b}) = P(\mathsf{a}|\mathsf{b}).$$

Proof. *We have*

$$E(F_{\mathsf{a}|\mathsf{b}}|\mathsf{b}) = \int_{\mathsf{f}} P(\mathsf{a}|\mathsf{b},\mathsf{f})\rho(\mathsf{f}|\mathsf{b})d\mathsf{f}$$
$$= P(\mathsf{a}|\mathsf{b}).$$

The second equality is due to the law of total probability. ∎

Since $P(\mathsf{a}|\mathsf{b})$ is the same for equivalent augmented Bayesian networks, the preceding theorem implies that the variances are the same whenever the expected values of the squares of the random variables are the same. We now give more examples comparing these expected values for equivalent augmented Bayesian networks.

Example 6.34 *Consider the augmented Bayesian networks in Figure 6.30 (a) and (b). Clearly, they are equivalent. For the network in (a) we have, due to Theorem 6.16, that*

$$E(F_{21}) = \frac{3}{3+1} = \frac{3}{4}$$

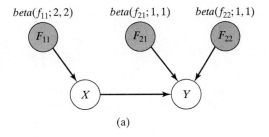

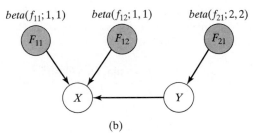

Figure 6.30: $E(F_{y1}^2) = 15/28$ regardless of which network we use to compute it.

$$E(F_{22}) = \frac{2}{2+1} = \frac{2}{3}$$

$$E(F_{11}^2) = \left(\frac{4+1}{4+3+1}\right)\left(\frac{4}{4+3}\right) = \frac{5}{14}$$

$$E(F_{21}^2) = \left(\frac{3+1}{3+1+1}\right)\left(\frac{3}{3+1}\right) = \frac{3}{5}$$

$$E(F_{22}^2) = \left(\frac{2+1}{2+1+1}\right)\left(\frac{2}{2+1}\right) = \frac{1}{2}$$

$$E([1 - F_{11}]^2) = \left(\frac{3+1}{4+3+1}\right)\left(\frac{3}{4+3}\right) = \frac{3}{14}$$

$$E(F_{11}[1 - F_{11}]) = \frac{(4)(3)}{(4+3+1)(4+3)} = \frac{3}{14}.$$

Therefore, due to Theorem 6.17,

$$
\begin{aligned}
E(F_{y1}^2) &= E(F_{21}^2)E(F_{11}^2) + 2E(F_{21})E(F_{22})E(F_{11}[1 - F_{11}]) \\
&\quad + E(F_{22}^2)E([1 - F_{11}]^2) \\
&= \left(\frac{3}{5}\right)\left(\frac{5}{14}\right) + 2\left(\frac{3}{4}\right)\left(\frac{2}{3}\right)\left(\frac{3}{14}\right) + \left(\frac{1}{2}\right)\left(\frac{3}{14}\right) = \frac{15}{28}.
\end{aligned}
$$

For the network in (b) we have, due to Theorem 6.16,

$$E(F_{y1}^2) = E(F_{21}^2) = \left(\frac{5+1}{5+2+1}\right)\left(\frac{5}{5+2}\right) = \frac{15}{28}.$$

The following theorem gives a formula for the expected value of the square of the random variable. We will use the formula in several examples.

Theorem 6.19 *Let a binomial augmented Bayesian network be given, and let* A *and* B *be two disjoint subsets of* V, *and* a *and* b *be values of the variables in these sets. Let* $F_{a|b}$ *be a random variable which assigns* $P(a|b, f)$ *to each set of values* f *of the variables in* F. *Then*

$$E(F_{a|b}^2|b) = \frac{1}{P(b)} \int_f \frac{[P(b|a, f)]^2 [P(a|f)]^2}{P(b|f)} \rho(f) df.$$

Proof. *We have*

$$
\begin{aligned}
E(F_{a|b}^2|b) &= \int_f [P(a|b, f)]^2 \rho(f|b) df \\
&= \int_f \frac{[P(b|a, f)]^2 [P(a|f)]^2}{[P(b|f)]^2} \frac{P(b|f)\rho(f)}{P(b)} df \\
&= \frac{1}{P(b)} \int_f \frac{[P(b|a, f)]^2 [P(a|f)]^2}{P(b|f)} \rho(f) df.
\end{aligned}
$$

Example 6.35 *Consider the network in Figure 6.29 (a). Let* $F_{x1|y1}$ *be a random variable which assigns* $P(x1|y1, f)$ *to each set of values* f *of the variables in* F. *Due to the preceding theorem, we have*

$$
\begin{aligned}
E(F_{x1|y1}^2|y1) &= \frac{1}{P(y1)} \int_f \frac{[P(y1|x1, f)]^2 [P(x1|f)]^2}{P(y1|f)} \rho(f) df \\
&= \frac{1}{1/2} \int_0^1 \int_0^1 \int_0^1 \frac{f_{21}^2 f_{11}^2}{f_{21}f_{11} + f_{22}(1 - f_{11})} \\
&\qquad beta(f_{11}; 2, 2)beta(f_{21}; 1, 1)beta(f_{22}; 1, 1)df_{11}df_{21}df_{22} \\
&= \frac{1}{3}.
\end{aligned}
$$

The integration was performed using the mathematics package Maple.

Consider next the augmented Bayesian network in Figure 6.29 (b), which is equivalent to the one in (a). Due to the fact that F_{11} *is independent of* Y *and Theorem 6.16, we have*

$$E(F_{x1|y1}^2|y1) = E(F_{11}^2) = \left(\frac{1+1}{1+1+1}\right)\left(\frac{1}{1+1}\right) = \frac{1}{3},$$

which is the same as the value obtained in the preceding calculation.

Example 6.36 *Consider the network in Figure 6.30 (a). Let $F_{x1|y1}$ and E_{y1} be as in the preceding example. Due to Theorem 6.19, we have*

$$
\begin{aligned}
E(F^2_{x1|y1}|y1) &= \frac{1}{P(x2[1])} \int_{\mathsf{f}} \frac{[P(y1|x1,\mathsf{f})]^2 [P(x1|\mathsf{f})]^2}{P(y1|\mathsf{f})} \rho(\mathsf{f}) df \\
&= \frac{1}{5/7} \int_0^1 \int_0^1 \int_0^1 \frac{f_{21}^2 f_{11}^2}{f_{21}f_{11} + f_{22}(1-f_{11})} \\
&\qquad beta(f_{11};4,3) beta(f_{21};3,1) beta(f_{22};2,1) df_{11} df_{21} df_{22} \\
&= \frac{2}{5}.
\end{aligned}
$$

The integration was performed using Maple.

Consider next the augmented Bayesian network in Figure 6.30 (b), which is equivalent to the one in (a). Due to the fact that F_{11} is independent of Y and Theorem 6.16, we have

$$
E(F^2_{x1|y1}|y1) = E(F^2_{11}) = \left(\frac{3+1}{3+2+1} \right) \left(\frac{3}{3+2} \right) = \frac{2}{5}.
$$

which is the same as the value obtained in the previous calculation.

Example 6.37 *Consider the augmented Bayesian network in Figure 6.31 (a). Let $F_{y1|x1,z1}$ be a random variable that assigns $P(y1|x1,z1,\mathsf{f})$ to each set of values f of the variables in $\mathbf{F}$. Due to Theorem 6.19, we have*

$$
E(F^2_{y1|x1,z1}|x1,z1)
$$

$$
\begin{aligned}
&= \frac{1}{P(x1,z1)} \int_{\mathsf{f}} \frac{[P(x1,z1|y1,\mathsf{f})]^2 [P(y1|\mathsf{f})]^2}{P(x1,z1|\mathsf{f})} \rho(\mathsf{f}) df \\
&= \frac{1}{P(x1,z1)} \int_{\mathsf{f}} \frac{[P(x1,z1|y1,\mathsf{f})]^2 [P(y1|\mathsf{f})]^2}{P(x1,z1|y1,\mathsf{f})P(y1|\mathsf{f}) + P(x1,z1|y2,\mathsf{f})P(y2|\mathsf{f})} \rho(\mathsf{f}) df \\
&= \frac{1}{P(x1,z1)} \int_{\mathsf{f}} \frac{[P(z1|y1\mathsf{f})]^2 [P(y1|x1,\mathsf{f})]^2 P(x1|\mathsf{f})}{P(z1|y1,\mathsf{f})P(y1|x1,\mathsf{f}) + P(z1|y2,\mathsf{f})P(y2|x1,\mathsf{f})} \rho(\mathsf{f}) df \\
&= \frac{1}{1/4} \int_0^1 \int_0^1 \int_0^1 \int_0^1 \frac{f_{31}^2 f_{21}^2 f_{11}}{f_{31}f_{21} + f_{32}(1-f_{21})} beta(f_{11};1,1) beta(f_{21};1,1) \\
&\qquad beta(f_{31};1,1) beta(f_{32};1,1) df_{11} df_{21} df_{31} df_{32} \\
&= .36.
\end{aligned}
$$

The third equality is obtained by exploiting the fact that X and Z are independent conditional on Y, using Bayes' theorem, and doing some manipulations. The integration was performed using Maple.

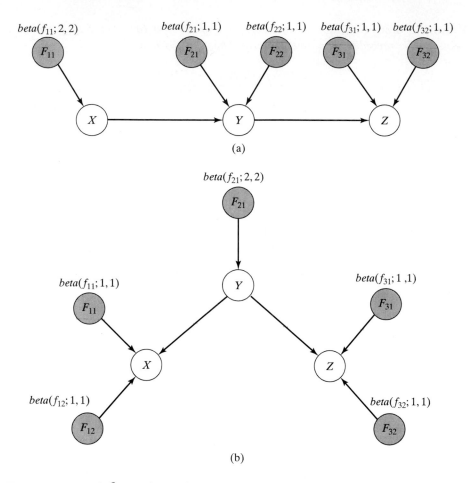

Figure 6.31: $E(F^2_{y1|x1,z1}|x1,z1) = .36$ regardless of which network we use to compute it.

Consider next the augmented Bayesian network in Figure 6.31 (b), which is equivalent to the one in (a). Due to Theorem 6.19, we have

$E(F^2_{y1|x1,z1}|x1,z1)$

$$= \frac{1}{P(x1,z1)} \int_{\mathsf{f}} \frac{[P(x1,z1|y1,\mathsf{f})]^2 [P(y1|\mathsf{f})]^2}{P(x1,z1|\mathsf{f})} \rho(\mathsf{f}) d\mathsf{f}$$

$$= \frac{1}{1/4} \int_0^1 \int_0^1 \int_0^1 \int_0^1 \int_0^1 \frac{f_{21}^2 f_{31}^2 f_{11}^2}{f_{21} f_{31} f_{11} + f_{22} f_{32}(1 - f_{11})} beta(f_{11}; 2, 2)$$

$$beta(f_{21}; 1, 1)beta(f_{22}; 1, 1)beta(f_{31}; 1, 1)beta(f_{32}; 1, 1)df_{11}df_{21}df_{22}df_{31}df_{32}$$

$$= .36,$$

which is the same as the value obtained previously. The integration was performed using Maple.

Due to the preceding examples, we offer the following conjecture:

Conjecture 6.1 *Suppose we have two equivalent binomial augmented Bayesian networks $(\mathbb{G}_1, \mathsf{F}_1, \rho_1)$ and $(\mathbb{G}_2, \mathsf{F}_2, \rho_2)$. Let A and B be two disjoint subsets of V, and a and b be values of the variables in these subsets. Furthermore, let $F_{1,\mathsf{a}|\mathsf{b}}$ be a random variable that assigns $P(\mathsf{a}|\mathsf{b}, \mathsf{f}_1)$ to each set of values f_1 of the variables in F_1, and let $F_{2,\mathsf{a}|\mathsf{b}}$ be a random variable that assigns $P(\mathsf{a}|\mathsf{b}, \mathsf{f}_2)$ to each set of values f_2 of the variables in F_2. Then*

$$E(F_{1,\mathsf{a}|\mathsf{b}}^2|\mathsf{b}) = E(F_{2,\mathsf{a}|\mathsf{b}}^2|\mathsf{b}).$$

Perhaps a proof technique, similar to the one in Heckerman et al. [1995], could be used to prove this conjecture.

6.6.3 Computing Variances in Larger Networks

So far we have computed variances involving only nodes that are touching each other. Next we show how to compute variances in larger networks. We start with an example.

Example 6.38 *Consider the augmented Bayesian network in Figure 6.31 (a). We already know how to compute $E(F_{x1}^2)$ and $E(F_{y1}^2)$. Let's compute $E(F_{z1}^2)$. We have*

$$P(z1|\mathsf{f}) = P(z1|y1,\mathsf{f})P(y1|\mathsf{f}) + P(z1|y2,\mathsf{f})P(y2|\mathsf{f}).$$

Therefore

$$F_{z1} = F_{31}F_{y1} + F_{32}(1 - F_{y1}).$$

This expression is like Expression 6.18 except that F_{y1} replaces F_{11}. So once we determine $E(F_{y1}^2)$, $E(F_{y1})$, $E([1 - F_{y1}]^2)$, and $E(F_{y1}[1 - F_{y1}]^2)$, we can apply the method in Example 6.30 to compute $E(F_{z1}^2)$. From Example 6.30, we have

$$E(F_{y1}^2) = \frac{3}{10} \qquad E(F_{y1}) = \frac{1}{2}.$$

Due to symmetry,

$$E([1 - F_{y1}]^2) = \frac{3}{10}.$$

Finally, we have

$$
\begin{aligned}
E(F_{y1}[1 - F_{y1}]^2) &= E([F_{21}F_{11} + F_{22}\{1 - F_{11}\}][1 - F_{21}F_{11} - F_{22}\{1 - F_{11}\}]) \\
&= \frac{1}{5}.
\end{aligned}
$$

The previous answer is obtained by multiplying out the expression on the right and applying Theorem 6.16.

Note that all the values obtained above are exactly the ones that would have been obtained if F_{y1} had the beta($f_{21}; 2, 2$) density function. Therefore, due to the result in Example 6.30,

$$E(F_{z1}^2) = \frac{3}{10},$$

which would be the value obtained if F_{z1} had the beta($f_{31}; 2, 2$) density function.

The result in the previous example is not surprising since, if we took the equivalent DAG that had the arrows reversed and used the same equivalent sample size, F_{z1} would have the beta($f_{21}; 2, 2$) density function. So the result is consistent with Conjecture 6.1.

The previous example gives us insight as to how we can compute all prior variances in a linked list. Starting from the root, at each node X, we compute $E(F_{x1}^2)$, $E(F_{x1})$, $E([1 - F_{x1}]^2)$, and $E(F_{x1}[1 - F_{x1}]^2)$ from information obtained from the node above it and from the distributions of the auxiliary parent nodes of X. Neapolitan and Kenevan [1991a], Neapolitan and Kenevan [1991b] extend this method to singly connected networks, and present a message-passing algorithm for computing all prior variances in such networks. The algorithm is similar to the one discussed in Section 3.2.2. They also show how to use Pearl's (Pearl [1988]) method of clustering to handle networks that are not singly connected networks.

The problem of computing variances conditional on instantiated variables is more difficult. Clearly, if an ancestor of a node is instantiated, the message-passing algorithm described above can be used to compute the conditional variance. However, if a descendent is instantiated, we must cope with the integral in Theorem 6.19. Che et al. [1993] discuss using numerical methods to approximate this integral.

6.6.4   When Do Variances Become Large?

Intuitively, we would expect the variance, in the random variable, whose possible values are a given conditional probability, could increase with the number of instantiated variables relevant to the computation of that conditional probability. The reason is that, as more variables are instantiated, the number of cases in the equivalent sample that have those instantiated values decreases. For example, in Figure 6.32, all 80 cases enter into the determination of $P(y1)$. However, only 5 cases have X, Z, W, and U instantiated for $x1$, $z1$, $w1$, and $u1$. Therefore, only 5 cases enter into the determination of $P(y1|x1, z1, w1, u1)$. The following table shows variances and 95% probability intervals given the network in Figure 6.32:

Random Variable	Expected Value	Variance	95% Probability Interval
F_{y1}	.5	.003	(.391, .609)
$F_{y1|x1,z1,w1,u1}$	.5	.042	(.123, .877)

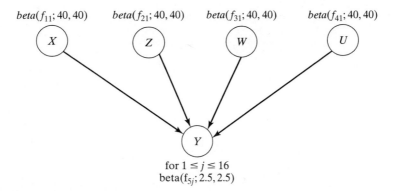

Figure 6.32: An augmented Bayesian network used to illustrate loss in confidence as variables are instantiated. Only the density functions for the auxiliary variables are shown.

Even though the expected value of the relative frequency with which $Y = y1$ remains at .5 when we instantiate Y's four parents, our confidence that it is .5 practically disappears.

When probabilities are nearly 1, we do not have as severe a problem concerning loss of confidence. The following theorem shows why.

Theorem 6.20 *Let F be a random variable whose values range between 0 and 1. Then*

$$V(F) \leq E(F)[1 - E(F)].$$

Proof. *We have*

$$
\begin{aligned}
V(F) &= E(F^2) - [E(F)]^2 \\
&\leq E(F) - [E(F)]^2 \\
&\leq E(F)[1 - E(F)]
\end{aligned}
$$

The first inequality is because $0 \leq f \leq 1$ implies $f \leq f^2$. ∎

Example 6.39 *Suppose $E(F) = .999$. Then, due to the preceding theorem,*

$$V(F) \leq .999(1 - .999) = .000999.$$

Using the normal approximation, we obtain that a 95% probability interval is contained in

$$(.937, 1.061).$$

Of course, F cannot exceed 1. This is only an approximation.

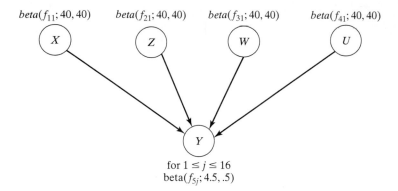

Figure 6.33: An augmented network used to illustrate loss in confidence as variables are instantiated. Only the density functions for the auxiliary variables are shown.

So regardless of how many variables are instantiated, if the conditional probability (expected value of the relative frequency) is .999, we can be confident that the actual relative frequency really is high. Intuitively, the reason is that a relative frequency estimate of .999 could not be based on a small sample.

However, if the probability is high but not extreme, we can lose a good deal of confidence when we instantiate variables. Given the network in Figure 6.33, we have the following variances and probability intervals:

Random Variable	Expected Value	Variance	95% Probability Interval
F_{y1}	.9	.001	$(.836, .964)$
$F_{y1\|x1,z1,w1,u1}$	.9	.015	$(.639, 1)$

Note that, when Y's four parents are instantiated, we are no longer confident that the relative frequency with which $Y = y1$ is high, even though the expected value of the relative frequency stays at .9.

When variables are instantiated from above, as in the previous illustrations, it is no surprise that the confidence becomes low because the confidence in specified relative frequencies was low to begin with. However, when variables are instantiated from below this is not the case. Consider the network in Figure 6.31 (b). As shown in Example 6.37, $E(F^2_{y1|x1,z1}|x1, z1) = .36$. Therefore,

$$\begin{aligned} V(F_{y1|x1,z1}|x1, z1) &= E(F^2_{y1|x1,z1}|x1, z1) - [E(F_{y1|x1,z1}|x1, z1)]^2 \\ &= .36 - (.5)^2 = .11. \end{aligned}$$

Yet the specified relative frequencies (i.e., F_{1i} and F_{3j}), in which we have least confidence, have the $beta(f; 1, 1)$ density function. So we have

$$V(F_{1i}) = V(F_{3j}) = .333 - (.5)^2 = .083.$$

So, even though $E(F_{y1|x1,z1}|x1, z1)$ is the same as the expected values of all relative frequencies specified in the network (namely .5), its variance is greater than any of their variances. It seems then that determination of variances may be quite important when variables are instantiated from below. In this case, we cannot assume that our confidence in specified relative frequencies gives us a bound on our confidence in inferred ones. On the other hand, Henrion et al. [1996] note that diagnosis using Bayesian networks is often insensitive to imprecision in probabilities. One reason they cite is that gold-standard posterior probabilities are often near zero or unity, and, as we noted, in the case of extreme probabilities, the variance is always small.

EXERCISES
Section 6.1

Exercise 6.1 *For some two-outcome experiment, which you can repeat indefinitely (such as the tossing of a thumbtack), determine the number of occurrences, a and b, of each outcome, that you feel your prior experience is equivalent to having seen. Then represent your belief concerning the relative frequency with the $beta(f; a, b)$ density function. Finally determine the probability of the first value occurring.*

Exercise 6.2 *Assume I feel that my prior experience concerning the relative frequency of smokers in a particular bar is equivalent to having seen 14 smokers and 6 nonsmokers. So I represent my beliefs concerning the relative frequency of smokers using the $beta(f; 14, 6)$ density function. Suppose I then decide to log whether or not individuals smoke. Compute the probability of my getting the data*

$$\{1, 2, 2, 2, 2, 1, 2, 2, 2, 1\},$$

where 1 means the individual smokes and 2 means the individual does not smoke.

Exercise 6.3 *Assuming the beliefs in Exercise 6.2, what is the probability that the first individual sampled smokes? If we obtain the data shown in that exercise, what is the updated beta density function representing my updated belief concerning the relative frequency of smokers? What is the probability that the next individual sampled smokes?*

Section 6.2

Exercise 6.4 *Suppose I am about to watch Sam and Dave race 10 times, and Sam looks substantially athletically inferior to Dave. So I give Sam a probability of .1 of winning the first race. However, I feel that if Sam wins once, he should usually win. So, given that Sam wins the first race, I give him a .8 probability of winning the next one. Using the technique shown in Example 6.10, determine the beta density function representing my prior belief concerning the relative frequency with which Sam will win. Determine my probability of Sam winning all 10 races.*

Suppose next that Sam wins the first two races. Determine the updated beta density function representing my updated belief concerning the relative frequency with which Sam will win. Determine my probability of him winning the next race and of winning all eight remaining races.

Section 6.3

Exercise 6.5 *Assuming the prior beliefs concerning the relative frequency of smokers shown in Exercise 6.2, determine a 95% for the $E(F)$ where F is a random variable representing my belief concerning the relative frequency of smokers. Do the determination exactly and using the normal approximation.*

Exercise 6.6 *Assuming the prior beliefs concerning the relative frequency of smokers shown in Exercise 6.2 and the data shown in that example, determine a 95% for the $E(F)$ where F is a random variable representing my updated belief concerning the relative frequency of smokers. Do the determination exactly and using the normal approximation.*

Section 6.4

Exercise 6.7 *Show the Bayesian network embedded in the augmented Bayesian network in Figure 6.34. Assume the random variables corresponding to the conditional relative frequencies are as follows:*

Parent Values	RandomVarable
$X_1 = 1, X_2 = 1$	F_{31}
$X_1 = 1, X_2 = 2$	F_{32}
$X_1 = 2, X_2 = 1$	F_{33}
$X_1 = 2, X_2 = 2$	F_{34}

Exercise 6.8 *Suppose we have a binomial Bayesian network sample whose parameter is the augmented Bayesian network in Figure 6.34, and we have these data* **d**:

Case	X_1	X_2	X_3
1	1	2	1
2	1	1	2
3	2	1	1
4	2	2	1
5	1	2	1
6	2	2	2
7	1	2	1
8	2	1	2
9	1	2	1
10	1	1	1

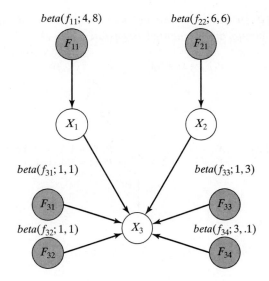

Figure 6.34: An augmented Bayesian network.

Compute $P(\mathsf{d})$ and $\rho(f_{ij}|\mathsf{d})$ for all i,j. Show the updated augmented Bayesian network and updated embedded Bayesian network. Determine $P(X_3 = 1)$ for the 11th case.

Exercise 6.9 *Does the augmented Bayesian network in Figure 6.34 have an equivalent sample size? If so, what is it?*

Exercise 6.10 *Complete the proof of Theorem 6.13.*

Exercise 6.11 *Use Theorem 6.13 to develop an augmented Bayesian network with equivalent sample sizes 1, 2, 4, and 10 for the DAG in Figure 6.35.*

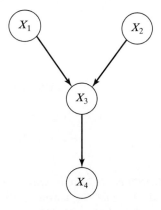

Figure 6.35: A DAG.

Exercise 6.12 *Given the Bayesian network in Figure 6.36 and $N = 36$, use Theorem 6.14 to create an augmented Bayesian network.*

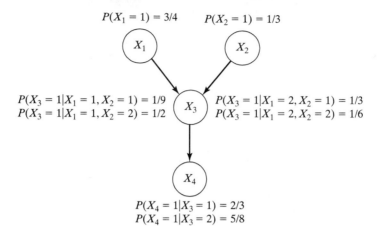

Figure 6.36: A Bayesian network.

Exercise 6.13 *Consider the augmented Bayesian network in Figure 6.37. What is its equivalent sample size? Determine all augmented Bayesian networks that are equivalent to it. Show that $P(\mathbf{d})$ is the same for every Bayesian network sample whose parameter is one of these augmented Bayesian networks, given the data $\mathbf{d}$ in Exercise 6.8.*

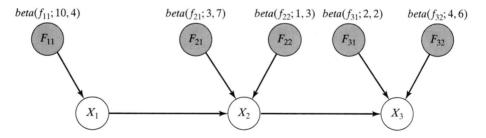

Figure 6.37: An augmented Bayesian network.

Section 6.5

Exercise 6.14 *In the text, we updated the augmented Bayesian network in Figure 6.28 (a) with the data $\mathbf{d}$ in Table 6.4 using two iterations of Algorithm 6.1 (Expectation–Maximization). Starting with the results in the text, perform the next two iterations.*

Section 6.6

Exercise 6.15 *Consider the augmented Bayesian network in Figure 6.37. Let F be a random variable representing our belief concerning the relative frequency with which X_2 equals 1. Compute $E(F^2)$ using that network and all networks equivalent to it. Are your values the same?*

Chapter 7

More Parameter Learning

Chapter 6 considered Bayesian networks in which the variables are all binary. In Section 7.1 we extend the theory presented in the previous chapter to multinomial variables. We provide fewer examples and intuitive explanations than usual and we leave proofs of theorems and lemmas as exercises. The reason is that the theory is a straightforward generalization of the theory for binary variables. The notation is merely more difficult. After that, Section 7.2 discusses learning parameters in the case of continuous variables.

7.1 Multinomial Variables

First, we present the method for learning a single parameter in the case of a multinomial variable; second, we further discuss the Dirichlet density function; third, we show how to compute probability intervals and regions; and fourth, we present the method for learning all the parameters in a Bayesian network in the case of multinomial variables. After all this, we close by briefly noting that the methods presented in Chapter 6 for learning parameters in the case of missing data items and for computing variances in computed relative frequencies can readily be extended to the case of multinomial variables.

7.1.1 Learning a Single Parameter

After discussing subjective probability distributions of relative frequencies in the case of multinomial variables, we generalize the method developed in Section 6.1.2 for estimating relative frequencies from data.

Probability Distributions of Relative Frequencies

We start with a definition.

Definition 7.1 *The **Dirichlet density function** with parameters $a_1, a_2, \ldots, a_r$,*

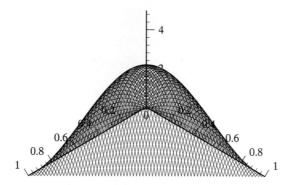

Figure 7.1: The $Dir(f_1, f_2; 2, 2, 2)$ density function.

$N = \sum_{k=1}^{r} a_k$, where $a_1, a_2, \dots, a_r$ are integers ≥ 1, is

$$\rho(f_1, f_2, \dots, f_{r-1}) = \frac{\Gamma(N)}{\prod\limits_{k=1}^{r} \Gamma(a_k)} f_1^{a_1-1} f_2^{a_2-1} \cdots f_r^{a_r-1} \quad 0 \leq f_k \leq 1, \ \sum_{k=1}^{r} f_k = 1.$$

*Random variables $F_1, F_2, \dots, F_r$, that have this density function, are said to have a **Dirichlet distribution**.*

The Dirichlet density function is denoted $Dir(f_1, f_2, \dots, f_{r-1}; a_1, a_2, \dots, a_r)$.

Note that the value of F_r is uniquely determined by the values of the first $r-1$ variables (i.e., $f_r = 1 - \sum_{h=1}^{r-1} f_h$). That is why ρ is only a function of $r-1$ variables. As shown in Section 6.2.3, the Dirichlet density function is a generalization of the beta density function. Figures 7.1 and 7.2 show Dirichlet density functions.

As discussed in Section 6.2.3, there are cogent arguments for using the Dirichlet distribution to model our beliefs concerning relative frequencies. Often we say the probability assessor's experience is equivalent to having seen the kth value occur a_k times in N trials.

We will need the following lemma concerning the Dirichlet density function:

Lemma 7.1 *If $F_1, F_2, \dots, F_r$ have a Dirichlet distribution with parameters $a_1, a_2, \dots, a_r$, $N = \sum a_k$, then, for $1 \leq k \leq r$,*

$$E(F_k) = \frac{a_k}{N}.$$

Proof. *The proof is left as an exercise.*   ■

Now suppose we have some r-outcome random process. Let X be a random variable whose space $\{1, 2, \dots, r\}$ contains the outcomes of the experiment, and for $1 \leq k \leq r$, let F_k be a random variable whose space is the interval $[0, 1]$.

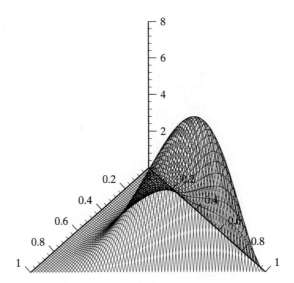

Figure 7.2: The $Dir(f_1, f_2; 4, 2, 2)$ density function.

The probability distribution of F_k represents our belief concerning the relative frequency with which $X = k$. Assume our beliefs are such that

$$P(X = k | f_k) = f_k.$$

That is, if we knew for a fact that the relative frequency of k was f_k, our belief concerning the occurrence of k in the first execution of the experiment would be f_k. Given this assumption, the theorem that follows obtains our subjective probability for the first trial.

Theorem 7.1 *Suppose X is a random variable with space $\{1, 2, \ldots, r\}$, and $F_1, F_2, \ldots, F_r$ are r random variables such that for all k,*

$$P(X = k | f_k) = f_k.$$

Then

$$P(X = k) = E(F_k).$$

Proof. *The proof is left as an exercise.* ∎

Corollary 7.1 *If the conditions in Theorem 7.1 hold, and if $F_1, F_2, \ldots, F_r$ have a Dirichlet distribution with parameters $a_1, a_2, \ldots, a_r, N = \sum a_k$, then*

$$P(X = k) = \frac{a_k}{N}.$$

Proof. *The proof follows immediately from Theorem 7.1 and Lemma 7.1.* ∎

Example 7.1 *Suppose I am going to repeatedly throw a strange lopsided die
with three sides. The shape is so odd that I have no reason to prefer one side
over the other, but due to my lack of experience with such a die, I do not feel
strongly that the relative frequencies are the same. So I model my beliefs with
the $Dir(f_1, f_2; 2, 2, 2)$ density function. We have*

$$Dir(f_1, f_2; 2, 2, 2) = \frac{\Gamma(6)}{\Gamma(2)\Gamma(2)\Gamma(2)} f_1^{2-1} f_2^{2-1} (1 - f_1 - f_2)^{2-1}$$
$$= 120 f_1 f_2 (1 - f_1 - f_2).$$

*This density function is shown in Figure 7.1. Due to the previous corollary, for
the first throw we have*

$$P(Side = 1) = \frac{2}{2 + 2 + 2} = \frac{1}{3}$$

$$P(Side = 2) = \frac{2}{2 + 2 + 2} = \frac{1}{3}$$

$$P(Side = 3) = \frac{2}{2 + 2 + 2} = \frac{1}{3}.$$

Example 7.2 *Suppose I am going to sample individuals in the United States,
and determine the relative frequency with which they wear colored, white, and
black socks. I think that about the same number of individuals wear black as
wear white socks, and about twice as many individuals wear colored socks. However, I do not feel strongly about this belief. So I model my beliefs with the
$Dir(f_1, f_2; 4, 2, 2)$ density function. We have*

$$Dir(f_1, f_2; 4, 2, 2) = \frac{\Gamma(8)}{\Gamma(4)\Gamma(2)\Gamma(2)} f_1^{4-1} f_2^{2-1} (1 - f_1 - f_2)^{2-1}$$
$$= 840 f_1^3 f_2 (1 - f_1 - f_2).$$

*This density function is shown in Figure 7.2. Due to the previous corollary, for
the first individual sampled,*

$$P(Socks = colored) = \frac{4}{4 + 2 + 2} = \frac{1}{2}$$

$$P(Socks = white) = \frac{2}{4 + 2 + 2} = \frac{1}{4}$$

$$P(Socks = black) = \frac{2}{4 + 2 + 2} = \frac{1}{4}.$$

Example 7.3 *Suppose I am going to repeatedly throw an ordinary six-sided die.
I am fairly confident all relative frequencies are the same. So I model my beliefs
with the $Dir(f_1, f_2, f_3, f_4, f_5; 50, 50, 50, 50, 50, 50)$ density function.*

Learning a Relative Frequency

We start with a definition.

Definition 7.2 *Suppose we have a sample of size M such that*

1. *each $X^{(h)}$ has space $\{1, 2, \ldots, r\}$;*

2. $\mathsf{F} = \{F_1, F_2, \ldots, F_r\}$, *and for $1 \leq h \leq M$ and $1 \leq k \leq r$*

$$P(X^{(h)} = k | f_1, \ldots, f_k, \ldots, f_r) = f_k.$$

*Then D is called a **multinomial sample** of size M with parameter F.*

Example 7.4 *Suppose we throw a strange lopsided die with three sides 10 times. Let k be the outcome if a k comes up, and let $X^{(h)}$'s value be the outcome of the hth throw. Furthermore, let the density function for the variables in F be $Dir(f_1, f_2; 2, 2, 2)$. Then $\mathsf{D} = \{X^{(1)}, X^2, \ldots, X^{(10)}\}$ is a multinomial sample of size 10 whose parameter has a Dirichlet distribution.*

Before developing theory that enables us to update our belief about the next trial from a multinomial sample, we present two more lemmas concerning the Dirichlet distribution.

Lemma 7.2 *Suppose $F_1, F_2, \ldots, F_r$ have a Dirichlet distribution with parameters $a_1, a_2, \ldots, a_r$, $N = \sum a_k$, $s_1, s_2, \ldots, s_r$ are r integers ≥ 0, and $M = \sum s_k$. Then*

$$E\left(\prod_{k=1}^{r} F_k^{s_k}\right) = \frac{\Gamma(N)}{\Gamma(N+M)} \prod_{k=1}^{r} \frac{\Gamma(a_k + s_k)}{\Gamma(a_k)}.$$

Proof. *The proof is left as an exercise.* ∎

Lemma 7.3 *Suppose $F_1, F_2, \ldots, F_r$ have a Dirichlet distribution with parameters $a_1, a_2, \ldots, a_r$, $N = \sum a_k$, and $s_1, s_2, \ldots, s_r$ are r integers ≥ 0. Then*

$$\frac{\left(\prod_{k=1}^{r} f^{s_k}\right) \rho(f_1, f_2, \ldots, f_{r-1})}{E\left(\prod_{k=1}^{r} F_k^{s_k}\right)} = Dir(f_1, f_2, \ldots, f_{r-1}; a_1 + s_1, a_2 + s_2, \ldots, a_r + s_r).$$

Proof. *The proof is left as an exercise.* ∎

Theorem 7.2 *Suppose*

1. D *is a multinomial sample of size M with parameter F;*

2. *we have a set of values (data)*

$$\mathsf{d} = \{x^{(1)}, x^{(2)}, \ldots, x^{(M)}\}$$

of the variables in D;

3. s_k is the number of variables in d *equal to k.*

Then

$$P(\mathsf{d}) = E\left(\prod_{k=1}^{r} F_k^{s_k}\right).$$

Proof. *The proof is left as an exercise.* ■

Corollary 7.2 *If the conditions in Theorem 7.2 hold, and $F_1, F_2, \ldots, F_r$ have a Dirichlet distribution with parameters $a_1, a_2, \ldots, a_r, N = \sum a_k$, then*

$$P(\mathsf{d}) = \frac{\Gamma(N)}{\Gamma(N+M)} \prod_{k=1}^{r} \frac{\Gamma(a_k + s_k)}{\Gamma(a_k)}.$$

Proof. *The proof follows immediately from Theorem 7.2 and Lemma 7.2.* ■

Example 7.5 *Suppose we have the multinomial sample in Example 7.4, and*

$$\mathsf{d} = \{1, 1, 3, 1, 1, 2, , 3, 1, 1, 1\}.$$

Then $a_1 = a_2 = a_3 = 2$, $N = 6$, $s_1 = 7$, $s_2 = 1$, $s_3 = 2$, $M = 10$, and due to the preceding corollary,

$$P(\mathsf{d}) = \frac{\Gamma(6)}{\Gamma(6+10)} \frac{\Gamma(2+7)}{\Gamma(2)} \frac{\Gamma(2+1)}{\Gamma(2)} \frac{\Gamma(2+2)}{\Gamma(2)} = 4.44 \times 10^{-5}.$$

Theorem 7.3 *If the conditions in Theorem 7.2 hold, then*

$$\rho(f_1, f_2, \ldots, f_{r-1}|\mathsf{d}) = \frac{\left(\prod_{k=1}^{r} f_k^{s_k}\right) \rho(f_1, f_2, \ldots, f_{r-1})}{E\left(\prod_{k=1}^{r} F_k^{s_k}\right)},$$

where $\rho(f_1, f_2, \ldots, f_{r-1}|\mathsf{d})$ denotes the conditional density function of $F_1, F_2, \ldots, F_r$ given $\mathsf{D} = \mathsf{d}$.
Proof. *The proof is left as an exercise.* ■

Corollary 7.3 *Suppose the conditions in Theorem 7.2 hold, and $F_1, F_2, \ldots, F_r$ have a Dirichlet distribution with parameters $a_1, a_2, \ldots, a_r$, $N = \sum a_k$. That is,*

$$\rho(f_1, f_2, \ldots, f_{r-1}) = Dir(f_1, f_2, \ldots, f_{r-1}; a_1, a_2, \ldots, a_r).$$

Then

$$\rho(f_1, f_2, \ldots, f_{r-1}|\mathsf{d}) = Dir(f_1, f_2, \ldots, f_{r-1}; a_1 + s_1, a_2 + s_2, \ldots, a_r + s_r).$$

Proof. *The proof follows immediately from Theorem 7.3 and Lemma 7.3.* ■

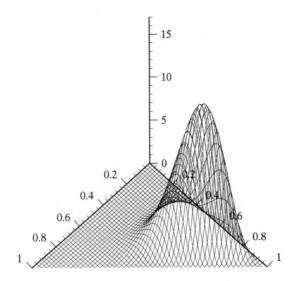

Figure 7.3: The $Dir(f_1, f_2; 9, 3, 4)$ density function.

The previous corollary shows that when we update a Dirichlet density function relative to a multinomial sample, we obtain another Dirichlet density function. For this reason, we say that the set of all Dirichlet density functions is a **conjugate family of density functions** for multinomial sampling.

Example 7.6 *Suppose we have the multinomial sample in Example 7.4 and the data in Example 7.5. Then $a_1 = a_2 = a_3 = 2$, $s_1 = 7$, $s_2 = 1$, and $s_3 = 2$. Due to the preceding corollary,*

$$\rho(f|\mathbf{d}) = Dir(f_1, f_2; 2+7, 2+1, 2+2) = Dir(f_1, f_2; 9, 3, 4).$$

Figure 7.1 shows the original density function and Figure 7.3 shows the updated density function.

Theorem 7.4 *Suppose the conditions in Theorem 7.2 hold. If we create a multinomial sample of size $M+1$ by adding variable $X^{(M+1)}$ to $\mathbf{D}$, then, for all k,*

$$P(X^{(M+1)} = k|\mathbf{d}) = E(F_k|\mathbf{d}).$$

Proof. *The proof is left as an exercise.* ∎

Corollary 7.4 *If the conditions in Theorem 7.2 hold, and $F_1, F_2, \ldots, F_r$ have a Dirichlet distribution with parameters $a_1, a_2, \ldots, a_r, N = \sum a_k$, then, for all k,*

$$P(X^{(M+1)} = k|\mathbf{d}) = \frac{a_k + s_k}{N + M}.$$

Proof. *The proof follows immediately from Theorem 7.4, Corollary 7.3, and Lemma 7.1.* ∎

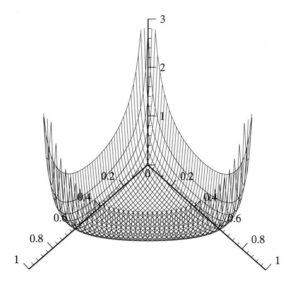

Figure 7.4: The $Dir(f_1, f_2; .2, .2, .2)$ density function.

Example 7.7 *Suppose we have the multinomial sample in Example 7.4 and the data in Example 7.5. Then $a_1 = a_2 = a_3 = 2, N = 6, s_1 = 7, s_2 = 1, s_3 = 2, M = 10$, and due to the preceding corollary,*

$$P(X^{(M+1)} = 1|\mathbf{d}) = \frac{2+7}{6+10} = .5625$$

$$P(X^{(M+1)} = 2|\mathbf{d}) = \frac{2+1}{6+10} = .1875$$

$$P(X^{(M+1)} = 3|\mathbf{d}) = \frac{2+2}{6+10} = .25.$$

7.1.2   More on the Dirichlet Density Function

After discussing the use of nonintegral values in the Dirichlet density function, we provide guidelines for assessing the values.

Nonintegral Values of a_k

So far we have shown only examples in which a_k is an integer ≥ 1 for each k. Figure 7.4 shows the $Dir(f_1, f_2; .2, .2, .2)$ density function. As that figure illustrates, as all a_k approach 0, we become increasingly certain that the relative frequency of one of the values is 1.

Assessing the Values of a_k

Next, we give some guidelines for choosing the size of a_k in the Dirichlet distribution, when we are assessing our beliefs concerning a relative frequency:

- $a_1 = a_2 = \cdots = a_r = 1$: These values mean that we consider all combinations of relative frequencies that sum to 1 equally probable. We would use these values when we feel we have no knowledge at all concerning the value of the relative frequency. We might also use these values to try to achieve objectivity in the sense that we impose none of our beliefs concerning the relative frequency on the learning algorithm. We impose only the fact that we know at most r things can happen. An example might be learning the probability of low, medium, and high blood pressure from data, which we want to communicate to the scientific community. The scientific community would not be interested in our prior belief, but in what the data had to say. Note that we might not actually believe a priori that all relative frequencies that sum to 1 are equally probable, but our goal is not to impose this belief on the learning algorithm. Essentially the posterior probability represents the belief of an agent that has no prior beliefs concerning the relative frequencies.

- $a_1 = a_2 = \cdots = a_r > 1$: These values mean that we feel it more probable that the relative frequency of the kth value is around a_k/N. The larger the values of a_k, the more we believe this. We would use such values when we want to impose our beliefs concerning the relative frequency on the learning algorithm. For example, if we were going to toss an ordinary die, we might take $a_1 = a_2 = \cdots = a_6 = 50$.

- $a_1 = a_2 = \cdots = a_r < 1$: These values mean that we feel that relative frequencies that result in not many different things happening are more probable. We would use such values when we want to impose our beliefs concerning the relative frequencies on the system. For example, suppose we know there are $1,000,000$ different species, and we are about to land on an uncharted island. We might feel it probable that not very many of the species are present. So, if we considered the relative frequencies with which we encountered different species, we would not consider relative frequencies that resulted in a lot of different species probable. Therefore, we might take $a_k = 1/1000,000$ for all k.

7.1.3   Computing Probability Intervals and Regions

We generalize the method for computing a probability interval developed in Section 6.3.

Suppose $F_1, F_2, \ldots, F_r$, have a Dirichlet distribution. That is, their density function is given by

$$\rho(f_1, f_2, \ldots, f_{r-1}) = \frac{\Gamma(N)}{\prod\limits_{k=1}^{r} \Gamma(a_k)} f_1^{a_1-1} f_2^{a_2-1} \cdots f_r^{a_r-1} \quad 0 \le f_k \le 1, \ \sum_{k=1}^{r} f_k = 1,$$

where $a_1, a_2, \ldots, a_r$ are integers ≥ 1, and $N = \sum_{k=1}^{r} a_k$. By integrating over the remaining variables, we find that the marginal density function of F_k is given by

$$\rho(f_k) = \frac{\Gamma(N)}{\Gamma(a_k)\Gamma(b_k)} f_k^{a_k-1}(1 - f_k)^{b_k-1},$$

where

$$b_k = N - a_k.$$

It is left an exercise to show this. So

$$\rho(f_k) = beta(f_k; a_k, b_k),$$

which means we can use all the techniques in Section 6.3 to compute a probability interval for F_k.

Example 7.8 *Consider the $Dir(f_1, f_2; 4, 2, 2)$ density function, which was used to model our beliefs concerning the color socks that people wear. We have $N = 4 + 2 + 2 = 8$. Therefore, due to Lemma 7.1, we have*

$$E(F_1) = \frac{a_1}{N} = \frac{4}{8} = .5.$$

Furthermore,

$$b_1 = 8 - 4 = 4.$$

A 95% probability interval for F_1 can therefore be found by solving the following equation for c:

$$\int_{.5-c}^{.5+c} \frac{\Gamma(8)}{\Gamma(4)\Gamma(4)} f_1^{4-1}(1 - f_1)^{4-1} df_1 = .95.$$

Using the mathematics package Maple, we obtain the solution $c = .316$. So our 95% probability interval for F_1 is

$$(.5 - .316, .5 + .316) = (.184, .816).$$

Similarly, a 95% probability interval for F_2 can be found by solving the following equation for c:

$$\int_{0}^{.25+c} \frac{\Gamma(8)}{\Gamma(2)\Gamma(6)} f_2^{2-1}(1 - f_2)^{6-1} df_2 = .95.$$

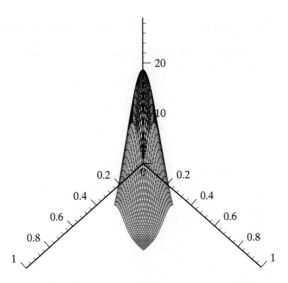

Figure 7.5: Given the $Dir(f_1, f_2; 8, 8, 16)$ density function, this is a 95% probability square for F_1 and F_2.

Using the mathematics package Maple, we obtain the solution $c = .271$. So our 95% probability interval for F_2 is

$$(0, .25 + .271) = (0, .521).$$

Clearly, this is also our 95% probability interval for F_3.

We can also obtain probability regions for two or more random variables. The following example illustrates this.

Example 7.9 *Suppose we have the $Dir(f_1, f_2; 8, 8, 16)$ density function. We can obtain a 95% probability square for F_1 and F_2 by solving the following equation for c:*

$$\int_{.25-c}^{.25+c} \int_{.25-c}^{.25+c} \frac{\Gamma(32)}{\Gamma(16)\Gamma(8)\Gamma(8)} f_1^{8-1} f_2^{8-1} (1 - f_1 - f_2)^{16-1} df_1 df_2 = .95.$$

Using the mathematics package Maple, the solution is $c = .167$. Since $.25 - .167 = .083$, and $.25 + .167 = .417$, the following are corners of a square, centered at $(.25, .25)$, that contains 95% of the probability mass:

$$(.167, 167) \quad (.417, .167) \quad (.167, .417) \quad (.417, .417).$$

Figure 7.5 shows this probability square.

When finding a region, as in the previous example, we must be careful not to cross the borders of where the density function is defined. For example, in the case of three values, we must not only be careful to not cross each axis, but also to not cross the line $f_1 + f_2 = 1$.

7.1.4   Learning Parameters in a Bayesian Network

Next we extend the theory for learning a single parameter to learning all the parameters in a Bayesian network.

Multinomial Augmented Bayesian Networks

We start by generalizing Definition 6.9 of a binomial augmented Bayesian network.

Definition 7.3 *A **multinomial augmented Bayesian network**$(\mathbb{G}, \mathsf{F}, \rho)$ is an augmented Bayesian network with the following properties:*

1. *For every i, X_i has space $\{1, 2, \ldots, r_i\}$.*

2. *For every i, there is an ordering $[\mathsf{pa}_{i1}, \mathsf{pa}_{i2}, \ldots, \mathsf{pa}_{iq_i}]$ of all instantiations of the parents PA_i in V of X_i, where q_i is the number of different instantiations of these parents. Furthermore, for every i,*

$$\mathsf{F}_i = \mathsf{F}_{i1} \cup \mathsf{F}_{i2} \cup \cdots \mathsf{F}_{iq_i},$$

   where

$$\mathsf{F}_{ij} = \{F_{ij1}, F_{ij2,\ldots}, F_{ijr_i}\}$$

   and each F_{ij} is a root, has no edge to any variable except X_i, and has density function

$$\rho_{ij}(\mathsf{f}_{ij}) = \rho(f_{ij1}, f_{ij2}, \ldots, f_{ij(r_i-1)}) \qquad 0 \leq f_{ijk} \leq 1, \sum_{k=1}^{r_i} f_{ijk} = 1.$$

3. *For every i, j and k, and all values $\mathsf{f}_{i1}, \ldots, \mathsf{f}_{ij}, \ldots, \mathsf{f}_{iq_i}$ of $\mathsf{F}_{i1}, \ldots, \mathsf{F}_{ij}, \ldots, \mathsf{F}_{iq_i}$,*

$$P(X_i = k | \mathsf{pa}_{ij}, \mathsf{f}_{i1}, \ldots, \mathsf{f}_{ij}, \ldots, \mathsf{f}_{iq_i}) = f_{ijk}.$$

Since the F_{ij}s are all roots in a Bayesian network, they are mutually independent. So besides the global parameter independence of the sets F_i, we have **local parameter independence** of their subsets F_{ij}. That is, for $1 \leq i \leq n$,

$$\rho(\mathsf{f}_{i1}, \mathsf{f}_{i2}, \ldots, \mathsf{f}_{iq_i}) = \rho(\mathsf{f}_{i1})\rho(\mathsf{f}_{i2}) \cdots \rho(\mathsf{f}_{iq_i}).$$

Global and local independence together imply that

$$\rho(\mathsf{f}_{11}, \mathsf{f}_{12}, \ldots, \mathsf{f}_{nq_n}) = \rho(\mathsf{f}_{11})\rho(\mathsf{f}_{12}) \cdots \rho(\mathsf{f}_{nq_n}). \tag{7.1}$$

Note that, again, to avoid clutter we did not subscript the density functions.

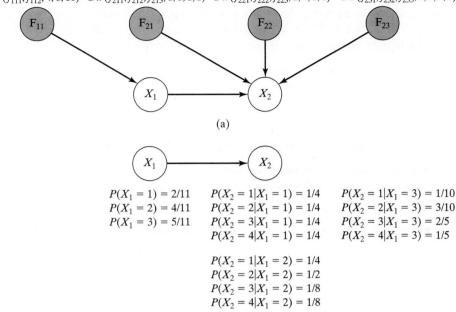

$Dir(f_{111}, f_{112}; 4, 8, 10)$ $Dir(f_{211}, f_{212}, f_{213}; 1, 1, 1, 1)$ $Dir(f_{221}, f_{222}, f_{223}; 2, 4, 1, 1)$ $Dir(f_{231}, f_{232}, f_{233}; 1, 3, 4, 2)$

(a)

$P(X_1 = 1) = 2/11$ $P(X_2 = 1 | X_1 = 1) = 1/4$ $P(X_2 = 1 | X_1 = 3) = 1/10$
$P(X_1 = 2) = 4/11$ $P(X_2 = 2 | X_1 = 1) = 1/4$ $P(X_2 = 2 | X_1 = 3) = 3/10$
$P(X_1 = 3) = 5/11$ $P(X_2 = 3 | X_1 = 1) = 1/4$ $P(X_2 = 3 | X_1 = 3) = 2/5$
$P(X_2 = 4 | X_1 = 1) = 1/4$ $P(X_2 = 4 | X_1 = 3) = 1/5$

$P(X_2 = 1 | X_1 = 2) = 1/4$
$P(X_2 = 2 | X_1 = 2) = 1/2$
$P(X_2 = 3 | X_1 = 2) = 1/8$
$P(X_2 = 4 | X_1 = 2) = 1/8$

(b)

Figure 7.6: A multinomial augmented Bayesian network is shown in (a), and its embedded Bayesian network is shown in (b).

Note that a binomial augmented Bayesian network is a multinomial augmented Bayesian network in which $r_i = 2$ for all i. Figure 7.6 shows a multinomial augmented Bayesian network that is not a binomial one. A multinomial augmented Bayesian network is a generalization of a binomial augmented Bayesian network, and has all the same properties. To that effect, we have the following theorem, which generalizes the corresponding theorem for binomial augmented Bayesian networks.

Theorem 7.5 *Let a multinomial augmented Bayesian network $(\mathbb{G}, \mathsf{F}, \rho)$ be given. Then, for every i and j, the ijth conditional distribution in $(\mathbb{G}, P)$ is given by*

$$P(X_i = k | \mathsf{pa}_{ij}) = E(F_{ijk}).$$

Proof. *The proof is left as an exercise.* ∎

Corollary 7.5 *Let a multinomial augmented Bayesian network be given. If the variables in each* F_{ij} *have a Dirichlet distribution with parameters* a_{ij1}, $a_{ij2}, \ldots, a_{ijr_i}$, $N_{ij} = \sum_k a_{ijk}$, *then for each* i *and each* j, *the* ij*th conditional distribution in the embedded network* $(\mathbb{G}, P)$ *is given by*

$$P(X_i = k|\mathsf{pa}_{ij}) = \frac{a_{ijk}}{N_{ij}}.$$

Proof. *The proof follows directly from Theorem 7.5 and Lemma 7.1.* ∎

Learning Using a Multinomial Augmented Bayesian Network

Next we give generalizations of the definitions and theorems in Section 6.4.3 to multinomial augmented Bayesian networks. You are referred to that section for discussions and examples, as we provide none here.

Definition 7.4 *Suppose we have a Bayesian network sample of size* M *such that*

1. *for every* i *each* $X_i^{(h)}$ *has space* $\{1, 2, \ldots, r_i\}$;

2. *its augmented Bayesian network* $(\mathbb{G}, \mathsf{F}, \rho)$ *is multinomial.*

Then D *is called a* **multinomial Bayesian network sample** *of size* M *with parameter* $(\mathbb{G}, \mathsf{F})$.

Theorem 7.6 *Suppose*

1. D *is a multinomial Bayesian network sample of size* M *with parameter* $(\mathbb{G}, \mathsf{F})$;

2. *we have a set of values (data) of the* $\mathbf{X}^{(h)}s$ *as follows:*

$$\mathbf{x}^{(1)} = \begin{pmatrix} x_1^{(11} \\ \vdots \\ x_n^{(1)} \end{pmatrix} \qquad \mathbf{x}^{(2)} = \begin{pmatrix} x_1^{(2)} \\ \vdots \\ x_n^{(2)} \end{pmatrix} \qquad \cdots \qquad \mathbf{x}^{(M)} = \begin{pmatrix} x_1^{(M)} \\ \vdots \\ x_n^{(M)} \end{pmatrix}$$

$$\mathsf{d} = \{\mathbf{x}^{(1)}, \mathbf{x}^{(2)}, \ldots, \mathbf{x}^{(M)}\};$$

3. M_{ij} *is the number of* $\mathbf{x}^{(h)}s$ *in which* X_i*'s parents are in their* j*th instantiation, and of these* M_{ij} *cases,* s_{ijk} *is the number in which* x_i *is equal to* k. *Then*

$$P(\mathsf{d}) = \prod_{i=1}^{n} \prod_{j=1}^{q_i} E\left(\prod_{k=1}^{r_i} F_{ijk}^{s_{ijk}}\right).$$

Proof. *The proof is left as an exercise.* ∎

Corollary 7.6 *Suppose we have the conditions in Theorem 7.6 and the variables in each* F_{ij} *have a Dirichlet distribution with parameters* $a_{ij1}, a_{ij2}, \ldots, a_{ijr_i}$, $N_{ij} = \sum_k a_{ijk}$. *Then*

$$P(\mathsf{d}) = \prod_{i=1}^{n} \prod_{j=1}^{q_i} \frac{\Gamma(N_{ij})}{\Gamma(N_{ij} + M_{ij})} \prod_{k=1}^{r_i} \frac{\Gamma(a_{ijk} + s_{ijk})}{\Gamma(a_{ijk})}.$$

Proof. *The proof follows immediately from Theorem 7.6 and Lemma 7.2.* ∎

Theorem 7.7 (Posterior Local Parameter Independence) *Suppose we have the conditions in Theorem 7.6. Then the* $F_{ij}s$ *are mutually independent conditional on* D. *That is,*

$$\rho(\mathsf{f}_{11}, \mathsf{f}_{12}, \ldots, \mathsf{f}_{nq_n} | \mathsf{d}) = \prod_{i=1}^{n} \prod_{j=1}^{q_i} \rho(\mathsf{f}_{ij} | \mathsf{d}).$$

Furthermore,

$$
\begin{aligned}
\rho(\mathsf{f}_{ij} | \mathsf{d}) &= \rho(f_{ij1}, f_{ij2}, \ldots, f_{ij(r_i-1)} | \mathsf{d}) \\
&= \frac{\left(\prod_{k=1}^{r_i} f_{ijk}^{s_{ijk}} \right) \rho(f_{ij1}, f_{ij2}, \ldots, f_{ij(r_1-1)})}{E\left(\prod_{k=1}^{r_i} F_{ijk}^{s_{ijk}} \right)}.
\end{aligned}
$$

Proof. *The proof is left as an exercise.* ∎

Corollary 7.7 *Suppose we have the conditions in Theorem 7.6 and the variables in each* F_{ij} *have a Dirichlet distribution with parameters* $a_{ij1}, a_{ij2}, \ldots, a_{ijr_i}$, $N_{ij} = \sum a_{ijk}$. *That is, for each i and each j,*

$$\rho(f_{ij1}, f_{ij2}, \ldots, f_{ij(r_i-1)}) = Dir(f_{ij1}, f_{ij2}, \ldots, f_{ij(r_i-1)}; a_{ij1}, a_{ij2}, \ldots, a_{ijr_i}).$$

Then

$$\rho(f_{ij1}, f_{ij2}, \ldots, f_{ij(r_i-1)} | \mathsf{d})$$

$$= Dir(f_{ij1}, f_{ij2}, \ldots, f_{ij(r_i-1)}; a_{ij1} + s_{ij1}, a_{ij2} + s_{ij2}, \ldots, a_{ijr_i} + s_{ijr_i}).$$

Proof. *The proof follows immediately from Theorem 7.7 and Lemma 7.3.* ∎

Using an Equivalent Sample Size

The results in Section 6.4.4 concerning equivalent sample sizes also hold for multinomial augmented Bayesian networks. We merely state the corresponding results here.

Prior Equivalent Sample Size   We start with a definition.

Definition 7.5 *Suppose we have a multinomial augmented Bayesian network in which the density functions are $Dir(f_{ij1}, f_{ij2}, \dots, f_{ij(r_i-1)}; a_{ij1}, a_{ij2}, \dots, a_{ijr_i})$ for all i and j. If there is a number N such that, for all i and j,*

$$N_{ij} = \sum_{k=1}^{r_i} a_{ijk} = P(\mathsf{pa}_{ij}) \times N,$$

*then the network is said to have **equivalent sample size** N.*

If a multinomial augmented Bayesian network has n nodes and equivalent sample size N, we have, for $1 \leq i \leq n$,

$$\sum_{j=1}^{q_i} N_{ij} = \sum_{j=1}^{q_i} \left[P(\mathsf{pa}_{ij}) \times N \right] = N \times \sum_{j=1}^{q_i} P(\mathsf{pa}_{ij}) = N.$$

It is unlikely we would arrive at a network with an equivalent sample size simply by making up values of a_{ijk}. The next two theorems give common ways for constructing one.

Theorem 7.8 *Suppose we specify* $\mathbb{G}$, F, *and* N *and assign, for all i, j, and k,*

$$a_{ijk} = \frac{N}{r_i q_i}.$$

Then the resultant augmented Bayesian network has equivalent sample size N, and the probability distribution in the resultant embedded Bayesian network is uniform.
Proof. *The proof is left as an exercise.*   ∎

Theorem 7.9 *Suppose we specify* $\mathbb{G}$, F, N, *a Bayesian network* $(\mathbb{G}, P)$, *and assign, for all i and j,*

$$a_{ijk} = P(X_i = k | \mathsf{pa}_{ij}) \times P(\mathsf{pa}_{ij}) \times N.$$

Then the resultant multinomial augmented Bayesian network has equivalent sample size N. Furthermore, it embeds the originally specified Bayesian network.
Proof. *The proof is left as an exercise.*   ∎

Definition 7.6 *Multinomial augmented Bayesian networks* $(\mathbb{G}_1, \mathsf{F}^{(\mathbb{G}_1)}, \rho|\mathbb{G}_1)$ *and* $(\mathbb{G}_2, \mathsf{F}^{(\mathbb{G}_2)}, \rho|\mathbb{G}_2)$ *are called* **equivalent** *if they satisfy the following:*

1. $\mathbb{G}_1$ *and* $\mathbb{G}_2$ *are Markov equivalent.*

2. *The probability distributions in their embedded Bayesian networks are the same.*

3. *The specified density functions in both are Dirichlet.*

4. *They have the same equivalent sample size.*

Lemma 7.4 *(**Likelihood Equivalence**) Suppose we have two equivalent multinomial augmented Bayesian networks* $(\mathbb{G}_1, \mathsf{F}^{(\mathbb{G}_1)}, \rho|\mathbb{G}_1)$ *and* $(\mathbb{G}_2, \mathsf{F}^{(\mathbb{G}_2)}, \rho|\mathbb{G}_2)$. *Let* D *be a set of random vectors as specified in Definition 7.4. Then, for every set* d *of values of the vectors in* D,

$$P(\mathsf{d}|\mathbb{G}_1) = P(\mathsf{d}|\mathbb{G}_2),$$

where $P(\mathsf{d}|\mathbb{G}_1)$ *and* $P(\mathsf{d}|\mathbb{G}_2)$ *are the probabilities of* d *when* D *is considered multinomial Bayesian network samples with parameters* $(\mathbb{G}_1, \mathsf{F}^{(\mathbb{G}_1)})$ *and* $(\mathbb{G}_2, \mathsf{F}^{(\mathbb{G}_2)})$, *respectively.*
Proof. *The proof can be found in Heckerman et al. [1995].* ∎

Theorem 7.10 *Suppose we have two equivalent multinomial augmented Bayesian networks* $(\mathbb{G}_1, \mathsf{F}^{(\mathbb{G}_1)}, \rho|\mathbb{G}_1)$ *and* $(\mathbb{G}_2, \mathsf{F}^{(\mathbb{G}_2)}, \rho|\mathbb{G}_2)$. *Let* D *be a set of random vectors as specified in Definition 7.4. Then, given any set* d *of values of the vectors in* D, *the updated embedded Bayesian network relative to* D *and the data* d, *obtained by considering* D *a binomial Bayesian network sample with parameter* $(\mathbb{G}_1, \mathsf{F}^{(\mathbb{G}_1)})$, *contains the same probability distribution as the one obtained by considering* D *a binomial Bayesian network sample with parameter* $(\mathbb{G}_2, \mathsf{F}^{(\mathbb{G}_2)})$.
Proof. *The proof is exactly like that of Theorem 6.15.* ∎

Corollary 7.8 *Suppose we have two equivalent multinomial augmented Bayesian networks* $(\mathbb{G}_1, \mathsf{F}^{(\mathbb{G}_1)}, \rho|\mathbb{G}_1)$ *and* $(\mathbb{G}_2, \mathsf{F}^{(\mathbb{G}_2)}, \rho|\mathbb{G}_2)$. *Then, given any set* d *of values of the variables in* D, *the updated embedded Bayesian network relative to* D *and the data* d, *obtained by considering* D *a binomial Bayesian network sample with parameter* $(\mathbb{G}_1, \mathsf{F}^{(\mathbb{G}_1)})$, *is equivalent to the one obtained by considering* D *a binomial Bayesian network sample with parameter* $(\mathbb{G}_2, \mathsf{F}^{(\mathbb{G}_2)})$.
Proof. *The proof follows easily from the preceding theorem.* ∎

Expressing Prior Indifference with a Prior Equivalent Sample Size
Recall that in Section 6.4.4 we suggested that perhaps the best way to express prior indifference when every variable has two values is simply to specify an equivalent sample size of two and, for each node, distribute the sample evenly among all specified values. If every variable has r values, this same argument suggests that we should use an equivalent sample size of r. However, in general, the variables do not have the same number of values. So what size should we

use in the general case? It seems that the most reasonable choice is to find the variable(s) with the greatest number of values $maxr$, and use $maxr$ as the equivalent sample size. This may seem a bit strange because, for example, if X is a root with two values and $maxr = 16$, then we specify a $beta(f; 8, 8)$ density function at X. It seems that we have become highly confident $P(X = 1)$ is equal to .5 just because we included X in a network with other variables. The following provides a reasonable intuitive justification for this. Suppose Y is a variable with $maxr$ values. In order to "know" Y has $maxr$ values, it is arguable that minimally our prior experience must be equivalent to having seen each of them occur once. Therefore, our prior sample size must be at least equal to $maxr$. Since X is in that prior sample, there are also $maxr$ observations of values of X.

Some Theoretical Results   In Section 6.4.4, we argued for an equivalent sample size on intuitive grounds. Furthermore, we proved that we get the kind of results we want when we use one. However, is there an axiomatic justification for assuming one? Heckerman et al. [1995] discuss learning the conditional independencies (and thereby a DAG pattern) among the variables from data, a subject we discuss in Chapters 8–11. However, their results are relevant to our considerations here—Namely, they show that if we make certain reasonable assumptions, then we must use an equivalent sample size. Their assumptions are the following: (1) we represent the belief that conditional independencies are present using a multinomial augmented Bayesian network whose DAG $\mathbb{G}$ entails all and only those conditional independencies; (2) the hypothesis that no conditional independencies are present has positive probability; (3) when X_i has the same set of parents in V in two multinomial augmented Bayesian networks, the density functions of F_{ij} for all j are the same in those networks (called **parameter modularity**); (4) if two multinomial augmented Bayesian networks $(\mathbb{G}_1, \mathsf{F}^{(\mathbb{G}_1)}, \rho|\mathbb{G}_1)$ and $(\mathbb{G}_2, \mathsf{F}^{(\mathbb{G}_2)}, \rho|\mathbb{G}_2)$ satisfy only the first two conditions in Definition 7.6, then we have **likelihood equivalence** (as defined in Lemma 7.4); and (5) all density functions are everywhere positive (i.e., the range of each function includes only numbers greater than zero). Given these assumptions, they prove the density functions must be Dirichlet, and there is some N such that each network has equivalent sample size N.

7.1.5   Learning with Missing Data Items

Algorithm 6.1, which appears in Section 6.5, extends immediately to one for learning in the case of multinomial Bayesian networks.

7.1.6   Variances in Computed Relative Frequencies

It is left as an exercise to consult the references mentioned in Section 6.6 in order to extend the results in that section to the case of multinomial variables. Here we state only a generalization of Theorem 6.16, which you will need to compute variances.

Theorem 7.11 *Suppose* $F_1, F_2, \ldots, F_r$ *have the* $Dir(f_1, f_2, \ldots, f_{r-1}; a_1, a_2, \ldots, a_r)$ *density function. Then*

$$E(F_m) = \frac{a_m}{\sum a_k}$$

$$E(F_m^2) = \left(\frac{a_m + 1}{\sum a_k + 1} \right) \left(\frac{a}{\sum a_k} \right)$$

$$E(F_l F_m) = \frac{a_l a_m}{(\sum a_k + 1) \sum a_k}.$$

Proof. *The proof is left as an exercise.*   ∎

7.2   Continuous Variables

Recall that in Section 4.1 we defined a Gaussian Bayesian network, and we developed an algorithm for doing inference in such a network. Here we present a method for learning parameters in Gaussian Bayesian networks. First, we discuss learning parameters for a normally distributed variable. Then we discuss learning parameters for variables that have the multivariate normal distribution. Finally, we apply the theory developed to learning parameters in a Gaussian Bayesian network.

7.2.1   Normally Distributed Variable

First, we assume the mean of the variable is unknown and the variance is known. Then we discuss the case in which the mean is known and the variance is unknown. Finally, we assume both are unknown.

   Before proceeding to do all this, we have the following definition:

Definition 7.7 *Suppose X has the normal density function $N(x; \mu, \sigma^2)$. Then the **precision** r of X is defined as follows:*

$$r = \frac{1}{\sigma^2}.$$

   Henceforth we show the normal distribution using the precision. The reason should become clear as we develop the theory.

The Case of Unknown Mean and Known Variance

Suppose X is normally distributed with unknown mean and known precision r. We represent our belief concerning the unknown mean with a random variable A (for average), which is normally distributed with mean μ and precision v. Note that the probability distribution of X is a relative frequency distribution

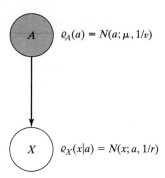

Figure 7.7: The probability distribution of A represents our belief concerning the mean of X.

that models a phenomenon in nature, while the probability distribution of A is our subjective probability concerning the value of X's mean. Owing to the discussion in Section 6.1.1, we represent this situation with the Bayesian network in Figure 7.7.

The following theorem gives the prior density function of X:

Theorem 7.12 *Suppose X and A are random variables such that*

the density function of A is

$$\rho_A(a) = N(a; \mu, 1/v),$$

and the conditional density function of X given $A = a$ is

$$\rho_X(x|a) = N(x; a, 1/r).$$

Then the prior density function of X is

$$\rho_X(x) = N\left(x; \mu, \frac{1}{r} + \frac{1}{v}\right).$$

Proof.

$$
\begin{aligned}
\rho_X(x) &= \int_a \rho_X(x|a)\rho_A(a)da \\[2mm]
&= \int_a N(x; a, 1/r)N(a; \mu, 1/v)da \\[2mm]
&= \int_a N(a; x, 1/r)N(a; \mu, 1/v)da \\[2mm]
&= N\left(x; \mu, \frac{1}{r} + \frac{1}{v}\right).
\end{aligned}
$$

The third equality is due to Equality 4.2 and the fourth is due to Equality 4.5. ∎

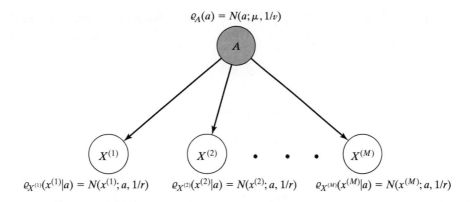

Figure 7.8: A Bayesian network representing a normal sample of size M with parameter $\{A, r\}$.

We see that X has a normal distribution with the same mean as A, but X has greater variability than A owing to the uncertainty in X conditional on A's value.

Suppose now that we perform M trials of a random process whose outcome is normally distributed with unknown mean and known precision r. Let $X^{(h)}$ be a random variable whose value is the outcome of the hth trial, and let A be a random variable representing our belief concerning the mean. Again assume A is normally distributed with mean μ and precision v. As discussed in Section 6.1.2, we assume that, if we knew the value a of A for certain, then we would feel that the $X^{(h)}$s are mutually independent, and our probability distribution for each trial would have mean a. That is, we have a sample defined as follows:

Definition 7.8 *Suppose we have a sample of size M such that*

1. *each $X^{(h)}$ has the reals as its space;*

2. $\mathsf{F} = \{A, r\}$,

$$\rho_A(a) = N(a; \mu, 1/v)$$

   and for $1 \leq h \leq M$,

$$\rho_{X^{(h)}}(x^{(h)} | a) = N(x^{(h)}; a, 1/r).$$

   *Then D is called a **normal sample** of size M with parameter $\{A, r\}$.*

We represent this sample with the Bayesian network in Figure 7.8.

Theorem 7.13 *Suppose*

1. D *is a normal sample of size M with parameter $\{A, r\}$ where $r > 0$, and A has precision $v > 0$;*

2. $\mathbf{d} = \{x^{(1)}, x^{(2)}, \dots, x^{(M)}\}$ *is a set of values (data) of the variables in* $\mathbf{D}$*,
and*

$$\overline{x} = \frac{\sum_{h=1}^{M} x^{(h)}}{M}.$$

Then the posterior density function of A *is*

$$\rho_A(a|\mathbf{d}) = N(a; \mu^*, 1/v^*),$$

where

$$\mu^* = \frac{v\mu + Mr\overline{x}}{v + Mr} \qquad and \qquad v^* = v + Mr. \qquad (7.2)$$

Proof. *It is left as exercises to show that (1)*

$$\rho_{\mathbf{D}}(\mathbf{d}|a) \simeq \exp\left[-\frac{r}{2}\sum_{h=1}^{M}(x^{(h)} - a)^2\right], \qquad (7.3)$$

where $exp(y)$ *denotes* e^y *and* $\simeq$ *means "is proportional to," and (2)*

$$\sum_{h=1}^{M}(x^{(h)} - a)^2 = M(a - \overline{x})^2 + \sum_{h=1}^{M}(x^{(h)} - \overline{x})^2. \qquad (7.4)$$

Since the far right term in Equality 7.4 does not contain a*, we may rewrite
Relation 7.3 as follows:*

$$\rho_{\mathbf{D}}(\mathbf{d}|a) \simeq \exp\left[-\frac{Mr}{2}(a - \overline{x})^2\right]. \qquad (7.5)$$

The prior density function of A *satisfies the following:*

$$\rho_A(a) \simeq \exp\left[-\frac{v}{2}(a - \mu)^2\right]. \qquad (7.6)$$

We have

$$\begin{aligned}\rho_A(a|\mathbf{d}) &\simeq \rho_{\mathbf{D}}(\mathbf{d}|a)\rho_A(a) \qquad\qquad\qquad\qquad\qquad (7.7)\\ &\simeq \exp\left[-\frac{v}{2}(a - \mu)^2\right]\exp\left[-\frac{Mr}{2}(a - \overline{x})^2\right].\end{aligned}$$

*The first proportionality in Relation 7.7 is due to Bayes' theorem, and the second
is due to Relations 7.5 and 7.6. It is left as an exercise to show that*

$$v(a - \mu)^2 + Mr(a - \overline{x})^2 = (v + Mr)(a - \mu^*)^2 + \frac{vMr(\overline{x} - \mu)^2}{v + Mr}. \qquad (7.8)$$

Since the final term in Equality 7.8 does not contain a, it can also be included in the proportionality factor. So we can rewrite Relation 7.7 as

$$\rho_A(a|\mathbf{d}) \simeq \exp\left[-\frac{v+Mr}{2}(a-\mu^*)^2\right]$$

$$\simeq \exp\left[-\frac{(a-\mu^*)^2}{2\,(1/v^*)}\right]$$

$$\simeq N(a;\mu^*,1/v^*). \qquad (7.9)$$

Since $\rho_A(a|\mathbf{d})$ and $N(a;\mu^*,1/v^*)$ are both density functions, their integrals over the real line must both equal 1. Therefore, owing to Relation 7.9, they must be the same function. ∎

Example 7.10 *Suppose* D *is a normal sample of size M with parameter $\{A,1\}$. That is, we represent our prior belief concerning A using a value of $r = 1$. Then, owing to the previous theorem, our posterior density function of A is given by*

$$\rho_A(a|\mathbf{d}) = N(a;\mu^*,1/v^*),$$

where

$$\mu^* = \frac{v\mu + M\bar{x}}{v+M} \qquad and \qquad v^* = v + M. \qquad (7.10)$$

From the previous example, we see that, when $r = 1$, if we consider the parameter μ the mean of the hypothetical sample on which we base our prior belief concerning the value of A and v its size, then μ^* would be the mean of the hypothetical sample combined with the actual sample, and v^* would be the size of this combined sample. Therefore, we can attach the following meaning to the parameters μ and v:

The parameter μ is the mean of the hypothetical sample upon which we base our prior belief concerning the value of A.

The parameter v is the size of the hypothetical sample on which we base our prior belief concerning the value of A.

Example 7.11 *Suppose $r = 1$, $v = 4$ and $\mu = 10$. Then we can consider our prior belief as being equivalent to having seen a sample of size 4 in which the mean was 10. Suppose next we sample three items, and we obtain $x^{(1)} = 4$, $x^{(2)} = 5$, $x^{(4)} = 6$. Then $M = 3$, $\bar{x} = (4+5+6)/3 = 5$, and, therefore, owing to Equality 7.10,*

$$\mu^* = \frac{v\mu + M\bar{x}}{v+M} = \frac{(4\times10)+(3\times5)}{4+3} = 7.86$$

and

$$v^* = 4 + 3 = 7.$$

Example 7.12 *Note that v must be greater than 0 because if v were 0, the variance of A would be infinite. We can take the limit as $v \to 0$ (i.e., as the variance approaches infinity) of the expressions for μ^* and v^* (Equality 7.2) to model the situation in which we have complete prior ignorance as to the value of A. Taking these limits, we have*

$$\mu^* = \lim_{v \to 0} \frac{v\mu + Mr\overline{x}}{v + Mr} = \overline{x}$$

and

$$v^* = \lim_{v \to 0} (v + Mr) = Mr.$$

*Alternatively, we could obtain the same result using an **improper prior density function**. It is called improper because it is not really a density function in that its integral is not finite. We obtain an improper density function by taking the limit of the prior density function as $v \to 0$. The prior density function appears in Equality 7.6. Taking the limit of that density function, we have*

$$\rho_A(a) \simeq \lim_{v \to 0} \left(\exp\left[-\frac{v}{2}(a - \mu)^2 \right] \right) = 1.$$

Note that this is only a formal result because we are ignoring the constant of proportionality which is approaching 0. This improper density function imparts a uniform distribution over the whole real line.

Using this improper prior density function and proceeding from Relation 7.7, we obtain

$$\rho_A(a|\mathbf{d}) = N(a; \overline{x}, 1/Mr),$$

which is the same as the result obtained by taking the limit as $v \to 0$ of the expressions for μ^* and v^*.

Assuming the improper prior density function, the posterior variance of A is σ^2/M, where $\sigma^2 = 1/r$ is the known variance of each X^i conditional on A. A posterior perc % probability interval for A is therefore given by

$$\left(\overline{x} - z_{perc} \frac{\sigma}{\sqrt{M}}, \overline{x} + z_{perc} \frac{\sigma}{\sqrt{M}} \right),$$

where z_{perc} is the z-score obtained from the standard normal table. (See Section 6.3 for a discussion of probability intervals and the z-score.) If you are familiar with "classical" statistics, you should notice that this probability interval is identical to the perc % confidence interval for the mean of a normal distribution with know variance σ^2.

Note that if we take $v = 0$, then the prior density function of X (obtained in Theorem 7.12) is also improper.

Next we give a theorem for the density function of $X^{(M+1)}$, the $M+1$st trial of the experiment.

Theorem 7.14 *Suppose we have the assumptions in Theorem 7.13. Then $X^{(M+1)}$ has the posterior density function*

$$\rho_{X^{(M+1)}}(x^{(M+1)}|\mathsf{d}) = N\left(x^{(M+1)}; \mu^*, \frac{1}{r} + \frac{1}{v^*}\right),$$

where the values of μ^* and v^* are those obtained in Theorem 7.13.
Proof. *The proof is left as an exercise.* ∎

The Case of Known Mean and Unknown Variance

Next we discuss the case in which the mean is known and the variance is unknown. First, we need to review the gamma distribution.

The Gamma Distribution We start with the following definition:

Definition 7.9 *The **gamma density function** with parameters α and β, where $\alpha > 0$ and $\beta > 0$, is*

$$\rho(x) = \frac{\beta^\alpha}{\Gamma(\alpha)} x^{\alpha-1} e^{-\beta x} \qquad x > 0$$

and is denoted gamma$(x; \alpha, \beta)$.
*A random variable X that has this density function is said to have a **gamma distribution**.*

If the random variable X has the gamma density function, then

$$E(X) = \frac{\alpha}{\beta} \qquad \text{and} \qquad V(X) = \frac{\alpha}{\beta^2}.$$

Definition 7.10 *The gamma density function is called the **chi-square (χ^2) density function** with k degrees of freedom, where k is a positive integer, when*

$$\alpha = \frac{k}{2} \qquad \text{and} \qquad \beta = \frac{1}{2},$$

and is denoted chi-square$(x; k)$ and $\chi_k^2(x)$.
*A random variable X that has this density function is said to have a **chi-square (χ^2) distribution** with k degrees of freedom.*

Example 7.13 *We have*

$$
\begin{aligned}
chi\text{-}square(x; 6) &= \frac{\beta^\alpha}{\Gamma(\alpha)} x^{\alpha-1} e^{-\beta x} \\
&= \frac{(1/2)^{6/2}}{\Gamma(6/2)} x^{6/2-1} e^{-(1/2)x} \\
&= \frac{1}{16} x^2 e^{-x/2}.
\end{aligned}
$$

Figure 7.9 shows this density function.

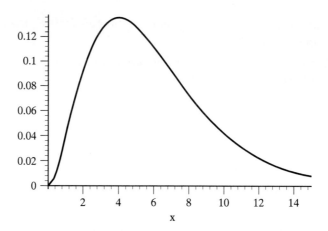

Figure 7.9: The chi-square density function with six degrees of freedom.

The following theorem is a well-known result concerning the gamma density function.

Theorem 7.15 *Suppose $X_1, X_2, \ldots, X_k$ are k independent random variables, each with the $N(x; 0, \sigma^2)$ density function. Then the random variable*

$$V = X_1^2 + X_2^2 + \cdots X_k^2$$

has the gamma$(v, k/2, 1/2\sigma^2)$ density function.
Proof. *The proof is left as an exercise.*   ■

Corollary 7.9 *Suppose $X_1, X_2, \ldots, X_k$ are k independent random variables, each with the standard normal density function. Then the random variable*

$$V = X_1^2 + X_2^2 + \cdots X_k^2$$

has the chi-square$(v; k)$ density function.
Proof. *The proof follows immediately from the preceding theorem.*   ■

Learning With Known Mean and Unknown Variance   Now we can discuss learning in the case of known mean and unknown variance. Our goal is to proceed quickly to the case in which both are unknown. So the only result we present here is a theorem that obtains the posterior distribution of the variance. We obtain this result because we refer to it in the next subsection.

Suppose we perform M trials of a random process whose outcome is normally distributed with known mean a and unknown variance, and we let $X^{(h)}$ be a random variable whose value is the outcome of the hth trial. We represent our belief concerning the unknown precision with a random variable R, which has the *gamma$(r; \alpha/2, \beta/2)$* density function. As in the earlier case, we assume that if we knew the value r of R for certain, then we would feel that the $X^{(h)}$s are mutually independent, and our probability distribution for each trial would have precision r. That is we have a sample defined as follows:

Definition 7.11 *Suppose we have a sample of size M such that*

1. *each $X^{(h)}$ has the reals as its space;*

2. $\mathsf{F} = \{a, R\}$,

$$\rho_R(r) = gamma\,(r; \alpha/2, \beta/2),$$

and, for $1 \le h \le M$,

$$\rho_{X^{(h)}}(x^{(h)}|r) = N(x^{(h)}; a, 1/r).$$

Then D *is called a **normal sample** of size M with parameter $\{a, R\}$.*

The following theorem obtains the updated distribution of R given this sample.

Theorem 7.16 *Suppose*

1. D *is a normal sample of size M with parameter $\{a, R\}$;*

2. $\mathsf{d} = \{x^{(1)}, x^{(2)}, \ldots, x^{(M)}\}$ *is a set of values of the variables in* D, *and*

$$s = \sum_{h=1}^{M} \left(x^{(h)} - a\right)^2.$$

Then the posterior density function of R is

$$\rho_R(r|\mathsf{d}) = gamma(r, \alpha^*/2, \beta^*/2),$$

where

$$\beta^* = \beta + s \qquad and \qquad \alpha^* = \alpha + M. \tag{7.11}$$

Proof. *The proof is left as an exercise.* ∎

Let's investigate the parameters α and β. Suppose $\hat{x}^{(1)}, \hat{x}^{(2)}, \ldots, \hat{x}^{(\alpha)}$ are the values in the hypothetical sample upon which we base our prior belief concerning the value of R, and β is the value of s for that sample. That is,

$$\beta = \sum_{i=1}^{\alpha} \left(\hat{x}^i - a\right)^2.$$

Then clearly, β^* would be the value of s for the combined sample. Therefore, we see that we can attach the following meaning to the parameters α and β:

The parameter β is the value of s in the hypothetical sample upon which we base our prior belief concerning the value of R.

The parameter α is the size of the hypothetical sample upon which we base our prior belief concerning the value of R.

Example 7.14 *We can take the limit as $\beta \to 0$ and $\alpha \to 0$ of the expressions for α^* and β^* to model the situation in which we have complete prior ignorance as to the value of R. Taking these limits, we have*

$$\beta^* = \lim_{\beta \to 0} (\beta + s) = s$$

$$\alpha^* = \lim_{\alpha \to 0} (\alpha + M) = M.$$

Alternatively, we could obtain the same result by taking the limit of the prior density function gamma $(r; \alpha/2, \beta/2)$ as $\beta \to 0$ and $\alpha \to 0$. Taking the limit of that density function, we have

$$\rho_R(r) \simeq \lim_{\alpha \to 0} \lim_{\beta \to 0} \left(r^{\alpha-1} e^{-\beta r} \right) = \frac{1}{r}.$$

This improper density function assigns a large probability to large variances (small values of r), and small probability to small variances.

Using this improper prior density function, it is left as an exercise to show that

$$\rho_R(r|\mathbf{d}) = gamma(r; M/2, s/2),$$

which is the same as the result obtained by taking the limit as $\beta \to 0$ and $\alpha \to 0$ of the expressions for β^* and α^*.

The Case of Unknown Mean and Unknown Variance

We now assume both the mean and the variance are unknown. First, we need to review the t distribution.

The t Distribution   We start with the following definition:

Definition 7.12 *The t **density function** with α degrees of freedom, where $\alpha > 0$, is*

$$\rho(x) = \left(\frac{1}{\alpha\pi} \right)^{1/2} \frac{\Gamma\left(\frac{\alpha+1}{2}\right)}{\Gamma\left(\frac{\alpha}{2}\right)} \left(1 + \frac{x^2}{\alpha} \right)^{-\frac{(\alpha+1)}{2}} \qquad -\infty < x < \infty \qquad (7.12)$$

and is denoted $t(x; \alpha)$.

*A random variable X that has this density function is said to have a t **distribution** with α degrees of freedom.*

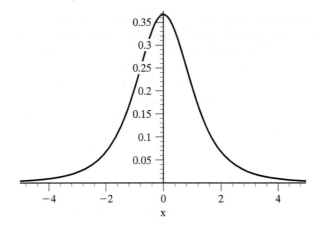

Figure 7.10: The t density function with three degrees of freedom.

If the random variable X has the $t(x; \alpha)$ density function and if $\alpha > 2$, then

$$E(X) = 0 \quad \text{and} \quad V(X) = \frac{\alpha}{\alpha - 2}.$$

Figure 7.10 shows the t density function with three degrees of freedom. Note its similarity to the standard normal density function. Indeed, it is possible to show that the standard normal density function is equal to the limit as α approaches infinity of the t distribution with α degrees of freedom.

The family of t distributions can be enlarged so that it includes every density function which can be obtained from a density function of the form shown in Equality 7.12 through an arbitrary translation and change of scale. We do that next.

Definition 7.13 *A random variable X has a t **distribution** with α degrees of freedom, where $\alpha > 0$, location parameter μ, where $-\infty < \mu < \infty$, and precision τ, where $\tau > 0$, if the random variable $\tau^{1/2}(X - \mu)$ has a t distribution with α degrees of freedom. The density function of X is*

$$\rho(x) = \left(\frac{\tau}{\alpha\pi}\right)^{\frac{1}{2}} \frac{\Gamma\left(\frac{\alpha+1}{2}\right)}{\Gamma\left(\frac{\alpha}{2}\right)} \left[1 + \frac{\tau}{\alpha}(x - \mu)^2\right]^{-\frac{(\alpha+1)}{2}} \qquad -\infty < x < \infty \quad (7.13)$$

and is denoted $t(x; \alpha, \mu, \tau)$.

If the random variable X has the $t(x; \alpha, \mu, \tau)$ density function and if $\alpha > 2$, then

$$E(X) = \mu \quad \text{and} \quad V(X) = \frac{\alpha}{\alpha - 2}\tau^{-1}.$$

Note that the precision in the t distribution does not exactly equal the inverse of the variance as it does in the normal distribution. The $N(x; \mu, 1/\tau)$ is equal to the limit as α approaches infinity of the $t(x; \alpha, \mu, \tau)$ density function. (See DeGroot [1970].)

Learning With Unknown Mean and Unknown Variance   Now we can discuss learning when both the mean and the variance are unknown. Suppose X is normally distributed with unknown mean and unknown precision. We again represent our belief concerning the unknown mean and unknown precision with the random variables A and R respectively. We assume R has the *gamma* $(r; \alpha/2, \beta/2)$ density function and A has the $N(a; \mu, 1/vr)$ conditional density function. The following theorem gives the prior density function of X.

Theorem 7.17 *Suppose X, A, and R are random variables such that*

the density function of R is

$$\rho_R(r) = gamma\,(r; \alpha/2, \beta/2)\,,$$

the conditional density function of A given $R = r$ is

$$\rho_A(a|r) = N\,(a; \mu, 1/vr)\,,$$

and the conditional density function of X given $A = a$ and $R = r$ is

$$\rho_X(x|a, r) = N(x; a, 1/r).$$

Then the prior density function of X is

$$\rho_X(x) = t\left(x; \alpha, \mu, \frac{v\alpha}{(v+1)\,\beta}\right). \tag{7.14}$$

Proof. *We have*

$$
\begin{aligned}
\rho_X(x) &= \int_a \int_r \rho_X(x|a, r)\rho_A(a|r)\rho_R(r)drda \\
&= \int_a \int_r N(x; a, 1/r)N\,(a; \mu, 1/vr)\,gamma\,(r; \alpha/2, \beta/2)\,drda.
\end{aligned}
$$

It is left as an exercise to perform this integration and obtain Equality 7.14.

∎

Suppose now that we perform M trials of a random process whose outcome is normally distributed with unknown mean and unknown variance. Let $X^{(h)}$ be a random variable whose values are the outcomes of the hth trial, and suppose we represent our belief concerning each trial as in Theorem 7.17. As before, we assume that, if we knew the values a and r of A and R for certain, then we would feel that the $X^{(h)}$s are mutually independent, and our probability distribution for each trial would have mean a and precision r. That is, we have a sample defined as follows:

Definition 7.14 *Suppose we have a sample of size M such that*

1. *each $X^{(h)}$ has the reals as its space*

2. *$\mathsf{F} = \{A, R\}$,*

$$\rho_R(r) = gamma\left(r; \alpha/2, \beta/2\right),$$

$$\rho_A(a|r) = N\left(a; \mu, 1/vr\right),$$

and, for $1 \le h \le M$,

$$\rho_{X^{(h)}}(x^{(h)}|a, r) = N(x^{(h)}; a, 1/r).$$

*Then D is called a **normal sample** of size M with parameter $\{A, R\}$.*

Theorem 7.18 *Suppose*

1. *D is a normal sample of size M with parameter $\{A, R\}$;*

2. *$\mathsf{d} = \{x^{(1)}, x^{(2)}, \dots, x^{(M)}\}$ is a set of values of the variables in D,*

$$\overline{x} = \frac{\sum_{h=1}^{M} x^{(h)}}{M}, \qquad and \qquad s = \sum_{h=1}^{M}\left(x^{(h)} - \overline{x}\right)^2.$$

Then the posterior density function of R is

$$\rho_R(r|\mathsf{d}) = gamma(r, \alpha^*/2, \beta^*/2),$$

where

$$\beta^* = \beta + s + \frac{vM(\overline{x} - \mu)^2}{v + M} \qquad and \qquad \alpha^* = \alpha + M, \qquad (7.15)$$

and the posterior conditional density function of A given $R = r$ is

$$\rho_A(a|r, \mathsf{d}) = N(a; \mu^*, 1/v^*r),$$

where

$$\mu^* = \frac{v\mu + M\overline{x}}{v + M} \qquad and \qquad v^* = v + M.$$

Proof. *It is left as exercises to show that*

$$\rho_{\mathsf{D}}(\mathsf{d}|a, r) \simeq r^{n/2} \exp\left[-\frac{r}{2}\sum_{h=1}^{M}(x^{(h)} - a)^2\right] \qquad (7.16)$$

and that

$$\rho_{A,R}(a,r) \quad = \quad \rho_A(a|r)\rho_R(r) \tag{7.17}$$

$$\simeq \quad r^{1/2}e^{-(vr/2)(a-\mu)^2}r^{\alpha/2-1}e^{-\beta r/2}.$$

Owing to Bayes' theorem, $\rho_{A,R}(a,r|\mathbf{d})$ is proportional to the product of the right sides of Relations 7.16 and 7.17. Using equalities similar to Equalities 7.4 and 7.8, it is left as an exercise to perform steps similar to those in Theorem 7.13 to obtain

$$\rho_{A,R}(a,r|\mathbf{d}) \simeq \left\{ r^{1/2}exp\left[\frac{v^*r}{2}(a-\mu^*)^2\right]\right\}\left\{r^{\alpha^*/2-1}e^{-\beta^*/2}\right\}.$$

This completes the proof. ∎

Based on a discussion similar to that following Example 7.10, we can attach the following meaning to the parameters μ and v:

The parameter μ is the mean of the hypothetical sample upon which we base our prior belief concerning the value of A.

The parameter v is the size of the hypothetical sample upon which we base our prior belief concerning the value of A.

Let's investigate the parameters α and β. Suppose $\hat{x}^{(1)}, \hat{x}^{(2)}, \ldots, \hat{x}^v$ are the values in the hypothetical sample upon which we base our prior belief concerning the value of A, μ is the mean of that sample, and β is the value of s in that sample. That is,

$$\beta = \sum_{i=1}^{v}\left(\hat{x}^i-\mu\right)^2. \tag{7.18}$$

Based on these assumptions, it is left as an exercise to use the left equality in Equalities 7.15 to show that

$$\beta^* = \sum_{i=1}^{v}\left(\hat{x}^i-\mu^*\right)^2 + \sum_{h=1}^{M}\left(x^{(h)}-\mu^*\right)^2, \tag{7.19}$$

which would be the value of s for the combined sample. Therefore, we see that we can attach the following meaning to the parameter β:

The parameter β is the value of s in the hypothetical sample upon which we base our prior belief concerning the value of A.

There does not seem to be a clear-cut meaning we can attach to the parameter α. Based on the right equality in Equality 7.15 and the result obtained in Section 7.2.1 for the case only the mean is known, we may want to say it is about equal to the size of the hypothetical sample upon which we base our prior belief concerning the value of R. However, Equality 7.18 indicates we should make v that size. These results suggest that we should make α about equal to v. Indeed, the next example shows that it is reasonable to make α equal to $v-1$.

Example 7.15 *Suppose we want to express complete prior ignorance as to the values of A and R by using the product of the improper density function when we knew only the value of the mean and the improper density function when we knew only the value of the variance. That is, we take the product of the uniform density function over the whole real line (which is simply 1) and the function $1/r$. We then have*

$$\rho_{A,R}(a,r) = \frac{1}{r}.$$

Recall Relation 7.17 says

$$\rho_{A,R}(a,r) \simeq r^{1/2}e^{-(vr/2)(a-\mu)^2}r^{\alpha/2-1}e^{-\beta r/2}.$$

In order for the limit of this expression to be equal to $1/r$, we would have to take the limit as $v \to 0$, $\beta \to 0$, and $\alpha \to -1$. If we use these values to model prior ignorance, we obtain

$$\beta^* = s \qquad and \qquad \alpha^* = M - 1,$$

$$\mu^* = \overline{x} \qquad and \qquad v^* = M,$$

the posterior density function of R is

$$\rho_R(r|\mathbf{d}) = gamma(r; (M-1)/2, s/2),$$

and the posterior conditional density function of A given $R = r$ is

$$\rho_A(a|r,\mathbf{d}) = N(a; \overline{x}, 1/Mr).$$

It is left as an exercise to show that this means $sr = s/\sigma^2$ is distributed $\chi^2(M-1)$. We therefore have

$$P\left[\chi^2_{P_1}(M-1) < \frac{s}{\sigma^2} < \chi^2_{P_2}(M-1)\right] = P_2 - P_1,$$

where $\chi^2_{P_i}(M-1)$ is the P_i fractional point of the $\chi^2(M-1)$ distribution. A few manipulations yields

$$P\left[\frac{s}{\chi^2_{P_2}(M-1)} < \sigma^2 < \frac{s}{\chi^2_{P_1}(M-1)}\right] = P_2 - P_1.$$

If you are familiar with "classical" statistics, you should notice that this $P_2 - P_1$ probability interval for σ^2 is identical to the $P_2 - P_1$ confidence interval for the variance of a normal distribution with unknown mean and unknown variance.

Next we give a theorem for the density function of $X^{(M+1)}$, the $M+1$st trial of the experiment:

Theorem 7.19 *Suppose we have the assumptions in Theorem 7.18. Then $X^{(M+1)}$ has the posterior density function*

$$\rho_{X^{(M+1)}}(x^{(M+1)}|\mathbf{d}) = t\left(x^{(M+1)}; \alpha^*, \mu^*, \frac{v^*\alpha^*}{(v^*+1)\beta^*}\right),$$

where the values of α^*, β^*, μ^*, and v^* are those obtained in Theorem 7.18.
Proof. *The proof is left as an exercise.* ∎

7.2.2   Multivariate Normally Distributed Variables

After reviewing the multivariate normal, the Wishart, and the multivariate t distributions, we obtain our result for learning parameters when variables have the multivariate normal distribution. We prove few results in this subsection. Most are generalizations of the results in the previous subsection.

The Multivariate Normal Distribution

Next we discuss the mulitivariate normal distribution, which is a generalization of the normal distribution to more than one variable. In this context, we call the normal distribution the **univariate normal distribution** and the distribution of two variables the bivariate normal distribution. We discuss this latter distribution first in order to make it easier to understand the general case.

Bivariate Normal Distribution Defined

Definition 7.15 *The **bivariate normal density function** with parameters* μ_1, σ_1, μ_2, σ_2, *and* p, *where* $-\infty < \mu_i < \infty$, $\sigma_i > 0$, *and* $|p| < 1$, *is*

$$\rho(x_1, x_2) =$$

$$\frac{1}{2\pi\sigma_1\sigma_2\left(1 - p^2\right)^{1/2}} \times$$

$$\exp\left\{-\frac{1}{2(1 - p^2)}\left[\left(\frac{x_1 - \mu_1}{\sigma_1}\right)^2 - 2p\frac{(x_1 - \mu_1)(x_2 - \mu_2)}{\sigma_1\sigma_2} + \left(\frac{x_2 - \mu_2}{\sigma_2}\right)^2\right]\right\}$$

$-\infty < x_i < \infty$, *and is denoted* $N(x_1, x_2; \mu_1, \sigma_1^2, \mu_2, \sigma_2^2, p)$.
   Random variables X_1 *and* X_2 *that have this density function are said to have the **bivariate normal distribution**.*

If the random variables X_1 and X_2 have the bivariate normal density function, then

$$E(X_1) = \mu_1 \quad \text{and} \quad V(X_1) = \sigma_1^2,$$

$$E(X_2) = \mu_2 \quad \text{and} \quad V(X_2) = \sigma_2^2,$$

and

$$p(X_1, X_2) = p,$$

where $p(X_1, X_2)$ denotes the correlation coefficient of X_1 and X_2.

Example 7.16 *We have*

$$N(x_1, x_2; 0, 1^2, 0, 1^2, 0) = \frac{1}{2\pi}\exp\left[-\frac{1}{2}\left(x_1^2 + x_2^2\right)\right]$$

$$= \frac{1}{\sqrt{2\pi}}e^{-\frac{x_1^2}{2}}\frac{1}{\sqrt{2\pi}}e^{-\frac{x_2^2}{2}},$$

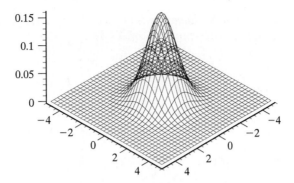

Figure 7.11: The $N(x_1, x_2; 0, 1, 0, 1, 0)$ density function.

*which is the product of two standard univariate normal density functions. This density function, which appears in Figure 7.11, is called the **bivariate standard normal density function**.*

Example 7.17 *We have*

$$N(x_1, x_2; 1, 2^2, 20, 12^2, .5) =$$

$$\frac{1}{2\pi(2)(12)(1 - .5^2)^{1/2}} \times$$

$$\exp\left\{ -\frac{1}{2(1 - .5^2)} \left[\left(\frac{x_1 - 1}{2} \right)^2 - 2(.5)\frac{(x_1 - 1)(x_2 - 20)}{(2)(12)} + \left(\frac{x_2 - 20}{12} \right)^2 \right] \right\}.$$

Figure 7.12 shows this density function.

In Figures 7.11 and 7.12, note the familiar bell-shaped curve which is characteristic of the normal density function. The following two theorems show the relationship between the bivariate normal and the normal density functions.

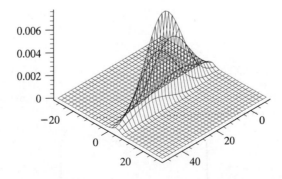

Figure 7.12: The $N(x_1, x_2; 1, 2, 20, 12, .5)$ density function.

Theorem 7.20 *If X_1 and X_2 have the $N(x_1, x_2; \mu_1, \sigma_1^2, \mu_2, \sigma_2^2, p)$ density function, then the marginal density function of X_1 is*

$$\rho_{X_1}(x_1) = N(x_1, ; \mu_1, \sigma_1^2).$$

Proof. *The proof is developed in the exercises.*   ∎

Theorem 7.21 *If X_1 and X_2 have the $N(x_1, x_2; \mu_1, \sigma_1^2, \mu_2, \sigma_2^2, p)$ density function, then the conditional density function of X_1 given $X_2 = x_2$ is*

$$\rho_{X_1}(x_1 | x_2) = N(x_1; \mu_{X_1|x_2}, \sigma_{X_1|x_2}^2),$$

where

$$\mu_{X_1|x_2} = \mu_1 + p \left(\frac{\sigma_1}{\sigma_2} \right) (x_2 - \mu_2)$$

and

$$\sigma_{X_1|x_2}^2 = (1 - p^2)\sigma_1^2.$$

Proof. *The proof is left as an exercise.*   ∎

More on Vectors and Matrices   Recall we defined random vector and random matrix in Section 5.3.1. Before proceeding, we discuss random vectors further. Similar to the discrete case, in the continuous case the joint density function of $X_1, \ldots,$ and X_n is represented using a random vector as follows:

$$\rho_{\mathbf{X}}(\mathbf{x}) \equiv \rho_{X_1, \ldots, X_n}(x_1, \ldots, x_n).$$

We call

$$E(\mathbf{X}) \equiv \begin{pmatrix} E(X_1) \\ \vdots \\ E(X_n) \end{pmatrix}$$

the **mean vector** of random vector $\mathbf{X}$, and

$$Cov(\mathbf{X}) \equiv \begin{pmatrix} V(X_1) & Cov(X_1, X_2) & \cdots & Cov(X_1, X_n) \\ Cov(X_2, X_1) & V(X_2) & \cdots & Cov(X_2, X_n) \\ \vdots & \vdots & \ddots & \vdots \\ Cov(X_n, X_1) & Cov(X_n, X_2) & \cdots & V(X_n, X_n) \end{pmatrix}$$

the **covariance matrix** of $\mathbf{X}$. Note that the covariance matrix is symmetric. We often denote a covariance matrix as follows:

$$\psi = \begin{pmatrix} \sigma_1^2 & \sigma_{12} & \cdots & \sigma_{1n} \\ \sigma_{21} & \sigma_2^2 & \cdots & \sigma_{2n} \\ \vdots & \vdots & \ddots & \vdots \\ \sigma_{n1} & \sigma_{n2} & \cdots & \sigma_n^2 \end{pmatrix}.$$

Recall that the **transpose** $\mathbf{X}^T$ of column vector $\mathbf{X}$ is the row vector defined as follows:

$$\mathbf{X}^T = (\ X_1 \quad \cdots \quad X_n \ ).$$

We have the following definitions:

Definition 7.16 *A symmetric $n \times n$ matrix $\mathbf{a}$ is called **positive definite** if*

$$\mathbf{x}^T \mathbf{ax} > 0$$

for all n-dimensional vectors $\mathbf{x} \neq \mathbf{0}$, where $\mathbf{0}$ is the vector with all 0 entries.

Definition 7.17 *A symmetric $n \times n$ matrix $\mathbf{a}$ is called **positive semidefinite** if*

$$\mathbf{x}^T \mathbf{ax} \geq 0$$

for all n-dimensional vectors $\mathbf{x}$.

Recall that a matrix $\mathbf{a}$ is called **nonsingular** if there exists a matrix $\mathbf{b}$ such that $\mathbf{ab} = \mathbf{I}$, where $\mathbf{I}$ is the identity matrix. Otherwise it is called **singular**. We have the following theorem:

Theorem 7.22 *If a matrix is positive definite, then it is nonsingular; and if a matrix is positive semidefinite but not positive definite, then it is singular.*
Proof. *The proof is left as an exercise.* ∎

Example 7.18 *The matrix*

$$\begin{pmatrix} 1 & 0 \\ 0 & 1 \end{pmatrix}$$

is positive definite. You should show this.

Example 7.19 *The matrix*

$$\begin{pmatrix} 1 & 1 \\ 1 & 1 \end{pmatrix}$$

is positive semidefinite but not positive definite. You should show this.

Multivariate Normal Distribution Defined   We can now define the multivariate normal distribution.

Definition 7.18 *Let*

$$\mathbf{X} = \begin{pmatrix} X_1 \\ \vdots \\ X_n \end{pmatrix}$$

be a random vector. We say **X** *has a **multivariate normal distribution** if, for every n-dimensional vector* $\mathbf{b}^T$,

$$\mathbf{b}^T\mathbf{X}$$

either has a univariate normal distribution or is constant.

The previous definition does not give much insight into multivariate normal distributions or even if one exists. The following theorems show that they do indeed exist.

Theorem 7.23 *For every n-dimensional vector* $\boldsymbol{\mu}$ *and* $n \times n$ *positive semidefinite symmetric matrix* $\boldsymbol{\psi}$, *there exists a unique multivariate normal distribution with mean vector* $\boldsymbol{\mu}$ *and covariance matrix* $\boldsymbol{\psi}$.
Proof. *The proof can be found in Muirhead [1982].*   ∎

Owing to the previous theorem, we need only specify a mean vector $\boldsymbol{\mu}$ and a positive semidefinite symmetric covariance matrix $\boldsymbol{\psi}$ to uniquely obtain a multivariate normal distribution. Theorem 7.22 implies that $\boldsymbol{\psi}$ is nonsingular if and only if it is positive definite. Therefore, if $\boldsymbol{\psi}$ is positive definite, we say the distribution is a **nonsingular multivariate normal distribution**, and otherwise we say it is a **singular multivariate normal distribution**. The next theorem gives us a density function for the nonsingular case.

Theorem 7.24 *Suppose the n-dimensional random vector* **X** *has a nonsingular multivariate normal distribution with mean vector* $\boldsymbol{\mu}$ *and covariance matrix* $\boldsymbol{\psi}$. *Then* **X** *has the density function*

$$\rho(\mathbf{x}) = \frac{1}{(2\pi)^{n/2}\,(\det \boldsymbol{\psi})^{1/2}}\,\exp\left[-\frac{1}{2}\Delta^2(\mathbf{x})\right],$$

where

$$\Delta^2(\mathbf{x}) = (\mathbf{x} - \boldsymbol{\mu})^T \boldsymbol{\psi}^{-1}(\mathbf{x} - \boldsymbol{\mu}).$$

This density function is denoted $N(\mathbf{x}; \boldsymbol{\mu}, \boldsymbol{\psi})$.
Proof. *The proof can be found in Flury [1997].*   ∎

The inverse matrix

$$\mathbf{T} = \boldsymbol{\psi}^{-1}$$

is called the **precision matrix** of $N(\mathbf{x}; \boldsymbol{\mu}, \boldsymbol{\psi})$. If $\boldsymbol{\mu} = \mathbf{0}$ and $\boldsymbol{\psi}$ is the identity matrix, $N(\mathbf{X}; \boldsymbol{\mu}, \boldsymbol{\psi})$ is called the **multivariate standard normal density function**.

Example 7.20 *Suppose* $n = 2$ *and we have the multivariate standard normal density function. That is,*

$$\boldsymbol{\mu} = \begin{pmatrix} 0 \\ 0 \end{pmatrix}$$

and

$$\psi = \begin{pmatrix} 1 & 0 \\ 0 & 1 \end{pmatrix}.$$

Then

$$\mathbf{T} = \psi^{-1} = \begin{pmatrix} 1 & 0 \\ 0 & 1 \end{pmatrix},$$

$$\begin{aligned} \Delta^2(\mathbf{x}) &= (\mathbf{x} - \boldsymbol{\mu})^T \psi^{-1}(\mathbf{x} - \boldsymbol{\mu}) \\ &= \begin{pmatrix} x_1 & x_2 \end{pmatrix} \begin{pmatrix} 1 & 0 \\ 0 & 1 \end{pmatrix} \begin{pmatrix} x_1 \\ x_2 \end{pmatrix} \\ &= x_1^2 + x_2^2, \end{aligned}$$

and

$$\begin{aligned} N(\mathbf{x}; \boldsymbol{\mu}, \psi) &= \frac{1}{(2\pi)^{n/2} (\det \psi)^{1/2}} \exp\left[-\frac{1}{2}\Delta^2(\mathbf{x})\right] \\ &= \frac{1}{(2\pi)^{2/2} (1)^{1/2}} \exp\left[-\frac{1}{2}\left(x_1^2 + x_2^2\right)\right] \\ &= \frac{1}{2\pi} \exp\left[-\frac{1}{2}\left(x_1^2 + x_2^2\right)\right] \\ &= N(x_1, x_2; 0, 1^2, 0, 1^2, 0), \end{aligned}$$

which is the bivariate standard normal density function.
It is left as an exercise to show that, in general, if

$$\boldsymbol{\mu} = \begin{pmatrix} \mu_1 \\ \mu_2 \end{pmatrix},$$

and

$$\psi = \begin{pmatrix} \sigma_1^2 & \sigma_{12} \\ \sigma_{21} & \sigma_2^2 \end{pmatrix}$$

is positive definite, then

$$N(\mathbf{x}; \boldsymbol{\mu}, \psi) = N(x_1, x_2; \mu_1, \sigma_1^2, \mu_2, \sigma_2^2, \sigma_{12}/\left[\sigma_1\sigma_2\right]).$$

Example 7.21 *Suppose*

$$\boldsymbol{\mu} = \begin{pmatrix} 3 \\ 3 \end{pmatrix}$$

and

$$\psi = \begin{pmatrix} 1 & 1 \\ 1 & 1 \end{pmatrix}.$$

Since ψ is not positive definite, Theorem 7.24 does not apply. However, since ψ is positive semidefinite, Theorem 7.23 says there is a unique multivariate normal distribution with this mean vector and covariance matrix. Consider the distribution of X_1 and X_2 determined by the following density function and equality:

$$\rho(x_1) = \frac{1}{\sqrt{2\pi}} e^{-\frac{(x_1-3)^2}{2}}$$

$$X_2 = X_1.$$

Clearly this distribution has the preceding mean vector and covariance matrix. Furthermore, it satisfies the condition in Definition 7.18. Therefore, it is the unique multivariate normal distribution that has this mean vector and covariance matrix.

Note that in the previous example $\mathbf{X}$ has a singular multivariate normal distribution, but X_1 has a nonsingular multivariate normal distribution. In general, if $\mathbf{X}$ has a singular multivariate normal distribution, there is some linear relationship among the components $X_1, \ldots, X_n$ of $\mathbf{X}$, and therefore these n random variables cannot have a joint n-dimensional density function. However, if some of the components are deleted until there are no linear relationships among the ones that remain, then the remaining components will have a nonsingular multivariate normal distribution.

Generalizations of Theorems 7.20 and 7.21 exist. That is, if $\mathbf{X}$ has the density function $N(\mathbf{X}; \boldsymbol{\mu}, \boldsymbol{\psi})$ and

$$\mathbf{X} = \left(\begin{array}{c} \mathbf{X}_1 \\ \mathbf{X}_2 \end{array} \right),$$

then the marginal distribution of $\mathbf{X}_1$ and the conditional distribution of $\mathbf{X}_1$ given $\mathbf{X}_2 = \mathbf{x}_2$ are both multivariate normal. You are referred to Flury [1997] for statements and proofs of these theorems.

The Wishart Distribution

We have the following definition:

Definition 7.19 *Suppose $\mathbf{X}_1, \mathbf{X}_2, \ldots, \mathbf{X}_k$ are k independent n-dimensional random vectors, each having the multivariate normal distribution with n-dimensional mean vector $\mathbf{0}$ and $n \times n$ covariance matrix ψ. Let $\mathbf{V}$ denote the random symmetric $k \times k$ matrix defined as follows:*

$$\mathbf{V} = \mathbf{X}_1\mathbf{X}_1^T + \mathbf{X}_2\mathbf{X}_2^T + \cdots \mathbf{X}_k\mathbf{X}_k^T.$$

*Then $\mathbf{V}$ is said to have a **Wishart distribution** with k degrees of freedom and parametric matrix ψ.*

Owing to Theorem 7.22, ψ is positive definite if and only if it is nonsingular. If $k > n - 1$ and ψ is positive definite, the Wishart distribution is called **nonsingular**. In this case, the precision matrix $\mathbf{T}$ of the distribution is defined as

$$\mathbf{T} = \psi^{-1}.$$

The following theorem obtains a density function in this case:

Theorem 7.25 *Suppose n-dimensional random vector $\mathbf{V}$ has the nonsingular Wishart distribution with k degrees of freedom and parametric matrix ψ. Then $\mathbf{V}$ has the density function*

$$\rho(\mathbf{v}) = c\,(n,k)\,|\psi|^{-k/2}|\mathbf{v}|^{(k-n-1)/2}\exp\left[-\frac{1}{2}tr\left(\psi^{-1}\mathbf{v}\right)\right],$$

where tr is the trace function and

$$c\,(n,k) = \left[2^{kn/2}\pi^{n(n-1)/4}\prod_{i=1}^{n}\Gamma\left(\frac{k+1-i}{2}\right)\right]^{-1}. \qquad (7.20)$$

This density function is denoted $Wishart(\mathbf{v}; k, \mathbf{T})$.
Proof. *The proof can be found in DeGroot [1970].* ∎

It is left as an exercise to show that if $n = 1$, then $Wishart(v; k, 1/\sigma^2) = gamma(v; k/2, 1/2\sigma^2)$. However, showing this is not really necessary because it follows from Theorem 7.15 and the definition of the Wishart distribution.

The Multivariate t Distribution

We have the following definition:

Definition 7.20 *Suppose n-dimensional random vector $\mathbf{Y}$ has the $N(\mathbf{Y}; \boldsymbol{\mu}, \psi)$ density function, $\mathbf{T} = \psi^{-1}$, random variable Z has the $chi-square(z; \alpha)$ density function, $\mathbf{Y}$ and Z are independent, and $\boldsymbol{\mu}$ is an arbitrary n-dimensional vector. Define the n-dimensional random vector $\mathbf{X}$ as follows: For $i = 1, \ldots, n$,*

$$X_i = Y_i\left(\frac{Z}{\alpha}\right)^{-1/2} + \mu_i.$$

*Then the distribution of $\mathbf{X}$ is called a **multivariate t distribution** with α degrees of freedom, location vector $\boldsymbol{\mu}$, and precision matrix $\mathbf{T}$.*

The following theorem obtains the density function for the multivariate t distribution.

Theorem 7.26 *Suppose n-dimensional random vector* $\mathbf{X}$ *has the multivariate t distribution with* α *degrees of freedom, location vector* $\boldsymbol{\mu}$, *and precision matrix* $\mathbf{T}$. *Then* $\mathbf{X}$ *has the density function*

$$\rho(\mathbf{x}) = b\,(n, \alpha) \left[1 + \frac{1}{\alpha}(\mathbf{x} - \boldsymbol{\mu})^T \mathbf{T}(\mathbf{x} - \boldsymbol{\mu}) \right]^{-(\alpha+n)/2}, \qquad (7.21)$$

where

$$b\,(n, \alpha) = \frac{\Gamma\left(\frac{\alpha+n}{2}\right) |\mathbf{T}|^{1/2}}{\Gamma\,(\alpha/2)\,(\alpha\pi)^{n/2}}.$$

This density function is denoted $t(\mathbf{x}; \alpha, \boldsymbol{\mu}, \mathbf{T})$.
Proof. *The proof can be found in DeGroot [1970].* ∎

It is left as an exercise to show that, in the case in which $n = 1$, the density function in Equality 7.21 is the univariate t density function that appears in Equality 7.13.

If the random vector $\mathbf{X}$ has the $t(\mathbf{x}; \alpha, \boldsymbol{\mu}, \mathbf{T})$ density function and if $\alpha > 2$, then

$$E(\mathbf{X}) = \mu \qquad \text{and} \qquad Cov(\mathbf{X}) = \frac{\alpha}{\alpha - 2} \mathbf{T}^{-1}.$$

Note that the precision matrix in the t distribution is not the inverse of the covariance matrix as it is in the normal distribution. The $N(\mathbf{x}; \boldsymbol{\mu}, \mathbf{T}^{-1})$ is equal to the limit as α approaches infinity of the $t(\mathbf{x}; \alpha, \boldsymbol{\mu}, \mathbf{T})$ density function. (See DeGroot [1970].)

Learning With Unknown Mean Vector and Unknown Covariance Matrix

We discuss the case where both the mean vector and the covariance matrix are unknown. Suppose $\mathbf{X}$ has a multivariate normal distribution with unknown mean vector and unknown precision matrix. We represent our belief concerning the unknown mean vector and unknown precision matrix with the random vector $\mathbf{A}$ and the random matrix $\mathbf{R}$ respectively. We assume that $\mathbf{R}$ has the $Wishart(\mathbf{r}; \alpha, \boldsymbol{\beta})$ density function and $\mathbf{A}$ has the $N\left(\mathbf{a}; \boldsymbol{\mu}, (v\mathbf{r})^{-1}\right)$ conditional density function. The following theorem gives the prior density function of $\mathbf{X}$.

Theorem 7.27 *Suppose* $\mathbf{X}$ *and* $\mathbf{A}$ *are n-dimensional random vectors, and* $\mathbf{R}$ *is an* $n \times n$ *random matrix such that*

(1) the density function of $\mathbf{R}$ *is*

$$\rho_{\mathbf{R}}(\mathbf{r}) = Wishart(\mathbf{r}; \alpha, \boldsymbol{\beta}),$$

where $\alpha > n - 1$ *and* $\boldsymbol{\beta}$ *is positive definite (i.e., the distribution is nonsingular).*

(2) the conditional density function of $\mathbf{A}$ *given* $\mathbf{R} = \mathbf{r}$ *is*

$$\rho_{\mathbf{A}}(\mathbf{a}|\mathbf{r}) = N\left(\mathbf{a}; \boldsymbol{\mu}, (v\mathbf{r})^{-1}\right),$$

where $v > 0$,

and (3) the conditional density function of $\mathbf{X}$ *given* $\mathbf{A} = \mathbf{a}$ *and* $\mathbf{R} = \mathbf{r}$ *is*

$$\rho_{\mathbf{X}}(\mathbf{x}|\mathbf{a}, \mathbf{r}) = N(\mathbf{x}; \mathbf{a}, \mathbf{r}^{-1}).$$

Then the prior density function of $\mathbf{X}$ *is*

$$\rho_{\mathbf{X}}(\mathbf{x}) = t\left(\mathbf{x}; \alpha - n + 1, \boldsymbol{\mu}, \frac{v(\alpha - n + 1)}{(v + 1)}\boldsymbol{\beta}^{-1}\right). \tag{7.22}$$

Proof. *The proof can be found in DeGroot [1970].* ∎

Suppose now that we perform M trials of a random process whose outcome has the multivariate normal distribution with unknown mean vector and unknown precision matrix. We let $\mathbf{X}^{(h)}$ be a random vector whose values are the outcomes of the hth trial, and we represent our belief concerning each trial as in Theorem 7.27. As before, we assume that if we knew the values $\mathbf{a}$ and $\mathbf{r}$ of $\mathbf{A}$ and $\mathbf{R}$ for certain, then we would feel that the $X^{(h)}$s are mutually independent, and our probability distribution for each trial would have mean vector $\mathbf{a}$ and precision matrix $\mathbf{r}$. That is, we have a sample defined as follows:

Definition 7.21 *Suppose we have a sample of size* M *as follows:*

1. *We have the n-dimensional random vectors*

$$\mathbf{X}^{(1)} = \begin{pmatrix} X_1^{(1)} \\ \vdots \\ X_n^{(1)} \end{pmatrix} \quad \mathbf{X}^{(2)} = \begin{pmatrix} X_1^{(2)} \\ \vdots \\ X_n^{(2)} \end{pmatrix} \quad \cdots \quad \mathbf{X}^{(M)} = \begin{pmatrix} X_1^{(M)} \\ \vdots \\ X_n^{(M)} \end{pmatrix}$$

$$\mathsf{D} = \{\mathbf{X}^{(1)}, \mathbf{X}^{(2)}, \ldots, \mathbf{X}^{(M)}\}$$

such that for every i, each $X_i^{(h)}$ *has the reals as its space.*

2. $\mathsf{F} = \{\mathbf{A}, \mathbf{R}\}$,

$$\rho_{\mathbf{R}}(\mathbf{r}) = Wishart(\mathbf{r}; \alpha, \boldsymbol{\beta}),$$

where $\alpha > n - 1$ *and* $\boldsymbol{\beta}$ *is positive definite,*

$$\rho_{\mathbf{A}}(\mathbf{a}|\mathbf{r}) = N\left(\mathbf{a}; \boldsymbol{\mu}, (v\mathbf{r})^{-1}\right),$$

where $v > 0$, *and, for* $1 \le h \le M$,

$$\rho_{\mathbf{X}^{(h)}}(\mathbf{x}^{(h)}|\mathbf{a}, \mathbf{r}) = N(\mathbf{x}^{(h)}; \mathbf{a}, \mathbf{r}^{-1}).$$

Then D *is called a* **multivariate normal sample** *of size* M *with parameter* $\{\mathbf{A}, \mathbf{R}\}$.

The following theorem obtains the updated distributions of $\mathbf{A}$ and $\mathbf{R}$ given this sample:

Theorem 7.28 *Suppose*

1. D *is a multivariate normal sample of size* M *with parameter* $\{\mathbf{A}, \mathbf{R}\}$;

2. $\mathsf{d} = \{\mathbf{x}^{(1)}, \mathbf{x}^{(2)}, \ldots, \mathbf{x}^{(M)}\}$ *is a set of values of the random vectors in* D,

$$\overline{\mathbf{x}} = \frac{\sum_{h=1}^{M} \mathbf{x}^{(h)}}{M} \qquad and \qquad \mathbf{s} = \sum_{h=1}^{M} \left(\mathbf{x}^{(h)} - \overline{\mathbf{x}}\right)\left(\mathbf{x}^{(h)} - \overline{\mathbf{x}}\right)^{T}.$$

Then the posterior density function of $\mathbf{R}$ *is*

$$\rho_{\mathbf{R}}(\mathbf{r}|\mathsf{d}) = Wishart(\mathbf{r}; \alpha^{*}, \boldsymbol{\beta}^{*}),$$

where

$$\boldsymbol{\beta}^{*} = \boldsymbol{\beta} + \mathbf{s} + \frac{vM}{v + M}(\overline{\mathbf{x}} - \boldsymbol{\mu})(\overline{\mathbf{x}} - \boldsymbol{\mu})^{T} \qquad and \qquad \alpha^{*} = \alpha + M, \qquad (7.23)$$

and the posterior conditional density function of $\mathbf{A}$ *given* $\mathbf{R} = \mathbf{r}$ *is*

$$\rho_{\mathbf{A}}(\mathbf{a}|\mathbf{r}, \mathsf{d}) = N(\mathbf{a}; \boldsymbol{\mu}^{*}, (v^{*}\mathbf{r})^{-1}),$$

where

$$\boldsymbol{\mu}^{*} = \frac{v\boldsymbol{\mu} + M\overline{\mathbf{x}}}{v + M} \qquad and \qquad v^{*} = v + M.$$

Proof. *The proof can be found in DeGroot [1970].* ∎

As in the univariate case discussed in Section 7.2.1, we can attach the following meaning to the parameters:

The parameter $\boldsymbol{\mu}$ is the mean vector in the hypothetical sample upon which we base our prior belief concerning the value of $\mathbf{A}$.

The parameter v is the size of the hypothetical sample upon which we base our prior belief concerning the value of $\mathbf{A}$.

The parameter $\boldsymbol{\beta}$ is the value of $\mathbf{s}$ in the hypothetical sample upon which we base our prior belief concerning the value of $\mathbf{A}$.

It seems reasonable to make α equal to $v - 1$.

As in to the univariate case, we can model prior ignorance by setting $v = 0$, $\boldsymbol{\beta} = \mathbf{0}$, and $\alpha = -1$ in the expressions for $\boldsymbol{\beta}^{*}$, α^{*}, $\boldsymbol{\mu}^{*}$, and v^{*}. However, we must also assume $M > n$. (See DeGroot [1970] for a complete discussion of this matter.) Doing so, we obtain

$$\boldsymbol{\beta}^{*} = \mathbf{s} \qquad and \qquad \alpha^{*} = M - 1,$$

and

$$\boldsymbol{\mu}^{*} = \overline{\mathbf{x}} \qquad and \qquad v^{*} = M.$$

Example 7.22 *Suppose $n = 3$, we model prior ignorance by setting $v = 0$, $\beta = \mathbf{0}$, and $\alpha = -1$, and we obtain the following data:*

Case	X_1	X_2	X_3
1	1	2	6
2	5	8	2
3	2	4	1
4	8	6	3

Then $M = 4$ and

$$\mathbf{x}^{(1)} = \begin{pmatrix} 1 \\ 2 \\ 6 \end{pmatrix} \qquad \mathbf{x}^{(2)} = \begin{pmatrix} 5 \\ 8 \\ 2 \end{pmatrix} \qquad \mathbf{x}^{(3)} = \begin{pmatrix} 2 \\ 4 \\ 1 \end{pmatrix} \qquad \mathbf{x}^{(4)} = \begin{pmatrix} 8 \\ 6 \\ 3 \end{pmatrix}.$$

So

$$\overline{\mathbf{x}} = \frac{\begin{pmatrix} 1 \\ 2 \\ 6 \end{pmatrix} + \begin{pmatrix} 5 \\ 8 \\ 2 \end{pmatrix} + \begin{pmatrix} 2 \\ 4 \\ 1 \end{pmatrix} + \begin{pmatrix} 8 \\ 6 \\ 3 \end{pmatrix}}{4}$$

$$= \begin{pmatrix} 4 \\ 5 \\ 3 \end{pmatrix}$$

and

$$\mathbf{s} = \begin{pmatrix} -3 \\ -3 \\ 3 \end{pmatrix} (\,-3 \ \ -3 \ \ 3\,) + \begin{pmatrix} 1 \\ 3 \\ -1 \end{pmatrix} (\,1 \ \ 3 \ \ -1\,)$$

$$+ \begin{pmatrix} -2 \\ -1 \\ -2 \end{pmatrix} (\,-2 \ \ -1 \ \ -2\,) + \begin{pmatrix} 4 \\ 1 \\ 0 \end{pmatrix} (\,4 \ \ 1 \ \ 0\,)$$

$$= \begin{pmatrix} 30 & 18 & -6 \\ 18 & 20 & -10 \\ -6 & -10 & 14 \end{pmatrix}.$$

So

$$\boldsymbol{\beta}^* = \mathbf{s} = \begin{pmatrix} 30 & 18 & -6 \\ 18 & 20 & -10 \\ -6 & -10 & 14 \end{pmatrix} \qquad and \qquad \alpha^* = M - 1 = 3,$$

and

$$\boldsymbol{\mu}^* = \overline{\mathbf{x}} = \begin{pmatrix} 4 \\ 5 \\ 3 \end{pmatrix} \qquad and \qquad v^* = M = 4.$$

Next we give a theorem for the density function of $\mathbf{X}^{(M+1)}$, the $M+1$st trial of the experiment.

Theorem 7.29 *Suppose we have the assumptions in Theorem 7.28.   Then* $\mathbf{X}^{(M+1)}$ *has the posterior density function*

$$\rho_{\mathbf{X}^{(M+1)}}(\mathbf{x}^{(M+1)}|\mathbf{d}) = t\left(\mathbf{x}^{(M+1)}; \alpha^* - n + 1, \boldsymbol{\mu}^*, \frac{v^*(\alpha^* - n + 1)}{(v^* + 1)}(\boldsymbol{\beta}^*)^{-1}\right),$$

where the values of α^*, $\boldsymbol{\beta}^*$, $\boldsymbol{\mu}^*$, and v^* are those obtained in Theorem 7.28.
Proof. *The proof is left as an exercise.*   ∎

7.2.3   Gaussian Bayesian Networks

A Gaussian Bayesian network uniquely determines a nonsingular multivariate normal distribution and vice versa. So, to learn parameters for a Gaussian Bayesian network we can apply the theory developed in the previous subsection. First we show the transformation; then we develop the method for learning parameters.

Transforming a Gaussian Bayesian Network to a Multivariate Normal Distribution

Recall that in Section 4.1.3 a Gaussian Bayesian network was defined as follows: If PA_X is the set of all parents of X, then

$$x = w_X + \sum_{Z \in \mathsf{PA}_X} b_{XZ} z, \tag{7.24}$$

where W_X has density function $N(w; 0, \sigma^2_{W_X})$, and W_X is independent of each Z. The variable W_X represents the uncertainty in X's value given values of X's parents. Recall further that $\sigma^2_{W_X}$ is the variance of X conditional on values of its parents. For each root X, its unconditional density function $N(x; \mu_X, \sigma^2_X)$ is specified.

We will show how to determine the multivariate normal distribution corresponding to a Gaussian Bayesian network; but first we develop a different method for specifying a Gaussian Bayesian network. We will consider a variation of the specification shown in Equality 7.24 in which each W_X does not necessarily have zero mean. That is, each W_X has density function $N(w; E(W_X), \sigma^2_{W_X})$. Note that a network, in which each of these variables has zero mean, can be obtained from a network specified in this manner by giving each node X an auxiliary parent Z, which has mean $E(W_X)$, zero variance, and for which $b_{XZ} = 1$. If the variable W_X in our new network is then given a normal density function with zero mean and the same variance as the corresponding variable in our original network, the two networks will contain the same probability distribution.

Recall that an **ancestral ordering** of the nodes in a directed graph is an ordering of the nodes such that, if Y is a descendent of Z, then Y follows

Z in the ordering. Now assume that we have a Gaussian Bayesian network determined by specifications as in Equality 7.24, but in which each W_X does not necessarily have zero mean. Assume that we have ordered the nodes in the network according to an ancestral ordering. Then each node is a linear function of the values of all the nodes that precede it in the ordering, where some of the coefficients may be 0. So we have

$$x_i = w_i + b_{i1}x_1 + b_{i2}x_2 + \cdots b_{i,i-1}x_{i-1},$$

where W_i has density function $N(w_i; E(W_i), \sigma_i^2)$, and $b_{ij} = 0$ if X_j is not a parent of X_i. Then the conditional density function of X_i is

$$\rho(x_i|\mathsf{pa}_i) = N(x_i; E(W_i) + \sum_{X_j \in \mathsf{PA}_i} b_{ij}x_j, \sigma_i^2). \qquad (7.25)$$

Since

$$E(X_i) = E(W_i) + \sum_{X_j \in \mathsf{PA}_i} b_{ij}E(X_j), \qquad (7.26)$$

we can specify the unconditional mean of each variable X_i instead of the unconditional mean of W_i. So our new way to specify a **Gaussian Bayesian network** is to show for each X_i its unconditional mean $\mu_i \equiv E(X_i)$ and its conditional variance σ_i^2. Owing to Equality 7.26, we then have

$$E(W_i) = \mu_i - \sum_{X_j \in \mathsf{PA}_i} b_{ij}\mu_j.$$

Substituting this expression for $E(W_i)$ into Equality 7.25, we obtain, for the conditional density function of X_i,

$$\rho(x_i|\mathsf{pa}_i) = N(x_i, \mu_i + \sum_{X_j \in \mathsf{PA}_i} b_{ij}(x_j - \mu_j), \sigma_i^2). \qquad (7.27)$$

Figures 7.13, 7.14, and 7.15 show examples of specifying Gaussian Bayesian networks in this manner.

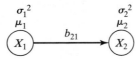

Figure 7.13: A Gaussian Bayesian network.

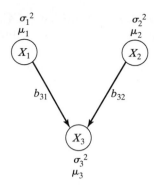

Figure 7.14: A Gaussian Bayesian network.

Next we show how we can generate the mean vector and the precision matrix for the multivariate normal distribution determined by a Gaussian Bayesian network. The method presented here is from Shachter and Kenley [1989]. Let

$$t_i = \frac{1}{\sigma_i^2},$$

and

$$\mathbf{b}_i = \begin{pmatrix} b_{i1} \\ \vdots \\ b_{i,i-1} \end{pmatrix}.$$

The mean vector in the multivariate normal distribution corresponding to a Gaussian Bayesian network is simply

$$\boldsymbol{\mu} = \begin{pmatrix} \mu_1 \\ \vdots \\ \mu_n \end{pmatrix}.$$

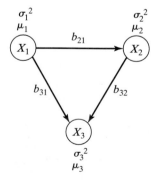

Figure 7.15: A complete Gaussian Bayesian network.

The following algorithm creates the precision matrix:

$$\mathbf{T}_1 = (t_1);$$
$$\textbf{for } (i = 2; i <= n; i++)$$
$$\mathbf{T}_i = \begin{pmatrix} \mathbf{T}_{i-1} + t_i \mathbf{b}_i \mathbf{b}_i^T & -t_i \mathbf{b}_i \\ -t_i \mathbf{b}_i^T & t_i \end{pmatrix};$$
$$\mathbf{T} = \mathbf{T}_n; \qquad // \text{ The precision matrix is } \mathbf{T}_n.$$

Example 7.23 *We apply the previous algorithm to the Gaussian Bayesian network in Figure 7.13. We have*

$$\mathbf{T}_1 = (t_1) = (1/\sigma_1)$$

$$
\begin{aligned}
\mathbf{T}_2 &= \begin{pmatrix} \mathbf{T}_1 + t_2 \mathbf{b}_2 \mathbf{b}_2^T & -t_2 \mathbf{b}_2 \\ -t_2 \mathbf{b}_2^T & t_2 \end{pmatrix} \\[2mm]
&= \begin{pmatrix} \frac{1}{\sigma_1^2} + \left(\frac{1}{\sigma_2^2}\right)(b_{21})(b_{21}) & -\left(\frac{1}{\sigma_2^2}\right)(b_{21}) \\ -\left(\frac{1}{\sigma_2^2}\right)(b_{21}) & \frac{1}{\sigma_2^2} \end{pmatrix} \\[2mm]
&= \begin{pmatrix} \frac{1}{\sigma_1^2} + \frac{b_{21}^2}{\sigma_2^2} & -\frac{b_{21}}{\sigma_2^2} \\ -\frac{b_{21}}{\sigma_2^2} & \frac{1}{\sigma_2^2} \end{pmatrix}.
\end{aligned}
$$

So, the multivariate normal distribution determined by this Gaussian Bayesian network has mean vector

$$\boldsymbol{\mu} = \begin{pmatrix} \mu_1 \\ \mu_2 \end{pmatrix}$$

and precision matrix

$$\mathbf{T} = \begin{pmatrix} \frac{1}{\sigma_1^2} + \frac{b_{21}^2}{\sigma_2^2} & -\frac{b_{21}}{\sigma_2^2} \\ -\frac{b_{21}}{\sigma_2^2} & \frac{1}{\sigma_2^2} \end{pmatrix}.$$

It is left as an exercise to show that the covariance matrix is

$$\psi = \mathbf{T}^{-1} = \begin{pmatrix} \sigma_1^2 & b_{21}\sigma_1^2 \\ b_{21}\sigma_1^2 & \sigma_2^2 + b_{21}^2\sigma_1^2 \end{pmatrix}. \tag{7.28}$$

Example 7.24 *We apply the preceding algorithm to the Gaussian Bayesian network in Figure 7.14. First, note that $b_{21} = 0$. We then have*

$$\mathbf{T}_1 = (t_1) = (1/\sigma_1)$$

$$\mathbf{T}_2 = \begin{pmatrix} \mathbf{T}_1 + t_2\mathbf{b}_2\mathbf{b}_2^T & -t_2\mathbf{b}_2 \\ -t_2\mathbf{b}_2^T & t_2 \end{pmatrix}$$

$$= \begin{pmatrix} \frac{1}{\sigma_1^2} + \left(\frac{1}{\sigma_2^2}\right)(b_{21})(b_{21}) & -\left(\frac{1}{\sigma_2^2}\right)(b_{21}) \\ -\left(\frac{1}{\sigma_2^2}\right)(b_{21}) & \frac{1}{\sigma_2^2} \end{pmatrix}$$

$$= \begin{pmatrix} \frac{1}{\sigma_1^2} + \left(\frac{1}{\sigma_2^2}\right)(0)(0) & -\left(\frac{1}{\sigma_2^2}\right)(0) \\ -\left(\frac{1}{\sigma_2^2}\right)(0) & \frac{1}{\sigma_2^2} \end{pmatrix}$$

$$= \begin{pmatrix} \frac{1}{\sigma_1^2} & 0 \\ 0 & \frac{1}{\sigma_2^2} \end{pmatrix}$$

$$\mathbf{T}_3 = \begin{pmatrix} \mathbf{T}_2 + t_3\mathbf{b}_3\mathbf{b}_3^T & -t_3\mathbf{b}_3 \\ -t_3\mathbf{b}_3^T & t_3 \end{pmatrix}$$

$$= \begin{pmatrix} \begin{pmatrix} \frac{1}{\sigma_1^2} & 0 \\ 0 & \frac{1}{\sigma_2^2} \end{pmatrix} + \left(\frac{1}{\sigma_3^2}\right)\begin{pmatrix} b_{31} \\ b_{32} \end{pmatrix}\begin{pmatrix} b_{31} & b_{32} \end{pmatrix} & -\left(\frac{1}{\sigma_3^2}\right)\begin{pmatrix} b_{31} \\ b_{32} \end{pmatrix} \\ -\left(\frac{1}{\sigma_3^2}\right)\begin{pmatrix} b_{31} & b_{32} \end{pmatrix} & \frac{1}{\sigma_3^2} \end{pmatrix}$$

$$= \begin{pmatrix} \begin{pmatrix} \frac{1}{\sigma_1^2} & 0 \\ 0 & \frac{1}{\sigma_2^2} \end{pmatrix} + \left(\frac{1}{\sigma_3^2}\right)\begin{pmatrix} b_{31}^2 & b_{31}b_{32} \\ b_{32}b_{31} & b_{32}^2 \end{pmatrix} & -\left(\frac{1}{\sigma_3^2}\right)\begin{pmatrix} b_{31} \\ b_{32} \end{pmatrix} \\ -\left(\frac{1}{\sigma_3^2}\right)\begin{pmatrix} b_{31} & b_{32} \end{pmatrix} & \frac{1}{\sigma_3^2} \end{pmatrix}$$

$$= \begin{pmatrix} \frac{1}{\sigma_1^2} + \frac{b_{31}^2}{\sigma_3^2} & \frac{b_{31}b_{32}}{\sigma_3^2} & -\frac{b_{31}}{\sigma_3^2} \\ \frac{b_{32}b_{31}}{\sigma_3^2} & \frac{1}{\sigma_2^2} + \frac{b_{32}^2}{\sigma_3^2} & -\frac{b_{32}}{\sigma_3^2} \\ -\frac{b_{31}}{\sigma_3^2} & -\frac{b_{32}}{\sigma_3^2} & \frac{1}{\sigma_3^2} \end{pmatrix}.$$

So the multivariate normal distribution determined by this Gaussian Bayesian network has mean vector

$$\boldsymbol{\mu} = \begin{pmatrix} \mu_1 \\ \mu_2 \\ \mu_3 \end{pmatrix}$$

and precision matrix

$$\mathbf{T} = \begin{pmatrix} \frac{1}{\sigma_1^2} + \frac{b_{31}^2}{\sigma_3^2} & \frac{b_{31}b_{32}}{\sigma_3^2} & -\frac{b_{31}}{\sigma_3^2} \\ \frac{b_{32}b_{31}}{\sigma_3^2} & \frac{1}{\sigma_2^2} + \frac{b_{32}^2}{\sigma_3^2} & -\frac{b_{32}}{\sigma_3^2} \\ -\frac{b_{31}}{\sigma_3^2} & -\frac{b_{32}}{\sigma_3^2} & \frac{1}{\sigma_3^2} \end{pmatrix}.$$

It is left as an exercise to show that the covariance matrix is

$$\boldsymbol{\psi} = \mathbf{T}^{-1} = \begin{pmatrix} \sigma_1^2 & 0 & b_{31}\sigma_1^2 \\ 0 & \sigma_2^2 & b_{32}\sigma_2^2 \\ b_{31}\sigma_1^2 & b_{32}\sigma_2^2 & b_{31}^2\sigma_1^2 + b_{32}^2\sigma_2^2 + \sigma_3^2 \end{pmatrix}. \qquad (7.29)$$

Example 7.25 *Suppose we have the Gaussian Bayesian network in Figure 7.15. It is left as an exercise to show that the multivariate normal distribution determined by this network has mean vector*

$$\mu = \begin{pmatrix} \mu_1 \\ \mu_2 \\ \mu_3 \end{pmatrix},$$

precision matrix

$$\mathbf{T} = \begin{pmatrix} \frac{1}{\sigma_1^2} + \frac{b_{21}^2}{\sigma_2^2} + \frac{b_{31}^2}{\sigma_3^2} & -\frac{b_{21}}{\sigma_2^2} + \frac{b_{31}b_{32}}{\sigma_3^2} & -\frac{b_{31}}{\sigma_3^2} \\ -\frac{b_{21}}{\sigma_2^2} + \frac{b_{32}b_{31}}{\sigma_3^2} & \frac{1}{\sigma_2^2} + \frac{b_{32}^2}{\sigma_3^2} & -\frac{b_{32}}{\sigma_3^2} \\ -\frac{b_{31}}{\sigma_3^2} & -\frac{b_{32}}{\sigma_3^2} & \frac{1}{\sigma_3^2} \end{pmatrix},$$

and covariance matrix

$$\psi = \mathbf{T}^{-1} =$$

$$\begin{pmatrix} \sigma_1^2 & b_{21}\sigma_1^2 & (b_{31} + b_{32}b_{21})\,\sigma_1^2 \\ b_{21}\sigma_1^2 & \sigma_2^2 + b_{21}^2\sigma_1^2 & \begin{array}{l} b_{32}\sigma_2^2 + \\ (b_{32}b_{21}^2 + b_{31}b_{21})\,\sigma_1^2 \end{array} \\ (b_{31} + b_{32}b_{21})\,\sigma_1^2 & \begin{array}{l} b_{32}\sigma_2^2 \\ + (b_{32}b_{21}^2 + b_{31}b_{21})\,\sigma_1^2 \end{array} & \begin{array}{l} \sigma_3^2 + b_{31}^2\sigma_1^2 + b_{32}^2\sigma_2^2 \\ + (b_{21}^2b_{32}^2 + 2b_{21}b_{31}b_{32})\,\sigma_1^2 \end{array} \end{pmatrix}.$$

$$(7.30)$$

Learning Parameters in a Gaussian Bayesian network

First we define a Gaussian augmented Bayesian network.

Definition 7.22 *A **Gaussian augmented Bayesian network** $(\mathbb{G}, \mathsf{F}, \rho)$ is an augmented Bayesian network with the following properties:*

1. *For every i, X_i is a continuous random variable.*

2. *For every i,*

$$\mathsf{F}_i = \{\mathbf{B}_i, M_i, \Sigma_i^2\},$$

where $\mathbf{B}_i^T = (B_{i1}, \dots, B_{i,i-1})$.

3. *For every i, for every value pa_i of the parents PA_i in V of X_i, and every value $\mathsf{f}_i = \{\mathbf{b}_i, \mu_i, \sigma_i^2\}$ of $\mathsf{F}_i = \{\mathbf{B}_i, M_i, \Sigma_i^2\}$,*

$$\rho(x_i | \mathsf{pa}_i, \mathsf{f}_i, \mathbb{G}) = N\left(x_i; \mu_i + \sum_{X_j \in \mathsf{PA}_i} b_{ij}(x_j - \mu_j), \sigma_i^2\right).$$

The method shown here first appeared in Geiger and Heckerman [1994]. We will update parameters relative to a multivariate normal sample using Theorem 7.28, and then convert the result to a Gaussian Bayesian network. However, as proven in Theorems 7.27 and 7.29, the prior and posterior distributions relative to a multivariate normal sample are t distributions rather than Gaussian. So, if we want our prior and updated distributions relative to the sample to be contained in Gaussian Bayesian networks, we can only approximately represent these distributions. We do this as follows: We develop a Gaussian Bayesian network that approximates our prior distribution. (We say approximates because, if our beliefs are represented by a multivariate normal sample, our prior distribution would have to be a t distribution.) Then we convert this network to the corresponding multivariate normal distribution, which has density function $N(\mathbf{x}; \boldsymbol{\mu}, \mathbf{T}^{-1})$. We approximate this distribution by a multivariate t distribution that has density function $t(\mathbf{x}; \alpha, \boldsymbol{\mu}, \mathbf{T})$, where the value of α must be assessed. This is our prior density function. After determining our prior values of α and v, we use Equality 7.22 to determine our prior value of $\boldsymbol{\beta}$. Next, we apply Theorem 7.28 to determine updated values $\boldsymbol{\mu}^*$, α^*, v^*, and $\boldsymbol{\beta}^*$. Then we use Equality 7.22 to determine the updated density function $t(\mathbf{x}; \alpha^*, \boldsymbol{\mu}^*, \mathbf{T}^*)$, and we approximate this density function by $N(\mathbf{x}; \boldsymbol{\mu}^*, (\mathbf{T}^*)^{-1})$. Finally, we convert this multivariate normal distribution back to a Gaussian Bayesian network. However, when we convert it back there is no guarantee that we will obtain a network entailing the same conditional independencies as our original network (which we assumed we know). Therefore, for each variable X_i we convert back to a complete Gaussian Bayesian network in which the set of parents of X_i are the same set of parents X_i has in our original Bayesian network. For each variable X_i the resultant updated values of b_{ij} and σ_i yield a density function, conditional on values of the parents of X_i, which approximates the actual density function conditional on values of the parents of X_i and the data. Therefore, if the conditional independencies entailed by the DAG in our original Gaussian Bayesian network are correct (i.e., they are the ones in the actual relative frequency distribution), the product of these conditional density functions approximates the joint density function of the variables conditional on the data. Note that if the conditional independencies entailed by that DAG are the ones in the relative frequency distribution of the variables, we will have convergence to that distribution.

Note further that we never actually assess probability distributions for the random variables F_i in an augmented Gaussian Bayesian network. Instead we assess distributions for the random variables $\mathbf{A}$ and $\mathbf{R}$ representing unknown mean vector and unknown precision matrix in a multivariate normal distribution. Our assumptions are actually those stated for a multivariate normal sample, and we use the Bayesian network only to obtain prior beliefs and to estimate the updated distribution.

We summarize our steps next. Suppose we have a multivariate normal sample $\mathsf{D} = \{\mathbf{X}^{(1)}, \mathbf{X}^{(2)}, \ldots, \mathbf{X}^{(M)}\}$ with unassessed values of the parameters $\boldsymbol{\mu}$, v, $\boldsymbol{\beta}$, and $\boldsymbol{\alpha}$, Then we assess values for these parameters and approximate the posterior density function $\rho_{\mathbf{X}^{(M+1)}}(\mathbf{x}^{(M+1)}|\mathsf{d})$ as follows:

1. Construct a prior Gaussian Bayesian network $(\mathbb{G}, P)$ containing, for $1 \leq i \leq n$, initial values of

$$\mu_i, \qquad \sigma_i^2, \qquad \text{and} \qquad b_{ij}.$$

2. Convert the Gaussian Bayesian network to the corresponding multivariate normal distribution using the algorithm in Section 7.2.3. Suppose the density function for that distribution is $N(\mathbf{x}; \boldsymbol{\mu}, \mathbf{T}^{-1})$.

3. Assess prior values of α and v. Recall that

   The parameter v is the size of the hypothetical sample upon which we base our prior belief concerning the value of the unknown mean.

   It seems reasonable to make α equal to $v - 1$.

4. Use Equality 7.22 to access the prior value of $\boldsymbol{\beta}$. That equality yields

$$\boldsymbol{\beta} = \frac{v(\alpha - n + 1)}{(v+1)} \mathbf{T}^{-1}.$$

5. Apply Theorem 7.28 to determine updated values $\boldsymbol{\beta}^*$, α^*, $\boldsymbol{\mu}^*$, and v^*.

   The components μ_i^* of the updated mean vector $\boldsymbol{\mu}^*$ are the updated unconditional means in our updated Gaussian Bayesian network.

6. Use Equality 7.22 to determine the updated value of $\mathbf{T}^*$. That equality yields

$$(\mathbf{T}^*)^{-1} = \frac{(v^* + 1)}{v^*(\alpha^* - n + 1)} \boldsymbol{\beta}^*.$$

7. For each variable X_i

   (a) Create an ordering of the variables such that all and only the parents of X_i in $\mathbb{G}$ are numbered before X_i.

   (b) Using the algorithm in Section 7.2.3 convert $N(\mathbf{x}^{(M+1)}; \boldsymbol{\mu}^*, (\mathbf{T}^*)^{-1})$ to a Gaussian Bayesian network yielding updated values

$$\sigma_i^{*2} \qquad \text{and} \qquad b_{ij}^*.$$

8. Estimate the distribution of $\mathbf{X}^{(M+1)}$ by the Gaussian Bayesian network containing the DAG $\mathbb{G}$ and the parameter values μ_i^*, σ_i^{*2}, and b_{ij}^*.

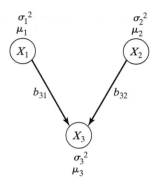

Figure 7.16: The prior Gaussian Bayesian network for Example 7.26.

Example 7.26 *Suppose we have three variables X_1, X_2, and X_3, we know that X_1 and X_2 are independent, and we obtain the following data:*

Case	X_1	X_2	X_3
1	1	2	6
2	5	8	2
3	2	4	1
4	8	6	3

We apply the previous steps to learn parameter values.

1. *Construct a prior Gaussian Bayesian network $(\mathbb{G}, P)$. Suppose it is the network in Figure 7.16, where all the parameters have arbitrary values. We will see that their values do not matter because we will set $v = 0$ to model prior ignorance.*

2. *Convert the Gaussian Bayesian network to the corresponding multivariate normal distribution using the algorithm in Section 7.2.3. We need only use Equality 7.29 to do this. We obtain the density function $N(\mathbf{x}; \boldsymbol{\mu}, \mathbf{T}^{-1})$, where*

$$\boldsymbol{\mu} = \begin{pmatrix} \mu_1 \\ \mu_2 \\ \mu_3 \end{pmatrix}$$

and

$$\mathbf{T}^{-1} = \begin{pmatrix} \sigma_1^2 & 0 & b_{31}\sigma_1^2 \\ 0 & \sigma_2^2 & b_{32}\sigma_2^2 \\ b_{31}\sigma_1^2 & b_{32}\sigma_2^2 & b_{31}^2\sigma_1^2 + b_{32}^2\sigma_2^2 + \sigma_3^2 \end{pmatrix}.$$

3. *Assess prior values of α and v. As discussed following Theorem 7.28, to model prior ignorance we set*

$$v = 0$$

$$\alpha = -1.$$

4. *Determine the prior value of β. We have*

$$\beta = \frac{v(\alpha - n + 1)}{(v + 1)} \mathbf{T}^{-1}$$

$$= \frac{0(-1 - 3 + 1)}{(0 + 1)} \begin{pmatrix} \sigma_1^2 & 0 & b_{31}\sigma_1^2 \\ 0 & \sigma_2^2 & b_{32}\sigma_2^2 \\ b_{31}\sigma_1^2 & b_{32}\sigma_2^2 & b_{31}^2\sigma_1^2 + b_{32}^2\sigma_2^2 + \sigma_3^2 \end{pmatrix} = \mathbf{0}.$$

Note that we obtained the value of β that we said we would use to model prior ignorance. (See the discussion following Theorem 7.28.) Note further that we would have obtained the same result if we had an arc from X_1 to X_2. In this case, the independence assumption matters only when we convert back to a Gaussian Bayesian network after learning.

5. *Apply Theorem 7.28 to determine updated values β^*, α^*, μ^*, and v^*. As obtained in Example 7.22,*

$$\beta^* = \begin{pmatrix} 30 & 18 & -6 \\ 18 & 20 & -10 \\ -6 & -10 & 14 \end{pmatrix} \quad and \quad \alpha^* = 3,$$

and

$$\mu^* = \begin{pmatrix} 4 \\ 5 \\ 3 \end{pmatrix} \quad and \quad v^* = 4.$$

So, in our updated Gaussian Bayesian network,

$$\mu_1^* = 4 \qquad \mu_2^* = 5 \qquad \mu_3^* = 3.$$

6. *Determine the updated value of $\mathbf{T}^*$. We have*

$$(\mathbf{T}^*)^{-1} = \frac{(v^* + 1)}{v^*(\alpha^* - n + 1)}\beta^*$$

$$= \frac{4 + 1}{4(3 - 3 + 1)} \begin{pmatrix} 30 & 18 & -6 \\ 18 & 20 & -10 \\ -6 & -10 & 14 \end{pmatrix}$$

$$= \begin{pmatrix} 37.5 & 22.5 & -7.5 \\ 22.5 & 25 & -12.5 \\ -7.5 & -12.5 & 17.5 \end{pmatrix}.$$

7. *For each variable X_i*

   (a) *Create an ordering of the variables such that all and only the parents of X_i in $\mathbb{G}$ are numbered before X_i.*

   (b) *Using the algorithm in Section 7.2.3 convert $N(\mathbf{x}^{(M+1)}; \boldsymbol{\mu}^*, (\mathbf{T}^*)^{-1})$ to a Gaussian Bayesian network yielding updated values*

$$\sigma_i^{*2} \qquad and \qquad b_{ij}^*.$$

For variables X_1 and X_3 we can use the ordering $[X_1, X_2, X_3]$. To transform our multivariate normal distribution to a Gaussian Bayesian network with this ordering, we need use only Equality 7.30. We obtain

$$\sigma_1^{*2} = 37.5 \qquad \sigma_2^{*2} = 11.5 \qquad \sigma_3^{*2} = 10.435$$

$$b_{21}^* = .6 \qquad b_{31}^* = .217 \qquad b_{32}^* = -.696.$$

The values of only σ_1^{*2}, σ_3^{*2}, b_{31}^*, and b_{32}^* are used in our updated Gaussian Bayesian network. To obtain the value of σ_2^{*2} we use an ordering in which X_2 is numbered first. It is left as an exercise to show that this value is 25.

Bernardo and Smith [1994] derive a formula for representing the updated t distribution of $\mathbf{X}$ in a Bayesian network exactly.

EXERCISES
Section 7.1

Exercise 7.1 *Find a rectangular block (not necessarily a cube) and label the sides. Given that you are going to throw the block repeatedly, determine a Dirichlet density function that represents your belief concerning the relative frequencies of the sides occurring and show the function. What is your probability of each side coming up on the first throw?*

Exercise 7.2 *Suppose we are going to sample individuals who have smoked two packs of cigarettes or more daily for the past 10 years. We will determine whether each individual's systolic blood pressure is ≤ 100, $101 - 120$, $121 - 140$, $141 - 160$, or ≥ 161. Ascertain a Dirichlet density function that represents your belief concerning the relative frequencies and show the function. What is your probability of each blood pressure range for the first individual sampled?*

Exercise 7.3 *Prove Lemma 7.1.*

Exercise 7.4 *Prove Theorem 7.1.*

Exercise 7.5 *Prove Lemma 7.2.*

Exercise 7.6 *Prove Lemma 7.3.*

Exercise 7.7 *Prove Theorem 7.2.*

Exercise 7.8 *Prove Theorem 7.3.*

Exercise 7.9 *Prove Theorem 7.4.*

Exercise 7.10 *Throw the block discussed in Exercise 7.1 100 times. Compute the probability of obtaining the data that occurs, the updated Dirichlet density function that represents your belief concerning the relative frequencies, and the probability of each side for the 101st throw.*

Exercise 7.11 *Suppose we sample 100 individuals after determining the blood pressure ranges in Exercise 7.2, and we obtain the following results:*

Blood Pressure Range	# of Individuals in this Range
≤ 100	2
$101 - 120$	15
$121 - 140$	23
$141 - 160$	25
≥ 161	35

Compute the probability of obtaining these data, the updated Dirichlet density function that represents your belief concerning the relative frequencies, and the probability of each blood pressure range for the next individual sampled.

Exercise 7.12 *Suppose $F_1, F_2, \ldots, F_r$, have a Dirichlet distribution. That is, their density function is given by*

$$\rho(f_1, f_2, \ldots, f_{r-1}) = \frac{\Gamma(N)}{\prod\limits_{k=1}^{r} \Gamma(a_k)} f_1^{a_1-1} f_2^{a_2-1} \cdots f_r^{a_r-1} \quad 0 \leq f_k \leq 1, \ \sum_{k=1}^{r} f_k = 1,$$

where $a_1, a_2, \ldots, a_r$ are integers ≥ 1, and $N = \sum_{k=1}^{r} a_k$. Show that, by integrating over the remaining variables, we obtain that the marginal density function of F_k is given by

$$\rho(f_k) = \frac{\Gamma(N)}{\Gamma(a_k)\Gamma(b_k)} f_k^{a_k-1} (1 - f_k)^{b_k-1},$$

where

$$b_k = N - a_k.$$

Exercise 7.13 *Using the Dirichlet density function you developed in Exercise 7.2, determine 95% probability intervals for the random variables that represent your prior belief concerning the relative frequencies of the five blood pressure ranges discussed in that exercise.*

Exercise 7.14 *Using the posterior Dirichlet density function obtained in Exercise 7.11, determine 95% probability intervals for the random variables that represent your posterior belief concerning the relative frequencies of the five blood pressure ranges discussed in that exercise.*

Exercise 7.15 *Using the Dirichlet density function you developed in Exercise 7.2, determine a 95% probability square for the random variables that represents your belief concerning the relative frequencies of the first two blood pressure ranges discussed in that exercise.*

Exercise 7.16 *Using the Dirichlet density function you developed in Exercise 7.2, determine a 95% probability cube for the random variables that represent your belief concerning the relative frequencies of the first three blood pressure ranges discussed in that exercise.*

Exercise 7.17 *Prove Theorem 7.5.*

Exercise 7.18 *Prove Theorem 7.6.*

Exercise 7.19 *Prove Theorem 7.7.*

Exercise 7.20 *Suppose we have the augmented Bayesian network in Figure 7.6 and these data:*

Case	X_1	X_2
1	1	2
2	1	3
3	2	1
4	2	2
5	3	4
6	2	2
7	3	3
8	2	1
9	3	4
10	1	1
11	1	4
12	2	1
13	3	2
14	2	3
15	1	1

Compute the following:

1. $P(\mathbf{d})$

2. $\rho(f_{111}, f_{112}|\mathbf{d})$

3. $\rho(f_{211}, f_{212}, f_{213}|\mathbf{d})$

    4. $\rho(f_{221}, f_{222}, f_{223}|\mathsf{d})$

    5. $\rho(f_{231}, f_{232}, f_{233}|\mathsf{d})$.

Show the updated augmented Bayesian network and the updated embedded Bayesian network. For $1 \leq k \leq 4$ determine $P(X_2 = k)$ for the 16th case.

Exercise 7.21 *Does the network in Figure 7.6 have an equivalent sample size? If so, what is it?*

Exercise 7.22 *Prove Theorem 7.8.*

Exercise 7.23 *Prove Theorem 7.9.*

Exercise 7.24 *Consult the references mentioned in Section 6.6 in order to extend the results in that section to the case of multinomial variables.*

Section 7.2

Exercise 7.25 *Establish Relation 7.3.*

Exercise 7.26 *Establish Relation 7.8.*

Exercise 7.27 *Prove Theorem 7.14.*

Exercise 7.28 *Prove Theorem 7.15.*

Exercise 7.29 *Prove Theorem 7.16.*

Exercise 7.30 *At the end of Example 7.14 it was left as an exercise to show $\rho_{R|d}(r) = gamma(r; M/2, s/2)$. Do this.*

Exercise 7.31 *Obtain Equality 7.14.*

Exercise 7.32 *Obtain Relation 7.16.*

Exercise 7.33 *Obtain Equality 7.19.*

Exercise 7.34 *Prove Theorem 7.19.*

Exercise 7.35 *In Example 7.15 it was left as an exercise to show that $sr = s/\sigma^2$ is distributed $\chi^2(M - 1)$. Do this.*

Exercise 7.36 *Prove Theorem 7.20. Hint: Show that*

$$
\begin{aligned}
N(x_1, x_2; 0, 1^2, 0, \sigma^2, p) &= \frac{1}{2\pi (1 - p^2)^{1/2}} \exp\left[-\frac{1}{2(1 - p^2)} \left(x_1^2 - 2px_1x_2 + x_2^2\right)\right] \\
&= \frac{1}{\sqrt{2\pi}} \exp\left[\frac{-x_1^2}{2}\right] \frac{1}{\sqrt{2\pi}(1 - p^2)^{1/2}} \exp\left[\frac{(x_2 - px_1)^2}{2(1 - p^2)}\right],
\end{aligned}
$$

and then integrate over x_2 to obtain the marginal density of X_1.

Exercise 7.37 *Prove Theorem 7.21.*

Exercise 7.38 *Show that the matrix*

$$\begin{pmatrix} 1 & 0 \\ 0 & 1 \end{pmatrix}$$

is positive definite.

Exercise 7.39 *Show that the matrix*

$$\begin{pmatrix} 1 & 1 \\ 1 & 1 \end{pmatrix}$$

is positive semidefinite, but not positive definite.

Exercise 7.40 *Show directly that if $n = 1$, then $Wishart(v; k, 1/\sigma^2)$ is equal to $gamma(v; k/2, 1/2\sigma^2)$.*

Exercise 7.41 *Show that, in the case in which $n = 1$, the density function in Equality 7.21 is the univariate t density function that appears in Equality 7.13.*

Exercise 7.42 *Prove Theorem 7.29.*

Exercise 7.43 *Obtain Equality 7.29.*

Exercise 7.44 *Obtain the covariance matrix in Example 7.23.*

Exercise 7.45 *Obtain the covariance matrix in Example 7.24.*

Exercise 7.46 *Obtain the results in Example 7.25.*

Exercise 7.47 *Show that the value of σ_2^{*2} is 25 in Example 7.26.*

Exercise 7.48 *Redo Example 7.26, using a prior Gaussian Bayesian network in which*

$$\sigma_1^2 = 1 \qquad \sigma_2^2 = 1 \qquad \sigma_3^2 = 1$$

$$b_{21} = 0 \qquad b_{31} = 1 \qquad b_{32} = 1$$

$$\mu_1 = 2 \qquad \mu_2 = 3 \qquad \mu_3 = 4.$$

Chapter 8

Bayesian Structure Learning

In Chapters 6 and 7 we assumed that we knew the structure of the DAG in a Bayesian network (i.e., the conditional independencies in the relative frequency distribution of a set of random variables). Then we developed a method for learning the parameters (estimates of the values of the relative frequencies). Here we assume only that we have a set of random variables with an unknown relative frequency distribution, and we develop a Bayesian method for learning DAG structure from data. Section 8.1 develops the basic structure learning methodology for the case of discrete variables. When a single structure is not found to be overwhelmingly most probable, averaging over structures is sometimes more appropriate. This topic is discussed in Section 8.2. Section 8.3 deals with learning structure when there are missing data items. Next, Section 8.4 discusses the problem of probabilistic model selection in a general setting, shows that our DAG structure learning problem is an example of probabilistic model selection, and further shows that the model selection method we developed satisfies an important criterion (namely, consistency) for a model selection methodology. Learning structure in the case of hidden variables is the focus of Section 8.5. Section 8.6 presents a method for learning structure in the case of continuous variables. The terms "probabilistic model" and "model selection" are defined rigorously in Section 8.4. In the first three sections, by **model** we always mean a candidate DAG (or DAG pattern), and we call the search for a DAG (or DAG pattern) that best fits some data **model selection**.

8.1 Learning Structure: Discrete Variables

Given a repeatable experiment, whose outcome determines the state of n random variables, in this section we assume the following:

1. The relative frequency distribution of the variables admits a faithful DAG representation.

2. Given that we believe the relative frequency distribution has all and only some set of conditional independencies, our beliefs concerning the probability of the outcome of M executions of the experiment is modeled by a multinomial Bayesian network sample with parameter $(\mathbb{G}, \mathsf{F})$ such that $\mathbb{G}$ entails all and only those conditional independencies.

In Example 2.10, we showed that, if a distribution has the conditional independencies

$$I_P(\{X\}, \{Z\}) \qquad I_P(\{X\}, \{Z\}|\{Y\}),$$

and only these conditional independencies, then the distribution does not admit a faithful DAG representation. In Example 2.11, we showed that, if a distribution has the conditional independencies

$$I_P(\{L\}, \{F, S\}) \qquad I_P(\{L\}, \{S\}) \qquad I_P(\{F\}, \{V\})$$
$$I_P(\{F\}, \{L, V\}) \qquad I_P(\{L\}, \{F\}),$$

and only these conditional independencies, then the distribution does not admit a faithful DAG representation. So, our first assumption is that conditional independencies like these are not the case for the relative frequency distribution.

The second assumption is simply the assumption we made in Chapters 6 and 7 when we were concerned with learning parameters.

After we develop a schema for learning structure based on these assumptions, we show how to learn structure using the schema. Then we show how to learn structure from a mixture of observational and experimental data. Finally, we discuss the complexity of structure learning.

8.1.1   Schema for Learning Structure

Recall from Section 2.3.1 that Markov equivalence divides the set of all DAGs containing the same nodes into disjoint equivalence classes, and all DAG in a given Markov equivalence class are faithful to the same probability distributions. Recall further that we can create a graph called a DAG pattern that represents each Markov equivalence class; and that, if a probability distribution admits a faithful DAG representation, then Theorem 2.6 says there is a unique DAG pattern that is faithful to that distribution. Therefore, although we cannot identify a unique DAG with the conditional independencies in the distribution, we can identify a unique DAG pattern with these conditional independencies. We will assume that the relative frequency distribution admits a faithful DAG representation, and we will develop a subjective probability distribution of the values of that distribution. Relative to our subjective probability distribution, we will use GP as a random variable whose possible values are DAG patterns gp. A DAG pattern event gp is the event that the DAG pattern gp is faithful to the relative frequency distribution.

In some situations we may consider DAGs events. For example, if an event is the causal structure among the variables, then $X_1 \rightarrow X_2$ represents the event that X_1 causes X_2, while $X_2 \rightarrow X_1$ represents the different event that X_2 causes X_1. However, unless otherwise stated, we will consider only DAG patterns events, and as in Section 6.4.4, the notation $\rho|\mathbb{G}$ denotes the density function in the augmented Bayesian network containing the DAG $\mathbb{G}$. It does not entail that the DAG $\mathbb{G}$ is an event.

We now have the following definition concerning learning structure:

Definition 8.1 *The following constitutes a **multinomial Bayesian network structure learning schema**:*

1. *n random variables $X_1, X_2, \ldots, X_n$ with discrete joint probability distribution P;*

2. *an equivalent sample size N;*

3. *for each DAG pattern gp containing the n variables, a multinomial augmented Bayesian network $(\mathbb{G}, \mathsf{F}^{(\mathbb{G})}, \rho|\mathbb{G})$ with equivalent sample size N, in which $\mathbb{G}$ is any member of the equivalence class represented by gp, such that P is the probability distribution in its embedded Bayesian network.*

Note that we have explicitly stated the dependence of F and ρ on $\mathbb{G}$ in the previous definition, whereas in Chapters 6 and 7 we did not. The reason is that now we are dealing with more than one DAG, whereas in Chapters 6 and 7 the DAG was part of our background knowledge.

Example 8.1 *We develop a multinomial Bayesian network structure learning schema containing two variables:*

1. *Specify two random variables X_1 and X_2, each having space $\{1, 2\}$, and assign*

$$P(X_1 = 1, X_2 = 1) = 1/4$$

$$P(X_1 = 1, X_2 = 2) = 1/4$$

$$P(X_1 = 2, X_2 = 1) = 1/4$$

$$P(X_1 = 2, X_2 = 2) = 1/4.$$

2. *Specify $N = 4$.*

3. *The two DAG patterns are shown in Figures 8.1 (a) and (c), and the augmented Bayesian networks are shown in Figures 8.1 (b) and (d).*

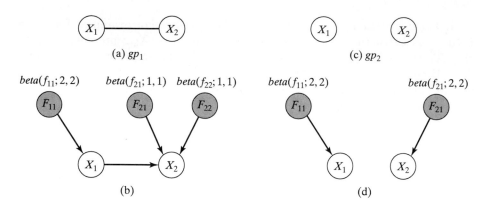

Figure 8.1: DAG patterns are shown in (a) and (c) and their respective augmented Bayesian network structures are shown in (b) and (d).

Recall $\mathbb{G}$ can be any element of the equivalence class represented by gp. So the DAG in Figure 8.1 (b) could be $X_1 \leftarrow X_2$. Note that gp_1 represents no independencies, while gp_2 represents $I_P(\{X_1\}, \{X_2\})$.

Note that there are assignments of values to the parameters in the augmented Bayesian network in Figure 8.1 (b) which make X_1 and X_2 independent; however, as discussed in Section 2.3.1, they form a set of measure zero. So, if we condition on DAG pattern event gp_1, the probability of X_1 and X_2 being independent is zero, which is what we want since gp_1 is the event that they are dependent.

In general, we do not directly assign a joint probability distribution because the number of values in the joint distribution grows exponentially with the number of variables. Rather we assign conditional distributions in all the augmented Bayesian networks such that the probability distributions in all the embedded Bayesian networks are the same. A common way to do this is to use Theorem 7.8 to construct, for each DAG pattern gp, an augmented Bayesian network with equivalent sample size N, whose embedded Bayesian network contains the uniform distribution. That is, for a given DAG pattern gp we first determine a DAG $\mathbb{G}$ in the equivalence class it represents. Then in the augmented Bayesian network corresponding to $\mathbb{G}$ for all i, j, and k we set

$$a_{ijk} = \frac{N}{r_i q_i}.$$

Recall that r_i is the number of possible values of X_i in $\mathbb{G}$, and q_i is the number of different instantiations of the parents of X_i in $\mathbb{G}$. This is how the networks in Figure 8.1 were created. Heckerman and Geiger [1995] discuss other methods for assessing priors.

8.1.2   Procedure for Learning Structure

Next we show how we can learn structure using a multinomial Bayesian network structure learning schema. We start with this definition:

Definition 8.2 *The following constitutes a **multinomial Bayesian network structure learning space**:*

1. *a multinomial Bayesian network structure learning schema containing the variables $X_1, X_2, \ldots, X_n$;*

2. *a random variable GP whose range consists of all DAG patterns containing the n variables, and for each value gp of GP, a prior probability $P(gp)$;*

3. *a set $\mathsf{D} = \{\mathbf{X}^{(1)}, \mathbf{X}^{(2)}, \ldots, \mathbf{X}^{(M)}\}$ of n-dimensional random vectors such that each $X_i^{(h)}$ has the same space as X_i (See Definition 7.4).*

   For each value gp of GP, D is a multinomial Bayesian network sample of size M with parameter $(\mathbb{G}, \mathsf{F}^{(\mathbb{G})})$, where $(\mathbb{G}, \mathsf{F}^{(\mathbb{G})}, \rho|\mathbb{G})$ is the multinomial augmented Bayesian network corresponding to gp in the specification of the schema.

Suppose we have such a space, and a set d (data) of values of the vectors in D. Owing to Corollary 7.6,

$$
P(\mathsf{d}|gp) = P(\mathsf{d}|\mathbb{G}) = \prod_{i=1}^{n} \prod_{j=1}^{q_i^{(\mathbb{G})}} \frac{\Gamma(N_{ij}^{(\mathbb{G})})}{\Gamma(N_{ij}^{(\mathbb{G})} + M_{ij}^{(\mathbb{G})})} \prod_{k=1}^{r_i} \frac{\Gamma(a_{ijk}^{(\mathbb{G})} + s_{ijk}^{(\mathbb{G})})}{\Gamma(a_{ijk}^{(\mathbb{G})})}, \tag{8.1}
$$

where $a_{ijk}^{(\mathbb{G})}$ and $s_{ijk}^{(\mathbb{G})}$ are their values in $(\mathbb{G}, \mathsf{F}^{(\mathbb{G})}, \rho|\mathbb{G})$.

A **scoring criterion** for a DAG (or DAG pattern) is a function that assigns a value to each DAG (or DAG pattern) under consideration based on the data. The expression in Equality 8.1 is called the **Bayesian scoring criterion** $score_B$, and is used to score both DAGs and DAG patterns. That is,

$$
score_B(\mathsf{d}, gp) = score_B(\mathsf{d}, \mathbb{G}) = P(\mathsf{d}|\mathbb{G}).
$$

Scoring criteria are discussed in a more general way in Section 8.4.

Note that in Equality 8.1 we condition on a DAG pattern to compute the probability that $\mathsf{D} = \mathsf{d}$, and in Chapters 6 and 7 we did not. Recall that in the previous two chapters we assumed we knew the DAG structure in all our computations. So this structure was part of the prior background knowledge in developing our probability space, and therefore we did not condition on it. Note further that, due to Lemma 7.4, this conditional probability is uniquely defined [i.e., it does depend on our choice of DAGs for $(\mathbb{G}, \mathsf{F}^{(\mathbb{G})}, \rho|\mathbb{G})$].

Given a multinomial Bayesian network structure learning space and data, **model selection** consists of determining and selecting the DAG patterns with maximum probability conditional on the data. (In general, there could be more than one maximizing DAG pattern.) The purpose of model selection is to learn a DAG pattern along with its parameter values (a model) that can be used for inference and decision making. Examples follow.

Example 8.2 *Suppose we are doing a study concerning individuals who were married by age* 30, *and we want to see if there is a correlation between graduating college and getting divorced. We first specify the following random variables:*

Variable	Value	When the Variable Takes this Value
X_1	1	*Individual graduated college*
	2	*Individual did not graduate college*
X_2	1	*Individual was divorced by age 50*
	2	*Individual was not divorced by age 50*

Next we represent our prior beliefs using the Bayesian network structure learning schema in Example 8.1. Then the DAG pattern gp_1 in Figure 8.1 (a) represents the event that they are correlated and the DAG pattern gp_2 in Figure 8.1 (b) represents the event that they are independent.

Suppose next that we obtain the data **d** *in the following table:*

Case	X_1	X_2
1	1	1
2	1	2
3	1	1
4	2	2
5	1	1
6	2	1
7	1	1
8	2	2

Then

$$P(\mathbf{d}|gp_1) = \left(\frac{\Gamma(4)}{\Gamma(4+8)}\frac{\Gamma(2+5)\Gamma(2+3)}{\Gamma(2)\Gamma(2)}\right)\left(\frac{\Gamma(2)}{\Gamma(2+5)}\frac{\Gamma(1+4)\Gamma(1+1)}{\Gamma(1)\Gamma(1)}\right)\left(\frac{\Gamma(2)}{\Gamma(2+3)}\frac{\Gamma(1+1)\Gamma(1+2)}{\Gamma(1)\Gamma(1)}\right)$$

$$= 7.2150 \times 10^{-6}$$

$$P(\mathbf{d}|gp_2) = \left(\frac{\Gamma(4)}{\Gamma(4+8)}\frac{\Gamma(2+5)\Gamma(2+3)}{\Gamma(2)\Gamma(2)}\right)\left(\frac{\Gamma(4)}{\Gamma(4+8)}\frac{\Gamma(2+5)\Gamma(2+3)}{\Gamma(2)\Gamma(2)}\right)$$

$$= 6.7465 \times 10^{-6}.$$

If we assign

$$P(gp_1) = P(gp_2) = .5,$$

then, owing to Bayes' theorem,

$$P(gp_1|\mathbf{d}) = \frac{P(\mathbf{d}|gp_1)P(gp_1)}{P(\mathbf{d})}$$

$$= \frac{7.2150 \times 10^{-6}(.5)}{P(\mathbf{d})}$$

$$= \alpha(3.6075 \times 10^{-6})$$

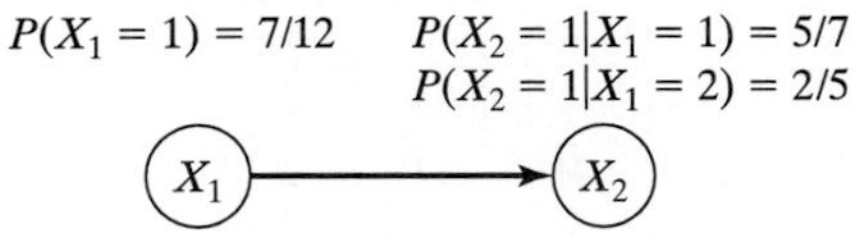

$$P(X_1 = 1) = 7/12 \qquad P(X_2 = 1 | X_1 = 1) = 5/7$$
$$P(X_2 = 1 | X_1 = 2) = 2/5$$

Figure 8.2: The Bayesian network developed in Example 8.2.

and

$$
\begin{aligned}
P(gp_2 | \mathbf{d}) &= \frac{P(\mathbf{d} | gp_1) P(gp_1)}{P(\mathbf{d})} \\
&= \frac{6.7465 \times 10^{-6}(.5)}{P(\mathbf{d})}. \\
&= \alpha(3.37325 \times 10^{-6}),
\end{aligned}
$$

where α is a normalizing constant equal to $1/P(\mathbf{d})$. Eliminating α we have

$$
\begin{aligned}
P(gp_1 | \mathbf{d}) &= \frac{3.6075 \times 10^{-6}}{3.6075 \times 10^{-6} + 3.37325 \times 10^{-6}} \\
&= .51678
\end{aligned}
$$

and

$$
\begin{aligned}
P(gp_2 | \mathbf{d}) &= \frac{3.37325 \times 10^{-6}}{3.6075 \times 10^{-6} + 3.37325 \times 10^{-6}} \\
&= .48322.
\end{aligned}
$$

We select DAG pattern gp_1 and conclude that it is more probable that college attendance and divorce are correlated.

Furthermore, we could develop a Bayesian network, whose DAG is in the equivalence class represented by gp_1, to do inference involving X_1 and X_2. Such a Bayesian network is shown in Figure 8.2. The parameter values in that network were learned using the technique developed in Chapter 6 (Corollary 6.7). For the ninth case, it could be used, for example, to compute

$$
\begin{aligned}
P(X_1 &= 2 | X_2 = 1) \\
&= \frac{P(X_2 = 1 | X_1 = 2) P(X_1 = 2)}{P(X_2 = 1 | X_1 = 1) P(X_1 = 1) + P(X_2 = 1 | X_1 = 2) P(X_1 = 2)} \\
&= \frac{(2/5)(5/12)}{(5/7)(7/12) + (2/5)(5/12)} = .28571.
\end{aligned}
$$

Example 8.3 Suppose we are doing the same study as in Example 8.1 and we obtain the data $\mathbf{d}$ in the following table:

Case	X_1	X_2
1	1	1
2	1	1
3	1	1
4	1	1
5	2	2
6	2	2
7	2	2
8	2	2

Then

$$P(\mathsf{d}|gp_1) = \left(\frac{\Gamma(4)}{\Gamma(4+8)} \frac{\Gamma(2+4)\Gamma(2+4)}{\Gamma(2)\Gamma(2)} \right) \left(\frac{\Gamma(2)}{\Gamma(2+4)} \frac{\Gamma(1+4)\Gamma(1+0)}{\Gamma(1)\Gamma(1)} \right) \left(\frac{\Gamma(2)}{\Gamma(2+4)} \frac{\Gamma(1+0)\Gamma(1+4)}{\Gamma(1)\Gamma(1)} \right)$$

$$= 8.6580 \times 10^{-5}$$

$$P(\mathsf{d}|gp_2) = \left(\frac{\Gamma(4)}{\Gamma(4+8)} \frac{\Gamma(2+4)\Gamma(2+4)}{\Gamma(2)\Gamma(2)} \right) \left(\frac{\Gamma(4)}{\Gamma(4+8)} \frac{\Gamma(2+4)\Gamma(2+4)}{\Gamma(2)\Gamma(2)} \right)$$

$$= 4.6851 \times 10^{-6}.$$

If we assign

$$P(gp_1) = P(gp_2) = .5,$$

then, proceeding as in Example 8.2, we obtain

$$P(gp_1|\mathsf{d}) = .94866$$

and

$$P(gp_2|\mathsf{d}) = .05134.$$

Notice that we become highly confident that the DAG pattern is the one with the dependency because in the data the variables are deterministically related. We conclude that college attendance and divorce are probably correlated.

Example 8.4 *Suppose we are doing the same study as in Example 8.1 and we obtain the data* **d** *in the following table:*

Case	X_1	X_2
1	1	1
2	1	1
3	1	2
4	1	2
5	2	1
6	2	1
7	2	2
8	2	2

Then

$$P(\mathsf{d}|gp_1) = \left(\frac{\Gamma(4)}{\Gamma(4+8)} \frac{\Gamma(2+4)\Gamma(2+4)}{\Gamma(2)\Gamma(2)} \right) \left(\frac{\Gamma(2)}{\Gamma(2+4)} \frac{\Gamma(1+2)\Gamma(1+2)}{\Gamma(1)\Gamma(1)} \right) \left(\frac{\Gamma(2)}{\Gamma(2+4)} \frac{\Gamma(1+2)\Gamma(1+2)}{\Gamma(1)\Gamma(1)} \right)$$

$$= 2.4050 \times 10^{-6}$$

$$P(\mathsf{d}|gp_2) = \left(\frac{\Gamma(4)}{\Gamma(4+8)} \frac{\Gamma(2+4)\Gamma(2+4)}{\Gamma(2)\Gamma(2)} \right) \left(\frac{\Gamma(4)}{\Gamma(4+8)} \frac{\Gamma(2+4)\Gamma(2+4)}{\Gamma(2)\Gamma(2)} \right)$$

$$= 4.6851 \times 10^{-6}.$$

If we assign

$$P(gp_1) = P(gp_2) = .5,$$

then proceeding as in Example 8.2 we obtain

$$P(gp_1|\mathsf{d}) = .33921$$

and

$$P(gp_2|\mathsf{d}) = .66079.$$

Notice that we become fairly confident the DAG pattern is the one with the independency because in the data the variables are independent. We conclude that it is more probable that college attendance and divorce are independent.

8.1.3 Learning From a Mixture of Observational and Experimental Data

Our Bayesian scoring criterion (Equality 8.1) was derived assuming that each case obtained its value according to the same probability distribution. So we can use it to learn structure only with all observational data. That is, we can use it when no values of any variables are obtained by performing a randomized control experiment (RCE). (See Section 1.5.1.) However, in general, we can have both observational data and experimental data (data obtained from an RCE) on a given set of variables. For example, in the medical domain, a great deal of observational data is contained in routinely collected electronic medical records. In addition, for certain variables of high clinical interest, we sometimes have data obtained from an RCE. Cooper and Yoo [1999] developed a method for using Equality 8.1 to score DAGs using a mixture of observational and experimental data. We describe their method next.

First we show Equality 8.1 again:

$$P(\mathsf{d}|gp) = P(\mathsf{d}|\mathbb{G}) = \prod_{i=1}^{n} \prod_{j=1}^{q_i^{(\mathbb{G})}} \frac{\Gamma(N_{ij}^{(\mathbb{G})})}{\Gamma(N_{ij}^{(\mathbb{G})} + M_{ij}^{(\mathbb{G})})} \prod_{k=1}^{r_i} \frac{\Gamma(a_{ijk}^{(\mathbb{G})} + s_{ijk}^{(\mathbb{G})})}{\Gamma(a_{ijk}^{(\mathbb{G})})}.$$

Note that for each variable X_i, for each value of the parent set of X_i, we have the term

$$\frac{\Gamma(N_{ij}^{(\mathrm{G})})}{\Gamma(N_{ij}^{(\mathrm{G})} + M_{ij}^{(\mathrm{G})})} \prod_{k=1}^{r_i} \frac{\Gamma(a_{ijk}^{(\mathrm{G})} + s_{ijk}^{(\mathrm{G})})}{\Gamma(a_{ijk}^{(\mathrm{G})})}.$$

When computing that term, we use all and only those cases in which the value of X_i was obtained from observational data, regardless of how the parents of X_i obtained their values. An example follows:

Example 8.5 *Suppose we have the data* d *in the following table, where the values obtained using manipulation appear boldfaced and primed:*

Case	X_1	X_2
1	2	2
2	2	1
3	2	2
4	1	1
5	1	2
6	**2′**	2
7	**1′**	1
8	2	**2′**
9	1	**2′**
10	2	**1′**
11	1	**1′**

The score of DAG pattern gp_1 in Figure 8.1 is as follows:

$$\begin{aligned}
P(\mathrm{d}|gp_1) &= \left(\frac{\Gamma(4)}{\Gamma(4+9)}\frac{\Gamma(2+4)\Gamma(2+5)}{\Gamma(2)\Gamma(2)}\right)\left(\frac{\Gamma(2)}{\Gamma(2+3)}\frac{\Gamma(1+2)\Gamma(1+1)}{\Gamma(1)\Gamma(1)}\right)\left(\frac{\Gamma(2)}{\Gamma(2+4)}\frac{\Gamma(1+1)\Gamma(1+3)}{\Gamma(1)\Gamma(1)}\right) \\
&= 4.509\,4 \times 10^{-6}.
\end{aligned}$$

Note that the term for X_1 is based on only nine cases. This is because Cases 6 and 7 obtained their values of X_1 via manipulation, and therefore they are not used in the computation of that term. Note further, that the terms for X_2 are based on only seven cases (three in which X_1 has value 1 and four in which it has value 2). This is because Cases 8, 9, 10 and 11 obtained their values of X_2 via manipulation, and therefore they are not used in the computation of those terms.

The scoring methodology just presented has been used in several algorithms and investigations Tong and Koller [2001], Pe'er et al. [2001]. We assumed the manipulation is deterministic. Cooper and Yoo [1999] discuss handling the situation in which the manipulation is stochastic. Cooper [2000] describes learning from a mixture of observational, experimental, and case-control (biased sample) data.

8.1.4 Complexity of Structure Learning

When there are only a few variables, we can exhaustively compute the probability of all possible DAG patterns as was done in the previous examples. We then select the values of gp that maximize $P(d|gp)$. (Note that there could be more than one maximizing pattern.) However, when the number of variables is not small, to find the maximizing DAG patterns by exhaustively considering all DAG patterns is computationally infeasible. We illustrate this next. Robinson [1977] has shown that the number of DAGs containing n nodes is given by the following recurrence:

$$f(n) = \sum_{i=1}^{n}(-1)^{i+1}\binom{n}{i}2^{i(n-i)}f(n-i) \qquad n > 2 \qquad (8.2)$$

$$f(0) = 1$$

$$f(1) = 1.$$

It is left as an exercise to show that $f(2) = 3$, $f(3) = 25$, $f(5) = 29,000$, and $f(10) = 4.2 \times 10^{18}$. There are fewer DAG patterns than there are DAGs, but this number also is forbiddingly large. Indeed, Gillispie and Pearlman [2001] show that an asymptotic ratio of the number of DAGs to DAG patterns equal to about 3.7 is reached when the number of nodes is only 10. Chickering [1996a] has proven that, for certain classes of prior distributions, the problem of finding the most probable DAG patterns is NP-hard.

One way to handle a problem like this is to develop heuristic search algorithms. Such algorithms are the focus of Section 9.1.

8.2 Model Averaging

Heckerman et al. [1999] illustrate that, when the number of variables is small and the amount of data is large, one structure can be orders of magnitude more likely than any other. In such cases, model selection yields good results. However, recall that in Example 8.2 we had little data, we obtained $P(gp_1|d) = .51678$ and $P(gp_2|d) = .48322$, we chose DAG pattern gp_1 because it was the more probable, and we used a Bayesian network based on this pattern to do inference for the 9th case. Since the probabilities of the two models are so close, it seems somewhat arbitrary to choose gp_1. So, model selection does not seem appropriate. Next we describe another approach.

Instead of choosing a single DAG pattern (model) and then using it to do inference, we could use the law of total probability to do the inference as follows: We perform the inference using each DAG pattern and multiply the result (a probability value) by the posterior probably of the structure. This is called **model averaging**.

Example 8.6 *Recall that, given the Bayesian network structure learning schema and data discussed in Example 8.2,*

$$P(gp_1|d) = .51678$$

and

$$P(gp_2|\mathsf{d}) = .48322.$$

Suppose we wish to compute $P(X_1 = 2|X_2 = 1)$ for the 9th trial. Since neither DAG structure is a clear "winner," we could compute this conditional probability by "averaging" over both models. To that end,

$$P(X_1^{(9)} = 2|X_2^{(9)} = 1, \mathsf{d}) = \sum_{i=1}^{2} P(X_1^{(9)} = 2|X_2^{(9)} = 1, gp_i, \mathsf{d})P(gp_i|X_2^{(9)} = 1, \mathsf{d}).$$

$$(8.3)$$

Note that we now explicitly show that this inference concerns the 9th case using a superscript. To compute this probability, we need $P(gp_i|X_2^{(9)} = 1, \mathsf{d})$, but we have $P(gp_i|\mathsf{d})$. We could either approximate the former probability by the latter one, or we could use the technique that will be discussed in Section 8.3 to compute it. For the sake of simplicity, we will approximate it by $P(gp_i|\mathsf{d})$. We have, then,

$$
\begin{aligned}
P(X_1^{(9)} = 2|X_2^{(9)} = 1, \mathsf{d}) &\approx \sum_{i=1}^{2} P(X_1^{(9)} = 2|X_2^{(9)} = 1, gp_i, \mathsf{d})P(gp_i|\mathsf{d}) \\
&= (.28571)(.51678) + (.41667)(.48322) \\
&= .34899.
\end{aligned}
$$

The result that $P(X_1^{(9)} = 2|X_2^{(9)} = 1, gp_1, \mathsf{d}) = .28571$ was obtained in Example 8.2. It is left as an exercise to show that $P(X_1^{(9)} = 2|X_2^{(9)} = 1, gp_2, \mathsf{d}) = .41667$. Note that we obtained a significantly different conditional probability using model averaging than that obtained using model selection in Example 8.2.

As is the case for model selection, when the number of possible structures is large, we cannot average over all structures. In these situations we heuristically search for high probability structures, and then we average over them. Such techniques are discussed in Section 9.2.

8.3　Learning Structure with Missing Data

Suppose now that our data set has data items missing at random as discussed in Section 6.5. Table 8.1 shows such a data set. The straightforward way to handle this situation is to apply the law of total probability and sum over all the variables with missing values. That is, if D is the set of random variables for which we have values, d is the set of these values, and M is the set of random variables whose values are missing, then, for a given DAG G,

$$score_B(\mathsf{d}, \mathbb{G}) = P(\mathsf{d}|\mathbb{G}) = \sum_{\mathsf{m}} P(\mathsf{d}, \mathsf{m}|\mathbb{G}). \tag{8.4}$$

Case	X_1	X_2	X_3
1	1	1	2
2	1	?	1
3	?	1	?
4	1	2	1
5	2	?	?

Table 8.1: Data on five cases with some data items missing

For example, if $\mathbf{X}^{(h)} = \left(\begin{array}{ccc} X_1^{(h)} & \cdots & X_n^{(h)} \end{array} \right)^T$ is a random vector whose value is the data for the hth case in Table 8.1, we have, for the data set in that table,

$$\mathsf{D} = \{X_1^{(1)}, X_2^{(1)}, X_3^{(1)}, X_1^{(2)}, X_3^{(2)}, X_2^{(3)}, X_1^{(4)}, X_2^{(4)}, X_3^{(4)}, X_1^{(5)}\}$$

and

$$\mathsf{M} = \{X_2^{(2)}, X_1^{(3)}, X_3^{(3)}, X_2^{(5)}, X_3^{(5)}\}.$$

We can compute each term in the sum in Equality 8.4 using Equality 8.1. Since this sum is over an exponential number of terms relative to the number of missing data items, we can use it only when the number of missing items is not large. To handle the case of a large number of missing items, we need approximation methods. One approximation method is to use Monte Carlo techniques. We discuss that method first. In practice, the number of calculations needed for this method to be acceptably accurate can be quite large. Another more efficient class of approximations uses large-sample properties of the probability distribution. We discuss that method second.

8.3.1 Monte Carlo Methods

We will use a Monte Carlo method called Gibbs' sampling to approximate the probability of data containing missing items. Gibbs' sampling is one variety of an approximation method called **Markov Chain Monte Carlo (MCMC)**, which we accordingly review first.

Review of Markov Chains and MCMC

First we review Markov chains; then we review MCMC; finally, we show the MCMC method called Gibbs' sampling.

Markov Chains   This exposition is only for the purpose of review. If you are unfamiliar with Markov chains, you should consult a complete introduction as can be found in Feller [1968]. We start with the definition:

Definition 8.3 *A **Markov chain** consists of the following:*

   1. A set of outcomes (states) $e_1, e_2, \ldots$.

Figure 8.3: An urn model of a Markov chain.

2. *For each pair of states e_i and e_j, a transition probability p_{ij} such that*

$$\sum_j p_{ij} = 1.$$

3. *A sequence of trials (random variables) $E^{(1)}, E^{(2)}, \ldots$, such that the outcome of each trial is one of the states and*

$$P(E^{(h+1)} = e_j | E^{(h)} = e_i) = p_{ij}.$$

To completely specify a probability space we need to define initial probabilities $P(E^{(0)} = e_j) = p_j$, but these probabilities are not necessary to our theory and will not be discussed further.

Example 8.7 *Any Markov chain can be represented by an urn model. One such model is shown in Figure 8.3. The Markov chain is obtained by choosing an initial urn according to some probability distribution, picking a ball at random from that urn, moving to the urn indicated on the ball chosen, picking a ball at random from the new urn, and so on.*

The transition probabilities p_{ij} are arranged in a matrix of transition probabilities as follows:

$$\mathbf{P} = \begin{pmatrix} p_{11} & p_{12} & p_{13} & \cdots \\ p_{21} & p_{22} & p_{23} & \cdots \\ p_{31} & p_{32} & p_{33} & \cdots \\ \vdots & \vdots & \vdots & \ddots \end{pmatrix}.$$

This matrix is called the **transition matrix** for the chain.

Example 8.8 *For the Markov chain determined by the urns in Figure 8.3, the transition matrix is*

$$\mathbf{P} = \begin{pmatrix} 1/6 & 1/2 & 1/3 \\ 2/9 & 4/9 & 1/3 \\ 1/2 & 1/3 & 1/6 \end{pmatrix}.$$

A Markov chain is called **finite** if it has a finite number of states. Clearly the chain represented by the urns in Figure 8.3 is finite. We denote by $p_{ij}^{(n)}$ **the probability of a transition from** e_i **to** e_j **in exactly** n **trials**. That is, $p_{ij}^{(n)}$ is the conditional probability of entering e_j at the nth trial given the initial state is e_i. We say e_j **is reachable from** e_i if there exists an $n \geq 0$ such that $p_{ij}^{(n)} > 0$. A Markov chain is called **irreducible** if every state is reachable from every other state.

Example 8.9 *Clearly, if $p_{ij} > 0$ for every i and j, the chain is irreducible.*

The state e_i has **period** $t > 1$ if $p_{ii}^{(n)} = 0$ unless $n = mt$ for some integer m, and t is the largest integer with this property. Such a state is called **periodic**. A state is **aperiodic** if no such $t > 1$ exists.

Example 8.10 *Clearly, if $p_{ii} > 0$, e_i is aperiodic.*

We denote by $f_{ij}^{(n)}$ the probability that starting from e_i, the first entry, to e_j occurs at the nth trial. Furthermore, we let

$$f_{ij} = \sum_{n=1}^{\infty} f_{ij}^{(n)}.$$

Clearly, $f_{ij} \leq 1$. When $f_{ij} = 1$, we call $P_{ij}(n) \equiv f_{ij}^{(n)}$ the **distribution of the first passage** for e_j starting at e_i. In particular, when $f_{ii} = 1$, we call $P_i(n) \equiv f_{ii}^{(n)}$ the **distribution of the recurrence times** for e_i, and we define the **mean recurrence time** for e_i to be

$$\mu_i = \sum_{n=1}^{\infty} n f_{ii}^{(n)}.$$

The state e_i is called **persistent** if $f_{ii} = 1$ and **transient** if $f_{ii} < 1$. A persistent state e_i is called **null** if its mean recurrence time $\mu_i = \infty$ and otherwise it is called **nonnull**.

Example 8.11 *It can be shown that every state in a finite irreducible chain is persistent (Ash [1970]), and that every persistent state in a finite chain is nonnull (Feller [1968]). Therefore, every state in a finite irreducible chain is persistent and nonnull.*

An aperiodic persistent nonnull state is called **ergodic**. A Markov chain is called **ergodic** if all its states are ergodic.

Example 8.12 *Owing to Examples 8.9, 8.10, and 8.11, if in a finite chain we have $p_{ij} > 0$ for every i and j, the chain is an irreducible ergodic chain.*

We have the following theorem concerning irreducible ergodic chains:

Theorem 8.1 *In an irreducible ergodic chain, the limits*

$$r_j = \lim_{n \to \infty} p_{ij}^{(n)} \tag{8.5}$$

exist and are independent of the initial state e_i. Furthermore, $r_j > 0$,

$$\sum_j r_j = 1, \tag{8.6}$$

$$r_j = \sum_i r_i p_{ij}, \tag{8.7}$$

and

$$r_j = \frac{1}{\mu_j},$$

where μ_j is the mean recurrence time of e_j.
    The probability distribution

$$P(E = e_j) \equiv r_j$$

*is called the **stationary distribution** of the Markov chain.*
    Conversely, suppose a chain is irreducible and aperiodic with transition matrix $\mathbf{P}$, and there exist numbers $r_j \geq 0$ satisfying Equalities 8.6 and 8.7. Then the chain is ergodic, and the r_js are given by Equality 8.5.
Proof. *The proof can be found in Feller [1968].*   ∎

We can write Equality 8.7 in the matrix/vector form

$$\mathbf{r}^T = \mathbf{r}^T \mathbf{P}. \tag{8.8}$$

That is,

$$\begin{pmatrix} r_1 & r_2 & r_3 & \cdots \end{pmatrix} = \begin{pmatrix} r_1 & r_2 & r_3 & \cdots \end{pmatrix} \begin{pmatrix} p_{11} & p_{12} & p_{13} & \cdots \\ p_{21} & p_{22} & p_{23} & \cdots \\ p_{31} & p_{32} & p_{33} & \cdots \\ \vdots & \vdots & \vdots & \ddots \end{pmatrix}.$$

Example 8.13 *Suppose we have the Markov chain determined by the urns in Figure 8.3. Then*

$$\begin{pmatrix} r_1 & r_2 & r_3 \end{pmatrix} = \begin{pmatrix} r_1 & r_2 & r_3 \end{pmatrix} \begin{pmatrix} 1/6 & 1/2 & 1/3 \\ 2/9 & 4/9 & 1/3 \\ 1/2 & 1/3 & 1/6 \end{pmatrix}. \tag{8.9}$$

Solving the system of equations determined by Equalities 8.6 and 8.9, we obtain

$$\begin{pmatrix} r_1 & r_2 & r_3 \end{pmatrix} = \begin{pmatrix} 2/7 & 3/7 & 2/7 \end{pmatrix}.$$

This means that for n large, the probabilities of being in states e_1, e_2, and e_3 are respectively about 2/7, 3/7, and 2/7, regardless of the initial state.

MCMC Again our coverage is cursory. See Hastings [1970] for a more thorough introduction.

Suppose that we have a finite set of states $\{e_1, e_2, \ldots, e_s\}$, and a probability distribution $P(E = e_j) \equiv r_j$ defined on the states such that $r_j > 0$ for all j. Suppose further that we have a function f defined on the states, and we wish to estimate

$$I = \sum_{j=1}^{s} f(e_j) r_j.$$

We can obtain an estimate as follows. Given that we have a Markov chain with transition matrix $\mathbf{P}$ such that $\mathbf{r}^T = \begin{pmatrix} r_1 & r_2 & r_3 & \cdots \end{pmatrix}$ is its stationary distribution, we simulate the chain for trials $1, 2, \ldots, M$. Then if k_i is the index of the state occupied at trial i, and

$$I' = \sum_{i=1}^{M} \frac{f(e_{k_i})}{M}, \tag{8.10}$$

the **ergodic theorem** says that $I' \to I$ with probability 1. (See Tierney [1996].) So we can estimate I by I'. This approximation method is called **Markov chain Monte Carlo**. To obtain more rapid convergence, in practice a "burn-in" number of iterations is used so that the probability of being in each state is approximately given by the stationary distribution. The sum in Expression 8.10 is then obtained over all iterations past the burn-in time. Methods for choosing a burn-in time and the number of iterations to use after burn-in are discussed in Gilks et al. [1996].

It is not hard to see why the approximation converges. After a sufficient burn-in time, the chain will be in state e_j about r_j fraction of the time. So, if we do M iterations after burn-in, we would have

$$\sum_{i=1}^{M} f(e_{k_i})/M \approx \sum_{j=1}^{s} \frac{f(e_j) r_j M}{M} = \sum_{j=1}^{s} f(e_j) r_j.$$

To apply this method for a given distribution $\mathbf{r}$, we need to construct a Markov chain with transition matrix $\mathbf{P}$ such that $\mathbf{r}$ is its stationary distribution. Next we show two ways for doing this.

Metropolis–Hastings Method Owing to Theorem 8.1, we see from Equality 8.8 that we need only find an irreducible aperiodic chain such that its transition matrix $\mathbf{P}$ satisfies

$$\mathbf{r}^T = \mathbf{r}^T \mathbf{P}. \tag{8.11}$$

It is not hard to see that if we determine values p_{ij}, such that for all i and j,

$$r_i p_{ij} = r_j p_{ji} \tag{8.12}$$

the resultant $\mathbf{P}$ satisfies Equality 8.11. To determine such values, let $\mathbf{Q}$ be the transition matrix of an arbitrary Markov chain whose states are the members of our given finite set of states $\{e_1, e_2, \ldots, e_s\}$, and let

$$
\alpha_{ij} = \begin{cases} \dfrac{s_{ij}}{1 + \dfrac{r_i q_{ij}}{r_j q_{ji}}} & q_{ij} \neq 0,\ q_{ji} \neq 0 \\[4ex] 0 & q_{ij} = 0 \text{ or } q_{ji} = 0 \end{cases} , \tag{8.13}
$$

where s_{ij} is a symmetric function of i and j chosen so that $0 \leq \alpha_{ij} \leq 1$ for all i and j. We then take

$$
\begin{aligned}
p_{ij} &= \alpha_{ij} q_{ij} & i \neq j \\
p_{ii} &= 1 - \sum_{j \neq i} p_{ij}.
\end{aligned} \tag{8.14}
$$

It is straightforward to show that the resultant values of p_{ij} satisfy Equality 8.12. The irreducibility of $\mathbf{P}$ must be checked in each application.

Hastings [1970] suggests the following way of choosing $\mathbf{s}$: If q_{ij} and q_{ji} are both nonzero, set

$$
s_{ij} = \begin{cases} 1 + \dfrac{r_i q_{ij}}{r_j q_{ji}} & \dfrac{r_j q_{ji}}{r_i q_{ij}} \geq 1 \\[4ex] 1 + \dfrac{r_j q_{ji}}{r_i q_{ij}} & \dfrac{r_j q_{ji}}{r_i q_{ij}} \leq 1 \end{cases} . \tag{8.15}
$$

Given this choice, we have

$$
\alpha_{ij} = \begin{cases} 1 & q_{ij} \neq 0,\ q_{ji} \neq 0,\ \dfrac{r_j q_{ji}}{r_i q_{ij}} \geq 1 \\[3ex] \dfrac{r_j q_{ji}}{r_i q_{ij}} & q_{ij} \neq 0,\ q_{ji} \neq 0,\ \dfrac{r_j q_{ji}}{r_i q_{ij}} \leq 1 \\[3ex] 0 & q_{ij} = 0 \text{ or } q_{ji} = 0 \end{cases} . \tag{8.16}
$$

If we make $\mathbf{Q}$ symmetric (i.e., $q_{ij} = q_{ji}$ for all i and j), we have the method devised by Metropolis et al. (1953). In this case,

$$
\alpha_{ij} = \begin{cases} 1 & q_{ij} \neq 0,\ r_j \geq r_i \\[2ex] r_j/r_i & q_{ij} \neq 0,\ r_j \leq r_i \\[2ex] 0 & q_{ij} = 0 \end{cases} . \tag{8.17}
$$

Note that with this choice if $\mathbf{Q}$ is irreducible so is $\mathbf{P}$.

Example 8.14 *Suppose* $\mathbf{r}^T = \begin{pmatrix} 1/8 & 3/8 & 1/2 \end{pmatrix}$. *Choose* $\mathbf{Q}$ *symmetric as follows:*

$$\mathbf{Q} = \begin{pmatrix} 1/3 & 1/3 & 1/3 \\ 1/3 & 1/3 & 1/3 \\ 1/3 & 1/3 & 1/3 \end{pmatrix}.$$

Choose s *according to Equality 8.15 so that* α *has the values in Equality 8.17. We then have*

$$\alpha = \begin{pmatrix} 1 & 1 & 1 \\ 1/3 & 1 & 1 \\ 1/4 & 3/4 & 1 \end{pmatrix}.$$

Using Equality 8.14, we have

$$\mathbf{P} = \begin{pmatrix} 1/3 & 1/3 & 1/3 \\ 1/9 & 5/9 & 1/3 \\ 1/12 & 1/4 & 2/3 \end{pmatrix}.$$

Notice that

$$\mathbf{r}^T\mathbf{P} = \begin{pmatrix} 1/8 & 3/8 & 1/2 \end{pmatrix} \begin{pmatrix} 1/3 & 1/3 & 1/3 \\ 1/9 & 5/9 & 1/3 \\ 1/12 & 1/4 & 2/3 \end{pmatrix}$$
$$= \begin{pmatrix} 1/8 & 3/8 & 1/2 \end{pmatrix} = \mathbf{r}^T,$$

as it should.

Once we have constructed matrices $\mathbf{Q}$ and α as discussed above, we can conduct the simulation as follows:

1. Given that the state occupied at the kth trial is e_i, choose a state using the probability distribution given by the ith row of $\mathbf{Q}$. Suppose that state is e_j.

2. Choose the state occupied at the $(k+1)$st trial to be e_j with probability α_{ij} and to be e_i with probability $1 - \alpha_{ij}$.

In this way, when state e_i is the current state, e_j will be chosen q_{ij} fraction of the time in Step (1), and of those times e_j will be chosen α_{ij} fraction of the time in Step (2). So overall, e_j will be chosen $\alpha_{ij}q_{ij} = p_{ij}$ fraction of the time (Equality 8.14), which is what we want.

Gibbs' Sampling Method   Next we show another method for creating a Markov chain whose stationary distribution is a particular distribution. The method is called **Gibbs' sampling**, and it deals with the case in which we have n random variables $X_1, X_2, \ldots, X_n$ and a joint probability distribution P of the variables (as in a Bayesian network). If we let $\mathbf{X} = \left(\begin{array}{ccc} X_1 & \cdots & X_n \end{array} \right)^T$, we want to approximate

$$\sum_{\mathbf{x}} f(\mathbf{x}) P(\mathbf{x}).$$

To approximate this sum using MCMC, we need to create a Markov chain whose set of states is all possible values of $\mathbf{X}$, and whose stationary distribution is $P(\mathbf{x})$. We do this as follows: The transition probability in our chain for going from state $\mathbf{x}'$ to $\mathbf{x}''$ is defined to be the product of these conditional probabilities:

$$P(x_1''|x_2', x_3', \ldots, x_n')$$
$$P(x_2''|x_1'', x_3', \ldots, x_n')$$
$$\vdots$$
$$P(x_k''|x_1'', \ldots, x_{k-1}'', x_{k+1}' \cdots, x_n')$$
$$\vdots$$
$$P(x_n''|x_1'', \ldots, , x_{n-1}'', x_n'').$$

We can implement these transition probabilities by choosing the event in each trial using n steps as follows. If we let $p_k(\mathbf{x}; \hat{\mathbf{x}})$ denote the transition probability from $\mathbf{x}$ to $\hat{\mathbf{x}}$ in the kth step, we set

$$p_k(\mathbf{x}; \hat{\mathbf{x}}) = \begin{cases} P(\hat{x}_k|\hat{x}_1, \ldots, \hat{x}_{k-1}, \hat{x}_{k+1} \cdots, \hat{x}_n) & \hat{x}_j = x_j \text{ for all } j \neq k \\ 0 & \text{otherwise.} \end{cases}$$

That is, we do the following for the hth trial:

Pick $x_1^{(h)}$ using the distribution $P(x_1|x_2^{(h-1)}, x_3^{(h-1)}, \ldots, x_n^{(h-1)})$.

Pick $x_2^{(h)}$ using the distribution $P(x_2|x_1^{(h)}, x_3^{(h-1)}, \ldots, x_n^{(h-1)})$.

$\vdots$

Pick $x_k^{(h)}$ using the distribution $P(x_k|x_1^{(h)}, \ldots, x_{k-1}^{(h)}, x_{k+1}^{(h-1)} \cdots, x_n^{(h-1)})$.

$\vdots$

Pick $x_n^{(h)}$ using the distribution $P(x_n|x_1^{(h)}, \ldots, , x_{n-1}^{(h)}, x_n^{(h-1)})$.

Notice that in the kth step, all variables except $x_k^{(h)}$ are unchanged, and the new value of $x_k^{(h)}$ is drawn from its distribution conditional on the current values of all the other variables.

As long as all conditional probabilities are nonzero, the chain is irreducible. Next we verify that $P(\mathbf{x})$ is the stationary distribution for the chain. If we let $p(\mathbf{x}; \hat{\mathbf{x}})$ denote the transition probability from $\mathbf{x}$ to $\hat{\mathbf{x}}$ in each trial, we need to show

$$P(\hat{\mathbf{x}}) = \sum_{\mathbf{x}} P(\mathbf{x}) p(\mathbf{x}; \hat{\mathbf{x}}). \tag{8.18}$$

It is not hard to see that it suffices to show that Equality 8.18 holds for each step of each trial. To that end, for the kth step, we have

$$\sum_{\mathbf{x}} P(\mathbf{x}) p_k(\mathbf{x}; \hat{\mathbf{x}})$$

$$= \sum_{x_1, \ldots, x_n} P(x_1, \ldots, x_n) p_k(x_1, \ldots, x_n; \hat{x}_1, \ldots, \hat{x}_n)$$

$$= \sum_{x_k} P(\hat{x}_1, \ldots, \hat{x}_{k-1}, x_k, \hat{x}_{k+1} \ldots, \hat{x}_n) P(\hat{x}_k | \hat{x}_1, \ldots, \hat{x}_{k-1}, \hat{x}_{k+1} \ldots, \hat{x}_n)$$

$$= P(\hat{x}_k | \hat{x}_1, \ldots, \hat{x}_{k-1}, \hat{x}_{k+1} \ldots, \hat{x}_n) \sum_{x_k} P(\hat{x}_1, \ldots, \hat{x}_{k-1}, x_k, \hat{x}_{k+1} \ldots, \hat{x}_n)$$

$$= P(\hat{x}_k | \hat{x}_1, \ldots, \hat{x}_{k-1}, \hat{x}_{k+1} \ldots, \hat{x}_n) P(\hat{x}_1, \ldots, \hat{x}_{k-1}, \hat{x}_{k+1} \ldots, \hat{x}_n)$$

$$= P(\hat{x}_1, \ldots, \hat{x}_{k-1}, \hat{x}_k, \hat{x}_{k+1} \ldots, \hat{x}_n)$$

$$= P(\hat{\mathbf{x}}).$$

The second step follows because $p_k(\mathbf{x}; \hat{\mathbf{x}}) = 0$ unless $\hat{x}_j = x_j$ for all $j \neq k$. See Geman and Geman [1984] for more on Gibbs' sampling.

Learning with Missing Data Using Gibbs' Sampling

The Gibbs' sampling approach we use is called the **Candidate method**. (See Chib [1995].) The approach proceeds as follows: Let $\mathbf{d}$ be the set of values of the variables for which we have values. By Bayes' theorem, we have

$$P(\mathbf{d}|\mathbb{G}) = \frac{P(\mathbf{d}|\check{\mathbf{f}}^{(\mathbb{G})}, \mathbb{G}) \rho(\check{\mathbf{f}}^{(\mathbb{G})}|\mathbb{G})}{\rho(\check{\mathbf{f}}^{(\mathbb{G})}|\mathbf{d}, \mathbb{G})}, \tag{8.19}$$

where $\check{\mathbf{f}}^{(\mathbb{G})}$ is an arbitrary assignment of values to the parameters in $\mathbb{G}$. To approximate $P(\mathbf{d}|\mathbb{G})$ we choose some value of $\check{\mathbf{f}}^{(\mathbb{G})}$, evaluate the numerator in Equality 8.19 exactly, and approximate the denominator using Gibbs' sampling. For the denominator, we have

$$\rho(\check{\mathbf{f}}^{(\mathbb{G})}|\mathbf{d}, \mathbb{G}) = \sum_{\mathbf{m}} \rho(\check{\mathbf{f}}^{(\mathbb{G})}|\mathbf{d}, \mathbf{m}, \mathbb{G}) P(\mathbf{m}|\mathbf{d}, \mathbb{G}),$$

where $\mathbf{M}$ is the set of variables that have missing values.

To approximate this sum using Gibbs' sampling we do the following:

1. Initialize the state of the unobserved variables to arbitrary values yielding a complete data set $\mathbf{d}_1$.

2. Choose some unobserved variable $X_i^{(h)}$ arbitrarily and obtain a value of $X_i^{(h)}$, using

$$P(x_i'^{(h)}|\mathsf{d}_1 - \{\check{x}_i^{(h)}\}, \mathbb{G}) = \frac{P(x_i'^{(h)}, \mathsf{d}_1 - \{\check{x}_i^{(h)}\}|\mathbb{G})}{\sum\limits_{x_i^{(h)}} P(x_i^{(h)}, \mathsf{d}_1 - \{\check{x}_i^{(h)}\}|\mathbb{G})},$$

where $\check{x}_i^{(h)}$ is the value of $X_i^{(h)}$ in d_1, and the sum is taken over all values in the space of $X_i^{(h)}$. The terms in the numerator and denominator can be computed using Equality 8.1.

3. Repeat step (2) for all the other unobserved variables, where the complete data set used in the $(k+1)$st iteration contains the values obtained in the previous k iterations.

   This will yield a new complete data set d_2.

4. Iterate the previous two steps some number R times, where the complete data set from the jth iteration is used in the $(j+1)$st iteration. In this manner R complete data sets will be generated. For each complete data set d_j, compute

$$\rho(\check{\mathsf{f}}^{(\mathbb{G})}|\mathsf{d}_j, \mathbb{G}),$$

   using Corollary 7.7.

5. Approximate

$$\rho(\check{\mathsf{f}}^{(\mathbb{G})}|\mathsf{d}, \mathbb{G}) \approx \frac{\sum_{j=1}^{R} \rho(\check{\mathsf{f}}^{(\mathbb{G})}|\mathsf{d}_j, \mathbb{G})}{R}.$$

Although the Candidate method can be applied with any value of $\check{\mathsf{f}}^{(\mathbb{G})}$ of the parameters, some assignments lead to faster convergence. Chickering and Heckerman [1997] discuss methods for choosing the value.

8.3.2   Large-Sample Approximations

Although Gibbs' sampling is accurate, the amount of computer time needed to achieve accuracy can be quite large. An alternative approach is the use of large-sample approximations. Large-sample approximations require only a single computation and choose the correct model in the limit. So they can be used when the size of the data set is large. We discuss four large-sample approximations next.

Before doing this, we need to further discuss the MAP and ML values of the parameter set. Recall that in Section 6.5 we introduced these values in a context specific to binomial Bayesian networks and in which we did not need to specify a DAG because the DAG was part of our background knowledge.

We now provide notation appropriate to this chapter. Given a multinomial augmented Bayesian network $(\mathbb{G}, \mathsf{F}^{(\mathbb{G})}, \rho | \mathbb{G})$, the **MAP** value $\tilde{\mathsf{f}}^{(\mathbb{G})}$ of $\mathsf{f}^{(\mathbb{G})}$ is the value that maximizes $\rho(\mathsf{f}^{(\mathbb{G})} | \mathsf{d}, \mathbb{G})$, and the **maximum likelihood (ML)** value $\hat{\mathsf{f}}^{(\mathbb{G})}$ of $\mathsf{f}^{(\mathbb{G})}$ is the value such that $P(\mathsf{d} | \mathsf{f}^{(\mathbb{G})}, \mathbb{G})$ is a maximum. In the case of missing data items, Algorithm 6.1 (EM-MAP-determination) can be used to obtain approximations to these values. That is, if we apply Algorithm 6.1 and we obtain the values $s_{ijk}'^{\mathbb{G}}$, then

$$\tilde{f}_{ijk}^{(\mathbb{G})} \approx \frac{a_{ijk}^{(\mathbb{G})} + s_{ijk}'^{(\mathbb{G})}}{\sum_{k=1}^{r_i} \left(a_{ijk}^{(\mathbb{G})} + s_{ijk}'^{(\mathbb{G})} \right)}.$$

Similarly, if we modify Algorithm 6.1 to estimate the ML value (as discussed after the algorithm) and we obtain the values $s_{ijk}'^{\mathbb{G}}$, then

$$\hat{f}_{ijk}^{(\mathbb{G})} \approx \frac{s_{ijk}'^{(\mathbb{G})}}{\sum_{k=1}^{r_i} s_{ijk}'^{(\mathbb{G})}}.$$

In the case of missing data items, these approximations are the ones that would be used to compute the MAP and ML values in the formulas we develop next.

The Laplace Approximation

First we derive the Laplace approximation. This approximation is based on the assumptions that $\rho(\mathsf{f}^{(\mathbb{G})} | \mathsf{d}, \mathbb{G})$ has a unique MAP value $\hat{\mathsf{f}}^{(\mathbb{G})}$ and its logarithm allows a Taylor series expansion about $\hat{\mathsf{f}}^{(\mathbb{G})}$. These conditions hold for multinomial augmented Bayesian networks. As we shall see in Section 8.5.3, they do not hold when we consider DAGs with hidden variables.

For the sake of notational simplicity, we do not show the dependence on $\mathbb{G}$ in this derivation. We have

$$P(\mathsf{d}) = \int P(\mathsf{d} | \mathsf{f}) \rho(\mathsf{f}) d\mathsf{f}. \tag{8.20}$$

Towards obtaining an approximation of this integral, let

$$g(\mathsf{f}) = \ln \left(P(\mathsf{d} | \mathsf{f}) \rho(\mathsf{f}) \right).$$

Owing to Bayes' theorem,

$$g(\mathsf{f}) = \ln \left(\alpha \rho(\mathsf{f} | \mathsf{d}) \right),$$

where α is a normalizing constant, which means that $g(\mathsf{f})$ achieves a maximum at the MAP value $\tilde{\mathsf{f}}$. Our derivation proceeds by taking the Taylor series expansion of $g(\mathsf{f})$ about $\tilde{\mathsf{f}}$. To write this expansion we denote f as a random vector $\mathbf{f}$. That is, $\mathbf{f}$ is the random vector whose components are the members of the set f. We denote $\tilde{\mathsf{f}}$ by $\tilde{\mathbf{f}}$. Discarding terms past the second derivative, this expansion is

$$g(\mathbf{f}) \approx g(\tilde{\mathbf{f}}) + (\mathbf{f} - \tilde{\mathbf{f}})^T g'(\tilde{\mathbf{f}}) + \frac{1}{2} (\mathbf{f} - \tilde{\mathbf{f}})^T g''(\tilde{\mathbf{f}}) (\mathbf{f} - \tilde{\mathbf{f}}),$$

where $g'(\mathbf{f})$ is the vector of first partial derivatives of $g(\mathbf{f})$ evaluated with respect to every parameter f_{ijk}, and $g''(\mathbf{f})$ is the **Hessian matrix** of second partial derivatives of $g(\mathbf{f})$ evaluated with respect to every pair of parameters $(f_{ijk}, f_{i'j'k'})$. That is,

$$g'(\mathbf{f}) = \left(\begin{array}{ccc} \frac{\partial g(\mathbf{f})}{\partial f_{111}} & \frac{\partial g(\mathbf{f})}{\partial f_{112}} & \cdots \end{array} \right)$$

and

$$g''(\mathbf{f}) = \left(\begin{array}{ccc} \frac{\partial^2 g(\mathbf{f})}{\partial f_{111}\partial f_{111}} & \frac{\partial^2 g(\mathbf{f})}{\partial f_{111}\partial f_{112}} & \cdots \\ \frac{\partial^2 g(\mathbf{f})}{\partial f_{112}\partial f_{111}} & \ddots & \cdots \\ \vdots & \vdots & \ddots \end{array} \right).$$

Now $g'(\tilde{\mathbf{f}}) = 0$ because $g(\mathbf{f})$ achieves a maximum at $\tilde{\mathbf{f}}$, which means its derivative is equal to zero at that point. Therefore,

$$g(\mathbf{f}) \approx g(\tilde{\mathbf{f}}) + \frac{1}{2}(\mathbf{f} - \tilde{\mathbf{f}})^T g''(\tilde{\mathbf{f}})(\mathbf{f} - \tilde{\mathbf{f}}). \tag{8.21}$$

By $\approx$ we mean "about equal to." The approximation in Equality 8.21 is guaranteed to be good only if $\mathbf{f}$ is close to $\tilde{\mathbf{f}}$. However, when the size of the data set is large, the value of $P(\mathbf{d}|\mathbf{f})$ declines fast as one moves away from $\tilde{\mathbf{f}}$, which means only values of $\mathbf{f}$ close to $\tilde{\mathbf{f}}$ contribute much to the integral in Equality 8.20. This argument is formalized in Tierney and Kadane [1986].

Owing to Equality 8.21, we have

$$\begin{aligned} P(\mathbf{d}) &= \int P(\mathbf{d}|\mathbf{f})\rho(\mathbf{f})d\mathbf{f} \\ &= \int \exp\left(g(\mathbf{f})\right) d\mathbf{f} \\ &\approx \exp\left(g(\tilde{\mathbf{f}})\right) \int \exp\left(\frac{1}{2}(\mathbf{f} - \tilde{\mathbf{f}})^T g''(\tilde{\mathbf{f}})(\mathbf{f} - \tilde{\mathbf{f}})\right) d\mathbf{f}. \end{aligned} \tag{8.22}$$

Recognizing that the expression inside the integral in Equality 8.22 is proportional to a multivariate normal density function (Section 7.2.2), we obtain that

$$P(\mathbf{d}) \approx \exp\left(g(\tilde{\mathbf{f}})\right) 2\pi^{d/2} |\mathbf{A}|^{-1/2} = \exp\left(P(\mathbf{d}|\tilde{\mathbf{f}})\rho(\tilde{\mathbf{f}})\right) 2\pi^{d/2} |\mathbf{A}|^{-1/2}, \tag{8.23}$$

where $\mathbf{A} = -g''(\tilde{\mathbf{f}})$, and d is the number of parameters in the network, which is $\sum_{i=1}^{n} q_i(r_i - 1)$. Recall that r_i is the number of states of X_i and q_i is the number of possible instantiations of the parents PA_i of X_i. In general, d is the **dimension** of the model given data $\mathbf{d}$ in the region of $\tilde{\mathbf{f}}$. If we do not make the assumptions leading to Equality 8.23, d is not necessarily the number of parameters in the network. We discuss such a case in Section 8.5.3. We have, then,

$$\ln\left(P(\mathbf{d})\right) \approx \ln\left(P(\mathbf{d}|\tilde{\mathbf{f}})\right) + \ln\left(\rho(\tilde{\mathbf{f}})\right) + \frac{d}{2}\ln(2\pi) - \frac{1}{2}\ln|\mathbf{A}|. \tag{8.24}$$

The expression in Equality 8.24 is called the **Laplace approximation** or **Laplace score**. Reverting back to showing the dependence on $\mathbb{G}$ and denoting the parameter set again as a set, we have that this approximation is given by

$$Laplace\,(\mathsf{d}, \mathbb{G}) \equiv \ln\left(P(\mathsf{d}|\tilde{\mathsf{f}}^{(\mathbb{G})}, \mathbb{G})\right) + \ln\left(\rho(\tilde{\mathsf{f}}^{(\mathbb{G})}|\mathbb{G})\right) + \frac{d}{2}\ln(2\pi) - \frac{1}{2}\ln|\mathbf{A}|.$$

(8.25)

To select a model using this approximation, we choose a DAG (and thereby the DAG pattern representing the equivalence class to which the DAG belongs) which maximizes $Laplace\,(\mathsf{d}, \mathbb{G})$. The value of $P(\mathsf{d}|\tilde{\mathsf{f}}^{(\mathbb{G})}, \mathbb{G})$ can be computed using a Bayesian network inference algorithm.

We say an approximation method for learning a DAG model is **asymptotically correct** if, for M (the sample size) sufficiently large, the DAG selected by the approximation method is one that maximizes $P(\mathsf{d}|\mathbb{G})$. Kass et al. [1988] show that under certain regularity conditions,

$$|\ln\left(P(\mathsf{d}|\mathbb{G})\right) - Laplace\,(\mathsf{d}, \mathbb{G})| \in O(1/M),$$

(8.26)

where M is the sample size and the constant depends on $\mathbb{G}$. For the sake of simplicity we have not shown the dependence of d on M. It is not hard to see that Relation 8.26 implies the Laplace approximation is asymptotically correct.

The BIC Approximation

It is computationally costly to determine the value of $|\mathbf{A}|$ in the Laplace approximation. A more efficient but less accurate approximation can be obtained by retaining only those terms in Equality 8.25 that are not bounded as M increases. Furthermore, as M approaches ∞, the determinant $|\mathbf{A}|$ approaches a constant times M^d, and the MAP value $\tilde{\mathsf{f}}^{(\mathbb{G})}$ approaches the ML value $\hat{\mathsf{f}}^{(\mathbb{G})}$. Retaining only the unbounded terms, replacing $|\mathbf{A}|$ by M^d, and using $\hat{\mathsf{f}}^{(\mathbb{G})}$ instead of $\tilde{\mathsf{f}}^{(\mathbb{G})}$, we obtain the **Bayesian information criterion(BIC) approximation** or **BIC score**, which is

$$BIC\,(\mathsf{d}, \mathbb{G}) \equiv \ln\left(P(\mathsf{d}|\hat{\mathsf{f}}^{(\mathbb{G})}, \mathbb{G})\right) - \frac{d}{2}\ln M.$$

Schwarz [1978] first derived the BIC approximation. It is not hard to see that Relation 8.26 implies that

$$|\ln\left(P(\mathsf{d}|\mathbb{G})\right) - BIC\,(\mathsf{d}, \mathbb{G})| \in O(1).$$

(8.27)

It is possible to show that the following two conditions hold for a multinomial Bayesian network structure learning space. (Note that we are now showing the dependence of d on M.)

1. If we assign proper prior distributions to the parameters, for every DAG $\mathbb{G}$ we have

$$\lim_{M\to\infty} P(\mathsf{d}_M|\mathbb{G}) = 0.$$

2. If $\mathbb{G}_M$ is a DAG that maximizes $P(\mathsf{d}_M|\mathbb{G})$, then for every $\mathbb{G}$ not in the same Markov equivalence class as $\mathbb{G}_M$,

$$\lim_{M \to \infty} \frac{P(\mathsf{d}_M|\mathbb{G})}{P(\mathsf{d}_M|\mathbb{G}_M)} = 0.$$

It is left as an exercise to show that these two facts, along with Relation 8.27, imply that the BIC approximation is asymptotically correct.

The BIC approximation is intuitively appealing because it contains (1) a term that shows how well the model predicts the data when the parameter set is equal to its ML value and (2) a term that punishes for model complexity. Another nice feature of the BIC is that it does not depend on the prior distribution of the parameters, which means there is no need to assess one.

The MLED Score

Recall that to handle missing values when learning parameter values we used Algorithm 6.1 (EM-MAP-determination) to estimate the MAP value $\tilde{\mathsf{f}}$ of the parameter set f. The fact that the MAP value maximizes the posterior distribution of the parameters suggests approximating the probability of d using a fictitious data set d' that is consistent with the MAP value. That is, we use the number of occurrences obtained in Algorithm 6.1 as the number of occurrences in an imaginary data set d' to obtain an approximation. We have, then,

$$MLED\,(\mathsf{d}, \mathbb{G}) \equiv P(\mathsf{d}'|\mathbb{G}) = \prod_{i=1}^{n} \prod_{j=1}^{q_i^{(\mathbb{G})}} \frac{\Gamma(N_{ij}^{(\mathbb{G})})}{\Gamma(N_{ij}^{(\mathbb{G})} + M_{ij}^{(\mathbb{G})})} \prod_{k=1}^{r_i} \frac{\Gamma(a_{ijk}^{(\mathbb{G})} + s_{ijk}'^{(\mathbb{G})})}{\Gamma(a_{ijk}^{(\mathbb{G})})},$$

where the values of $s_{ijk}'^{(\mathbb{G})}$ are obtained using Algorithm 6.1. We call this approximation the **marginal likelihood of the expected data (MLED) score**. Note that we do not call MLED an approximation because it computes the probability of fictitious data set d', and d' could be substantially larger than d, which means it could have a much smaller probability. So MLED could be used only to select a DAG pattern, not to approximate the probability of data given a DAG pattern.

Using MLED, we select a DAG pattern that maximizes $P(\mathsf{d}'|\mathbb{G})$. However, as discussed in Chickering and Heckerman [1996], a problem with MLED is that it is not asymptotically correct. Next we develop an adjustment to it that is asymptotically correct.

The Cheeseman–Stutz Approximation

The **Cheeseman–Stutz approximation** or **CS score**, which was originally proposed in Cheeseman and Stutz [1995], is given by

$$CS(\mathsf{d}, \mathbb{G}) \equiv \ln\left(P(\mathsf{d}'|\mathbb{G})\right) - \ln\left(P(\mathsf{d}'|\hat{\mathsf{f}}^{(\mathbb{G})}, \mathbb{G})\right) + \ln\left(P(\mathsf{d}|\hat{\mathsf{f}}^{(\mathbb{G})}, \mathbb{G})\right),$$

where d' is the imaginary data set introduced in the previous subsection. The value of $P(\mathsf{d}'|\hat{\mathsf{f}}^{(\mathbb{G})}, \mathbb{G})$ can readily be computed using Lemma 6.11. The formula in that lemma extends immediately to multinomial Bayesian networks.

Next we show that the CS approximation is asymptotically correct. We have

$$
\begin{aligned}
CS(\mathsf{d}, \mathbb{G}) &\equiv \ln\left(P(\mathsf{d}'|\mathbb{G})\right) - \ln\left(P(\mathsf{d}'|\hat{\mathsf{f}}^{(\mathbb{G})}, \mathbb{G})\right) + \ln\left(P(\mathsf{d}|\hat{\mathsf{f}}^{(\mathbb{G})}, \mathbb{G})\right) \\
&= \ln\left(P(\mathsf{d}'|\mathbb{G})\right) - \left[BIC\left(\mathsf{d}', \mathbb{G}\right) + \frac{d}{2}\ln M\right] + \left[BIC\left(\mathsf{d}, \mathbb{G}\right) + \frac{d}{2}\ln M\right] \\
&= \ln\left(P(\mathsf{d}'|\mathbb{G})\right) - BIC\left(\mathsf{d}', \mathbb{G}\right) + BIC\left(\mathsf{d}, \mathbb{G}\right).
\end{aligned}
$$

So

$$
\begin{aligned}
&\ln\left(P(\mathsf{d}|\mathbb{G})\right) - CS(\mathsf{d}, \mathbb{G}) \\
&\qquad = \left[\ln\left(P(\mathsf{d}|\mathbb{G})\right) - BIC\left(\mathsf{d}, \mathbb{G}\right)\right] + \left[BIC\left(\mathsf{d}', \mathbb{G}\right) - \ln\left(P(\mathsf{d}'|\mathbb{G})\right)\right]. \qquad (8.28)
\end{aligned}
$$

Relation 8.27 and Equality 8.28 imply that

$$
\left|\ln\left(P(\mathsf{d}|\mathbb{G})\right) - CS\left(\mathsf{d}, \mathbb{G}\right)\right| \in O(1),
$$

which means that the CS approximation is asymptotically correct.

The CS approximation is intuitively appealing for the following reason. If we use this approximation to actually estimate the value of $\ln(P(\mathsf{d}|\mathbb{G}))$, then our estimate of $P(\mathsf{d}|\mathbb{G})$ is given by

$$
P(\mathsf{d}|\mathbb{G}) \approx \left[\frac{P(\mathsf{d}'|\mathbb{G})}{P(\mathsf{d}'|\hat{\mathsf{f}}^{(\mathbb{G})}, \mathbb{G})}\right] P(\mathsf{d}|\hat{\mathsf{f}}^{(\mathbb{G})}, \mathbb{G}).
$$

That is, we approximate the probability of the data by its probability given the ML value of the parameter set, but with an adjustment based on d'.

A Comparison of the Approximations

Chickering and Heckerman [1997] compared the accuracy and computer processing times of the approximations methods. Their analysis is very detailed, and you should consult the original source for a complete understanding of their results. Briefly, they used a model to generate data, and then compared the results of the Laplace, BIC, and CS approximations to those of the Gibbs' sampling Candidate method. That is, this latter method was considered the gold standard. Furthermore, they used both MAP and ML values in the BIC and CS. (We presented them with ML values.)

First, they used the Laplace, BIC, and CS approximations as approximations of the probability of the data given candidate models. They compared these results with the probabilities obtained using the Candidate method. They found that the CS approximation was more accurate with the MAP values, but the BIC approximation was more accurate with the ML values. Furthermore, with the MAP values, the CS approximation was about as accurate as the Laplace approximation, and both were significantly more accurate than the BIC approximation. This result is not unexpected since the BIC approximation includes a constant term.

In the case of model selection, we are really concerned only with how well the method selects the correct model. Chickering and Heckerman [1997] also compared the models selected by the approximation methods with that selected by the Candidate method. They found that the CS and Laplace approximations both selected models which were very close to that selected by the Candidate method, and the BIC approximation did somewhat worse. Again the CS approximation performed better with the MAP values.

As for computer time usage, the order is as we would expect. If we consider the time used by the EM algorithm separately, the time usage, in increasing order is as follows: (1) BIC/CS, (2) EM, (3) Laplace, (4) Candidate. Furthermore, the time usage increased significantly with model dimension for the Laplace algorithm, whereas it hardly increased for the BIC, CS, and EM algorithms. As the dimension went from 130 to 780, the time usage for the Laplace algorithm increased over 10 fold to over 100 seconds and approached that of the Candidate algorithm. On the other hand, the time usage for the BIC and CS algorithms stayed close to 1 second, and the time usage for the EM algorithm stayed close to 10 seconds.

Given the preceding, of the approximation methods presented here, the CS approximation seems to be the method of choice. Chickering and Heckerman [1996], Chickering and Heckerman [1997] discuss other approximations based on the Laplace approximation, which fared about as well as the CS approximation in their studies.

8.4   Probabilistic Model Selection

The structure learning problem discussed in Section 8.1 is an example of a more general problem called probabilistic model selection. After defining "probabilistic model," we discuss the general problem of model selection. Finally we show that the selection method we developed satisfies an important criterion (namely consistency) for a model selection methodology.

8.4.1   Probabilistic Models

A **probabilistic model** $\mathcal{M}$ for a set V of random variables is a set of joint probability distributions of the variables. Ordinarily, a model is specified using a parameter set F and combinatoric rules for determining the joint probability distribution from the parameter set. Each member of the model is then obtained by assigning values to the members of F and applying the rules. If probability distribution P is a member of model $\mathcal{M}$, we say P is **included** in $\mathcal{M}$. If the probability distributions in a model are obtained by assignments of values to the members of a parameter set F, this means that there is some assignment of values to the parameters that yields the probability distribution. Note that this definition of "included" is a generalization of the one in Section 2.3.2. An example of a probabilistic model follows.

Example 8.15 *Suppose we are going to toss a die and a coin, neither of which is known to be fair. Let X be a random variable whose value is the outcome of the die toss, and let Y be a random variable whose value is the outcome of the coin toss. Then the space of X is $\{1, 2, 3, 4, 5, 6\}$ and the space of Y is $\{heads, tails\}$. The following is a probabilistic model $\mathcal{M}$ for the joint probability distribution of X and Y:*

1. $\mathsf{F} = \{f_{11}, f_{12}, f_{13}, f_{14}, f_{15}, f_{16}, f_{21}, f_{22}\}$, $0 \leq f_{ij} \leq 1$, $\sum_{j=1}^{6} f_{1j} = 1$, $\sum_{j=1}^{2} f_{2j} = 1$.

2. *For each permissible combination of the parameters in F, obtain a member of $\mathcal{M}$ as follows:*

$$P(X = i, Y = heads) = f_{1i} f_{21}$$

$$P(X = i, Y = tails) = f_{1i} f_{22}.$$

Any probability distribution of X and Y for which X and Y are independent is included in $\mathcal{M}$; any probability distribution of X and Y for which X and Y are not independent is not included $\mathcal{M}$.

A **Bayesian network model** (also called a **DAG model**) consists of a DAG $\mathbb{G} = (\mathsf{V}, \mathsf{E})$, where V is a set of random variables, and a parameter set F whose members determine conditional probability distributions for the DAG, such that for every permissible assignment of values to the members of F, the joint probability distribution of V is given by the product of these conditional distributions and this joint probability distribution satisfies the Markov condition with the DAG. Theorem 1.5 shows that, if F determines discrete probability distributions, the product of the conditional distributions will satisfy the Markov condition. After this theorem, we noted that the result also holds if F determines Gaussian distributions. For simplicity, we ordinarily denote a Bayesian network model using only $\mathbb{G}$ (i.e., we do not show F). Note that an augmented Bayesian network (Definition 6.8) is based on a Bayesian network model. That is, given an augmented Bayesian network $(\mathbb{G}, \mathsf{F}^{(\mathbb{G})}, \rho | \mathbb{G})$, $(\mathbb{G}, \mathsf{F}^{(\mathbb{G})})$ is a Bayesian network model. We say the augmented Bayesian network **contains** the Bayesian network model.

Example 8.16 *Bayesian network models appear in Figures 8.4 (a) and (b). The probability distribution contained in the Bayesian network in Figure 8.4 (c) is included in both models, whereas the one in the Bayesian network in Figure 8.4 (d) is included only in the model in Figure 8.4 (b).*

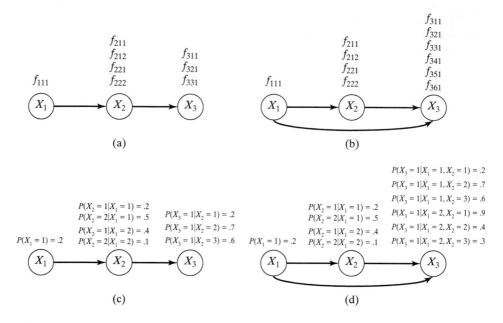

Figure 8.4: Bayesian network models appear in (a) and (b). The probability distribution in the Bayesian network in (c) is included in both models, whereas the one in (d) is included only in the model in (b).

A set of models, each of which is for the same set of random variables, is called a **class** of models.

Example 8.17 *The set of Bayesian network models contained in the set of all multinomial augmented Bayesian networks containing the same variables is a class of models. We call this class a **multinomial Bayesian network model class**. Figure 8.4 shows models from the class when* $V = \{X_1, X_2, X_3\}$, X_1 *and* X_3 *are binary, and* X_2 *has space size three.*

A conditional independency common to all probability distributions included in model $\mathcal{M}$ is said to be **in** $\mathcal{M}$. We have the following theorem:

Theorem 8.2 *In the case of a Bayesian network model* $\mathbb{G}$, *the set of conditional independencies in model* $\mathbb{G}$ *is the set of all conditional independencies entailed by d-separation in DAG* $\mathbb{G}$.
Proof. *The proof follows immediately from Theorems 2.1.*   ■

Model $\mathcal{M}_1$ is **distributionally included** in model $\mathcal{M}_2$ (denoted $\mathcal{M}_1 \leq_D \mathcal{M}_2$) if every distribution included in $\mathcal{M}_1$ is included in $\mathcal{M}_2$. If $\mathcal{M}_1$ is distributionally included in $\mathcal{M}_2$ and there exists a probability distribution that is included in $\mathcal{M}_2$ and not in $\mathcal{M}_1$, we say $\mathcal{M}_1$ is **strictly distributionally included** in $\mathcal{M}_2$ (denoted $\mathcal{M}_1 <_D \mathcal{M}_2$). If $\mathcal{M}_1$ is distributionally included in $\mathcal{M}_2$ and no such probability distribution exists, we say they are **distributionally**

equivalent (denoted $\mathcal{M}_1 \approx_D \mathcal{M}_2$). Model $\mathcal{M}_1$ is **independence included** in model $\mathcal{M}_2$ (denoted $\mathcal{M}_1 \leq_I \mathcal{M}_2$) if every conditional independency in $\mathcal{M}_2$ is in $\mathcal{M}_1$. If $\mathcal{M}_1$ is both distributionally included and independence included in $\mathcal{M}_2$, we simply say $\mathcal{M}_1$ is **included** in $\mathcal{M}_2$ (denoted $\mathcal{M}_1 \leq \mathcal{M}_2$). Definitions analogous to those for distributional inclusion hold for **strictly independence included**, **independence equivalent**, **strictly included**, and **equivalent**.

Theorem 8.3 *For a multinomial Bayesian network class, $\mathbb{G}_1$ is distributionally included in $\mathbb{G}_2$ if and only if $\mathbb{G}_1$ is independence included in $\mathbb{G}_2$.*
Proof. *Suppose $\mathbb{G}_1$ is independence included in $\mathbb{G}_2$. Let P be a distribution included in $\mathbb{G}_1$. Then every conditional independency in $\mathbb{G}_1$ is a conditional independency in P, which means every conditional independency in $\mathbb{G}_2$ is a conditional independency in P. Owing to Theorem 8.2, this means every d-separation in DAG $\mathbb{G}_2$ is a conditional independency in P, which means P satisfies the Markov condition with DAG $\mathbb{G}_2$. Theorem 1.4 therefore implies that P is equal to the product of its conditional distributions in DAG $\mathbb{G}_2$. The inclusion of P in $\mathbb{G}_2$ now follows from the fact that for this class there is an assignment of values to the parameters in $\mathbb{G}_2$ that yields these conditional distributions.*

In the other direction, suppose $\mathbb{G}_1$ is not independence included in $\mathbb{G}_2$. Then there exists some conditional independence (d-separation) I in $\mathbb{G}_2$ that is not in $\mathbb{G}_1$. Let P be a probability distribution included in $\mathbb{G}_1$ that is faithful to $\mathbb{G}_1$. (As mentioned following Example 2.9, almost all assignments of values to the conditional distributions will yield such a P.) This P does not have conditional independence I, which means P is not included in $\mathbb{G}_2$. Therefore, $\mathbb{G}_1$ is not distributionally included in $\mathbb{G}_2$. ∎

Due to the previous theorem, when we discuss models from a multinomial Bayesian network class, we speak only of inclusion. Note that in this case models are equivalent if and only if their DAGs are Markov equivalent.

Example 8.18 *Suppose our models are from a multinomial Bayesian network class. Model $\mathbb{G}_1$, whose DAG contains the three variables X_1, X_2, and X_3 and whose only edge is $X_1 \rightarrow X_2$, is strictly included in model $\mathbb{G}_2 = X_1 \rightarrow X_2 \rightarrow X_3$ because $\mathbb{G}_1$ contains more conditional independencies. Therefore, $\mathbb{G}_1 < \mathbb{G}_2$.*

Example 8.19 *Suppose our models are from a multinomial Bayesian network class. Model $X_1 \rightarrow X_2 \rightarrow X_3$ is equivalent to model $X_1 \leftarrow X_2 \leftarrow X_3$ since models in this class are equivalent if and only if their DAGs are Markov equivalence.*

Given some class of models, if $\mathcal{M}_2$ includes P and there exists no $\mathcal{M}_1$ in the class such that $\mathcal{M}_1$ includes P and $\mathcal{M}_1 <_D \mathcal{M}_2$, then $\mathcal{M}_2$ is called a **distributionally inclusion optimal map**. Analogous definitions hold for **independence inclusion optimal map** and **inclusion optimal map**.

Suppose we have a multinomial Bayesian network class of models for a set of random variables V. Then, if a probability distribution P of V admits a faithful DAG representation, DAG $\mathbb{G}$ is faithful to P if and only if model $\mathbb{G}$ is an inclusion optimal map of P. However, if DAG $\mathbb{G}$ satisfies the minimality condition with

P, model $\mathbb{G}$ is not necessarily an inclusion optimal map. For example, the DAG $\mathbb{G}$ in Figure 2.18 (c) on page 97 satisfies the minimality condition with the DAG referenced in that figure, but model $\mathbb{G}$ is not an inclusion optimal map since the model containing the DAG in Figure 2.18 (a) is strictly included in it. On the other hand, if model $\mathbb{G}$ is an inclusion optimal map of P, then DAG $\mathbb{G}$ satisfies the minimality condition with P. Section 8.4.3 discusses a model $\mathbb{G}$ that is an inclusion optimal map of P but DAG $\mathbb{G}$ is not faithful to P.

Given some class of models, if $\mathcal{M}_2$ includes probability distribution P and there exists no $\mathcal{M}_1$ in the class such that $\mathcal{M}_1$ includes P, and $\mathcal{M}_1$ has smaller dimension than $\mathcal{M}_2$, then $\mathcal{M}_2$ is called a **parameter optimal map** of P. In the case of Bayesian network models (DAG models), the **dimension** of the model is the number of parameters in the model. However, as we shall see in Section 8.5.3, this is not always the case. Theorem 8.6 will show that, in the case of a multinomial Bayesian network class, a parameter optimal map is an inclusion optimal map.

8.4.2   The Model Selection Problem

In general, the problem of **model selection** is to find a concise model which, based on a random sample of observations from the population that determines a relative frequency distribution P, includes P. As before, we use $\mathbf{d}$ to represent the set of values (data) of the sample. To perform model selection, we develop a scoring function *score* (called a scoring criterion) which assigns a value $score(\mathbf{d}, \mathcal{M})$ to each model under consideration based on the data. We make the standard assumption from classical statistics that the random vectors, whose values are our data, are independent and each has distribution P. We then have the following definition concerning scoring criteria:

Definition 8.4 *Let $\mathbf{d}_M$ be a set of values (data) of a set of M mutually independent random vectors, each with probability distribution P, and let P_M be the probability function determined by the joint distribution of the M random vectors. Furthermore, let score be a scoring criterion over some class of models for the random variables that constitute each vector. We say score is **consistent** for the class of models if the following two properties hold:*

1. If $\mathcal{M}_1$ includes P and $\mathcal{M}_2$ does not, then

$$\lim_{M \to \infty} P_M\left(score(\mathbf{d}_M, \mathcal{M}_1) > score(\mathbf{d}_M, \mathcal{M}_2)\right) = 1.$$

2. If $\mathcal{M}_1$ and $\mathcal{M}_2$ both include P and $\mathcal{M}_1$ has smaller dimension than $\mathcal{M}_2$, then

$$\lim_{M \to \infty} P_M\left(score(\mathbf{d}_M, \mathcal{M}_1) > score(\mathbf{d}_M, \mathcal{M}_2)\right) = 1.$$

We call P the **generative distribution**. The limit, as the size of the data set approaches infinity, of the probability of a consistent scoring criterion choosing a parameter optimal map of P is 1.

8.4.3   Using the Bayesian Scoring Criterion for Model Selection

First we show that the Bayesian scoring criterion is consistent. Then we discuss using it when the faithfulness assumption is not warranted.

Consistency of Bayesian Scoring

If the generative distribution P admits a faithful DAG representation, our goal is to find a DAG (and its corresponding DAG pattern) which is faithful to that distribution. If it does not admit a faithful DAG representation , we would want to find a DAG $\mathbb{G}$ such that model $\mathbb{G}$ is a parameter optimal independence map of that distribution. We can be highly confident that a consistent scoring criterion (Definition 8.4) will accomplish the latter task when the size of the data set is large. Next we show that the Bayesian scoring criterion is consistent. After that, we show that, in the case of DAGs, if the data set is sufficiently large, then with high probability, a consistent scoring criterion will find a DAG faithful to P.

Lemma 8.1 *In the case of a multinomial Bayesian network class, the BIC scoring criterion (Section 8.3.2) is consistent for scoring DAGs.*
Proof. *Haughton [1988] shows that this lemma holds for a class consisting of curved exponential models. Geiger et al. [1998] show that a multinomial Bayesian network class is such a class.* ∎

Theorem 8.4 *In the case of a multinomial Bayesian network class, the Bayesian scoring criterion* $score_B(\mathbf{d}, \mathbb{G}) = P(\mathbf{d}|\mathbb{G})$ *is consistent for scoring DAGs.*
Proof. *The Bayesian scoring criterion scores a model $\mathbb{G}$ in a multinomial Bayesian network class by computing $P(\mathbf{d}|\mathbb{G})$ using a multinomial augmented Bayesian network containing $\mathbb{G}$. In Section 8.3.2 we showed that, for multinomial augmented Bayesian networks, the BIC score is asymptotically correct, which means that for M (the sample size) sufficiently large, the model selected by the BIC score is one that maximizes $P(\mathbf{d}|\mathbb{G})$. The proof now follows from the previous lemma.* ∎

Before proceeding, we need the definitions and lemmas that follow.

Definition 8.5 *We say edge $X \rightarrow Y$ is covered in DAG $\mathbb{G}$ if X and Y have the same parents in $\mathbb{G}$ except X is not a parent of itself.*

Definition 8.6 *If we reverse a covered edge in a DAG, we call it a **covered edge reversal**.*

Clearly, if we perform a covered edge reversal on a DAG $\mathbb{G}$ we obtain a DAG in the same Markov equivalence class as $\mathbb{G}$.

Theorem 8.5 *Suppose we have a class of Bayesian network models such that if you add or reverse an edge to a member of the class you obtain another member. Suppose further $\mathbb{G}_1$ and $\mathbb{G}_2$ are members of the class such that $\mathbb{G}_1 \leq_I \mathbb{G}_2$. Let r be the number of links in $\mathbb{G}_2$ that have opposite orientation in $\mathbb{G}_1$, and let m be the number of links in $\mathbb{G}_2$ that do not exist in $\mathbb{G}_1$ in either orientation. There exists a sequence of at most $r + 2m$ distinct operations to $\mathbb{G}_1$, where each operation is either an edge addition or a covered edge reversal, such that*

1. *after each operation $\mathbb{G}_1$ is a DAG and $\mathbb{G}_1 \leq_I \mathbb{G}_2$;*

2. *after all the operations $\mathbb{G}_1 = \mathbb{G}_2$.*

Proof. *The proof can be found in Chickering [2002].*   ∎

Definition 8.7 *Size Equivalence holds for a class of Bayesian network models if*

1. *Models containing Markov equivalent DAGs have the same dimension.*

2. *If every edge in DAG $\mathbb{G}_1$ is in DAG $\mathbb{G}_2$ and $\mathbb{G}_2$ has at least one edge not in $\mathbb{G}_1$, then model $\mathbb{G}_2$ has greater dimension than model $\mathbb{G}_1$.*

It is not hard to see that size equivalence holds for a multinomial Bayesian network class.

Theorem 8.6 *Suppose we have a class of Bayesian network models such that if you add or reverse an edge to a member of the class you obtain another member. Suppose further size equivalence holds for the class. Then a parameter optimal map of a probability distribution P is an independence inclusion optimal map of P.*

Proof. *Let $\mathbb{G}_2$ be a parameter optimal map of P. If $\mathbb{G}_2$ is not an independence inclusion optimal map of P, there is some model $\mathbb{G}_1$ that includes P and*

$$\mathbb{G}_1 <_I \mathbb{G}_2.$$

Owing to Theorem 8.5, we can transform $\mathbb{G}_1$ to $\mathbb{G}_2$ with a sequence of edge additions and covered edge reversals. If there are no edge additions, $\mathbb{G}_1$ and $\mathbb{G}_2$ are in the same Markov equivalence class, which means $\mathbb{G}_1 \not<_I \mathbb{G}_2$. So, there must be at least one edge addition, which, owing to size equivalence, strictly increases the size of the model. Again owing to size equivalence, covered edge reversals leave the size of the model unchanged. We conclude that the model containing $\mathbb{G}_2$ has greater dimension than the model containing $\mathbb{G}_1$, which contradicts the fact that $\mathbb{G}_2$ is a parameter optimal map of P.   ∎

The converse of the preceding theorem does not hold. That is, an independence inclusion optimal map is not necessarily a parameter optimal map. Section 9.1.2 presents an example illustrating this.

Corollary 8.1 *Given a multinomial Bayesian network class, if a model is a parameter optimal map of P and P admits a faithful DAG representation, then the DAG in the model is faithful to P.*
Proof. *Clearly, size equivalence holds for this class. Therefore, owing to the previous theorem, a parameter optimal map of P is an independence inclusion optimal map of P. It is not hard to see that for this class, if P admits a faithful DAG representation then, if model* $\mathbb{G}$ *is an independence optimal inclusion map of P, DAG* $\mathbb{G}$ *must be faithful to P.*   ∎

Theorem 8.7 *In the case of a multinomial Bayesian network class, the limit, as the size of the data set approaches infinity, of the probability of a consistent scoring criterion choosing an inclusion optimal map of the generative distribution P is 1. If P admits a faithful DAG representation, and an inclusion optimal map is chosen, the DAG in the chosen model is faithful to P.*
Proof. *The proof follows from the definition of consistency, Theorem 8.6, and Corollary 8.1.*   ∎

Results When the Faithfulness Assumption Is Not Warranted

Recall from Section 8.1 that our structure learning methodology assumes the relative frequency distribution of the variables admits a faithful DAG representation. Suppose we have the following random variables:

Variable	Value	When the Variable Takes this Value
T	$t1$	Patient has tuberculosis
	$t2$	Patient does not have tuberculosis
N	$n1$	Patient's job requires night plane travel
	$n2$	Patient job does not require night plane travel
L	$l1$	Patient has lung cancer
	$l2$	Patient does not have lung cancer
F	$f1$	Patient is fatigued
	$f2$	Patient is not fatigued
C	$c1$	Patient has a positive chest X-ray
	$c2$	Patient has a negative chest X-ray

Suppose further that lung cancer and the job requiring night plane travel each cause fatigue, lung cancer and tuberculosis each cause a positive chest X-ray, there are no other causal relationships among the variables, and there are no hidden common causes. Then, due to the argument in Section 2.6, we would expect the relative frequency distribution of the five variables to be faithful to the DAG in Figure 8.5. Assume this is the case. Then owing to the result in Example 2.11, the marginal distribution of N, F, C, and T is not faithful to any DAG. Assume next that we are observing only these four variables and we obtain data on them. That is, assume we know nothing about lung cancer, indeed we have not even identified it as a feature of humans. Then the assumption of faithfulness is not valid. Suppose we score

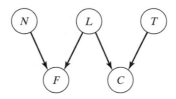

Figure 8.5: We assume that the probability distribution of job requring night plane travel (N), lung cancer (L), tuberculosis (T), fatigue (F), and a positive chest X-ray (C) is faithful to this DAG.

models using the Bayesian scoring criterion (Equality 8.1). Owing to Theorems 8.4 and 8.7, if the data set is sufficiently large, with high probability a parameter optimal independence map, which is also an inclusion optimal map, of the generative distribution P will be chosen. Assuming this happens, the DAG in the model will be one from the Markov equivalence class represented by the DAG pattern in either Figure 8.6 (a) or Figure 8.6 (b). Say it is a model containing a DAG $\mathbb{G}$ from the equivalence class represented in Figure 8.6 (a). DAG $\mathbb{G}$ does not entail $I_P(\{N\}, \{C\})$, which holds for the actual relative frequency distribution. Nevertheless, since P is included in model $\mathbb{G}$, DAG $\mathbb{G}$ is an independence map of P, which means we can use DAG $\mathbb{G}$ in a Bayesian network containing the variables. We can then use our inference algorithms for Bayesian networks to do inference with the variables.

You may ask what determines whether a model corresponding to Figure 8.6 (a) or one corresponding to Figure 8.6 (b) is chosen. It depends on the size of the models. For example, suppose all variables are binary except F, which has space size three. Then a model containing a DAG in the equivalence class represented in Figure 8.6 (a) has smaller dimension, and therefore such a model will be chosen. If all variables are binary, the dimension is the same regardless of the equivalence class and therefore the Bayesian score is the same.

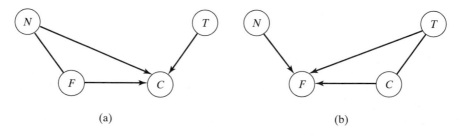

(a)   (b)

Figure 8.6: If P is faithful to the DAG in Figure 8.5, both DAG patterns represent inclusion optimal models.

8.5 Hidden Variable DAG Models

Next, we discuss DAG models containing hidden variables. A **hidden variable DAG model** is a DAG model containing a DAG $\mathbb{G} = (V \cup H, E)$, where $V = \{X_1, X_2, \ldots, X_n\}$ and $H = \{H_1, H_2, \ldots, H_k\}$ are disjoint sets of random variables. The variables in V are called **observable variables**, while the variables in H are called **hidden variables**. In practice we obtain data only on the variables in V. By using hidden variables, we can obtain more models for V than we could if we considered only DAG models containing DAGs of the form $\mathbb{G} = (V, E)$.

After discussing hidden variable DAG models in which the DAG entails more conditional independencies than any DAG containing only the observables, we present hidden variable DAG models in which the DAG entails the same conditional independencies as one containing only the observables. Next, we discuss computing the dimension of a hidden variable DAG model. Then we illustrate how changing the space sizes of the hidden variables changes the model. Finally, we address efficient methods for scoring hidden variable DAG models.

8.5.1 Models Containing More Conditional Independencies than DAG Models

Recall that in Section 8.4.3 we showed that, if the generative distribution P is faithful to the DAG in Figure 8.5, the Bayesian scoring criterion will probably choose (when the data set is sufficiently large) a model whose DAG is in one of the equivalence classes represented in Figure 8.6. The DAG in the model does not entail all the conditional independencies in P. However, if we consider only DAGs containing the four observable variables, this is the best we can do because the probability distribution of these four variables does not admit a faithful DAG representation. Alternatively, we could also consider a hidden variable DAG model $\mathbb{G}_H$ containing the DAG in Figure 8.7. The variable H is a hidden variable because it is not one of the four variables on which we have data. (Notice that we shade nodes representing hidden variables.) This variable does not represent lung cancer. (Recall that we are assuming that we have not even identified lung cancer as a feature of humans.) Rather, it is a hypothesized variable about which we have no knowledge. We could give H any size space we wish. For the current discussion, assume it is binary. Mathematically, this is

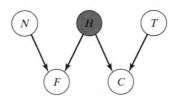

Figure 8.7: A DAG containing a hidden variable.

really a case of missing data items. We simply have all data items missing for H. So we can compute $P(\mathbf{d}|\mathbb{G}_H)$ in the same way as we computed the probability of data with missing data items in Equality 8.4 on page 444 . That is,

$$score_B(\mathbf{d}, \mathbb{G}_H) = P(\mathbf{d}|\mathbb{G}_H) = \sum_{i=1}^{2^M} P(\mathbf{d}_i|\mathbb{G}_H), \qquad (8.29)$$

where M is the size of the sample, and $\mathbf{d}_i$ is data on the five variables, N, F, C, T, and H, with the values of N, F, C, and T being their actual ones and those of H ranging over all of their 2^M possibilities.

For example, suppose we have the data $\mathbf{d}$ in the following actual table:

Case	N	F	C	T
1	$n1$	$f1$	$c2$	$t2$
2	$n1$	$f2$	$c1$	$t2$
3	$n2$	$f1$	$c2$	$t2$
4	$n2$	$f2$	$c2$	$t1$
5	$n1$	$f1$	$c1$	$t1$
6	$n2$	$f1$	$c2$	$t2$
7	$n2$	$f1$	$c1$	$t1$
8	$n2$	$f1$	$c1$	$t2$
9	$n2$	$f1$	$c2$	$t1$

Then $\mathbf{d}_1$ and an arbitrary intermediate $\mathbf{d}_i$ are respectively the data in the following tables:

$\mathbf{d}_1$

Case	N	F	C	T	H
1	$n1$	$f1$	$c2$	$t2$	$h1$
2	$n1$	$f2$	$c1$	$t2$	$h1$
3	$n2$	$f1$	$c2$	$t2$	$h1$
4	$n2$	$f2$	$c2$	$t1$	$h1$
5	$n1$	$f1$	$c1$	$t1$	$h1$
6	$n2$	$f1$	$c2$	$t2$	$h1$
7	$n2$	$f1$	$c1$	$t1$	$h1$
8	$n2$	$f1$	$c1$	$t2$	$h1$
9	$n2$	$f1$	$c2$	$t1$	$h1$

$\mathbf{d}_i$

Case	N	F	C	T	H
1	$n1$	$f1$	$c2$	$t2$	$h1$
2	$n1$	$f2$	$c1$	$t2$	$h2$
3	$n2$	$f1$	$c2$	$t2$	$h2$
4	$n2$	$f2$	$c2$	$t1$	$h1$
5	$n1$	$f1$	$c1$	$t1$	$h2$
6	$n2$	$f1$	$c2$	$t2$	$h1$
7	$n2$	$f1$	$c1$	$t1$	$h2$
8	$n2$	$f1$	$c1$	$t2$	$h2$
9	$n2$	$f1$	$c2$	$t1$	$h1$

Given that we score all the possible DAG models containing only the variables N, F, C, and T using the standard Bayesian scoring criterion, and we score the hidden variable DAG model $\mathbb{G}_H$ we've discussed using Equality 8.29, you may ask which model should win when the sample size is large. Theorem 8.4 is not applicable because it assumes that the class consists of curved exponential models, and Geiger et al. [1998] show that a hidden variable DAG model $\mathbb{G} = (\mathsf{V} \cup \mathsf{H}, \mathsf{E})$ is not a curved exponential model for V. Rather it is a stratified exponential model. For hidden variable DAG models, Meek [1997] sketched a proof showing that the Bayesian scoring criterion satisfies the first requirement in a consistent scoring criterion. That is, he illustrated that, if the hidden variable model $\mathbb{G}_H$ includes the generative distribution P and model $\mathbb{G}$ does not, then with high probability the Bayesian scoring criterion will score $\mathbb{G}_H$ higher than $\mathbb{G}$ when the data set is sufficiently large. Furthermore, Rusakov and Geiger [2002] proved that the BIC and Bayesian scoring criterion satisfy both requirements for consistency (i.e., they show that BIC and the Bayesian scoring criterion are consistent) in the case of **naive hidden variable DAG models**, which are models with the following properties: There is a single hidden variable H, all observables are children of H, and there are no edges between any observables. Model $\mathbb{G}_H$ is not a naive hidden variable DAG model. However, it seems that the Bayesian scoring criterion is consistent in the case of more general hidden variable DAG models. If it is consistent in the case of model $\mathbb{G}_H$ and if the relative frequency distribution is faithful to the DAG in Figure 8.5, then $\mathbb{G}_H$ will probably be chosen when the data set is large. It is left an exercise to test this conjecture by generating data and scoring the models.

A problem with using this technique lies in identifying which hidden variable DAG models to consider. That is, why should we suspect that the joint distribution of N, F, C, and T does not admit a faithful DAG representation, and, even if we did suspect this, why should we choose the correct hidden variable DAG model? Chapter 10 presents an algorithm for determining whether a probability distribution admits a faithful DAG representation, and it develops a method for discovering hidden variables when this is not the case. Furthermore, that chapter discusses applying the theory to causal learning, and it shows that in many applications the variable H in Figure 8.7 can be considered a hidden common cause of F and C.

8.5.2 Models Containing the Same Conditional Independencies as DAG Models

Recall that Example 2.14 on page 104 showed that it is possible to embed a distribution P faithfully in two DAGs, and yet P is included in only one of the DAGs. Owing to this fact, data can sometimes distinguish a hidden variable DAG model from a DAG model containing no hidden variables, even when both models contain the same conditional independencies. First we illustrate this. Then we discuss an application to learning causal influences.

Distinguishing a Hidden Variable Model From a DAG Model

When a hidden variable DAG model and a DAG model that has no hidden variables contain the same conditional independencies, the hidden variables are somewhat obscure entities. To impart intuition for them we develop a lengthy urn example. Please bear with us as the outcome should be worth the effort.

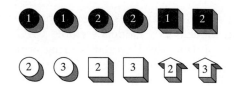

Figure 8.8: Value and shape are not independent, but they are conditionally independent give color.

Suppose we have an urn containing the objects in Figure 8.8. Let random variables V, S, and C be defined as follows:

Variable	Value	Outcomes Mapped to this Value
V	$v1$	All objects containing a "1"
	$v2$	All objects containing a "2"
	$v3$	All objects containing a "3"
S	$s1$	All circular objects
	$s2$	All square objects
	$s3$	All arrow objects
C	$c1$	All black objects
	$c2$	All white objects

Suppose further that we sample with replacement from the urn. Assuming that the generative distribution is the same as the distribution obtained by applying the principle of indifference to the objects in the urn, clearly, we have

$$\neg I_P(V, S) \qquad \text{and} \qquad I_P(V, S|C),$$

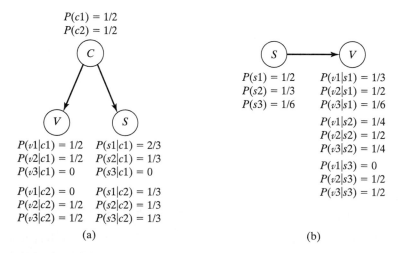

Figure 8.9: The probability distribution of V and S obtained by sampling from the objects in Figure 8.8 is contained in both Bayesian networks.

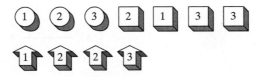

Figure 8.10: There is no apparent division of the objects into two groups which renders value and shape independent.

where P denotes the generative distribution. It is not hard to see then that the probability distribution of V, S, and C is contained in the Bayesian network in Figure 8.9 (a), and that the probability distribution of only V and S is contained in the Bayesian networks in both Figure 8.9 (a) and Figure 8.9 (b).

Suppose next that we have an urn containing the objects in Figure 8.10. Let random variables V and S be defined as before. If we sample from this urn and the generative distribution is the same as that obtained by applying the principle of indifference to the objects, this distribution is contained in the Bayesian network in Figure 8.11. Could the distribution also be contained in a Bayesian network like the one in Figure 8.9 (a)? That is, is there some division of the objects into two groups that renders V and S independent in each group? Note that the coloring of the objects in Figure 8.8 was only for emphasis. It is the fact that they could be divided into two groups such that V and S are independent in each group that enabled us to represent the probability distribution of V and S using the Bayesian network in Figure 8.9 (a).

Towards answering the question just posed, consider the two models in Figure 8.12. The Bayesian network in Figure 8.9 (a) is obtained from the model in Figure 8.12 (a) by assigning values to the parameters in the model. The only difference is that we labeled the root C instead of H in the DAG in Figure 8.9 (a) because at that time we were identifying color. The Bayesian networks in Figure 8.9 (b) and Figure 8.11 are obtained from the model in Figure 8.12 (b) by assigning values to the parameters in the model. The question posed in the

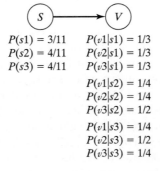

$$P(s1) = 3/11 \quad P(v1|s1) = 1/3$$
$$P(s2) = 4/11 \quad P(v2|s1) = 1/3$$
$$P(s3) = 4/11 \quad P(v3|s1) = 1/3$$
$$P(v1|s2) = 1/4$$
$$P(v2|s2) = 1/4$$
$$P(v3|s2) = 1/2$$
$$P(v1|s3) = 1/4$$
$$P(v2|s3) = 1/2$$
$$P(v3|s3) = 1/4$$

Figure 8.11: The probability distribution of V and S obtained by sampling from the objects in Figure 8.10 is contained in this Bayesian network.

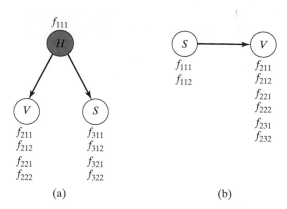

Figure 8.12: A hidden variable DAG model for V and S is in (a) and a DAG model for V and S is in (b).

previous paragraph can now be stated as follows: Is the probability distribution in the Bayesian network in Figure 8.11 included in the hidden variable DAG model in Figure 8.12 (a)? It is very unlikely for the following reason. Although the model in Figure 8.12 (a) has more parameters than the one in Figure 8.12 (b), some of the parameters are redundant. As a result, it effectively has fewer parameters and its dimension is smaller. This is discussed much more in Section 8.5.3. As a result of its dimension being smaller, it includes far less distributions. Specifically, every distribution included in the model in Figure 8.12 (a) is clearly included in the model in Figure 8.12 (b). However, if we consider the space consisting of the set of all possible permissible assignments to the parameters in the model in Figure 8.12 (b), the subset, whose members yield joint distributions included in the model in Figure 8.12 (a), has Lebesgue measure zero. In summary, if we let $\mathbb{G}_H$ be the model in Figure 8.12 (a) and $\mathbb{G}$ be the model in Figure 8.12 (b), it is the case that $\mathbb{G}_H <_D \mathbb{G}$.

Suppose we now randomly select either model $\mathbb{G}_H$ or model $\mathbb{G}$, we randomly assign permissible values to the parameters, and we generate a very large amount of data on V and S using the resultant Bayesian network. You are then given the data and have the task of deciding which model we selected. To accomplish this, you could score each model using the Bayesian scoring criterion and select the one with the higher score. Recall from Section 8.5.1 that the Bayesian scoring criterion is consistent in the case of naive hidden variable DAG models. Clearly, model $\mathbb{G}_H$ is a naive hidden variable model. So the Bayesian scoring criterion is consistent when choosing between models $\mathbb{G}_H$ and $\mathbb{G}$. Therefore, for a sufficiently large data set, with high probability it will choose model $\mathbb{G}$ over $\mathbb{G}_H$ if and only if the generative distribution is not included in model $\mathbb{G}_H$. This means that, if we generated the large data set using model $\mathbb{G}_H$ (with arbitrary assignment of values to its parameters), the Bayesian scoring criterion will probably correctly choose $\mathbb{G}_H$ over $\mathbb{G}$. On the other hand if we generated the large data set using model $\mathbb{G}$ (with arbitrary assignment of values to its

Case	Sex	Height (inches)	Wage ($)
1	*female*	64	30, 000
2	*female*	64	30, 000
3	*female*	64	40, 000
4	*female*	64	40, 000
5	*female*	68	30, 000
6	*female*	68	40, 000
7	*male*	64	40, 000
8	*male*	64	50, 000
9	*male*	68	40, 000
10	*male*	68	50, 000
11	*male*	70	40, 000
12	*male*	70	50, 000

Table 8.2: Possible data on sex, height, and wage

parameters), almost for certain the generative distribution is not included $\mathbb{G}_H$. So the Bayesian scoring criterion will probably correctly choose $\mathbb{G}$ over $\mathbb{G}_H$.

Note that whenever you discover that a "hidden variable" exists in the previous experiment, you are really discovering that there is a division of the objects into two groups such that V and S are independent in each group.

Application to Causal Learning

The value of urn problems is that they shed light on interpreting results obtained when we model situations in the external world. Next, we discuss such a situation.

Recall Example 1.15 in which we had the data in Table 8.2. In Exercise 1.12, we showed that if *Sex*, *Height*, and *Wage* are random variables representing sex, height, and wage respectively, then, if this small sample is indicative of the probabilistic relationships P among the variables in some population, we have

$$I_P(Height, Wage|Sex).$$

Note that the distribution determined by the objects in Figure 8.8 is the same as the distribution in Table 8.2 if we make the following associations:

$$black/female \quad white/male \quad circle/64 \quad square/68$$
$$arrow/70 \quad 1/30,000 \quad 2/40,000 \quad 3/50,000$$

Now suppose we have the data in Table 8.2, but we are not able to detect the sex of the individuals. Sex is then a **hidden variable** in that it is a property of the entities being investigated that renders two measured variables independent. Owing to the discussion in the previous section, if we obtain a large amount of data on height and wage reflecting the distribution in Table 8.2, the Bayesian scoring criterion will probably choose the hidden variable DAG model $\mathbb{G}_H$ in

Figure 8.12 (a) over the DAG model $\mathbb{G}$ in Figure 8.12 (b), and we obtain evidence for the existence of a hidden common cause of height and wage.

There are several reasons we say only that we obtain evidence for the existence of a hidden common cause. First of all, the DAGs $X \to H \to Y$ and $X \leftarrow H \leftarrow Y$ are Markov equivalent to $X \leftarrow H \to Y$. So the division of the data into subsets that render *Height* and *Wage* independent in each subset could be due to an intermediate cause. Furthermore, in real applications, features such as height and wage are actually continuous, and we create discrete variables by imposing cutoff points in the data. For example, we may classify height as $68 \leq height < 69$, $69 \leq height < 70$, and so forth, and wage as $30,000 \leq wage < 40,000$, $40,000 \leq wage < 50,000$, and so forth. With these cutoff points, we may obtain a division of the data that render height and wage independent, whereas with other cutoff points we may not.

The same cautionary note holds concerning the conclusion of the absence of a hidden clause. Suppose model $\mathbb{G}$ were chosen over model $\mathbb{G}_H$. A different choice of cutoff points may result in $\mathbb{G}_H$ being chosen. Furthermore, if there is a hidden common cause, it may be better modeled with a hidden variable that has a larger space. Clearly, if we increase the space size of the hidden variable sufficiently, $\mathbb{G}_H$ will have the same dimension as $\mathbb{G}$, and the data will not be able to distinguish between the two models.

8.5.3   Dimension of Hidden Variable DAG Models

Recall that in Section 8.5.2 we mentioned that although the model in Figure 8.12 (a) has more parameters than the one in Figure 8.12 (b), some of the parameters are redundant. As a result, it effectively has fewer parameters and its dimension is smaller. Next we discuss the calculation of the dimension of hidden variable DAG models.

Let d be the dimension (size) of the model given data d in the region of the MAP (or ML) value of the parameters. Recall that in Equality 8.23 d equals the number of parameters in the model. That equality was obtained by assuming that the expression inside the integral in Equality 8.22 is proportional to a multivariate normal density function. This assumption requires that there be a unique MAP (and therefore ML) value of the parameters, and that the probability of the data is peaked at that value. This assumption holds for multinomial Bayesian network models. We show next that it does not hold for hidden variable DAG models, and therefore we cannot consider the number of parameters in such a model the dimension of the model.

Consider the hidden variable DAG model in Figure 8.13 (a) and the trivial DAG model in Figure 8.13 (b). Clearly, they include the same distributions of X, and the dimension of the trivial DAG model is 1. We will show that the dimension of the hidden variable DAG model is also 1. Let $\mathsf{f} = \{f_{111}, f_{211}, f_{221}\}$ and f_X be a parameter representing the probability that X equals its first value. Then

$$f_X = f_{211} f_{111} + f_{221}(1 - f_{111}).$$

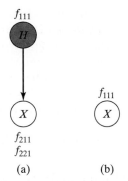

Figure 8.13: The effective dimension of the model in (a) is the same as the dimension of the model in (b).

The probability of data on X is uniquely determined by the value of f_X. That is, if we let $\mathbf{d}$ be a set of M values (data) of X, s be the number of times X equals its first value, and t be the number of times X equals its second value, then

$$P(\mathbf{d}|\mathbf{f}) = P(\mathbf{d}|f_X) = f_X^s(1 - f_X)^t.$$

The unique maximum likelihood value of f is

$$\hat{f}_X = \frac{s}{M}.$$

Any values of the parameters in the network such

$$\frac{s}{M} = f_{211}f_{111} + f_{221}(1 - f_{111})$$

will yield this value. So, the probability of the data does not reach a peak at a unique value of $\mathbf{f}$; rather, it reaches a ridge at a set of values. In this sense, the model has only one nonredundant parameter, and the dimension of the model is 1.

Geiger et al. [1996] discuss this matter more formally, and they show that, if we determine the dimension d of the model as just illustrated, the scores discussed in Section 8.3.2 approximate the Bayesian score in the case of hidden variable DAG models. Furthermore, they compute the dimension of some interesting hidden variable DAG models. The following table shows the dimension of naive hidden variable DAG models when all variables are binary:

Number (n) of Observables	Dimension (d) of Hidden Variable DAG Model
1	1
2	3
$3 \le n \le 7$	$2n + 1$
$n > 7$	$2n \le d \le 2n + 1$

For $n > 7$ they obtained only the bounds shown. Note that when n is 1 or 2, the dimension of the hidden variable DAG model is less than the number of parameters in the model, when $3 \leq n \leq 7$ its dimension is the same as the number of parameters, and for $n > 7$ its dimension is bounded above by the number of parameters. Note further that when n is 1, 2, or 3 the dimension of the hidden variable DAG model is the same as the dimension of the complete DAG model, and when $n \geq 4$ it is smaller. Therefore, owing to the fact that the Bayesian scoring criterion is consistent in the case of naive hidden variable DAG models (discussed in Section 8.5.1), using that criterion we can distinguish the models from data when $n \geq 4$.

Let's discuss the naive hidden variable DAG model in which H is binary and there are two nonbinary observables. Let r be the space size of both observables. If $r \geq 4$, the number of parameters in the hidden variable DAG model is less than the number in the complete DAG model; so clearly its dimension is smaller. It is possible to show that the dimension is smaller even when $r = 3$. (See Kocka and Zhang [2002].)

Finally, consider the hidden variable DAG model $X \rightarrow Y \leftarrow H \rightarrow Z \leftarrow W$, where H is the hidden variable. If all variables are binary, the number of parameters in the model is 11. However, Geiger et al. [1996] show that the dimension is only 9. Tomas Kocka [private correspondence] showed if the observables are binary, and H has space size greater than 2, the dimension is 10.

8.5.4   Number of Models and Hidden Variables

At the end of the last section, we discussed varying the space size of the hidden variable, while leaving the number of states of the observable fixed. In the case of hidden variable DAG models, a DAG containing observables with fixed space sizes, can be contained in different models because we can assign different space sizes to a hidden variable. An example is AutoClass, which was developed by Cheeseman and Stutz [1995].

Autoclass is a classification program for unsupervised learning of clusters. The cluster learning problem is as follows: Given a collection of unclassified entities and the features of those entities, organize the entities into classes that in some sense maximize the similarity of the features of the entities in the same class. For example, we may want to create classes of observed creatures. Autoclass models this problem using the hidden variable DAG model in Figure 8.14. In that figure, the hidden variable is discrete, and its possible values correspond to the underlying classes of entities. The model assumes that the features represented by discrete variables (in the figure D_1, D_2, and D_3), and sets of features represented by continuous variables (in the figure $\{C_1, C_2, C_3, C_4\}$ and $\{C_5, C_6\}$) are mutually independent given H. Given a data set containing values of the features, Autoclass searches over variants of

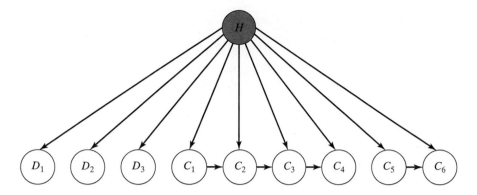

Figure 8.14: An example of a hidden variable DAG model used in Autoclass.

this model, including the number of possible values of the hidden variable, and it selects a variant so as to approximately maximize the posterior probability of the variant.

The comparison studies discussed in Section 8.3.2 were performed using this model with all variables being discrete.

8.5.5 Efficient Model Scoring

In the case of hidden variable DAG models, the determination of $score_B(\mathsf{d}, \mathbb{G}_H)$ requires an exponential number of calculations. First we develop a more efficient way to do this calculation in certain cases. Then we discuss approximating the score.

A More Efficient Calculation

Recall that in the case of binary variables, Equality 8.29 gives the Bayesian score

$$score_B(\mathsf{d}, \mathbb{G}_H) = P(\mathsf{d}|\mathbb{G}_H) = \sum_{i=1}^{2^M} P(\mathsf{d}_i|\mathbb{G}_H), \qquad (8.30)$$

where M is the size of the sample. Clearly, this method has exponential time complexity in terms of M. Next, we show how to do this calculation more efficiently.

One Hidden Variable Suppose $\mathbb{G}_H$ is $S \leftarrow H \rightarrow V$ where H is hidden, all variables are binary, we have the data d in the following table, and we wish to score $\mathbb{G}_H$ based on these data:

Case	S	V
1	$s1$	$v1$
2	$s1$	$v2$
3	$s2$	$v1$
4	$s2$	$v2$
5	$s1$	$v1$
6	$s2$	$v1$
7	$s2$	$v1$
8	$s2$	$v1$
9	$s2$	$v1$

Consider the d_is, represented by the following tables, which would appear in the sum in Equality 8.30:

Case	H	S	V
1	$h2$	$s1$	$v1$
2	$h1$	$s1$	$v2$
3	$h2$	$s2$	$v1$
4	$h2$	$s2$	$v2$
5	$h1$	$s1$	$v1$
6	$h2$	$s2$	$v1$
7	$h1$	$s2$	$v1$
8	$h2$	$s2$	$v1$
9	$h1$	$s2$	$v1$

Case	H	S	V
1	$h1$	$s1$	$v1$
2	$h1$	$s1$	$v2$
3	$h2$	$s2$	$v1$
4	$h2$	$s2$	$v2$
5	$h2$	$s1$	$v1$
6	$h2$	$s2$	$v1$
7	$h1$	$s2$	$v1$
8	$h2$	$s2$	$v1$
9	$h1$	$s2$	$v1$

They are identical, except that in the table on the left we have

$$\text{Case } 1 = (\ h2 \quad s1 \quad v1\ )$$

$$\text{Case } 5 = (\ h1 \quad s1 \quad v1\ ),$$

and in the table on the right we have

$$\text{Case } 1 = (\ h1 \quad s1 \quad v1\ )$$

$$\text{Case } 5 = (\ h2 \quad s1 \quad v1\ ).$$

Clearly, $P(d_i|\mathbb{G}_H)$ will be the same for the these two d_is since the value in Corollary 6.6 does not depend on the order of the data. Similarly if, for example, we flip around Case 2 and Case 3, we will not affect the result of the computation. So, in general, for all d_is which have the same data but in different order, we need only compute $P(d_i|\mathbb{G}_H)$ once, and then multiply this value by the number of such d_is. As an example, consider again the d_i in the following table:

Case	H	S	V
1	$h2$	$s1$	$v1$
2	$h1$	$s1$	$v2$
3	$h2$	$s2$	$v1$
4	$h2$	$s2$	$v2$
5	$h1$	$s1$	$v1$
6	$h2$	$s2$	$v1$
7	$h1$	$s2$	$v1$
8	$h2$	$s2$	$v1$
9	$h1$	$s2$	$v1$

In this table, we have the following:

Value	# of Cases with this Value	# of Cases with H Equal to $h1$
($s1$ $v1$)	2	1
($s1$ $v2$)	1	1
($s2$ $v1$)	5	2
($s2$ $v2$)	1	0

So there are $\binom{2}{1}\binom{1}{1}\binom{5}{2}\binom{1}{0} = 20$ d_is that have the same data as the one just discussed, except in a different order. This means that we need compute only $P(\mathsf{d}_i|\mathbb{G}_H)$ for the d_i above, and multiply this result by 20.

Using this methodology, the following pseudocode shows the algorithm that replaces the sum in Equality 8.30:

$total = 0;$
for $(k1 = 0; k1 <= M1; k1 + +)$ // $M1 =$ # of ($s1$ $v1$).
  for $(k2 = 0; k2 <= M2; k2 + +)$ // $M2 =$ # of ($s1$ $v2$).
    for $(k3 = 0; k3 <= M3; k3 + +)$ // $M3 =$ # of ($s2$ $v1$).
      for $(k4 = 0; k4 <= M4; k4 + +)$ // $M4 =$ # of ($s2$ $v2$).
        $total = total + \binom{M1}{k1}\binom{M2}{k2}\binom{M3}{k3}\binom{M4}{k4}P(\mathsf{d}_i|\mathbb{G}_H);$

// d_i is any data that has the following:

// $k1$ occurrences of $h1$ in the cases with ($s1$ $v1$)
// $k2$ occurrences of $h1$ in the cases with ($s1$ $v2$)
// $k3$ occurrences of $h1$ in the cases with ($s1$ $v2$)
// $k4$ occurrences of $h1$ in the cases with ($s2$ $v2$).

We have replaced exponential time complexity with quadratic time complexity. Given the data shown at the beginning of this subsection, we compute $3 \times 2 \times 6 \times 2 = 72$ values instead of $2^9 = 512$ values.

Cooper [1995b] presents a general algorithm based on the method just presented that allows for more than two observables and allows variables (including the hidden variable) to have arbitrary discrete space sizes. Letting

n = number of variables in the network other than the single hidden variable

r = maximum space size of all variables

M = number of cases in the data

f = number of different instantiations of the variables,

he shows that the number of values computed is in

$$O\left(\left(\tfrac{M}{f} + r - 1\right)^{f(r-1)}\right). \tag{8.31}$$

In Cooper and Herskovits [1992], it is shown that the time complexity to compute any one term (i.e., $P(\mathsf{d}_i|\mathbb{G}_H)$) is in

$$O\left(Mn^2r\right).$$

For example, in the case of the data presented at the beginning of this subsection,

$$
\begin{aligned}
n &= 2 \\
r &= 2 \\
M &= 9 \\
f &= 4.
\end{aligned}
$$

So, the number of terms computed is in

$$O((M/4 + 2 - 1)^{4(2-1)}) = O(M^4),$$

which is quadratic in terms of M as we have already noted.

Although the time complexity shown in Expression 8.31 is polynomial, the degree of the polynomial is large if either f or r is large.

More than One Hidden Variable   So far we have considered only one hidden variable. Cooper [1995b] discusses extending the method just presented to the case in which we postulate more than one hidden variable.

Approximation Methods

The more efficient method for determining the Bayesian score of a hidden variable DAG model, which was developed in the previous subsection, is still computationally intensive. So approximation methods are sometimes more appropriate. Clearly, the Monte Carlo methods developed in Section 8.3.1 can be used to approximate the Bayesian score of a hidden variable DAG model. Furthermore, recall from Section 8.5.3 that Geiger et al. [1996] show that, if we determine the dimension d of the model as illustrated in that section, the scores discussed in Section 8.3.2 approximate the Bayesian score in the case of hidden variable DAG models. However, one score we developed must be modified. Recall that in Section 8.3.2 we showed that the Cheeseman–Stutz approximation is asymptotically correct by showing that

$$
\begin{aligned}
CS(\mathsf{d}, \mathbb{G}) &\equiv \ln\left(P(\mathsf{d}'|\mathbb{G})\right) - \ln\left(P(\mathsf{d}'|\hat{\mathsf{f}}^{(\mathbb{G})}, \mathbb{G})\right) + \ln\left(P(\mathsf{d}|\hat{\mathsf{f}}^{(\mathbb{G})}, \mathbb{G})\right) \\
&= \ln\left(P(\mathsf{d}'|\mathbb{G})\right) - \left[BIC(\mathsf{d}', \mathbb{G}) + \frac{d}{2}\ln M\right] + \left[BIC(\mathsf{d}, \mathbb{G}) + \frac{d}{2}\ln M\right] \\
&= \ln\left(P(\mathsf{d}'|\mathbb{G})\right) - BIC(\mathsf{d}', \mathbb{G}) + BIC(\mathsf{d}, \mathbb{G}).
\end{aligned}
$$

In this development, we assumed that the dimension d' of the model given data d' in the region of $\tilde{\mathsf{f}}^{(\mathbb{G})}$ is equal to the dimension d of the model given data d in the region of $\tilde{\mathsf{f}}^{(\mathbb{G})}$, and so the dimensions cancelled out. However, in the case of hidden variable DAG models, d' is the dimension of the model in which the hidden variables are not hidden, while d is the dimension of the model in which they are. As discussed in Section 8.5.3, we may have $d' > d$. So, in the case of hidden variable DAG models, our Cheeseman–Stutz approximation must be as follows:

$$
CS(\mathsf{d}, \mathbb{G}) \equiv \ln\left(P(\mathsf{d}'|\mathbb{G})\right) - \ln\left(P(\mathsf{d}'|\hat{\mathsf{f}}^{(\mathbb{G})}, \mathbb{G})\right) + \frac{d'}{2}\ln M + \ln\left(P(\mathsf{d}|\hat{\mathsf{f}}^{(\mathbb{G})}, \mathbb{G})\right) - \frac{d}{2}\ln M.
$$

8.6 Learning Structure: Continuous Variables

An algorithm for doing inference in Gaussian Bayesian networks was developed in Section 4.1. A method for learning parameters in such networks appears in Section 7.2. Presently, we develop a method for learning structure assuming a Gaussian Bayesian network.

Recall that, given a set $\mathsf{D} = \{\mathbf{X}^{(1)}, \mathbf{X}^{(2)}, \dots, \mathbf{X}^{(M)}\}$ of M random vectors such that for every i all $X_i^{(h)}$ have the same space and a set d of values of the vectors in D, in order to learn structure, we need, for each value gp of GP, the conditional density function

$$
\rho(\mathsf{d}|gp).
$$

First we develop a method for obtaining the density function of D in the case of a multivariate normal sample. Then we apply this result to determine the density function of D given a DAG pattern gp.

8.6.1 The Density Function of D

Recall the definition of a multivariate normal sample (Definition 7.21) and Theorem 7.28. This theorem says that, for a multivariate normal sample $\mathsf{D} = \{\mathbf{X}^{(1)}, \mathbf{X}^{(2)}, \dots, \mathbf{X}^{(M)}\}$ with prior parameter values $\boldsymbol{\beta}$, α, $\boldsymbol{\mu}$, and v, and data

$\mathsf{d} = \{\mathbf{x}^{(1)}, \mathbf{x}^{(2)}, \ldots, \mathbf{x}^{(M)}\}$, the updated parameter values $\boldsymbol{\beta}^*$, α^*, $\boldsymbol{\mu}^*$, and v^* are as follows. If we let

$$\overline{\mathbf{x}} = \frac{\sum_{h=1}^{M} \mathbf{x}^{(h)}}{M} \qquad \text{and} \qquad \mathsf{s} = \sum_{h=1}^{M} \left(\mathbf{x}^{(h)} - \overline{\mathbf{x}}\right)\left(\mathbf{x}^{(h)} - \overline{\mathbf{x}}\right)^T,$$

then

$$\boldsymbol{\beta}^* = \boldsymbol{\beta} + \mathsf{s} + \frac{vM}{v + M}(\overline{\mathbf{x}} - \boldsymbol{\mu})(\overline{\mathbf{x}} - \boldsymbol{\mu})^T \qquad \text{and} \qquad \alpha^* = \alpha + M, \qquad (8.32)$$

and

$$\boldsymbol{\mu}^* = \frac{v\boldsymbol{\mu} + M\overline{\mathbf{x}}}{v + M} \qquad \text{and} \qquad v^* = v + M.$$

Now let $\mathsf{d}_h = \{\mathbf{x}^{(1)}, \mathbf{x}^{(2)}, \ldots, \mathbf{x}^{(h)}\}$ where $1 \leq h \leq M$. Denote the updated parameters based on this subset of the data by $\boldsymbol{\beta}_h$, α_h, $\boldsymbol{\mu}_h$, and v_h. Owing to the result in Theorem 7.28, if we let

$$\overline{\mathbf{x}} = \frac{\sum_{i=1}^{h} \mathbf{x}^{(i)}}{h} \qquad \text{and} \qquad \mathsf{s} = \sum_{i=1}^{h} \left(\mathbf{x}^{(i)} - \overline{\mathbf{x}}\right)\left(\mathbf{x}^{(i)} - \overline{\mathbf{x}}\right)^T,$$

then

$$\boldsymbol{\beta}_h = \boldsymbol{\beta} + \mathsf{s} + \frac{vh}{v + h}(\overline{\mathbf{x}} - \boldsymbol{\mu})(\overline{\mathbf{x}} - \boldsymbol{\mu})^T \qquad \text{and} \qquad \alpha_h = \alpha + h, \qquad (8.33)$$

and

$$\boldsymbol{\mu}_h = \frac{v\boldsymbol{\mu} + h\overline{\mathbf{x}}}{v + h} \qquad \text{and} \qquad v_h = v + h.$$

We have the following lemma:

Lemma 8.2 *Given a multivariate normal sample* D *with prior parameter values* $\boldsymbol{\beta}$, α, $\boldsymbol{\mu}$, *and* v,

$$\boldsymbol{\beta}_{h+1} = \boldsymbol{\beta}_h + \left(\frac{v}{v + 1}\right)(\mathbf{x}^{(h+1)} - \boldsymbol{\mu})(\mathbf{x}^{(h+1)} - \boldsymbol{\mu})^T.$$

Proof. *The proof is left as an exercise.* ∎

We also need this lemma, which establishes a less traditional form of the t density function.

Lemma 8.3 *Suppose* $\mathbf{X}$ *is an* n-*dimensional random vector with density function*

$$\rho(\mathbf{X}) = t\left(\mathbf{x}; \alpha - n + 1, \boldsymbol{\mu}, \frac{v(\alpha - n + 1)}{(v + 1)}\boldsymbol{\beta}^{-1}\right).$$

Then

$$\rho(\mathbf{X}) = \left(\frac{1}{2\pi}\right)^{\frac{n}{2}} \left(\frac{v}{v+1}\right)^{\frac{n}{2}} \left(\frac{c(n,\alpha)}{c(n,\alpha+1)}\right) \left(\frac{|\beta|^{\frac{\alpha}{2}}}{|\hat{\beta}|^{\frac{\alpha+1}{2}}}\right),$$

where

$$\hat{\beta} = \beta + \left(\frac{v}{v+1}\right)(\mathbf{x}-\boldsymbol{\mu})(\mathbf{x}-\boldsymbol{\mu})^{T}$$

and

$$c(n,\alpha) = \left[2^{\alpha n/2}\pi^{n(n-1)/4}\prod_{i=1}^{n}\Gamma\left(\frac{\alpha+1-i}{2}\right)\right]^{-1}. \tag{8.34}$$

Note that the function $c(n,\alpha)$ is the one obtained for the Wishart density function in Theorem 7.25.

Proof. *The proof can be found in Box and Tiao [1973].* ∎

Now we can prove the theorem which gives the density function of D.

Theorem 8.8 *Suppose we have a multivariate normal sample* $\mathsf{D} = \{\mathbf{X}^{(1)}, \mathbf{X}^{(2)}, \dots, \mathbf{X}^{(M)}\}$, *where the* $\mathbf{X}^{(h)}s$ *are n-dimensional, with prior parameter values* β, α, $\boldsymbol{\mu}$, *and* v, *and data* $\mathsf{d} = \{\mathbf{x}^{(1)}, \mathbf{x}^{(2)}, \dots, \mathbf{x}^{(M)}\}$. *Then*

$$\rho(\mathsf{d}) = \left(\frac{1}{2\pi}\right)^{\frac{Mn}{2}} \left(\frac{v}{v+M}\right)^{\frac{n}{2}} \left(\frac{c(n,\alpha)}{c(n,\alpha+M)}\right) \left(\frac{|\beta|^{\frac{\alpha}{2}}}{|\beta^{*}|^{\frac{\alpha+M}{2}}}\right),$$

where β^{*} is given by Equality 8.32 and $c(n,\alpha)$ is given by Equality 8.34. Note that we do not condition on a DAG pattern because we now are talking only about a multivariate normal sample.

Proof. *Owing to the chain rule and Theorem 7.29, we have*

$$
\begin{aligned}
\rho(\mathsf{d}) &= \sum \rho(\mathbf{x}^{(1)}, \dots, \mathbf{x}^{(M)}) \\
&= \prod_{h=0}^{M-1} \rho(\mathbf{x}^{(h+1)} | \mathbf{x}^{(1)}, \dots, \mathbf{x}^{(h)}) \\
&= \prod_{h=0}^{M-1} t\left(\mathbf{x}^{(h+1)}; \alpha_{h}-n+1, \boldsymbol{\mu}_{h}, \frac{v_{h}(\alpha_{h}-n+1)}{(v_{h}+1)}(\beta_{h})^{-1}\right) \\
&= \prod_{h=0}^{M-1} t\left(\mathbf{x}^{(h+1)}; \alpha+h-n+1, \boldsymbol{\mu}_{h}, \frac{(v+h)(\alpha+h-n+1)}{(v+h+1)}(\beta_{h})^{-1}\right),
\end{aligned}
$$

where α_0, $\boldsymbol{\mu}_0$, v_0, and $\boldsymbol{\beta}_0$ denote the initial values α, $\boldsymbol{\mu}$, v, and $\boldsymbol{\beta}$. The last equality is due to the right equality in Equality 8.33. Owing to Lemmas 8.2 and 8.3, we have

$$\rho(\mathsf{d}) = \prod_{h=0}^{M-1} \left(\frac{1}{2\pi}\right)^{\frac{n}{2}} \left(\frac{v+h}{v+h+1}\right)^{\frac{n}{2}} \left(\frac{c(n,\alpha+h)}{c(n,\alpha+h+1)}\right) \left(\frac{|\boldsymbol{\beta}_h|^{\frac{\alpha+h}{2}}}{|\boldsymbol{\beta}_{h+1}|^{\frac{\alpha+h+1}{2}}}\right).$$

Simplifying this product completes the proof.   ∎

We state one more theorem, which will be needed in the next subsection. However, before stating it, we need to develop some notation. If $\mathsf{V} = \{X_1, \ldots, X_n\}$, $\mathsf{W} \subseteq \mathsf{V}$, and $\mathbf{M}$ is an $n \times n$ matrix, then

$$\mathbf{M}^{(\mathsf{W})}$$

denotes the submatrix of $\mathbf{M}$ containing entries M_{ij} such that $X_i, X_j \in \mathsf{W}$. We now have the following theorem:

Theorem 8.9 *Suppose we have a multivariate normal sample $\mathsf{D} = \{\mathbf{X}^{(1)}, \mathbf{X}^{(2)}, \ldots, \mathbf{X}^{(M)}\}$, where the $\mathbf{X}^{(h)}$s are n-dimensional, with prior parameter values $\boldsymbol{\beta}$, α, $\boldsymbol{\mu}$, and v, and data $\mathsf{d} = \{\mathbf{x}^{(1)}, \mathbf{x}^{(2)}, \ldots, \mathbf{x}^{(M)}\}$. Let $\mathsf{V} = \{X_1, \ldots, X_n\}$. For $\mathsf{W} \subseteq \mathsf{V}$ let*

$$\boldsymbol{\beta}_{\mathsf{W}} = \left(\left(\boldsymbol{\beta}^{-1}\right)^{(\mathsf{W})}\right)^{-1},$$

$$\boldsymbol{\beta}_{\mathsf{W}}^* = \boldsymbol{\beta}_{\mathsf{W}} + \mathsf{s}_{\mathsf{W}} + \frac{vM}{v+M}(\overline{\mathbf{x}}_{\mathsf{W}} - \boldsymbol{\mu})(\overline{\mathbf{x}}_{\mathsf{W}} - \boldsymbol{\mu})^T,$$

where subscripting s_{W} and $\overline{\mathbf{x}}_{\mathsf{W}}$ with W means that the quantities are computed for the data restricted to the variables in W,

$$\alpha_{\mathsf{W}} = \alpha - n + l_{\mathsf{W}},$$

where l_{W} is the number if elements in W, and

$$\mathsf{d}_{\mathsf{W}}$$

denote the data d restricted to the variables in W. Then

$$\rho(\mathsf{d}_{\mathsf{W}}) = \left(\frac{1}{2\pi}\right)^{\frac{Ml_{\mathsf{W}}}{2}} \left(\frac{v}{v+M}\right)^{\frac{l_{\mathsf{W}}}{2}} \left(\frac{c(l_{\mathsf{W}}, \alpha_{\mathsf{W}})}{c(l_{\mathsf{W}}, \alpha_{\mathsf{W}} + M)}\right) \left(\frac{|\boldsymbol{\beta}_{\mathsf{W}}|^{\frac{\alpha_{\mathsf{W}}}{2}}}{|\boldsymbol{\beta}_{\mathsf{W}}^*|^{\frac{\alpha_{\mathsf{W}}+M}{2}}}\right).$$

Proof. *The proof can be found in Heckerman and Geiger [1995].*   ∎

Note that subscripting with W restricts the components of the vectors, not the data items. For example, if

$$
d = \left\{ \begin{pmatrix} x_1^{(1)} \\ x_2^{(1)} \\ x_3^{(1)} \end{pmatrix}, \begin{pmatrix} x_1^{(2)} \\ x_2^{(2)} \\ x_3^{(2)} \end{pmatrix}, \begin{pmatrix} x_1^{(2)} \\ x_2^{(2)} \\ x_3^{(2)} \end{pmatrix} \right\},
$$

and $W = \{x_1, x_3\}$, then

$$
d_W = \left\{ \begin{pmatrix} x_1^{(1)} \\ x_3^{(1)} \end{pmatrix}, \begin{pmatrix} x_1^{(2)} \\ x_3^{(2)} \end{pmatrix}, \begin{pmatrix} x_1^{(2)} \\ x_3^{(2)} \end{pmatrix} \right\}.
$$

8.6.2 The Density function of D Given a DAG pattern

First, we obtain further results for augmented Bayesian networks in general. Then we apply our results to learning structure.

Further Results for Augmented Bayesian Networks

We will use the notation ρ when referring to the joint distribution embedded in an augmented Bayesian network because we will be applying these results to continuous variables. We start with a lemma.

Lemma 8.4 *Let an augmented Bayesian network* $(\mathbb{G}, F^{(\mathbb{G})}, \rho|\mathbb{G})$ *be given where* $\mathbb{G} = (V, E)$ *and* $V = \{X_1, X_2, \ldots, X_n\}$. *Then*

$$
\rho(x_1, x_2, \ldots, x_n | f, \mathbb{G}) = \prod_{i=1}^{n} \rho(x_i | pa_i, f_i | \mathbb{G}).
$$

Proof. *The proof is left as an exercise.* ∎

We have the following definitions:

Definition 8.8 *Suppose we have a set of augmented Bayesian networks such that*

1. *every DAG* $\mathbb{G}$ *in each of the networks contains the same set of variables* $\{X_1, X_2, \ldots, X_n\}$;

2. *for every* i, *if* $(\mathbb{G}_1, F^{(\mathbb{G}_1)}, \rho|\mathbb{G}_1)$ *and* $(\mathbb{G}_2, F^{(\mathbb{G}_2)}, \rho|\mathbb{G}_2)$ *are two networks in the set such that* X_i *has the same parents in* $\mathbb{G}_1$ *and* $\mathbb{G}_2$, *then* $F_i^{(\mathbb{G}_1)} = F_i^{(\mathbb{G}_2)}$,

where $F_i^{(\mathbb{G}_i)}$ *is the parameter set associated with* X_i *in* $\mathbb{G}_i$.
*Then the set is called a **class** of augmented Bayesian networks.*

Example 8.20 *Any subset of all multinomial augmented Bayesian networks such that the DAGs in the networks all contain the same variables is a class of augmented Bayesian networks. Such a class is called a **multinomial augmented Bayesian network class**.*

Example 8.21 *Any subset of all Gaussian augmented Bayesian networks such that the DAGs in the networks all contain the same variables is a class of augmented Bayesian networks. Such a class is called a **Gaussian augmented Bayesian network class**.*

Definition 8.9 *Likelihood modularity holds for a class of augmented Bayesian networks if, for every two networks $(\mathbb{G}_1, \mathsf{F}^{(\mathbb{G}_1)}, \rho|\mathbb{G}_1)$ and $(\mathbb{G}_2, \mathsf{F}^{(\mathbb{G}_2)}, \rho|\mathbb{G}_2)$ in the class and every i, if X_i has the same parents in $\mathbb{G}_1$ and $\mathbb{G}_2$, then for all values pa_i and all values f_i,*

$$\rho(x_i|\mathsf{pa}_i, \mathsf{f}_i, \mathbb{G}_1) = \rho(x_i|\mathsf{pa}_i, \mathsf{f}_i, \mathbb{G}_2). \tag{8.35}$$

where PA_i is the parent set of X_i in the two DAGs, and F_i is the parameter set associated with X_i in the two DAGs.

Example 8.22 *It is left as an exercise to show that likelihood modularity holds for any multinomial augmented Bayesian network class.*

Example 8.23 *It is left as an exercise to show that likelihood modularity holds for any Gaussian augmented Bayesian network class.*

Definition 8.10 *Parameter modularity holds for a class of augmented Bayesian networks if, for every two networks $(\mathbb{G}_1, \mathsf{F}^{(\mathbb{G}_1)}, \rho|\mathbb{G}_1)$ and $(\mathbb{G}_2, \mathsf{F}^{(\mathbb{G}_2)}, \rho|\mathbb{G}_2)$ in the class and every i, if X_i has the same parents in $\mathbb{G}_1$ and $\mathbb{G}_2$, then*

$$\rho(\mathsf{f}_i|\mathbb{G}_1) = \rho(\mathsf{f}_i|\mathbb{G}_2), \tag{8.36}$$

where F_i is the parameter set associated with X_i in the two DAGs.

To illustrate parameter modularity suppose $\mathbb{G}_1$ is $X_1 \rightarrow X_2 \leftarrow X_3$ and $\mathbb{G}_2$ is $X_1 \rightarrow X_2 \rightarrow X_3$. Since X_1 has the same parents in both (none), parameter modularity would imply $\rho(\mathsf{f}_1|\mathbb{G}_1) = \rho(\mathsf{f}_1|\mathbb{G}_2)$. Clearly, parameter modularity does not hold for every multinomial augmented Bayesian network class or for every Gaussian augmented Bayesian network class. However, we do have the following:

Example 8.24 *It is left as an exercise to show that parameter modularity holds for any multinomial augmented Bayesian network class satisfying the following:*

1. *The probability distributions in all the embedded Bayesian networks are the same.*

2. *The specified density functions are all Dirichlet.*

3. *All the augmented networks have the same equivalent sample size.*

Owing to the previous example, we see that parameter modularity holds for the class of augmented Bayesian networks in a multinomial Bayesian network structure learning schema. (See Definition 8.1.) Recall that size equivalence (Definition 8.7) was defined on page 466 for a class of Bayseian network models. Of course, the definition can be stated for a class of augmented Bayesian networks. In the same way, the following definition could be stated using only the Bayesian network models contained in augmented Bayesian networks:

Definition 8.11 *Distribution equivalence holds for a class of augmented Bayesian networks if, for every two networks* $(\mathbb{G}_1, \mathsf{F}^{(\mathbb{G}_1)}, \rho|\mathbb{G}_1)$ *and* $(\mathbb{G}_2, \mathsf{F}^{(\mathbb{G}_2)}, \rho|\mathbb{G}_2)$ *such that* $\mathbb{G}_1$ *and* $\mathbb{G}_2$ *are Markov equivalent, for every value* $\mathsf{f}^{(\mathbb{G}_1)}$ *of* $\mathsf{F}^{(\mathbb{G}_1)}$, *there exists a value* $\mathsf{f}^{(\mathbb{G}_2)}$ *of* $\mathsf{F}^{(\mathbb{G}_2)}$ *such that*

$$\rho(x_1, x_2, \ldots, x_n | \mathsf{f}^{(\mathbb{G}_1)}, \mathbb{G}_1) = \rho(x_1, x_2, \ldots, x_n | \mathsf{f}^{(\mathbb{G}_2)}, \mathbb{G}_2).$$

Example 8.25 *It is left as an exercise to show that distribution equivalence holds for any multinomial augmented Bayesian network class.*

Example 8.26 *Shachter and Kenley [1989] show that distribution equivalence holds for any Gaussian augmented Bayesian network class.*

Example 8.27 *Suppose we have a class of augmented Bayesian networks whose set of variables consists of three or more binary variables, for each* i $\mathsf{F}_i^{(\mathbb{G})} = (A_i, \mathbf{B}_i)$ *and*

$$\rho(X_i = 1 | \mathsf{pa}_i, a_i, \mathbf{b}_i, \mathbb{G}) = \frac{1}{1 + \exp(a_i + \sum_{X_j \in \mathsf{PA}_i} b_{ij} x_j)}.$$

We did not show the dependence of A_i *and* $\mathbf{B}_i$ *on* $\mathbb{G}$ *for the sake of simplicity. Distribution equivalence does not hold for this class. For example, if* $\mathbb{G}_1$ *contains the edges* $X_1 \to X_2$, $X_2 \to X_3$, *and* $X_1 \to X_3$, *and* $\mathbb{G}_2$ *contains the edges* $X_1 \to X_2$, $X_3 \to X_2$, *and* $X_1 \to X_3$, *then clearly* $\mathbb{G}_1$ *and* $\mathbb{G}_2$ *are Markov equivalent. It is left as an exercise to show that there are joint distributions which can be obtained from a value of* $\mathsf{F}^{(\mathbb{G}_1)}$ *but not from a value of* $\mathsf{F}^{(\mathbb{G}_2)}$ *and vice versa.*

Suppose now that we have a class of augmented Bayesian networks such that the DAG $\mathbb{G}$ in each network contains the variables $\{X_1, X_2, \ldots, X_n\}$. Suppose further that we have a set $\mathsf{D} = \{\mathbf{X}^{(1)}, \mathbf{X}^{(2)}, \ldots, \mathbf{X}^{(M)}\}$ of n-dimensional random vectors such that each $X_i^{(h)}$ has the same space as X_i. (Definitions 6.11 and 7.4) and a set d of values of the vectors in D (data). Then, for any member $(\mathbb{G}, \mathsf{F}^{(\mathbb{G})}, \rho|\mathbb{G})$ of the class, we can update relative to d by considering D a Bayesian network sample with parameter $(\mathbb{G}, \mathsf{F}^{(\mathbb{G})})$. We have the following definition, lemmas, and theorem concerning updating:

Definition 8.12 *Suppose we have a class of augmented Bayesian networks for which distribution equivalence holds. Suppose further that for all data* d, *for every two networks* $(\mathbb{G}_1, \mathsf{F}^{(\mathbb{G}_1)}, \rho | \mathbb{G}_1)$ *and* $(\mathbb{G}_2, \mathsf{F}^{(\mathbb{G}_2)}, \rho | \mathbb{G}_2)$ *in the class such that* $\mathbb{G}_1$ *and* $\mathbb{G}_2$ *are Markov equivalent,*

$$\rho(\mathsf{d}|\mathbb{G}_1) = \rho(\mathsf{d}|\mathbb{G}_2),$$

where $\rho(\mathsf{d}|\mathbb{G}_1)$ *and* $\rho(\mathsf{d}|\mathbb{G}_2)$ *are the density functions of* d *when* D *is considered a Bayesian network sample with parameters* $(\mathbb{G}_1, \mathsf{F}^{(\mathbb{G}_1)})$ *and* $(\mathbb{G}_2, \mathsf{F}^{(\mathbb{G}_2)})$, *respectively. Then we say that **likelihood equivalence** holds for the class.*

Example 8.28 *Heckerman et al. [1995] show that likelihood equivalence holds for any multinomial augmented Bayesian network class satisfying the following:*

1. *The probability distributions in all the embedded Bayesian networks are the same.*

2. *The specified density functions are all Dirichlet.*

3. *All the augmented networks have the same equivalent sample size.*

The result in the previous example is the same result as in Lemma 7.4.

Lemma 8.5 *(**Posterior Parameter Modularity**) Suppose we have a class of augmented Bayesian networks for which likelihood modularity and parameter modularity hold. Then the parameters remain modular when we update relative to data* d. *That is, for every two networks* $(\mathbb{G}_1, \mathsf{F}^{(\mathbb{G}_1)}, \rho | \mathbb{G}_1)$ *and* $(\mathbb{G}_2, \mathsf{F}^{(\mathbb{G}_2)}, \rho | \mathbb{G}_2)$ *in the class, for every* i, *if* X_i *has the same parents in* $\mathbb{G}_1$ *and* $\mathbb{G}_2$, *then*

$$\rho(\mathsf{f}_i|\mathsf{d}, \mathbb{G}_1) = \rho(\mathsf{f}_i|\mathsf{d}, \mathbb{G}_2).$$

Proof. *It is left as an exercise to use Equalities 6.6, 8.35, and 8.36 to obtain the proof.* ∎

Lemma 8.6 *Suppose that we have a class of augmented Bayesian networks for which likelihood modularity holds. Suppose further that the DAG* $\mathbb{G}$ *in each network in the class contains the variables in* V. *For* $\mathsf{W} \subseteq \mathsf{V}$ *let* $(\mathbb{G}_\mathsf{W}, \mathsf{F}^{(\mathbb{G}_\mathsf{W})}, \rho | \mathbb{G}_\mathsf{W})$ *be a member of the class for which* $\mathbb{G}_\mathsf{W}$ *is a complete DAG in which all variables in* W *are ordered first. That is, no variable in* $\mathsf{V} - \mathsf{W}$ *has an edge to a variable in* W. *Then, for any data* d,

$$\rho(\mathsf{W}|\mathsf{d}, \mathbb{G}_\mathsf{W}) = \rho(\mathsf{W}|\mathsf{d}_\mathsf{W}, \mathbb{G}_\mathsf{W}).$$

As before, d_W *denotes the data* d *restricted to variables in* W.
Proof. *It is left as an exercise to use Equalities 6.6, and 8.35 to obtain the proof.* ∎

Theorem 8.10 *Suppose that we have a class of augmented Bayesian networks for which likelihood modularity, parameter modularity, and likelihood equivalence hold. Suppose further that* $(\mathbb{G}_C, \mathsf{F}^{(\mathbb{G}_C)}, \rho|\mathbb{G}_C)$ *is a member of the class containing a complete DAG* $\mathbb{G}_C$. *Then, for any member* $(\mathbb{G}, \mathsf{F}^{(\mathbb{G})}, \rho|\mathbb{G})$ *of the class and data* $\mathsf{d} = \{\mathbf{x}^{(1)}, \mathbf{x}^{(2)}, \dots, \mathbf{x}^{(M)}\}$,

$$\rho(\mathsf{d}|\mathbb{G}) = \prod_{i=1}^{n} \frac{\rho(\mathsf{d}_{\mathsf{PA}_i^{(\mathbb{G})} \cup \{x_i\}}|\mathbb{G}_C)}{\rho(\mathsf{d}_{\mathsf{PA}_i^{(\mathbb{G})}}|\mathbb{G}_C)}, \tag{8.37}$$

where $\mathsf{PA}_i^{(\mathbb{G})}$ *is the set of parents of* X_i *in* $\mathbb{G}$.

Proof. *For the sake of notational simplicity, we do not superscript parent sets with a DAG in this proof. Let*

$$\mathsf{d}^{(h)} = \{\mathbf{x}^{(1)}, \dots, \mathbf{x}^{(h-1)}\}.$$

Owing to the chain rule, we have

$$
\begin{aligned}
\rho(\mathsf{d}|\mathbb{G}) &= \prod_{h=1}^{M} \rho(\mathbf{x}^{(h)}|\mathsf{d}^{(h)}, \mathbb{G}) \\
&= \prod_{h=1}^{M} \int \rho(\mathbf{x}^{(h)}|\mathsf{f}^{(\mathbb{G})}, \mathsf{d}^{(h)}, \mathbb{G})\rho(\mathsf{f}^{(\mathbb{G})}|\mathsf{d}^{(h)}, \mathbb{G})d\mathsf{f}^{(\mathbb{G})} \\
&= \prod_{h=1}^{M} \int \rho(\mathbf{x}^{(h)}|\mathsf{f}^{(\mathbb{G})}, \mathbb{G})\rho(\mathsf{f}^{(\mathbb{G})}|\mathsf{d}^{(h)}, \mathbb{G})d\mathsf{f}^{(\mathbb{G})} \\
&= \prod_{h=1}^{M} \int \left[\prod_{i=1}^{n} \rho(x_i^{(h)}|\mathsf{pa}_i^{(h)}, \mathsf{f}_i^{(\mathbb{G})}, \mathbb{G})\right] \rho(\mathsf{f}^{(\mathbb{G})}|\mathsf{d}^{(h)}, \mathbb{G})d\mathsf{f}^{(\mathbb{G})} \\
&= \prod_{h=1}^{M} \int \left[\prod_{i=1}^{n} \rho(x_i^{(h)}|\mathsf{pa}_i^{(h)}, \mathsf{f}_i^{(\mathbb{G})}, \mathbb{G})\rho(\mathsf{f}_i^{(\mathbb{G})}|\mathsf{d}^{(h)}, \mathbb{G})\right] d\mathsf{f}^{(\mathbb{G})} \\
&= \prod_{h=1}^{M} \prod_{i=1}^{n} \int \rho(x_i^{(h)}|\mathsf{pa}_i^{(h)}, \mathsf{f}_i^{(\mathbb{G})}, \mathbb{G})\rho(\mathsf{f}_i^{(\mathbb{G})}|\mathsf{d}^{(h)}, \mathbb{G})d\mathsf{f}_i^{(\mathbb{G})} \\
&= \prod_{h=1}^{M} \prod_{i=1}^{n} \int \rho(x_i^{(h)}|\mathsf{pa}_i^{(h)}, \mathsf{f}_i^{(\mathbb{G})}, \mathbb{G}_i)\rho(\mathsf{f}_i^{(\mathbb{G})}|\mathsf{d}^{(h)}, \mathbb{G}_i)d\mathsf{f}^{(\mathbb{G})}, \tag{8.38}
\end{aligned}
$$

where $\mathbb{G}_i$ *is a complete DAG in which all variables in* PA_i *are ordered first, followed by* X_i *and then by the remaining variables. The third equality is true because the* $\mathbf{X}^{(h)}$*s are mutually independent conditional on* $\mathsf{f}^{(\mathbb{G})}$, *the fourth equality is true due to Lemma 8.4, the fifth equality is true due to Theorem 6.9, and the seventh equality follows from Equality 8.35 and Lemma 8.5.*

We have, after performing the integration in Equality 8.38,

$$
\begin{aligned}
\rho(\mathsf{d}|\mathbb{G}) &= \prod_{h=1}^{M}\prod_{i=1}^{n}\rho(x_i^{(h)}|\mathsf{pa}_i^{(h)},\mathsf{d}^{(h)},\mathbb{G}_i) \\[2mm]
&= \prod_{h=1}^{M}\prod_{i=1}^{n}\frac{\rho(x_i^{(h)},\mathsf{pa}_i^{(h)}|\mathsf{d}^{(h)},\mathbb{G}_i)}{\rho(\mathsf{pa}_i^{(h)}|\mathsf{d}^{(h)},\mathbb{G}_i)} \\[2mm]
&= \prod_{h=1}^{M}\prod_{i=1}^{n}\frac{\rho(x_i^{(h)},\mathsf{pa}_i^{(h)}|\mathsf{d}_{\mathsf{PA}_i\cup\{X_i\}}^{(h)},\mathbb{G}_i)}{\rho(\mathsf{pa}_i^{(h)}|\mathsf{d}_{\mathsf{PA}_i}^{(h)},\mathbb{G}_i)} \\[2mm]
&= \prod_{i=1}^{n}\prod_{h=1}^{M}\frac{\rho(x_i^{(h)},\mathsf{pa}_i^{(h)}|\mathsf{pa}_i^{(1)},x_i^{(1)},\dots,\mathsf{pa}_i^{(h-1)},x_i^{(h-1)},\mathbb{G}_i)}{\rho(\mathsf{pa}_i^{(h)}|\mathsf{pa}_i^{(1)},\dots,\mathsf{pa}_i^{(h-1)},\mathbb{G}_i)} \\[2mm]
&= \prod_{i=1}^{n}\frac{\rho(\mathsf{pa}_i^{(1)},x_i^{(1)},\dots,\mathsf{pa}_i^{(M)},x_i^{(M)}|\mathbb{G}_i)}{\rho(\mathsf{pa}_i^{(1)},\dots,\mathsf{pa}_i^{(M)}|\mathbb{G}_i)} \\[2mm]
&= \prod_{i=1}^{n}\frac{\rho(\mathsf{d}_{\mathsf{PA}_i\cup\{X_i\}}|\mathbb{G}_i)}{\rho(\mathsf{d}_{\mathsf{PA}_i}|\mathbb{G}_i)}. \qquad\qquad (8.39)
\end{aligned}
$$

The third equality is true due to Lemma 8.6, the fourth is obtained by writing the elements of the sets $\mathsf{d}_{\mathsf{PA}_i}^{(h)}$ and $\mathsf{d}_{\mathsf{PA}_i\cup\{X_i\}}^{(h)}$, and the fifth is true due to the chain rule.

Due to likelihood equivalence, we have, for $1 \le i \le n$,

$$\rho(\mathsf{d}|\mathbb{G}_i) = \rho(\mathsf{d}|\mathbb{G}_C).$$

So for any subset $\mathsf{W} \subseteq \mathsf{V}$, by summing over all values of the variables in $\mathsf{D}_{\mathsf{V-W}}$, we obtain for $1 \le i \le n$,

$$\rho(\mathsf{d}_\mathsf{W}|\mathbb{G}_i) = \rho(\mathsf{d}_\mathsf{W}|\mathbb{G}_C).$$

Applying this result to Equality 8.39 completes the proof.   ∎

Example 8.29 *Owing to Examples 8.22, 8.24, and 8.28, likelihood modularity, parameter modularity, and likelihood equivalence hold for any multinomial augmented Bayesian network class satisfying the following:*

1. *The probability distributions in all the embedded Bayesian networks are the same.*

2. *The specified density functions are all Dirichlet.*

3. *All the augmented networks have the same equivalent sample size.*

Therefore, the result in the previous theorem holds for this class. Heckerman and Geiger [1995] use that fact to obtain the result in Corollary 7.6, which we obtained directly.

Learning Structure

First we show how to compute the density of d given a complete DAG pattern. Then we show how to do it for an arbitrary DAG pattern.

A Complete DAG pattern Recall from Section 8.1.1 that a DAG pattern event is the event that all and only the d-separations in the pattern are conditional independencies in the relative frequency distribution of the variables. Recall further that a multivariate normal sample (Definition 7.21) makes no assumptions of conditional independencies. So, we assume that given the event that no conditional independencies are present, we have a multivariate normal sample. Since the complete DAG pattern event gp_C is the event that no conditional independencies are present, owing to Theorem 8.8, we have

$$\rho(\mathsf{d}|gp_C) = \left(\frac{1}{2\pi}\right)^{\frac{Mn}{2}} \left(\frac{v}{v+M}\right)^{\frac{n}{2}} \left(\frac{c(n,\alpha)}{c(n,\alpha+M)}\right) \left(\frac{|\beta|^{\frac{\alpha}{2}}}{|\beta^*|^{\frac{\alpha+M}{2}}}\right), \quad (8.40)$$

where

$$c(n,\alpha) = \left[2^{\alpha n/2}\pi^{n(n-1)/4}\prod_{i=1}^{n}\Gamma\left(\frac{\alpha+1-i}{2}\right)\right]^{-1}.$$

To compute the density function of the data given this pattern, we first use Steps 1–5 in Section 7.2.3 to determine the values needed in Theorem 8.8. Then we apply that theorem to obtain our density function. An example follows.

Example 8.30 *Suppose we have variables X_1 and X_2 and these data* d:

Case	X_1	X_2
1	2	4
2	2	8
3	6	4
4	6	8

To compute the density of the data given the complete DAG pattern, we first use Steps 1–5 in Section 7.2.3 to determine the values needed in Theorem 8.8:

1. *Construct a prior Gaussian Bayesian network* $(\mathbb{G}, P)$. *Suppose it is the network in Figure 8.15.*

2. *Convert the Gaussian Bayesian network to the corresponding multivariate normal distribution, using the algorithm in Section 7.2.3. We need use only Equality 7.28 to do this. We obtain the density function* $N(\mathbf{x}; \boldsymbol{\mu}, \mathbf{T}^{-1})$, *where*

$$\boldsymbol{\mu} = \begin{pmatrix} 0 \\ 0 \end{pmatrix}$$

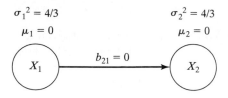

Figure 8.15: A Gaussian Bayesian network

and

$$\mathbf{T}^{-1} = \begin{pmatrix} 4/3 & 0 \\ 0 & 4/3 \end{pmatrix}.$$

3. *Assess prior values of α and.v. We assess*

$$v = 3 \qquad and \qquad \alpha = 2.$$

4. *Compute the prior value of $\boldsymbol{\beta}$. We have*

$$
\begin{aligned}
\boldsymbol{\beta} &= \frac{v(\alpha - n + 1)}{(v+1)}\mathbf{T}^{-1} \\
&= \frac{3(2 - 2 + 1)}{(3+1)} \begin{pmatrix} 4/3 & 0 \\ 0 & 4/3 \end{pmatrix} = \begin{pmatrix} 1 & 0 \\ 0 & 1 \end{pmatrix}.
\end{aligned}
$$

Note that we could not model prior ignorance by taking $v = 0$, $\alpha = -1$, and $\boldsymbol{\beta} = \mathbf{0}$ (as discussed following Theorem 7.28). The function $c(n,\alpha)$ is not defined for $\alpha = -1$, and the expression on the right in Equality 8.40 would be 0 if $\boldsymbol{\beta}$ were $\mathbf{0}$. The reason this happens is that the density function of $\mathbf{X}$ is improper if we use the values that represent prior ignorance. (See Theorem 7.27.) So, we have chosen the smallest "legal" value of α, and a prior Gaussian Bayesian network that yields the identity matrix for $\boldsymbol{\beta}$.

5. *Apply Theorem 7.28 to compute the updated value $\boldsymbol{\beta}^*$. We obtain*

$$\boldsymbol{\beta}^* = \begin{pmatrix} \frac{311}{7} & \frac{288}{7} \\ \frac{288}{7} & \frac{551}{7} \end{pmatrix}. \tag{8.41}$$

We now have

$$\rho(\mathsf{d}|gp_C)$$

$$
= \left(\frac{1}{2\pi}\right)^{\frac{Mn}{2}} \left(\frac{v}{v+M}\right)^{\frac{n}{2}} \left(\frac{c(n,\alpha)}{c(n,\alpha+M)}\right) \left(\frac{|\boldsymbol{\beta}|^{\frac{\alpha}{2}}}{|\boldsymbol{\beta}^*|^{\frac{\alpha+M}{2}}}\right)
$$

$$
= \left(\frac{1}{2\pi}\right)^{\frac{4\times 2}{2}} \left(\frac{3}{3+4}\right)^{\frac{2}{2}} \left(\frac{c(2,2)}{c(2,2+4)}\right) \left|\begin{pmatrix} 1 & 0 \\ 0 & 1 \end{pmatrix}\right|^{\frac{2}{2}} \left|\begin{pmatrix} \frac{311}{7} & \frac{288}{7} \\ \frac{288}{7} & \frac{551}{7} \end{pmatrix}\right|^{-\left(\frac{2+4}{2}\right)}
$$

$$= \left(\frac{1}{2\pi}\right)^{\frac{4\times2}{2}} \left(\frac{3}{3+4}\right)^{\frac{2}{2}} \left(\frac{1/4\pi}{1/96\pi}\right) \left|\begin{pmatrix} 1 & 0 \\ 0 & 1 \end{pmatrix}\right|^{\frac{2}{2}} \left|\begin{pmatrix} \frac{311}{7} & \frac{288}{7} \\ \frac{288}{7} & \frac{551}{7} \end{pmatrix}\right|^{-\left(\frac{2+4}{2}\right)}$$

$$= 1.12 \times 10^{-12}.$$

An Arbitrary DAG Pattern   It is reasonable to construct a class of augmented Bayesian networks, which is used to learn structure, so that likelihood modularity, parameter modularity, and likelihood equivalence all hold. Examples 8.22, 8.24, and 8.28 show that they do indeed hold for the class of augmented Bayesian networks in a multinomial Bayesian network structure learning schema. Assuming these three conditions, Theorem 8.10 gives us the means to calculate the conditional probability of d given an arbitrary DAG from the conditional probability of d given the complete DAG pattern. However, as is the case for learning parameters in Gaussian Bayesian networks, which is discussed in Section 7.2.3, we do not actually develop augmented Gaussian Bayesian networks when we learn structure. However, we use the result in Theorem 8.10 to motivate our structure learning methodology. That is, we compute the probability given the complete DAG pattern as shown in the previous subsection, and then we define the probability given an arbitrary DAG pattern by Equality 8.37. Since this equality involves DAGs and not DAG patterns, we need to show that it yields the same result for Markov equivalent DAGs. The following theorem implies that this is the case:

Theorem 8.11 *Suppose* $\mathbb{G}_1$ *and* $\mathbb{G}_2$ *are Markov equivalent DAGs containing n nodes* $\{X_1, X_2, \ldots, X_n\}$. *Then, for any function* f,

$$\prod_{i=1}^{n} \frac{f(\mathsf{PA}_i^{(\mathbb{G}_1)} \cup \{x_i\})}{f(\mathsf{PA}_i^{(\mathbb{G}_1)})} = \prod_{i=1}^{n} \frac{f(\mathsf{PA}_i^{(\mathbb{G}_2)} \cup \{x_i\})}{f(\mathsf{PA}_i^{(\mathbb{G}_2)})}.$$

Proof. *The proof can be found in Geiger and Heckerman [1994].*   ∎

So, if gp is not the complete DAG pattern, we proceed as follows: We first compute $\rho(d|gp_C)$ as shown in the previous subsection. We then specify some DAG $\mathbb{G}$ in the equivalence class represented by gp, and we define

$$\rho(\mathsf{d}|gp) = \rho(\mathsf{d}|\mathbb{G}) \equiv \prod_{i=1}^{n} \frac{\rho(\mathsf{d}_{\mathsf{PA}_i^{(\mathbb{G})} \cup \{x_i\}}|gp_C)}{\rho(\mathsf{d}_{\mathsf{PA}_i^{(\mathbb{G})}}|gp_C)}, \tag{8.42}$$

where $\mathsf{PA}_i^{(\mathbb{G})}$ is the set of parents of X_i in $\mathbb{G}$. The values in Equality 8.42 can be computed using Theorem 8.9. Recall that in that theorem we did not condition on a DAG pattern. However, we have assumed the assumptions in that theorem constitute the hypothesis of a complete DAG pattern. As was the case for discrete variables, we call the expression in Equality 8.42 the **Bayesian scoring criterion** $score_B$, and it is used to score both DAGs and DAG patterns.

Example 8.31 *Suppose we have the data in Example 8.30. Let gp_I be the pattern in which there is no edge between X_1 and X_2. Then Equality 8.42 becomes*

$$\rho(\mathsf{d}|gp_I) = \rho\left(\mathsf{d}_{\{X_1\}}|gp_C\right)\rho\left(\mathsf{d}_{\{X_2\}}|gp_C\right).$$

We will apply Theorem 8.9 to compute this value. First, we need to compute $\boldsymbol{\beta}_{\{X_1\}}$, $\boldsymbol{\beta}_{\{X_2\}}$, $\boldsymbol{\beta}^*_{\{X_1\}}$, and $\boldsymbol{\beta}^*_{\{X_2\}}$. We have

$$\left(\boldsymbol{\beta}^{-1}\right) = \begin{pmatrix} 1 & 0 \\ 0 & 1 \end{pmatrix}^{-1} = \begin{pmatrix} 1 & 0 \\ 0 & 1 \end{pmatrix}.$$

So

$$\left(\boldsymbol{\beta}^{-1}\right)^{\{X_1\}} = (1)$$

and

$$\boldsymbol{\beta}_{\{X_1\}} = \left(\left(\boldsymbol{\beta}^{-1}\right)^{\{X_1\}}\right)^{-1} = (1)^{-1} = (1).$$

Given this result, it is not hard to see that $\boldsymbol{\beta}^*_{\{X_1\}}$ is simply (β^*_{11}). Similarly, $\boldsymbol{\beta}^*_{\{X_2\}}$ is (β^*_{22}). So, by looking at Equality 8.41, we ascertain that

$$\boldsymbol{\beta}^*_{\{X_1\}} = \left(\frac{311}{7}\right) \qquad and \qquad \boldsymbol{\beta}^*_{\{X_2\}} = \left(\frac{551}{7}\right).$$

Owing to Theorem 8.9, we now have

$$\rho\left(\mathsf{d}_{\{X_1\}}\right)$$

$$= \left(\frac{1}{2\pi}\right)^{\frac{Ml_{\{X_1\}}}{2}} \left(\frac{v}{v+M}\right)^{\frac{l_{\{X_1\}}}{2}} \left(\frac{c(l_{\{X_1\}},\alpha_{\{X_1\}})}{c(l_{\{X_1\}},\alpha_{\{X_1\}}+M)}\right) \left(\frac{|\boldsymbol{\beta}_{\{X_1\}}|^{\frac{\alpha_{\{X_1\}}}{2}}}{|\boldsymbol{\beta}^*_{\{X_1\}}|^{\frac{\alpha_{\{X_1\}}+M}{2}}}\right)$$

$$= \left(\frac{1}{2\pi}\right)^{\frac{4\times1}{2}} \left(\frac{3}{3+4}\right)^{\frac{1}{2}} \left(\frac{c(1,1)}{c(1,1+4)}\right) |1|^{\frac{1}{2}} \left|\left(\frac{311}{7}\right)\right|^{-\left(\frac{1+4}{2}\right)}$$

$$= \left(\frac{1}{2\pi}\right)^{\frac{4\times1}{2}} \left(\frac{3}{3+4}\right)^{\frac{1}{2}} \left(\frac{1/\left(\sqrt{2}\sqrt{\pi}\right)}{1/\left(3\sqrt{2}\sqrt{\pi}\right)}\right) |1|^{\frac{1}{2}} \left|\left(\frac{311}{7}\right)\right|^{-\left(\frac{1+4}{2}\right)}$$

$$= 3.78 \times 10^{-6}$$

$$\rho\left(\mathbf{d}_{\{X_2\}}\right)$$

$$
= \left(\frac{1}{2\pi}\right)^{\frac{Ml_{\{X_2\}}}{2}} \left(\frac{v}{v+M}\right)^{\frac{l_{\{X_2\}}}{2}} \left(\frac{c(l_{\{X_2\}},\alpha_{\{X_2\}})}{c(l_{\{X_2\}},\alpha_{\{X_2\}}+M)}\right) \left(\frac{|\boldsymbol{\beta}_{\{X_2\}}|^{\frac{\alpha_{\{X_2\}}}{2}}}{|\boldsymbol{\beta}^{*}_{\{X_2\}}|^{\frac{\alpha_{\{X_2\}}+M}{2}}}\right)
$$

$$
= \left(\frac{1}{2\pi}\right)^{\frac{4\times1}{2}} \left(\frac{3}{3+4}\right)^{\frac{1}{2}} \left(\frac{c(1,1)}{c(1,1+4)}\right) |1|^{\frac{1}{2}} \left|\left(\frac{551}{7}\right)\right|^{-\left(\frac{1+4}{2}\right)}
$$

$$
= \left(\frac{1}{2\pi}\right)^{\frac{4\times1}{2}} \left(\frac{3}{3+4}\right)^{\frac{1}{2}} \left(\frac{1/\left(\sqrt{2}\sqrt{\pi}\right)}{1/\left(3\sqrt{2}\sqrt{\pi}\right)}\right) |1|^{\frac{1}{2}} \left|\left(\frac{551}{7}\right)\right|^{-\left(\frac{1+4}{2}\right)}
$$

$$
= 9.05 \times 10^{-7}.
$$

We therefore have

$$
\begin{aligned}
\rho(\mathbf{d}|gp_I) &= \rho\left(\mathbf{d}_{\{X_1\}}\right)\rho\left(\mathbf{d}_{\{X_2\}}\right) \\
&= \left(3.78 \times 10^{-6}\right)\left(9.05 \times 10^{-7}\right) \\
&= 3.42 \times 10^{-12}.
\end{aligned}
$$

Recall from Example 8.30 that

$$
\rho(\mathbf{d}|gp_C) = 1.12 \times 10^{-12}.
$$

Note that gp_I is about three times as likely as gp_C. This is reasonable since the data exhibit independence.

Example 8.32 *Suppose we have two variables, X_1 and X_2, and these data $\mathbf{d}$:*

Case	X_1	X_2
1	1	1
2	2	2
3	4	4
4	5	5

To compute the density function of the data given the complete DAG pattern, we first use Steps 1–5 in Section 7.2.3 to determine the values needed in Theorem 8.8. Suppose we use the same prior values as in Example 8.30. It is left as an exercise to show that

$$
\rho(\mathbf{d}|gp_C) = 4.73 \times 10^{-8}
$$

$$
\rho(\mathbf{d}|gp_I) = 1.92 \times 10^{-10}.
$$

Notice that gp_C is much more likely. This is not surprising, since the data exhibit complete dependence.

Finally, we define the schema for learning structure in the case of Gaussian Bayesian networks. Given this schema definition, the definition of a Gaussian **Bayesian network structure learning space** is analogous to Definition 8.2.

Definition 8.13 *A **Gaussian Bayesian network structure learning schema** consists of the following:*

1. *a prior Gaussian Bayesian network $(\mathbb{G}, P)$;*

2. *values of α and v for a multivariate normal sample;*

3. *for each DAG pattern gp' containing the variables in $\mathbb{G}$ a DAG $\mathbb{G}'$ which is any member of the equivalence class represented by gp'.*

Monti [1999] contains a Bayesian method for learning structure when the network contains both discrete and continuous variables.

8.7   Learning Dynamic Bayesian Networks

Friedman et al. [1998] developed methods for learning the structure of dynamic Bayesian networks which mirror our results for Bayesian networks.

EXERCISES
Section 8.1

Exercise 8.1 *Figure 9.6 on 524 shows the 11 DAG patterns containing three variables X_1, X_2, and X_3. Create a Bayesian network structure learning schema for three variables by assigning, for each variable X_i and each set of parents pa_{ij} of X_i, a Dirichlet distribution of the variables in F_{ij} such that for each k,*

$$a_{ijk} = \frac{N}{q_i r_i},$$

where r_i is the number of possible values of X_i, and q_i is the number of different instantiations of the parents of X_i. Do this for $N = 1, 2$, and 4. For each value of N, create a schema with $r_1 = r_2 = r_3 = 2$ and with $r_1 = 2, r_2 = 3, r_3 = 4$. Assign each DAG pattern a prior probability of $1/11$.

Exercise 8.2 *Suppose we create the joint probability distribution in a multinomial Bayesian network structure learning schema by assigning, for each variable X_i and each set of parents pa_{ij} of X_i, a Dirichlet distribution of the variables in F_{ij} such that for each k,*

$$a_{ijk} = \frac{N}{q_i r_i}.$$

Show that this results in the same probability being assigned to all combinations of values of the X_is.

Exercise 8.3 *Suppose we have the Bayesian network learning schema in Exercise 8.1 with $r_1 = r_2 = r_3 = 2$, and the following data:*

Case	X_1	X_2	X_3
1	1	1	1
2	1	1	1
3	1	1	1
4	1	1	1
5	1	1	1
6	1	1	1
7	1	2	1
8	1	2	1
9	1	2	1
10	2	1	1
11	2	1	1
12	2	2	1
13	1	1	2
14	1	2	2
15	2	1	2
16	2	2	2

Compute $P(\text{gp}|\text{d})$ for each DAG pattern gp for each of the values of N. Is the same DAG pattern most probable for all values of N? Determine which, if any, conditional independencies, hold for the data. Compare your determination to the most probable DAG pattern(s).

Exercise 8.4 *Suppose we have the Bayesian network learning schema in Exercise 8.1 with $r_1 = r_2 = r_3 = 2$, and the following data:*

Case	X_1	X_2	X_3
1	1	1	1
2	1	1	2
3	1	1	2
4	1	1	1
5	1	1	2
6	1	1	1
7	1	1	1
8	1	1	1
9	1	1	2
10	1	2	1
11	1	2	1
12	1	2	1
13	2	1	2
14	2	1	2
15	2	1	2
16	2	2	2

Compute $P(gp|d)$ for each DAG pattern gp and for each of the values of N. Is the same DAG pattern most probable for all values of N? Determine which, if any, conditional independencies, hold for the data. Compare your determination to the most probable DAG pattern(s).

Exercise 8.5 *Show for recurrence 8.2 that $f(2) = 3$, $f(3) = 25$, $f(5) = 29,000$, and $f(10) = 4.2 \times 10^{18}$.*

Section 8.2

Exercise 8.6 *Show for the problem instance discussed in Example 8.6 that $P(X_1^{(9)} = 2|X_2^{(9)} = 1, gp_2, \mathbf{d}) = .41667$.*

Exercise 8.7 *Using model averaging, compute $P(X_1^{(9)} = 2|X_2^{(9)} = 1, \mathbf{d})$ given the Bayesian network structure learning schema and data discussed a) in Example 8.3; and b) in Example 8.4.*

Section 8.3

Exercise 8.8 *Suppose we have a Markov chain with the following transition matrix:*

$$\begin{pmatrix} 1/5 & 2/5 & 2/5 \\ 1/7 & 4/7 & 2/7 \\ 3/8 & 1/8 & 1/2 \end{pmatrix}.$$

Determine the stationary distribution for the chain.

Exercise 8.9 *Suppose we have the distribution $\mathbf{r}^T = (\ 1/9\ \ 2/3\ \ 2/9\ )$. Using the Metropolis–Hastings method, find a transition matrix for a Markov chain that has this as its stationary distribution. Do it both with a matrix $\mathbf{Q}$ that is symmetric and with one that is not.*

Exercise 8.10 *Implement the Candidate method, the Laplace approximation, the BIC approximation, the MLED score, and the Cheeseman–Stutz approximation in the computer language of your choice, and compare their performance using various data sets.*

Section 8.5

Exercise 8.11 *Use a probability distribution, which is faithful to the DAG in Figure 8.7, to generate data containing values of N, F, C, and T, and determine the Bayesian scores of models containing the DAGs in the equivalence classes represented in Figure 8.6 and a model containing the DAG in Figure 8.7. Do this for various sizes of the data set.*

Section 8.6

Exercise 8.12 *Prove Lemma 8.2.*

Exercise 8.13 *Prove Lemma 8.4.*

Exercise 8.14 *Show that likelihood modularity holds for any multinomial augmented Bayesian network class.*

Exercise 8.15 *Show that likelihood modularity holds for any Gaussian augmented Bayesian network class.*

Exercise 8.16 *Show that parameter modularity holds for any multinomial augmented Bayesian network class satisfying the following:*

1. *The probability distributions in all the embedded Bayesian networks are the same.*

2. *The specified density functions are all Dirichlet.*

3. *All the augmented networks have the same equivalent sample size.*

Exercise 8.17 *Show that distribution equivalence holds for any multinomial augmented Bayesian network class.*

Exercise 8.18 *Prove Lemma 8.5.*

Exercise 8.19 *Prove Lemma 8.6.*

Exercise 8.20 *Show that $\boldsymbol{\beta}^*_{\{X_1\}} = (\beta^*_{11})$ in Example 8.31.*

Exercise 8.21 *Obtain the results in Example 8.32.*

Exercise 8.22 *Suppose we have variables X_1 and X_2 and these data* **d***:*

Case	X_1	X_2
1	4	1
2	4	3
3	2	1
4	2	5

Making the assumptions for a Gaussian Bayesian network and assuming the priors in Example 8.30, determine the density of the data given the complete DAG pattern and the DAG pattern with an edge between the variables.

Exercise 8.23 *Given the data in Example 8.22 and the assumptions for a Gaussian Bayesian network, ascertain priors different than those in Example 8.30, and determine the density of the data given the complete DAG pattern and the DAG pattern with an edge between the variables.*

Exercise 8.24 *Suppose we have variables X_1, X_2, and X_3, and these data* d:

Case	X_1	X_2	X_3
1	1	5	3
2	1	6	4
3	2	7	3
4	2	8	4

Making the assumptions for a Gaussian Bayesian network, ascertain priors which come as close as possible to modeling prior ignorance, and determine the density of the data given all possible DAG patterns.

Chapter 9

Approximate Bayesian Structure Learning

As discussed in Section 8.1.4, when the number of variables is not small, to find the maximizing DAG pattern(s) by exhaustively considering all DAG patterns is computationally infeasible. Furthermore, in this case it is not possible to average over all DAG patterns either. Section 9.1 discusses approximation algorithms for finding the most probable structure, while Section 9.2 presents algorithms for doing approximate model averaging.

9.1 Approximate Model Selection

Recall that the problem of finding the most probable structure is called **model selection**, and that the purpose of model selection is to learn a DAG pattern that can be used for inference and decision making. Given that we assign equal prior probabilities to all DAG patterns, this amounts to finding the values of gp that maximize $P(\mathsf{d}|gp)$, which we call the Bayesian score $score_B(\mathsf{d}, gp)$. There could be more than one such pattern. However, to simplify our discussion, we assume there is a unique one. As mentioned above, to find this DAG pattern by exhaustively considering all DAG patterns is computationally infeasible when the number of variables is not small.

One way to handle a problem like this is to develop a heuristic search algorithm. Heuristic search algorithms are algorithms that search for a solution which is not guaranteed to be optimal (in this case the value of gp that maximizes $score_B(\mathsf{d}, gp)$), but rather, they often find solutions that are reasonably close to optimal. A search algorithm requires a **search space** which contains all candidate solutions, and a **set of operations** that transforms one candidate solution to another. In the case of learning Bayesian networks, perhaps the simplest search space consists of all DAGs containing the n variables. We first present a heuristic search algorithm whose search space is the set of such DAGs and that requires a prior ordering of the variables. Then we present an algorithm that does not have the restriction of a prior ordering, but whose search space is still a set of DAGs. Since we are really concerned with learning DAG patterns, we then present an algorithm whose search space is all DAG patterns containing the n variables. Finally, we present an approximate model selection algorithm specifically for the cases of missing data and hidden variables.

Before proceeding, we review the formulas we've developed for $score_B(\mathsf{d}, gp)$, and we develop an expression that shows this score as a product of local scores. In the case of discrete variables, Equality 8.1 gives $score_B(\mathsf{d}, gp)$. Recall that this equality says that

$$score_B(\mathsf{d}, gp) = score_B(\mathsf{d}, \mathbb{G}) = \prod_{i=1}^{n} \prod_{j=1}^{q_i^{(\mathbb{G})}} \frac{\Gamma(N_{ij}^{(\mathbb{G})})}{\Gamma(N_{ij}^{(\mathbb{G})} + M_{ij}^{(\mathbb{G})})} \prod_{k=1}^{r_i} \frac{\Gamma(a_{ijk}^{(\mathbb{G})} + s_{ijk}^{(\mathbb{G})})}{\Gamma(a_{ijk}^{(\mathbb{G})})},$$

$$(9.1)$$

where $a_{ij1}^{(\mathbb{G})}, a_{ij2}^{(\mathbb{G})}, \dots, a_{ijr_i}^{(\mathbb{G})}$, and $N_{ij}^{(\mathbb{G})} = \sum_k a_{ijk}^{(\mathbb{G})}$ are their values in the multinomial augmented Bayesian network $(\mathbb{G}, \mathsf{F}^{(\mathbb{G})}, \rho|\mathbb{G})$ corresponding to gp.

In the case of continuous variables, Equality 8.42 gives $\rho(\mathsf{d}|gp)$. Recall that this equality says

$$score_B(\mathsf{d}, gp) = score_B(\mathsf{d}, \mathbb{G}) = \prod_{i=1}^{n} \frac{\rho(\mathsf{d}_{\mathsf{PA}_i^{(\mathbb{G})} \cup \{x_i\}} | gp_C)}{\rho(\mathsf{d}_{\mathsf{PA}_i^{(\mathbb{G})}} | gp_C)},$$

$$(9.2)$$

where $\mathbb{G}$ is any DAG in the equivalence class represented by gp, $\mathsf{PA}_i^{(\mathbb{G})}$ is the set of parents of X_i in $\mathbb{G}$, and gp_C is the complete DAG pattern.

The score of a DAG or DAG pattern is the product of factors that locally score each node paired with the node's parents in the DAG. We show this next. In the discrete case, for a given node X_i and parent set PA, set

$$score_B(\mathsf{d}, X_i, \mathsf{PA}) = \prod_{j=1}^{q^{(\mathsf{PA})}} \frac{\Gamma(\sum_k a_{ijk}^{(\mathsf{PA})})}{\Gamma(\sum_k a_{ijk}^{(\mathsf{PA})} + \sum_k s_{ijk}^{(\mathsf{PA})})} \prod_{k=1}^{r_i} \frac{\Gamma(a_{ijk}^{(\mathsf{PA})} + s_{ijk}^{(\mathsf{PA})})}{\Gamma(a_{ijk}^{(\mathsf{PA})})}, \quad (9.3)$$

where $q^{(\mathsf{PA})}$ is the number of different instantiations of the variables in PA, $s_{ijk}^{(\mathsf{PA})}$ is the number of cases in which $X_i = k$ and in which the variables in PA are in their jth instantiation, and so forth. Note that $a_{ijk}^{(\mathsf{PA})}$ depends only on i, j, and k and a parent set PA; it does not depend on a DAG. This follows from parameter modularity. (See Definition 8.10.) Similarly, in the continuous case, set

$$score_B(\mathsf{d}, X_i, \mathsf{PA}) = \frac{\rho(\mathsf{d}_{\mathsf{PA} \cup \{x_i\}} | gp_C)}{\rho(\mathsf{d}_{\mathsf{PA}} | gp_C)}.$$

$$(9.4)$$

In both the discrete and continuous cases, we then have

$$score_B(\mathsf{d}, gp) = score_B(\mathsf{d}, \mathbb{G}) = \prod_{i=1}^{n} score_B(\mathsf{d}, X_i, \mathsf{PA}_i^{(\mathbb{G})}),$$

where $\mathsf{PA}_i^{(\mathbb{G})}$ is the set of parents of X_i in $\mathbb{G}$.

9.1.1 Algorithms That Search over DAGs

We present two algorithms in which the search space consists of DAGs.

The K2 Algorithm

First, we give the algorithm. Then, we show an example in which it was applied.

The Algorithm Cooper and Herskovits [1992] developed a greedy search algorithm that searches for a DAG $\mathbb{G}'$ that approximates maximizing $score_B(\mathsf{d}, \mathbb{G})$. That is, the search space is the set of all DAGs containing the n variables. Towards approximately maximizing the $score_B(\mathsf{d}, \mathbb{G})$, for each i they locally find a value PA_i that approximately maximizes $score_B(\mathsf{d}, X_i, \mathsf{PA})$. The single operation in this search algorithm is the addition of a parent to a node. The algorithm proceeds as follows: We assume an ordering of the nodes such that, if X_i precedes X_j in the order, an arc from X_j to X_i is not allowed. Let $Pred(X_i)$ be the set of nodes that precede X_i in the ordering, We initially set the parents PA_i of X_i to empty and compute $score_B(\mathsf{d}, X_i, \mathsf{PA})$. Next we visit the nodes in sequence according to the ordering. When we visit X_i, we determine the node in $Pred(X_i)$ which most increases $score_B(\mathsf{d}, X_i, \mathsf{PA})$. We "greedily" add this node to PA_i. We continue doing this until the addition of no node increases $score_B(\mathsf{d}, X_i, \mathsf{PA})$. Pseudocode for this algorithm follows. The algorithm is called K2 because it evolved from a system name Kutató (Herskovits and Cooper [1991]).

Algorithm 9.1 K2

Problem: Find a DAG $\mathbb{G}'$ that approximates maximizing $score_B(\mathsf{d}, \mathbb{G})$.

Inputs: A Bayesian network structure learning schema BL containing n variables, an upper bound u on the number of parents a node may have, data d.

Outputs: n sets of parent nodes PA_i, where $1 \leq i \leq n$, in a DAG that approximates maximizing $score_B(\mathsf{d}, \mathbb{G})$.

```
void K2   (Bayes_net_struct_learn_schema BL, int u,
              data d, for 1 ≤ i ≤ n parent_set& PAᵢ)
{
   for (i = 1; i <= n; i + +) {            // n is the number of nodes.
      PAᵢ = ∅;
      P_old = score_B(d, Xᵢ, PAᵢ);
      findmore = true;
      while (findmore && |PAᵢ| < u) {    // | | returns the size of a set.
```

Z = node in $Pred(X_i) - \mathsf{PA}_i$ that maximizes $score_B(\mathsf{d}, X_i, \mathsf{PA}_i \cup \{Z\})$;
$P_{new} = score_B(\mathsf{d}, X_i, \mathsf{PA}_i \cup \{Z\})$;
if $(P_{new} > P_{old})$ {
    $P_{old} = P_{new}$;
    $\mathsf{PA}_i = \mathsf{PA}_i \cup \{Z\}$;
}
else
    $findmore$ = false;
}
}
}

Next we analyze the algorithm:

Analysis of Algorithm 9.1 (K2)

Let

n	=	number of variables (nodes)
r	=	maximum number of values for any one variable
u	=	upper bound on number of parents a node may have
M	=	number of cases in the data
L	=	$maximum(N_{ij})$

We assume the values of the gamma functions in Equality 9.3 are first computed and stored in an array. There are no such values greater than $\Gamma(L+M)$ in Equality 9.3 because M_{ij} can have no value greater than M. The time complexity of computing and storing the factorials of the integers from 1 to $L + M - 1$ is in

$$O(L + M - 1).$$

In each iteration of the **while** loop, the determination of the value of Z requires at most $n-1$ computations of g because each node has at most $n-1$ predecessors. Cooper and Herskovits [1992] show that the time complexity to compute g once is in $O(Mur)$. Therefore, the time complexity to compute the value of Z once is in $O(nMur)$. The other statements in the **while** loop require constant time. There are always at most u iterations of the **while** loop and n iterations of the **for** loop. Therefore, the time complexity of the **for** loop is in $O(n^2Mu^2r)$. Since $u \leq n$, this time complexity of the **for** loop is in

$$O(n^4Mr).$$

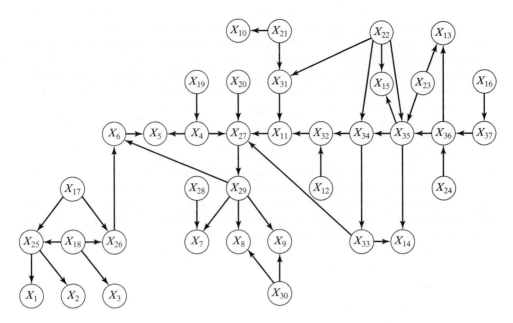

Figure 9.1: The DAG in the ALARM Bayesian network.

You might wonder where we could obtain the ordering required by Algorithm 9.1. Such an ordering could be obtained from domain knowledge such as a time ordering of the variables. For example, we might know that in patients, smoking precedes bronchitis and lung cancer, and that each of these conditions precedes fatigue and a positive chest X-ray.

An Example: The ALARM Network Cooper and Herskovits [1992] tested the K2 algorithm in the following way. They randomly generated 10,000 cases from the ALARM Bayesian network, used the K2 algorithm to learn a DAG from the generated data, and then they compared the resultant DAG with the one in the ALARM Bayesian network. We discuss their results next.

The ALARM Bayesian network (Beinlich et al. [1989]) is an expert system for identifying anesthesia problems in the operating room. It is shown in Figure 9.1. For the sake of brevity, we identify only a few values of the variables. You are referred to the original source for the entire network. We identify the following:

Variable	Value	Outcome Mapped to this Value
X_8	1	EKG shows the patient has an increased heart rate.
X_{20}	1	Patient is receiving insufficient anesthesia or analgesia.
X_{27}	1	Patient has an increased level of adrenaline.
X_{29}	1	Patient has an increased heart rate.

There are 37 nodes and 46 edges in the network. Of these 37 nodes, 8 are diagnostic problems, 16 are findings, and 13 are intermediate variables connecting diagnostic problems to findings. Each node has from two to four possible values. Beinlich constructed the network from his personal domain knowledge of the relationships among the variables.

Cooper and Herskovits [1992] generated 10,000 cases from the ALARM network using a Monte Carlo technique developed in Henrion [1988]. Their Monte Carlo technique is an unbiased generator of cases in that the probability of a particular case being generated is equal to the probability of that case according to the Bayesian network. They supplied the K2 algorithm with the 10,000 cases and an ordering of the nodes that is consistent with the partial ordering of the nodes according to the DAG in the ALARM Bayesian network. For example, X_{21} must appear before X_{10} in the ordering because there is an edge from X_{21} to X_{10}. However, they need not be consecutive. Indeed, X_{21} could be first and X_{10} could be last. They manually generated the ordering by adding a node to the list only when the node's parents were already in the list. In their decision as to where to place the nodes in the list, no regard was given to the meaning of the nodes. Their resultant ordering is as follows (we list only the numbers of the nodes):

$$12, 16, 17, 18, 19, 20, 21, 22, 23, 24, 25, 26, 28, 30, 31, 37, 1,$$
$$2, 3, 4, 10, 36, 13, 35, 15, 34, 32, 33, 11, 14, 27, 29, 6, 7, 8, 9, 5$$

From this ordering and the 10,000 cases, the K2 Algorithm constructed a DAG identical to the one in the ALARM network, except that the edge from X_{12} to X_{32} was missing, and an edge from X_{15} to X_{34} was added. Subsequent analysis showed that the edge X_{12} to X_{32} was not strongly supported by the 10,000 cases. Cooper and Herskovits [1992] presented the K2 algorithm with the 100, 200, 500, 1000, 2000, and 3000 cases in the 10,000 case data file. They found that the algorithm learned the same DAG from the first 3000 cases as it learned from the entire file.

An Algorithm Without a Prior Ordering

First we present the algorithm; then we discuss improving it.

The Algorithm We present a straightforward greedy search that does not require a time ordering. The search space is again the set of all DAGs containing the n variables, and the set DAGOPS of operations is as follows:

1. If two nodes are not adjacent, add an edge between them in either direction.

2. If two nodes are adjacent, remove the edge between them.

3. If two nodes are adjacent, reverse the edge between them.

All operations are subject to the constraint that the resultant graph does not contain a cycle. The set of all DAGs that can be obtained from $\mathbb{G}$ by applying one of the operations is called $\mathsf{Nbhd}(\mathbb{G})$. If $\mathbb{G}' \in \mathsf{Nbhd}(\mathbb{G})$, we say $\mathbb{G}'$ is in the **neighborhood** of $\mathbb{G}$. Clearly, this set of operations is **complete** for the search space. That is, for any two DAGs $\mathbb{G}$ and $\mathbb{G}'$ there exists a sequence of operations that transforms $\mathbb{G}$ to $\mathbb{G}'$. The reverse edge operation is not needed for the operations to be complete, but it increases the connectivity of the space without adding too much complexity, which typically leads to better search. Furthermore, when using a greedy search algorithm, including edge reversals seems to often lead to a better local maximum.

The algorithm proceeds as follows: We start with a DAG with no edges. At each step of the search, of all those DAGs in the neighborhood of our current DAG, we "greedily" choose the one that maximizes $score_B(\mathsf{d}, \mathbb{G})$. We halt when no operation increases this score. Note that in each step, if an edge to X_i is added or deleted, we need only reevaluate $score_B(\mathsf{d}, X_i, \mathsf{PA}_i)$. (See Equalities 9.3 and 9.4.) If an edge between X_i and X_j is reversed, we need only re-evaluate $score_B(\mathsf{d}, X_i, \mathsf{PA}_i)$ and $score_B(\mathsf{d}, X_j, \mathsf{PA}_j)$. When a model searching algorithm need only locally recompute a few scores to determine the score for the next model under consideration, we say the algorithm has **local scoring updating**. A model with local scoring updating is considerably more efficient than one without it. Note that Algorithm 9.1 also has local scoring updating. The algorithm follows:

Algorithm 9.2 DAG Search

Problem: Find a DAG $\mathbb{G}$ that approximates maximizing $score_B(\mathsf{d}, \mathbb{G})$.

Inputs: A Bayesian network structure learning schema BL containing n variables, data d.

Outputs: A set of edges E in a DAG that approximates maximizing $score_B(\mathsf{d}, \mathbb{G})$.

```
void DAG_search  (Bayes_net_struct_learn_schema BL,
                  data d,
                  set_of_edges& E)
{
   E = ∅; G = (V, E);
   do
      if (any DAG in the neighborhood of our current DAG
      increases scoreB(d, G))
         modify E according to the one that increases scoreB(d, G) the most;
   while (some operation increases scoreB(d, G));
}
```

An Improvement to the Algorithm A problem with a greedy search algorithm is that it could halt at a candidate solution that locally maximizes the objective function rather than globally maximizing it. (See Xiang et al. [1996].) One way of dealing with this problem is iterated hill-climbing. In iterated hill-climbing, local search is done until a local maximum is obtained. Then, the current structure is randomly perturbed, and the process is repeated. Finally, the maximum over local maxima is used. Other methods for attempting to avoid local maxima include simulated annealing Metropolis et al. [1953], best-first search Korf [1993], and Gibb's sampling (discussed in Section 8.3.1).

9.1.2 Algorithms That Search over DAG Patterns

Although Algorithms 9.1 and 9.2 find a DAG $\mathbb{G}$ rather than a DAG pattern, we can use them to find a DAG pattern by determining the DAG pattern gp representing the Markov equivalence class to which $\mathbb{G}$ belongs. Since $score_B(\mathsf{d}, gp) = score_B(\mathsf{d}, \mathbb{G})$, we have approximated maximizing $score_B(\mathsf{d}, gp)$. However, as discussed in Anderson et al. [1995], there are a number of potential problems in searching for a DAG instead of a DAG pattern. Briefly, we discuss two of the problems. The first is efficiency. By searching over DAGs, the algorithm can waste time encountering and rescoring DAGs in the same Markov equivalence class. A second problem has to do with priors. If we search over DAGs, we are implicitly assigning equal priors to all DAGs, which means DAG patterns containing more DAGs will have higher prior probability. For example, if there are n nodes, the complete DAG pattern (representing no conditional independencies) contains $n!$ DAGs, whereas the pattern with no edges (representing all variables are mutually independent) contains just one DAG. On the other hand, recall from Section 8.1.4 that Gillispie and Pearlman [2001] show that an asymptotic ratio of the number of DAGs to DAG patterns equal to about 3.7 is reached when the number of nodes is only 10. Therefore, on the average, the number of DAGs in a given equivalence class is small and perhaps our concern about searching over DAGs is not necessary. Contrariwise, in simulations performed by Chickering [2001] the average number of DAGs, in the equivalence classes over which his algorithm searched, were always greater than 8.5 and in one case was 9.7×10^{19}.

When performing model selection, assigning equal priors to DAGs is not necessarily a serious problem, since we will finally select a high-scoring DAG that corresponds to a high-scoring DAG pattern. However, as discussed in Section 9.2.2 (which follows), it can be a serious problem in the case of model averaging.

After presenting an algorithm that searches over DAG patterns, we improve the algorithm.

A Basic Algorithm

Chickering [1996b] developed an algorithm that searches over DAG patterns. After presenting the algorithm, we compare its results with those of Algorithm 9.2.

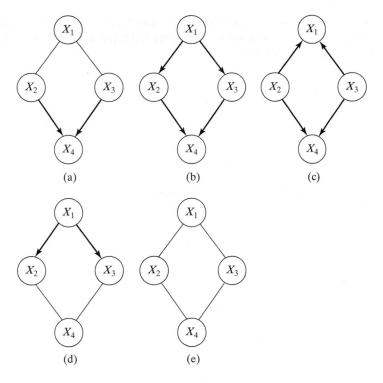

Figure 9.2: The DAG in (b) is a consistent extension of the PDAG in (a), while the DAG in (c) is not. Each of the PDAGs in (d) and (e) does not admit a consistent extension.

First we need some definitions. A **PDAG** (partially directed DAG) gp is a graph containing both directed and undirected edges. A DAG $\mathbb{G}$ is called a **consistent extension** of PDAG gp if $\mathbb{G}$ has the same nodes and links (edges without regard to direction) as gp, all edges directed in gp are directed in $\mathbb{G}$, and $\mathbb{G}$ does not contain any uncoupled head-to-head meetings that are not in gp. PDAG gp admits a consistent extension if there is at least one consistent extension of gp. Notice that a DAG pattern (defined at the end of Section 2.2) is a PDAG, and any DAG in the Markov equivalence class it represents is a consistent extension of it.

Example 9.1 *The DAG in Figure 9.2 (b) is a consistent extension of the PDAG in Figure 9.2 (a), while the DAG in Figure 9.2 (c) is not because it contains the uncoupled head-to-head meeting $X_2 \to X_1 \leftarrow X_3$. The PDAG in Figure 9.2 (d) does not admit a consistent extension because it is not possible to direct the edges so as to have no new uncoupled head-to-head meetings, and the PDAG in Figure 9.2 (e) does not admit a consistent extension because it is not possible to direct the edges so as to have no new uncoupled head-to-head meetings without creating a cycle.*

Now we can describe the algorithm. The search space is the set of all DAG patterns containing the n variables. We start with the following set of operations, which we call **PDAGOPS**:

1. If two nodes are not adjacent, add an edge between them that is undirected or is directed in either direction.

2. If there is an undirected edge, delete it.

3. If there is a directed edge, delete it or reverse it.

4. If there is an uncoupled undirected meeting $X_i - X_j - X_k$, add the uncoupled head-to-head meeting $X_i \rightarrow X_j \leftarrow X_k$.

Anderson et al. [1995] showed that this set of operators is complete for the search space. That is, for any two DAG patterns gp_1 and gp_2 there exists a sequence of operations that transforms gp_1 to gp_2. As is the case for DAGs, the reverse edge operation is not needed for the operations to be complete.

Note that the operations in **PDAGOPS** do not necessarily yield a PDAG that is a DAG pattern. Next we show how to obtain a DAG pattern after applying one of these operations. Assume that we have the following two routines:

void $find\_DAG$ (**PDAG** gp, **DAG&** $\mathbb{G}$, **bool&** $switch$)

void $find\_DAG\_pattern$(**DAG** $\mathbb{G}$, **DAG–pattern&** gp)

If gp admits a consistent extension, routine $find\_DAG$ returns a consistent extension $\mathbb{G}$ and sets $switch$ to true; otherwise, it sets $switch$ to false. Routine $find\_DAG\_pattern$ returns the DAG pattern that represents the Markov equivalence class to which $\mathbb{G}$ belongs. A $\theta(nm)$ algorithm, where n is the number of nodes and m is the number of edges, for $find\_DAG$ appears in Dor and Tarsi [1992]. To obtain a $\theta(m)$ algorithm for $find\_DAG\_pattern$, where m is the number of edges in $\mathbb{G}$, we first change all the edges in $\mathbb{G}$, that are not involved in an uncoupled head-to-head meeting, to undirected edges, and then we apply the **while** loop in Algorithm 10.1 in Section 10.1.

We use the preceding two routines to perform an operation that transforms DAG pattern gp to DAG pattern gp'' as follows:

Apply one of the operations in **PDAGOPS** to gp to obtain gp';
$find\_DAG$ (gp', $\mathbb{G}$, $switch$);
if ($switch$)
  $find\_DAG\_pattern$($\mathbb{G}$, gp'');

Now, if an edge insertion results in a DAG pattern, but the edge in the DAG pattern does not have the same direction as it had when inserted, we do not

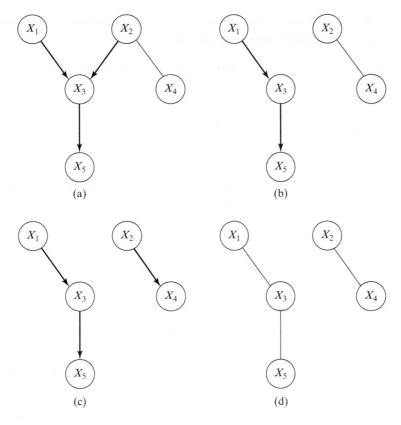

Figure 9.3: An initial DAG pattern gp is shown in (a), the result gp' of deleting the edge $X_2 \to X_3$ is displayed in (b), the output $\mathbb{G}$ of $find\_DAG$ is shown in (c), and the output gp'' of $find\_DAG\_pattern$ is illustrated in (d).

want to allow the operation. That is, if the inserted edge is undirected it must be undirected in the resultant DAG pattern, and if it is directed it must be directed in the resultant DAG pattern. With this restriction, a DAG pattern cannot directly yield another DAG pattern in two different ways. The set of all allowable DAG patterns that can be obtained from gp is called $\mathsf{Nbhd}(gp)$.

Figure 9.3 shows an applications of one operation. That is, Figure 9.3 (a) shows an initial DAG pattern gp, Figure 9.3 (b) shows the result gp' of deleting the edge $X_2 \to X_3$, Figure 9.3 (c) shows the output $\mathbb{G}$ of $find\_DAG$, and Figure 9.3 (d) shows the output gp'' of $find\_DAG\_pattern$. Owing to our restriction, we would not allow the edge $X_1 \to X_5$ to be added to the DAG pattern in Figure 9.3 (d) because it would end up being undirected in the resultant DAG pattern. However, we would allow the edge $X_1 \to X_5$ to be added to the DAG pattern in Figure 9.3 (a) because it would end up being directed in the resultant DAG pattern.

Next we show the algorithm.

Algorithm 9.3 DAG Pattern Search

Problem: Find a DAG pattern gp that approximates maximizing $score_B(\mathsf{d}, gp)$.

Inputs: A Bayesian network structure learning schema BL containing n variables, data d.

Outputs: A set of edges E in a DAG pattern that approximates maximizing $score_B(\mathsf{d}, gp)$.

> **void** $DAG\_pattern\_search$ (**Bayes_net_struct_learn_schema** BL,
> **data** d,
> **set_of_edges&** E)
> {
> $\mathsf{E} = \varnothing;\ gp = (\mathsf{V}, \mathsf{E})$;
>   **do**
>   **if** (any DAG pattern in the neighborhood of our current DAG pattern increases $score_B(\mathsf{d}, gp)$)
>   modify E according to the one that increases $score_B(\mathsf{d}, gp)$ the most;
>   **while** (some operation increases $score(gp)$);
> }

Note that the output $\mathbb{G}$ of $find\_DAG$ can be used to compute the conditional probability of the output gp'' of $find\_DAG\_pattern$. Note further that, when we apply an operator to obtain a new element of the search space, we can get a DAG pattern which is globally quite different from the previous pattern. The example in Figure 9.3 illustrates this. That is, the algorithm does not have local scoring updating. Recall that Algorithm 9.2 does have local scoring updating.

Chickering [1996b] compared Algorithms 9.2 and 9.3. The performance results appear in Tables 9.1 and 9.2. We discuss these results next. A gold standard Bayesian network containing binary variables, whose DAG contained the number of nodes indicated, was used to generate data items. Using a structure learning schema in which the equivalent sample size was 8, Algorithms 9.2 and

# of Nodes	Alg 9.3 Score	Alg 9.2 Score	Score Diff.	Alg 9.3 Struct.	Alg 9.2 Struct.	Struct. Diff.
5	−1326.64	−1327.06	0.42	0.78	1.44	0.66
10	−2745.55	−2764.95	18.50	4.44	10.56	6.12
15	−3665.29	−3677.17	11.88	17.67	21.89	4.22
20	−5372.94	−5408.67	35.73	25.11	30.78	5.67
25	−6786.83	−6860.24	73.41	32.67	47.11	14.44

Table 9.1: A comparison of performance of Algorithms 9.2 and 9.3. Each entry is the average over nine random data sets consisting of 500 items each.

Alg 9.3 Score	Alg 9.2 Score	Score Diff.	Alg 9.3 Struct.	Alg 9.2 Struct.	Struct. Diff.
-101004	-101255	251	36.3	51.5	15.2

Table 9.2: A comparison of performance of Algorithms 9.2 and 9.3 for the ALARM Network. Each entry is the average over 10 random data bases consisting of 10,000 items each.

9.3 were then used to learn a DAG and a DAG pattern, respectively. The DAG pattern, representing the Markov equivalence class to which the gold standard DAG belongs, was then compared to the DAG pattern, representing the Markov equivalence class to which the DAG learned by Algorithm 9.2 belongs, and to the DAG pattern learned by Algorithm 9.3. For each pair of nodes, if the edges between these two nodes were different in the two DAG patterns, one was added to the structural difference. This was done for nine random data sets, and the averages appear in Table 9.1 in the columns labeled Alg 9.2 Struct. and Alg 9.3 Struct. The structural difference appearing in the last column of the table is the structural difference for Algorithm 9.2 minus the structural difference for Algorithm 9.3. So, a positive structural difference indicates that Algorithm 9.3 learned structures closer to that of the gold standard. The scores appearing in the table are the averages of the logs of the probabilities of the data given the structures learned. The score difference is the score of Alg. 9.3 minus the score of Alg. 9.2. So, a positive score difference indicates that Algorithm 9.3 learned structures which make the data more probable. We see that in every case Algorithm 9.3 outperformed Algorithm 9.2 according to both criteria. Table 9.2 contains the same information for the case in which the ALARM network was used to generate the data. Again, Algorithm 9.3 outperformed Algorithm 9.2. Note however that Algorithm 9.3 performed somewhat worse than the K2 algorithm (Algorithm 9.1) relative to the ALARM network. That is, Algorithm 9.3 had a structure difference of 36.3 compared with 2 (Section 9.1.1) for the K2 algorithm. This is not surprising since the K2 algorithm has the benefit of a prior ordering.

# of Nodes	Alg 9.3 Time	Alg 9.2 Time	Time Ratio
5	1	0	—
10	18.11	1.67	10.84
15	70.44	6.22	11.32
20	184.67	11.78	15.68
25	487.33	22.56	21.60

Table 9.3: A comparison of time usage of Algorithms 9.2 and 9.3. Each entry is the average over nine random data bases consisting of 500 items each.

Operation	Change in Score
Insert $X - Y$	$score_B(\mathsf{d}, Y, N_{X,Y}^{+X} \cup \mathsf{PA}_Y) - score_B(\mathsf{d}, Y, N_{X,Y} \cup \mathsf{PA}_Y)$
Insert $X \to Y$	$score_B(\mathsf{d}, Y, \Omega_{X,Y} \cup \mathsf{PA}_Y^{+X}) - score_B(\mathsf{d}, Y, \Omega_{X,Y} \cup \mathsf{PA}_Y)$
Delete $X - Y$	$score_B(\mathsf{d}, Y, N_{X,Y} \cup \mathsf{PA}_Y) - score_B(\mathsf{d}, Y, N_{X,Y}^{+X} \cup \mathsf{PA}_Y)$
Delete $X \to Y$	$score_B(\mathsf{d}, Y, N_Y \cup \mathsf{PA}_Y^{-X}) - score_B(\mathsf{d}, Y, N_Y \cup \mathsf{PA}_Y)$
Reverse $X \to Y$	$score_B(\mathsf{d}, Y, \mathsf{PA}_Y^{-X}) + score_B(\mathsf{d}, X, \mathsf{PA}_X^{+Y} \cup \Omega_{Y,X})$ $-score_B(\mathsf{d}, Y, \mathsf{PA}_Y) - score_B(\mathsf{d}, X, \mathsf{PA}_X \cup \Omega_{Y,X})$
Insert $X \to Z \leftarrow Y$	$score_B(\mathsf{d}, Z, N_{X,Y}^{-Z+X} \cup \mathsf{PA}_Z^{+Y}) + score_B(\mathsf{d}, Y, N_{X,Y}^{-Z} \cup \mathsf{PA}_Y)$ $-score_B(\mathsf{d}, Z, N_{X,Y}^{-Z+X} \cup \mathsf{PA}_Z) + score_B(\mathsf{d}, Y, N_{X,Y} \cup \mathsf{PA}_Y)$

Table 9.4: Local change in score for each operation in PDAGOPS.

Table 9.3 shows results of the Chickering [1996b] time performance comparison of the two algorithms. Recall that both algorithms terminate when no operation increases the score. The time shown in the table is the time until that happens. It is not surprising that Algorithm 9.3 takes significantly longer. First, Algorithm 9.2 need only consider $n(n-1)$ node pairs in each step, while Algorithm 9.3 needs to consider $n(n-1)$ node pairs plus $2e(n-2)$ uncoupled head-to-head meetings in each step. Second, Algorithm 9.3 requires additional overhead by calling *find_DAG* and *find_DAG_pattern*. Third, Algorithm 9.3 does not have local scoring updating, whereas Algorithm 9.2 does. This last problem is removed with the improvement in the next subsection.

Spirtes and Meek [1995] also develop a heuristic algorithm that searches for a DAG pattern.

An Improvement to the Algorithm

A problem with Algorithm 9.3 is that it does not have local scoring updating. In 2001 Chickering improved the algorithm by determining a way to update the score locally. Table 9.4 shows the local change that is needed after each operation is performed. You should consult the original source for a proof that the changes indicated in Table 9.4 are correct. We explain only the notation in the table. In a PDAG, nodes X and Y are called **neighbors** if there is an undirected edge between them. In Table 9.4, PA_X denotes the set of parents of X, N_X denotes the set of neighbors of X, $N_{X,Y}$ denotes the set of common neighbors of X and Y, and $\Omega_{X,Y}$ denotes $\mathsf{PA}_X \cap N_Y$. Furthermore, for any set M, M^{+X} is shorthand for $\mathsf{M} \cup \{X\}$ and M^{-X} is shorthand for $\mathsf{M} - \{X\}$. Chickering [2001] also develops necessary and sufficient conditions for each operation to be valid (that is, the operation yields a DAG pattern). The score in Table 9.4 is the expression in either Equality 9.3 or Equality 9.4.

When we use Table 9.4 to update the score of the new DAG pattern in Algorithm 9.3, we call this the improved Algorithm 9.3. Chickering [2001] compared the improved Algorithm 9.3 to Algorithm 9.2 using six real-life data sets. Table 9.5 shows the results of the time comparisons. We see that in four of six cases the improved Algorithm 9.3 terminated more rapidly, and in two of those

Data set	Time Ratio
MS Web	.95
Nielsen	.96
Each Movie	2.90
Media Metrix	1.49
House Votes	1.27
Mushroom	2.81

Table 9.5: The ratio of the time usage of Algorithm 9.2 to that of improved Algorithm 9.3.

cases it terminated almost three times as fast. Chickering [2001] also found that the improved Algorithm 9.3 outperformed Algorithm 9.2 as far as the patterns they learned.

An Optimal Algorithm

As discussed in Section 9.1.1, a problem with a greedy search algorithm is that it could halt at a candidate solution that locally maximizes the objective function rather than globally maximizing it, and we can deal with this problem using techniques such as iterated hill-climbing. However, these techniques improve only our search; they do not guarantee that we will find an optimal solution. In 1997, Meek developed an algorithm called **GES** (greedy equivalent search) that has the following property: If a perfect map of the generative distribution P exists, the limit, as the size of the data set approaches infinity, of the probability of finding a perfect map of P is equal to 1. In 2002, Chickering proved that this is the case. We describe the algorithm next.

In what follows, we denote the equivalence class represented by DAG pattern gp by **gp**. GES is a two-phase algorithm that searches over DAG patterns. In the first phase, DAG pattern gp' is in the neighborhood of DAG pattern gp, denoted $\mathsf{Nbhd}^+(gp)$, if there is some DAG $\mathbb{G} \in \mathbf{gp}$ for which a single edge addition results in a DAG $\mathbb{G}' \in \mathbf{gp}'$. Starting the DAG pattern containing no edges, we repeatedly replace the current DAG pattern gp with the DAG pattern in $\mathsf{Nbhd}^+(gp)$ that has the highest score of all DAG patterns in $\mathsf{Nbhd}^+(gp)$. We do this until there is no DAG pattern in $\mathsf{Nbhd}^+(gp)$ that increases the score.

The second phase is completely analogous to the first phase. In this phase, DAG pattern gp' is in the neighborhood of DAG pattern gp, denoted $\mathsf{Nbhd}^-(gp)$, if there is some DAG $\mathbb{G} \in \mathbf{gp}$ for which a single edge deletion results in a DAG $\mathbb{G}' \in \mathbf{gp}'$. Starting with the DAG pattern obtained in the first phase, we repeatedly replace the current DAG pattern gp with the DAG pattern in $\mathsf{Nbhd}^-(gp)$ that has the highest score of all DAG patterns in $\mathsf{Nbhd}^-(gp)$. We do this until there is no DAG pattern in $\mathsf{Nbhd}^-(gp)$ that increases the score.

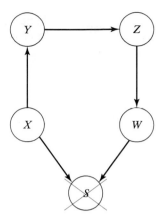

Figure 9.4: Selection bias is present.

Proof of Optimality   We do not show an algorithm for GES since its structure is analogous to that of Algorithm 9.3. Rather, we prove its optimality via the two theorems that follow. First we need a definition:

Definition 9.1 *Let P be a joint probability distribution of the random variables in a set* V*. If, for every variable* $X \in \mathsf{V}$ *and every two subsets* $\mathsf{S}, \mathsf{T} \subseteq \mathsf{V}$ *, whenever* $I_P(\{X\}, \mathsf{S}|\mathsf{T})$ *is not the case, there exists a* $Y \in \mathsf{S}$ *such that* $I_P(\{X\}, \{Y\}|\mathsf{T})$ *is not the case, then we say the **composition property** holds for* P*.*

Theorem 9.1 *Given a class of augmented Bayesian networks for which size equivalence holds, if we have a consistent scoring criterion for DAGs, and if the generative distribution P satisfies the composition property, then the limit, as the size of the data set approaches infinity, of the probability of the first phase of GES yielding an independence map of P is equal to 1.*
Proof.   *The proof can be found in Chickering [2002].*   ∎

The proof of the preceding theorem assumes that the composition property holds for the probability distribution. This property holds for many important probability distributions. Chickering and Meek [2002] show that it holds for all probability distributions that admit embedded faithful DAG representations. They show further that it holds in the case of selection bias even if the distribution does not admit an embedded faithful DAG representation. Recall Figure 2.33, which appears again as Figure 9.4. In Exercise 2.35, we discussed that if the probability distribution of X, Y, Z, W, and S is faithful to the DAG in Figure 9.4, then the probability distribution of X, Y, Z, and W conditional on $S = s$ does not admit an embedded faithful DAG representation. This situation might happen when selection bias is present. (See Section 1.5.1.) Chickering and Meek [2002] show that the composition property holds for such conditional distributions. Specifically, they show that if we have a probability distribution of a set of variables W which admits a faithful DAG representation, $\mathsf{V} \subseteq \mathsf{W}$, $\mathsf{O} \subseteq \mathsf{V}$, and $\mathsf{S} = \mathsf{V} - \mathsf{O}$, then the composition property holds for the probability distribution of O conditional on $\mathsf{S} = \mathsf{s}$.

Theorem 9.2 *Given a class of augmented Bayesian networks for which size equivalence holds, if we have a consistent scoring criterion for DAGs, and the second phase of GES starts with an independence map of the generative distribution P, then the limit, as the size of the data set approaches infinity, of the probability of the second phase of GES yielding an independence inclusion optimal map of P is equal to 1.*

Proof. *The proof is similar to that of Theorem 8.7 on page 467 and is left as an exercise.* ∎

Note that, for the second phase to yield an independence inclusion optimal map, it can start with any independence map. Therefore, it could simply start with the complete DAG pattern. The problem of course with the complete DAG pattern is that, in general, it would require a prohibitively large number of parameters. The purpose of the first phase is that hopefully it will identify a simple independence map.

Theorem 9.3 *Given a class of augmented Bayesian networks for which size equivalence holds, if we have a consistent scoring criterion for DAGs, and if the generative distribution P admits a faithful DAG representation, then the limit, as the size of the data set approaches infinity, of the probability of GES yielding the DAG pattern which is a perfect map of P is 1.*

Proof. *The proof follows from the previous theorems, and the fact that, if P admits a faithful DAG representation, then P satisfies the composition property.* ∎

Time Complexity Chickering [2002] developed a method for efficiently generating the members of $\mathsf{Nbhd}(gp)$ and for updating the score locally. The updating is similar to that shown in Section 9.1.2. In the first phase of the algorithm, at most $\theta(n^2)$ edges can be added and in the second phase at most $\theta(n^2)$ edges can be deleted, where n is the number of nodes. So, in terms of states visited, we have a quadratic time algorithm. Recall from Section 9.1 that Chickering [1996a] has proven that for certain classes of prior distributions the problem of finding the most probable DAG pattern is NP-hard. Therefore, it is unlikely that we have a polynomial-time algorithm. The nonpolynomial-time behavior of this algorithm is in the possible number of members of $\mathsf{Nbhd}(gp)$ that must be investigated in each step. For example, if in gp there is an edge between X and Y and Y has k neighbors that are not adjacent to X, there may be at least $\theta(2^k)$ members of $\mathsf{Nbhd}(gp)$. In experiments performed by Chickering [2002] the density of the search space was never found to be a problem. If it did become a problem in some real-world application, a heuristically-selected subset of $\mathsf{Nbhd}(gp)$ could be investigated at each step; however, the large-sample optimality guarantee would be lost in this case.

Comparison with Algorithms 9.2 and 9.3 Chickering [2002] compared the GES algorithm with Algorithm 9.2 and the improved Algorithm 9.3. When 100 different gold standard Bayesian networks were used to generate data sets,

GES learned the equivalence classes to which the gold standards belongs much more often than Algorithm 9.2 or 9.3. On the other hand, when the algorithms were applied to the six real-life data sets shown in Table 9.5, there was no significant difference in the scores of the DAG patterns learned by Algorithm 9.3 and GES. Indeed, in the case of Media Metrix and Mushroom, the algorithms learned the exact same pattern, which contained no directed links. In all cases the patterns learned were fairly sparse. Since in these experiments the local maxima can be identified by applying many operators that create uncoupled head-to-head meetings, the algorithms essentially traversed the same set of states. Chickering [2002] suspects that, in domains in which there are more complicated dependencies, the GES algorithm will identify different patterns, and, given the results using the gold standards, better patterns. Finally, Chickering [2002] suggests using the GES algorithm as follows. First run a simple, fast DAG-based greedy algorithm like Algorithm 9.2. If the resultant pattern is sparse and contains few compelled edges, a more sophisticated algorithm will probably not find a better solution. On the other hand, if the model is fairly complicated, try the GES algorithm.

Are There Other Optimality Properties? Given that the GES algorithm terminates in a reasonable amount of time, without having to resort to a heuristic, there are two things that could prevent us from finding an optimal solution. The first is that the sample size is not sufficiently large (or it is sufficiently large but an extremely unlikely event occurs). There is nothing we can do about this other than to find a larger data set. The second is that the generative distribution P does not admit a faithful DAG representation. An interesting question is whether the GES algorithm has other optimal properties in this case. We know that, for a large data set, with high probability it finds an independence inclusion optimal map. However, does it also find a parameter optimal map? Chickering and Meek [2002] ran an experiment indicating that it does not. We describe their results next.

Suppose P is faithful to the DAG in Figure 9.4, and all variables are binary except for X, which has space size 4. Representative DAGs from the two DAG patterns, which are inclusion optimal maps of $P|s$ (the distribution of X, Y, Z, and W conditional on $S = s$), appear in Figure 9.5. The DAG model containing the DAG in Figure 9.5 (a) has 23 parameters and is not a parameter optimal map of $P|s$, while the DAG model containing the DAG in Figure 9.5 (b) contains 19 parameters and is. Owing to size equivalence, every DAG in the equivalence class containing the DAG in Figure 9.5 (a) yields a DAG model with 23 parameters. Similarly, DAGs from the equivalence class containing the DAG in Figure 9.5 (b) yield DAG models with 19 parameters. Chickering and Meek [2002] generated many Bayesian networks (each time with a different probability distribution) containing the DAG in Figure 9.4 and with all variables binary except for X, which has space size 4. For each network, they instantiated S to its first value, generated large data sets, and used the GES algorithm to learn a DAG pattern containing the other four variables. They found that the

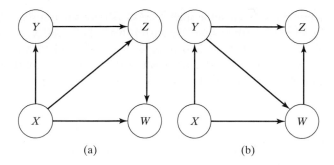

Figure 9.5: Two independence inclusion optimal maps of $P|s$, when P is faithful to the DAG in Figure 9.4 and all variables are binary except for X, which has space size 4. Only the one in (b) is parameter optimal.

GES algorithm learned each DAG pattern about half the time, indicating that a parameter optimal map is not almost always learned when the data set is large.

The experiment just described was conducted using a probability distribution that did not admit an embedded faithful DAG representation. If we assume embedded faithfulness, does the GES algorithm always identify a parameter optimal map for large data sets? Apparently not. Chickering and Meek [2002] performed an experiment, similar to the one just illustrated, in which P admits an embedded faithful DAG representation. They found a parameter optimal map was learned about three-fourths of the time. Another possibility is that, even though GES does not almost always identify a parameter optimal map, it might almost always identify an independence inclusion optimal map containing the maximal number of conditional independencies. That is, there is no independence map containing more conditional independencies. Future research might investigate this possibility.

9.1.3 An Algorithm Assuming Missing Data or Hidden Variables

The algorithms developed so far can be used when we have missing data or hidden variables. In this case we would use as our scoring function an approximate value obtained using one of the methods in Section 8.3.1 or 8.3.2. However, we have a problem in that with these scoring functions we no longer have local scoring updating. So we must do a new expensive computation for each candidate model we consider, which means we must do many expensive computations before we can make a single change in the model. Next we present the **Structural EM Algorithm** Friedman [1998], which only does an expensive computation each time we change the model. We show the algorithm as a modification of Algorithm 9.2, which means that it searches for DAGs. It is straightforward to also modify Algorithm 9.3 and search for DAG patterns. Furthermore, the method holds for discrete and continuous variables, but for simplicity we develop it using notation for discrete variables.

The algorithm starts with some initial DAG $\mathbb{G}$ (say the empty DAG), and it computes (actually estimates using Algorithm 6.1) the MAP value $\tilde{f}^{(\mathbb{G})}$ of $f^{(\mathbb{G})}$ relative to the data. That is, it determines the value of $f^{(\mathbb{G})}$ that maximizes $\rho(f^{(\mathbb{G})}|d, \mathbb{G})$. For a given X_i and parent set PA, the algorithm then scores as follows (the notation used in this formula is discussed after Equality 9.3):

$$score'_B(d, X_i, \mathsf{PA}) = \prod_{j=1}^{q^{(\mathsf{PA})}} \frac{\Gamma(\sum_k a_{ijk}^{(\mathsf{PA})})}{\Gamma(\sum_k a_{ijk}^{(\mathsf{PA})} + \sum_k s_{ijk}'^{(\mathsf{PA})})} \prod_{k=1}^{r_i} \frac{\Gamma(a_{ijk}^{(\mathsf{PA})} + s_{ijk}'^{(\mathsf{PA})})}{\Gamma(a_{ijk}^{(\mathsf{PA})})}, \quad (9.5)$$

In this equality

$$s_{ijk}'^{(\mathsf{PA})} = E(s_{ijk}^{(\mathsf{PA})}|d, \tilde{f}^{(\mathbb{G})}) = \sum_{h=1}^{M} P(X_i^{(h)} = k, \mathsf{pa}_j|\mathbf{x}^{(h)}, \tilde{f}^{(\mathbb{G})}).$$

That is, the calculation is the same as the one used in Algorithm 6.1 (EM MAP determination) except that the probability distribution used to compute the expected value is the MAP value of the parameter set for $\mathbb{G}$. The algorithm scores each candidate DAG $\mathbb{G}''$ as the product of the scores of its variables paired with their parents in $\mathbb{G}''$. Using this scoring methodology, it proceeds exactly as in Algorithm 9.2 except that in each iteration, it scores using the MAP value $\tilde{f}^{(\mathbb{G})}$ where $\mathbb{G}$ is the DAG chosen in the previous iteration.

Algorithm 9.4 Structural EM

Problem: Find a DAG $\mathbb{G}$ that approximates maximizing $score'_B(d, \mathbb{G})$ as given by Equality 9.5.

Inputs: A Bayesian network structure learning schema BL containing n variables, data d with missing values or hidden variables.

Outputs: A set of edges E in a DAG that approximates maximizing $score'_B(d, \mathbb{G})$.

```
void Struct_EM  (Bayes_net_struct_learn_schema BL,
                 data d, set_of_edges& E)
{
    E = ∅; G = (V, E);
    do                                    // This is MAP Value.
        f̃^(G) = value that maximizes ρ(f^(G)|d, G);   // Use Algorithm 6.1.
        compute score'_B(d, G);
        if (any application of an operation in DAGOPS increases score'_B(d, G))
            modify E according to the one that increases score'_B(d, G) the most;
    while (some operation increases score'_B(d, G));
}
```

The preceding algorithm is intuitively appealing for two reasons: (1) if there are no missing data, it reduce to Algorithm 8.2; and (2) it computes the score using expected values relative to the MAP value of the parameter set for the most recent best DAG. However, is there a theoretical justification for it? We discuss such a justification next. Suppose we score each variable and parent set pairing, using

$$
E\left[\ln(score_B(\mathsf{d}, X_i, \mathsf{PA}))\right] = E\left[\ln\left(\prod_{j=1}^{q^{(\mathsf{PA})}} \frac{\Gamma(N_j^{(\mathsf{PA})})}{\Gamma(N_j^{(\mathsf{PA})} + M_j^{(\mathsf{PA})})} \prod_{k=1}^{r_i} \frac{\Gamma(a_{ijk}^{(\mathsf{PA})} + s_{ijk}^{(\mathsf{PA})})}{\Gamma(a_{ijk}^{(\mathsf{PA})})}\right)\right],
$$

where the expected value is again relative to the MAP value of the parameter set for the DAG from the previous iteration. The score of a DAG is then the sum of the scores of the variables paired with their parents in the DAG. Friedman [1998] shows that, if we use this scoring methodology in Algorithm 9.4, we are approximating a method that improves the actual score (probability of the data given the model) in each step. A simple approximation of $E\left[\ln(score_B(\mathsf{d}, X_i, \mathsf{PA}_i))\right]$ is $\ln(score'(X_i, \mathsf{PA}_i))$. That is, we move the expectation inside the logarithm. This approximation is what we used in Algorithm 9.4. Friedman [1998] shows that Equality 9.5 is a good approximation when the expected counts are far from 0. Furthermore, Friedman [1998] develops more complex approximations for cases in which Equality 9.5 is not appropriate.

9.2 Approximate Model Averaging

As mentioned in Section 8.2, Heckerman et al. [1999] illustrate that when the number of variables is small and the amount of data is large, one structure can be orders of magnitude more likely than any other. In such cases, approximate model selection yields good results. However, if the amount of data is not large, it seems more appropriate to do inference by averaging over models as illustrated in the Example 8.6. Another application of model averaging would be to learn partial structure when the amount of data is small relative to the number of variables. For example, Friedman et al. [2000] discuss learning the mechanism by which genes in a cell produce proteins, which then cause other genes to express themselves. In this case, there are thousands of genes, but typically we have only a few hundred data items. In such cases, there are often many structures that are equally likely. So, choosing one particular structure is somewhat arbitrary. However, in these cases we are not always interested in learning the entire structure. That is, rather than needing the structure for inference and decision making, we are interested only in learning relationships among some of the variables. In particular, in the gene expression example, we are interested in the dependence and causal relationships among the expression

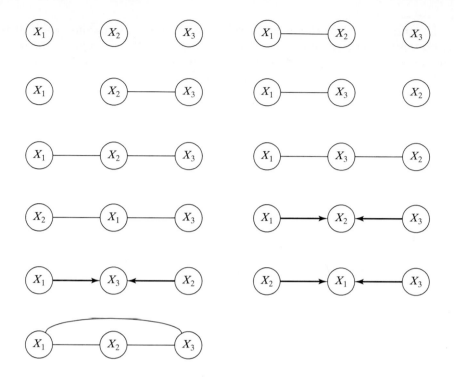

Figure 9.6: The 11 DAG patterns when there are three nodes.

levels of certain genes (See Lander [1999].) Model averaging would be useful in this case. That is, by averaging over the highly probable structures, we may reliably learn that there is a dependence among the expression levels of certain genes.

Madigan and Rafferty [1994] developed an algorithm called **Occam's Window** that does approximate model averaging. Madigan and York [1995] developed another approach that uses the Markov Chain Monte Carlo (MCMC) method. That is the approach discussed here.

After presenting an example of using model averaging to learn partial structure, we develop MCMC algorithms for approximate model averaging.

9.2.1   A Model Averaging Example

Example 8.6 on page 443 illustrated the use of model averaging to do inference. The following example illustrates its use to learn partial structure (as in the gene expression application discussed earlier):

Example 9.2 *Suppose we have three random variables X_1, X_2, and X_3. Then the possible DAG patterns are the ones in Figure 9.6. We may be interested in the probability that a feature of the DAG pattern is present. For example, we may be interested in the probability that there is an edge between X_1 and X_2.*

Given the five DAG patterns in which there is an edge, this probability is 1, and given the six DAG pattern in which there is no edge, this probability is 0. In general, if we let F be a random variable whose value is present if a feature is present,

$$P(F = present|\mathbf{d}) = \sum_{gp} P(F = present|gp, \mathbf{d})P(gp|\mathbf{d})$$

$$= \sum_{gp} P(F = present|gp)P(gp|\mathbf{d}),$$

where

$$P(F = present|gp) = \begin{cases} 1 & \text{if the feature is present in gp} \\ 0 & \text{if the feature is not present in gp.} \end{cases}$$

You may wonder what event a feature represents. For example, what event does an edge between X_1 and X_2 represent? This feature is the event that X_1 and X_2 are not independent and are not conditionally independent given X_3 in the actual relative frequency distribution of the variables. Another possible feature is that there is a directed edge from X_1 to X_2. This feature is the event that, assuming that the relative frequency distribution admits a faithful DAG representation, there is a directed edge from X_1 to X_2 in the DAG pattern faithful to that distribution. Similarly, the feature that there is a directed path from X_1 to X_2 represents the event that there is a directed path from X_1 to X_2 in the DAG pattern faithful to that distribution. Given that we are discussing only the relative frequency distribution, these events are ordinarily not of great interest. However, if we are discussing causality, they tell us something about the causal relationships among the variables. This matter is discussed in Section 10.2.5.

9.2.2 Approximate Model Averaging Using MCMC

As mentioned at the beginning of this section, when the number of possible structures is large, we cannot average over all structures. In these situations we heuristically search for high probability structures, and then we average over them. Next we discuss doing this using the Markov Chain Monte Carlo (MCMC) method.

Recall our two examples of model averaging (Examples 8.6 and 9.2). The first involved computing a conditional probability over all possible DAG patterns. That is, we wish to compute

$$P(\mathsf{a}|\mathsf{b}, \mathsf{d}) = \sum_{gp} P(\mathsf{a}|\mathsf{b}, gp, \mathsf{d})P(gp|\mathsf{a}, \mathsf{d}).$$

The second involved computing the probability that a feature is present as follows:

$$P(F = present|\mathsf{d}) = \sum_{gp} P(F = present|gp)P(gp|\mathsf{d}).$$

In general, these problems involve some function of the DAG pattern and possibly the data, and a probability distribution of the patterns conditional on the data. So we can represent the general problem to be the determination of

$$\sum_{gp} f(gp, \mathsf{d}) P(gp|\mathsf{d}),\tag{9.6}$$

where f is some function of gp and possibly d, and P is some probability distribution of the DAG patterns.

To approximate the value of Expression 9.6 using MCMC, our stationary distribution $\mathbf{r}$ is $P(gp|\mathsf{d})$. Ordinarily, we can compute $P(\mathsf{d}|gp)$ but not $P(gp|\mathsf{d})$. However, if we assume that the prior probability $P(gp)$ is the same for all DAG patterns, then

$$
\begin{aligned}
P(gp|\mathsf{d}) &= \frac{P(\mathsf{d}|gp)P(gp)}{P(\mathsf{d})} \\
&= kP(\mathsf{d}|gp)P(gp),
\end{aligned}
$$

where k does not depend on gp. If we use Equality 8.16 or 8.17 on page 450 as our expression for $\boldsymbol{\alpha}$, k cancels out of the expression, which means that we can use $P(\mathsf{d}|gp)$ in the expression for $\boldsymbol{\alpha}$. Note that we do not have to assign equal prior probabilities to all DAG patterns. That is, we could also use $P(\mathsf{d}|gp)P(gp)$ in the expression for $\boldsymbol{\alpha}$.

If we average over DAGs instead of DAG patterns, the problem is the determination of

$$\sum_{\mathbb{G}} f(\mathbb{G}, \mathsf{d}) P(\mathbb{G}|\mathsf{d}),$$

where f is some function of $\mathbb{G}$ and possibly d, and P is some probability distribution of the DAGs. As is the case for DAG patterns, if we assume that the prior probability $P(\mathbb{G})$ is the same for all DAGs, then $P(\mathbb{G}|\mathsf{d}) = kP(\mathsf{d}|\mathbb{G})$, and we can use $P(\mathsf{d}|\mathbb{G})$ in the expression for $\boldsymbol{\alpha}$. However, we must realize what this assumption entails. If we assign equal prior probabilities to all DAGs, DAG patterns containing more DAGs will have higher prior probability. As noted in Section 9.1.2, when performing model selection, assigning equal prior probabilities to DAGs is not necessarily a serious problem, since we will finally select a high-scoring DAG that corresponds to a high-scoring DAG pattern. However, when performing model averaging, a given DAG pattern will be included in the average according to the number of DAGs in the pattern. For example, there are three DAGs corresponding to the DAG pattern $X - Y - Z$ but only one corresponding to DAG pattern $X \to Y \leftarrow Z$. So by assuming that all DAGs have the same prior probability, we are assuming that the prior probability that the actual relative frequency distribution has the set of conditional independencies $\{I_P(X, Z|Y)\}$ is three times the prior probability that it has the set of conditional independencies $\{I_P(X, Z)\}$. Even more dramatic is the fact that there are $n!$ DAGs corresponding to the complete DAG pattern and only one corresponding to the DAG pattern with no edges. So, we are assuming that the prior probability that there are no conditional independencies is far greater than the prior probability that the variables are mutually independent. This assumption has consequences as follows: Suppose, for example, there are two variables X and Y, the correct DAG pattern is the one without an edge, and we are interested in the feature $I_P(X, Y)$. If we average over DAGs and assign all DAGs equal prior probability, the posterior probability of the pattern $X - Y$ will be larger than it would be if we averaged over patterns and assigned all patterns equal prior probability. Therefore, the feature is less probable if we averaged over DAGs than if we averaged over patterns, which means averaging over patterns has a better result. On the other hand, if the correct pattern is $X - Y$ and the feature of interest is $\neg I_P(X, Y)$, we will confirm the feature more if we average over DAGs. So averaging over DAGs has a better result. We see then that we need to look at the ensemble of all relative frequency distributions rather than at any particular one to discuss which method may be "correct." If relative frequency distributions are distributed uniformly in nature and we assign equal prior probabilities to all DAG patterns, then $P(F = present|\mathbf{d})$, obtained by averaging over DAG patterns, is the relative frequency with which we are investigating a relative frequency distribution with this feature when we are observing these data. So, averaging over DAG patterns is "correct." On the other hand, if relative frequency distributions are distributed in nature according to the number of DAGs in DAG patterns and we assign equal prior probabilities to all DAGs, then $P(F = present|\mathbf{d})$, obtained by averaging over DAGs, is the relative frequency with which we are investigating a relative frequency distribution with this feature when we are observing these data. So averaging over DAGs is "correct." Although it seems reasonable to assume that relative frequency distributions are distributed uniformly in nature, some feel a relative frequency distribution, represented by a DAG pattern containing a larger number of DAGs, may occur more often because there are more causal relationships that can give rise to it.

After developing methods for averaging over DAGs, we develop a method for averaging over DAG patterns.

Averaging over DAGs

After presenting a straightforward algorithm, we simplify it.

A Straightforward Algorithm We show how to use MCMC to approximate averaging over DAGs. Our set of states is the set of all possible DAGs containing the variables in the application, and our stationary distribution is $P(\mathbb{G}|\mathbf{d})$, but as noted previously, we can use $P(\mathbf{d}|\mathbb{G})$ in our expression for $\boldsymbol{\alpha}$. Recall from Section 9.1.1 that $\mathsf{Nbhd}(\mathbb{G})$ is the set of all DAGs which differ from $\mathbb{G}$ by one edge addition, one edge deletion, or one edge reversal. Clearly $\mathbb{G}_j \in \mathsf{Nbhd}(\mathbb{G}_i)$ if and only if $\mathbb{G}_i \in \mathsf{Nbhd}(\mathbb{G}_j)$. However, since adding or reversing an edge can create a cycle, if $\mathbb{G}_j \in \mathsf{Nbhd}(\mathbb{G}_i)$ it is not necessarily true that $\mathsf{Nbhd}(\mathbb{G}_i)$ and $\mathsf{Nbhd}(\mathbb{G}_j)$ contain the same number of elements. For example, if $\mathbb{G}_i$ and $\mathbb{G}_j$

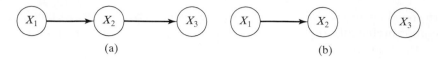

(a)   (b)

Figure 9.7: These DAGs are in each other's neighborhoods, but their neighborhoods do not contain the same number of elements.

are the DAGs in Figures 9.7 (a) and (b), respectively, then $\mathbb{G}_j \in \mathsf{Nbhd}(\mathbb{G}_i)$. However, $\mathsf{Nbhd}(\mathbb{G}_i)$ contains five elements because adding the edge $X_3 \to X_1$ would create a cycle, whereas $\mathsf{Nbhd}(\mathbb{G}_j)$ contains six elements. We create our transition matrix $\mathbf{Q}$ as follows: For each pair of states $\mathbb{G}_i$ and $\mathbb{G}_j$, we set

$$
q_{ij} = \begin{cases} \dfrac{1}{|\mathsf{Nbhd}(\mathbb{G}_i)|} & \mathbb{G}_j \in \mathsf{Nbhd}(\mathbb{G}_i) \\[2mm] 0 & \mathbb{G}_j \notin \mathsf{Nbhd}(\mathbb{G}_i) \end{cases},
$$

where $|\mathsf{Nbhd}(\mathbb{G}_i)|$ returns the number of elements in the set. Since $\mathbf{Q}$ is not symmetric, we use Equality 8.16 rather than Equality 8.17 to compute α_{ij}. Specifically, our steps are as follows:

1. If the DAG at the kth trial is $\mathbb{G}_i$ choose a DAG uniformly from $\mathsf{Nbhd}(\mathbb{G}_i)$. Suppose that DAG is $\mathbb{G}_j$.

2. Choose the DAG for the $(k+1)$st trial to be $\mathbb{G}_j$ with probability

$$
\alpha_{ij} = \begin{cases} 1 & \dfrac{P(d|\mathbb{G}_j) \times |\mathsf{Nbhd}(\mathbb{G}_i)|}{P(d|\mathbb{G}_i) \times |\mathsf{Nbhd}(\mathbb{G}_j)|} \geq 1 \\[4mm] \dfrac{P(d|\mathbb{G}_j) \, |\mathsf{Nbhd}(\mathbb{G}_i)|}{P(d|\mathbb{G}_i) \, |\mathsf{Nbhd}(\mathbb{G}_j)|} & \dfrac{P(d|\mathbb{G}_j) \times |\mathsf{Nbhd}(\mathbb{G}_i)|}{P(d|\mathbb{G}_i) \times |\mathsf{Nbhd}(\mathbb{G}_j)|} \leq 1 \end{cases},
$$

and to be $\mathbb{G}_i$ with probability $1 - \alpha_{ij}$.

A Simplification   It is burdensome to compute the sizes of the neighborhoods of the DAGs in each step. Alternatively, we could include DAGs with cycles in the neighborhoods. That is, $\mathsf{Nbhd}(\mathbb{G}_i)$ is the set of all graphs (including ones with cycles) that differ from $\mathbb{G}_i$ by one edge addition, one edge deletion, or one edge reversal. It is not hard to see that then the size of every neighborhood is equal $n(n-1)$. We therefore define

$$
q_{ij} = \begin{cases} \dfrac{1}{n(n-1)} & \mathbb{G}_j \in \mathsf{Nbhd}(\mathbb{G}_i) \\[2mm] 0 & \mathbb{G}_j \notin \mathsf{Nbhd}(\mathbb{G}_i) \end{cases}.
$$

If we are currently in state $\mathbb{G}_i$ and we obtain a graph $\mathbb{G}_j$ which is not a DAG, we set $P(\mathsf{d}|\mathbb{G}_j) = 0$ (effectively making r_j zero). In this way α_{ij} is zero, the graph is not chosen, and we stay at $\mathbb{G}_i$ in this step. Since $\mathbf{Q}$ is now symmetric, we can use Equality 8.17 to compute α_{ij}. Notice that our theory was developed assuming all values in the stationary distribution are positive, which is not currently the case. However, Tierney [1995] shows convergence also follows if we allow 0 values as discussed here.

Averaging over DAG Patterns

Next we develop an algorithm that approximates averaging over DAG patterns.

Recall from Section 9.1.2 that we developed the following complete set of operations (PDAGOPS) for searching over DAG patterns:

1. If two nodes are not adjacent, add an edge between them that is undirected or is directed in either direction.

2. If there is an undirected edge, delete it.

3. If there is a directed edge, delete it or reverse it.

4. If there is an uncoupled undirected meeting $X_i - X_j - X_k$, add the uncoupled head-to-head meeting $X_i \rightarrow X_j \leftarrow X_k$.

After applying one of these operations, our strategy was to find a consistent DAG extension of the new PDAG if one exists, and then determine the DAG pattern corresponding to the DAG extension. Recall further that the operations in PDAGOPS do not always yield a PDAG that results in a new DAG pattern being chosen. Sometimes an operation yields a PDAG that does not admit a consistent extension; and other times an edge insertion yields a PDAG that admits a consistent extension, but the edge does not have the same direction in the resultant DAG pattern as it had when inserted, which we do not allow. In Section 9.1.2 we called $\mathsf{Nbhd}(gp)$ the set of all allowable DAG patterns that can be obtained from DAG pattern gp. The determination of the sizes of these neighborhoods is not straightforward. For the purpose of model averaging, we can instead let $\mathsf{Nbhd}(gp)$ be the set of all PDAGs that result from applying one of the operations in PDAGOPS to gp. However, $\mathsf{Nbhd}(gp)$ will then contain some PDAGs that do not result in a new DAG pattern being chosen. We can solve this problem using the simplified method shown in at the end of the previous section. That is, if we obtain a PDAG gp' in $\mathsf{Nbhd}(gp)$ that does not result in a DAG pattern being chosen, we stay at gp in this step. Note that, due to our restriction concerning edge direction, each DAG pattern obtainable from gp is chosen in only one way. So, if we choose uniformly from all PDAGs in $\mathsf{Nbhd}(gp)$, we will be choosing each such DAG pattern with probability $1/|\mathsf{Nbhd}(gp)|$. The situation is not as simple as the one concerning DAGs, because the transition Matrix $\mathbf{Q}$ is not symmetric. For example, if gp is the DAG pattern in Figure 9.8 (a), $\mathsf{Nbhd}(gp)$ is the set of PDAGs in Figure 9.8 (c). Yet if gp' is the DAG pattern in Figure 9.8 (b), which clearly results from a member of $\mathsf{Nbhd}(gp)$, $\mathsf{Nbhd}(gp')$

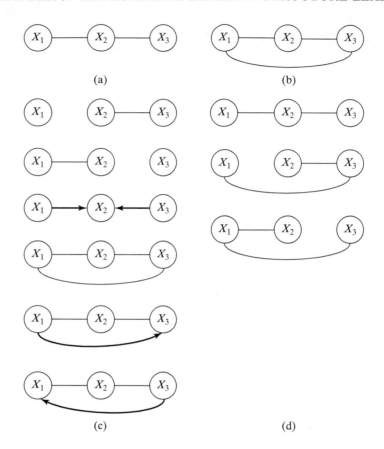

Figure 9.8: The PDAGs in the neighborhood of the DAG patterns in (a) and (b) are shown in (c) and (d), respectively.

contains the PDAGs in Figure 9.8 (d). We can solve this problem using the method discussed at the top of page 528. That is, we count the number of PDAGs in $\mathsf{Nbhd}(gp_i)$ and use that value to determine the values of q_{ij}. In summary, we set

$$
q_{ij} = \begin{cases} \dfrac{1}{|\mathsf{Nbhd}(gp_i)|} & gp_j \in \mathsf{Nbhd}(gp_i) \\[2ex] 0 & gp_j \notin \mathsf{Nbhd}(gp_i) \end{cases},
$$

and if we are currently in state gp_i and obtain a PDAG gp_j which does result in a new DAG pattern being chosen, we stay at gp_i in this step.

Next we discuss determining the size of the neighborhoods. We can do that fairly efficiently as follows: The reverse edge operation is not necessary for our set of operations to be complete. First, we remove this operation. Then the number of possible operations on each edge is unity, regardless of the direction of the edge (namely, to delete it). For a given DAG pattern gp_i, let

$$m \quad = \quad \text{number of edges}$$
$$r \quad = \quad \text{number of uncoupled undirected meetings.}$$

Then

$$\begin{aligned} |\mathsf{Nbhd}(gp_i)| \quad &= \quad 3\left[n(n-1)/2 - (m)\right] + m + r \\ &= \quad 3n(n-1)/2 - 2m + r. \end{aligned}$$

If we start with the DAG pattern with no edges, initially $m = r = 0$. Each time our next pattern results from an edge addition we add 1 to m, and each time it results from an edge deletion we subtract 1 from m. Each time our next pattern results from an edge addition or deletion, we determine if any uncoupled undirected meetings are added or eliminated, and we adjust r accordingly. Finally, each time our next pattern results from an uncoupled head-to-head meeting insertion, we determine how uncoupled undirected meetings have been eliminated. (We know there is at least one.) We then subtract that number from r. Note that this bookkeeping can be done while we construct the DAG pattern, providing little additional overhead. Alternatively, we could not remove the reverse edge operation and perform a little more bookkeeping.

Madigan et al. [1996] developed a method that averages over DAG patterns by introducing an auxiliary variable that takes values in the set of total orderings of the nodes. Friedman and Koller [2000] developed a method that averages over orderings of the nodes instead of over DAGs or DAG patterns. They found this method to be well correlated with averaging over DAG patterns in the case of small networks in which they were able to compute the averages exactly. Furthermore, they found their method outperformed averaging over DAGs in experiments involving recovering features from large data sets.

EXERCISES

Section 9.1

Exercise 9.1 *Does the PDAG in Figure 9.9 admit a consistent extension? If so, find one.*

Exercise 9.2 *Implement Algorithms 9.1, 9.2 and 9.3, and the GES algorithm in the programming language of your choice. Next, develop a Bayesian network in some domain in which you are familiar, use the Monte Carlo technique to generate cases from that network, and finally use your algorithms to approximate learning the most probable DAG pattern. Compare the DAG patterns learned to the DAG pattern representing the Markov equivalence class to which your original DAG belongs.*

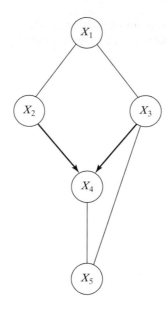

Figure 9.9: A PDAG.

Section 9.2

Exercise 9.3 *Assuming there are three variables X_1, X_2, and X_3, and that all DAG patterns have the same posterior probability (1/11), compute the probability of the following features being present (assuming faithfulness):*

1. *$I_p(X_1, X_2)$.*

2. *$\neg I_p(X_1, X_2)$.*

3. *$I_p(X_1, X_2 | X_3)$ and $\neg I_p(X_1, X_2)$.*

4. *$\neg I_p(X_1, X_2 | X_3)$ and $I_p(X_1, X_2)$.*

Exercise 9.4 *Implement the algorithms for averaging over DAGs and for averaging over DAG patterns and compare their performance on various data sets.*

Chapter 10

Constraint-Based Learning

In Chapters 8 and 9, we assumed that we had a set of variables with an unknown relative frequency distribution, and we developed methods for learning the DAG structure from data by computing the probability of the data given different DAG patterns. Here we take a different approach. Given the set of conditional independencies in a probability distribution, we try to find a DAG for which the Markov condition entails all and only those conditional independencies. This is called **constraint-based learning**. Chapter 11 discusses the relative advantages of the two approaches and shows how, in practice, they can be used together.

We assume that we are able to determine (or at least estimate) the conditional independencies IND_P in a probability distribution P. Usually we do this from data. Since (owing to Lemma 2.2) we need concern ourselves only with conditional independencies among disjoint sets, henceforth we will assume IND_P contains all and only these conditional independencies. Recall Theorem 2.1 which says that the Markov condition entails all and only those conditional independencies that are identified by d-separation. So, our goal is to find a DAG whose d-separations are the same as IND_P. As discussed in Section 8.1.1, since we cannot distinguish DAGs in the same Markov equivalence class from the conditional independencies in P, we can only learn the DAG pattern whose d-separations are the same as IND_P from those conditional independencies. We will use the term "probability" rather than "relative frequency" in this chapter because, although in practice the conditional independencies ordinarily come from a relative frequency distribution, this is not a necessity.

It is possible to find a DAG pattern whose d-separations are the same as IND_P only when P admits a faithful DAG representation. Section 10.1 develops algorithms for finding such a DAG pattern assuming P admits a faithful DAG representation. In Section 10.2, this assumption is relaxed; that is, it is assumed only that the set of conditional independencies can be embedded faithfully in a DAG. Section 10.3 deals with obtaining the set of conditional independencies from data. Finally, in Section 10.4 we discuss the relationship between constraint-based learning and human causal reasoning.

10.1   Algorithms Assuming Faithfulness

Since we are looking for a DAG that has the same d-separations as a set of conditional independencies, our search has nothing to do with numeric probability, which means the theory can be developed without involving the notion of probability. Therefore, we obtain our results by discussing only DAG properties. To do this, we need to first define faithfulness without involving probability.

By a **set of d-separations** IND amongst a set of nodes V we mean a set containing statements of d-separation for the members of V. For example,

$$\mathsf{IND} = \{I(\{X\}, \{Y\}), I(\{X\}, \{Y\}|\{Z\})\} \tag{10.1}$$

is a set of d-separations amongst $V = \{X, Y, Z\}$. In general, such a set does not entail that there actually is a DAG with the d-separations. Indeed, there is no DAG containing the d-separations in Equality 10.1. Note that we do not subscript the set or the d-separations in the set with a DAG because we do not know if there is a DAG with the d-separations. IND simply represents a set of statements as shown in Equality 10.1. We say a set of d-separations IND is **faithful** to DAG $\mathbb{G}$ if IND contains all and only the d-separations in $\mathbb{G}$ and therefore, in all DAGs Markov equivalent to $\mathbb{G}$. When IND is faithful to some DAG, we say IND **admits a faithful DAG representation.** Recall that a DAG pattern gp has the same links as every DAG in the Markov equivalence class represented by the pattern, and Definition 2.8 says that two sets of nodes are d-separated in gp by a third set of nodes if they are d-separated by that set in any (and therefore every) DAG $\mathbb{G}$ in the Markov equivalence class represented by gp. When a set of d-separations IND admits a faithful DAG representation, we say IND is **faithful** to the DAG pattern representing the DAGs with which IND is faithful. Clearly, gp is unique.

We show an algorithm that determines this unique DAG pattern from a set of d-separations when the set admits a faithful DAG representation. First, we give some examples introducing the methodology used in the algorithm; then we present the algorithm. After that, we develop an algorithm for determining whether a given set of d-separations admits a faithful DAG representation. Finally, we apply our results to probability.

10.1.1   Simple Examples

Next we present several examples illustrating constraint-based learning.

Example 10.1 *Suppose* $V = \{X, Y\}$ *and*

$$\mathsf{IND} = \{I(\{X\}, \{Y\})\}.$$

Owing to Lemma 2.7 on page 95, if IND *admits a faithful DAG representation, the DAG pattern faithful to* IND *must not have a link (edge without regard for direction). So we can conclude that only the DAG pattern in Figure 10.1 could be correct. It is left as an exercise to show that* IND *is faithful to this DAG pattern.*

Figure 10.1: Given the d-separation in Example 10.1, this must be the DAG pattern.

Example 10.2 *Suppose* $V = \{X, Y\}$ *and*

$$\text{IND} = \varnothing.$$

Owing to Lemma 2.7, if IND *admits a faithful DAG representation, the DAG pattern faithful to* IND *must have the link* $X - Y$. *So we can conclude that only the DAG pattern in Figure 10.2 could be correct. It is left as an exercise to show that* IND *is faithful to this DAG pattern.*

Example 10.3 *Suppose* $V = \{X, Y, Z\}$ *and*

$$\text{IND} = \{I(\{X\}, \{Y\}|\{Z\})\}.$$

Owing to Lemma 2.7, if IND *admits a faithful DAG representation, the DAG pattern faithful to* IND *must have the links* $X - Z$ *and* $Y - Z$ *and only these links. This means our DAG pattern can only be one of the patterns in Figure 10.3 (a) or (b). Since we have* $I(\{X\}, \{Y\}|\{Z\})$, *Lemma 2.8 says that the meeting* $X - Z - Y$ *must not be head-to-head. So we can conclude that only the DAG pattern in Figure 10.3 (a) could be correct. It is left as an exercise to show that* IND *is faithful to this DAG pattern.*

Example 10.4 *Suppose* $V = \{X, Y, Z\}$ *and*

$$\text{IND} = \{I(\{X\}, \{Y\})\}.$$

Owing to Lemma 2.7, if IND *admits a faithful DAG representation, the DAG pattern faithful to* IND *must have the links* $X - Z$ *and* $Y - Z$ *and only these links. This means that our DAG pattern can only be one of the patterns in Figure 10.3 (a) or (b). Since we have* $I(\{X\}, \{Y\})$, *Lemma 2.8 says the meeting* $X - Z - Y$ *must be head-to-head. So we can conclude only that the DAG pattern in Figure 10.3 (b) could be correct. It is left as an exercise to show that* IND *is faithful to this DAG pattern.*

Figure 10.2: Given the d-separation in Example 10.2, this must be the DAG pattern.

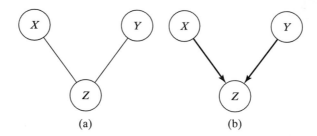

(a)   (b)

Figure 10.3: Given the d-separation in Example 10.3, the DAG pattern must be the one in (a). Given the d-separation in Example 10.4, the DAG pattern must be the one in (b).

Example 10.5 *Suppose* $V = \{X, Y, Z, W\}$ *and our set* IND *of d-separations contains all and only the d-separations entailed by the d-separations in the following set:*

$$\{I(\{X\}, \{Y\}\})\qquad I(\{X, Y\}, \{W\}|\{Z\})\}.$$

For example, IND *also contains the d-separation* $I(\{X\}, \{W\}|\{Z\})$ *because it is entailed by* $I(\{X, Y\}, \{W\}|\{Z\})$. *Owing to Lemma 2.7, our DAG pattern must have the links in Figure 10.4 (a). Since we have* $I(\{X\}, \{Y\})$, *Lemma 2.8 says that the meeting* $X-Z-Y$ *must be head-to-head. Since we have* $I(\{X\}, \{W\}|\{Z\})$, *Lemma 2.8 says that the meeting* $X - Z - W$ *must not be head-to-head. Since we have already concluded that the link* $X - Z$ *must be* $X \rightarrow Z$, *we can therefore conclude that the link* $Z - W$ *must be* $Z \rightarrow W$. *Figure 10.4 (b) shows the resultant DAG pattern. It is left as an exercise to show that* IND *is faithful to this DAG pattern.*

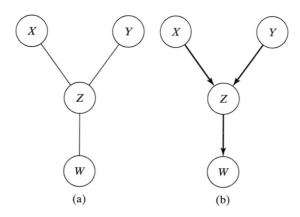

(a)   (b)

Figure 10.4: Given the d-separations in Example 10.5, the links must be as shown in (a) and the DAG pattern must be the one in (b).

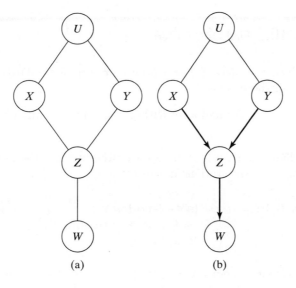

Figure 10.5: Given the d-separations in Example 10.6, the links must be as shown in (a) and the DAG pattern must be the one in (b).

Example 10.6 *Suppose* $V = \{X, Y, Z, U, W\}$, *and our set* IND *of d-separations contains all and only the d-separations entailed by the d-separations in the following set:*

$$\{I(\{X\}, \{Y\}|\{U\}) \qquad I(\{U\}, \{Z, W\}|\{X, Y\}) \qquad I(\{X, Y, U\}, \{W\}|\{Z\})\}.$$

Owing to Lemma 2.7, our DAG pattern must have the links in Figure 10.5 (a). Since we have $I(\{X\}, \{Y\}|\{U\})$, Lemma 2.8 says that the meeting $X - Z - Y$ must not be head-to-head. The other links must all be directed as in Example 10.5 for the reasons given in that example. Figure 10.5 (b) shows the resultant DAG pattern. It is left as an exercise to show that IND *is faithful to this DAG pattern.*

10.1.2   Algorithms for Finding Faithful DAG Patterns

Using the methodology illustrated in the examples in the previous subsection, we next develop algorithms that determine a DAG pattern from the d-separations in the pattern. After giving a basic algorithm, we improve it.

A Basic Algorithm

First we give the algorithm and prove its correctness. Then we give some examples applying it. Finally, we analyze it.

Algorithm 10.1 Find DAG Pattern

Problem: Given a set IND of d-separations, determine the DAG pattern faithful to IND if there is one.

Inputs: a set V of nodes and a set IND of d-separations among subsets of the nodes.

Outputs: If IND admits a faithful DAG representation, the DAG pattern gp containing the d-separations in this set.

```
void find_DAG_pattern (set-of-nodes V,
                       set-of-d-separations IND,
                       graph& gp)
{
    for (each pair of nodes X, Y ∈ V) {          // Use Algorithm 2.2.
        search for a subset S_XY ⊆ V
        such that I({X},{Y}|S_XY);
        if (no such set can be found) {
            create the link X − Y in gp;          // Step 1
        }
    for (each uncoupled meeting X − Z − Y)
        if (Z ∉ S_XY)
            orient X − Z − Y as X → Z ← Y;        // Step 2
    while (more edges can be oriented) {
        for (each uncoupled meeting X → Z − Y );
            orient Z − Y as Z → Y;                // Step 3
        for (each link X − Y
        such that there is a path from X to Y)
            orient X − Y as X → Y;                // Step 4

        for (each uncoupled meeting X − Z − Y
        such that X → W, Y → W, and Z − W)
            orient Z − W as Z → W;                // Step 5
    }
}
```

In an implementation of the algorithm we do not actually input a set of d-separations. Rather, they usually come from a probability distribution.

Next we prove the correctness of the algorithm.

Lemma 10.1 *If the set of d-separations, which are the input to Algorithm 10.1, admit a faithful DAG representation, the algorithm creates a link between X and Y if and only if there is a link between X and Y in the DAG pattern gp containing the d-separations in this set.*

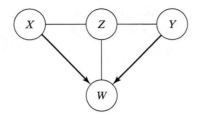

Figure 10.6: The link $Z - W$ must be $Z \to W$.

Proof. *The algorithm produces a link if and only if X and Y are not d-separated by any subset of V, which, owing to Lemma 2.7, is the case if and only if X and Y are adjacent in gp.* ∎

Lemma 10.2 *(soundness) If the set of d-separations, which are the input to Algorithm 10.1, admit a faithful DAG representation, then any directed edge created by the algorithm is a directed edge in the DAG pattern containing the d-separations in this set.*
Proof. *We consider the directed edges created in each step in turn:*

Step 2: *The fact that such edges must be directed follows from Lemma 2.8.*

Step 3: *If the uncoupled meeting $X \to Z - Y$ were $X \to Z \leftarrow Y$, Z would not be in any set that d-separates X and Y due to Lemma 2.8, which means we would have created the orientation $X \to Z \leftarrow Y$ in Step 2. Therefore, $X \to Z - Y$ must be $X \to Z \to Y$.*

Step 4: *If $X - Y$ were $X \leftarrow Y$, we would have a directed cycle. Therefore, it must be $X \to Y$.*

Step 5: *The situation in Step 5 is depicted in Figure 10.6. If $Z - W$ were $Z \leftarrow W$, then $X - Z - Y$ would have to be $X \to Z \leftarrow Y$ because otherwise we would have a directed cycle. But if this were the case, we would have created the orientation $X \to Z \leftarrow Y$ in Step 2. (See the analysis of Step 3.) So $Z - W$ must be $Z \to W$.* ∎

Lemma 10.3 *(completeness) If the set of d-separations, which are the input to Algorithm 10.1, admit a faithful DAG representation, all the directed edges, in the DAG pattern containing the d-separations in this set, are directed by the algorithm.*
Proof. *The proof can be found in Meek [1995b].* ∎

Theorem 10.1 *If the set of d-separations, which are the input to Algorithm 10.1, admit a faithful DAG representation, the algorithm creates the DAG pattern containing the d-separations in this set.*
Proof. *The proof follows from the preceding three lemmas.* ∎

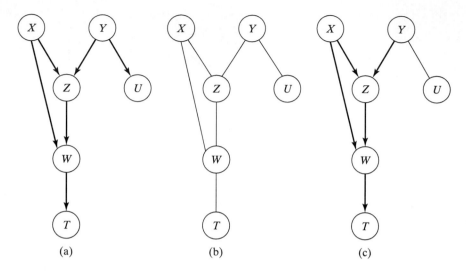

Figure 10.7: Given the d-separations in the DAG in (a), Algorithm 10.1 creates the links in (b) and the directed edges in (c).

Some of the examples that follow involve cases in which IND is fairly large. So, rather than explicitly listing the d-separations in IND, we show d-separations using a DAG.

Example 10.7 *Suppose* $V = \{X, Y, Z, U, T, W\}$ *and* IND *consists of the d-separations in the DAG in Figure 10.7 (a). Given this input, Algorithm 10.1 does the following:*

Step 1 produces the links in Figure 10.7 (b).

Step 2 orients $X - Z - Y$ *as* $X \to Z \leftarrow Y$.

Step 3 orients $Z—W$ *as* $Z \to W$.

Step 4 orients $X - W$ *as* $X \to W$.

Step 3 orients $W - T$ *as* $W \to T$.

   The resultant DAG pattern appears in Figure 10.7 (c).

Example 10.8 *Suppose* $V = \{X, Y, Z, T, W\}$ *and* IND *consists of the d-separations in the DAG in Figure 10.8 (a). Given this input, Algorithm 10.1 does the following:*

Step 1 produces the links in Figure 10.8 (b).

Step 2 orients $X - W - Y$ *as* $X \to W \leftarrow Y$.

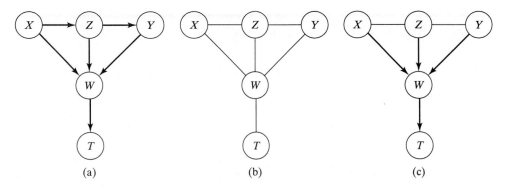

Figure 10.8: Given the d-separations in the DAG in (a), Algorithm 10.1 produces the links in (b) and the directed edges in (c).

Step 3 orients $W - T$ as $W \to T$.

Step 5 orients $Z - W$ as $Z \to W$.

The resultant DAG pattern appears in Figure 10.8 (c).

An implementation of Algorithm 10.1 could prove to be very inefficient because, to determine whether there is a set d-separating X and Y in Step 1, we might search all 2^{n-2} subsets of V not including X and Y. The algorithm given next improves on this performance on the average.

An Improvement to the Algorithm

In the worst case, any algorithm would have to search all 2^{n-2} subsets of $V - \{X, Y\}$ to determine whether X and Y are d-separated. The reason is that, given a subset $U \subset V - \{X, Y\}$, X and Y could be d-separated not by U, but by some superset or subset of U. Therefore, in general we only eliminate one set each time we test for d-separation. However, in the case of sparse DAGs, we can improve things significantly by considering small subsets first. Recall Corollary 2.2, which says that if X and Y are d-separated in DAG $\mathbb{G}$, then either they are d-separated by the parents of X in $\mathbb{G}$ or by the parents of Y in $\mathbb{G}$. This means that we need consider only subsets of ADJ_X in gp and subsets of ADJ_Y in gp when determining whether X and Y are d-separated in gp. By ADJ_X we mean the subset of V consisting of all nodes adjacent to X. Next, we show an algorithm that does this. The algorithm looks first at subsets of size 0, then at subsets of size 1, then at subset of size 2, and so on.

First, we give the algorithm, then we show an example, and finally we discuss its efficiency. We call it the PC algorithm because that is the name given it by its developers in Spirtes et al. [1993, 2000].

Algorithm 10.2 PC Find DAG Pattern

Problem: Given a set IND of d-separations, determine the DAG pattern faithful to IND if there is one.

Inputs: a set V of nodes and a set IND of d-separations among subsets of the nodes.

Outputs: If IND admits a faithful DAG representation, the DAG pattern gp containing the d-separations in this set.

```
void PC (set-of-nodes V,
           set-of-d-separations IND,
           graph& gp)
{
   form the complete undirected graph gp over V;
   i = 0;
   repeat
      for (each X ∈ V)
         for (each Y ∈ ADJ_X) {
            determine if there is a set S ⊆ ADJ_X − {Y}
            such that |S| = i and I({X}, {Y}|S) ∈ IND;     // | | returns
            if such a set S is found {                      // size of set.
               S_XY = S;
               remove the edge X − Y from gp;              // Step 1
            }
         }
      i = i + 1;
   until (|ADJ_X| <= i for all X ∈ V);
   for (each uncoupled meeting X − Z − Y)
      if (Z ∉ S_XY)
         orient X − Z − Y as X → Z ← Y;                    // Step 2

   while (more edges can be oriented) {
      for (each uncoupled meeting X → Z − Y );
         orient Z − Y as Z → Y;                            // Step 3
      for (each X − Y
      such that there is a path from X to Y)
         orient X − Y as X → Y;                            // Step 4
      for (each uncoupled meeting X − Z − Y
      such that X → W, Y → W, and Z − W)
         orient Z − W as Z → W;                            // Step 5
   }
}
```

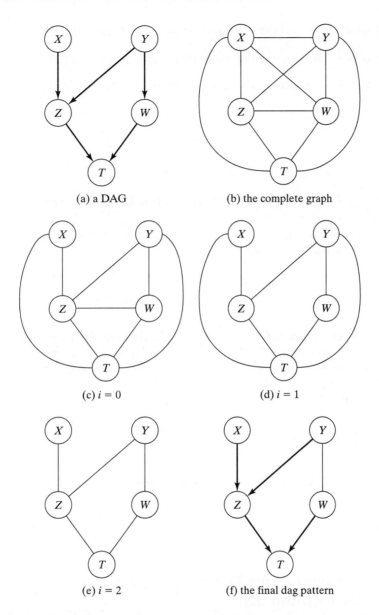

Figure 10.9: Given the d-separations in the DAG in (a), the steps in Algorithm 10.2 produce the graphs in (b)–(f).

Before analyzing the preceding algorithm, we show an example of applying it.

Example 10.9 *Suppose* V $=$ $\{X, Y, Z, T, W\}$ *and* IND *consists of the d-separations in the DAG in Figure 10.9 (a). Given this input, Algorithm 10.2 does the following:*

Step 1 produces the complete undirected graph in Figure 10.9 (b)

Step 2 with i = 0 produces the undirected graph in Figure 10.9 (c);

Step 2 with i = 1 produces the undirected graph in Figure 10.9 (d);

Step 2 with i = 2 produces the undirected graph in Figure 10.9 (e);

Steps 3–6 produce the DAG pattern in Figure 10.9 (f).

Next we analyze the algorithm:

Analysis of Algorithm 10.2 (PC Find DAG Pattern)

We will determine a bound $W(n)$ for the number of d-separation tests required in the **repeat-until** loop. Let

$$n \;=\; \text{number of nodes in } \mathsf{V}$$
$$k \;=\; \text{maximum size of } \mathsf{ADJ}_X \text{ in } gp \text{ over all } X \in \mathsf{V}.$$

There are n choices for the value of X in the first **for** loop. Once X is chosen, there are $n - 1$ choices for Y. For given values of X, Y, and i, we must check at most $\binom{n-2}{i}$ subsets for d-separating X and Y. The values of i, which are considered, are at most from 0 to k. So we have

$$W(n) \leq n(n-1) \sum_{i=0}^{k} \binom{n-2}{i} \leq \frac{n^2(k+1)(n-2)^k}{k!}.$$

It is left as an exercise to derive the second inequality.

So we see, if the DAG pattern is sparse (i.e., no node is adjacent to very many other nodes), the algorithm is reasonably efficient. Of course, in general it is not.

10.1.3   Algorithm for Determining Admission of Faithfulness

Algorithms 10.1 and 10.2 do not check whether the set of d-separations, which is their input, admits a faithful DAG representation. They are guaranteed just to produce the correct DAG pattern if it does. In Examples 10.7, 10.8, and 10.9 the d-separations come from a DAG; so we know they are the d-separations in a DAG pattern. However, in general this is not the case. For example, in the next subsection we will obtain the d-separations from a probability distribution. So, in general we need to check whether the outputs of Algorithms 10.1 and 10.2 are DAG patterns. Next, we discuss how to determine whether this is the case. First, we give examples in which it is not.

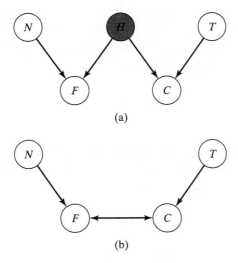

(a)

(b)

Figure 10.10: Given $V = \{N, F, C, T\}$ and IND, consisting of the d-separations in the DAG in (a) restricted to these variables, Algorithms 10.1 and 10.2 will produce the graph in (b).

Example 10.10 *Suppose* $V = \{N, F, C, T\}$ *and* IND *consists of the d-separations in the DAG in Figure 10.10 (a) restricted to these variables. Given this input, it is left as an exercise to show that Algorithms 10.1 and 10.2 produce the graph in Figure 10.10 (b). This graph is not a DAG pattern because it contains a directed cycle. Theorem 10.1 says that, if the set of d-separations, which is the input to Algorithm 10.1, admits a faithful DAG representation, the algorithm creates that DAG pattern faithful to that set. Since the algorithm produced something that is not a DAG pattern, we can conclude* IND *does not admit a faithful DAG representation.*

Note that Figure 10.10 (a) is the same as Figure 8.7 in Section 8.5.1. In that section we said that the variable H is a hidden variable because it is not one of the four variables on which we have data, and we shade nodes representing such variables. Here we are using H only to facilitate showing a set of d-separations amongst N, F, C and T, and there is no need to call it a hidden variable. However, in Section 10.2 we will develop methods for learning a DAG pattern, in which a set of d-separations amongst V is embedded faithfully, when the set does not admit a faithful DAG representation. Using these methods, from the set IND in Example 10.10 we can learn a DAG pattern containing the DAG in Figure 10.10 (a). This pattern will contain a variable other than those in V, and it is hidden in the same way H is hidden in the situation discussed in Section 8.5.1. That is, it is not one of the four variables for which we have "data." When we apply the theory to probability, not having d-separations involving a variable is the same as not having data on the variable. We shade the node now and call it H for consistency.

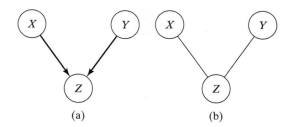

Figure 10.11: Given the d-separations in Example 10.11, Algorithm 10.2 will produce the DAG pattern in (a) and Algorithm 10.1 could produce either DAG pattern.

Example 10.11 *Suppose* $V = \{X, Y, Z\}$ *and*

$$IND = \{I(\{X\}, \{Y\}), I(\{X\}, \{Y\}|\{Z\})\}.$$

Given this input, Algorithm 10.2 produces the DAG pattern in Figure 10.11 (a), while Algorithm 10.1 produces either the one in Figure 10.11 (a) or the one Figure 10.11 (b) depending on whether $I(\{X\}, \{Y\})$ or $I(\{X\}, \{Y\}|\{Z\})$ is found first. It is left as an exercise to show that neither DAG pattern contains both d-separations. Owing to Theorem 10.1, we can conclude that IND does not admit a faithful DAG representation.

The previous example shows that, even if Algorithm 10.1 or Algorithm 10.2 produces a DAG pattern, we cannot assume that this pattern contains the d-separations which are the input to the algorithm. A straightforward way to determine whether this is the case is to check whether the output DAG pattern has all and only the input d-separations (as was done in Example 10.11). Next, we develop an algorithm for doing this.

Recall that a DAG pattern gp has the same d-separations as any DAG $\mathbb{G}$ in the equivalence class represented by that DAG pattern. We can check whether a DAG $\mathbb{G}$ contains all and only a given set IND of d-separations as follows: It is straightforward to check if every d-separation in $\mathbb{G}$ is in IND. (We discuss how to do this after presenting Algorithm 10.4.) We can then use Algorithm 2.2 in Section 2.1.3 to determine whether every d-separation in IND is a d-separation in $\mathbb{G}$. So, if we first construct a DAG in the Markov equivalence class represented by a given DAG pattern from that pattern, we can test whether the pattern has a given set of d-separations. An algorithm for constructing such a DAG follows.

Algorithm 10.3 Construct DAG

Problem: Given a DAG pattern, construct any DAG in the equivalence class represented by that pattern.

Inputs: a graph gp.

Outputs: if *gp* is a DAG pattern, a DAG $\mathbb{G}$ in the equivalence class represented by *gp*.

```
void construct_DAG (graph gp,
                    graph& G)

{
   while there are unoriented edges {
      choose an unoriented edge X − Y;
      orient X − Y as X → Y;                          // Step 1
      while (more edges can be oriented) {
         if (X → Z − Y is an uncoupled meeting);
         orient Z − Y as Z → Y;                       // Step 2
         if (X − Y && there is a path from X to Y)
            orient X − Y as X → Y;                    // Step 3
         for (each uncoupled meeting X − Z − Y
         such that X → W, Y → W, and Z − W)
            orient Z − W as Z → W;                    // Step 4
         for (each X → Y → Z − W − X such that
         Y and W are linked, and Z and X are not linked)
            orient W − Z as W → Z;                    // Step 5
      }
   }
}
```

Theorem 10.2 *If its input is a DAG pattern gp, Algorithm 10.3 produces a DAG in the Markov equivalence class represented by gp.*
Proof. *The proof can be found in Meek [1995b].* ∎

Notice that the rules for orienting edges in Algorithm 10.3 are the same as those in Algorithms 10.1 and 10.2 except that we have the additional rule in Step 5. Let's discuss that rule. The situation it concerns is shown in Figure 10.12. The dotted line means that the link between Y and W could be $Y − W$, $Y → W$, or $W → Y$. Step 5 says that, in this situation, $W − Z$ must be $W → Z$. The reason is as follows. If we have $W → Y$, then $Z → W$ would create a directed cycle. So we must have $W → Z$. If we have $Y → W$, then $W → X$ would create a directed cycle. So, we must have $X → W$, and therefore, since $Z—W—X$ is an uncoupled meeting, we must have $W → Z$. You may wonder why we do not need this rule in Algorithms 10.1 and 10.2. The reason is that, when we start only with edges oriented from uncoupled meetings, the first three steps always end up orienting $W − Z$ as $W → Z$ in this situation. It is left as an exercise to show this.

It is not hard to modify Algorithm 10.3 so that it determines whether a consistent extension of any PDAG exists and, if so, it produces one. It is left as an exercise to do so. Dor and Tarsi [1992] develop a quite different algorithm

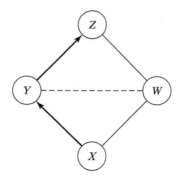

Figure 10.12: Given this situation, $W - Z$ must be $W \rightarrow Z$. The dotted line means the link between Y and W could be $Y - W$, $Y \rightarrow W$, or $W \rightarrow Y$.

that also accomplishes this, and which therefore could also be used for our purposes here.

We have the following theorem, which enables us to create a DAG faithful to IND when IND admits a faithful DAG representation.

Theorem 10.3 *Suppose we have a set of d-separations which admits a faithful DAG representation, and gp is the DAG pattern that has the d-separations in this set. Then, if this set is the input to Algorithm 10.1 or 10.2, and the output of the algorithm is the input to Algorithm 10.3, this algorithm produces a DAG that is a member of the Markov equivalence class represented by gp.*
Proof. *The proof follows immediately from Theorems 10.1 and 10.2.*

We can now test whether a given set IND of d-separations admits a faithful DAG representation as follows: We first use IND as the input to Algorithm 10.2. Then we use the output of Algorithm 10.2 as the input to Algorithm 10.3. Finally, we test whether the output of Algorithm 10.3 is a DAG containing all and only the d-separations in IND. If it is, we've shown there is a DAG pattern containing all and only the d-separations in the set, while if it is not, the preceding theorem implies there is no such DAG pattern. The algorithm follows:

Algorithm 10.4 Determine Faithful

Problem: Determine whether a set of d-separations admits a faithful DAG representation.

Inputs: A set of nodes V and a set of d-separations IND.

Outputs: A boolean variable *switch* and a graph $\mathbb{G}$. If IND admits a faithful DAG representation, *switch*'s value is true and $\mathbb{G}$ is a DAG faithful to IND. If IND does not admit a faithful DAG representation, *switch*'s value is false.

```
void determine_faithful  (set-of-nodes V,
                          set-of-d-separations IND,
                          graph& G,
                          bool& switch)

{
    graph gp;

    switch = false;
    PC(V, IND, gp);                          // Call Algorithm 10.2.
    construct_DAG(gp, G);                     // Call Algorithm 10.3.
       if (G does not contain a directed cycle)
          if (set of d-separations in G ⊆ IND)
             if (IND ⊆ set of d-separations in G)   // Use Algorithm 2.2
                switch = true;                        // to check this.
}
```

As discussed in Section 10.1.4, we are interested in the case in which IND is the set of conditional independencies IND_P in a probability distribution P. In this case, to determine whether every d-separation in G is in IND, we need only check whether the Markov condition is satisfied. That is, for each node X, if we denote the sets of parents and nondescendents of X in G by PA_X and ND_X respectively, we need to check whether

$$I_P(\{X\}, ND_X - PA_X | PA_X).$$

The reason is that Lemma 2.1 then implies that every d-separation in G is a conditional independency in P. It turns out that we can even improve on this. Order the nodes so that for each X all the ancestors of X in G are numbered before X. Let R_X be the set of nodes that precede X in this ordering. It is left as an exercise to show that for each X we need only check whether

$$I_P(\{X\}, R_X - PA_X | PA_X).$$

Example 10.12 *Suppose* $V = \{X, Y, Z, W, T\}$ *and* IND *consists of the d-separations in the DAG in Figure 10.13 (a). Given this as the input to Algorithm 10.4, Algorithm 10.2 will produce the DAG pattern in Figure 10.13 (b). After that, Algorithm 10.3 will do the steps shown in Figure 10.13 (c), (d), (e), and (f). Of course, if other edges are chosen in Step 1, we could get a different DAG (e.g., the one in (a)). The fact that the output of Algorithm 10.3 is a DAG does not necessarily mean that* IND *admits a faithful DAG representation. Algorithm 10.4 still must check this. It is left as an exercise for you to do this using the DAG in Figure 10.13 (f). Of course, we already knew the result because we started with the DAG in Figure 10.13 (a).*

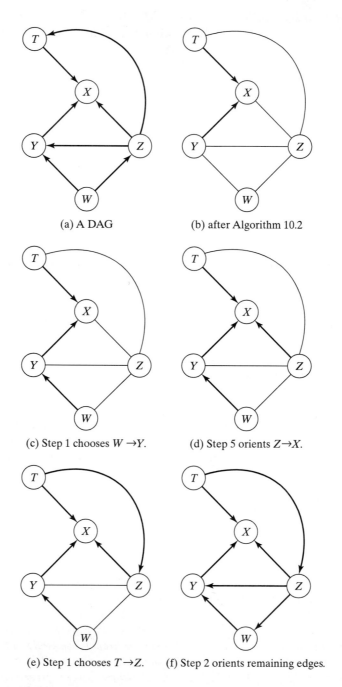

(a) A DAG   (b) after Algorithm 10.2

(c) Step 1 chooses $W \rightarrow Y$.   (d) Step 5 orients $Z \rightarrow X$.

(e) Step 1 chooses $T \rightarrow Z$.   (f) Step 2 orients remaining edges.

Figure 10.13: Given the d-separations in the DAG in (a), the steps in Algorithm 10.4 are shown in (b)–(f)). The steps in (c)–(f) refer to those in Algorithm 10.3.

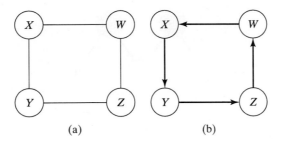

Figure 10.14: Given the d-separations in Example 10.13, Algorithm 10.4 will first call Algorithm 10.2 to produce the graph in (a). After that, it will call Algorithm 10.3 to produce the directed graph in (b) (or one with the arrows reversed).

Example 10.13 *Suppose* $V = \{X, Y, Z, W\}$ *and*

$$\mathsf{IND} = \{I(\{X\}, \{Z\}|\{Y, W\}), I(\{Y\}, \{W\}|\{X, Z\})\}.$$

Given this as the input to Algorithm 10.4, it is left as an exercise to show that Algorithm 10.2 will produce the graph in Figure 10.14 (a); then, Algorithm 10.3 will produce either the directed graph in Figure 10.14 (b) or one containing a directed cycle with the direction of the arrows reversed. Since this graph contains a directed cycle, it is not a DAG. So, Theorem 10.3 implies that there is no DAG pattern containing d-separations in this set.

The previous example shows a case in which the output of Algorithm 10.4 is not a DAG, which immediately enables us to conclude that there is no DAG pattern containing the d-separations. Example 10.10 also shows a case in which the output of Algorithm 10.4 would not be a DAG. Example 10.11 shows a case in which the output of Algorithm 10.4 would be a DAG, and the set of d-separations in the DAG is a subset of IND. However, IND is not a subset of the d-separations in the DAG, which enables us to conclude that there is no DAG pattern containing the d-separations. The next example shows a situation in which the output of Algorithm 10.4 is a DAG, but the set of d-separations in the DAG is not a subset of IND.

Example 10.14 *Suppose* $V = \{X, Y, Z, W, T\}$ *and* IND *consists of the d-separations in the DAG in Figure 10.15 (a) restricted to these variables. Given this input, it is left as an exercise to show that Algorithm 10.4 will produce the DAG in Figure 10.15 (b) or one with $W \rightarrow T$ instead of $W \leftarrow T$. It is further left as an exercise to show that we have $I(\{X\}, \{T\}|\{Y, Z, W\})$ in the DAG in Figure 10.15 (b) but not in the one in Figure 10.15 (a). Therefore, the set of d-separations in the DAG in Figure 10.15 (b) is not a subset of IND, which means that, due to Theorem 10.3, IND does not admit a faithful DAG representation.*

As in Figure 10.10 (a), nodes are shaded in Figure 10.15 (a) for consistency with the figures in Section 10.2.

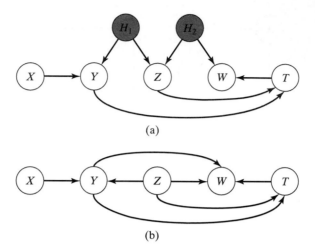

(a)

(b)

Figure 10.15: Given $V = \{X, Y, Z, W, T\}$ and IND consists of the d-separations in the DAG in (a) restricted to these variables, Algorithm 10.4 will produce the DAG in (b) or one with $W \to T$ instead of $W \leftarrow T$.

10.1.4   Application to Probability

Suppose we have a joint probability distribution P of the random variables in a set V. Recall that Theorem 2.6 on page 99 says that if P admits a faithful DAG representation, then the d-separations in the DAG pattern gp faithful to P identify all and only conditional independencies in P. So, assuming P admits a faithful DAG representation, we can find the DAG pattern gp faithful to P by using the conditional independencies IND_P in P as the input to Algorithms 10.1 and 10.2. That is, we do the following:

> $IND = IND_P$;
> $PC(V, IND, gp)$;

Again, in an implementation of the algorithm, we do not actually input a set of d-separations. This code means the d-separations are obtained from the conditional independencies in the probability distribution.

Furthermore, to determine whether a given probability distribution P admits a faithful DAG representation, we can call Algorithm 10.4 as follows:

> $IND = IND_P$;
> $determine\_faithful(V, IND, \mathbb{G}, switch)$;

If P admits a faithful DAG representation, $switch$ will be true and $\mathbb{G}$ will be a DAG faithful to P. If P does not, $switch$ will be false.

Given the preceding, we can use Examples 10.10, 10.11, 10.13, and 10.14 to illustrate applications to probability. That is, suppose the d-separations in these examples are the conditional independencies in a probability distribution P. Then, Examples 10.10 and 10.13 show cases in which we can conclude that P does not admit a faithful DAG representation because the output of Algorithm 10.4 is not a DAG. Recall that a probability distribution, that has the conditional independencies that are the d-separations in Example 10.13, is shown in Exercise 2.19. Example 10.11 shows a case in which the output of Algorithm 10.4 is a DAG, but P still does not admit a faithful DAG representation. Recall that Figure 2.6 on page 80 shows a probability distribution which has these conditional independencies, and Example 2.13 on page 103 shows that such a probability distribution does not even admit an embedded faithful DAG representation. Example 10.14 shows a case in which P does admit an embedded faithful DAG representation, and the output of Algorithm 10.4 is a DAG, but yet P is not faithful to this DAG. Indeed, P does not even satisfy the Markov condition with this DAG. This example shows that, even if we assume that P admits an embedded faithful DAG representation, the fact that Algorithm 10.4 produces a DAG does not necessarily mean that P admits a faithful DAG representation.

10.2 Assuming Only Embedded Faithfulness

In Example 10.11, we noticed that Algorithm 10.1 does not even produce a unique output. As previously noted, a probability distribution that has the conditional independencies which are the d-separations in that example not only does not admit a faithful DAG representation, but does not even admit an embedded faithful DAG representation. However, such distributions seem rare. (See the discussions of causation in Section 2.6 and of the results in Meek [1995a] in Section 2.3.1.) Example 10.14 involved a P that does not admit a faithful DAG representation, but does admit an embedded faithful DAG representation. In that example, we saw that, in that case, P does not necessarily even satisfy the Markov condition with the DAG produced by Algorithm 10.4. Therefore, we can conclude that, when we assume only embedded faithfulness, Algorithm 10.4 (and therefore Algorithms 10.1 and 10.2) cannot tell us much about P.

In this section, given the assumption of embedded faithfulness, we develop algorithms for learning about the DAGs in which P is embedded faithfully. Again, we obtain our results by discussing DAGs. To do this we need to first define embedded faithfulness without involving probability.

Let IND be a set of d-separations amongst the set V of nodes. We say IND **is embedded faithfully** in DAG $\mathbb{G}$ if $\mathbb{G} = (W, E)$, $V \subseteq W$, and all and only the d-separations in IND are d-separations in $\mathbb{G}$ restricted to elements of V. We say IND **admits an embedded faithful DAG representation** if there is some DAG in which IND is embedded faithfully. If IND admits an embedded faithful DAG representation, it is embedded faithfully in an infinite number of DAGs.

We will develop algorithms that determine common features of every DAG in which IND is embedded faithfully. After developing a basic algorithm, we improve it. Then we apply our results to probability, and finally we show an application to learning causal influences. Before we can do any of this, we need to develop theory concerning inducing chains.

10.2.1   Inducing Chains

First we introduce some notation. Let $\mathbb{G} = (\mathsf{V}, \mathsf{E})$ be a directed graph. Given a chain $\rho = [X_1, X_2, \ldots, X_k]$ in $\mathbb{G}$, we denote the subchain $[X_i, X_{i+1}, \ldots, X_j]$ of ρ between X_i and X_j by $\rho(X_i, X_j)$ and by $\rho(X_j, X_i)$. Given chains $\rho = [X_1, \ldots X_j]$ and $\gamma = [Y_1, \ldots, Y_k]$ in $\mathbb{G}$ such that $X_j = Y_1$, the chain $[X_1, \ldots, X_j, Y_2, \ldots, Y_k]$ is called the **concatenation** of ρ and γ. We denote it as $\rho \oplus \gamma$ or $\gamma \oplus \rho$. Let ρ be a chain between X and Y in $\mathbb{G}$. We say ρ is **out of** X if the edge touching X on ρ has its tail at X; we say ρ is **into** X if the edge touching X on ρ has its head at X. If Z is an interior node on ρ, and we have $X \to Z \leftarrow Y$ on ρ, then Z is called a **collider** on ρ; and otherwise Z is called a **noncollider** on ρ.

A **hidden node DAG** is a DAG $\mathbb{G} = (\mathsf{V} \cup \mathsf{H}, \mathsf{E})$, where V and H are disjoint sets. The nodes in V are called **observable nodes**, while the nodes in H are called **hidden nodes**. We denote members of H by H or H_i, while we denote members of V by all other letters of the alphabet (e.g. X, Y, Z, and so forth). Note that this definition corresponds to the definition of a hidden variable DAG model given in Section 8.5. We say "hidden node" instead of "hidden variable" because we are currently discussing only DAG properties. We shade hidden nodes.

Example 10.15 *A hidden node DAG appears in Figure 10.16. In that DAG, the chain $\rho = [X, H_1, H_2, H_3, Y, Z]$ is out of Z and into X. The nodes Y and H_2 are colliders on ρ, while all other nodes on ρ are noncolliders.*

We now have the following definition:

Definition 10.1 *Suppose $\mathbb{G} = (\mathsf{V} \cup \mathsf{H}, \mathsf{E})$ is a hidden node DAG. For $X, Z \in \mathsf{V}$, $X \neq Z$, an **inducing chain**[1] ρ over V in $\mathbb{G}$ between X and Z is a chain between X and Z satisfying the following:*

 1. *If $Y \in \mathsf{V}$ and Y is an interior node on ρ, then Y is a collider on ρ.*

 2. *If $W \in \mathsf{V} \cup \mathsf{H}$ is a collider on ρ, then W is an ancestor in $\mathbb{G}$ of either X or Z. That is, there is a path from W to either X or Z.*

Example 10.16 *Let $\mathsf{H} = \{H_1, H_2, H_3\}$ and $\mathsf{V} = \{X, Y, Z, T\}$. Consider the hidden node DAG $\mathbb{G}$ in Figure 10.16. The chain $\rho = [X, H_1, H_2, H_3, Y, Z]$ is an inducing chain over V in $\mathbb{G}$ between X and Z. We see that as follows: The interior node Y is a collider on ρ, the collider Y is an ancestor in $\mathbb{G}$ of X, and the collider H_2 is an ancestor in $\mathbb{G}$ of Z.*

Notice that it is not possible to d-separate X and Z using only a subset of V. That is, if $\mathsf{S} \subseteq \mathsf{V}$ is to d-separate X and Z, we need both T and $Y \in \mathsf{S}$ to block the chains $[X, H_1, H_2, T, Z]$ and $[X, Y, Z]$ respectively. However including T and Y in S unblocks the chain $[X, H_1, H_2, H_3, Y, Z]$.

---

[1]An inducing chain is traditionally called an "inducing path" because that is how it was originally defined in Verma [1992]. However, we use terminology consistent with the rest of this text.

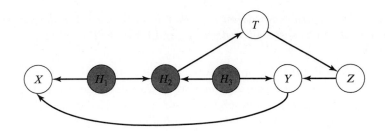

Figure 10.16: The chain $[X, H_1, H_2, H_3, Y, Z]$ is an inducing chain over V in $\mathbb{G}$ between X and Z, where $\mathsf{V} = \{X, Y, Z, T\}$.

The definition of an inducing chain allows cycles. However, the following lemma shows that, when there is an inducing chain, we can assume there is one without cycles.

Lemma 10.4 *Suppose* $\mathbb{G} = (\mathsf{V} \cup \mathsf{H}, \mathsf{E})$ *is a hidden node DAG, and* $X, Z \in \mathsf{V}$. *Suppose there is an inducing chain over* V *in* $\mathbb{G}$ *between* X *and* Z *that is into/out of* X *and into/out of* Z. *Then, there is a simple (one without cycles) inducing chain between* X *and* Z, *which is into/out of* X *and into/out of* Z.
Proof. *Assume there is at least one inducing chain between* X *and* Z, *which is into/out of* X *and into/out of* Y. *Let* $\rho = [V_1, \dots, V_k]$ *be the one with the least number* m *of cyclic subpaths. Note that* $X = V_1$ *and* $Z = V_k$. *If* $m = 0$, *we are done. Otherwise, there are some* i *and* j, $i \neq j$, *such that* $V_i = V_j$. *Let* γ *be* $[V_1, \dots, V_i] \oplus [V_j, \dots, V_k]$. *Clearly, any cyclic subchain of* γ *is a cyclic subchain of* ρ, *and* ρ *contains at least one cyclic subchain that* γ *does not. Therefore,* γ *contains less cyclic subchains than* ρ. *It is left as an exercise to show that* γ *is an inducing chain over* V *in* $\mathbb{G}$ *between* X *and* Z, *and that the edges touching* X *and* Z *on* γ *have the same direction as the ones touching* X *and* Z *on* ρ. *This contradiction proves the lemma.* ∎

Example 10.16 illustrates the importance of inducing chains. Namely, in that example, we noticed that the inducing chain between X and Z made it impossible for any subset of V to d-separate X and Z. This is a general property of inducing chains. We will give a theorem to that effect shortly. First, we need some lemmas.

Lemma 10.5 *Suppose* $\mathbb{G} = (\mathsf{V} \cup \mathsf{H}, \mathsf{E})$ *is a hidden node DAG,* $X, Z \in \mathsf{V}$, *and there is an inducing chain* ρ *over* V *in* $\mathbb{G}$ *between* X *and* Z *that is out of* X *and into* Z. *Then, given any set* $\mathsf{S} \subseteq \mathsf{V} - \{X, Z\}$, *there exists a chain between* X *and* Z *that is out of* X *and into* Z *and that is not blocked by* S.
Proof. *We have two cases:*

1. *If every collider on* ρ *either is in* S *or has a descendent in* S, *then* ρ *itself satisfies the conditions of the lemma.*

2. *At least one head-to-head on ρ neither is in S nor has a descendent in S. Let Y be the closest such node to X, and let W be the collider on ρ closest to X.*

   If $Y = W$, Y cannot be an ancestor of X because we would have a directed cycle. So, there is a path λ from Y to Z that does not contain X. Let δ be $\rho(X, Y) \oplus \lambda$. Since δ contains no head-to-head meetings and no nodes in S, and δ is out of X and into Z, δ satisfies the conditions of the lemma.

   If $Y \neq W$, W is in S or has a descendent in S. Furthermore, since W is the collider on ρ closest to X, and ρ is out of X, W is a descendent of X. Therefore, every collider on ρ, which is an ancestor of X, has a descendent in S. So Y cannot be an ancestor of X, which means there is a path λ from Y to Z that does not contain X. Since Y has no descendents in S, λ contains no nodes in S. All colliders on $\rho(X, Y)$ either are in S or have a descendent in S. Let δ be $\rho(X, Y) \oplus \lambda$. All colliders on δ either are in S or have a descendent in S, and δ contains no nodes in S that are not head-to-head. Furthermore, δ is out of X and into Z. So δ satisfies the conditions of the lemma. ∎

Lemma 10.6 *Suppose $\mathbb{G} = (V \cup H, E)$ is a hidden node DAG, $X, Z \in V$, and there is an inducing chain ρ over V in $\mathbb{G}$ between X and Z that is into X and into Z. Then, given any set $S \subseteq V - \{X, Z\}$, there exists a chain between X and Z that is into X and into Z and that is not blocked by S.*

Proof. *The proof is similar to that of the preceding lemma and is left as an exercise.* ∎

Before proceeding, we introduce more notation. Given a DAG $\mathbb{G} = (W, E)$, $X, Z \in W$, we denote the union of the ancestors of X and the ancestors of Y by ANC_{XY}.

Lemma 10.7 *Suppose $\mathbb{G} = (V \cup H, E)$ is a hidden node DAG, and $X, Z \in V$. If ρ is a chain between X and Z that is not blocked by $\mathsf{ANC}_{XY} \cap V$, ρ is an inducing chain over V in $\mathbb{G}$ between X and Z.*

Proof. *Since ρ is not blocked by $\mathsf{ANC}_{XY} \cap V$, every collider on ρ is either in $\mathsf{ANC}_{XY} \cap V$ or is an ancestor of a node in $\mathsf{ANC}_{XY} \cap V$, which means that every collider on ρ is in ANC_{XY}.*

Next we show that every node in V, which is an internal node on ρ, is a collider on ρ. To that end, since every collider on ρ is in ANC_{XY}, every internal node on ρ is also in ANC_{XY}. This means that the set of nodes in V, which are internal nodes on ρ, is a subset of $\mathsf{ANC}_{XY} \cap V$. However, since ρ is not blocked by $\mathsf{ANC}_{XY} \cap V$, every member of $\mathsf{ANC}_{XY} \cap V$ on ρ is a collider on ρ. This establishes our result. ∎

Lemma 10.8 *Suppose $\mathbb{G} = (V \cup H, E)$ is a hidden node DAG, and $X, Z \in V$. Suppose there is an inducing chain ρ over V in $\mathbb{G}$ between X and Z that is out of X. Then there is a path from X to Z. Furthermore, the inducing chain ρ is into Z.*

Proof. *If there are no colliders on ρ, then ρ itself is a path from X to Z. If there are colliders on ρ, let Y be the one closest to X. If Y were an ancestor of X, we'd have a directed cycle. So Y must be an ancestor of Z. If we let γ be the path from Y to Z, $\rho(X, Y) \oplus \gamma$ is then a path from X to Z.*

As to the second part of the lemma, it is left as an exercise to show that we would have a directed cycle if the inducing chain were also out of Z. ∎

Corollary 10.1 *Suppose $\mathbb{G} = (\mathsf{V} \cup \mathsf{H}, \mathsf{E})$ is a hidden node DAG, and $X, Z \in \mathsf{V}$. Then there is no inducing chain ρ over V in $\mathbb{G}$ between X and Z that is both out of X and out of Z.*

Proof. *The proof follows immediately from the preceding corollary.* ∎

Lemma 10.9 *Suppose $\mathbb{G} = (\mathsf{V} \cup \mathsf{H}, \mathsf{E})$ is a hidden node DAG. Suppose there is an inducing chain ρ over V in $\mathbb{G}$ between X and Z which is out of X. Then every inducing chain over V in $\mathbb{G}$ between X and Z is into Z.*

Proof. *Owing to Lemma 10.8, there is a path from X to Z. If there were an inducing chain over V in $\mathbb{G}$ between X and Z that was out of Z, that lemma would also imply there is a path from Z to X. The concatenation of these paths would be a directed cycle. This contradiction proves the lemma.* ∎

Next we give the theorem to which we alluded earlier.

Theorem 10.4 *Suppose $\mathbb{G} = (\mathsf{V} \cup \mathsf{H}, \mathsf{E})$ is a hidden node DAG. For $X, Z \in \mathsf{V}$, $X \neq Z$, there is an inducing chain over V in $\mathbb{G}$ between X and Z if and only if no subset of V d-separates X and Z.*

Proof. *Suppose there is an inducing chain over V in $\mathbb{G}$ between X and Z. Owing to Corollary 10.1 and Lemmas 10.5, and 10.6, given any set $\mathsf{S} \subseteq \mathsf{V} - \{X, Z\}$, there exists a chain between X and Z that is not blocked by S. This means that X and Z are not d-separated by any subset of V.*

In the other direction, suppose X and Z are not d-separated by any subset of V. Then X and Z are not d-separated by $\mathrm{ANC}_{XY} \cap \mathsf{V}$, which means that there is some chain ρ between X and Z which is not blocked by $\mathrm{ANC}_{XY} \cap \mathsf{V}$. Lemma 10.7 therefore implies that ρ is an inducing chain over V in $\mathbb{G}$ between X and Z. ∎

We close with some further lemmas that will be needed in the next subsection.

Lemma 10.10 *Suppose $\mathbb{G} = (\mathsf{V} \cup \mathsf{H}, \mathsf{E})$ is a hidden node DAG, and there is an inducing chain ρ over V in $\mathbb{G}$ between X and Z that is into Z. Then, given any set $\mathsf{S} \subseteq \mathsf{V} - \{X, Z\}$, there exists a chain between X and Z that is into Z and that is not blocked by S.*

Proof. *The proof follows from Lemmas 10.5 and 10.6.* ∎

Lemma 10.11 *Suppose* $\mathbb{G} = (\mathsf{V} \cup \mathsf{H}, \mathsf{E})$ *is a hidden node DAG,* $X, Y, Z \in \mathsf{V}$, *and we have the following:*

1. *There is an inducing chain* ρ *over* V *in* $\mathbb{G}$ *between* X *and* Z *that is into* Z.

2. *There is an inducing chain* γ *over* V *in* $\mathbb{G}$ *between* Z *and* Y *that is into* Z.

Then X *and* Y *are not d-separated by any subset of* V *containing* Z.

Proof. Suppose X and Y are d-separated by $\mathsf{S} \subseteq \mathsf{V} - \{X, Y\}$ and $Z \in \mathsf{S}$. Lemma 10.10 says there is a chain δ between X and Z that is into Z and that is not blocked by $\mathsf{S} - \{Z\}$, and there is a chain λ between Z and Y that is into Z and that is not blocked by $\mathsf{S} - \{Z\}$. Let σ be $\delta \oplus \lambda$. The chain σ is not blocked by S at Z because Z is a collider on σ and $Z \in \mathsf{S}$. If σ were blocked by S somewhere between X and Z, then δ would be blocked by $\mathsf{S} - \{Z\}$, and if σ were blocked by S somewhere between Z and Y, then λ would be blocked by $\mathsf{S} - \{Z\}$. So σ cannot be blocked anywhere by S, which means that X and Y are not d-separated by S. This contradiction proves the lemma. ∎

Before proceeding, we develop more notation. Given a hidden node DAG $\mathbb{G}$ = $(\mathsf{V} \cup \mathsf{H}, \mathsf{E})$, and $X, Z \in \mathsf{V}$,

$$X \leftarrow \cdots H \cdots \rightarrow Z \text{ represents a chain that}$$

1. has no head-to-head meetings;
2. has a tail-to-tail meeting at some node $H \in \mathsf{H}$;

$$X \cdots \rightarrow Z \text{ represents a path from } X \text{ to } Z.$$

Lemma 10.12 *Suppose* $\mathbb{G} = (\mathsf{V} \cup \mathsf{H}, \mathsf{E})$ *is a hidden node DAG,* $X, Z \in \mathsf{V}$, *and there is an inducing chain over* V *in* $\mathbb{G}$ *between* X *and* Z *that is into* Z. *Then at least one of the following holds:*

(a) *There is a path* $X \cdots \rightarrow Z$.

(b) *There is a simple chain* $X \leftarrow \cdots H \cdots \rightarrow Z$.

The possibilities are depicted in Figure 10.17 (a) and (b).

Proof. Owing to Lemma 10.4 there is a simple inducing chain ρ over V in $\mathbb{G}$ between X and Z that is into Z. We have three cases:

1. *There are no head-to-head meetings on* ρ. *In this case* ρ *itself satisfies property (a) or (b).*

2. *There are head-to-head meetings on* ρ, *and no colliders on* ρ *are ancestors of* Z. *Let* Y *be the collider closest to* Z *on* ρ. *There is a path* γ *from* Y *to* X *that does not go through* Z. *Note that this path must be simple because it is in a DAG. Let* W *be the node on* γ *that is closest to* Z *on* ρ. *Then* $\gamma(X, W) \oplus \rho(W, Z)$ *satisfies property (b).*

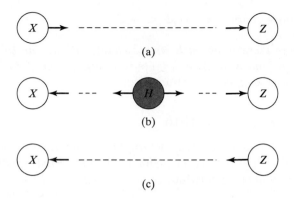

Figure 10.17: If there is an inducing chain ρ over V in $\mathbb{G}$ between X and Z, we must have one of these situations.

3. *There are head-to-head meetings on ρ, and at least one collider is an ancestor of Z. Let Y be the closest such node to X. There is a path γ from Y to Z. If γ goes through X, then there is a path from X to Z and property (a) is satisfied. So, suppose γ does not go through X. Let W be the node on γ that is closet to X on ρ. If there are no head-head nodes between X and W on ρ, the chain $\rho(X, W) \oplus \gamma(W, Z)$ satisfies either property (a) or (b). If there are head-head nodes between X and W on ρ, let T be the one closest to W on ρ. There is a path δ from T to X that does not go through Z. Let U be the node on δ that is closest to W on ρ. Then chain $\delta(X, U) \oplus \rho(U, W) \oplus \gamma(W, Z)$ satisfies property (b).* ∎

Lemma 10.13 *Suppose $\mathbb{G} = (\mathsf{V} \cup \mathsf{H}, \mathsf{E})$ is a hidden node DAG, $X, Z \in \mathsf{V}$, and there is an inducing chain ρ over V in $\mathbb{G}$ between X and Z. Then at least one of the following holds:*

a) *There is a path $X \cdots \to Z$.*

b) *There is a simple chain $X \leftarrow \cdots \mathsf{H} \cdots \to Z$.*

c) *There is a path $Z \cdots \to X$.*

The possibilities are depicted in Figure 10.17.
   Furthermore, (a) and (c) cannot both hold.
Proof. *The first part of the lemma follows from Corollary 10.1 and Lemma 10.12. As to (a) and (c) both holding, we would have a directed cycle if this were the case.* ∎

Lemma 10.14 *Suppose $\mathbb{G} = (\mathsf{V} \cup \mathsf{H}, \mathsf{E})$ is a hidden node DAG, $X, Z \in \mathsf{V}$, there is an inducing chain over V in $\mathbb{G}$ between X and Z that is into Z, and there is an inducing chain over V in $\mathbb{G}$ between X and Z that is into X. Then the following holds:*

There is a simple chain $X \leftarrow \cdots H \cdots \rightarrow Z$.

Proof. *Suppose there is no such simple chain. Then, due to Lemma 10.12, there is a path λ from X to Z, and there is a path γ from Z to X. Since $\lambda \oplus \gamma$ is a directed cycle, we have a contradiction.* ∎

10.2.2   A Basic Algorithm

Next we develop an algorithm that determines common features of every DAG in which a set of d-separations is embedded faithfully. First, we discuss the links and notation used in the algorithm:

- There is a new kind of link $X \rightarrowtail Z$.

- It is possible for the algorithm to produce the links $X \rightarrow Z$ and $X \leftarrow Z$. When this is the case, we write $X \leftrightarrow Z$.

- Some meetings are marked as follows: $X-Z-Y$. They are called **marked meetings**.

- The symbol $*$ is used to denote any of the possible edge endings that may be touching the node. For example,

  $X* \rightarrow Y$ means the link could be $X \rightarrow Y$, $X \rightarrowtail Y$, or $X \leftrightarrow Y$.

- By a **directed path**, we mean a path in which all the links are of the form $X \rightarrowtail Z$.

We prove theorems concerning the meaning of the links after presenting the algorithm. The algorithm produces a graph, which we call a **hidden node DAG pattern**. Later we will formally define this term.

Algorithm 10.5 Learn Embedded Faithfulness

Problem: Given a set IND of d-separations, determine common features of every DAG in which IND is embedded faithfully.

Inputs: a set V of nodes and a set IND of d-separations amongst the nodes.

Outputs: If IND admits an embedded faithful DAG representation, a hidden node DAG pattern *gp* showing common features of every DAG in which IND is embedded faithfully.

> **void** *learn_embedded* (**set-of-nodes** V,
>   **set-of-d-separations** IND,
>   **graph&** *gp*)

```
{
    for (each pair of nodes X, Y ∈ V) {
        search for a subset S_XY ⊆ V such that
        I({X}, {Y}|S_XY) ∈ IND;
        if (no such set can be found) {
            create the link X − Y in gp;                    // Step 1
        }
    }
    for (each uncoupled meeting X − Z − Y)
        if (Z ∉ S_XY)
            orient X − Z − Y as X → Z ← Y;                  // Step 2
        else
            mark X − Z − Y as X−Z−Y;

    while (more edges can be oriented) {
        for (each marked meeting X∗ → Z − ∗Y );
            orient Z − ∗Y as Z ⟼ Y;                        // Step 3
        for (each link X ∗ −Y)
            if (there is a directed path from X to Y)
                orient X ∗ −Y as X∗ → Y;                    // Step 4
        for (each head-to-head meeting X∗ → W ← ∗Y)
            if (Z ∗ −W && Z ∈ S_XY)
                orient Z ∗ −W as Z∗ → W;                    // Step 5
    }
}
```

As shown by the following lemmas and theorems, the graph produced by the preceding algorithm tells us common features of every DAG in which IND is embedded faithfully.

Lemma 10.15 *Suppose* IND *is a set of d-separations amongst a set of nodes* V, *and* IND *is embedded faithfully in DAG* $\mathbb{G} = (V \cup H, E)$. *If* IND *is the input to Algorithm 10.5, that algorithm creates a link between* X *and* Z *if and only if no subset of* V *d-separates* X *and* Z *in* $\mathbb{G}$.

Proof. *Since* IND *is embedded faithfully in DAG* $\mathbb{G}$, *all and only the d-separations in* $\mathbb{G}$ *restricted to elements of* V *are in* IND. *Algorithm 10.5 creates a link between* X *and* Z *if and only if there is no d-separation in* IND *for* X *and* Z, *which means no subset of* V *d-separates* X *and* Z *in* $\mathbb{G}$. ∎

Lemma 10.16 *Suppose* IND *is a set of d-separations amongst a set of nodes* V, *and* IND *is embedded faithfully in DAG* $\mathbb{G} = (V \cup H, E)$. *If* IND *is the input to Algorithm 10.5, that algorithm creates a link between* X *and* Z *if and only if there is an inducing chain over* V *in* $\mathbb{G}$ *between* X *and* Z.

Proof. *The proof follows from Lemma 10.15 and Theorem 10.4.* ∎

Theorem 10.5 *Suppose* IND *is a set of d-separations amongst a set of nodes* V, *and* IND *admits an embedded faithful DAG representation. If* IND *is the input*

Prp.	Link	Meaning (inducing chains are over V in $\mathbb{G} = (V \cup H, E)$)
1	X and Y not linked	No inducing chain between X and Y.
2	$X - Y$	Inducing chain between X and Y.
3	$X \rightarrow Y$	Inducing chain between X and Y into Y, and no path $Y \cdots \rightarrow X$.
4	$X \rightarrowtail Y$	Inducing chain between X and Y out of X/into Y, and no inducing chain between X and Y into X.
5	$X \leftrightarrow Y$	Inducing chain between X and Y into X/into Y, and no path $Y \cdots \rightarrow X$, and no path $X \cdots \rightarrow Y$.
6	$X * - * Z * - * Y$	Inducing chain between Z and X out of Z/into X, and no inducing chain between Z and X into Z; or inducing chain between Z and Y out of Z/into Y, and no inducing chain between Z and Y into Z.

Table 10.1: The meaning of the links created by Algorithm 10.5 for any DAG in which a set of d-separations is embedded faithfully. The "or" is inclusive.

to Algorithm 10.5, the links created by the algorithm have the meaning shown in Table 10.1 for any DAG $\mathbb{G} = (V \cup H, E)$ in which IND *is embedded faithfully.*
Proof. *Let $\mathbb{G}$ be a DAG in which* IND *is embedded faithfully. We prove each of the properties in turn:*

- *Properties 1 and 2 were proven in Lemma 10.16.*

- *Properties 3 and 4 will be established using induction on the links created by the algorithm.*

  Induction base : *The initial arrowheads created are due to uncoupled meetings such as $X \rightarrow Z \leftarrow Y$, where $I(\{X\}, \{Y\} | S_{XY}) \in$ IND, and $Z \notin S_{XY}$. If no such arrowheads are created, then the algorithm will create no arrowheads and we are done. So, assume k such arrowheads are created where $k \geq 2$. Lemma 10.16 says there is an inducing chain ρ over V in $\mathbb{G}$ between X and Z, and there is an inducing chain δ over V in $\mathbb{G}$ between Z and Y. Suppose there is a path $Z \cdots \rightarrow X$ in $\mathbb{G}$. Then all ancestors of Z are also ancestors of X, which means $\rho \oplus \delta$ is an inducing chain over $V - \{Z\}$ in $\mathbb{G}$ between X and Y. Theorem 10.4 therefore implies that no subset of $V - \{Z\}$ can d-separate X and Y. This contradiction establishes that there can be no path $Z \cdots \rightarrow X$ in $\mathbb{G}$, and therefore Lemma 10.8 implies that there can be no inducing chain over V in $\mathbb{G}$ between X and Z which is out of Z. So, ρ is into Z. Similarly, there can be no path $Z \cdots \rightarrow Y$ and δ is into Z.*

  Induction hypothesis : *Suppose for the first m links created, where $m \geq k$, the links $X \rightarrow Y$ and $X \rightarrowtail Y$ have the meaning in Table 10.1.*

Induction step : *Consider the* $(m+1)st$ *link created. We consider each of the possible steps that could create it in turn:*

> *Suppose Step 3 creates the link* $Z \rightarrowtail Y$. *The link is created because there is a marked meeting* $X* \to Z - *Y$, *which means that it is an uncoupled meeting* $X* \to Z - *Y$. *Due to the induction hypothesis, there is an inducing chain* ρ *over* V *in* $\mathbb{G}$ *between* X *and* Z *that is into* Z. *Since Algorithm 10.5 did not create a link between* X *and* Y, *there is some subset* $\mathsf{S}_{XY} \subseteq \mathsf{V}$ *that d-separates them. If* Z *were not in* S_{XY}, *Algorithm 10.5 would have oriented* $X \to Z \leftarrow Y$. *So,* $Z \in \mathsf{S}_{XY}$. *Therefore,* S_{XY} *is a set containing* Z *that d-separates* X *and* Y *in* $\mathbb{G}$. *Lemma 10.11 therefore says that there cannot be an inducing chain over* V *in* $\mathbb{G}$ *between* Z *and* Y, *which is into* Z, *which proves the second part of the property. Lemma 10.16 says there is some inducing chain* γ *over* V *in* $\mathbb{G}$ *between* Z *and* Y. *So,* γ *must be out of* Z. *The first part of the property now follows from Lemma 10.8.*

> *Suppose Step 4 creates the link* $X* \to Y$. *Since there is a directed path from* X *to* Y *in the pattern created by Algorithm 10.5, due to the induction hypothesis and Lemma 10.8, there is a path* $X \cdots \to Y$ *in* $\mathbb{G}$. *This implies, again due to Lemma 10.8, that there cannot be an inducing chain over* V *in* $\mathbb{G}$ *between* X *and* Y *that is out of* Y. *Lemma 10.16 says that there is some inducing chain* γ *over* V *in* $\mathbb{G}$ *between* X *and* Y. *So,* γ *must be into* Y. *Finally, if there were a path* $Y \cdots \to X$ *in* $\mathbb{G}$, *we'd have a directed cycle in* $\mathbb{G}$.

> *Suppose Step 5 creates the link* $Z* \to W$. *We know that* X *and* Y *are d-separated by* S_{XY} *where* $Z \in \mathsf{S}_{XY}$. *This means that, due to Theorem 2.5, every chain in* $\mathbb{G}$ *between* X *and* Y *must be blocked by* S_{XY}. *Since we have* $X* \to W \leftarrow *Y$, *due to the induction hypothesis and Lemma 10.10, there is a chain* ψ *in* $\mathbb{G}$ *between* X *and* W *that is into* W, *and a chain* δ *in* $\mathbb{G}$ *between* Y *and* W *that is into* W, *and neither chain is blocked by* S_{XY}. *Consider the chain* $\psi \oplus \delta$ *between* X *and* Y. *Clearly it cannot be blocked by* S_{XY} *at an interior node on* ψ *or on* δ. *Therefore, it must be blocked at* W. *If there were a path* $W \cdots \to Z$ *in* $\mathbb{G}$, *then* $\psi \oplus \delta$ *would not be blocked by* S_{XY} *at* W *because* $Z \in \mathsf{S}_{XY}$. *We conclude that there can be no path* $W \cdots \to Z$ *in* $\mathbb{G}$, *and due to Lemma 10.8, no inducing chain over* V *in* $\mathbb{G}$ *between* W *and* Z *that is out of* W. *However, Lemma 10.16 says that there is some inducing chain* γ *over* V *in* $\mathbb{G}$ *between* Z *and* W. *So,* γ *is into* W.

- *Next consider Property 5. Such a link* $X \leftrightarrow Y$ *means that the algorithm created the links* $X \to Y$ *and* $X \leftarrow Y$. *First, we show that there is an inducing chain over* V *in* $\mathbb{G}$ *between* X *and* Y *which is into* X *and into* Y. *Owing to Property 3, we know that there is an inducing chain* ρ *over* V *in* $\mathbb{G}$ *between* X *and* Y *which is into* Y *and an inducing chain* γ *over* V *in* $\mathbb{G}$ *between* X *and* Y *which is into* X. *Suppose* ρ *is out of* X *and* γ *is out*

Prp.	Link	Meaning
1	X and Y not linked	Any chain between X and Y containing only hidden nodes has a head-to-head meeting on it.
2	$X - Y$	Path $X \cdots \rightarrow Y$ (exclusive) or path $Y \cdots \rightarrow X$; or simple chain $X \leftarrow \cdots H \cdots \rightarrow Y$.
3	$X \rightarrow Y$	Path $X \cdots \rightarrow Y$ or simple chain $X \leftarrow \cdots H \cdots \rightarrow Y$; and no path $Y \cdots \rightarrow X$.
4	$X \rightarrowtail Y$	Path $X \cdots \rightarrow Y$ and no chain $X \leftarrow \cdots H \cdots \rightarrow Y$ containing only hidden nodes.
5	$X \leftrightarrow Y$	Simple chain $X \leftarrow \cdots H \cdots \rightarrow Y$ and no path $Y \cdots \rightarrow X$ and no path $X \cdots \rightarrow Y$.
6	$\underline{X * - * Z * - *Y}$	Path $Z \cdots \rightarrow X$ and no chain $X \leftarrow \cdots H \cdots \rightarrow Z$ containing only hidden nodes; or path $Z \cdots \rightarrow Y$ and no chain $Z \leftarrow \cdots H \cdots \rightarrow Y$ containing only hidden nodes.

Table 10.2: The high-level meaning of the links created by Algorithm 10.5 for any DAG in which a set of d-separations is embedded faithfully. When we say a chain "contains only hidden nodes," we mean on its interior. "Or's" are inclusive unless denoted as exclusive.

> of Y. Then Lemma 10.8 implies that there is a path from X to Y in $\mathbb{G}$ and a path from Y to X in $\mathbb{G}$. But, in this case, we would have a directed cycle. Therefore, either ρ or γ must be both into X and into Y. As to the second part of Property 5, the fact that there can be no such paths follows directly from Property 3.

> - Finally, consider Property 6. Such a marked meeting is created only if we have $I(\{X\}, \{Y\}|\mathsf{S}_{XY})$ where $Z \in \mathsf{S}_{XY}$. Suppose there is an inducing chain over V in $\mathbb{G}$ between X and Z that is into Z and an inducing chain over V in $\mathbb{G}$ between Z and Y that is into Z. Then, due to Lemma 10.11, X and Y are not d-separated by any subset of V containing Z. This contradiction shows that there is either no inducing chain over V in $\mathbb{G}$ between X and Z which is into Z or no inducing chain over V in $\mathbb{G}$ between Z and Y which is into Z. Without loss of generality, suppose the former is true. Lemma 10.16 says that there is some inducing chain ρ over V in $\mathbb{G}$ between X and Z. So, ρ must be out of Z, and due to Lemma 10.8, ρ must be into X, which completes the proof. ∎

Next we give a theorem concerning higher level meaning of the links created by Algorithm 10.5.

Theorem 10.6 *Suppose* IND *is a set of d-separations amongst a set of nodes* V, *and* IND *admits an embedded faithful DAG representation. If* IND *is the input to*

Algorithm 10.5, the links created by the algorithm have the higher level meaning shown in Table 10.2 for any DAG $\mathbb{G} = (V \cup H, E)$ in which IND is embedded faithfully.

Proof. *We prove each property in turn:*

1. *If a chain, which contains only hidden nodes on its interior, did not have a head-to-head meeting on it, it would be an inducing chain over V in $\mathbb{G}$ between X and Y. However, Property 1 in Theorem 10.5 says that there can be no inducing chain over V in $\mathbb{G}$ between X and Y.*

2. *Property 2 follows from Property 2 in Theorem 10.5 and Lemma 10.13.*

3. *Property 3 follows from Property 3 in Theorem 10.5 and Lemma 10.12.*

4. *The first part of Property 4 follows from the first part of Property 4 in Theorem 10.5 and Lemma 10.8. As to the second part, the second part of Property 4 in Theorem 10.5 says that there can be no inducing chain over V between X and Y that is into X. However, a chain $X \leftarrow \cdots H \cdots \rightarrow Y$, containing only hidden nodes on its interior, is such an inducing chain.*

5. *Property 5 follows from Property 5 in Theorem 10.5 and Lemma 10.14.*

6. *The proof of Property 6 is just like that of Property 4.* ∎

Next we give some examples.

Example 10.17 *Suppose* $V = \{N, F, C, T\}$ *and* IND *consists of the d-separations in the DAG in Figure 10.18 (a) restricted to these nodes. Given this input, Algorithm 10.5 will produce the hidden node DAG pattern in Figure 10.18 (b). From Table 10.2, we see that* IND *could not be embedded faithfully in the DAGs in 10.18 (e) and (f). It is left as an exercise to show that* IND *is embedded faithfully in the DAGs in Figures (a), (c), and (d). Of course, it is embedded faithfully in many more DAGs (indeed, an infinite number).*

Example 10.18 *Suppose* $V = \{N, F, C, T, A, D\}$ *and* IND *consists of the d-separations in the DAG in Figure 10.19 (a) restricted to these nodes. Given this input, Algorithm 10.5 will produce the hidden node DAG pattern in Figure 10.19 (b). In this and all future figures, we do not show marked meetings that are apparent from the arrowheads. For example, the meeting $N \rightarrow F \rightarrowtail D$ is marked as $N \xrightarrow{*} F \xrightarrow{*} D$, but we do not show this in the figure because it is apparent from the link $F \rightarrowtail D$.*

Owing to Property 6 in Table 10.2, in any DAG in which IND *is embedded faithfully, either*

there is a path $A \cdots \rightarrow N$ and

there is no simple chain $A \leftarrow \cdots H \cdots \rightarrow N$ containing only hidden nodes on its interior;

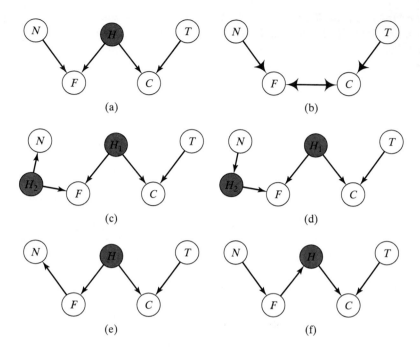

Figure 10.18: Given $V = \{N, F, C, T\}$ and IND consists of the d-separations in the DAG in (a) restricted to these nodes, Algorithm 10.5 will produce the hidden node DAG pattern in (b). IND is embedded faithfully in the DAGs in (a), (c) and (d), but it is not embedded faithfully in the DAGs in (e) and (f).

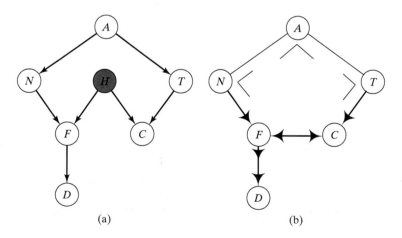

Figure 10.19: Given $V = \{N, F, C, T, A, D\}$ and IND consists of the d-separations in the DAG in (a) restricted to these nodes, Algorithm 10.5 will produce the hidden node DAG pattern in (b).

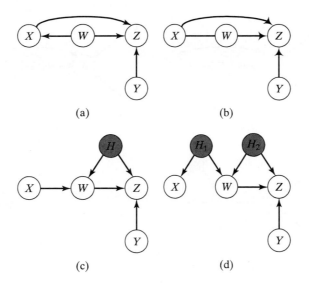

Figure 10.20: Given $\mathsf{V} = \{X, Y, Z, W\}$ and IND consists of the d-separations in the DAG in (a) restricted to these nodes, Algorithm 10.5 will produce the hidden node DAG pattern in (b). IND is embedded faithfully in the DAGs in (c) and (d).

or

there is a path $A \cdots \to T$ and

there is no simple chain $A \leftarrow \cdots H \cdots \to T$ containing only hidden nodes on its interior.

Furthermore, if, for example, we have the first condition (i.e., a path $A \cdots \to N$, and so forth.), then, again owing to Property 6 in Table 10.2, we know that

there is a path $N \cdots \to F$ and

there is no simple chain $N \leftarrow \cdots H \cdots \to F$ containing only hidden nodes on its interior.

Example 10.19 *Suppose $\mathsf{V} = \{X, Y, Z, W\}$ and IND consists of the d-separations in the DAG in Figure 10.20 (a) restricted to these nodes. Given this input, Algorithm 10.5 will produce the hidden node DAG pattern in Figure 10.20 (b). It is not hard to see that IND is embedded faithfully in the DAGs in Figures 10.20 (c) and (d). This example shows that, when Algorithm 10.5 creates an edge $X \to Z$, Property 3 in Table 10.2 does not entail that there must be a path $X \cdots \to Z$ or a simple chain $X \leftarrow \cdots H \cdots \to Z$ containing only hidden nodes on its interior (or no nodes). In Figure 10.20 (c) we have only the path $X \to W \to Z$ satisfying that property, and in Figure 10.20 (d) we have only the simple chain $X \leftarrow H_1 \to W \to Z$ satisfying that property.*

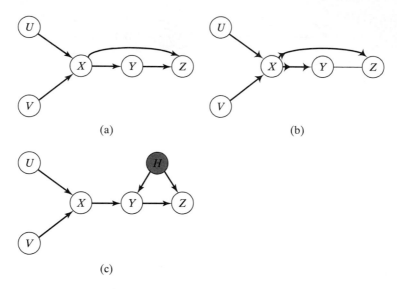

(a)

(b)

(c)

Figure 10.21: Given $\mathsf{V} = \{X, Y, Z, U, V\}$ and IND consists of the d-separations in the DAG in (a) restricted to these nodes, Algorithm 10.5 will produce the hidden node DAG pattern in (b). IND is embedded faithfully in the DAG in (c).

Example 10.20 *Suppose* $\mathsf{V} = \{X, Y, Z, U, V\}$ *and* IND *consists of the d-separations in the DAG in Figure 10.21 (a) restricted to these nodes. Given this input, Algorithm 10.5 will produce the hidden node DAG pattern in Figure 10.21 (b). It is not hard to see that* IND *is embedded faithfully in the DAG in Figure 10.21 (c). This example shows that, when Algorithm 10.5 creates an edge* $X \rightarrowtail Z$, *Property 4 in Table 10.2 does not entail that there must be a path* $X \cdots \rightarrow Z$ *containing only hidden nodes on its interior (or no nodes). In Figure 10.21 (c) we have only the path* $X \rightarrow Y \rightarrow Z$ *satisfying that property.*

Example 10.21 *Suppose* $\mathsf{V} = \{X, Y, Z, W, T\}$ *and* IND *consists of the d-separations in the DAG in Figure 10.22 (a) restricted to these nodes. Given this input, Algorithm 10.5 will produce the hidden node DAG pattern in Figure 10.22 (b). Clearly* IND *is embedded faithfully in the DAG in Figure 10.22 (a). This example shows that, when Algorithm 10.5 creates an edge* $X \leftrightarrow Z$, *Property 5 in Table 10.2 does not entail that there must be a chain* $X \leftarrow \cdots H \cdots \rightarrow Z$ *containing only hidden nodes on its interior. In Figure 10.22 (a) we have only the chain* $X \leftarrow H_1 \rightarrow Y \rightarrow Z$ *satisfying that property.*

Example 10.22 *Suppose* $\mathsf{V} = \{X, Y, Z, U, V, W\}$ *and* IND *consists of the d-separations in the DAG in Figure 10.23 (a) restricted to these nodes. Given this input, Algorithm 10.5 will produce the hidden node DAG pattern in Figure 10.23 (b). It is not hard to see that* IND *is embedded faithfully in the DAG in Figure 10.23 (c). This example shows that, when Algorithm 10.5 creates an*

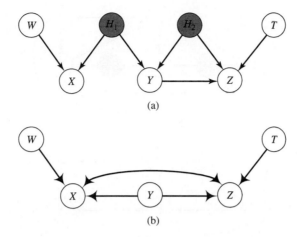

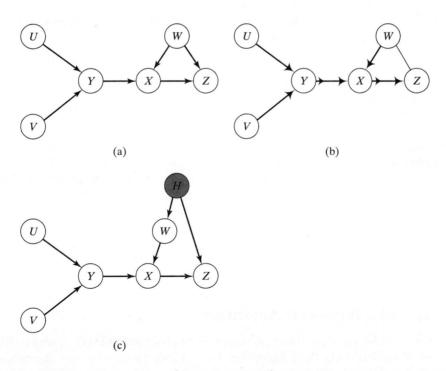

Figure 10.22: Given $V = \{X, Y, Z, W, T\}$ and IND consists of the d-separations in the DAG in (a) restricted to these nodes, Algorithm 10.5 will produce the hidden node DAG pattern in (b).

Figure 10.23: Given $V = \{X, Y, Z, U, V, W\}$ and IND consists of the d-separations in the DAG in (a) restricted to these nodes, Algorithm 10.5 will produce the hidden node DAG pattern in (b). IND is embedded faithfully in the DAG in (c).

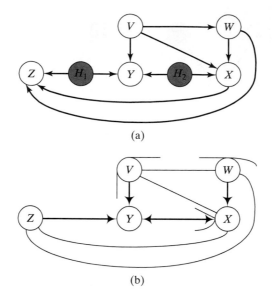

(a)

(b)

Figure 10.24: Given $V = \{X, Y, Z, V, W\}$ and IND consists of the d-separations in the DAG in (a) restricted to these nodes, Algorithm 10.5 will produce the hidden node DAG pattern in (b).

edge $X \rightarrowtail Z$, there can still be a chain $X \leftarrow \cdots H \cdots \rightarrow Z$ that does not contain only hidden nodes on its interior.

Example 10.23 *Suppose* $V = \{X, Y, Z, V, W\}$ *and* IND *consists of the d-separations in the DAG in Figure 10.24 (a) restricted to these nodes. Given this input, Algorithm 10.5 will produce the hidden node DAG pattern in Figure 10.24 (b). This example shows that it is not correct to direct arrows to avoid directed cycles when arrows in the path are of the form* $\rightarrow$. *When Step 4 is encountered, Step 5 has not yet directed* $Y \rightarrow X$ *as* $Y \longleftrightarrow X$. *So, if we directed* $Z - X$ *as* $Z \rightarrow X$ *due to the path* $Z \rightarrow Y \rightarrow X$, *it would mean that* IND *is not embedded faithfully in any DAG with a path from* X *to* Z. *Clearly, the DAG in Figure 10.24 (a) is such a DAG.*

10.2.3   An Improved Algorithm

Next we develop an algorithm that learns more about every DAG in which IND is embedded faithfully than Algorithm 10.5. First, we develop the algorithm; then, we improve its efficiency.

The Algorithm

We start by formally defining "hidden node DAG pattern."

Definition 10.2 *A **hidden node DAG pattern** is a graph with links and marked meetings like those shown in Table 10.1.*

Definition 10.3 *Suppose* IND *is a set of d-separations amongst a set* V *of nodes that admits an embedded faithful DAG representation. We say* IND *is **embedded** in hidden node DAG pattern gp if the links in gp have the meanings shown in Table 10.1 (and, therefore, the high-level meanings shown in Table 10.2) for any DAG* G *in which* IND *is embedded faithfully.*

It is clear that Algorithm 10.5 creates a hidden node DAG pattern in which IND is embedded.

Consider two hidden node DAG patterns gp_1 and gp_2 in which IND is embedded. Suppose there is no link between X and Y in gp_1. Then, owing to Property 1 in Table 10.1, there is no inducing chain over V between X and Y in any DAG in which IND is embedded faithfully. If there were a link between X and Y in gp_2, then owing to Properties 2–6 in Table 10.1, there would be an inducing chain over V between X and Y in any DAG in which IND is embedded faithfully. So there can be no link between X and Y in gp_2. We conclude that all hidden node DAG patterns in which IND is embedded have the same links. The difference is in the arrowheads and marked meetings.

Definition 10.4 *Suppose* IND *is a set of d-separations amongst a set* V *of nodes which admits an embedded faithful DAG representation. We say that* IND *is **maximally embedded** in hidden node DAG pattern gp if* IND *is embedded in gp and there is no hidden node DAG pattern, in which* IND *is embedded, which has either*

1. *more links marked with arrowheads (either at the beginning or end) or*

2. *more marked meetings $X* - *Z * -*Y$.*

Example 10.24 *Suppose* V $= \{N, F, C, T\}$ *and* IND *consists of the d-separations in the DAG in Figure 10.25 (a) restricted to these nodes. Then* IND *is embedded in the hidden node DAG patterns in Figure 10.25 (b), (c), and (d). Clearly,* IND *is not maximally embedded in the patterns Figure 10.25 (c) or (d). Is* IND *maximally embedded in the pattern in Figure 10.25 (b)? If* IND *were not, there would have to be a hidden node DAG pattern, in which* IND *is embedded, with more arrows than the one in Figure 10.25 (b). That pattern would have to have $N \rightarrowtail F$ or $T \rightarrowtail C$. A pattern with $N \rightarrowtail F$ is shown in Figure 10.25 (e). However, as shown in Example 10.17,* IND *is embedded faithfully in the DAG in Figure 10.25 (f). This DAG does not have a path $N \cdots \rightarrow F$, and it has a chain $N \leftarrow \cdots H \cdots \rightarrow F$ containing only hidden nodes. Table 10.2 says neither of these is allowed if we have $N \rightarrowtail F$. Similarly, we cannot have $T \rightarrowtail C$. So,* IND *is maximally embedded in the hidden node DAG pattern in Figure 10.25 (b).*

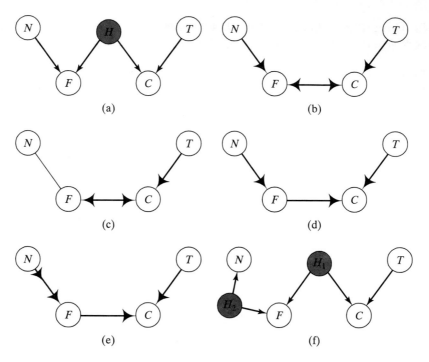

Figure 10.25: Given $\mathsf{V} = \{N, F, C, T\}$ and IND consists of the d-separations in the DAG in (a) restricted to these nodes, IND is embedded in the hidden node DAG patterns in (b), (c), and (d), and IND is maximally embedded in the hidden node DAG pattern in (b). IND is not embedded in the hidden node DAG pattern in (e).

As shown in Example 10.17, Algorithm 10.5 produces the hidden variable DAG pattern in Figure 10.25 (b) when IND consists of the d-separations in the DAG in Figure 10.25 (a). So, in this case, Algorithm 10.5 created a hidden node DAG pattern in which IND is maximally embedded. Is this always the case? Consider the following example.

Example 10.25 *Suppose* $\mathsf{V} = \{X, Y, Z, U, V, W\}$ *and* IND *consists of the d-separations in the DAG in Figure 10.26 (a) restricted to these nodes. Given this input, Algorithm 10.5 will produce the hidden node DAG pattern gp in Figure 10.26 (b). Next we show that* IND *is not maximally embedded in that pattern. To that end, let* $\mathbb{G}$ *be a DAG in which* IND *is embedded faithfully. Suppose there is a path* $\rho = Z \leftarrow \cdots Y$ *in* $\mathbb{G}$. *Since* IND *is embedded in gp, owing to Table 10.2 the link* $X \rightarrowtail W$ *in gp means that we must have a path* $\gamma = X \cdots \rightarrow W$ *in* $\mathbb{G}$, *and the link* $W \rightarrowtail Y$ *in gp means that we must have a path* $\delta = W \cdots \rightarrow Y$ *in* $\mathbb{G}$. *Consider the chain* $\gamma \oplus \delta \oplus \rho$ *between* X *and* Z. *This chain is not blocked by* $\varnothing$. *Yet, since* IND *is embedded faithfully in the DAG in*

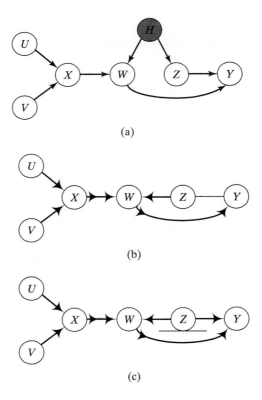

(a)

(b)

(c)

Figure 10.26: Given $V = \{X, Y, Z, U, V, W\}$ and IND consists of the d-separations in the DAG in (a) restricted to these nodes, Algorithm 10.5, will produce the hidden node DAG pattern in (b). IND is maximally embedded in the hidden node DAG pattern in (c).

Figure 10.26 (a), clearly we have $I(\{X\}, \{Z\})$. This contradiction shows that there can be no such path ρ. Due to Table 10.2, we can therefore orient the link $Z - Y$ in gp as $Z \to Y$. It is left as an exercise to show that we can also mark $W \leftarrow Z \to Y$ in gp as $W \underline{\leftarrow} Z \underline{\to} Y$. So IND is embedded in the hidden node DAG pattern in Figure 10.26 (c). It is also left as an exercise to show that IND is maximally embedded in this pattern.

Based on considerations such as those in Example 10.25, Spirtes et al. [1993, 2000] developed an algorithm that creates more arrowheads and marked meetings than Algorithm 10.5. The algorithm requires the concept of a definite discriminating chain, which is defined shortly. First we need some preliminary definitions. Let *gp* be a hidden node DAG pattern, ρ be a chain in *gp*, Z be an interior node on ρ, and X and Y the nodes adjacent to Z on ρ. Then Z is called a **collider** on ρ if we have $X * \to Z \leftarrow *Y$ on ρ, and Z is called a **definite noncollider** on ρ if we have $X * \underline{\hspace{0.3em}} - *Z * \underline{\hspace{0.3em}} - *Y$ on ρ.

Definition 10.5 *Let gp be a hidden node DAG pattern and ρ be chain between X and Y. Then ρ is a **definite discriminating chain** for Z in gp if the following hold:*

1. *X and Y are not adjacent in gp.*

2. *Z is an interior node on ρ.*

3. *Every interior node on ρ, except for Z, is a collider or definite non-collider.*

4. *If U and V are adjacent on ρ and V is between U and Z on ρ, then*

$$U* \rightarrow V \ \ on \ \rho.$$

5. *If V is between X and Z, then*

   if V is a collider on ρ,

   $$V \rightarrowtail Y \ \ in \ g\rho,$$

   else

   $$V \leftarrow *Y \ \ in \ g\rho.$$

6. *If V is between Y and Z, then*

   if V is a collider on ρ,

   $$V \rightarrowtail X \ \ in \ g\rho,$$

   else

   $$V \leftarrow *X \ \ in \ g\rho.$$

Example 10.26 *Consider the hidden node DAG pattern gp in Figure 10.26 (b). The chain $X \rightarrowtail W \rightarrowtail Y - Z$ is a definite discriminating chain for Y in gp. The chain $X \rightarrowtail W \leftarrow Z - Y$ is a definite discriminating chain for Z in gp.*

In Example 10.25 it was the definite discriminating chain $X \rightarrowtail W \rightarrowtail Y - Z$ for Y in gp that enabled us to conclude that we could orient the link $Z - Y$ in gp as $Z \rightarrow Y$. Note that we have $I(\{X\}, \{Z\})$ and $Y \notin \varnothing$. Furthermore, it was the definite discriminating chain $X \rightarrowtail W \leftarrow Z - Y$ for Z in gp that enabled us to mark $W \leftarrow Z \rightarrow Y$ in gp as $W \leftarrow Z \rightarrow Y$. Note that we have $I(\{X\}, \{Y\}|\{W, Z\})$ and $Z \in \{W, Z\}$. These situations illustrate general properties of discriminating chains. Specifically, we have the following theorem:

Theorem 10.7 *Suppose* IND *is a set of d-separations amongst a set* V *of nodes that admits an embedded faithful DAG representation. Suppose further that gp is a hidden node DAG pattern in which* IND *is embedded and ρ is a chain between X and Y in gp, which is a definite discriminating chain for Z in gp. Let* U *and* V *be the nodes adjacent to Z on ρ, and let S_{XY} be a subset of* V *such that $I(\{X\}, \{Y\}|S_{XY})$. Then if* U *and* V *are adjacent in ρ,* IND *is embedded in hidden node DAG pattern gp', where gp' has the same arrowheads and marked meeting as gp and also the following ones:*

1. $U* - *Z * -*V$ if $Z \in \mathsf{S}_{XY}$.

2. $U* \rightarrow Z \leftarrow *V$ if $Z \notin \mathsf{S}_{XY}$.

Proof. *The proof can be found in Spirtes et al. [1993, 2000].* ∎

Example 10.27 *Suppose again that* $\mathsf{V} = \{X, Y, Z, U, V, W\}$ *and* IND *consists of the d-separations in the DAG in Figure 10.26 (a) restricted to these nodes. Recall that, if we use this distribution as the input to Algorithm 10.5, we obtain the hidden node DAG pattern gp in Figure 10.26 (b), and the chain* $X \rightarrowtail W \rightarrowtail Y - Z$ *is a definite discriminating chain for* Y *in gp. Clearly, we have* $I(\{X\}, \{Z\})$. *Owing to Theorem 10.7,* IND *is embedded in the hidden node DAG pattern gp′ obtained from gp by marking* $W \rightarrowtail Y - Z$ *as* $W \rightarrowtail Y \leftarrow Z$. *Similarly, since* $X \rightarrowtail W \leftarrow Z \rightarrow Y$ *is a definite discriminating chain for* Z *in gp′ and we have* $I(\{X\}, \{Y\}|\{W, Z\})$, *we can then mark* $W \leftarrow Z \rightarrow Y$ *as* $W \underline{\leftarrow Z \rightarrow} Y$. *The final pattern appears in Figure 10.26 (c).*

Next, we give the improvement to Algorithm 10.5. The correctness of this algorithm follows directly from Theorem 10.7.

Algorithm 10.6 Learn Embedded Faithfulness2

Problem: Given a set IND of d-separations, determine common features of every DAG in which IND is embedded faithfully.

Inputs: a set V of nodes and a set IND of d-separations amongst the nodes.

Outputs: If IND admits an embedded faithful DAG representation, a hidden node DAG pattern *gp* showing common features of every DAG in which IND is embedded faithfully.

```
void learn_embedded_2 (set-of-nodes V, set-of-d-separations IND,
                       graph& gp)
{
   for (each pair of nodes X, Y ∈ V) {
      search for a subset S_XY ⊆ V such that
      I({X}, {Y}|S_XY) ∈ IND;
      if (no such set can be found) {
         create the link X − Y in gp;                    // Step 1
      }
   for (each uncoupled meeting X − Z − Y)
      if (Z ∉ S_XY)
         orient X − Z − Y as X → Z ← Y;                  // Step 2
      else
         mark X − Z − Y as X−Z−Y;
```

```
while (more edges can be oriented) {
    for (each marked meeting X* → Z − *Y);
        orient Z − *Y as Z ⟼ Y;                          // Step 3
    for (each link X * −Y)
        if (there is a directed path from X to Y)
            orient X * −Y as X* → Y;                      // Step 4
    for (each head-to-head meeting X* → W ← *Y)
        if (Z * −W && Z ∈ S_XY)
            orient Z * −W as Z* → W;                      // Step 5
    for (each definite discriminating chain ρ
    between X and Y for Z)
        if (U and V are adjacent to Z on ρ
        && U and V are adjacent)
            if (Z ∈ S_XY)                                 // Step 6
                mark U * − * Z * − * Y as U* − *Z * −*V;
            else
                orient U * − * Z * − * Y as U* → Z ← *V;
}
}
```

Example 10.28 *Suppose* $V = \{I, P, S, C, D, L, B\}$ *and* IND *consists of the d-separations in the DAG in Figure 10.27 (a) restricted to these nodes. Given this input, Algorithms 10.5 and 10.6 will produce the hidden node DAG patterns in Figure 10.27 (b) and (c), respectively. It is left as an exercise to show that* IND *is maximally embedded in the pattern in Figure 10.27 (c).*

In the previous example, Algorithm 10.6 created a hidden node DAG pattern in which IND is maximally embedded. Is this always the case? No one has ever proven this, but no one has ever developed an example in which it did not. So we offer the following conjecture:

Conjecture 10.1 *Suppose* IND *is a set of d-separations amongst a set* V *of nodes that admits an embedded faithful DAG representation. If we use this distribution as the input to Algorithm 10.6, we obtain a hidden node DAG pattern in which* IND *is maximally embedded.*

Improving the Efficiency of the Algorithm

A problem with Algorithm 10.6 (and Algorithm 10.5) is the same problem we had with Algorithm 10.1—namely, that the average case performance is no better than the worst case. Recall from the beginning of Section 10.1.2 that, in the worst case, any algorithm would have to search all 2^{n-2} subsets of V to determine whether X and Y are d-separated. However, in the case of sparse DAGs, we realized that we could improve on this performance by considering small subsets first. Recall that in Algorithm 10.2 we exploited the fact that, if X

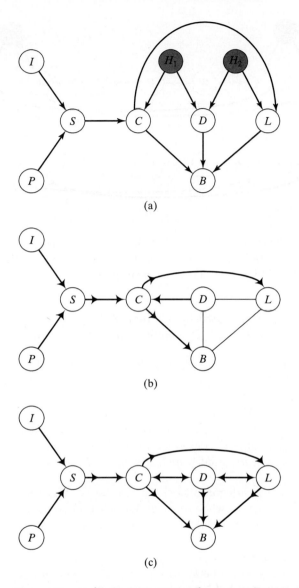

Figure 10.27: Given $V = \{I, P, S, C, D, L, B\}$ and IND consists of the d-separations in the DAG in (a) restricted to these variables, Algorithms 10.5 and 10.6 will produce the hidden node DAG patterns in (b) and (c), respectively. IND is maximally embedded in the pattern in (c).

and Y are d-separated, then they are d-separated by the parents of X or by the parents of Y. That is, in that algorithm we considered only subsets of ADJ_X and subsets of ADJ_Y when determining whether X and Y are d-separated. Things are not as simple here. That is, X and Y could be d-separated by some subset

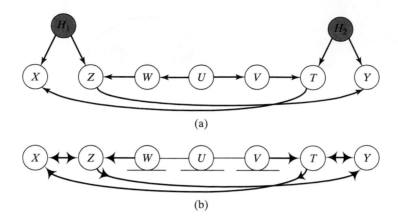

(a)

(b)

Figure 10.28: Given $V = \{X, Y, Z, W, U, V, T\}$ and IND consists of the d-separations in the DAG in (a) restricted to these variables, IND is maximally embedded in the hidden node DAG pattern in (b).

of V without being d-separated by a subset of ADJ_X or ADJ_Y in some hidden node DAG pattern in which IND is embedded. Consider the following example:

Example 10.29 *Suppose* $V = \{X, Y, Z, W, U, V, T\}$ *and* IND *consists of the d-separations in the DAG in Figure 10.28 (a). Then* IND *is maximally embedded in the hidden node DAG pattern in Figure 10.28 (b). In that pattern* $\text{ADJ}_X = \{Z, T\}$, $\text{ADJ}_Y = \{Z, T\}$, *and we do not have* $I(\{X\}, \{Y\}|\{Z, T\})$. *We need to add* W, U, *or* V *to* $\{Z, T\}$ *for the conditional independency to hold. The problem is that some of the nodes adjacent to* X *and* Y, *in a DAG in which* IND *is embedded faithfully, are hidden and, therefore, do not appear in the pattern.*

So we see it is not adequate to check only nodes adjacent to X or Y in a hidden node DAG pattern when determining whether some subset of V renders X and Y independent. Fortunately, in many cases, it is still possible to eliminate quite a few nodes from consideration. Consider again the hidden node DAG pattern in Figure 10.28 (b). Let $\mathbb{G}$ be a DAG in which IND is embedded faithfully. Owing to Property 1 in Table 10.2, other than chains containing head-to-head meetings at hidden nodes, any chain in $\mathbb{G}$ between X and Y, which passes through U, must pass through Z, then through W, and then through U. Owing to Properties 1 and 6 in Table 10.2, other than chains containing head-to-head meetings at hidden nodes, there cannot be chains in $\mathbb{G}$ between Z and W and between W and U, both of which are into W. We can conclude then that all chains between X and Y, which pass through U, are blocked by $\{W\}$. Furthermore, it is not hard to see that W does not unblock any chain in $\mathbb{G}$ between X and Y. This means that we need not consider U when looking for a set that renders X and Y independent. The general statement of this result is given by the following theorem:

Theorem 10.8 *Suppose* IND *is a set of d-separations amongst a set* V *of nodes that admits an embedded faithful DAG representation. Suppose further that gp is a hidden node DAG pattern in which* IND *is embedded. Let* C_X *be the set of all nodes V such that there is at least one chain in gp between X and V which contains no definite noncolliders. Then, if X and Y are conditionally independent given some subset of* V, *they are conditionally independent given a subset of either* $C_X - \{Y\}$ *or* $C_Y - \{X\}$.

Proof. *The proof can be found in Spirtes et al. [1993, 2000].* ∎

Example 10.30 *Suppose* V $= \{X, Y, Z, W, U, V, T\}$ *and* IND *consists of the d-separations in the DAG in Figure 10.28 (a). Consider again the hidden node DAG pattern gp in Figure 10.28 (b) in which* IND *is embedded. In gp,* $C_X = \{Z, T, W, Y\}$ *and* $C_Y = \{Z, T, V, X\}$. *Theorem 10.8 says that if X and Y are conditionally independent given some subset of* V, *they are conditionally independent given a subset of either* $C_X - \{Y\}$ *or* $C_Y - \{X\}$. *It turns out they are conditionally independent given both sets themselves.*

Based on the previous considerations, we have the following algorithm for determining the links in any hidden node DAG pattern in which IND is embedded. This algorithm replaces Step 1 in Algorithm 10.6. After calling this algorithm, we would call an algorithm containing Steps 2–6 of Algorithm 10.6 to find a hidden node DAG pattern in which IND is embedded. Note that Step 1 in this algorithm is the same as Step 1 in Algorithm 10.2 (PC Find DAG Pattern). However, as illustrated in Example 10.29, we do not necessarily find all d-separations by looking only at adjacent vertices. So, we use Step 1 to find as many as possible, and then, in Step 4, we find the remaining ones using the result in Theorem 10.8.

Algorithm 10.7 Determine Links

Problem: Given a set IND of d-separations, determine common features of every DAG in which IND is embedded faithfully.

Inputs: a set V of nodes and a set IND of d-separations amongst the nodes.

Outputs: If IND admits an embedded faithful DAG representation, a hidden node DAG pattern *gp* showing common features of every DAG in which IND is embedded faithfully.

```
void determine_links (set-of-nodes V,
                      set-of-d-separations IND,
                      graph& gp)
```

```
{
    form the complete undirected graph gp
    containing the nodes in V;
    i = 0;
    repeat
        for (each X ∈ V)
            for (each Y ∈ ADJ_X) {
                determine if there is a set S ⊆ ADJ_X − {Y}
                such that |S| = i and I({X}, {Y}|S) ∈ IND;
                if such a set S is found {
                    S_XY = S;
                    remove the edge X − Y from gp;              // Step 1
                }
            }
        i = i + 1;
    until (|ADJ_X| < i for all X ∈ V);


    for (each uncoupled meeting X − Z − Y)
        if (Z ∈ S_XY)
            mark X − Z − Y as X−Z−Y;                          // Step 2


    for (all X ∈ V)
        C_X = set of all nodes V such that                    // Step 3
        there is a chain between X and V
        containing no marked meetings;


    for (each X ∈ V)
        for (each Y ∈ ADJ_X) {
            determine if there is an S ⊆ C_X − {Y} or
            an S ⊆ C_Y − {X} such that I({X}, {Y}|S) ∈ IND;
            if such a set S is found {
                S_XY = S;
                remove the edge X − Y from gp;                 // Step 4
            }
        }
}
```

Example 10.31 *Suppose* $V = \{X, Y, Z, W, U, V, T\}$ *and* IND *consists of the d-separations in the DAG Figure 10.29 (a) (which is the same DAG as in Figure 10.28 (a)) restricted to these nodes. Then Steps 1 and 2 of Algorithm 10.7 create the graph in Figure 10.29 (b); and Step 3 creates the graph in Figure 10.29 (c). Step 1 leaves a link between* X *and* Y *because no subset of* ADJ$_X$ *or* ADJ$_Y$ *in the graph in Figure 10.29 (b) d-separates* X *and* Y *in the DAG in Figure 10.29 (a). However,* $C_X − \{Y\} = \{Z, T, W\}$ *and* $C_Y − \{X\} = \{Z, T, V\}$

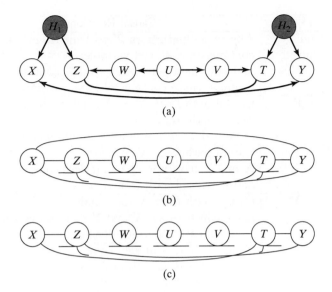

(a)

(b)

(c)

Figure 10.29: Given $V = \{X, Y, Z, W, U, V, T\}$ and IND consists of the d-separations in the DAG in (a) restricted to these variables, Steps 1 and 2 of Algorithm 10.7 produce the graph in (b), and Step 3 produces the graph in Figure (c).

in the graph in Figure 10.29 (b), and both of these sets d-separate X and Y in the DAG in Figure 10.29 (a). So, Step 3 removes the link between X and Y.

10.2.4   Application to Probability

Suppose we have a joint probability distribution P of the random variables in a set V. Recall that Theorem 2.9 says $(\mathbb{G}, P)$ satisfies the embedded faithfulness condition if and only if all and only conditional independencies in P are identified by d-separation in $\mathbb{G}$ restricted to elements of V. So, assuming that P admits an embedded faithful DAG representation, we can find common features of every DAG in which P is embedded faithfully by using the conditional independencies IND_P in P as the input to Algorithm 10.5, 10.6, or 10.7. That is, we do the following:

> IND = IND_P;
> *learn_embedded*(V, IND, gp);

Again, in an implementation of the algorithm we do not actually input a set of d-separations. This code means that the d-separations are obtained from the conditional independencies in the probability distribution.

Given the preceding, all the examples in this section pertain to learning structure from conditional probabilities.

Prp.	Link	Causal Relationship
1	X and Y not linked	Any causal path from X to Y or from Y to X contains an observed variable; and any chain between X and Y containing a hidden common cause contains observed variables.
2	$X - Y$	Causal path from X to Y (exclusive) or causal path from Y to X; or X and Y have a hidden common cause.
3	$X \to Y$	Causal path from X to Y or X and Y have a hidden common cause; and no causal path from Y to X.
4	$X \rightarrowtail Y$	Causal path from X to Y and any chain between X and Y containing a hidden common cause contains observed variables.
5	$X \leftrightarrow Y$	X and Y have a hidden common cause and no causal path from X to Y and no causal path from Y to X.
6	$X * - *Z * -*Y$	Causal path from Z to X and any chain between X and Z containing a hidden common cause contains observed variables; or causal path from Z to Y and any chain between Z and Y containing a hidden common cause contains observed variables.

Table 10.3: Causal relationships entailed by the links in a hidden node DAG pattern.

10.2.5 Application to Learning Causal Influences[2]

First we discuss learning causal influences assuming selection bias is absent; then we remove this assumption.

Assuming No Selection Bias

In Section 2.6.3, we argued that the causal embedded faithfulness assumption is often justified when we can assume selection bias is not present. Given this assumption, let's investigate how much Algorithms 10.5, 10.6, and 10.7 can tell us about the causal relationships among variables from passive data (i.e., the conditional independencies in the observed probability distribution). To this end, we have rewritten Table 10.2 using causality terminology. The result is Table 10.3. We will show two examples that use the algorithms and this table to conclude causal relationships.

---

[2]The relationships in the examples in this section are largely fictitious.

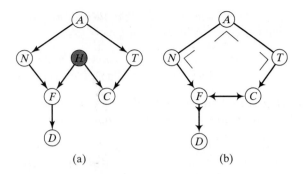

Figure 10.30: If $V = \{N, F, C, T, A, D\}$ and P is the marginal distribution of a distribution faithful to the DAG in (a), Algorithms 10.5 and 10.6 will produce the hidden node DAG pattern in (b).

Example 10.32 *Suppose we have the following random variables:*

Variable	Value	When the Variable Takes this Value
T	$t1$	*Patient has tuberculosis*
	$t2$	*Patient does not have tuberculosis*
N	$n1$	*Patient's job requires night plane travel*
	$n2$	*Patient's job does not require night plane travel*
F	$f1$	*Patient is fatigued*
	$f2$	*Patient is not fatigued*
C	$c1$	*Patient has a positive chest X-ray*
	$c2$	*Patient has a negative chest X-ray*
A	$a1$	*Visit to Asia*
	$a1$	*No visit to Asia*
D	$d1$	*Driving impairment*
	$d2$	*No driving impairment*

Suppose further that the probability distribution of the variables is the marginal distribution of a distribution faithful to the DAG in Figure 10.30 (a) (which is the same as the DAG in Figure 10.19 (a)). We stress that we are not saying this is a causal DAG; rather, it is just a succinct way to represent conditional independencies that in practice would be obtained from data. As noted in Example 10.18, if we use d-separations, which are the same as the conditional independencies in this marginal distribution, as the input to Algorithm 10.5 or 10.6, we obtain the hidden node DAG pattern in Figure 10.30 (b). If we assume that the probability distribution of the variables can be embedded faithfully in a causal DAG containing those variables, we can draw the following conclusions from Table 10.3 and Figure 10.30 (b):

- *Property (4) says that fatigue has a causal influence on impaired driving.*

- *Property (4) says that fatigue and impaired driving do not have a hidden common cause other than through other observed variables.*

- *Properties (1) and (4) together say that fatigue and impaired driving do not have a hidden common cause at all.*

- *Property (3) says that either the job requiring night plane travel has a causal influence on fatigue or they have a hidden common cause.*

- *Property (3) says that either tuberculosis has a causal influence on a positive chest X-ray or they have a hidden common cause.*

- *Property (5) says that fatigue and a positive chest X-ray have a hidden common cause. In Section 8.4.3, we noted lung cancer as that hidden common cause.*

- *Property (2) says that a visit to Asia has a causal influence on tuberculosis, or tuberculosis has a causal influence on visiting Asia, or they have a hidden common cause.*

- *Property (2) says that a visit to Asia has a causal influence on the job requiring night plane travel or the job requiring night plane travel has a causal influence on visiting Asia, or they have a hidden common cause.*

- *From domain knowledge, we suspect that the job requiring night plane travel could cause the patient to visit Asia. Given this, Property (6) says that a visit to Asia has a causal influence on tuberculosis and they do not have a hidden common cause other than through observed variables. Properties (1) and (6) together say that they do not have a hidden common cause at all. These same properties enable us to then draw the same conclusions about tuberculosis relative to a positive chest X-ray.*

Example 10.33 *Suppose we have the following random variables, which are not necessarily binary:*

Variable	What the Variable Represents
I	Patent's income
S	Patient's smoking history
P	Patient's parents smoking history
C	Patient's level of cilia damage
D	Patient's level of heart disease
L	Patient's lung capacity
B	Patient's level of breathing dysfunction

Suppose further that the probability distribution of the variables is the marginal distribution of a distribution faithful to the DAG in Figure 10.31 (a) (which is the same as the DAG in Figure 10.27 (a)). We stress that we are not saying this DAG is a causal DAG; rather it is just a succinct way to represent conditional independencies that in practice would be obtained from data. As noted in Example 10.28, if we use the d-separations, which are the same as the conditional independencies in this marginal distribution, as the input to Algorithm 10.6, we

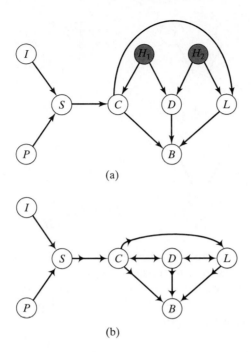

Figure 10.31: Suppose $V = \{I, P, S, C, D, L, B\}$, and P is faithful to the DAG in (a). If we use this distribution as the input to Algorithm 10.6, we obtain the hidden node DAG pattern in (b).

obtain the hidden node DAG pattern in Figure 10.31 (b). If we assume that the probability distribution of the variables can be embedded faithfully in a causal DAG containing those variables, we can draw the following conclusions from Table 10.3 and Figure 10.31 (b):

- *Property (5) says that cilia damage and heart disease have a hidden common cause. This hidden cause could be environmental pollution.*

- *Property (5) says that heart disease and lung capacity have a hidden common cause. This hidden cause could be genotype.*

It is left as an exercise to draw more conclusions.

Note that the technique outlined here gives a way to infer causal influences without manipulation. However, as is the case for all statistical inference, we can only become confident the causal influence exists.

Assuming Selection Bias May Be Present

Recall our discussion concerning selection bias at the beginning of Section 1.5.1. We assumed that neither F (finasteride) nor G (hair growth) causes the other

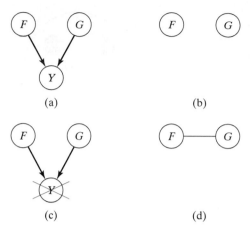

Figure 10.32: Given the causal relationships in (a), the probability distribution of F and G should be faithful to the causal DAG in (b). However, if our sample come from a subpopulation in which every member has Y equal to *true*, as indicated in (c), the observed probability distribution of F and G should be faithful to the DAG pattern in (d).

and that both have a causal influence on Y (hypertension). So the causal relationships are represented by the DAG in Figure 10.32 (a). Assuming that there are no hidden common causes, the causal embedded faithfulness assumption would entail that the observed probability distribution of F and G is faithful to the causal DAG in Figure 10.32 (b). However, if our sample comes from a subpopulation of individuals who have hypertension, Y will be equal to *true* for all members of the subpopulation. This instantiation is shown in Figure 10.32 (c). So, the observed probability distribution (the distribution according to which we sample) of F and G will have a dependency between F and G and will be faithful to the DAG pattern in Figure 10.32 (d). As discussed in Section 1.5.1, this type of dependency is called selection bias. We see then that the causal embedded faithfulness assumption does not hold owing to selection bias.

In general, we can model selection bias as follows: We assume that, relative to some population, the probability distribution P of a set V of observed variables is embedded faithfully in a causal DAG containing these variables. We assume further that we are sampling from a subpopulation of that population. We create an auxiliary **selection variable** S which takes the value *true* for all cases in that subpopulation and *false* otherwise. If S is not independent of all observed variables, then $P'(V = v) \equiv P(V = v | S = true) \neq P(V = v)$ and we say **selection bias** is present. When this is the case, our sample will give us an estimate of P' instead of an estimate of P.

In our original version of the finasteride/hair regrowth example, $S = true$ if and only if $Y = true$. So they can be collapsed to one variable. In a more sophisticated version, we assume the subpopulation consists of individuals hospitalized for hypertension. However, it is not necessarily the case that everyone hospi-

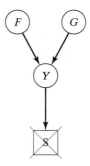

Figure 10.33: A causal DAG with a selection variable representing the situation in which the sample comes from individuals hospitalized for hypertension.

talized for hypertension actually has hypertension. So $P(Y = true | S = true)$ should be greater than $P(Y = true)$ but it is not necessarily equal to 1. Figure 10.33 shows a causal DAG describing this version. The selection variable is shown as a square node and is instantiated. Thus, the figure represents the probability distribution of F, G, and Y in our subpopulation.

If we assume that the probability distribution P of the observed variables, relative to some population, is embedded faithfully in a causal DAG containing these variables and all hidden common causes, but that possibly selection bias is present when we sample, we say we are making the **causal embedded faithfulness assumption with selection bias**. When we make the causal embedded faithfulness assumption with selection bias, the observed probability distribution will not necessarily be the same as P. So, some of the links produced by Algorithms 10.5, 10.6, and 10.7 can represent causal relationships besides those shown in Table 10.3. The other possibilities are shown in Table 10.4. The causal relationships in Table 10.4 could be present instead of, or in addition to, the ones in Table 10.3. Furthermore, the restrictions in Table 10.3 still hold. Notice that the link $X \rightarrowtail Y$ still means X has a causal influence on Y. The reason should become apparent from the examples that follow.

Prp.	Link	Causal Relationship
2	$X - Y$	(Causal path from X to S or X and S have a hidden common cause) and (causal path from Y to S or Y and S have a hidden common cause).
3	$X \rightarrow Y$	(Causal path from X to S or X and S have a hidden common cause) and Y and S have a hidden common cause).
5	$X \leftrightarrow Y$	X and S have a hidden common cause and Y and S have a hidden common cause.

Table 10.4: Additional possible causal relationships given the links in a hidden node DAG pattern when selection bias may be present. S is the selection variable.

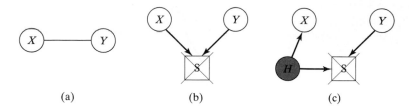

Figure 10.34: If Algorithms 10.5–10.7 produced the hidden node DAG pattern in (a), the probability distribution of X and Y could be embedded faithfully in the causal DAGs in (b) and (c).

Example 10.34 *Suppose* $\mathsf{V} = \{X, Y\}$ *and* X *and* Y *are not independent in our observed probability distribution (the distribution according to which we sample). Suppose further that our sample correctly represents that distribution. Then our algorithms will produce the hidden node DAG pattern in Figure 10.34 (a). Assuming the causal embedded faithfulness assumption with selection bias, the probability distribution* P *of* X *and* Y, *relative to the entire population, could be embedded faithfully in the causal DAGs in Figures 10.34 (b) and (c). Note that the figures represent the observed probability distribution, which is the conditional distribution of* P *given* $S = true$.

Example 10.35 *Suppose* $\mathsf{V} = \{X, Y, Z, W\}$, *and our set of conditional independencies in our observed probability distribution contains all and only the ones entailed by the conditional independencies in the following set:*

$$\{I_{P'}(\{X\}, \{Z\}) \qquad I_{P'}(\{W\}, \{X, Z\}|\{Y\}).$$

Note that we used P' *to denote our observed distribution. Suppose further that our sample correctly represents that distribution. Then our algorithms will produce the hidden node DAG pattern in Figure 10.35 (a). Assuming the causal embedded faithfulness assumption with selection bias, the probability distribution* P *of* X, Y, Z, *and* W, *relative to the entire population, could be embedded faithfully in the causal DAG in Figure 10.35 (b), but it could not be embedded faithfully in the causal DAG in Figure 10.35 (c), (d), or (e). It could not be imbedded faithfully in the causal DAGs in (c) or (d) because those DAGs do not entail* $I_P(\{X\}, \{Z\}|\{S\})$ *and we observed* $I_{P'}(\{X\}, \{Z\})$. *It could not be imbedded faithfully in the causal DAG in (e) because that DAG entails* $I_P(\{X, Z\}, \{W\}|\{S\})$ *and we did not observe* $I_{P'}(\{X, Z\}, \{W\})$.

Example 10.36 *This example is taken from Spirtes et al. [1995]. Suppose we have the following variables:*

Variable	What the Variable Represents
A	Age
I	Intelligence
L	Libido (Sex drive)
C	College student

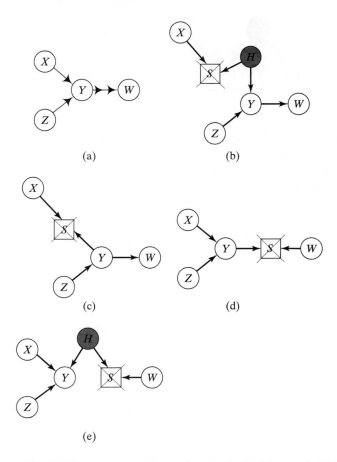

Figure 10.35: If algorithms 10.5–10.7 produced the hidden node DAG pattern in (a), the probability distribution P of X, Y, Z, and W could be embedded faithfully in the causal DAG in (b), but it could not be embedded faithfully in the causal DAGs in (c), (d), or (e).

The variable C takes on the value true if the subject is a college student and false otherwise. Suppose further that the causal relationships among the variables are those shown in Figure 10.36 (a). Finally, suppose that Professor Morris is interested in investigating whether there is a relationship between intelligence and libido, and so he decides to survey the students at his college concerning these two variables. If we make the causal embedded faithfulness assumption with selection bias and the survey correctly represents the probability distribution, he will find that the variables are correlated and our algorithms will produce the hidden node DAG pattern in Figure 10.36 (b). This is a case in which there is both a hidden common cause (Age) and a variable responsible for selection bias (College student).

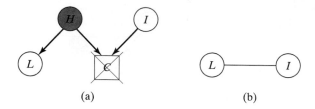

(a)   (b)

Figure 10.36: If the causal relationships are those shown in (a), Algorithms 10.5–10.7 will produce the hidden node DAG pattern in (b), based on a sample of only the values of L and I, which was taken from a subpopulation in which C was instantiated for true.

Samples like the one discussed in the previous example are called **convenience samples** because they are obtained from a population convenient to the researcher. Convenience samples often contain selection bias. Another common source of selection bias is when two or more variables in the study have a causal relationship on whether the subject chooses to complete the survey. For example, suppose we are investigating racial incidents in the military, and two variables of interest are "race" and "military responsible for incident." It seems that both of these variables may have a causal influence on whether subjects complete the survey.

10.3   Obtaining the d-separations

In general, our set of d-separations IND can come from any source whatsoever. However, when IND represents a set of conditional independencies IND_P in a probability distribution P, ordinarily we estimate whether a conditional independency is present using a statistical test on a sample. Next, we describe the statistical tests used in Tetrad II Scheines et al. [1994], which contains an implementation of Algorithm 10.2 (PC Find DAG Pattern). We discuss the tests used when learning discrete Bayesian networks and Gaussian Bayesian networks in turn.

10.3.1   Discrete Bayesian Networks

First we discuss testing for global independencies. Suppose our sample contains M data items. Let S_i^a be a random variable whose value is the number of times $X_i = a$ in the sample, and S_{ij}^{ab} be a random variable whose value is the number of times simultaneously $X_i = a$ and $X_j = b$ in the sample. Then it is not hard to show that if X_i and X_j are independent, it follows that

$$E(S_{ij}^{ab}|S_i^a = s_i^a, S_j^b = s_j^b) = \frac{s_i^a s_j^b}{M}.$$

The statistic used in Tetrad II to test for the independence of X_i and X_j is

$$
\begin{aligned}
G^2 &= 2 \sum_{a,b} s_{ij}^{ab} \ln \left(\frac{s_{ij}^{ab}}{E(S_{ij}^{ab}|S_i^a = s_i^a, S_j^b = s_j^b)} \right) \\
&= 2 \sum_{a,b} s_{ij}^{ab} \ln \left(\frac{s_{ij}^{ab} M}{s_i^a s_j^b} \right),
\end{aligned}
$$

which asymptotically has the chi-square (χ^2) distribution with appropriate degrees of freedom. It is not hard to see that G^2 increases as the data shows increased dependence. The number of degrees of freedom f in the test is

$$
f = (r_i - 1)(r_j - 1),
$$

where r_i is the size of X_i's space.

Example 10.37 *Suppose X_1 and X_2 each have space $\{1, 2\}$, and we have these data:*

Case	X_1	X_2
1	1	2
2	1	1
3	2	1
4	2	2
5	2	1
6	2	1
7	1	2
8	2	2

Then,

$$
\begin{aligned}
G^2 &= 2 \sum_{a,b} s_{ij}^{ab} \ln \left(\frac{s_{ij}^{ab} M}{s_i^a s_j^b} \right) \\
&= 2 \left[1 \ln \left(\frac{1 \times 8}{3 \times 4} \right) + 2 \ln \left(\frac{2 \times 8}{3 \times 4} \right) + 3 \ln \left(\frac{3 \times 8}{5 \times 4} \right) + 2 \ln \left(\frac{2 \times 8}{5 \times 4} \right) \right] \\
&= 0.54.
\end{aligned}
$$

Furthermore, $f = (2 - 1)(2 - 1) = 1$. From a table for the fractional points of the χ^2 distribution, if U has the χ^2 distribution with 1 degree of freedom, then

$$
P(U > .54) \approx .47.
$$

So, we can reject the hypothesis that X_1 and X_2 are independent at all and only significance levels greater than .47. This means we would not reject this hypothesis at any standard level significance (e.g., 05), and we would conclude that X_1 and X_2 are independent.

Example 10.38 *Suppose X_1 and X_2 each have space $\{1, 2\}$, and we have these data:*

Case	X_1	X_2
1	1	1
2	1	1
3	1	2
4	1	2
5	2	1
6	2	1
7	2	2
8	2	2

Then

$$
\begin{aligned}
G^2 &= 2 \sum_{a,b} s_{ij}^{ab} \ln \left(\frac{s_{ij}^{ab} M}{s_i^a s_j^b} \right) \\
&= 2 \left[2 \ln \left(\frac{2 \times 8}{4 \times 4} \right) + 2 \ln \left(\frac{2 \times 8}{4 \times 4} \right) + 2 \ln \left(\frac{2 \times 8}{4 \times 4} \right) + 2 \ln \left(\frac{2 \times 8}{4 \times 4} \right) \right] \\
&= 0.
\end{aligned}
$$

Furthermore, $f = (2 - 1)(2 - 1) = 1$. From a table for the fractional points of the χ^2 distribution, if U has the χ^2 distribution with 1 degree of freedom, then

$$
P(U > 0) = 1.
$$

So we cannot reject the hypothesis that X_1 and X_2 are independent at any significance level. We would not reject the hypothesis.

Example 10.39 *Suppose X_1 and X_2 each have space $\{1, 2\}$, and we have these data:*

Case	X_1	X_2
1	1	1
2	1	1
3	1	1
4	1	1
5	2	2
6	2	2
7	2	2
8	2	2

Then

$$
\begin{aligned}
G^2 &= 2 \sum_{a,b} s_{ij}^{ab} \ln \left(\frac{s_{ij}^{ab} M}{s_i^a s_j^b} \right) \\
&= 2 \left[4 \ln \left(\frac{4 \times 8}{4 \times 4} \right) + 4 \ln \left(\frac{4 \times 8}{4 \times 4} \right) + 0 \ln \left(\frac{0 \times 8}{4 \times 4} \right) + 0 \ln \left(\frac{0 \times 8}{4 \times 4} \right) \right] \\
&= 11.09.
\end{aligned}
$$

Furthermore, $f = (2 - 1)(2 - 1) = 1$. From a table for the fractional points of the χ^2 distribution, if U has the χ^2 distribution with 1 degree of freedom, then

$$P(U > 11.09) \approx .001.$$

So we can reject the hypothesis that X_1 and X_2 are independent at all and only significance levels greater than .001. Ordinarily we would reject the hypothesis.

In the previous example, two of the counts had value 0. In general, Tetrad II uses the heuristic to reduce the number of degrees of freedom by one for each count that is 0. In this example, that was not possible because $f = 1$. In general, there does not seem to be an exact rule for determining the reduction in the number of degrees of freedom given zero counts. See Bishop et al. [1975].

The method just described extends easily to testing for conditional independencies. If we let S_{ijk}^{abc} be a random variable whose value is the is the number of times simultaneously $X_i = a$, $X_j = b$, and $X_k = c$ in the sample, then if X_i and X_j are conditionally independent given X_k, it follows that

$$E(S_{ijk}^{abc}|S_{ik}^{ac} = s_{ik}^{ac}, S_{jk}^{bc} = s_{jk}^{bc}) = \frac{s_{ik}^{ac} s_{jk}^{bc}}{s_k^c}.$$

In this case,

$$G^2 = 2 \sum_{a,b} s_{ijk}^{abc} \ln \left(\frac{s_{ijk}^{abc} s_k^c}{s_{ik}^{ac} s_{jk}^{bc}} \right).$$

These formulas readily extend to the case in which X_i and X_j are conditionally independent given a set of variables.

In general, when we are testing for the conditional independence of X_i and X_j given a set of variables S, the number of degrees of freedom used in the test is

$$df = (r_i - 1)(r_j - 1) \prod_{Z_k \in \mathsf{S}} r_k,$$

where r_i is the size of X_i's space.

The Tetrad II system allows the user to enter the significance level. Often significance levels of .01 or .05 are used. A significance level of α means the probability of rejecting a conditional independency hypothesis, when it it is true, is α. Therefore, the smaller the value α, the less likely we are to reject a conditional independency, and therefore the sparser our resultant graph. Note that the system uses hypothesis testing in a nonstandard way. That is, if the null hypothesis (a particular conditional independency) is not rejected, it is accepted and the edge is removed. The standard use of significance tests is to reject the null hypothesis if the observation falls in a critical region with small probability (the significance level) assuming the null hypothesis. If the null hypothesis is not true, there must be some alternate hypothesis that is true. This is fundamentally different than accepting the null hypothesis when the observation does not fall in the critical region. If the observation is not in the critical region, then it lies in a more probable region assuming the null hypothesis, but this is a weaker statement. It tells us nothing about the likelihood of the observation assuming some alternate hypotheses. The power π of the test is the probability of the observation falling in the region of rejection when the alternate hypothesis is true, and $1 - \pi$ is the probability of the observation falling in the region of acceptance when the alternate hypothesis is true. To accept the null hypothesis, we want to feel that the alternative hypothesis is unlikely, which means that we want $1 - \pi$ to be small. Spirtes et al. [1993, 2000] argue that this is less of a concern as sample size increases. When the sample size is large, for a nontrivial alternate hypothesis, if the observation falls in a region where we could reject the null hypothesis only if α is large (so we would not reject the null hypothesis), then $1 - \pi$ is small, which means that we would want to reject the alternate hypothesis. However, when the sample size is small, $1 - \pi$ may be large even when we would not reject the null hypothesis, and the interpretation of nonrejection of the null hypothesis becomes ambiguous.

Furthermore, the significance level cannot be given its usual interpretation. That is, it is not the limiting frequency with which a true null hypothesis will be rejected. The reason is that, to determine whether an edge between X and Y should be removed, there are repeated tests of conditional independencies given different sets, each using the same significance level. However, the significance level is the probability that each hypothesis will be rejected when it is true; it is not the probability that some true hypotheses will be rejected when at least one of them is true. This latter probability could be much higher than the significance level. Spirtes et al. [1993, 2000] discuss this matter in more detail.

Finally, Druzdzel and Glymour [1999] note that Tetrad II is much more reliable in determining the existence of edges than in determining their orientation.

10.3.2   Gaussian Bayesian Networks

In the case of Gaussian Bayesian networks, Tetrad II tests for a conditional independency by testing if the partial correlation coefficient is zero. It does this as follows: Suppose we are testing whether the partial correlation coefficient ρ of X_i and X_j given S is zero. The so-called Fisher's Z is given by

$$Z = \frac{1}{2}\sqrt{M - |\mathsf{S}| - 3}\left(\ln\frac{1 + R}{1 - R}\right),$$

where M is the size of the sample, and R is a random variable whose value is the sample partial correlation coefficient of X_i and X_j given S. If we let

$$\zeta = \frac{1}{2}\sqrt{M - |\mathsf{S}| - 3}\left(\ln\frac{1 + \rho}{1 - \rho}\right),$$

then asymptotically $Z - \zeta$ has the standard normal distribution.

Suppose we wish to test the hypothesis that the partial correlation coefficient of X_i and X_j given S is ρ' against the alternative hypothesis that it is not. We compute the value r of R, then the value z of Z, and let

$$\zeta' = \frac{1}{2}\sqrt{M - |S| - 3}\left(\ln\frac{1+\rho'}{1-\rho'}\right). \qquad (10.2)$$

To test that the partial correlation coefficient is zero, we let $\rho' = 0$ in Expression 10.2, which means that $\zeta' = 0$.

Example 10.40 *Suppose we are testing whether $I_P(\{X_1\}, \{X_2\}|\{X_3\})$, and the sample partial correlation coefficient of X_1 and X_2 given $\{X_3\}$ is .097 in a sample of size* 20. *Then*

$$z = \frac{1}{2}\sqrt{20 - 1 - 3}\left(\ln\frac{1+.097}{1-.097}\right) = .389$$

and

$$|z - \zeta'| = |.389 - 0| = .389.$$

From a table for the standard normal distribution, if U has the standard normal distribution, then

$$P(|U| > .389) \approx .7,$$

which means that we can reject the conditional independency at all and only significance levels greater than .7. For example, we could not reject it at a significance level of .05.

10.4 Relationship to Human Reasoning

Neapolitan et al. [1997] argue that perhaps the concept of causation in humans has its genesis in observations of statistical relationships similar to those discussed in this chapter. Before presenting their argument, we develop some necessary background theory.

10.4.1 Background Theory

Similar to the way in which theory was developed in earlier sections, the following theorem could be stated for a set of d-separations that admits an embedded faithful DAG representation, instead of a probability distribution that admits one. However, presently we are concerned only with probability and its relationship to causality. So, we develop the theory directly for probability distributions.

Theorem 10.9 *Suppose* V *is a set of random variables and* P *is a probability distribution of these variables that admits an embedded faithful DAG representation. Suppose further that for* $X, Y, Z \in \mathsf{V}$, $\mathbb{G} = (\mathsf{V} \cup \mathsf{H}, \mathsf{E})$ *is a DAG, in which* P *is embedded faithfully, such that there is a subset* $\mathsf{S}_{XY} \subseteq \mathsf{V}$ *satisfying the following conditions:*

1. $\neg I_P(Z, Y | \mathsf{S}_{XY})$.

2. $I_P(Z, Y | \mathsf{S}_{XY} \cup \{X\})$.

3. Z *and all elements of* S_{XY} *are not descendents of* X *in* $\mathbb{G}$.

Then there is a path from X *to* Y *in* $\mathbb{G}$.
Proof. *Since* P *is embedded faithfully in* $\mathbb{G}$, *owing to Theorem 2.5, we have*

1. $\neg I_{\mathbb{G}}(Z, Y | \mathsf{S}_{XY})$;

2. $I_{\mathbb{G}}(Z, Y | \mathsf{S}_{XY} \cup \{X\})$.

Therefore, it is clear that there must be a chain ρ *between* Z *and* Y *which is blocked by* $\mathsf{S}_{XY} \cup \{X\}$ *at* X *and which is not blocked by* $\mathsf{S}_{XY} \cup \{X\}$ *at any element of* S_{XY}. *So* X *must be a noncollider on* ρ. *Consider the subchain* α *of* ρ *between* Z *and* X. *Suppose* α *is out of* X. *Then there must be at least one collider on* α *because otherwise* Z *would be a descendent of* X. *Let* W *be the collider on* α *closest to* X *on* α. *Since* W *is a descendent of* X, *we must have* $W \notin \mathsf{S}_{XY}$. *But if this were the case,* ρ *would be blocked by* S_{XY} *at* W. *This contradiction shows that* α *must be into* X. *Let* β *be the subchain of* ρ *between* X *and* Y. *Since* X *is noncollider on* ρ, β *is out of* X. *Suppose there is a collider on* β. *Let* U *be the collider on* β *closest to* X *on* β. *Since* U *is a descendent of* X, *we must have* $U \notin \mathsf{S}_{XY}$. *But, if this were the case,* ρ *would be blocked by* S_{XY} *at* U. *This contradiction shows that there can be no colliders on* β, *which proves the theorem.* ∎

Suppose the probability distribution of the observed variables can be embedded faithfully in a causal DAG $\mathbb{G}$ containing the variables. Suppose further that we have a time ordering of the occurrences of the variables. If we assume that an effect cannot precede its cause in time, then any variable occurring before X in time cannot be an effect of X. Since all descendents of X in $\mathbb{G}$ are effects of X, this means that any variable occurring before X in time cannot be a descendent of X in $\mathbb{G}$. So condition (3) in Theorem 10.9 holds if we require only that Z and all elements of S_{XY} occur before X in time. We can therefore conclude the following:

> Assume that an effect cannot precede its cause in time. Suppose V is a set of random variables, and P is a probability distribution of these variables for which we make the causal embedded faithfulness assumption. Suppose further that $X, Y, Z \in \mathsf{V}$ and $\mathsf{S}_{XY} \subseteq \mathsf{V}$ satisfy the following conditions:

1. $\neg I_P(Z, Y | \mathsf{S}_{XY})$.

2. $I_P(Z, Y | \mathsf{S}_{XY} \cup \{X\})$.

3. Z and all elements of S_{XY} occur before X in time.

   Then X causes Y.

This method for learning causes first appeared in Pearl and Verma [1991]. Using the method, we can statistically learn a causal relationship by observing just three variables.

10.4.2   A Statistical Notion of Causality

Christensen [1990, p. 279] claims that "causation is not something that can be established by data analysis. Establishing causation requires logical arguments that go beyond the realm of numerical manipulation." This chapter has done much to refute this claim. However, we now go a step further, and offer the hypothesis that perhaps the concept of causation finds its genesis in the observation of statistical relationships.

Many of the researchers who developed the theory presented in this chapter, offer no definition of causality. Rather, they just assume that the probability distribution satisfies the causal faithfulness assumption. Spirtes et al. [1993, 2000, p. 41] state, "we advocate no definition of causation," while Pearl and Verma [1991, p. 2] say "nature possesses stable causal mechanisms which, on a microscopic level are deterministic functional relationships between variables, some of which are unobservable."

There have been many efforts to define causality. Notable among these are the Salmon [1997] definition in terms of processes and the Cartwright [1989] definition in terms of capacities. Furthermore, there are means for identifying causal relationships such as the manipulation method given in Section 1.5. However, none of these methods tries to identify how humans develop the concept of causality. That is the approach taken here.

What is this relationship among variables that the notion of causality embodies? Pearl and Verma [1991, p. 2] assume "that most human knowledge derives from statistical observations." If we accept this assumption, then it seems a causal relationship recapitulates some statistical observation among variables. Should we look at the adult to learn what this statistical observation might be? As Piaget and Inhelder [1969, p. 157] note, "Adult thought might seem to provide a preestablished model, but the child does not understand adult thought until he has reconstructed it, and thought is itself the result of an evolution carried on by several generations, each of which has gone through childhood." The intellectual concept of causality has been developed through many generations and knowledge of many, if not most, cause–effect relationship are passed on to individuals by previous generations. Piaget and Inhelder [1969, p. ix] note further, "While the adult educates the child by means of multiple social transmissions, every adult, even if he is a creative genius, begins as a small child." So, we will look to the small child, indeed to the infant, for the genesis of the concept of causality. We will discuss results of studies by Piaget. We will show how these results can lead us to a definition of causality as a statistical relationship among an individual's observed variables.

The Genesis of the Concept of Causality

Piaget [1952, 1954] established a theory of the development of sensori-motor intelligence in infants from birth until about age two. He distinguished six stages within the sensori-motor period. Our purpose here is not to recount these stages, but rather to discuss some observations Piaget made concerning several stages, which might shed light on what observed relationships the concept of causality recapitulates.

Piaget argues that the mechanism of learning "consists in assimilation; meaning that reality data are treated or modified in such a way as to become incorporated into the structure ... According to this view, the organizing activity of the subject must be considered just as important as the connections inherent in the external stimuli" [Piaget and Inhelder 1969, p. 5]. We will investigate how the infant organizes external stimuli into cause–effect relationships.

The third sensori-motor stage goes from about the age of four months to nine months. Here is a description of what Piaget observed in infants in this stage (taken from Drescher [1991, p. 27]):

> Secondary circular reactions are characteristic of third stage behavior; these consist of the repetition of actions in order to reproduce fortuitously-discovered effects on objects. For example:

> - The infant's hand hits a hanging toy. The infant sees it bob about, then repeats the gesture several times, later applying it to other objects as well, developing a striking schema for striking.

> - The infant pulls a string hanging from the bassinet hood and notices a toy, also connected to the hood, shakes in response. The infant again grasps and pulls the string, already watching the toy rather than the string. Again, the spatial and causal nature of the connection between the objects is not well understood; the infant will generalize the gesture to inappropriate situations.

Piaget and Inhelder [1969, p. 10] discuss these inappropriate situations:

> Later you need only hang a new toy from the top of the cradle for the child to look for the cord, which constitutes the beginning of a differentiation between means and end. In the days that follow, when you swing an object from a pole two yards from the crib, and even when you produce unexpected and mechanical sounds behind a screen, after these sights or sounds have ceased the child will look for and pull the magic cord. Although the child's actions seem to reflect

a sort of magical belief in causality without any material connection, his use of the same means to try to achieve different ends indicates that he is on the threshold of intelligence.

Piger and Inhelder [1969, p. 18] note, "This early notion of causality may be called magical phenomenalist; 'phenomenalist'; because the phenomenal contiguity of two events is sufficient to make them appear causally related." At this point, the notion of causality in the infant's model entails a primitive cause–effect relationship between actions and results. For example, if

$$Z \quad = \quad \text{"pull string hanging from bassinet hood"}$$
$$Y \quad = \quad \text{"toy shakes,"}$$

the infant's model contains the causal relationship $Z \to Y$. The infant extends this relationship to believe there may be an arrow from Z to other desired results even when they were not preceded by Z. Drescher [1991, p. 28] states that the "causal nature of the connection between the objects is not well understood." Since our goal here is to determine what relationships the concept of causality recapitulates, we do not want to assume there is a "causal nature of the connection" that is actually out there. Rather, we could say that at this stage an infant is only capable of forming two-variable relationships. The infant cannot see how a third variable may enter into the relationship between any two. For example, the infant cannot develop the notion that the hand is moving the bassinet hood, which in turn makes the toy shake. Note that, at this point, the infant is learning relationships only through the use of manipulation. At this point the infant's universe is entirely centered on its own body, and anything it learns only concerns itself.

Although there are advances in the fourth stage (about age nine months to one year), the infant's model still only includes two-variable relationships during this stage. Consider the following account taken from Drescher [1991, p. 32]:

> The infant plays with a toy that is then taken away and hidden under a pillow at the left. The infant raises the pillow and reclaims the object. Once again, the toy is taken and hidden, this time under a blanket at the right. The infant promptly raises, not the blanket, but the pillow again, and appears surprised and puzzled not to find the toy ... So the relationships among objects are yet understood only in terms of pairwise transitions, as in the cycle of hiding and uncovering a toy. The intervention of a third object is not properly taken into account.

It is in the fifth stage (commencing at about one year of age) that the infant sees a bigger picture. Here is an account by Drescher [1991, p. 34] of what can happen in this stage:

> You may recall that some secondary circular reactions involved influencing one object by pulling another connected to the first by a

string. But that effect was discovered entirely by accident, and with no appreciation of the physical connection. During the present stage, the infant wishing to influence a remote object learns to search for an attached string, visually tracing the path of connection.

Piaget and Inhelder [1969, p. 19] describe this fifth stage behavior as follows:

> In the behavior patterns of the support, the string, and the stick, for example, it is clear that the movements of the rug, the string, or the stick are believed to influence those of the subject (independently of the author of the displacement).

If we let

$$
\begin{aligned}
Z &= \text{``pull string hanging from bassinet hood''} \\
X &= \text{``bassinet hood moves''} \\
Y &= \text{``toy shakes,''}
\end{aligned}
$$

at this stage the infant develops the relationship that Z is connected to Y through X. At this point, the infant's model entails that Z and Y are dependent, but that X is a causal mediary and that they are independent given X. Using our previous notation, this relationship is expressed as follows:

$$
\neg I_P(Z, Y) \qquad\qquad I_P(Z, Y | X). \tag{10.3}
$$

The fifth-stage infant shows no signs of mentally simulating the relationship between objects and learning from the simulation instead of from actual experimentation. So it can form causal relationships only by repeated experiments. Furthermore, although it seems to recognize the conditional independence, it does not seem to recognize a causal relationship between X and Y that is merely learned via Z. Because it learns only from actual experiments, the third variable is always part of the relationship. This changes in the sixth stage. Piaget and Inhelder [1969], [p. 11] Piager and Inhelder [1969, p. 11] describe this stage as follows:

> Finally, a sixth stage marks the end of the sensori-motor period and the transition to the following period. In this stage the child becomes capable of finding new means not only by external or physical groping but also by internalized combinations that culminate in sudden comprehension or *insight*.

Drescher [1991, p. 35] gives the following example of what can happen at this stage:

> An infant who reaches the sixth stage without happening to have learned about (say) using a stick may invent that behavior (in response to a problem that requires it) quite suddenly.

It is in the sixth stage that the infant recognizes that an object will move as long as something hits it (e.g., the stick); that there need be no specific learned sequence of events. Therefore, at this point the infant recognizes the movement of the bassinet hood as a *cause* of the toy shaking, and that the toy will shake if the hood is moved by any means whatsoever. Note that, at this point, manipulation is no longer necessary for the infant to learn relationships. Rather, the infant realizes that external variables can affect other external variables. So, at the time the infant formulates a concept, which we might call *causality*, the infant is observing that external variables satisfy certain relationships to each other. We conjecture that the infant develops this concept to describe the statistical relationships in Expression 10.3. We conjecture this because (1) the infant started to accurately model the exterior when it first realized those relationships in the fifth stage; and (2) the concept seems to develop at the time the infant is observing and not merely manipulating.

The argument is not that the two-year-old child has causal notions like the adult. Rather, it is that they are as described by Piaget and Inhelder [1969, p. 13]:

> It organizes reality by constructing the broad categories of action which are the schemes of the permanent object, space, time, and causality, substructures of the notions that will later correspond to them. None of these categories is given at the outset, and the child's initial universe is entirely centered on his own body and action in an egocentrism as total as it is unconscious (for lack of consciousness of the self). In the course of the first eighteen months, however, there occurs a kind of Copernican revolution, or, more simply, a kind of general decentering process whereby the child eventually comes to regard himself as an object among others in a universe that is made up of permanent objects and in which there is at work a causality that is both localized in space and objectified in things.

Piget and Inhelder [1969, p. 90] feel that these early notions are the foundations of the concepts developed later in life:

> The roots of logic are to be sought in the general coordination of actions (including verbal behavior) beginning with the sensori-motor level, whose schemes are of fundamental importance. This schematism continues thereafter to develop and to structure thought, even verbal thought, in terms of the progress of actions, until the formation of the logico-mathematical operations.

Piaget found that the development of the intellectual notion of causality mirrors the development of the infant's notion. Drescher [1991, p. 110] discusses this as follows:

> The stars "were born when we were born," says the boy of six, "because before that there was no need for sunlight ... " Interestingly

enough, this precausality is close to the initial sensori-motor forms of causality, which we called "magical-phenomenalist" in Chapter 1. Like those, it results from a systematic assimilation of physical processes to the child's own action, an assimilation which sometimes leads to quasi-magical attitudes (for instance, many subjects between four and six believe that the moon follows them . . . .) But, just as sensori-motor precausality makes way (after Stages 4 to 6 of infancy) for an objectified and spacialized causality, so representative precausality, which is essentially an assimilation to actions, is gradually, at the level of concrete operations, transformed into a rational causality by assimilation no longer to the child's own action in their egocentric orientation but to the operations as general coordination of actions.

In the period of concrete operations (between the ages of seven and eleven), the child develops the adult concept of causality. According to Piaget, that concept has its foundations in the notion of objective causality developed at the end of the sensori-motor period.

In summary, we have offered the hypothesis that the concept of causality develops in the individual, starting in infancy, through the observation of statistical relationships among variables and we have given supportive evidence for that hypothesis. But what of the properties of *actual causal relationships* that a statistical explanation does not seem to address? For example, consider the child who moves the toy by pulling the rug on which it is situated. We said that the child develops the causal relationship that the moving rug causes the toy to move. An adult, in particularly a physicist, would have a far more detailed explanation. For example, the explanation might say that the toy is sufficiently massive to cause a downward force on the rug so that the rug does not slide from underneath the toy, and so forth. However, such an explanation is not unlike that of the child's; it simply contains more variables because the adult makes keener observations and has already developed the intellectual concept of causality. Piaget and Inhelder [1969, p. 19] note that even the stage-five infant requires physical contact between the toy and rug to infer causality:

> If the object is placed beside the rug and not on it, the child at Stage 5 will not pull the supporting object, whereas the child at Stage 3 or even 4 who has been trained to make use of the supporting object will still pull the rug even if the object no longer maintains with it the spatial relationship "placed upon."

This physical contact is a necessary component to the child forming the causal link, but it is not the mechanism by which the link develops. The hypothesis here is that this mechanism is the observed statistical relationships among the variables. A discussion of *actual causal relationships* does not apply in a psychological investigation into the genesis of the concept of causality because that concept is part of the human model; not part of reality itself. As Kant [1787] noted long ago, we cannot truly gain access to what is "out there." What does apply is how humans assimilate reality into the concept of causality. Assuming we are realists, we maintain that there is something external unfolding. Perhaps it is something similar to the Pearl and Verma [1991, p. 2] claim that "nature possesses stable causal mechanisms which, on a microscopic level are deterministic functional relationships between variables, some of which are unobservable." However, consistent with the argument presented here, we should strike the words "cause" and "variable" from this claim. We've argued that these concepts developed to describe what we can observe; so it seems presumptuous to apply them to that which we cannot. Rather, we should say that our need and effort to understand and predict results in our developing (1) the notion of variables, which describe observable chunks of our perceptions; and (2) the notion of causality, which describes how these variables relate to each other. We are hypothesizing that this latter notion developed to describe the observed statistical relationships among variables shown in this section.

A Definition of Causality

We've offered the argument that the concept of causality developed to describe the statistical relationships in Expression 10.3. We therefore offer these statistical relationships as a definition of causality. Since the variables are specific to an individual's observations, this is a subjective definition of causation not unlike the subjective definition of probability. Indeed, since it is based on statistical relationships, one could say it is expressed in terms of that definition. According to this view, there are no objective causes as such. Rather a cause–effect relationship is relative to an individual. For example, consider again selection bias. Recall from Section 1.5, that if D and S are both "causes" of Y, and we happen to be observing individuals hospitalized for treatment of Y, we would observe a correlation between D and S even when they have no "causal" relationship to each other. If some "cause" of D were also present and we were not aware of the selection bias, we would conclude that D causes S. An individual who was aware of the selection bias, would not draw this conclusion and would apparently have a model that more accurately describes reality. But this does not diminish the fact that D causes S as far as the first individual is concerned. As is the case for relative frequencies in probability theory, we call cause–effect relationships objective when we all seem to agree on them.

Russell [1913] long ago noted that causation played no role in physics and wanted to eliminate the word from science. Similarly, Pearson [1911] wanted it removed from statistics. Whether this would be appropriate for these disciplines is another issue. However, the concept is important in psychology and artificial intelligence because humans do model the exterior in terms of causation. We have suggested that the genesis of the concept lies in the statistical relationship discussed above. If this is so, for the purposes of these disciplines, the statistical definition would be accurate. This definition simplifies the task of researchers in artificial intelligence, as they need not engage in metaphysical wrangling about causality. They need only enable an agent to learn causes statistically from the agent's personally observed variables.

The definition of causation presented here is consistent with other efforts to define causation as a human concept rather than as something objectively occurring in the exterior world. These include the Hume [1748] claim that causation has to do with a habit of expecting conjunctions in the future, rather than with any objective relations really existing between things in the world, and the Freeman [1989] conclusion that "the psychological basis for our human conception of cause and effect lies in the mechanism of reafference; namely, that each intended action is accompanied by motor command ('cause') and expected consequence ('effect') so that the notion of causality lies at the most fundamental level of our capacity for acting and knowing."

Testing How Humans Learn Causes

Although the definition of causation presented here was motivated by observing behavior in infants, its accuracy could be tested using both small children and adults. Studies indicate that humans learn causes to satisfy a need for prediction and control of their environment. (See Heider [1944], Kelly [1967].) Putting people into an artificial environment, with a large number of cues, and forcing them to predict and control the environment should produce the same types of causal reasoning that occurs naturally. One option is some sort of computer game. A study in Berry and Broadbent [1988] has taken this approach. Subjects would be given a scenario and a goal (e.g., predicting the stock market or killing aliens). There would be a large variance in how the rules of the game operated. For example, some rules would function according to the independencies/dependencies in Expression 10.3; some rules would not function according to those independencies/dependencies; some rules would appear nonsensical according to cause–effect relationships included in the subject's background knowledge; and some rules would have no value to success in the game.

EXERCISES
Section 10.1

Exercise 10.1 *In Examples 10.1, 10.2, 10.3, 10.4, 10.5, and 10.6 it was left as an exercise to show that* IND *is faithful to the DAG patterns developed in those examples. Do this.*

Exercise 10.2 *Show that for all $n \geq 2$ and all $k \geq 0$,*

$$n(n-1) \sum_{i=0}^{k} \binom{n-2}{i} \leq \frac{n^2(k+1)(n-2)^k}{k!}.$$

Exercise 10.3 *Given the d-separations amongst the variables N, F, C, and T in the DAG in Figure 10.10 (a), show that Algorithms 10.1 and 10.2 will produce the graph in Figure 10.10 (b).*

Exercise 10.4 *Show that the DAG patterns in Figures 10.11 (a) and (b) each do not contain both of the following d-separations:*

$$I(\{X\},\{Y\}) \qquad I(\{X\},\{Y\}|\{Z\}).$$

Exercise 10.5 *Suppose Algorithm 10.2 has constructed the chain $X \to Y \to Z - W - X$, where Y and W are linked, and Z and X are not linked. Show that it will orient $W - Z$ as $W \to Z$.*

Exercise 10.6 *Let P be a probability distribution of the variables in V and $G = (V, E)$ be a DAG. For each $X \in V$, denote the sets of parents and nondescendents of X in G by PA_X and ND_X respectively. Order the nodes so that, for each X, all the ancestors of X in G are numbered before X. Let R_X be the set of nodes that precede X in this ordering. Show that, to determine whether every d-separation in G is a conditional independency in P, for each $X \in V$ we need only check whether*

$$I_P(\{X\}, R_X - PA_X | PA_X).$$

Exercise 10.7 *Modify Algorithm 10.3 so that it determines whether a consistent extension of any PDAG exists and, if so, produces one.*

Exercise 10.8 *Suppose $V = \{X, Y, Z, W, T, V, R\}$ is a set of random variables, and IND contains all and only the d-separations entailed by the following set of d-separations:*

$$\{I(\{X\},\{Y\}|\{Z\}) \qquad I(\{T\},\{X, Y, Z, V\}|\{W\})$$

$$I(\{V\},\{X, Z, W, T\}|\{Y\}) \qquad I(\{R\},\{X, Y, Z, W\}|\{T, V\})).$$

1. *Show the output if IND is the input to Algorithm 10.4.*

2. *Does IND admit a faithful DAG representation?*

Exercise 10.9 *Show what was left as an exercise in Example 10.12.*

Exercise 10.10 *Show what was left as an exercise in Example 10.13.*

Exercise 10.11 *Show what was left as an exercise in Example 10.14.*

Section 10.2

Exercise 10.12 *In Lemma 10.4 it was left as an exercise to show that γ is an inducing chain over V in G between X and Z, and that the edges touching X and Z on γ have the same direction as the ones touching X and Z on ρ. Do this.*

Exercise 10.13 *Prove Lemma 10.6.*

Exercise 10.14 *Prove the second part of Lemma 10.8 by showing that we would have a directed cycle if the inducing chain were also out of Z.*

Exercise 10.15 *Show that the probability distribution discussed in Example 10.17 is embedded faithfully in the DAGs in 10.18 (b), (c), and (d).*

Exercise 10.16 *In Example 10.25 it was left as exercises to show the following:*

1. *We can also mark $W \leftarrow Z \rightarrow Y$ in gp as $W \underline{\leftarrow} Z \rightarrow Y$.*

2. *IND is maximally embedded in the hidden node DAG pattern in Figure 10.26 (c).*

Show both of these.

Exercise 10.17 *In Example 10.28, it was left as an exercise to show that P is maximally embedded in the pattern in Figure 10.27 (c). Show this.*

Exercise 10.18 *Suppose $V = \{U, V, W, X, Y, Z\}$ and IND consists of the d-separatins in the DAG in Figure 10.37 restricted to these nodes.*

1. *Show the resultant hidden node DAG pattern when IND is the input to Algorithm 10.5. Is IND maximally imbedded in this pattern?*

2. *Show the resultant hidden node DAG pattern when IND is the input to Algorithm 10.6. Is IND maximally imbedded in this pattern?*

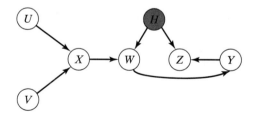

Figure 10.37: The DAG used in Exercise 10.18.

Exercise 10.19 *Suppose $V = \{R, S, U, V, W, X, Y, Z\}$ and IND consists of the d-separations in the DAG in Figure 10.38 restricted to these nodes.*

1. *Show the resultant hidden node DAG pattern when IND is the input to Algorithm 10.5. Is IND maximally imbedded in this pattern?*

2. *Show the resultant hidden node DAG pattern when IND is the input to Algorithm 10.6. Is IND maximally imbedded in this pattern?*

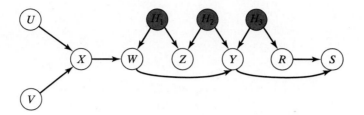

Figure 10.38: The DAG used in Exercise 10.19.

Exercise 10.20 *Draw all conclusions you can concerning the causal relationships among the variables discussed in Example 10.33.*

Chapter 11

More Structure Learning

We've presented the following two methods for learning structure from data: (1) Bayesian method; (2) constraint-based method. They are quite different in that the second finds a unique model based on categorical information about conditional independencies obtained by performing statistical tests on the data, while the first computes the conditional probability of each model given the data and ranks the models. Given this difference, each method may have particular advantages over the other. In Section 11.1 we discuss these advantages by applying both methods to the same learning problems. Section 11.2 references scoring criteria based on data compression, which are an alternative to the Bayesian scoring criterion, while Section 11.3 references algorithms for parallel learning of Bayesian networks. Finally, Section 11.4 shows examples in which the methods have been applied to real data sets in interesting applications.

11.1 Comparing the Methods

Much of this section is based on a discussion in Heckerman et al. [1999]. The constraint-based method uses a statistical analysis to test the presence of a conditional independency. If it cannot reject a conditional independency at some level of significance (typically .05), it categorically accepts it. On the other hand, the Bayesian method ranks models by their conditional probabilities given the data. As a result, the Bayesian method has three advantages:

1. The Bayesian method can avoid making incorrect categorical decisions about conditional independencies, whereas the constraint-based method is quite susceptible to this when the size of the data set is small. That is, the Bayesian method can do model averaging in the case of very small data sets, whereas the constraint-based method must still categorically choose one model.

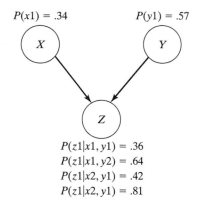

$P(x1) = .34$ $P(y1) = .57$

$P(z1|x1, y1) = .36$
$P(z1|x1, y2) = .64$
$P(z1|x2, y1) = .42$
$P(z1|x2, y1) = .81$

Figure 11.1: A Bayesian network.

2. The Bayesian method can handle missing data items. On the other hand, the constraint-based method typically throws out a case containing a missing data item.

3. The Bayesian method can distinguish among models that the constraint-based method cannot. (We will see a case of this in Section 11.1.2.)

After showing two examples illustrating some of these advantages, we discuss an advantage of the constraint-based method and draw some final conclusions.

11.1.1   A Simple Example

Heckerman et al. [1999] selected the DAG $X \rightarrow Z \leftarrow Y$, assigned a space of size two to each variable, and randomly sampled each conditional probability according to the uniform distribution. Figure 11.1 shows the resultant Bayesian network. They then sampled from this Bayesian network. Table 11.1 shows the resultant data for the first 150, 250, 500, 1000, and 2000 cases sampled. Based on these data, they investigated how well the Bayesian model selection, Bayesian modeling averaging, and the constraint-based method (in particular, Algorithm 10.2) learned that the edge $X \rightarrow Z$ is present. If we give the problem a causal interpretation (as was done by the authors) and make the causal

#cases in d	# $x1y1z1$	# $x1y1z2$	# $x1y2z1$	# $x1y2z2$	# $x2y1z1$	# $x2y1z2$	# $x2y2z1$	# $x2y2z2$
150	10	23	16	7	15	38	36	5
250	21	41	25	15	27	51	60	10
500	44	79	44	19	67	103	121	23
1000	75	134	80	51	152	222	242	44
2000	145	264	180	105	311	431	476	88

Table 11.1: The data generated using the Bayesian network in Figure 11.1.

#cases in d	Model Averaging $P(X \rightarrow Z$ is present$\|$d$)$	Output of Model Selection	Output of Algorithm 10.2
150	.036	X and Z independent	X and Z independent
250	.123	X and Z independent	$X \rightarrow Z$
500	.141	$X \rightarrow Z$ or $Z \rightarrow X$	Inconsistency
1000	.593	$X \rightarrow Z$	$X \rightarrow Z$
2000	.926	$X \rightarrow Z$	$X \rightarrow Z$

Table 11.2: The results of applying Bayeisan model selection, Bayesian, model averaging and the constraint-based method to data obtained by sampling from the Bayesian network in Figure 11.1.

faithfulness assumption, we are learning whether X causes Z. For Bayesian model averaging and selection, they used a prior equivalent sample size of 1 and a uniform distribution for the prior joint distribution of X, Y, and Z. They averaged over DAGs and assigned a prior probability of 1/25 to each of the 25 possible DAGs. Since the problem was given a causal interpretation, averaging over DAGs seems reasonable. That is, if we say X causes Z if and only if the feature $X \rightarrow Z$ is present and we averaged over patterns, the probability of the feature would be 0 given the pattern $X - Z - Y$ even though this pattern allows that X could cause Z. We could remedy this problem by assigning a nonzero probability to "X causes Z" given the pattern $X - Z - Y$. However, we must also consider the meaning of the prior probabilities. (See the beginning of Section 9.2.2.) Heckerman et al. [1999] also performed model selection by assigning a probability of 1/25 to each of the 25 possible DAGs. For the constraint-based method, they used the implementation of Algorithm 10.2 (PC Find DAG Pattern) which is part of the Tetrad II system Scheines et al. [1994].

Table 11.2 shows the results. In that table, "X and Z independent" means that they obtained a DAG which entails that X and Z are independent, and $X \rightarrow Z$ means they obtained a DAG which has the edge $X \rightarrow Z$. Note that in the case of model selection, when $N = 500$ they say "$X \rightarrow Z$ or $Z \rightarrow X$." Recall that they did selection by DAGs, not by DAG patterns. So, this does not mean they obtained a pattern with the edge $X - Z$. Rather, three DAGs had the highest posterior probability, two of them had $X \rightarrow Z$ and one had $Z \rightarrow X$. Note further that the output of Algorithm 10.2, in the case in which the sample size is 500, is that there is an inconsistency. In this case, the independence tests yielded (1) X and Z are dependent; (2) Y and Z are dependent; (3) X and Y are independent given Z; and (4) X and Z are independent given Y. This set of conditional independencies does not admit a faithful DAG representation, which is an assumption in Algorithm 10.2. So we say there is an inconsistency. Indeed, the set of conditional independencies does not even admit an embedded faithful DAG representation.

This example illustrates two advantage of the Bayesian model averaging method over both the Bayesian model selection method and the constraint-based method. First, the latter two methods give a categorical output with no indication as to strength of the conclusion. Second, this categorical output can

4	349	13	64	9	207	33	72	12	126	38	54	10	67	49	43
2	232	27	84	7	201	64	95	12	115	93	92	17	79	119	59
8	166	47	91	6	120	74	110	17	92	148	100	6	42	198	73
4	48	39	57	5	47	123	90	9	41	224	65	8	17	414	54
5	454	9	44	5	312	14	47	8	216	20	35	13	96	28	24
11	285	29	61	19	236	47	88	12	164	62	85	15	113	72	50
7	163	36	72	13	193	75	90	12	174	91	100	20	81	142	77
6	50	36	58	5	70	110	76	12	48	230	81	13	49	360	98

Table 11.3: The data obtained in the Sewell and Shah [1968] study.

be incorrect. On the other hand, in the case of model averaging we become increasingly certain that $X \to Z$ is present as the sample size becomes larger.

11.1.2 Learning College Attendance Influences

This example is also taken from Heckerman et al. [1999]. In 1968, Sewell and Shah studied the variables that influenced the decision of high school students concerning attending college. For 10,318 Wisconsin high school seniors they determined the values of the following variables:

Variable	Values
Sex	*male, female*
SeS (socioeconomic status)	*low, lower middle, upper middle, high*
IQ (intelligent quotient)	*low, lower middle, upper middle, high*
PE (parental encouragement)	*low, high*
CP (College plans)	*yes, no*

There are $2 \times 4 \times 4 \times 2 \times 2 = 128$ possible configurations of the values of the variables. Table 11.3 shows the number of students with each configuration. In that table, the entry in the first row and column corresponds to *Sex = male*, *Ses = low*, *IQ = low*, *PE = low*, and *CP = yes*. The remaining entries correspond to the configurations obtained by cycling through the values of the variables in the order that *Sex* varies the slowest and *CP* varies the fastest. For example, the upper half of the table contains the data on all the male students.

Heckerman et al. [1999] developed a multinomial Bayesian network structure learning space. (See Section 8.1.) containing the five variables in which the equivalent sample size was 5, the prior distribution of the variables was uniform, and all the DAG patterns had the same prior probability, except they eliminated any pattern in which *Sex* has parents, or *Ses* has parents, or *CP* has children (inclusive or). They then determined the posterior probability of the patterns using the method illustrated in Example 8.2 on page 438. The two most probable patterns are shown in Figure 11.2. Note that the posterior probability of the pattern in Figure 11.2 (a) is essentially 1, which means model averaging is unnecessary. The only difference between the second most probable pattern

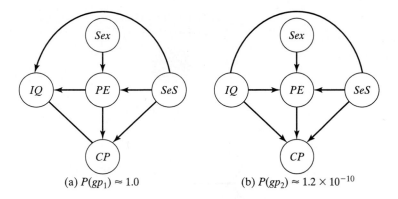

(a) $P(gp_1) \approx 1.0$ (b) $P(gp_2) \approx 1.2 \times 10^{-10}$

Figure 11.2: The two most probable DAG patterns given the data in Table 11.3.

and the most probable one is that *Sex* and *IQ* are independent in the second most probable pattern, whereas they are conditionally independent given *SeS* and *PE* in the most probable one.

Assuming that the probability distribution admits a faithful DAG representation and using the constraint-based method (in particular, Algorithm 10.2), Spirtes et al. [1993, 2000] obtained the pattern in Figure 11.2 (b). Algorithm 10.2 (PC Find DAG Pattern) chooses this pattern due to its greedy nature. After it decides that *Sex* and *IQ* are independent, it never investigates the conditional independence of *Sex* and *IQ* given *SeS* and *PE*.

In Section 2.6.3 we argued that the causal embedded faithfulness assumption is often justified. If we make this assumption and further assume that there are no hidden common causes, then the probability distribution of the observed variables is faithful to the causal DAG containing only those variables. That is, we can make the causal faithfulness assumption. Making this assumption, then all the edges in Figure 11.2 (a) represent direct causal influences (also assuming that we have correctly learned the DAG pattern faithful to the probability distribution). Some results are not surprising. For example, it seems reasonable that socioeconomic status would have a direct causal influence on college plans. Furthermore, Sex influences college plans only indirectly through parental influence.

Heckerman et al. [1999] maintain that it does not seem as reasonable that socioeconomic status has a direct causal influence on *IQ*. To investigate this, they eliminated the assumption that there are no hidden common causes (i.e., they made only the causal embedded faithfulness assumption) and investigated the presence of a hidden variable connecting *IQ* and *SeS*. That is, they obtained new DAGs from the one in Figure 11.2 (a) by adding a hidden variable. In particular, they investigated DAGs in which there is a hidden variable pointing to *IQ* and *SeS*, and ones in which there is a hidden variable pointing to *IQ*, *SeS*, and *PE*. In both cases, they considered DAGs in which none, one, or both of the links $SeS \rightarrow PE$ and $PE \rightarrow IQ$ are removed. They varied the number of values of the hidden variable from two to six. Besides the DAG in

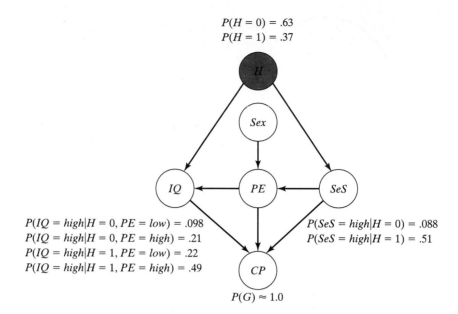

Figure 11.3: The most probable DAG given the data in Table 11.3 when we consider hidden variables. Only some conditional probabilities are shown.

Figure 11.2 (a), these are the only DAGs they considered possible. Note that they directly specified DAGs rather than DAG patterns.

Heckerman et al. [1999] computed the probabilities of the DAGs given the data using the Cheeseman–Stutz approximation discussed in Section 8.5.5. The DAG with the highest posterior probability appears in Figure 11.3. Some of the learned conditional probabilities also appear in that figure. The posterior probability of this DAG is 2×10^{10} times that of the DAG in Figure 11.2 (a). Furthermore, it is 2×10^8 as probable as the next most probable DAG with a hidden variable, which is the one that also has an edge from the hidden variable to PE.

Note that the DAG in Figure 11.3 entails the same conditional independencies (among all the variables including the hidden variable) as one with the edge $SeS \rightarrow H$. So the pattern learned actually has the edge $SeS - H$. As discussed in Section 8.5.2, the existence of a hidden variable enables us only to conclude that the causal DAG is either $SeS \leftarrow H \rightarrow IQ$ (there is a hidden common cause influencing IQ and SeS and they each have no direct causal influence on each other) or $SeS \rightarrow H \rightarrow IQ$ (SeS has a causal influence on IQ through an unobserved variable). However, even though we cannot conclude that $SeS \leftarrow H \rightarrow IQ$, the existence of a hidden variable tells us that the causal DAG is not $SeS \rightarrow IQ$ with no intermediate variable mediating this influence. This eliminates one way SeS could cause IQ and therefore lends support to the causal DAG being $SeS \leftarrow H \rightarrow IQ$. Note that IQ and SeS are both more probable to be high when H has value 1. Heckerman et al. [1999] state that this suggests that, if there is a hidden common cause, it may be "parent quality."

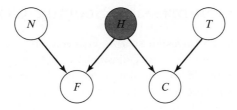

Figure 11.4: A DAG pattern containing a hidden variable.

Note further that the causal DAGs in Figure 11.2 (a) and Figure 11.3 entail the same conditional independencies among the observed variables. So the constraint-based method could not distinguish between them. Although the Bayesian method was not able to distinguish $SeS \leftarrow H \rightarrow IQ$ from $SeS \rightarrow H \rightarrow IQ$, it was able to conclude $SeS - H \rightarrow IQ$ and eliminate $SeS \rightarrow IQ$, and thereby lend support to the existence of a hidden common cause.

Before closing, we mention another explanation for the Bayesian method choosing the pattern with the hidden variable. As discussed in Section 8.5.2, it could be that by making SeS and IQ discrete, we organize the data in such a way that the resultant probability distribution can be included in the hidden variable model. So, the existence of a hidden variable could be an artifact of this process.

11.1.3   Conclusions

We've shown some advantages of the Bayesian method over the constraint-based method. On the other hand, the case in which the probability distribution admits an embedded faithful DAG representation but not a faithful DAG representation (i.e., the case of hidden variables) poses a problem to the Bayesian method. For example, suppose the probability distribution is faithful to the DAG pattern in Figure 8.7, which appears again in Figure 11.4. Then, the Bayesian model selection method could not obtain the correct result without considering hidden variables. However, even if we restrict ourselves to patterns that entail different conditional independencies among the observed variables, the number of patterns with hidden variables can be much larger than the number of patterns containing only the observed variables. The constraint-based method, however, can discover DAG patterns in which the probability distribution of the observed variables is embedded faithfully. That is, it can discover hidden variables (nodes). Section 10.2 contains many examples illustrating this. Given this, a reasonable method would be to use the constraint-based method to suggest an initial set of plausible solutions, and then use the Bayesian method to analyze the models in this set. If we are concerned with learning causal influences, we would finally use the conditional independencies in the model learned as the input to Algorithm 10.7 to obtain a hidden node DAG pattern.

11.2   Data Compression Scoring Criteria

As an alternative to the Bayesian scoring criterion, Rissanen [1987], Lam and Bacchus [1994], and Friedman and Goldszmidt [1996] developed and discussed a scoring criterion called **MDL** (minimum description length). The MDL principle frames model learning in terms of data compression. The MDL objective is to determine the model that provides the shortest description of the data set. You should consult the references above for the derivation of the MDL scoring criterion. Although this derivation is based on different principles than the derivation of the BIC scoring criterion (See Section 8.3.2.), it turns out that the MDL scoring criterion is simply the additive inverse of the BIC scoring criterion. All the techniques developed in Chapters 8 and 9 can be applied using the MDL scoring criterion instead of the Bayesian scoring criterion. As discussed in Section 8.4.3, this scoring criterion is also consistent for multinomial and Gaussian augmented Bayesian networks. In Section 8.3.2 we discussed using it when learning structure in the case of missing data values.

Wallace and Korb [1999] developed a data compression scoring criterion called **MML** (minimum message length), which more carefully determines the message length for encoding the parameters in the case of Gaussian Bayesian networks.

11.3   Parallel Learning of Bayesian Networks

Algorithms for parallel learning of Bayesian networks from data can be found in Lam and Segre [2002] and Mechling and Valtorta [1994].

11.4   Examples

There are two ways that Bayesian structure learning can be applied. The first is to learn a structure that can be used for inference concerning future cases. We use model selection to do this. The second is to learn something about the (often causal) relationships involving some or all of the variables in the domain. Both model selection and model averaging can be used for this. First, we show examples of learning useful structures; then we show examples of inferring causal relationships.

11.4.1   Structure Learning

We show several examples in which useful Bayesian networks were learned from data.

Cervical Spinal-Cord Trauma

Physicians face the problem of assessing cervical spinal-cord trauma. To learn a Bayesian network that could assist physicians in this task, Herskovits and

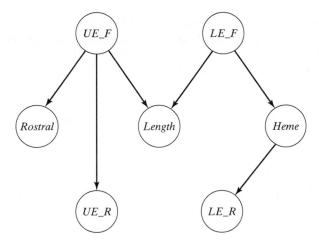

Figure 11.5: The structure learned by Cogito for assesseing cervical spinal-cord trauma.

Dagher [1997] obtained a data set from the Regional Spinal Cord Injury Center of the Delaware Valley. The data set consisted of 104 cases of patients with spine injury, who were evaluated acutely and at one year follow-up. Each case consisted of the following seven variables:

Variable	What the Variable Represents
UE_F	Upper extremity functional score
LE_F	Lower extremity functional score
$Rostral$	Most superior point of cord edema as demonstrated by MRI
$Length$	Length of cord edema as demonstrated by MRI
$Heme$	Cord hemorrhage as demonstrated by MRI
UE_R	Upper extremity recovery at one year
LE_R	Lower extremity recovery at one year

They represented the data as discrete values and used the Bayesian network learning program Cogito^{TM} to learn a Bayesian network containing these variables. Cogito, which was developed by E. H. Herskovits and A.P. Dagher, does model selection using the Bayesian method presented in this text. The structure learned is shown in Figure 11.5.

Herskovits and Dagher [1997] compared the performance of their learned Bayesian network with that of a regression model that had independently been developed by other researchers from the same data set (Flanders et al. [1996]). The other researchers did not render the data discrete , but rather, they assumed that it followed a normal distribution. The comparison consisted of evaluating 40 new cases not present in the original data set. They entered the values of all variables except the outcome variables, which are UE_R (upper extremity recovery at one year) and LE_R (lower extremity recovery at one year), and used the Bayesian network inference program Ergo^{TM} (Beinlich and Herskovits [1990]) to predict the values of the outcome variables. They also used the regression model to predict these values. Finally, they compared the predictions of both models with the actual values for each case. They found that the Bayesian network correctly predicted the degree of upper-extremity recovery three times as often as the regression model. They attributed part of this result to the fact that the original data did not follow a normal distribution, which the regression model assumed. An advantage of Bayesian networks is that they need not assume any particular distribution and therefore can accommodate unusual distributions.

Forecasting Sea Breezes

Next we describe Bayesian networks that were developed by Kennett et al. [2001] for forecasting sea breezes. They describe the sea breeze prediction problem as follows:

> Sea breezes occur because of the unequal heating and cooling of neighboring sea and land areas. As warm air rises over the land, cool air is drawn in from the sea. The ascending air returns seaward in the upper current, building a cycle and spreading the effect over a large area. If wind currents are weak, a sea breeze will usually commence soon after the temperature of the land exceeds that of the sea, peaking in mid-afternoon. A moderate to strong prevailing offshore wind will delay or prevent a sea breeze from developing, while a light to moderate prevailing offshore wind at 900 meters (known as the gradient level) will reinforce a developing sea breeze. The sea breeze process is affected by time of day, prevailing weather, seasonal changes, and geography.

Kennett et al. [2001] note that forecasting in the Sydney area was currently being done using a simple rule-based system. The rule is as follows:

If the wind is offshore
and the wind is less than 23 knots
and part of the timeslice falls in the afternoon,
then a sea breeze is likely to occur.

The Australian Bureau of Meteorology (BOM) provides a data set of meteorological information obtained from three different sensor sites in the Sydney area. Kennett et al. [2001] used 30 MB of data obtained from October, 1997 to October, 1999. Data on ground level wind speed (ws) and direction (wd) at 30 minute intervals (date and time stamped) were obtained from automatic weather stations (AWS). Olympic sites provided ground level wind speed (ws), wind direction (wd), gust strength, temperature, dew temperature, and rainfall. Weather balloon data from Sydney airport, collected at 5 A.M. and 11 P.M. daily, provided vertical readings for gradient-level wind speed (gws) and direction (gdw), temperature, and rainfall. Predicted variables are wind speed prediction (*wsp*) and wind direction prediction (*wdp*). The variables used in the networks are summarized in the following table:

Variable	What the Variable Represents
gwd	Gradient-level wind direction
gws	Gradient-level wind speed
wd	Wind direction
ws	Wind speed
date	Date
time	Time
wdp	Wind direction prediction (predicted variable)
wsp	Wind speed prediction (predicted variable)

From this data set, Kennett et al. [2001] used Tetrad II, both with and without a prior temporal ordering, to learn a Bayesian network, They also learned a Bayesian network by searching the space of causal models and using MML (discussed in Section 11.2) to score DAGs. They called this method **CaMML** (causal MML). Furthermore, they constructed a Bayesian network using expert elicitation with meteorologists at the BOM. The links between the variables represent the experts' beliefs concerning the causal relationships among the variables. The networks learned using CaMML, Tetrad II with a prior temporal ordering, and expert elicitation are shown in Figure 11.6.

Next Kennett et al. [2001] learned the values of the parameters in each Bayesian network by inputting 80% of the data from 1997 and 1998 to the learning package Netica (Norsys [2000]). Netica uses the techniques discussed in Chapters 6 and 7 for learning parameters from data. Finally, they evaluated the predictive accuracy of all four networks and the rule-based system using the remaining 20% of the data. All four Bayesian networks had almost identical predictive accuracies, and all significantly outperformed the rule-based system. Figure 11.7 plots the predictive accuracy of CaMML and the rule-based system. Note the periodicity in the prediction rates, and the extreme fluctuations for the rule-based system.

MENTOR

Mani et al. [1997] developed MENTOR, a system that predicts the risk of mental retardation (MR) in infants. Specifically, the system can determine the probabilities of the child later obtaining scores in four different ranges on the Raven Progressive Matrices Test, which is a test of cognitive function. The probabilities are conditional on values of variables such as the mother's age at time of birth, whether the mother had recently had an X-ray, whether labor was induced, and so forth.

Developing the Network The structure of the Bayesian network used in MENTOR was created in the following three steps:

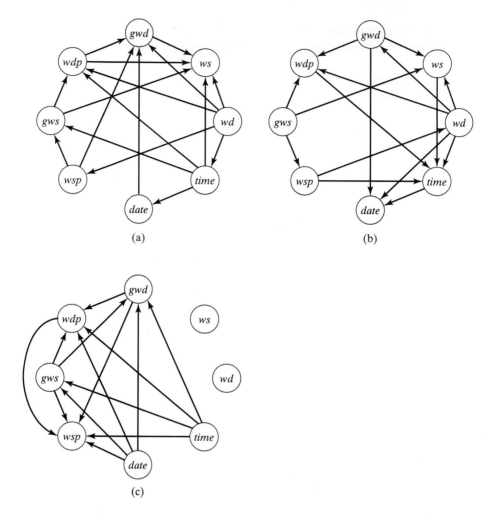

Figure 11.6:   The sea breeze forecasting Bayesian networks learned by
(a) CaMML; (b) Tetrad II with a prior temporal ordering; and (c) expert elicitation.

1. Mani et al. [1997] obtained the Child Health and Development Study
   (CHDS) data set, which is the data set developed in a study concerning pregnant mothers and their children. The children were monitored
   through their teen years and were given numerous questionnaires, physical and psychological exams, and special tests. The study was conducted
   by the University of California at Berkeley and the Kaiser Foundation. It
   started in 1959 and continued into the 1980s. There are approximately
   6000 children and 3000 mothers with IQ scores in the data set. The
   children were either five years old or nine years old when their IQs were
   tested. The IQ test used for the children was the Raven Progressive Ma-

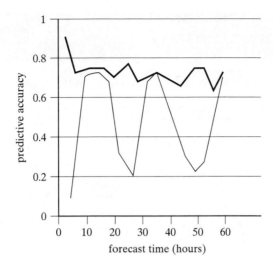

Figure 11.7: The thick curve represents the predictive accuracy of CaMML, and the thin one represents that of the rule-based system.

trices Test. The mothers' IQs were also tested, and the test used was the Peabody Picture Vocabulary Test.

Initially, Mani et al. [1997] identified 50 variables in the data set that were thought to play a role in the causal mechanism of mental retardation. However, they eliminated those with weak associations to the Raven score, and finally used only 23 in their model. The variables used are shown in Table 11.4.

After the variables were identified, they used the CB algorithm to learn a network structure from the data set. The **CB** Algorithm, which is discussed in Singh and Valtorta [1995], uses the constraint-based method to propose a total ordering of the nodes, and then uses a modified version of Algorithm 9.1 (K2) to learn a DAG structure.

2. Mani et al. [1997] decided that they wanted the network to be a causal network. So, next they modified the DAG according to the following three rules:

   (a) Rule of Chronology: An event cannot be the parent of a second event that preceded the first event in time. For example, CHILD_HPRB (child's health problem) cannot be the parent of MOM_DIS (mother's disease).

   (b) Rule of Commonsense: The causal links should not go against common sense. For example, DAD_EDU (father's education) cannot be a cause of MOM_RACE (mother's race).

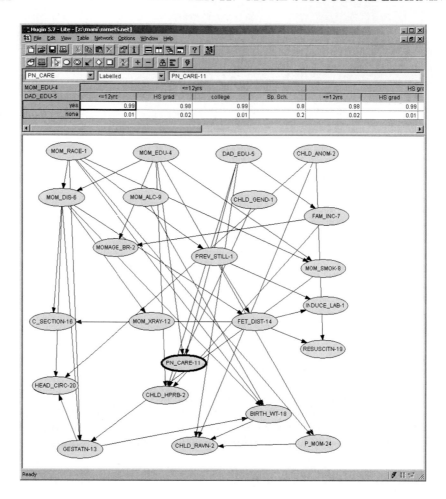

Figure 11.8: The DAG used in MENTOR (displayed using HUGIN).

   (c) Domain Rule: The causal links should not violate established do-
      main rules. For example, PN_CARE (prenatal care) should not cause
      MOM_SMOK (maternal smoking).

3. Finally, the DAG was refined by an expert. The expert was a clinician
   who had 20 years experience with children with mental retardation and
   other developmental disabilities. When the expert stated that there was
   no relationship between variables with a causal link, the link was removed
   and new ones were incorporated to capture knowledge of the domain causal
   mechanisms.

The final DAG specifications were input to HUGIN (Olesen et al. [1992]), using the HUGIN graphic interface. The output is the DAG shown in Figure 11.8.

Variable	What the Variable Represents
MOM_RACE	Mother's race classified as White (European or White and American Indian or others considered to be of white stock) or nonWhite (Mexican, Black, Oriental, interracial mixture, South-East Asian).
MOMAGE_BR	Mother's age at time of child's birth categorized as 14–19 years, 20–34 years, or $\geq$ 35 years.
MOM_EDU	Mother's education categorized as $\leq$ 12 and did not graduate high school, graduated high school, and > high school (attended college or trade school).
DAD_EDU	Father's education categorized same as mother's.
MOM_DIS	Yes, if mother had one or more of lung trouble, heart trouble, high blood pressure, kidney trouble, convulsions, diabetes, thyroid trouble, anemia, tumors, bacterial disease, measles, chicken pox, herpes simplex, eclampsia, placenta previa, any type of epilepsy, or malnutrition; no, otherwise.
FAM_INC	Family income categorized as < \$10,000 or $\geq$ \$10,000.
MOM_SMOK	Yes, if mother smoked during pregnancy; no, otherwise.
MOM_ALC	Mother's alcoholic drinking level classified as mild (0–6 drinks per week), moderate (7–20), or severe (>20).
PREV_STILL	Yes, if mother previously had a stillbirth; no, otherwise.
PN_CARE	Yes, if mother had prenatal care; no, otherwise.
MOM_XRAY	Yes, if mother had been X-rayed in the year prior to or during the pregnancy; no, otherwise.
GESTATN	Period of gestation categorized as premature ($\leq$ 258 days), or normal (259–294 days), or postmature ($\geq$ 295 days).
FET_DIST	Fetal distress classified as yes if there was prolapse of cord, mother had a history of uterine surgery, there was uterine rupture or fever at or just before delivery, or there was an abnormal fetal heart rate; no, otherwise.
INDUCE_LAB	Yes, if mother had induced labor; no, otherwise.
C_SECTION	Yes, if delivery was a caesarean section; no, if it was vaginal.
CHLD_GEND	Gender of child (male or female).
BIRTH_WT	Birth weight categorized as low < 2500 g) or normal ($\geq$ 2500 g).
RESUSCITN	Yes, if child had resuscitation; no, otherwise.
HEAD_CIRC	Normal, if head circumference is 20 or 21; abnormal, otherwise.
CHLD_ANOM	Child anomaly classified as yes if child has cerebral palsy, hypothyroidism, spina binfida, Down's syndrome, chromosomal abnormality, anencephaly, hydrocephalus, epilepsy, Turner's syndrome, cerbellar ataxia, speech defect, Klinefelter's syndrome, or convulsions; no, otherwise.
CHILD_HPRB	Child's health problem categorized as having a physical problem, having a behavior problem, having both a physical and a behavioral problem, or having no problem.
CHLD_RAVN	Child's cognitive level, measured by the Raven test, categorized as mild MR, borderline MR, normal, or superior.
P_MOM	Mother's cognitive level, measured by the Peabody test, categorized as mild MR, borderline MR, normal, or superior.

Table 11.4: The variables used in MENTOR.

Cognitive Level	Avg. Probability for Controls ($n = 13019$)	Avg. Probability for Subjects ($n = 3598$)
Mild MR	.06	.09
Borderline MR	.12	.16
Mild or Borderline MR	.18	.25

Table 11.5: Average probabilities, as determined by MENTOR, of having mental retardation for controls (children identified as having normal cognitive functioning at age 8) and subjects (children identified as having mild or borderline MR at age 8).

After the DAG was developed the conditional probability distributions were learned from the CHDS data set using the techniques shown in Chapters 6 and 7. After that, they too were modified by the expert, resulting finally in the Bayesian network in MENTOR.

Validating the Model   Mani et al. [1997] tested their model in a number of different ways. We present two of their results.

The National Collaborative Perinatal Project (NCPP), of the National Institute of Neurological and Communicative Disorders and Strokes, developed a data set containing information on pregnancies between 1959 and 1974 and eight years of follow-up for live-born children. For each case in the data set, the values of all 22 variables except CHLD_RAVN (child's cognitive level as measured by the Raven test) were entered, and the conditional probabilities of each of the four values of CHLD_RAVN were computed. Table 11.5 shows the average values of $P(\text{CHLD\_RAVN} = mildMR|\mathbf{d})$ and $P(\text{CHLD\_RAVN} = borderlineMR|\mathbf{d})$, where $\mathbf{d}$ is the set of values of the other 22 variables, for both the controls (children in the study with normal cognitive function at age 8) and the subjects (children in the study with mild or borderline MR at age 8).

In actual clinical cases, the diagnosis of mental retardation is rarely made after only a review of history and physical examination. Therefore, we cannot expect MENTOR to do more than indicate a risk of mental retardation by computing the probability of it. The higher the probability the greater the risk. Table 11.5 shows that, on the average, children who were later determined to have mental retardation were found to be at greater risk than those who were not. MENTOR can confirm a clinician's assessment by reporting the probability of mental retardation.

As another test of the model, Mani et al. [1997] developed a strategy for comparing the results of MENTOR with the judgments of an expert. They generated nine cases, each with some set of variables instantiated to certain values, and let MENTOR compute the conditional probability of the values of CHLD_RAVN. The generated values for three of the cases are shown in Table 11.6, while the conditional probabilities of the values of CHLD_RAVN for those cases are shown in Table 11.7.

Variable	Case 1 Variable Value	Case 2 Variable Value	Case 3 Variable Value
MOM_RACE	nonWhite	White	White
MOMAGE_BR	14–19		≥ 35
MOM_EDU	≤ 12	> high school	≤ 12
DAD_EDU	≤ 12	> high school	high school
MOM_DIS			no
FAM_INC	< \$10,000		< \$10,000
MOM_SMOK			yes
MOM_ALC			moderate
PREV_STILL			
PN_CARE		yes	
MOM_XRAY			yes
GESTATN	normal	normal	premature
FET_DIST		no	yes
INDUCE_LAB			
C_SECTION			
CHLD_GEND			
BIRTH_WT	low	normal	low
RESUSCITN			
HEAD_CIRC			abnormal
CHLD_ANOM		no	
CHILD_HPRB			both
CHLD_RAVN			
P_MOM	normal	superior	borderline

Table 11.6: Generated values for three cases.

The expert was in agreement with MENTOR's assessments (conditional probabilities) in seven of the nine cases. In the two cases in which the expert was not in complete agreement, there were problems in the child. In one case the child had a congenital anomaly, while in the other the child had a health problem. In both these cases a review of the medical chart would indicate the exact nature of the problem and this information would then be used by the expert to determine the probabilities. It is possible that MENTOR's conditional

Value of CHLD_RAVN and Prior Probability	Case 1 Posterior Probability	Case 2 Posterior Probability	Case 3 Posterior Probability
mild MR (.056)	.101	.010	.200
borderline MR (.124)	.300	.040	.400
normal (.731)	.559	.690	.380
superior (.089)	.040	.260	.200

Table 11.7: Posterior probabilities for three cases.

probabilities are accurate given the current information, and the domain expert could not accurately determine probabilities without the additional information.

11.4.2   Inferring Causal Relationships

Next we show examples of learning something about causal relationships among the variables in the domain.

University Student Retention

Using the data collected by the *U.S. News and World Record* magazine for the purpose of college ranking, Druzdzel and Glymour [1999] analyzed the influences that affect university student retention rate. By "student retention rate," we mean the percent of entering freshmen who end up graduating from the university at which they initially matriculate. Low student retention rate is a major concern at many American universities since the mean retention rate over all American universities is only 55%.

The data set provided by the *U.S. News and World Record* magazine contains records for 204 United States universities and colleges identified as major research institutions. Each record consists of over 100 variables. The data were collected separately for the years 1992 and 1993. Druzdzel and Glymour [1999] selected the following eight variables as being most relevant to their study:

Variable	What the Variable Represents
grad	Fraction of entering students who graduate from the institution
rejr	Fraction of applicants who are not offered admission
tstsc	Average standardized score of incoming students
*tp*10	Fraction of incoming students in the top 10% of high school class
acpt	Fraction of students who accept the institution's admission offer
spnd	Average educational and general expenses per student
sfrat	Student/faculty ratio
salar	Average faculty salary

From the 204 universities they removed any universities that had missing data for any of these variables. This resulted in 178 universities in the 1992 study and 173 universities in the 1993 study. Table 11.8 shows exemplary records for six of the universities.

Druzdzel and Glymour [1999] used the implementation of Algorithm 10.7 in the Tetrad II (Scheines et al. [1994]) to learn a hidden node DAG pattern from the data. Tetrad II allows the user to specify a "temporal" ordering of the variables. If variable Y precedes X in this order, the algorithm assumes there can be no path from X to Y in any DAG in which the probability distribution of the variables is embedded faithfully. It is called a temporal ordering because in applications to causality if Y precedes X in time, we would assume X could not cause Y. Druzdzel and Glymour [1999] specified the following temporal ordering for the variables in this study:

Univ.	grad	rejr	tstsc	tp10	acpt	spnd	sfrat	salar
1	52.5	29.47	65.06	15	36.89	9855	12.0	60800
2	64.25	22.31	71.06	36	30.97	10527	12.8	63900
3	57.00	11.30	67.19	23	40.29	6601	17.0	51200
4	65.25	26.91	70.75	42	28.28	15287	14.4	71738
5	77.75	26.69	75.94	48	27.19	16848	9.2	63000
6	91.00	76.68	80.63	87	51.16	18211	12.8	74400

Table 11.8: Records for six universities.

spnd, sfrat, salar
rejr, acpt
tstsc, tp10
grad

Their reasons for this ordering are as follows: They believed the average spending per student (*spnd*), the student/teacher ratio (*sfrat*), and faculty salary (*salar*) are determined based on budget considerations and are not influenced by the other five variables. Furthermore, they placed the rejection rate (*rejr*) and the fraction of students who accept the institution's admission offer (*acpt*) before the average test scores (*tstsc*) and the class standing (*tp*10) because the values of these latter two variables are obtained only from matriculating students. Finally, they assumed that graduate rate (*grad*) does not cause any of the other variables.

Recall from Section 10.3 that Tetrad II allows the user to enter a significance level. A significance level of α means that the probability of rejecting a conditional independency hypothesis, when it is true, is α. Therefore, the smaller the value α, the less likely we are to reject a conditional independency, and therefore the sparser our resultant graph. Figure 11.9 shows the hidden node DAG patterns that Druzdzel and Glymour [1999] obtained from *U.S. News and World Report's* 1992 data set using significance levels of .2, .1, .05, and .01.

Although different hidden node DAG patterns were obtained at different levels of significance, all the hidden node DAG patterns in Figure 11.9 show that standardized test scores (*tstsc*) has a direct causal influence on graduation rate (*grad*), and no other variable has a direct causal influence on *grad*. The results for the 1993 data set were not as overwhelming, but they too indicated *tstsc* to be the only direct causal influence of *grad*.

To test whether the causal structure may be different for top research universities, Druzdzel and Glymour [1999] repeated the study using only the top 50 universities according to the ranking of *U.S. News and World Report*. The results were similar to those for the complete data sets.

These result indicate that, although factors such as spending per student and faculty salary may have an influence on graduation rates, they do this only indirectly by affecting the standardized test scores of matriculating students. If the results correctly model reality, retention rate can be improved by bringing in students with higher test scores in any way whatsoever. Indeed, in 1994

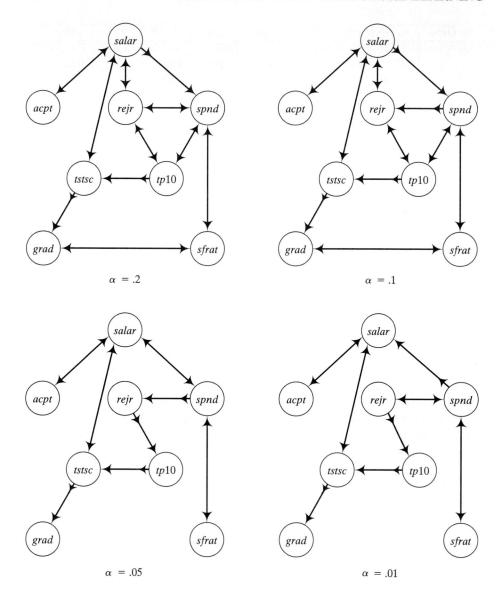

Figure 11.9: The hidden node DAG patterns obtained from *U.S. News and World Record*'s 1992 data base.

Carnegie Mellon changed its financial aid policies to assign a portion of its scholarship fund on the basis of academic merit. Druzdzel and Glymour [1999] note that this resulted in an increase in the average test scores of matriculating freshman classes and an increase in freshman retention.

Before closing, we note that the notion that test score has a causal influence on graduation rate does not fit into our manipulation definition of causation discussed in Section 1.5.1. For example, if we manipulated an individual's test score by accessing the testing agency's database and changing it to a much higher score, we would not expect the individual's chances of graduating to become that of individuals who obtained the same score legitimately. Rather, this study indicates that test score is a near perfect indicator of some other variable, which we can call "graduation potential," and, if we manipulated an individual in such a way that the individual scored higher on the test, it is actually this variable that is being manipulated.

Analyzing Gene Expression Data

Recall that at the beginning of Section 9.2, we mentioned that genes in a cell produce proteins, which then cause other genes to express themselves. Furthermore, there are thousands of genes, but typically we have only a few hundred data items. So, although model selection is not feasible, we can still use approximate model averaging to learn something about the dependence and causal relationships between the expression levels of certain genes. Next we give detailed results of doing this using a nonBayesian method called the "bootstrap" method Friedman et al. [1999]; and we give preliminary analyses comparing results obtained using approximate model averaging with MCMC to results obtained using the bootstrap method.

Results Obtained Using the Bootstrap Method First, let's discuss the mechanism of gene regulation in more detail. A **chromosome** is an extremely long threadlike molecule consisting of deoxyribonucleic acid, abbreviated **DNA**. Each cell in an organism has one or two copies of a set of chromosomes, called a **genome**. A **gene** is a section of a chromosome. In complex organisms, chromosomes number in the order of tens, whereas genes number in the order of tens of thousands. The genes are the functional area of the chromosomes, and are responsible for both the structure and processes of the organism. Stated simply, a gene does this by synthesizing **mRNA**, a process called **transcription**. The information in the mRNA is eventually translated into a protein. Each gene codes for a separate protein, each with a specific function either within the cell or for export to other parts of the organism. Although cells in an organism contain the same genetic code, their protein composition is quite different. This difference is owing to regulation. Regulation occurs largely in mRNA transcription. During this process, proteins bind to regulatory regions along the DNA, affecting the mRNA transcription of certain genes. Thus, the proteins produced by one gene have a causal effect on the level of mRNA (called the **gene expression level**) of another gene. We see then that the expression level of one gene has a causal influence on the expression levels of other genes. A goal of molecular biology is to determine the gene regulation process, which includes the causal relationships among the genes.

In recent years, microarray technology has enabled researchers to measure the expression level of all genes in an organism, thereby providing us with the data to investigate the causal relationships among the genes. Classical experiments had previously been able to determine the expression levels of only a few genes. Microarray data provide us with the opportunity to learn much about the gene regulation process from passive data.

Early tools for analyzing microarray data used clustering algorithms. (See e.g., Spellman et al. [1998].) These algorithms determine groups of genes that have similar expression levels in a given experiment. Thus, they determine correlation but tell us nothing of the causal pattern. By modeling gene interaction using a Bayesian network, Friedman et al. [2000] learned something about the causal pattern. We discuss their results next.

Making the causal faithfulness assumption, Friedman et al. [2000] investigated the presence of two types of features in the causal network containing the expression levels of the genes for a given species. See Section 9.2 for a discussion of features. The first type of feature, called a **Markov relation**, is whether Y is in the Markov boundary (Section 2.5) of X. Clearly, this relationship is symmetric. This relationship holds if two genes are related in a biological interaction. The second type of feature, called an **order relation**, is whether X is an ancestor of Y in the DAG pattern representing the Markov equivalence class to which the causal network belongs. If this feature is present, X has a causal influence on Y. (However, as discussed at the beginning of Section 11.1.1, X could have a causal influence on Y without this feature being present.) Friedman et al. [2000] note that the faithfulness assumption is not necessarily justified in this domain due to the possibility of hidden variables. So, for both the Markov and causal relations, they take their results to be indicative, rather than evidence, that the relationship holds for the genes.

As an alternative to using model averaging to determine the probability that a feature is present, Friedman et al. [2000] used the nonBayesian bootstrap method to determine the confidence that a feature is present. A discussion of this method appears in Friedman et al. [1999]. They applied this method to the data set provided in Spellman et al. [1998], which contains data on gene expression levels of *s. cerevisiae*. For each case (data item) in the data set, the variables measured are the expression levels of 800 genes along with the current cell cycle phase. There are 76 cases in the data set. The cell cycle phase was forced to be a root in all the networks, allowing the modeling of the dependency of expression levels on the cell cycle phase.

They performed their analysis by (1) representing the data as discrete values and using Equality 9.1 to compute the probability of the data given candidate DAGs; and by (2) assuming continuously distributed variables and using Equality 9.2 to compute the probability of the data given candidate DAGs. They represented the data discretely using the three categories *underexpressed, normal,* and *overexpressed*, depending on whether the expression rate is, respectively, significantly lower than, similar to, or greater than control. The results of their analysis contained sensible relations between genes of known function. We show the results of the order relation analysis and Markov relation analysis in turn.

Gene	Cont. d_score	Discrete d_score	Comment
MCD1	525	550	Mitotic chromosome determinant
MSH6	508	292	Required for mismatch repair in mitosis
CS12	497	444	Cell wall maintenance, chitin synthesis
CLN2	454	497	Role in cell cycle start
YLR183C	448	551	Contains fork-headed associated domain
RFA2	423	456	Involved in nucleotide excision repair
RSR1	395	352	Involved in bud site selection
CDC45	394	-	Role in chromosome replication initiation
RAD43	383	60	Cell cycle control, checkpoint function
CDC5	353	209	Cell cycle control, needed for mitosis exit
POL30	321	376	Needed for DNA replication and repair
YOX1	291	400	Homeodomain protein
SRO4	239	463	Role in cellular polarization during budding
CLN1	-	324	Role in cell cycle start
YBR089W	-	298	

Table 11.9: The dominant genes in the order relation.

Analysis of Order Relations For a given variable X, they determined a dominance score for X based on the confidence that X is an ancestor of Y summed over all other variables Y. That is,

$$d\_score(X) = \sum_{Y:C(X,Y)>t} (C(X,Y))^k,$$

where $C(X,Y)$ is the confidence that X is an ancestor of Y, k is a constant rewarding high confidence terms, and t is a threshold discarding low confidence terms. They found the dominant genes are not sensitive to the values of t and k. The highest scoring genes appear in Table 11.9. This table shows some interesting results. First, the set of high scoring genes includes genes involved in initiation of the cell-cycle and its control. They are CLN1, CLN2, CDC5, and RAD43. The functional relationship of these genes has been established (Cvrckova and Nasmyth [1993]). Furthermore, the genes MCD1, RFA2, CDC45, RAD53, CDC5, and POL30 have been found to be essential in cell functions (Guacci et al. [1997]). In particular, the genes CDC5 and POL30 are components of prereplication complexes, and the genes RFA2, POL30, and MSH6 are involved in DNA repair. DNA repair is known to be associated with transcription initiation, and DNA areas that are more active in transcription are repaired more frequently (McGregor [1999]).

Analysis of Markov Relations The top scoring Markov relations in the discrete analysis are shown in Table 11.10. In that table, all pairings involving known genes make sense biologically. When one of the genes is unknown, searches using Psi–Blast (Altschul et al. [1997]) have revealed firm homologies

Conf.	Gene-1	Gene-2	Comment
1.0	YKL163W-PIR3	YKL164C-PIR1	Close locality on chromosome
.985	PRY2	YKR012C	Close locality on chromosome
.985	MCD1	MSH6	Both bind to DNA during mitosis
.98	PHO11	PHO12	Nearly identical acid phosphatases
.975	HHT1	HTB1	Both are histones
.97	HTB2	HTA1	Both are histones
.94	YNL057W	YNL058C	Close locality on chromosome
.94	YHR143W	CTS1	Both involved in cytokinesis
.92	YOR263C	YOR264W	Close locality on chromosome
.91	YGR086	SIC1	Both involved in nuclear function
.9	FAR1	ASH1	Both part of a mating type switch
.89	CLN2	SVS1	Function of SVS1 unknown
.88	YDR033W	NCE2	Both involved in protein secretion
.86	STE2	MFA2	A mating factor and receptor
.85	HHF1	HHF2	Both are histones
.85	MET10	ECM17	Both are sulfite reductases
.85	CDC9	RAD27	Both involved in fragment processing

Table 11.10: The highest ranking Markov relations in the discrete analysis.

to proteins functionally related to the other gene in the pair. Several of the unknown pairs are physically close on the chromosome and therefore perhaps are regulated by the same mechanism. Overall, there are 19 biologically sensible pairs out of the 20 top scoring relations.

Comparison with Clustering   Friedman et al. [2000] determined conditional independencies that are beyond the capabilities of the clustering method. For example, CLN2, RNR3, SVS1, SRO4, and RAD51 all appear in the same cluster according to the analysis done by Spellman et al. [1998]. From this, we can conclude only that they are correlated. Friedman et al. [2000] found with high confidence that CLN2 is a parent of the other four and that there are no other causal paths between them. This means that each of the other four is conditionally independent of the remaining three given CLN2. This agrees with biological knowledge because it is known that CLN2 has a central role in each cell cycle control, and there is no known biological relationship among the other four.

Comparison with Approximate Model Averaging with MCMC   Friedman and Koller [2000] developed an order-based MCMC method for approximate model averaging, which they call order-MCMC. They compared the use of order-MCMC to analyze gene expression data with the use of the bootstrap method. Their comparison proceeded as follows: Given a threshold $t \in [0.1]$, we say a feature F is present if $P(F = present|\mathsf{d}) > t$ and otherwise we say it is absent. If a method says a feature is present when it is absent, we call that a **false positive error**, whereas if a method says a feature is absent when it is present, we call that a **false negative error**. Clearly, as t increases, the number of false negative errors increases whereas the number of false positive errors decreases. So there is a tradeoff between the two types of errors. Friedman and Koller used Bayesian model selection to learn a DAG $\mathbb{G}$ from the data set provided in Spellman et al. [1998]. They then used the order-MCMC method and the bootstrap method to learn Markov features from $\mathbb{G}$. Using the presence of a feature in $\mathbb{G}$ as the gold standard, they determined the false positive and false negative rates for both methods for various values of t. Finally, for both methods they plotted the false negative rates versus the false positive rates. For each method, each value of t determined a point on its graph. They used the same procedure to learn order features from $\mathbb{G}$. In the cases both of Markov and order features, the graph for the order-MCMC method was significantly below the graph of the bootstrap method, indicating that the order-MCMC method makes fewer errors.

Friedman and Koller [2000] caution that their learned DAG is probably much simpler than the DAG in the underlying structure because it was learned from a small data set relative to the number of genes. Nevertheless, their results are indicative of the fact that the order-MCMC method is more reliable in this domain.

A Cautionary Note

Next we present another example concerning inference of causes from data obtained from a survey, which illustrates problems one can encounter when using such data to infer causation.

Scarville et al. [1999] provide a data set obtained from a survey in 1996 of experiences of racial harassment and discrimination of military personnel in the United States Armed Forces. Surveys were distributed to 73,496 members of the U.S. Army, Navy, Marine Corps, Air Force and Coast Guard. The survey sample was selected using a nonproportional stratified random sample in order to ensure adequate representation of all subgroups. Usable surveys were received from 39,855 service members (54%). The survey consisted of 81 questions related to experiences of racial harassment, discrimination, and job attitudes. Respondents were asked to report incidents that had occurred during the previous 12 months. The questionnaire asked participants to indicate the occurrence of 57 different types of racial/ethnic harassment or discrimination. Incidents ranged from telling offensive jokes to physical violence, and included harassment by military personnel as well as the surrounding community. Harassment experienced by family members was also included.

Neapolitan and Morris [2003] used Tetrad III to attempt to learn causal influences from the data set. For their analysis, 9640 records (13%) that had no missing data on the variables of interest were selected. The analysis was initially based on eight variables. Similar to the situation discussed in Section 11.4.2 concerning university retention rates, they found one causal relationship to be present regardless of the significance level. That is, they found that whether the individual held the military responsible for the racial incident had a direct causal influence on the race of the individual. Since this result made no sense, they investigated which variables were involved in Tetrad III learning this causal influence. The five variables involved are the following:

Variable	What the Variable Represents
race	Respondent's race/ethnicity
yos	Respondent's years of military service
inc	Whether respondent reported a racial incident
rept	Whether the incident was reported to military personnel
resp	Whether respondent held the military responsible for the incident

The variable *race* consisted of five categories: White, Black, Hispanic, Asian or Pacific Islander, and Native American or Alaskan Native. Respondents who reported Hispanic ethnicity were classified as Hispanic, regardless of race. Respondents were classified based on self-identification at the time of the survey. Missing data were replaced with data from administrative records. The variable *yos* was classified into four categories: 6 years or less, 7–11 years, 12–19 years, and 20 years or more. The variable *inc* was coded dichotomously to indicate whether any type of harassment was reported on the survey. The variable *rept* indicates responses to a single question concerning whether the incident was reported to military and/or civilian authorities. This variable was coded 1 if an incident had been reported to military officials. Individuals who experienced no incident, did not report the incident, or only reported the incident to civilian officials were coded 0. The variable *resp* indicates responses to a single question concerning whether the respondent believed the military to be responsible for an incident of harassment. This variable was coded 1 if the respondent indicated that the military was responsible for some or all of a reported incident. If the respondent indicated no incident, unknown responsibility, or that the military was not responsible, the variable was coded 0.

Neapolitan and Morris [2003] reran the experiment using only these five variables, and again at all levels of significance, they found that *resp* had a direct causal influence on *race*. In all cases, this causal influence was learned because *rept* and *yos* were found to be probabilistically independent, and there was no edge between *race* and *inc*. That is, the causal connection between *race* and *inc* is mediated by other variables. Figure 11.10 shows the hidden node DAG pattern obtained at the .01 significance level. The edges *yos → inc* and *rept → inc* are directed towards *inc* because *yos* and *rept* were found to be independent. The edge *yos → inc* resulted in the edge *inc ⟶ resp* being directed the way it was, which in turn resulted in *resp ⟶ race* being directed the way it was. If there had been an edge between *inc* and *race*, the edge between responsible and race would not have been directed.

It seems suspicious that no direct causal connection between *race* and *inc* was found. Recall, however, that these are the probabilistic relationships among the responses; they are not necessarily the probabilistic relationships among the

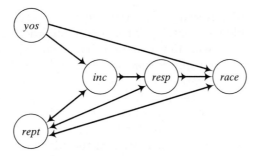

Figure 11.10: The hidden node DAG pattern Tetrad III learned from the racial harassment survey at the .01 significance level.

actual events. There is a problem with using responses on surveys to represent occurrences in nature because subjects may not respond accurately. Let's assume race is recorded accurately. The actual causal relationship between *race*, *inc*, and *says_inc* may be as shown in Figure 11.11. By *inc* we now mean whether there really was an incident, and by *says_inc* we mean the survey response. It could be that races which experienced higher rates of harassment were less likely to report the incident, and the causal influence of *race* on *says_inc* through *inc* was negated by the direct influence of *race* on *inc*. This would be a case in which faithfulness is violated, similar to the situation involving finasteride discussed in Section 2.6.2. The previous conjecture is substantiated by another study. Stangor et al. [2002] found that minority members were more likely to attribute a negative outcome to discrimination when responses were recorded privately, but less likely to report discrimination when they had to express their opinion publicly and there was a member of the nonminority group present. Although the survey of military personnel was intended to be confidential, minority members in the military may have had similar feelings about reporting discrimination to the army as the subjects in the study in Stangor et al. [2002] had about reporting it in the presence of a nonminority individual.

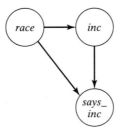

Figure 11.11: Possible causal relationships among race, incidence of harassment, and saying there is an incident of harassment.

As noted previously, Tetrad II (and III) allows the user to enter a temporal ordering. So, one could have put *race* first in such an ordering to avoid it being an effect of another variable. However, one should do this with caution. The fact that the data strongly support that race as an effect indicates that there is something wrong with the data, which means we should be dubious of drawing any conclusions from it. In the present example, Tetrad III actually informed us that we cannot draw causal conclusions from the data when we make *race* a root. That is, when Neapolitan and Morris [2003] made *race* a root, Tetrad III concluded there is no consistent orientation of the edge between *race* and *resp*, which means the probability distribution does not admit an embedded faithful DAG representation unless the edge is directed towards *race*.

Part IV

Applications

Chapter 12

Applications

In this chapter, we first discuss some real-world applications that are based on Bayesian networks; then we examine an application that uses a model which goes beyond Bayesian networks.

12.1 Applications Based on Bayesian Networks

A list of applications based on Bayesian networks follows. It includes applications in which structure was learned from data and ones in which the Bayesian network was constructed manually. Some of the applications have already been discussed in the previous chapters. The list is by no means meant to be exhaustive.

Academics

- The Learning Research and Development Center at the University of Pittsburgh developed Andes (www.pitt.edu/~vanlehn/andes.html), an intelligent tutoring system for physics. Andes infers a student's plan as the student works on a physics problem, and it assesses and tracks the student's domain knowledge over time. Andes is used by approximately 100 students/year.

- Royalty et al. [2002] developed POET, which is an academic advising tool that models the evolution of a student's transcripts. Most of the variables represent course grades and take values from the set of grades plus the values "NotTaken" and "Withdrawn." This and related papers can be found at www.cs.uky.edu/~goldsmit/papers/papers.html.

Biology

- Friedman et al. [2000] developed a technique for learning causal relationships among genes by analyzing gene expression data. This technique is a result of the "Project for Using Bayesian Networks to Analyze Gene Expression," which is described at www.cs.huji.ac.il/labs/compbio/expression.

- Friedman et al. [2002] developed a method for phylogenetic tree reconstruction. The method is used in SEMPHY, which is a tool for maximum likelihood phylogenetic reconstruction. More on it can be found at www.cs.huji.ac.il/labs/compbio/semphy/.

Business and Finance

- Data Digest (www.data-digest.com) modeled and predicted customer behavior in a variety of business settings.

- The Bayesian Belief Network Application Group (www.soc.staffs.ac.uk/~cmtaa/bbnag.htm) developed applications in the financial sector. One application concerned the segmentation of a bank's customers. Business segmentation rules, which determine the classification of a bank's customers, had previously been implemented using an expert systems rule-based approach. This group developed a Bayesian network implementation of the rules. The developers say the Bayesian network was demonstrated to senior operational management within Barclays Bank, and that these management personnel readily understood its reasoning. A second application concerned the assessment of risk in a loan applicant.

Capital Equipment

- Knowledge Industries, Inc. (KI; www.kic.com) developed a relatively large number of applications during the 1990s. Most of them are used in internal applications by their licensees and are not publicly available. KI applications in capital equipment include locomotives, gas-turbine engines for aircraft and land-based power production, the space shuttle, and office equipment.

Causal Learning

- Applications to causal learning are discussed in Spirtes et al. [1993, 2000].

- Causal learning applications also appear in Glymour and Cooper [1999].

Computer Games

- Valadares [2002] developed a computer game that models the evolution of a simulated world.

Computer Vision

- The Reading and Leeds Computer Vision Groups developed an integrated traffic and pedestrian model-based vision system. Information concerning this system can be found at www.cvg.cs.rdg.ac.uk/~imv.

- Huang et al. [1994] analyzed freeway traffic using computer vision.

- Pham et al. [2002] developed a face detection system.

Computer Hardware

- Intel Corporation (www.intel.com) developed a system for processor fault diagnosis. Specifically, given end-of-line tests on semiconductor chips, it infers possible processing problems. They began developing their system in 1990 and, after many years of "evolution," they say it is now pretty stable. The network has three levels and a few hundred nodes. One difficulty they had was obtaining and tuning the prior probability values. The newer parts of the diagnosis system are now being developed using a fuzzy-rule system, which they found to be easier to build and tune.

Computer Software

- Microsoft Research (research.microsoft.com) has developed a number of applications. Since 1995, Microsoft Office's AnswerWizard has used a naive-Bayesian network to select help topics based on queries. Also, since 1995, there are about 10 troubleshooters in Windows that use Bayesian networks. (See Heckerman et al. [1994].)

- Burnell and Horvitz [1995] describe a system, which was developed by UT-Arlington and American Airlines (AA), for diagnosing problems with legacy software, specifically the Sabre airline reservation system used by AA. Given the information in a dump file, this diagnostic system identifies which sequences of instructions may have led to the system error.

Data Mining

- Margaritis et al. [2001] developed NetCube, a system for computing counts of records with desired characteristics from a database, which is a common task in the areas of decision support systems and data mining. The method can quickly compute counts from a database with billions of records. See www.cs.cmu.edu/~dmarg/Papers for this and related papers.

Medicine

- Knowledge Industries, Inc. (KI; www.kic.com) developed a relatively large number of applications during the 1990s. Most of them are used in internal applications by their licensees and are not publicly available. KI applications in medicine include sleep disorders, pathology, trauma care, hand and wrist evaluations, dermatology, and home-based health evaluations. They have the demonstration site www.Symptomedix.com, which is a site for the interactive diagnosis of headaches. It was designed and built to show the principles of operation of a Bayesian network in a medical application. It is medically correct for the domain of interest and has been tested in clinical application. The diagnostic system core was built with the KI DXpress Solution Series Software and has been widely used to demonstrate the use of Bayesian networks for diagnosis over the web.

- Heckerman et al. [1992] describe Pathfinder, which is a system that assists community pathologists with the diagnosis of lymph node pathology. Pathfinder has been integrated with videodiscs to form the commercial system Intellipath.

- Nicholson [1996] modeled the stepping patterns of the elderly to diagnose falls.

- Mani et al. [1997] developed MENTOR, which is a system that predicts mental retardation in newborns.

- Herskovits and Dagher [1997] learned from data a system for assessing cervical spinal-cord trauma.

- Chevrolat et al. [1998] modeled behavioral syndromes, in particular depression.

- Sakellaropoulos et al. [1999] developed a system for the prognosis of head injuries.

- Onisko, [2001] describes Hepar II, which is a system for diagnosing liver disorders.

- Ogunyemi et al. [2002] developed TraumaSCAN, which assesses conditions arising from ballistic penetrating trauma to the chest and abdomen. It accomplishes this by integrating three-dimensional geometric reasoning about anatomic likelihood of injury with probabilistic reasoning about injury consequences.

- Galán et al. [2002] created NasoNet, which is a system that performs diagnosis and prognosis of nasopharyngeal cancer (cancer concerning the nasal passages).

Natural Language Processing

- The University of Utah School of Medicine's Department of Medical Informatics developed SymText, which uses a Bayesian network to (1) represent semantic content; (2) relate words used to express concepts; (3) disambiguate constituent meaning and structure; (4) infer terms omitted due to ellipsis, errors, or context-dependent background knowledge; and (5) various other natural language processing tasks.

  The developers say the system is used constantly.

  So far four networks have been developed, each with 14 to 30 nodes, 3 to 4 layers, and containing an average of 1000 probability values. Each network models a "context" of information targeted for extraction. Three networks exhibit a simple tree structure, while one uses multiple parents to model differences between positive and negated language patterns. The developers say the model has proven to be very valuable, but carries two difficulties. First, the knowledge engineering tasks to create the network are costly and time consuming. Second, inference in the network carries a high computational cost. Methods are being explored for dealing with these issues. The developers say the model serves as an extremely robust backbone to the NLP engine.

Planning

- Dean and Wellman [1991] applied dynamic Bayesian networks to planning and control under uncertainty.

- Cozman and Krotkov [1996] developed quasi-Bayesian strategies for efficient plan generation.

Psychology

- Glymour [2001] discusses applications to cognitive psychology.

Reliability Analysis

- Torres-Toledano and Sucar [1998] developed a system for reliability analysis in power plants. This paper and related ones can be found at the site w3.mor.itesm.mx/~esucar/Proyectos/redes-bayes.html.

- The Centre for Software Reliability at Agena Ltd. (www.agena.co.uk) developed TRACS (Transport Reliability Assessment and Calculation System), which is a tool for predicting the reliability of military vehicles. The tool is used by the United Kingdom's Defense Research and Evaluation Agency (DERA) to assess vehicle reliability at all stages of the design and development life cycle. The TRACS tool is in daily use and is being applied by DERA to help solve the following problems:

  1. Identify the most likely top vehicles from a number of tenders before prototype development and testing begins.
  2. Calculate reliability of future high-technology concept vehicles at the requirements stage.
  3. Reduce the amount of resources devoted to testing vehicles on test tracks.
  4. Model the effects of poor quality design and manufacturing processes on vehicle reliability.
  5. Identify likely causes of unreliability and perform "what-if?" analyses to investigate the most profitable process improvements.

The TRACS tool is built on a modular architecture consisting of the following five major Bayesian networks:

  1. An updating network used to predict the reliability of subsystems based on failure data from historically similar subsystems.

2. A recursive network used to coalesce subsystem reliability probability distributions in order to achieve a vehicle level prediction.

3. A design quality network used to estimate design unreliability caused by poor quality design processes.

4. A manufacturing quality network used to estimate unreliability caused by poor quality manufacturing processes.

5. A vehicle testing network that uses failure data gained from vehicle testing to infer vehicle reliability.

The TRACS tool can model vehicles with an arbitrarily large number of subsystems. Each subsystem network consists of over 1 million state combinations generated using a hierarchical Bayesian model with standard statistical distributions. The design and manufacturing quality networks contain 35 nodes, many of which have conditional probability distributions elicited directly from DERA engineering experts.

The TRACS tool was built using the SERENE tool and the Hugin API (www.hugin.dk), and it was written in VB using the MSAccess database engine. The SERENE method (www.hugin.dk/serene) was used to develop the Bayesian network structures and generate the conditional probability tables. A full description of the TRACS tool can be found at www.agena.co.uk/tracs/index.html.

Scheduling

- MITRE Corporation (www.mitre.org) developed a system for real-time weapons scheduling for ship self defense. Used by the United States Navy (NSWC-DD), the system can handle multiple target, multiple weapon problems in under two seconds on a Sparc laptop.

Speech Recognition

- Bilmes [2000] applied dynamic Bayesian multinets to speech recognition. Further work in the area can be found at ssli.ee.washington.edu/~bilmes.

- Nefian et al. [2002] developed a system for audiovisual speech recognition. This and related research done by Intel Corporation on speech and face recognition can be found at www.intel.com/research/mrl/research/opencv and at www.intel.com/research/mrl/research/avcsr.htm.

Vehicle Control and Malfunction Diagnosis

- Automotive Information Systems (AIS; www.PartsAmerica.com) developed over 600 Bayesian networks which diagnose 15 common automotive problems for about 10,000 different vehicles. Each network has one hundred or more nodes. Their product, Auto Fix, is built with the DXpress software package available from Knowledge Industries, Inc. (KI). Auto Fix is the reasoning engine behind the Diagnosis/SmartFix feature available at the www.PartsAmerica.com web site. SmartFix is a free service that AIS provides as an enticement to its customers. AIS and KI say they have teamed together to solve a number of very interesting problems in order to deliver "industrial strength" Bayesian networks. More details about how this was achieved can be found in the article "Web Deployment of Bayesian Network Based Vehicle Diagnostics," which is available through the Society of Automotive Engineers, Inc. Go to www.sae.org/servlets/search and search for paper 2001-01-0603.

- Microsoft Research developed Vista, which is a decision–theoretic system used at NASA Mission Control Center in Houston. The system uses Bayesian networks to interpret live telemetry, and it provides advice on the likelihood of alternative failures of the space shuttle's propulsion systems. It also considers time criticality and recommends actions of the highest expected utility. Furthermore, the Vista system employs decision–theoretic methods for controlling the display of information to dynamically identify the most important information to highlight. Information on Vista can be found at research.microsoft.com/research/dtg/horvitz/vista.htm.

- Morjaia et al. [1993] developed a system for locomotive diagnostics.

Weather Forecasting

- From data, Kennett et al. [2001] learned a system that predicts sea breezes.

12.2 Beyond Bayesian Networks

A Bayesian network requires that the graph be directed and acyclic. As mentioned in Section 1.5.1, the assumption that there are no cycles is sometimes not warranted. To accommodate cycles, Heckerman et al. [2000] developed a graphical model for probabilistic relationships called a **dependency network**. The graph in a dependency network is potentially cyclic. They show that dependency networks are useful for collaborative filtering (predicting preferences) and visualization of acausal predictive relationships. Microsoft Research developed a tool, called DNetViewer, which learns a dependency network from data. Furthermore, dependency networks are learned from data in two of Microsoft's products, namely SQL Server 2000 and Commerce Server 2000.

Bibliography

[Ackerman, 1987] Ackerman, P.L., "Individual Differences in Skill Learning: An Integration of Psychometric and Information Processing Perspectives," *Psychological Bulletin*, Vol. 102, 1987.

[Altschul et al., 1997] Altschul, S., L. Thomas, A. Schaffer, J. Zhang, W. Miller, and D. Lipman, "Gapped Blast and Psi-blast: a new Generation of Protein Database Search Programs," *Nucleic Acids Research*, Vol. 25, 1997.

[Anderson et al., 1995] Anderson, S.A., D. Madigan, and M.D. Perlman, *A Characterization of Markov Equivalence Classes for Acyclic Digraphs*, Technical Report # 287, Department of Statistics, University of Washington, Seattle, Washington, 1995 (also in Annals of Statistics, Vol. 25, 1997).

[Ash, 1970] Ash, R.B., *Basic Probability Theory*, Wiley, New York, 1970.

[Basye et al., 1993] Basye, K., T. Dean, J. Kirman, and M. Lejter, "A Decision-Theoretic Approach to Planning, Perception and Control," *IEEE Expert*, Vol. 7, No. 4, 1993.

[Bauer et al., 1997] Bauer, E., D. Koller, and Y. Singer, "Update Rules for Parameter Estimation in Bayesian Networks," in Geiger, D., and P. Shenoy (Eds.): *Uncertainty in Artificial Intelligence; Proceedings of the Thirteenth Conference*, Morgan Kaufmann, San Mateo, California, 1997.

[Beinlich and Herskovits, 1990] Beinlich, I.A., and E. H. Herskovits, "A Graphical Environment for Constructing Bayesian Belief Networks," *proceeding of the Conference on Uncertainty in Artificail Intelligence*, Cambridge, Massachusetts, 1990.

[Beinlich et al., 1989] Beinlich, I.A., H.J. Suermondt, R.M. Chavez, and G.F. Cooper, "The ALARM Monitoring System: A Case Study with Two Probabilistic Inference Techniques for Belief Networks," *Proceedings of the Second European Conference on Artificial Intelligence in Medicine*, London, England, 1989.

[Bentler, 1980] Bentler, P.N., "Multivariate Analysis with Latent Variables," *Review of Psychology*, Vol. 31, 1980.

[Bernardo and Smith, 1994] Bernado, J., and A. Smith, *Bayesian Theory*, Wiley, New York, 1994.

[Berry, 1996] Berry, D.A., *Statistics, A Bayesian Perspective*, Wadsworth, Belmont, California, 1996.

[Berry and Broadbent, 1988] Berry, D.C., and D.E. Broadbent, "Interactive Tasks and the Implicit-Explicit Distinction," *British Journal of Psychology*, Vol. 79, 1988.

[Bilmes, 2000] Bilmes, J.A., "Dynamic Bayesian Multinets," in Boutilier, C. and M. Goldszmidt (Eds.): *Uncertainty in Artificial Intelligence; Proceedings of the Sixteenth Conference*, Morgan Kaufmann, San Mateo, California, 2000.

[Bishop et al., 1975] Bishop, Y., S. Feinberg, and P. Holland, *Discrete Multivariate Statistics: Theory and Practice*, MIT Press, Cambridge, Massachusetts, 1975.

[Bloemeke and Valtora, 1998] Bloemeke, M., and M. Valtora, "A Hybrid Algorithm to Compute Marginal and Joint Beliefs in Bayesian Networks and Its Complexity," in Cooper, G.F., and S. Moral (Eds.): *Uncertainty in Artificial Intelligence; Proceedings of the Fourteenth Conference*, Morgan Kaufmann, San Mateo, California, 1998.

[Box and Tiao, 1973] Box, G., and G. Tiao, *Bayesian Inference in Statistical Analysis*, McGraw-Hill, New York, 1973.

[Brownlee, 1965] Brownlee, K.A., *Statistical Theory and Methodology*, Wiley, New York, 1965.

[Bryk and Raudnebush, 1992] Bryk, A.S., and S.W. Raudenbush, *Hierarchical Linear Models: Application and Data Analysis Methods*, Sage, Thousand Oaks, California, 1992.

[Burnell and Horvitz, 1995] Burnell, L., and E. Horvitz, "Structure and Chance: Melding Logic and Probability for Software Debugging," *CACM*, March, 1995.

[Cartwright, 1989] Cartwright, N., *Nature's Capacities and Their Measurement*, Clarendon Press, Oxford, 1989.

[Castillo et al., 1997] Castillo, E., J.M. Gutiérrez, and A.S. Hadi, *Expert Systems and Probabilistic Network Models*, Springer-Verlag, New York, 1997.

[Charniak, 1983] Charniak, E., "The Bayesian Basis of Common Sense Medical Diagnosis," *Proceedings of AAAI*, Washington, D.C., 1983.

[Che et al., 1993] Che, P., R.E. Neapolitan, J.R. Kenevan, and M. Evens, "An implementation of a Method for Computing the Uncertainty in Inferred Probabilities in Belief Networks." in Heckerman, D., and A. Mamdani (Eds.): *Uncertainty in Artificial Intelligence; Proceedings of the Ninth Conference*, Morgan Kaufmann, San Mateo, California, 1993.

[Chevrolat et al., 1998] Chevrolat, J., J. Golmard, S. Ammar, R. Jouvent, and J. Boisvieux, "Modeling Behavior Syndromes Using Bayesian Networks," *Artificial Intelligence in Medicine*, Vol. 14, 1998.

[Cheeseman and Stutz, 1995] Cheeseman, P., and J. Stutz, "Bayesian Classification (Autoclass): Theory and Results," in Fayyad, D., G. Piatesky-Shapiro, P. Smyth, and R. Uthurusamy (Eds.): *Advances in Knowledge Discovery and Data Mining*, AAAI Press, Menlo Park, California, 1995.

[Chib, 1995] Chib, S., "Marginal Likelihood from the Gibb's Output," *Journal of the American Statistical Association*, Vol. 90, 1995.

[Chickering, 1996a] Chickering, D., "Learning Bayesian Networks is NP-Complete," In Fisher, D., and H. Lenz (Eds.): *Learning From Data*, Springer-Verlag, New York, 1996.

[Chickering, 1996b] Chickering, D., "Learning Equivalence Classes of Bayesian-Network Structures," in Horvitz, E., and F. Jensen (Eds.): *Uncertainty in Artificial Intelligence; Proceedings of the Twelfth Conference*, Morgan Kaufmann, San Mateo, California, 1996.

[Chickering, 2001] Chickering, D., *Learning Equivalence Classes of Bayesian Networks*, Technical Report # MSR-TR-2001-65, Microsoft Research, Redmond, Washington, 2001.

[Chickering, 2002] Chickering, D., "Optimal Structure Identification with Greedy Search," submitted to *JMLR*, 2002.

[Chickering and Heckerman, 1996] Chickering, D., and D. Heckerman, "Efficient Approximation for the Marginal Likelihood of Incomplete Data Given a Bayesian Network," in Horvitz, E., and F. Jensen (Eds.): *Uncertainty in Artificial Intelligence; Proceedings of the Twelfth Conference*, Morgan Kaufmann, San Mateo, California, 1996.

[Chickering and Heckerman, 1997] Chickering, D., and D. Heckerman, *Efficient Approximation for the Marginal Likelihood of Bayesian Networks with Hidden Variables*, Technical Report # MSR-TR-96-08, Microsoft Research, Redmond, Washington, 1997.

[Chickering and Meek, 2002] Chickering, D., and C. Meek, "Finding Optimal Bayesian Networks," in Darwiche, A., and N. Friedman (Eds.): *Uncertainty in Artificial Intelligence; Proceedings of the Eighteenth Conference*, Morgan Kaufmann, San Mateo, California, 2002.

[Christensen, 1990] Christensen, R., *Log-Linear Models*, Springer-Verlag, New York, 1990.

[Chung, 1960] Chung, K.L., *Markov Processes with Stationary Transition Probabilities*, Springer-Verlag, Heidelberg, 1960.

[Clemen, 1996] Clemen, R.T., *Making Hard Decisions*, PWS-KENT, Boston, Massachusetts, 1996.

[Cooper, 1984] Cooper, G.F., "NESTOR: A Computer-based Medical Diagnostic that Integrates Causal and Probabilistic Knowledge," *Technical Report HPP-84-48*, Stanford University, Stanford, California, 1984.

[Cooper, 1990] Cooper, G.F., "The Computational Complexity of Probabilistic Inference Using Bayesian Belief Networks," *Artificial Intelligence*, Vol. 33, 1990.

[Cooper, 1995a] Cooper, G.F., "Causal Discovery From Data in the Presence of Selection Bias," *Proceedings of the Fifth International Workshop on Artificial Intelligence and Statistics*, Fort Lauderdale, Florida, 1995.

[Cooper, 1995b] Cooper, G.F., "A Bayesian Method for Learning Belief Networks that Contain Hidden Variables," *Journal of Intelligent Systems*, Vol. 4, 1995.

[Cooper, 1999] Cooper, G.F., "An Overview of the Representation and Discovery of Causal Relationships Using Bayesian Networks," in Glymour, C., and G.F. Cooper (Eds.): *Computation, Causation, and Discovery*, AAAI Press, Menlo Park, California, 1999.

[Cooper, 2000] Cooper, G.F., "A Bayesian Method for Causal Modeling and Discovery Under Selection," in Boutilier, C. and M. Goldszmidt (Eds.): *Uncertainty in Artificial Intelligence; Proceedings of the Sixteenth Conference*, Morgan Kaufmann, San Mateo, California, 2000.

[Cooper and Herskovits, 1992] Cooper, G.F., and E. Herskovits, "A Bayesian Method for the Induction of Probabilistic Networks from Data," *Machine Learning*, Vol. 9, 1992.

[Cooper and Yoo, 1999] Cooper, G.F., and C. Yoo, "Causal Discovery From a Mixture of Experimental and Observational Data," in Laskey, K.B., and H. Prade (Eds.): *Uncertainty in Artificial Intelligence; Proceedings of the Fifteenth Conference*, Morgan Kaufmann, San Mateo, California, 1999.

[Cozman and Krotkov, 1996] Cozman, F., and E. Krotkov, "Quasi-Bayesian Strategies for Efficient Plan Generation: Application to the Planning to Observe Problem," in Horvitz, E., and F. Jensen (Eds.): *Uncertainty in Artificial Intelligence; Proceedings of the Twelfth Conference*, Morgan Kaufmann, San Mateo, California, 1996.

[Cunningham and Hirshkowitz, 1995] Cunningham, G.R., and M. Hirshkowitz, "Inhibition of Steroid 5 Alpha-reductase with Finasteride: Sleep-related Erections, Potency, and Libido in Healthy Men," *Journal of Clinical Endocrinology and Metabolism*, Vol. 80, No. 5, 1995.

[Cvrckova and Nasmyth, 1993] Cvrckova, F., and K. Nasmyth, "Yeast GI Cyclins CLN1 and CLN2 and a GAP-like Protein have a Role in Bud Formation," *EMBO. J.*, Vol 12, 1993.

[Dagum and Chavez, 1993] Dagum, P., and R.M. Chavez, "Approximate Probabilistic Inference in Bayesian Belief Networks," *IEEE Transactions on Pattern Analysis and Machine Intelligence*, Vol. 15, No. 3, 1993.

[Dagum and Luby, 1993] Dagum, P., and M. Luby, "Approximate Probabilistic Inference in Bayesian Belief Networks in NP-hard," *Artificial Intelligence*, Vol. 60, No. 1, 1993.

[Dawid, 1979] Dawid, A.P., "Conditional Independencies in Statistical Theory," *Journal of the Royal Statistical Society*, Series B 41, No. 1, 1979.

[Dawid and Studeny, 1999] Dawid, A.P., and M. Studeny, "Conditional Products, an Alternative Approach to Conditional Independence," in Heckerman, D., and J. Whitaker (Eds.): *Artificial Intelligence and Statistics*, Morgan Kaufmann, San Mateo, California, 1999.

[Dean and Wellman, 1991] Dean, T., and M. Wellman, *Planning and Control*, Morgan Kaufmann, San Mateo, California, 1991.

[de Finetti, 1937] de Finetti, B., "La prévision: See Lois Logiques, ses Sources Subjectives," *Annales de l'Institut Henri Poincaré*, Vol. 7, 1937.

[DeGroot, 1970] Degroot, M.H., *Optimal Statistical Decisions*, McGraw-Hill, New York, 1970.

[Dempster et al., 1977] Dempster, A, N. Laird, and D. Rubin, "Maximum Likelihood from Incomplete Data via the EM Algorithm," *Journal of the Royal Statistical Society B*, Vol. 39, No. 1, 1977.

[Dor and Tarsi, 1992] Dor, D., and M. Tarsi, *A Simple Algorithm to Construct a Consistent Extension of a Partially Oriented Graph*, Technical Report # R-185, UCLA Cognitive Science LAB, Los Angeles, California, 1992.

[Drescher, 1991] Drescher, G.L., *Made-up Minds*, MIT Press, Cambridge, Massachusetts, 1991.

[Druzdzel and Glymour, 1999] Druzdzel, M.J., and C. Glymour, "Causal Inferences from Databases: Why Universities Lose Students," in Glymour, C., and G.F. Cooper (Eds.): *Computation, Causation, and Discovery*, AAAI Press, Menlo Park, California, 1999.

[Eells, 1991] Eells, E., Probabilistic Causality, Cambridge University Press, London, 1991.

[Einhorn and Hogarth, 1983] Einhorn, H., and R. Hogarth, *A Theory of Diagnostic Inference: Judging Causality* (memorandum), Center for Decision Research, University of Chicago, Chicago, Illinois, 1983.

[Feller, 1968] Feller, W., *An Introduction to Probability Theory and its Applications*, Wiley, New York, 1968.

[Flanders et al., 1996] Flanders, A.E., C.M. Spettell, L.M. Tartaglino, D.P. Friedman, and G.J. Herbison, "Forecasting Motor Recovery after Cervical Spinal Cord Injury: Value of MRI," *Radiology*, Vol. 201, 1996.

[Flury, 1997] Flury, B., *A First Course in Multivariate Statistics*, Springer-Verlag, New York, 1997.

[Freeman, 1989] Freeman, W.E., "On the Fallacy of Assigning an Origin to Consciousness," *Proceedings of the First International Conference on Machinery of the Mind*, Havana City, Cuba. Feb/March, 1989.

[Friedman, 1998] Friedman, N., "The Bayesian Structural EM Algorithm," in Cooper, G.F., and S. Moral (Eds.): *Uncertainty in Artificial Intelligence; Proceedings of the Fourteenth Conference*, Morgan Kaufmann, San Mateo, California, 1998.

[Friedman and Goldszmidt, 1996] Friedman, N., and M. Goldszmidt, "Building Classifiers and Bayesian Networks," *Proceedings of the National Conference on Artificial Intelligence*, AAAI Press, Menlo Park, California, 1996.

[Friedman and Koller, 2000] Friedman, N., and K. Koller, "Being Bayesian about Network Structure," in Boutilier, C. and M. Goldszmidt (Eds.): *Uncertainty in Artificial Intelligence; Proceedings of the Sixteenth Conference*, Morgan Kaufmann, San Mateo, California, 2000.

[Friedman et al., 1998] Friedman, N., K. Murphy, and S. Russell, "Learning the Structure of Dynamic Probabilistic Networks," in Cooper, G.F., and S. Moral (Eds.): *Uncertainty in Artificial Intelligence; Proceedings of the Fourteenth Conference*, Morgan Kaufmann, San Mateo, California, 1998.

[Friedman et al., 1999] Friedman, N., M. Goldszmidt, and A. Wyner, "Data Analysis with Bayesian Networks: a Bootstrap Approach," in Laskey, K.B., and H. Prade (Eds.): *Uncertainty in Artificial Intelligence; Proceedings of the Fifteenth Conference*, Morgan Kaufmann, San Mateo, California, 1999.

[Friedman et al., 2000] Friedman, N., M. Linial, I. Nachman, and D. Pe'er, "Using Bayesian Networks to Analyze Expression Data," in *Proceedings of the Fourth Annual International Conference on Computational Molecular Biology*, 2000.

[Friedman et al., 2002] Friedman, N., M. Ninio, I. Pe'er, and T. Pupko, "A Structural EM Algorithm for Phylogenetic Inference, *Journal of Computational Biology*, 2002.

[Fung and Chang, 1990] Fung, R., and K. Chang, "Weighing and Integrating Evidence for Stochastic Simulation in Bayesian Networks," in Henrion, M., R.D. Shachter, L.N. Kanal, and J.F. Lemmer (Eds.): *Uncertainty in Artificial Intelligence; Proceeding of the Fifth Conference*, North-Holland, Amsterdam, 1990.

[Galán et al., 2002] Galán, S.F., and F. Aguado, F.J. Díez, and J. Mira, "NasoNet, Modeling the Spread of Nasopharyngeal Cancer with Networks of Probabilistic Events in Discrete Time," *Artificial Intelligence in Medicine*, Vol. 25, 2002.

[Geiger and Heckerman, 1994] Geiger, D., and D. Heckerman, "Learning Gaussian Networks," in de Mantras, R.L., and D. Poole (Eds.): *Uncertainty in Artificial Intelligence; Proceedings of the Tenth Conference*, Morgan Kaufmann, San Mateo, California, 1994.

[Geiger and Heckerman, 1997] Geiger, D., and D. Heckerman, "A Characterization of the Dirichlet Distribution Through Global and Local Independence," *Annals of Statistics*, Vol. 23, No. 3, 1997.

[Geiger and Pearl, 1990] Geiger, D., and J. Pearl, "On the Logic of Causal Models," in Shachter, R.D., T.S. Levitt, L.N. Kanal, and J.F. Lemmer (Eds.): *Uncertainty in Artificial Intelligence; Proceedings of the Fourth Conference*, North-Holland, Amsterdam, 1990.

[Geiger et al., 1990a] Geiger, D., T. Verma, and J. Pearl, "d-separation: From Theorems to Algorithms," in Henrion, M., R.D. Shachter, L.N. Kanal, and J.F. Lemmer (Eds.): *Uncertainty in Artificial Intelligence; Proceeding of the Fifth Conference*, North Holland, Amsterdam, 1990.

[Geiger et al., 1990b] Geiger, D., T. Verma, and J. Pearl, "Identifying Independence in Bayesian Networks," *Networks*, Vol. 20, No. 5, 1990.

[Geiger et al., 1996] Geiger, D., D. Heckerman, and C. Meek, "Asymptotic Model Selection for Directed Networks with Hidden Variables," in Horvitz, E., and F. Jensen (Eds.): *Uncertainty in Artificial Intelligence; Proceedings of the Twelfth Conference*, Morgan Kaufmann, San Mateo, California, 1996.

[Geiger et al., 1998] Geiger, D., D. Heckerman, H. King, and C. Meek, *Stratified Exponential Families: Graphical Models and Model Selection*, Technical Report # MSR-TR-98-31, Microsoft Research, Redmond, Washington, 1998.

[Geman and Geman, 1984] Geman, S., and D. Geman, "Stochastic Relaxation, Gibb's Distributions and the Bayesian Restoration of Images," *IEEE Transactions on Pattern Analysis and Machine Intelligence*, Vol. 6, 1984.

[Gilbert et al., 1988] Gilbert. D.T., B.W. Pelham, and D.S. Krull, "On Cognitive Business: When Person Perceivers meet Persons Perceived," *Journal of Personality and Social Psychology*, Vol. 54, 1988.

[Gilks et al., 1996] Gilks, W.R., S. Richardson, and D.J. Spiegelhalter (Eds.): *Markov Chain Monte Carlo in Practice*, Chapman & Hall/CRC, Boca Raton, Florida, 1996.

[Gillispie and Pearlman, 2001] Gillispie, S.B., and M.D. Pearlman, "Enumerating Markov Equivalence Classes of Acyclic Digraph Models," in Koller, D., and J. Breese (Eds.): *Uncertainty in Artificial Intelligence; Proceedings of the Seventeenth Conference*, Morgan Kaufmann, San Mateo, California, 2001.

[Glymour, 2001] Glymour, C., *The Mind's Arrows: Bayes Nets and Graphical Causal Models in Psychology*, MIT Press, Cambridge, Massachusetts, 2001.

[Glymour and Cooper, 1999] Glymour, C., and G. Cooper, *Computation, Causation, and Discovery*, MIT Press, Cambridge, Massachusetts 1999.

[Good, 1965] Good, I., *The Estimation of Probability*, MIT Press, Cambridge, Massachusetts, 1965.

[Good, 1983] Good, I.J., *Good Thinking*, University of Minnesota Press, Minneapolis, Minnesota, 1983.

[Guacci et al., 1997] Guacci, V., D. Koshland, and A. Strunnikov, "A Direct Link between Sister Chromatid Cohesion and Chromosome Condensation Revealed through the Analysis of MCDI in *s. cerevisiae*, *Cell*, Vol. 9, No. 1, 1997.

[Hardy, 1889] Hardy, G.F., Letter, *Insurance Record* (reprinted in *Transactions of Actuaries*, Vol. 8, 1920).

[Hastings, 1970] Hastings, W.K., "Monte Carlo Sampling Methods Using Markov Chains and their Applications," *Biometrika*, Vol. 57, No. 1, 1970.

[Haughton, 1988] Haughton, D., "On the Choice of a Model to Fit Data from an Exponential Family," *The Annals of Statistics*, Vol. 16, No. 1, 1988.

[Heckerman, 1996] Heckerman, D., *A Tutorial on Learning with Bayesian Networks*, Technical Report # MSR-TR-95-06, Microsoft Research, Redmond, Washington, 1996.

[Heckerman and Geiger, 1995] Heckerman, D., and D. Geiger, *Likelihoods and Parameter Priors for Bayesian Networks*, Technical Report MSR-TR-95-54, Microsoft Research, Redmond, Washington, 1995.

[Heckerman and Meek, 1997] Heckerman, D., and C. Meek, *Embedded Bayesian Network Classifiers*, Technical Report MSR-TR-97-06, Microsoft Research, Redmond, Washington, 1997.

[Heckerman et al., 1992] Heckerman, D., E. Horvitz, and B. Nathwani, "Toward Normative Expert Systems: Part I The Pathfinder Project," *Methods of Information in Medicine*, Vol 31, 1992.

[Heckerman et al., 1994] Heckerman, D., J. Breese, and K. Rommelse, *Troubleshooting under Uncertainty*, Technical Report MSR-TR-94-07, Microsoft Research, Redmond, Washington, 1994.

[Heckerman et al., 1995] Heckerman, D., D. Geiger, and D. Chickering, *Learning Bayesian Networks: The Combination of Knowledge and Statistical Data*, Technical Report MSR-TR-94-09, Microsoft Research, Redmond, Washington, 1995.

[Heckerman et al., 1999] Heckerman, D., C. Meek, and G. Cooper, "A Bayesian Approach to Causal Discovery," in Glymour, C., and G.F. Cooper (Eds.): *Computation, Causation, and Discovery*, AAAI Press, Menlo Park, California, 1999.

[Heckerman et al., 2000] Heckerman, D., D. Chickering, C. Meek, R. Rounthwaite, and C. Kadie, "Dependency Networks for Inference, Collaborate Filtering, and Data Visualization," *Journal of Machine Learning Inference*, Vol. 1, 2000.

[Heider, 1944] Heider, F., "Social Perception and Phenomenal Causality," *Psychological Review*, Vol. 51, 1944.

[Henrion, 1988] Henrion, M., "Propagating Uncertainty in Bayesian Networks by Logic Sampling," in Lemmer, J.F. and L.N. Kanal (Eds.): *Uncertainty in Artificial Intelligence; Proceedings of the Second Conference*, North-Holland, Amsterdam, 1988.

[Henrion et al., 1996] Henrion, M., M. Pradhan, B. Del Favero, K. Huang, G. Provan, and P. O'Rorke, "Why is Diagnosis Using Belief Networks Insensitive to Imprecision in Probabilities?" in Horvitz, E., and F. Jensen (Eds.): *Uncertainty in Artificial Intelligence; Proceedings of the Twelfth Conference*, Morgan Kaufmann, San Mateo, California, 1996.

[Herskovits and Cooper, 1991] Herskovits, E.H., and G.F. Cooper, "Kutató: An Entropy-Driven System for the Construction of Probabilistic Expert Systems from Databases," in Bonissone, P.P., M. Henrion, L.N. Kanal, and J.F. Lemmer (Eds.): *Uncertainty in Artificial Intelligence; Proceedings of the Sixth Conference*, North-Holland, Amsterdam, 1991.

[Herskovits and Dagher, 1997] Herskovits, E.H., and A.P. Dagher, *Applications of Bayesian Networks to Health Care*, Technical Report NSI-TR-1997-02, Noetic Systems Incorporated, Baltimore, Maryland, 1997.

[Hogg and Craig, 1972] Hogg, R.V., and A.T. Craig, *Introduction to Mathematical Statistics*, Macmillan, New York, 1972.

[Huang et al., 1994] Huang, T., D. Koller, J. Malik, G. Ogasawara, B. Rao, S. Russell, and J. Weber, "Automatic Symbolic Traffic Scene Analysis Using Belief Networks," *Proceedings of the Twelfth National Conference on Artificial Intelligence (AAAI94)*, AAAI Press, Seattle, Washington, 1994.

[Hume, 1748] Hume, D., *An Inquiry Concerning Human Understanding*, Prometheus, Amhurst, New York, 1988 (originally published in 1748).

[Iversen et al., 1971] Iversen, G.R., W.H. Longcor, F. Mosteller, J.P. Gilbert, and C. Youtz, "Bias and Runs in Dice Throwing and Recording: A Few Million Throws," *Psychometrika*, Vol. 36, 1971.

[Jensen, 1996] Jensen, F.V., *An Introduction to Bayesian Networks*, Springer-Verlag, New York, 1996.

[Jensen et al., 1990] Jensen, F.V., S.L. Lauritzen, and K.G. Olesen, "Bayesian Updating in Causal Probabilistic Networks by Local Computation," *Computational Statistical Quarterly*, Vol. 4, 1990.

[Jensen et al., 1994] Jensen, F., F.V. Jensen, and S.L. Dittmer, "From Influence Diagrams to Junction Trees," in de Mantras, R.L., and D. Poole (Eds.): *Uncertainty in Artificial Intelligence; Proceedings of the Tenth Conference*, Morgan Kaufmann, San Mateo, California, 1994.

[Joereskog, 1982] Joereskog, K.G., *Systems Under Indirect Observation*, North Holland, Amsterdam, 1982.

[Jones, 1979] Jones, E.E., "The Rocky Road From Acts to Dispositions," *American Psychologist*, Vol. 34, 1979.

[Kahneman et al., 1982] Kahneman, D., P. Slovic, and A. Tversky, *Judgment Under Uncertainty: Heuristics and Biases*, Cambridge University Press, Cambridge, New York, 1982.

[Kanouse, 1972] Kanouse, D.E., "Language, Labeling, and Attribution," in Jones, E.E., D.E. Kanouse, H.H. Kelly, R.S. Nisbett, S. Valins, and B. Weiner (Eds.): *Attribution: Perceiving the Causes of Behavior*, General Learning Press, Morristown, New Jersey, 1972.

[Kant, 1787] Kant, I., *Kritik der reinen Vernunft (Critique of Pure Reason)*, reprinted in 1968, Suhrkamp Taschenbücher Wissenschaft, Frankfurt, 1787.

[Kass et al., 1988] Kass, R., L. Tierney, and J. Kadane, "Asymptotics in Bayesian Computation," in Bernardo, J., M. DeGroot, D. Lindley, and A. Smith (Eds.): *Bayesian Statistics 3*, Oxford University Press, Oxford, England, 1988.

[Kelly, 1967] Kelly, H.H., "Attribution Theory in Social Psychology," in Levine, D. (Ed.): *Nebraska Symposium on Motivation*, University of Nebraska Press, Lincoln, Nebraska, 1967.

[Kelly, 1972] Kelly, H.H., "Causal Schema and the Attribution Process," in Jones, E.E., D.E. Kanouse, H.H. Kelly, R.S. Nisbett, S. Valins, and B. Weiner (Eds.): *Attribution: Perceiving the Causes of Behavior*, General Learning Press, Morristown, New Jersey, 1972.

[Kennett et al., 2001] Kennett, R., K. Korb, and A. Nicholson, "Seabreeze Prediction Using Bayesian Networks: A Case Study," *Proceedings of the 5th Pacific-Asia Conference on Advances in Knowledge Discovery and Data Mining —PAKDD*, Springer-Verlag, New York, 2001.

[Kenny, 1979] Kenny, D.A., *Correlation and Causality*, Wiley, New York, 1979.

[Kerrich, 1946] Kerrich, J.E., *An Experimental Introduction to the Theory of Probability*, Einer Munksgaard, Copenhagen, 1946.

[Keynes, 1921] Keynes, J.M, *A Treatise on Probability*, Macmillan, London, 1948 (originally published in 1921).

[Kocka and Zhang, 2002] Kocka, T, and N. L. Zhang, "Dimension Correction for Hierarchical Latent Class Models," in Darwiche, A., and N. Friedman (Eds.): *Uncertainty in Artificial Intelligence; Proceedings of the Eighteenth Conference*, Morgan Kaufmann, San Mateo, California, 2002.

[Kolmogorov, 1933] Kolmogorov, A.N., *Foundations of the Theory of Probability*, Chelsea, New York, 1950 (originally published in 1933 as *Grundbegriffe der Wahrscheinlichkeitsrechnung*, Springer, Berlin).

[Korf, 1993] Korf, R., "Linear-space Best-first Search," *Artificial Intelligence*, Vol. 62, 1993.

[Lam and Segre, 2002] Lam, W., and M. Segre, "A Parallel Learning Algorithm for Bayesian Inference Networks," *IEEE Transactions on Knowledge and Data Engineering*, Vol. 14, No. 1, 2002.

[Lam and Bacchus, 1994] Lam, W., and F. Bacchus, "Learning Bayesian Belief Networks; An Approach Based in the MDL Principle," *Computational Intelligence*, Vol. 10, 1994.

[Lander, 1999] Lander, E., "Array of Hope," *Nature Genetics*, Vol. 21, No. 1, 1999.

[Lauritzen and Spiegelhalter, 1988] Lauritzen, S.L., and D.J. Spiegelhalter, "Local Computation with Probabilities in Graphical Structures and Their Applications to Expert Systems," *Journal of the Royal Statistical Society B*, Vol. 50, No. 2, 1988.

[Li and D'Ambrosio, 1994] Li, Z., and B. D'Ambrosio, "Efficient Inference in Bayes' Networks as a Combinatorial Optimization Problem," International Journal of Approximate Inference, Vol. 11, 1994.

[Lindley, 1985] Lindley, D.V., *Introduction to Probability and Statistics from a Bayesian Viewpoint*, Cambridge University Press, London, 1985.

[Lugg et al., 1995] Lugg, J.A., J. Raifer, and C.N.F. González, "Dihydrotestosterone is the Active Androgen in the Maintenance of Nitric Oxide-Mediated Penile Erection in the Rat," *Endocrinology*, Vol. 136, No. 4, 1995.

[Madigan and Rafferty, 1994] Madigan, D., and A. Rafferty, "Model Selection and Accounting for Model Uncertainty in Graphical Models Using Occam's Window," *Journal of the American Statistical Society*, Vol. 89, 1994.

[Madigan and York, 1995] Madigan, D., and J. York, "Bayesian Graphical Methods for Discrete Data," *International Statistical Review*, Vol. 63, No. 2, 1995.

[Madigan et al., 1996] Madigan, D., S. Anderson, M. Perlman, and C. Volinsky, "Bayesian Model Averaging and Model Selection for Markov Equivalence Classes of Acyclic Graphs," *Communications in Statistics: Theory and Methods*, Vol. 25, 1996.

[Mani et al., 1997] Mani, S., S. McDermott, and M. Valtorta, "MENTOR: A Bayesian Model for Prediction of Mental Retardation in Newborns," *Research in Developmental Disabilities*, Vol. 8, No.5, 1997.

[Margaritis et al., 2001] Margaritis, D., C. Faloutsos, and S. Thrun, "NetCube: A Scalable Tool for Fast Data Mining and Compression," *Proceedings of the 27th VLB Conference*, Rome, Italy, 2001.

[McClennan and Markham, 1999] McClennan, K.J., and A. Markham, "Finasteride: A review of its Use in Male Pattern Baldness," *Drugs*, Vol. 57, No. 1, 1999.

[McClure, 1989] McClure, J., *Discounting Causes of Behavior: Two Decades of Research,* unpublished manuscript, University of Wellington, Wellington, New Zealand, 1989.

[McCullagh and Neider, 1983] McCullagh, P., and J. Neider, *Generalized Linear Models*, Chapman & Hall, 1983.

[McGregor, 1999] McGregor, W.G., "DNA Repair, DNA Replication, and UV Mutagenesis," *J. Investig. Determotol. Symp. Proc.*, Vol. 4, 1999.

[McLachlan and Krishnan, 1997] McLachlan, G.J., and T. Krishnan, *The EM Algorithm and its Extensions*, Wiley, New York, 1997.

[Mechling and Valtorta, 1994] Mechling, R., and M. Valtorta, "A Parallel Constructor of Markov Networks," in Cheeseman, P., and R. Oldford (Eds.): *Selecting Models from Data: Artificial Intelligence and Statistics IV*, Springer-Verlag, New York, 1994.

[Meek, 1995a] Meek, C., "Strong Completeness and Faithfulness in Bayesian Networks," in Besnard, P., and S. Hanks (Eds.): *Uncertainty in Artificial Intelligence; Proceedings of the Eleventh Conference*, Morgan Kaufmann, San Mateo, California, 1995.

[Meek, 1995b] Meek, C., "Causal Influence and Causal Explanation with Background Knowledge," in Besnard, P., and S. Hanks (Eds.): *Uncertainty in Artificial Intelligence; Proceedings of the Eleventh Conference*, Morgan Kaufmann, San Mateo, California, 1995.

[Meek, 1997] Meek, C., "Graphical Models: Selecting Causal and Statistical Models," Ph.D. thesis, Carnegie Mellon University, 1997.

[Metropolis et al., 1953] Metropolis, N., A. Rosenbluth, M. Rosenbluth, A. Teller, and E. Teller, "Equation of State Calculation by Fast Computing Machines," *Journal of Chemical Physics*, Vol. 21, 1953.

[Mill, 1843] Mill, J.S., *A System of Logic Ratiocinative and Inductive*, reprinted in 1974, University of Toronto Press, Toronto, Canada, 1843.

[Monti, 1999] Monti, S., "Learning Hybrid Bayesian Networks from Data," Ph.D. Thesis, University of Pittsburgh, 1999.

[Morjaia et al., 1993] Morjaia, M., F. Rink, W. Smith, G. Klempner, C. Burns, and J. Stein, "Commercialization of EPRI's Generator Expert Monitoring System (GEMS)," in *Expert System Application for the Electric Power Industry*, EPRI, Phoenix, Arizona, 1993.

[Morris and Larrick, 1995] Morris, M.W., and R.P. Larrick, "When One Cause Casts Doubt on Another: A Normative Analysis of Discounting in Causal Attribution," *Psychological Review*, Vol. 102, No. 2, 1995.

[Morris and Neapolitan, 2000] Morris, S. B., and R.E. Neapolitan, "Examination of a Bayesian Network Model of Human Causal Reasoning," in M. H. Hamza (Ed.): *Applied Simulation and Modeling: Proceedings of the IASTED International Conference*, IASTED/ACTA Press, Anaheim, California, 2000.

[Muirhead, 1982] Muirhead, R.J., *Aspects of Mutivariate Statistical Theory*, Wiley, New York, 1982.

[Mulaik et al., 1997] Mulaik, S.A., N.S. Raju, and R.A. Harshman, "There is a Time and Place for Significance Testing," in Harlow, L.L, S. A. Mulaik, and J. H. Steiger (Eds.) *What if There Were no Significance Tests?* Lawrence Erlbaum Associates, Mahwaw, New Jersey, 1997.

[Neal, 1992] Neal, R., "Connectionist Learning of Belief Networks," *Artificial Intelligence*, Vol. 56, 1992.

[Neapolitan, 1990] Neapolitan, R.E., *Probabilistic Reasoning in Expert Systems*, Wiley, New York, 1990.

[Neapolitan, 1992] Neapolitan, R.E., "A Limiting Frequency Approach to Probability Based on the Weak Law of Large Numbers," *Philosophy of Science*, Vol. 59, No. 3, 1992.

[Neapolitan, 1996] Neapolitan, R.E., "Is Higher-Order Uncertainty Needed?" in *IEEE Transactions on Systems, Man, and Cybernetics Part A: Systems and Humans*, Vol. 26, No. 3, 1996.

[Neapolitan and Kenevan, 1991a] Neapolitan, R.E., and J.R. Kenevan, "Computation of Variances in Causal Networks," in Bonnissone, P.P., M. Henrion, L.N. Kanal, and J.F. Lemmer (Eds.): *Uncertainty in Artificial Intelligence; Proceedings of the Sixth Conference*, North-Holland, Amsterdam, 1991.

[Neapolitan and Kenevan, 1991b] Neapolitan, R.E., and J.R. Kenevan, "Investigation of Variances in Belief Networks," in D'Ambrosio, B., P. Smets, and P.P. Bonissone (Eds.): *Uncertainty in Artificial Intelligence; Proceedings of the Seventh Conference*, North Holland, Amsterdam, 1991.

[Neapolitan and Morris, 2003] Neapolitan, R.E., and S. Morris, "Probabilistic Modeling Using Bayesian Networks," in D. Kaplan (Ed.): *Handbook of Quantitative Methodology in the Social Sciences*, Sage, Thousand Oaks, California, 2003.

[Neapolitan et al., 1997] Neapolitan, R.E., S. Morris, and D. Cork, "The Cognitive Processing of Causal Knowledge," in Geiger, G., and P.P. Shenoy (Eds.): *Uncertainty in Artificial Intelligence; Proceedings of the Thirteenth Conference*, Morgan Kaufmann, San Mateo, California, 1997.

[Neapolitan and Naimipour, 1998] Neapolitan, R.E., and K. Naimipour, *Foundations of Algorithms Using C++ Pseudocode*, Jones and Bartlett, Sudbury, Massachusetts, 1998.

[Nease and Owens, 1997] Nease, R.F., and D.K. Owens, "Use of Influence Diagrams to Structure Medical Decisions," *Medical Decision Making*, Vol. 17, 1997.

[Nefian et al., 2002] Nefian, A.F., L. H. Liang, X.X. Liu, X. Pi. and K. Murphy, "Dynamic Bayesian Networks for Audio-Visual Speech Recognition," *Journal of Applied Signal Processing, Special issue on Joint Audio–Visual Speech Processing*, 2002.

[Nicholson, 1996] Nicholson, A.E., "Fall Diagnosis Using Dynamic Belief Networks," in *Proceedings of the 4th Pacific Rim International Conference on Artificial Intelligence (PRICAI-96)*, Cairns, Australia, 1996.

[Nisbett and Ross, 1980] Nisbett, R.E., and L. Ross, *Human Inference: Strategies and Shortcomings of Social Judgment*, Prentice Hall, Englewood Cliffs, New Jersey, 1980.

[Norsys, 2000] Netica, http://www.norsys.com, 2000.

[Ogunyemi et al., 2002] Ogunyemi, O., J. Clarke, N. Ash, and B. Webber, "Combining Geometric and Probabilistic Reasoning for Computer-Based Penetrating-Trauma Assessment," *Journal of the American Medical Informatics Association*, Vol. 9, No. 3, 2002.

[Olesen et al., 1992] Olesen, K.G., S.L. Lauritzen, and F.V. Jensen, "HUGIN: A System Creating Adaptive Causal Probabilistic Networks," in Dubois, D., M.P. Wellman, B. D'Ambrosio, and P. Smets (Eds.): *Uncertainty in Artificial Intelligence; Proceedings of the Eighth Conference*, North Holland, Amsterdam, 1992.

[Onisko,, 2001] Onisko, A., "Evaluation of the Hepar II System for Diagnosis of Liver Disorders," *Working Notes on the European Conference on Artificial Intelligence in Medicine (AIME-01): Workshop Bayesian Models in Medicine*, Cascais, Portugal, 2001.

[Pearl,, 1986] Pearl, J. "Fusion, Propagation, and Structuring in Belief Networks," *Artificial Intelligence*, Vol. 29, 1986.

[Pearl, 1988] Pearl, J., *Probabilistic Reasoning in Intelligent Systems*, Morgan Kaufmann, San Mateo, California, 1988.

[Pearl, 1995] Pearl, J., "Bayesian networks," in M. Arbib (Ed.): *Handbook of Brain Theory and Neural Networks*, MIT Press, Cambridge, Massachusetts, 1995.

[Pearl and Verma, 1991] Pearl, J., and T.S. Verma, "A Theory of Inferred Causation," in Allen, J.A., R. Fikes, and E. Sandewall (Eds.): *Principles of Knowledge Representation and Reasoning: Proceedings of the Second International Conference*, Morgan Kaufmann, San Mateo, California, 1991.

[Pearl et al., 1989] Pearl, J., D. Geiger, and T.S. Verma, "The Logic of Influence Diagrams," in R.M. Oliver and J.Q. Smith (Eds): *Influence Diagrams, Belief Networks and Decision Analysis*, Wiley Ltd., Sussex, England, 1990 (a shorter version originally appeared in *Kybernetica*, Vol. 25, No. 2, 1989).

[Pearson, 1911] Pearson, K., *Grammar of Science*, A. and C. Black, London, 1911.

[Pe'er et al., 2001] Pe'er, D., A. Regev, G. Elidan and N. Friedman, "Inferring Subnetworks from Perturbed Expression Profiles," *Proceedings of the Ninth International Conference on Intelligent Systems for Molecular Biology (ISMB)*, Copenhagen, Denmark, 2001.

[Petty and Cacioppo, 1986] Petty, R.E., and J.T. Cacioppo, "The Elaboration Likelihood Model of Persuasion," in M. Zanna (Ed.): *Advances in
Experimental Social Psychology*, Vol. 19, 1986.

[Pham et al., 2002] Pham, T.V., M. Worring, and A. W. Smeulders, "Face Detection by Aggregated Bayesian Network Classifiers," *Pattern Recognition
Letters*, Vol. 23. No. 4, 2002.

[Piaget, 1952] Piaget, J., *The Origins of Intelligence in Children*, Norton, New
York, 1952.

[Piaget, 1954] Piaget, J., *The Construction of Reality in the Child*, Ballentine,
New York, 1954.

[Piaget, 1966] Piaget, J., *The Child's Conception of Physical Causality*,
Routledge and Kegan Paul, London, 1966.

[Piaget and Inhelder, 1969] Piaget, J., and B. Inhelder, *The Psychology of the
Child*, Basic Books, 1969.

[Plach, 1997] Plach, M., "Using Bayesian Networks to Model Probabilistic
Inferences About the Likelihood of Traffic Congestion," in D. Harris
(Ed.): *Engineering Psychology and Cognitive Ergonomics*, Vol. 1, Ashgate,
Aldershot, 1997.

[Popper, 1975] Popper, K.R., *Logic of Scientific Discovery*, Hutchinson & Co,
1975. (originally published in 1935).

[Popper, 1983] Popper, K.R., *Realism and the Aim of Science*, Rowman &
Littlefield, Totowa, New Jersey, 1983.

[Pradham and Dagum, 1996] Pradham, M., and P. Dagum, "Optimal Monte
Carlo Estimation of Belief Network Inference," in Horvitz, E., and F.
Jensen (Eds.): *Uncertainty in Artificial Intelligence; Proceedings of the
Twelfth Conference*, Morgan Kaufmann, San Mateo, California, 1996.

[Quattrone, 1982] Quattrone, G.A., "Overattribution and Unit Formation:
When Behavior Engulfs the Person," *Journal of Personality and Social
Psychology*, Vol. 42, 1982.

[Raftery, 1995] Raftery, A., "Bayesian Model Selection in Social Research," in
Marsden, P. (Ed.): *Sociological Methodology 1995*, Blackwells, Cambridge,
Massachusetts, 1995.

[Ramoni and Sebastiani, 1999] Ramoni, M., and P. Sebastiani, "Learning
Conditional Probabilities from Incomplete Data: An Experimental Com-
parison," in Heckerman, D, and J. Whittaker (Eds.): *Proceedings of the
Seventh International Workshop on Artificial Intelligence and Statistics*,
Morgan Kaufman, San Mateo, California, 1999.

[Richardson and Spirtes, 1999] Richardson, T., and P. Spirtes, "Automated Discovery of Linear Feedback Models," in Glymour, C., and G.F. Cooper (Eds.): *Computation, Causation, and Discovery*, AAAI Press, Menlo Park, California, 1999.

[Rissanen, 1987] Rissanen, J., "Stochastic Complexity (with discussion)," *Journal of the Royal Statistical Society*, Series B, Vol. 49, 1987.

[Robinson, 1977] Robinson, R.W., "Counting Unlabeled Acyclic Digraphs," in C.H.C. Little (Ed.): *Lecture Notes in Mathematics, 622: Combinatorial Mathematics V*, Springer-Verlag, New York, 1977.

[Royalty et al., 2002] Royalty, J., R. Holland, A. Dekhtyar, and J. Goldsmith, "POET, The Online Preference Elicitation Tool," submitted for publication, 2002.

[Rusakov and Geiger, 2002] Rusakov, D., and D. Geiger, "Bayesian Model Selection for Naive Bayes Models," in Darwiche, A., and N. Friedman (Eds.): *Uncertainty in Artificial Intelligence; Proceedings of the Eighteenth Conference*, Morgan Kaufmann, San Mateo, California, 2002.

[Russell, 1913] Russell, B., "On the Notion of Cause," *Proceedings of the Aristotelian Society*, Vol. 13, 1913.

[Russell and Norvig, 1995] Russell, S., and P. Norvig, *Artificial Intelligence A Modern Approach*, Prentice Hall, Upper Saddle River, New Jersey, 1995.

[Sakellaropoulos et al., 1999] Sakellaropoulos, G.C., and G.C. Nikiforidis, "Development of a Bayesian Network in the Prognosis of Head Injuries using Graphical Model Selection Techniques," *Methods of Information in Medicine*, Vol. 38, 1999.

[Salmon, 1994] Salmon, W.C., "Causality without Counterfactuals," *Philosophy of Science*, Vol. 61, 1994.

[Salmon, 1997] Salmon, W., *Causality and Explanation*, Oxford University Press, New York, 1997.

[Scarville et al., 1999] Scarville, J., S.B. Button, J.E. Edwards, A.R. Lancaster, and T.W. Elig, "Armed Forces 1996 Equal Opportunity Survey," Defense Manpower Data Center, Arlington, VA. DMDC Report No. 97-027, 1999.

[Scheines et al., 1994] Scheines, R., P. Spirtes, C. Glymour, and C. Meek, *Tetrad II: User Manual*, Lawrence Erlbaum, Hillsdale, New Jersery, 1994.

[Schwarz, 1978] Schwarz, G., "Estimating the Dimension of a Model," *Annals of Statistics*, Vol. 6, 1978.

[Sewell and Shah, 1968] Sewell, W., and V. Shah, "Social Class, Parental Encouragement, and Educational Aspirations," *American Jurnal of Sociology*, Vol. 73, 1968.

[Shachter, 1988] Shachter, R.D., "Probabilistic Inference and Influence Diagrams," *Operations Research*, Vol. 36, 1988.

[Shachter and Kenley, 1989] Shachter, R.D., and Kenley, "Gaussian Influence Diagrams," *Management Science*, Vol. 35, 1989.

[Shachter and Ndilikijlikeshav, 1993] Shachter, R.D., and Ndilikijlikeshav, P., "Using Potential Influence Diagrams for Probabilistic Inference and Decision Making," in Heckerman, D., and A. Mamdani (Eds.): *Uncertainty in Artificial Intelligence; Proceedings of the Ninth Conference*, Morgan Kaufmann, San Mateo, California, 1993.

[Shachter and Peot, 1990] Shachter, R.D., and M. Peot, "Simulation Approaches to General Probabilistic Inference in Bayesian Networks," in Henrion, M., R.D. Shachter, L.N. Kanal, and J.F. Lemmer (Eds.): *Uncertainty in Artificial Intelligence; Proceedings at the Fifth Conference*, North Holland, Amsterdam, 1990.

[Shenoy, 1992] Shenoy, P.P. "Valuation-Based Systems for Bayesian Decision Analysis," *Operations Research*, Vol. 40, No. 3, 1992.

[Simon, 1955] Simon, H.A., "A Behavioral Model of Rational Choice," *Quarterly Journal of Economics*, Vol. 69, 1955.

[Singh and Valtorta, 1995] Singh, M., and M. Valtorta, "Construction of Bayesian Network Structures from Data: a Brief Survey and an Efficient Algorithm," *International Journal of Approximate Reasoning*, Vol. 12, 1995.

[Spellman et al., 1998] Spellman, P., G. Sherlock, M. Zhang, V. Iyer, K. Anders, M. Eisen, P. Brown, D. Botstein, and B. Futcher, "Comprehensive Identification of Cell Cycle-regulated Genes of the Yeast *sacccharomomyces cerevisiae* by Microarray Hybridization," *Molecular Biology of the Cell*, Vol. 9, 1998.

[Spirtes and Meek, 1995] Sprites, P., and C. Meek, "Learning Bayesian Networks with Discrete Variables from Data," In *Proceedings of the First International Conference on Knowledge Discovery and Data Mining*, Morgan Kaufmann, San Mateo, California, 1995.

[Spirtes et al., 1993, 2000] Spirtes, P., C. Glymour, and R. Scheines, *Causation, Prediction, and Search*, Springer-Verlag, New York, 1993; 2nd ed.: MIT Press, Cambridge, Massachusetts, 2000.

[Spirtes et al., 1995] Spirtes, P., C. Meek, and T. Richardson, "Causal Inference in the Presence of Latent Variables and Selection Bias," in Besnard, P., and S. Hanks (Eds.): *Uncertainty in Artificial Intelligence; Proceedings of the Eleventh Conference*, Morgan Kaufmann, San Mateo, California, 1995.

[Srinivas, 1993] Srinivas, S., "A Generalization of the Noisy OR Model," in Heckerman, D., and A. Mamdani (Eds.): *Uncertainty in Artificial Intelligence; Proceedings of the Ninth Conference*, Morgan Kaufmann, San Mateo, California, 1993.

[Stangor et al., 2002] Stangor, C., J.K. Swim, K.L. Van Allen, and G.B. Sechrist, "Reporting Discrimination in Public and Private Contexts," *Journal of Personality and Social Psychology*, Vol. 82, 2002.

[Suermondt and Cooper, 1990] Suermondt, H.J., and G.F. Cooper, "Probabilistic Inference in Multiply Connect Belief Networks Using Loop Cutsets," *International Journal of Approximate Inference*, Vol. 4, 1990.

[Suermondt and Cooper, 1991] Suermondt, H.J., and G.F. Cooper, "Initialization for the Method of Conditioning in Bayesian Belief Networks, *Artificial Intelligence*," Vol. 50, No. 83, 1991.

[Tierney, 1995] Tierney, L., "Markov Chains for Exploring Posterior Distributions," *Annals of Statistics*, Vol. 22, 1995.

[Tierney, 1996] Tierney, L., "Introduction to General State Space Markov Chain Theory," in Gilks, W.R., S. Richardson, and D.J. Spiegelhalter (Eds.): *Markov Chain Monte Carlo in Practice*, Chapman & Hall/CRC, Boca Raton, Florida, 1996.

[Tierney and Kadane, 1986] Tierney, L., and J. Kadane, "Accurate Approximations for Posterior Moments and Marginal Densities," *Journal of the American Statistical Association*, Vol. 81, 1986.

[Tong and Koller, 2001] Tong, S., and D. Koller, "Active Learning for Structure in Bayesian Networks," *Proceedings of the Seventeenth International Joint Conference on Artificial Intelligence (IJCAI)*, Seattle, Washington, August 2001.

[Torres-Toledano and Sucar, 1998] Torres-Toledano, J.G and L.E. Sucar, "Bayesian Networks for Reliability Analysis of Complex Systems," in Coelho, H. (Ed.): *Progress in Artificial Intelligence - IBERAMIA 98*, Springer-Verlag, Berlin, 1998.

[Valadares, 2002] Valadares, J. "Modeling Complex Management Games with Bayesian Networks: The FutSim Case Study," *Proceeding of Agents in Computer Games, a Workshop at the 3rd International Conference on Computers and Games (CG'02)*, Edmonton, Canada, 2002.

[van Lambalgen, 1987] van Lambalgen, M., *Random Sequences*, Ph.D. Thesis, University of Amsterdam, 1987.

[Verma, 1992] Verma, T. *Graphical Aspects of Causal Models*, Technical Report R-191, UCLA Cognitive Science LAB, Los Angeles, California, 1992.

[Verma and Pearl, 1990] Verma, T., and J. Pearl, "Causal Networks: Semantics and Expressiveness," in Shachter, R.D., T.S. Levitt, L.N. Kanal, and J.F. Lemmer (Eds.): *Uncertainty in Artificial Intelligence; Proceedings of the Fourth Conference*, North-Holland, Amsterdam, 1990.

[Verma and Pearl, 1991] Verma, T., and J. Pearl, "Equivalence and Synthesis of Causal Models," in Bonissone, P.P., M. Henrion, L.N. Kanal, and J.F. Lemmer (Eds.): *Uncertainty in Artificial Intelligence; Proceedings of the Sixth Conference*, North-Holland, Amsterdam, 1991.

[von Mises, 1919] von Mises, R., "Grundlagen der Wahrscheinlichkeitsrechnung," *Mathematische Zeitschrift*, Vol. 5, 1919.

[von Mises, 1928] von Mises, R., *Probability, Statistics, and Truth*, Allen & Unwin, London, 1957 (originally published in 1928).

[Wallace and Korb, 1999] Wallace, C.S., and K. Korb, "Learning Linear Causal Models by MML Sampling," in Gammerman, A. (Ed.): *Causal Models and Intelligent Data Mining*, Springer-Verlag, New York, 1999.

[Whitworth, 1897] Whitworth, W.A., *DCC Exercise in Choice and Chance*, 1897 (reprinted by Hafner, New York, 1965).

[Wright, 1921] Wright, S., "Correlation and Causation," *Journal of Agricultural Research*, Vol. 20, 1921.

[Xiang et al., 1996] Xiang, Y., S.K.M. Wong, and N. Cercone, "Critical Remarks on Single Link Search in Learning Belief Networks," in Horvitz, E., and F. Jensen (Eds.): *Uncertainty in Artificial Intelligence; Proceedings of the Twelfth Conference*, Morgan Kaufmann, San Mateo, California, 1996.

[Zabell, 1982] Zabell, S.L., "W.E. Johnson's 'Sufficientness' Postulate," *The Annals of Statistics*, Vol. 10, No. 4. 1982.

[Zabell, 1996] Zabell, S.L., "The Continuum of Inductive Methods Revisited," in Earman, J., and J. Norton (Eds.): *The Cosmos of Science*, University of Pittsburgh Series in the History and Philosophy of Science, 1996.

[Zhaoyu and D'Ambrosio, 1993] Zhaoyu, L., and B. D'Ambrosio, "An Efficient Approach for Finding the MPE in Belief Networks," in Heckerman, D., and A. Mamdani (Eds.): *Uncertainty in Artificial Intelligence; Proceedings of the Ninth Conference*, Morgan Kaufmann, San Mateo, California, 1993.

[Zhaoyu and D'Ambrosio, 1994] Zhaoyu, L., and B. D'Ambrosio, "Efficient Inference in Bayes Networks as a Combinatorial Optimization Problem," *International Journal of Approximate Inference*, Vol. 11, 1994.

Index